Management Information Systems

MANAGING THE DIGITAL FIRM

FOURTEENTH EDITION

Management Information Systems

MANAGING THE DIGITAL FIRM

FOURTEENTH EDITION

Kenneth C. Laudon
New York University

Jane P. Laudon
Azimuth Information Systems

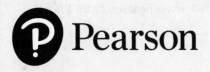

Authorized adaptation from the United States edition, entitled *Management Information Systems: Managing the Digital Firm, 14 Edition*, ISBN 978-0-13-389816-3 Laudon, Kenneth C; and Laudon, Jane P., published by Pearson Education Inc., publishing as Prentice Hall, Copyright © 2012 Pearson Education, Inc.

Indian Subcontinent Adaptation

ISBN 978-93-325-4890-9

First Impression, 2016
Third Impression, 2017
Fourth Impression,

This edition is manufactured in India and is authorized for sale only in India, Bangladesh, Bhutan, Pakistan, Nepal, Sri Lanka and the Maldives. Circulation of this edition outside of these territories is UNAUTHORIZED.

Published by Pearson India Education Services Pvt. Ltd, CIN: U72200TN2005PTC057128, formerly known as TutorVista Global Pvt. Ltd, licensee of Pearson Education in South Asia.

Head Office: A-8(A), 7th Floor, Knowledge Boulevard, Sector 62, Noida 201 309, Uttar Pradesh, India.

Registered Office: 4th floor, Software Block, Elnet Software City, TS 140 Block 2 & 9, Rajiv Gandhi Salai, Taramani, Chennai - 600 113, Tamil Nadu, India. Fax: 080-30461003, Phone: 080-30461060 www.pearson.co.in, Email: companysecretary.india@pearson.com

Printed in India by Thomson Press India Ltd.

About the Authors

Kenneth C. Laudon is a Professor of Information Systems at New York University's Stern School of Business. He holds a B.A. in Economics from Stanford and a Ph.D. from Columbia University. He has authored twelve books dealing with electronic commerce, information systems, organizations, and society. Professor Laudon has also written over forty articles concerned with the social, organizational, and management impacts of information systems, privacy, ethics, and multimedia technology.

Professor Laudon's current research is on the planning and management of large-scale information systems and multimedia information technology. He has received grants from the National Science Foundation to study the evolution of national information systems at the Social Security Administration, the IRS, and the FBI. Ken's research focuses on enterprise system implementation, computer-related organizational and occupational changes in large organizations, changes in management ideology, changes in public policy, and understanding productivity change in the knowledge sector.

Ken Laudon has testified as an expert before the United States Congress. He has been a researcher and consultant to the Office of Technology Assessment (United States Congress), Department of Homeland Security, and to the Office of the President, several executive branch agencies, and Congressional Committees. Professor Laudon also acts as an in-house educator for several consulting firms and as a consultant on systems planning and strategy to several Fortune 500 firms.

At NYU's Stern School of Business, Ken Laudon teaches courses on Managing the Digital Firm, Information Technology and Corporate Strategy, Professional Responsibility (Ethics), and Electronic Commerce and Digital Markets. Ken Laudon's hobby is sailing.

Jane Price Laudon is a management consultant in the information systems area and the author of seven books. Her special interests include systems analysis, data management, MIS auditing, software evaluation, and teaching business professionals how to design and use information systems.

Jane received her Ph.D. from Columbia University, her M.A. from Harvard University, and her B.A. from Barnard College. She has taught at Columbia University and the New York University Graduate School of Business. She maintains a lifelong interest in Oriental languages and civilizations.

The Laudons have two daughters, Erica and Elisabeth, to whom this book is dedicated.

Brief Contents

Complete Contents

Chapter 4   Ethical and Social Issues in Information Systems 130

Part Two   Information Technology Infrastructure 177

Chapter 5   IT Infrastructure and Emerging Technologies 178

Chapter 7

Telecommunications, the Internet, and Wireless Technology 268

Chapter 8 Securing Information Systems 320

Chapter 10   E-commerce: Digital Markets, Digital Goods 404

Part Four Building and Managing Systems 531

Chapter 13 Building Information Systems 532

Chapter 15   Managing Global Systems 612

Preface

We wrote this book for business school students who wanted an in-depth look at how today's business firms use information technologies and systems to achieve corporate objectives. Information systems are one of the major tools available to business managers for achieving operational excellence, developing new products and services, improving decision making, and achieving competitive advantage. Students will find here the most up-to-date and comprehensive overview of information systems used by business firms today. After reading this book, we expect students will be able to participate in, and even lead, management discussions of information systems for their firms.

When interviewing potential employees, business firms often look for new hires who know how to use information systems and technologies for achieving bottom-line business results. Regardless of whether you are an accounting, finance, management, operations management, marketing, or information systems major, the knowledge and information you find in this book will be valuable throughout your business career.

WHAT'S NEW IN THIS EDITION

CURRENCY

The 14th edition features all new opening, closing and Interactive Session cases. The text, figures, tables, and cases have been updated through October 2014 with the latest sources from industry and MIS research.

This Indian edition of *Management Information Systems, 14e*, is a balanced attempt to retain the strengths of the original edition while attempting to make it closer to the requirements of the Indian students and instructors. At multiple places throughout the book, the text has been adapted to fit the Indian industries. Accordingly, changes were made in this respect to chapters 2, 3, and 9. One of the highlights of this book is the way in which the cases are segmented into different categories of opening case, Interactive Session, and end-of-chapter case. India is fast emerging as a global IT hub and a number of organizations are implementing information system either to enhance core competency or to gain competitive advantage. Considering these facts, in every chapter at least one category of case is substituted with an Indian equivalent. As every country has its own unique features which also influence how an organization perceives and implements the information system. Hence, the inclusion of Indian case studies will definitely help readers to get acclimatized to the workings of various information systems and the circumstances under which an organization decides to implement an information system. Considering the wide range of application areas of information system, an effort has been made to include all the important aspects of information systems from an Indian perspective in the form of case studies and revised text.

NEW TOPICS

- **Social, Mobile, Local:**   New e-commerce content in Chapter 10 describing how social tools, mobile technology, and location-based services are transforming marketing and advertising.
- **Big Data:**   Chapter 6 on Databases and Information Management updated to provide in-depth coverage of Big Data and new data management technologies, including Hadoop, in-memory computing, non-relational databases, and analytic platforms.
- **Cloud Computing:**   Updated coverage of cloud computing in Chapter 5 (IT Infrastructure), with more detail on types of cloud services, private and public clouds, hybrid clouds, managing cloud services, and a new Interactive Session on using cloud services. Cloud computing also covered in Chapter 6 (databases in the cloud); Chapter 8 (cloud security); Chapter 9 (cloud-based CRM and ERP); Chapter 10 (e-commerce); and Chapter 13 (cloud-based systems development).
- **Social Business:**   Extensive coverage of social business, introduced in Chapter 2 and discussed in throughout the text. Detailed discussions of enterprise (internal corporate) social networking as well as social networking in e-commerce.
- Consumerization of IT and BYOD
- Internet of Things
- Visual Web
- Location analytics
- Location-based services (geosocial, geoadvertising, geoinformation services)
- Building an e-commerce presence
- Wearable computers
- Mobile application development, mobile and native apps
- Operational intelligence
- Expanded coverage of business analytics including big data analytics
- Software-defined networking
- 3-D printing
- Quantum computing
- Two-factor authentication
- Ransomware
- Chief data officer
- MOOCs

NEW CASES IN THE INDIAN CONTEXT

- Employee Pick-ups and Drop-offs at Convergys; The Domino's PULSE™ System: Reading the Pulse of the Customer   (*Chapter 1*)
- Azure Medical System: Integrating Departments Using Enterprise System; HDFC Banking on Business Intelligence and Analytics Technology; Ranbaxy: Taking the ERP Pill   (*Chapter 2*)
- AirAsia: Saving on Operational Costs through Effective; Information Systems; Securing Flipkart   (*Chapter 3*)
- Ethical Issues of Google Earth   (*Chapter 4*)
- Establishing Global Classrooms through WebEx; Wipro on the Cloud   (*Chapter 5*)
- The Gym Database   (*Chapter 6*)
- RFID-enabled LSmart Library Management System   (*Chapter 7*)
- SAS Helping SEBI Check Equities-trading Malpractices; Securing Information: the HSBC Way   (*Chapter 8*)
- Optimizing Operations at QuarkCity: A Move Away from Legacy Systems; CRM Tools Aid Airtel in the Efficient Handling of Customer Support Processes; Social CRM: Connecting with Customers through Social Networks   (*Chapter 9*)
- Social Media Analytics in Indian Politics; Mobile Commerce with Airtel Money   (*Chapter 10*)
- Connecting Unisys Globally through Social Collaboration Information Systems   (*Chapter 11*)
- The Analytics behind Matrimony.com   (*Chapter 12*)
- Centralization of Operations at Tata Power   (*Chapter 13*)
- Reliance Installing the 4G Project in India   (*Chapter 14*)
- One Organization, One Data, One Information: ONGC's Global System   (*Chapter 15*)

WHAT'S NEW IN MIS?

Plenty. In fact, there's a whole new world of doing business using new technologies for managing and organizing. What makes the MIS field the most exciting area of study in schools of business is the continuous change in technology, management, and business processes. (Chapter 1 describes these changes in more detail.)

IT Innovations.   A continuing stream of information technology innovations is transforming the traditional business world. Examples include the emergence of cloud computing, the growth of a mobile digital business platform based on smartphones and tablet computers, and not least, the use of social networks by managers to achieve business objectives. Most of these changes have occurred in the last few years. These innovations enabling entrepreneurs and innovative traditional firms to create new products and services, develop new business models, and transform the day-to-day conduct of business. In the process, some old businesses, even industries, are being destroyed while new businesses are springing up.

New Business Models.   For instance, the emergence of online video stores like Netflix for streaming, and Apple iTunes for downloading, has forever changed how premium video is distributed, and even created. Netflix in 2013 attracted 30 million subscribers to its DVD rental and streaming movie business. Netflix now accounts for 90 percent of streaming premium movies and TV shows, and consumes an estimated 33 percent of Internet bandwidth in the United States. Netflix has moved into premium TV show production with House of Cards, and Arrested Development, challenging cable networks like HBO, and potentially disrupting the cable channels dominance of TV show production. Apple's iTunes now accounts for 67 percent of movie and TV show downloads and has struck deals with major Hollywood studios for recent movies and TV shows. A growing trickle of viewers are unplugging from cable and using only the Internet for entertainment.

E-commerce Expanding.   E-commerce will generate an estimated $470 billion in revenues in 2014, and is estimated to grow to nearly $700 billion in 2018. Amazon's revenues grew 21 percent to $74 billion in 2013, despite a slowly expanding economy growing at 2 percent annually, while offline retail grew by only 5 percent. E-commerce is changing how firms design, produce and deliver their products and services. E-commerce has reinvented itself again, disrupting the traditional marketing and advertising industry and putting major media and content firms in jeopardy. Facebook and other social networking sites such as YouTube, Twitter, and Tumblr, exemplify the new face of e-commerce in the 21st Century. They sell services. When we think of e-commerce we tend to think of a selling physical products. While this iconic vision of e-commerce is still very powerful and the fastest growing form of retail in the U.S., growing up alongside is a whole new value stream based on selling services, not goods. It's a services model of e-commerce. Growth in social commerce is spurred by powerful growth of the mobile platform: 60 percent of Facebook's users access the service from mobile phones and tablets. Information systems and technologies are the foundation of this new services-based e-commerce.

Management Changes.   Likewise, the management of business firms has changed: With new mobile smartphones, high-speed wireless Wi-Fi networks, and wireless laptop computers, remote salespeople on the road are only seconds away from their managers' questions and oversight. Managers on the move are in direct, continuous contact with their employees. The growth of enterprise-wide information systems with extraordinarily rich data means that managers no longer operate in a fog of confusion, but instead have online, nearly instant, access to the really important information they need for accurate and timely decisions. In addition to their public uses on the Web, wikis and blogs are becoming important corporate tools for communication, collaboration, and information sharing.

Changes in Firms and Organizations: Compared to industrial organizations of the previous century, new fast-growing 21st Century business firms put less emphasis on hierarchy and structure, and more emphasis on employees taking on multiple roles and tasks. They put greater emphasis on competency and skills rather than position in the hierarchy. They emphasize higher speed and more accurate decision making based on data and analysis. They are more aware of changes in technology, consumer attitudes, and culture. They use social media to enter into conversations with consumers, and demonstrate a greater willingness to listen to consumers, in part because they have no choice. They show better understanding of the importance of information technology in creating and managing business firms and other organizations. To the extent organizations and business firms demonstrate these characteristics, they are 21st Century digital firms.

THE 14TH EDITION: THE COMPREHENSIVE SOLUTION FOR THE MIS CURRICULUM

Since its inception, this text has helped to define the MIS course around the globe. This edition continues to be authoritative, but is also more customizable, flexible, and geared to meeting the needs of different colleges, universities, and individual instructors.

The core text consists of 15 chapters with hands-on projects covering the most essential topics in MIS.

THE CORE TEXT

The core text provides an overview of fundamental MIS concepts using an integrated framework for describing and analyzing information systems. This framework shows information systems composed of people, organization, and technology elements and is reinforced in student projects and case studies.

Chapter Organization

Each chapter contains the following elements:

- A Chapter Outline based on Learning Objectives
- A chapter-opening case describing a real-world organization to establish the theme and importance of the chapter
- A diagram analyzing the opening case in terms of the management, organization, and technology model used throughout the text
- At least two Interactive Sessions with Case Study Questions
- A Review Summary keyed to the Student Learning Objectives
- A list of Key Terms that students can use to review concepts
- Review questions for students to test their comprehension of chapter material
- Discussion questions raised by the broader themes of the chapter.
- A series of Hands-on MIS Projects
- A chapter-ending case study for students to apply chapter concepts
- Two assisted-graded writing questions with prebuilt grading rubrics
- Chapter references

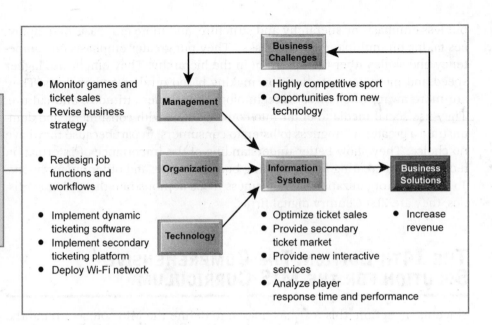

A diagram accompanying each chapter-opening case graphically illustrates how management, organization, and technology elements work together to create an information system solution to the business challenges discussed in the case.

KEY FEATURES

We have enhanced the text to make it more interactive, leading-edge, and appealing to both students and instructors. The features and learning tools are described in the following sections:

Business-Driven with Real-World Business Cases and Examples

The text helps students see the direct connection between information systems and business performance. It describes the main business objectives driving the use of information systems and technologies in corporations all over the world: operational excellence; new products and services; customer and supplier intimacy; improved decision making; competitive advantage; and survival. In-text examples and case studies show students how specific companies use information systems to achieve these objectives.

We use only current (2014) examples from business and public organizations throughout the text to illustrate the important concepts in each chapter. All the case studies describe companies or organizations that are familiar to students, such as The San Francisco Giants, Facebook, Walmart, and Google.

Interactivity

There's no better way to learn about MIS than by doing MIS! We provide different kinds of hands-on projects where students can work with real-world business scenarios and data, and learn firsthand what MIS is all about. These projects heighten student involvement in this exciting subject.

- **Interactive Sessions.**   At least two short cases in each chapter have been redesigned as Interactive Sessions to be used in the classroom (or on Internet discussion boards) to stimulate student interest and active learning. Each case concludes with case study questions. The case

Chapter 9 Achieving Operational Excellence and Customer Intimacy: Enterprise Applications **381**

INTERACTIVE SESSION: MANAGEMENT

SCOTTS MIRACLE-GRO CULTIVATES SUPPLY CHAIN PROFICIENCY

When you have to make nearly all of your annual sales of 10 billion pounds of lawn fertilizer and other gardening products in a 10- to 14- week seasonal window, you realize the importance of an optimized supply chain. As the world's principal supplier of lawn and garden care products, the Scotts Miracle-Gro Company, headquartered in Marysville, Ohio, needed to optimize its entire supply chain—from shelf to supplier—in order to meet the needs of its seasonal, weather-dependent business.

When lawn care company, Scotts, and top gardening brand, Miracle-Gro, merged in 1995, a number of challenges arose. Customer lists overlapped, causing duplication of sales force efforts. Multiple supply chain designs conflicted, incompatible invoicing systems clashed, and multiple IT systems could not be coordinated to resolve the discord. The result was that despite holding the leading gardening and lawn care brands in the United States (Roundup and Ortho) in addition to the two that comprise its masthead, the Scotts Miracle-Gro Company suffered declining productivity and deteriorating customer service.

With execution during its peak-demand season suffering, the company embarked on an initiative

Two key factors enabled Scotts Miracle-Gro to better respond to rapid changes in market conditions: the ability to create POS forecasts and an increased adeptness at responding to weather events.

POS forecasts at the store level are the basis for Scott's demand planning, which then incorporates promotions, media and advertising campaigns, and stockout planning. These plans are further honed by integrating safety-stock settings, on-hand quantities, and on-order quantities for each store. Scotts Miracle-Gro's supply chain is segmented by warehouse. The individualized store replenishment plans are aggregated for each warehouse so that enough product is produced to properly stock them.

Weather-related impacts are translated into plans of action for each zip code on a day-by-day and weekly basis. JDA Demand is integrated with business weather intelligence pioneer Planalytics' database of regional and seasonal weather patterns and analytical program. The improved ability to anticipate weather patterns and make sound inventory decisions also ensures that promotions are properly timed to maximize revenue increases for the company's retail partners and market share for the company.

In addition to supply chain segmentation by

> Each chapter contains Interactive Sessions on Management, Organizations, or Technology using real-world companies to illustrate chapter concepts and issues.

CASE STUDY QUESTIONS

1. Identify the supply chain management problems faced by Scotts Miracle-Gro. What was the business impact of not being able to manage the company's supply chain well?

2. What management, organization, and technology factors contributed to Scotts Miracle-Gro's supply chain problems?

3. How did implementing JDA Software solutions change the way Scotts Miracle-Gro ran its business?

4. How did the new supply chain systems improve management decision making? Describe two decisions that were improved by the new system solution.

> Case Study Questions encourage students to apply chapter concepts to real-world companies in class discussions, student presentations, or writing assignments.

study questions provide topics for class discussion, Internet discussion, or written assignments.

- **Hands-on MIS Projects.** Every chapter concludes with a Hands-on MIS Projects section containing either of these three types of projects: two Management Decision Problems, a hands-on application software exercise using Microsoft Excel, Access, or Web page and blog creation tools, and a project that develops Internet business skills.

- **Collaboration and Teamwork Projects.** Each chapter features a collaborative project that encourages students working in teams to use Google Drive, Google Docs, or other open-source collaboration tools.

Assessment and AACSB Assessment Guidelines

The Association to Advance Collegiate Schools of Business (AACSB) is a not-for-profit corporation of educational institutions, corporations and other organizations that seeks to improve business education primarily by

Real-world business scenarios per chapter provide opportunities for students to apply chapter concepts and practice management decision making.

Management Decision Problems

3-8 Macy's, Inc., through its subsidiaries, operates approximately 840 department stores in the United States. Its retail stores sell a range of merchandise, including apparel, home furnishings, and house-wares. Senior management has decided that Macy's needs to tailor merchandise more to local tastes, and that the colors, sizes, brands, and styles of clothing and other merchandise should be based on the sales patterns in each individual Macy's store. How could information systems help Macy's man-agement implement this new strategy? What pieces of data should these systems collect to help man-agement make merchandising decisions that support this strategy?

3-9 Despite aggressive campaigns to attract customers with lower mobile phone prices, T-Mobile has been losing large numbers of its most lucrative two-year contract subscribers. Management wants to know why so many customers are leaving T-Mobile and what can be done to entice them back. Are customers deserting because of poor customer service, uneven network coverage, wireless service charges, or competition from carriers with Apple iPhone service? How can the company use infor-mation systems to help find the answer? What management decisions could be made using informa-tion from these systems?

The chapters also feature a project to develop Internet skills for accessing informa-tion, conducting research, and performing online calculations and analysis.

Improving Decision Making: Using Web Tools to Configure and Price an Automobile

Software skills: Internet-based software
Business skills: Researching product information and pricing

3-10 In this exercise, you will use software at car Web sites to find product information about a car of your choice and use that information to make an important purchase decision. You will also evaluate two of these sites as selling tools.

You are interested in purchasing a new Ford Escape (or some other car of your choice). Go to the Web site of CarsDirect (www.carsdirect.com) and begin your investigation. Locate the Ford Escape. Research the various Escape models, choose one you prefer in terms of price, features, and safety rat-ings. Locate and read at least two reviews. Surf the Web site of the manufacturer, in this case Ford (www. ford.com). Compare the information available on Ford's Web site with that of CarsDirect for the Ford Escape. Try to locate the lowest price for the car you want in a local dealer's inventory. Suggest improve-ments for CarsDirect.com and Ford.com.

accrediting university business programs. As a part of its accreditation activi-ties, the AACSB has developed an Assurance of Learning Program designed to ensure that schools do in fact teach students what they promise. Schools are required to state a clear mission, develop a coherent business program, identify student learning objectives, and then prove that students do in fact achieve the objectives.

We have attempted in this book to support AACSB efforts to encourage assessment-based education. The back end papers of this edition identify student learning objectives and anticipated outcomes for our Hands-on MIS projects. The authors will provide custom advice on how to use this text in their colleges with different missions and assessment needs. Please e-mail the authors or contact your local Pearson representative for contact information.

Annotated Slides

The authors have prepared a comprehensive collection of fifty PowerPoint slides to be used in your lectures. Many of these slides are the same as used by Ken Laudon in his MIS classes and executive education presentations. Each of the slides is annotated with teaching suggestions for asking students questions, developing in-class lists that illustrate key concepts, and recom-mending other firms as examples in addition to those provided in the text. The annotations are like an Instructor's Manual built into the slides and make it easier to teach the course effectively.

Student Learning-focused

Student Learning Objectives are organized around a set of study questions to focus student attention. Each chapter concludes with a Review Summary and Review Questions organized around these study questions, and each major chapter section is based on a Learning Objective.

Career Resources

The Instructor Resources for this text include extensive Career Resources, including job-hunting guides and instructions on how to build a Digital Portfolio demonstrating the business knowledge, application software proficiency, and Internet skills acquired from using the text. The portfolio can be included in a resume or job application or used as a learning assessment tool for instructors.

INSTRUCTOR RESOURCES

The following supplements are available to adopting instructors at www.pearson.co.in/laudon.

- Instructor's Resource Manual
- PowerPoint Presentation

ACKNOWLEDGEMENTS

The production of any book involves valued contributions from a number of persons. We would like to thank all of our editors for encouragement, insight, and strong support for many years. We thank our editor Nicole Sam, Program Manager Denise Vaughn, and Project Manager Karalyn Holland for their role in managing the project. We remain grateful to Bob Horan for all his years of editorial guidance.

Our special thanks go to our supplement authors for their work: John Hupp, Columbus State University; Robert J. Mills, Utah State University; John P. Russo, Wentworth Institute of Technology; and Michael L. Smith, SUNY Oswego. We are indebted to Robin Pickering for her assistance with writing and to William Anderson and Megan Miller for their help during production. We thank Diana R. Craig for her assistance with database and software topics.

Special thanks to colleagues at the Stern School of Business at New York University; to Professor Werner Schenk, Simon School of Business, University of Rochester; to Professor Mark Gillenson, Fogelman College of Business and Economics, University of Memphis; to Robert Kostrubanic, CIO and Director of Information Technology Services Indiana-Purdue University Fort Wayne; to Professor Lawrence Andrew of Western Illinois University; to Professor Detlef Schoder of the University of Cologne; to Professor Walter Brenner of the University of St. Gallen; to Professor Lutz Kolbe of the University of Gottingen; to Professor Donald Marchand of the International Institute for Management Development; and to Professor

Daniel Botha of Stellenbosch University who provided additional suggestions for improvement. Thank you to Professor Ken Kraemer, University of California at Irvine, and Professor John King, University of Michigan, for more than a decade's long discussion of information systems and organizations. And a special remembrance and dedication to Professor Rob Kling, University of Indiana, for being my friend and colleague over so many years.

We also want to especially thank all our reviewers whose suggestions helped improve our texts. Reviewers for Managing the Digital Firm include the following:

Brad Allen, Plymouth State University
Dawit Demissie: University of Albany
Anne Formalarie, Plymouth State University
Bin Gu, University of Texas – Austin
Essia Hamouda, University of California – Riverside
Linda Lau: Longwood University
Kimberly L. Merritt, Oklahoma Christian University
James W. Miller, Dominican University
Fiona Nah, University of Nebraska – Lincoln
M.K. Raja: University of Texas Arlington
Thomas Schambach, Illinois State University
Shawn Weisfeld: Florida Institute of Technology

K.C.L.
J.P.L.

The publisher would like to thank Dr Sahil Raj, who is a faculty in the School of Management Studies at Punjabi University (Patiala), for his valuable suggestions and inputs in enhancing the content of this book to suit the requirements of Indian universities.

Dr Raj has multifarious background with experience in the industry, teaching, and research spanning over a decade. He holds an engineering as well as MBA (Information Technology) degree. Dr Raj did his doctoral research in the field of information systems. He has authored four books on information systems.

PART ONE

Organizations, Management, and the Networked Enterprise

Part One introduces the major themes of this book, raising a series of important questions: What is an information system and what are its management, organization, and technology dimensions? Why are information systems so essential in businesses today? Why are systems for collaboration and social business so important? How can information systems help businesses become more competitive? What broader ethical and social issues are raised by widespread use of information systems?

Information Systems in Global Business Today

CHAPTER 1

LEARNING OBJECTIVES

After reading this chapter, you will be able to answer the following questions:

1. How are information systems transforming business, and why are they so essential for running and managing a business today?

2. What is an information system? How does it work? What are its management, organization, and technology components and why are complementary assets essential for ensuring that information systems provide genuine value for organizations?

3. What academic disciplines are used to study information systems and how does each contribute to an understanding of information systems?

CHAPTER CASES

The San Francisco Giants Win Big with Information Technology

Employee Pick-ups and Drop-offs at Convergys

UPS Competes Globally with Information Technology

The Domino's PULSE™ System: Reading the Pulse of the Customer

THE SAN FRANCISCO GIANTS WIN BIG WITH INFORMATION TECHNOLOGY

The San Francisco Giants are one of the oldest U.S. baseball teams, and one of the most successful as well. They have won the most games of any team in the history of American baseball and any North American professional sports team. The Giants have captured 23 National League pennants and appeared in 20 World Series competitions— both records in the National League. Their most recent triumph was winning the 2014 World Series. The Giants have outstanding players (with the most Hall of Fame players in all of professional baseball) and coaches, but some of their success, both as a team and as a business, can be attributed to their use of information technology.

Baseball is very much a game of statistics, and all the major teams are constantly analyzing their data on player performance and optimal positioning on the field. But the Giants are doing more. They have started to use a video system from Sportsvision called FIELDf/x which digitally records the position of all players and hit balls in real time. The system generates defensive statistics such as the difficulty of a catch and the probability of a particular fielder making that catch. Information produced by the system on player speed and response time, such as how quickly an outfielder comes in for a ball or reacts to line drives, will enable the Giants to make player data analysis much more precise. In some cases, it will provide information that didn't exist before on players'

© Cynthia Lindow/Alamy.

defensive skills and other skills. FIELDf/x generates a million records per game. That amounts to 5 billion records in three years, the amount of time required to provide a high level of confidence in the data. In addition to player and team statistics, the Giants are starting to collect data about fans, including ticket purchases and social media activity.

Under the leadership of chief information officer (CIO) Bill Schlough, the San Francisco Giants have pioneered dynamic ticket pricing, based on software from Qcue, in which the price of a ticket fluctuates according to the level of demand for a particular ball game. It's similar to the dynamic ticket pricing used in the airline industry. If a game is part of a crucial series, the Giants are playing an in-division rival, or the game appears to be selling out especially fast, ticket prices will rise. If the game isn't a big draw, ticket prices fall. The Giants have sold out 100 percent of their home games since October 2010, and have increased season ticket sales from 21,000 in 2010 to 29,000 in 2012.

Season ticket-holders don't normally attend every game, and this can lose revenue for a team. Every time a fan with a season ticket decides to stay home from a game, the sports franchise loses an average of $20 in concession and merchandise sales. To make sure stadium seats are always filled, the Giants created a secondary online ticket market where season ticket holders can resell tickets they are not using over the Internet. The Giants's information technology specialists found a way to activate and deactivate the bar codes on tickets so that they can be resold. The system is also a way for the Giants to provide additional service to customers.

The Giants have also taken advantage of wireless technology to enhance their fans' experience. A network extends from the seats to the concession stands to areas outside the stadium, and is one of the largest public wireless networks in the world. The stadium, AT&T Park, has a giant high-speed wireless network, which fans can use to check scores and video highlights, update their social networks, and do e-mail.

Sources: http://www.sportvision.com/baseball/fieldfx, accessed January 16, 2014; http://www.sanfranciscogiants.mlb.com, accessed February 12, 2014; Kenneth Corbin, "Federal CIOs Look to Speed Tech Development Cycle," CIO, December 17, 2013; Peter High, "Interview with World Champion San Francisco Giants CIO and San Jose Giants Chairman, Bill Schlough," *Forbes*, February 4, 2013; and Fritz Nelson, "Chief of the Year," *Information Week*, December 17, 2012.

The challenges facing the San Francisco Giants and other baseball teams show why information systems are so essential today. Major league baseball is a business as well as a sport, and teams such as the Giants need to take in revenue from games in order to stay in business. Major league baseball is also a business where what matters above all is winning, and any way of using information to improve player performance is a competitive edge.

The chapter-opening diagram calls attention to important points raised by this case and this chapter. To increase stadium revenue, the San Francisco Giants developed a dynamic ticket pricing system designed to adjust ticket prices to customer demand and to sell seats at the optimum price. The team developed another ticketing system that enables existing ticketholders to sell their tickets easily online to someone else. An additional way of

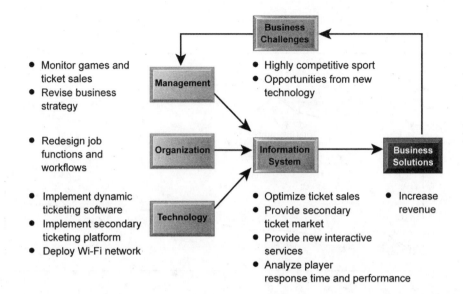

- Monitor games and ticket sales
- Revise business strategy

- Redesign job functions and workflows

- Implement dynamic ticketing software
- Implement secondary ticketing platform
- Deploy Wi-Fi network

Business Challenges

Management

- Highly competitive sport
- Opportunities from new technology

Organization

Information System

- Optimize ticket sales
- Provide secondary ticket market
- Provide new interactive services
- Analyze player response time and performance

Technology

Business Solutions

- Increase revenue

cultivating customers is to deploy modern information technology at AT&T Park, including a massive Wi-Fi wireless network with interactive services. To improve player performance, the Giants implemented a system that captures video on players and then uses the data to analyze player defensive statistics, including speed and reaction times.

Here are some questions to think about: What role does technology play in the San Francisco Giants' success as a baseball team? Assess the contributions of the systems described in this case study.

1.1 HOW ARE INFORMATION SYSTEMS TRANSFORMING BUSINESS, AND WHY ARE THEY SO ESSENTIAL FOR RUNNING AND MANAGING A BUSINESS TODAY?

It's not business as usual in America anymore, or the rest of the global economy. In 2014, American businesses will spend an estimated $817 billion on information systems hardware, software, and telecommunications equipment. In addition, they will spend another $230 billion on business and management consulting and services—much of which involves redesigning firms' business operations to take advantage of these new technologies. Figure 1.1 shows that between 1999 and 2013, private business investment in information technology consisting of hardware, software, and communications equipment grew from 14 percent to 33 percent of all invested capital.

As managers, most of you will work for firms that are intensively using information systems and making large investments in information technology. You will certainly want to know how to invest this money wisely. If you make wise choices, your firm can outperform competitors. If you make poor choices, you will be wasting valuable capital. This book is dedicated to helping you make wise decisions about information technology and information systems.

FIGURE 1.1 INFORMATION TECHNOLOGY CAPITAL INVESTMENT

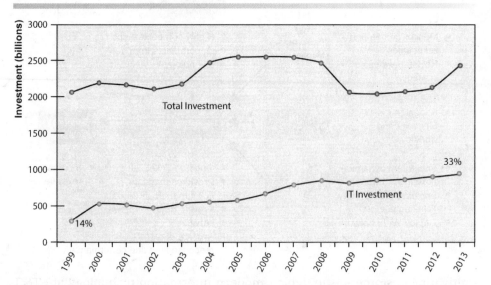

Information technology capital investment, defined as hardware, software, and communications equipment, grew from 14 percent to 33 percent of all invested capital between 1999 and 2013.

Source: Based on data in U.S. Department of Commerce, Bureau of Economic Analysis, *National Income and Product Accounts,* 2014.

HOW INFORMATION SYSTEMS ARE TRANSFORMING BUSINESS

You can see the results of this massive spending around you every day by observing how people conduct business. Changes in technology, and new innovative business models, have transformed social life and business practices. Over 247 million Americans have mobile phones (67% of the population), and 167 million of these people access the Internet using smartphones and tablets. 46% of the entire population now use tablet computers whose sales have soared. 172 million Americans use online social networks, 150 million use Facebook, while 48 million use Twitter. Smartphones, social networking, texting, emailing, and Webinars have all become essential tools of business because that's where your customers, suppliers, and colleagues can be found. (eMarketer, 2014).

By June 2014, more than 114 million businesses worldwide had dot-com Internet sites registered (Domain Tools, 2014). Today, 196 million Americans shop online, and 163 million will purchase online. Every day about 90 million Americans go online to research a product or service. (eMarketer, 2014).

In 2013, FedEx moved about 3.5 million packages daily to 220 countries and territories around the world, mostly overnight, and the United Parcel Service (UPS) moved over 16 million packages daily worldwide. Businesses are using information technology to sense and respond to rapidly changing customer demand, reduce inventories to the lowest possible levels, and achieve higher levels of operational efficiency. Supply chains have become more fast-paced, with companies of all sizes depending on just-in-time inventory to reduce their overhead costs and get to market faster.

As newspaper print readership continues to decline, more than 168 million people read a newspaper online, and millions more read other news sites. About 83 million people watch a video online every day, 66 million read a blog, and 25 million post to blogs, creating an explosion of new writers and new forms of customer feedback that did not exist five years ago (eMarketer, 2014). Social networking site Facebook attracted 152 million monthly visitors in 2014 in the United States, and over 1 billion worldwide. Google + has attracted over 130 million users in the United States. Businesses are starting to use social networking tools to connect their employees, customers, and managers worldwide. Many Fortune 500 companies now have Facebook pages, Twitter accounts, and Tumblr sites.

E-commerce and Internet advertising continue to expand. Google's online ad revenues surpassed $17 billion in 2013, and Internet advertising continues to grow at more than 15 percent a year, reaching more than $43 billion in revenues in 2013 (eMarketer, 2014).

New federal security and accounting laws, requiring many businesses to keep e-mail messages for five years, coupled with existing occupational and health laws requiring firms to store employee chemical exposure data for up to 60 years, are spurring the annual growth of digital information at the estimated rate of 5 exabytes annually, equivalent to 37,000 new Libraries of Congress.

WHAT'S NEW IN MANAGEMENT INFORMATION SYSTEMS?

Lots! What makes management information systems the most exciting topic in business is the continual change in technology, management use of the technology, business models and the impact on business success. New businesses and industries appear, old ones decline, and successful firms are those that learn how to use the new technologies. Table 1.1 summarizes the major new themes in business uses of information systems. These themes will appear throughout the book in all the chapters, so it might be a good idea to take some time now and discuss these with your professor and other students.

There are three interrelated changes in the technology area: (1) the widespread adoption of the mobile computing platform, (2) the growing business use of "big data," and (3) the growth in "cloud computing," where more and more business software runs over the Internet.

IPhones, iPads, Android tablets, and smartphones are not just gadgets or entertainment outlets. They represent new emerging computing platforms based on an array of new hardware and software technologies. More and more business computing is moving from PCs and desktop machines to these mobile devices. Managers are increasingly using these devices to coordinate work, communicate with employees, and provide information for decision making. We call these developments the "mobile digital platform."

Managers routinely use online collaboration and social technologies in order to make better, faster decisions. As management behavior changes,

TABLE 1.1 WHAT'S NEW IN MIS

CHANGE	BUSINESS IMPACT
TECHNOLOGY	
Cloud computing platform emerges as a major business area of innovation	A flexible collection of computers on the Internet begins to perform tasks traditionally performed on corporate computers. Major business applications are delivered online as an Internet service (Software as a Service, or SaaS).
Big data	Businesses look for insights from huge volumes of data from Web traffic, e-mail messages, social media content, and machines (sensors) that require new data management tools to capture, store, and analyze.
A mobile digital platform emerges to compete with the PC as a business system	The Apple iPhone and tablet computers and Android mobile devices are able to download hundreds of thousands of applications to support collaboration, location-based services, and communication with colleagues. Small tablet computers, including the iPad and Kindle Fire, challenge conventional laptops as platforms for consumer and corporate computing.
MANAGEMENT	
Managers adopt online collaboration and social networking software to improve coordination, collaboration, and knowledge sharing	Google Apps, Google Sites, Microsoft Windows SharePoint Services, and IBM Lotus Connections are used by over 100 million business professionals worldwide to support blogs, project management, online meetings, personal profiles, social bookmarks, and online communities.
Business intelligence applications accelerate	More powerful data analytics and interactive dashboards provide real-time performance information to managers to enhance decision making.
Virtual meetings proliferate	Managers adopt telepresence videoconferencing and Web conferencing technologies to reduce travel time, and cost, while improving collaboration and decision making.
ORGANIZATIONS	
Social business	Businesses use social networking platforms, including Facebook, Twitter, and internal corporate social tools, to deepen interactions with employees, customers, and suppliers. Employees use blogs, wikis, e-mail texting, and SMS messaging to interact in online communities.
Telework gains momentum in the workplace	The Internet, wireless laptops, smartphones, and tablet computers make it possible for growing numbers of people to work away from the traditional office. Fifty-five percent of U.S. businesses have some form of remote work program.
Co-creation of business value	Sources of business value shift from products to solutions and experiences, and from internal sources to networks of suppliers and collaboration with customers. Supply chains and product development become more global and collaborative; customer interactions help firms define new products and services.

INTERACTIVE SESSION: MANAGEMENT

EMPLOYEE PICK-UPS AND DROP-OFFS AT CONVERGYS

Convergys is a leading provider of customer management solutions for organizations across India. It started business in 2009, when the BPO industry was still in its infancy. But owing to the sky-rocketing prices of real estate in Delhi, it decided to build its center outside the city. The Delhi National Capital Region (NCR) was still developing at that time and property prices were significantly more economical in Gurgaon as compared to Delhi. So, the firm decided to set up its main Indian headquarters in Gurgaon. But limited connectivity to this new place, coupled with poor residential facilities, proved to be a challenge for the employees of Convergys, who had to commute from Delhi to work. This led the management to announce pick-up and drop-off facilities for all its workers.

Coordinating the logistics of the pick-ups and drop-offs went well initially. But over a decade of aggressive expansions in operations, staff (now over 10,000 strong), as well as centers (with three facilities in Gurgaon, and one each in Bangalore, Thane, and Pune), Convergys had to arrange around 200 pick-ups and drops-offs every day.

In addition to the cost burden of this activity, Convergys had to deal with the challenges of managing the pick-ups and drop-offs. The transport desk manually decided on the shortest route for every ride so that employees could reach the offices in time for work. But with over 1,000 cabs sourced from 40 vendors, managing 44 different shift timings was a herculean task. Ipinder Singh, the technical director at Convergys, tried looking into some off-the-shelf software to see if they could meet his company's requirements. But even with the deployment of these software, Singh found that a lot of the tasks would have to be done manually. He finally decided to design a solution in-house.

In order to automate tasks, the processes involved with running the existing system needed to be understood. Every week, supervisors (over 100 in number) would send complete information about their team's shift timings, addresses, contact numbers, and leave status for the following week to the transport department. The team at this department sorted through the sheets they received and made a plan for the coming week. The whole process was time consuming. Once the plan was frozen, no changes could be made unless the whole plan was overhauled. This meant that in case an employee took unexpected leave, there was a problem. Moreover, if there was a change in the employee's address or phone number, or if an employee quit in the middle of a week, the pick-up vans would keep waiting for that employee, adding to the company's transportation expenses.

Singh's team of developers built an automated application that had all the parameters and metrics preloaded in the system, so that it could generate costs by department and employee. Singh integrated the transport application with the human resource information system. This helped him get updated information regarding change in address, phone number, leave, or resignation status of employees. Further, Convergys automated a lot of the transport department's manual tasks. For example, earlier, cab drivers were required to fill out a sheet after every trip, stating the distance covered. The transport department would then enter this information into Excel sheets to compute the costs for the different types of vehicles. This function is now handled almost entirely by the new application.

In spite of all these developments, one pressing issue still remained. How to find the most optimal route for each of the cabs so that the staff can reach the office on time? There are two aspects to this question. First, considering that the vendors charge on the basis of the kilometers covered by their cars, going a longer route significantly increases the costs to company. Second, late arrival of employees to work translates to losses for the firm. So, it was imperative that Singh finds a solution to the optimal route challenge as quickly as possible.

Singh decided to buy a generic routing solution with 10–12 built-in algorithms, and layered it with a digital version of the Eicher world maps.

The software was further customized by feeding in additional information about the cab capabilities, average speed on various roads, locations of employees, and so on. With all this done, the software could now select the optimum route, as well as reschedule the ride in case an employee fell sick. In doing so, Convergys was able to save 30 to 40 per cent of its transportation costs.

Convergys now also allows employees to change or cancel the status of their pick-up or drop-off through a self-service portal. This has reduced dependency on the transport helpdesk. Using this portal, employees can also get information about their routes and pick-up time without any delay or difficulty.

Sources: Roy, Debarati: "Convergys Boosts its Fleet Management", Cio.In (2012). Retrieved from http://www.cio.in/case-study/convergys-turns-course-its-fleet-management; Convergys. Retrieved from http://www.convergysindia.in/

CASE STUDY QUESTIONS

1. Why did Convergys need an information system to manage the transportation of employees?

2. What were the problems in the manual process of fleet management?

3. What was the benefit of integrating human resource data with the transportation information system?

4. Discuss the role of the routing solution and self-service portals.

how work gets organized, coordinated, and measured also changes. By connecting employees working on teams and projects, the social network is where works gets done, where plans are executed, and where managers manage. Collaboration spaces are where employees meet one another—even when they are separated by continents and time zones.

iPhone and iPad Applications for Business

1. Salesforce1
2. Cisco WebEx
3. SAP Business ByDesign
4. iWork
5. Evernote
6. Adobe Reader
7. Oracle Business Intelligence
8. Dropbox

© STANCA SANDA/Alamy.

Whether it's attending an online meeting, checking orders, working with files and documents, or obtaining business intelligence, Apple's iPhone and iPad offer unlimited possibilities for business users. A stunning multi-touch display, full Internet browsing, and capabilities for messaging, video and audio transmission, and document management, make each an all-purpose platform for mobile computing.

The strength of cloud computing and the growth of the mobile digital platform allow organizations to rely more on telework, remote work, and distributed decision making. This same platform means firms can outsource more work, and rely on markets (rather than employees) to build value. It also means that firms can collaborate with suppliers and customers to create new products, or make existing products more efficiently.

Millions of managers rely heavily on the mobile digital platform to coordinate suppliers and shipments, satisfy customers, and manage their employees. A business day without these mobile devices or Internet access would be unthinkable.

GLOBALIZATION CHALLENGES AND OPPORTUNITIES: A FLATTENED WORLD

In 1492, Columbus reaffirmed what astronomers were long saying: the world was round and the seas could be safely sailed. As it turned out, the world was populated by peoples and languages living in isolation from one another, with great disparities in economic and scientific development. The world trade that ensued after Columbus's voyages has brought these peoples and cultures closer. The "industrial revolution" was really a world-wide phenomenon energized by expansion of trade among nations and the emergence of the first global economy.

In 2005, journalist Thomas Friedman wrote an influential book declaring the world was now "flat," by which he meant that the Internet and global communications had greatly reduced the economic and cultural advantages of developed countries. Friedman argued that the U.S. and European countries were in a fight for their economic lives, competing for jobs, markets, resources, and even ideas with highly educated, motivated populations in low-wage areas in the less developed world (Friedman, 2007). This "globalization" presents both challenges and opportunities for business firms.

A growing percentage of the economy of the United States and other advanced industrial countries in Europe and Asia depends on imports and exports. In 2013, more than 33 percent of the U.S. economy resulted from foreign trade, both imports and exports. In Europe and Asia, the number exceeded 50 percent. Many Fortune 500 U.S. firms derive half their revenues from foreign operations. For instance, 85 percent of Intel's revenues in 2013 came from overseas sales of its microprocessors. Eighty percent of the toys sold in the United States are manufactured in China, while about 90 percent of the PCs manufactured in China use American-made Intel or Advanced Micro Design (AMD) chips. The microprocessor chips are shipped from the United States to China for assembly into devices. In the severe recession of 2008-2011, all the world's economies were negatively impacted.

It's not just goods that move across borders. So too do jobs, some of them high-level jobs that pay well and require a college degree. In the past decade, the United States lost several million manufacturing jobs to offshore, low-wage producers. But manufacturing is now a very small part of U.S.

employment (less than 12 percent and declining). In a normal year, about 300,000 service jobs move offshore to lower wage countries. Many of the jobs are in less-skilled information system occupations, but some are "tradable service" jobs in architecture, financial services, customer call centers, consulting, engineering, and even radiology.

On the plus side, the U.S. economy creates over 3.5 million new jobs in a normal, non-recessionary year. However, only 1.1 million private sector jobs were created due to slow recovery in 2011, but by 2014 2.5 million jobs were added. Employment in information systems and the other service occupations is expanding, and wages are stable. Outsourcing has actually accelerated the development of new systems in the United States and worldwide.

The challenge for you as a business student is to develop high-level skills through education and on-the-job experience that cannot be outsourced. The challenge for your business is to avoid markets for goods and services that can be produced offshore much less expensively. The opportunities are equally immense. Throughout this book, you will find examples of companies and individuals who either failed or succeeded in using information systems to adapt to this new global environment.

What does globalization have to do with management information systems? That's simple: everything. The emergence of the Internet into a full-blown international communications system has drastically reduced the costs of operating and transacting on a global scale. Communication between a factory floor in Shanghai and a distribution center in Rapid City, South Dakota, is now instant and virtually free. Customers can now shop in a worldwide marketplace, obtaining price and quality information reliably 24 hours a day. Firms producing goods and services on a global scale achieve extraordinary cost reductions by finding low-cost suppliers and managing production facilities in other countries. Internet service firms, such as Google and eBay, are able to replicate their business models and services in multiple countries without having to redesign their expensive fixed-cost information systems infrastructure. Half of the revenue of eBay (as well as General Motors) originates outside the United States. Briefly, information systems enable globalization.

THE EMERGING DIGITAL FIRM

All of the changes we have just described, coupled with equally significant organizational redesign, have created the conditions for a fully digital firm. A digital firm can be defined along several dimensions. A **digital firm** is one in which nearly all of the organization's *significant business relationships* with customers, suppliers, and employees are digitally enabled and mediated. *Core business processes* are accomplished through digital networks spanning the entire organization or linking multiple organizations.

Business processes refer to the set of logically related tasks and behaviors that organizations develop over time to produce specific business results and the unique manner in which these activities are organized and coordinated. Developing a new product, generating and fulfilling an order, creating a marketing plan, and hiring an employee are examples of business processes, and the ways organizations accomplish their business processes can be a source of competitive strength. (A detailed discussion of business processes can be found in Chapter 2.)

Key corporate assets—intellectual property, core competencies, and financial and human assets—are managed through digital means. In a digital firm, any piece of information required to support key business decisions is available at any time and anywhere in the firm.

Digital firms sense and respond to their environments far more rapidly than traditional firms, giving them more flexibility to survive in turbulent times. Digital firms offer extraordinary opportunities for more flexible global organization and management. In digital firms, both time shifting and space shifting are the norm. *Time shifting* refers to business being conducted continuously, 24/7, rather than in narrow "work day" time bands of 9 a.m. to 5 p.m. *Space shifting* means that work takes place in a global workshop, as well as within national boundaries. Work is accomplished physically wherever in the world it is best accomplished.

Many firms, such as Cisco Systems, 3M, and IBM, are close to becoming digital firms, using the Internet to drive every aspect of their business. Most other companies are not fully digital, but they are moving toward close digital integration with suppliers, customers, and employees.

STRATEGIC BUSINESS OBJECTIVES OF INFORMATION SYSTEMS

What makes information systems so essential today? Why are businesses investing so much in information systems and technologies? In the United States, more than 21 million managers and 154 million workers in the information and knowledge sectors in the labor force rely on information systems to conduct business. Information systems are essential for conducting day-to-day business in the United States and most other advanced countries, as well as achieving strategic business objectives.

Entire sectors of the economy are nearly inconceivable without substantial investments in information systems. E-commerce firms such as Amazon, eBay, Google, and E*Trade simply would not exist. Today's service industries—finance, insurance, and real estate, as well as personal services such as travel, medicine, and education—could not operate without information systems. Similarly, retail firms such as Walmart and Sears and manufacturing firms such as General Motors and General Electric require information systems to survive and prosper. Just as offices, telephones, filing cabinets, and efficient tall buildings with elevators were once the foundations of business in the twentieth century, information technology is a foundation for business in the twenty-first century.

There is a growing interdependence between a firm's ability to use information technology and its ability to implement corporate strategies and achieve corporate goals (see Figure 1.2). What a business would like to do in five years often depends on what its systems will be able to do. Increasing market share, becoming the high-quality or low-cost producer, developing new products, and

FIGURE 1.2 THE INTERDEPENDENCE BETWEEN ORGANIZATIONS AND INFORMATION SYSTEMS

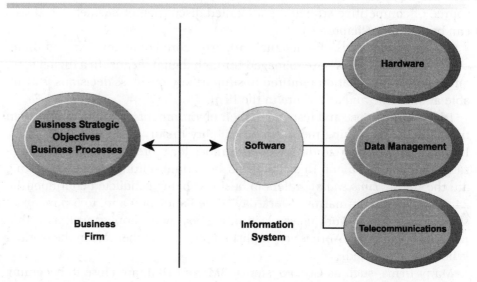

In contemporary systems, there is a growing interdependence between a firm's information systems and its business capabilities. Changes in strategy, rules, and business processes increasingly require changes in hardware, software, databases, and telecommunications. Often, what the organization would like to do depends on what its systems will permit it to do.

increasing employee productivity depend more and more on the kinds and quality of information systems in the organization. The more you understand about this relationship, the more valuable you will be as a manager.

Specifically, business firms invest heavily in information systems to achieve six strategic business objectives: operational excellence; new products, services, and business models; customer and supplier intimacy; improved decision making; competitive advantage; and survival.

Operational Excellence

Businesses continuously seek to improve the efficiency of their operations in order to achieve higher profitability. Information systems and technologies are some of the most important tools available to managers for achieving higher levels of efficiency and productivity in business operations, especially when coupled with changes in business practices and management behavior.

Walmart, the largest retailer on earth, exemplifies the power of information systems coupled with brilliant business practices and supportive management to achieve world-class operational efficiency. In fiscal year 2014, Walmart achieved $473 billion in sales—nearly one-tenth of retail sales in the United States—in large part because of its Retail Link system, which digitally links its suppliers to every one of Walmart's stores. As soon as a customer purchases an item, the supplier monitoring the item knows to ship a replacement to the shelf. Walmart is the most efficient retail store in the industry, achieving sales of more than $428 per square foot, compared to its closest competitor, Target, at $295 a square foot. Other less efficient general merchandise stores generate from $150 to $200 a square foot.

New Products, Services, and Business Models

Information systems and technologies are a major enabling tool for firms to create new products and services, as well as entirely new business models. A **business model** describes how a company produces, delivers, and sells a product or service to create wealth.

Today's music industry is vastly different from the industry a decade ago. Apple Inc. transformed an old business model of music distribution based on vinyl records, tapes, and CDs into an online, legal distribution model based on its own iPod technology platform. Apple has prospered from a continuing stream of iPod innovations, including the iTunes music service, the iPad, and the iPhone.

Customer and Supplier Intimacy

When a business really knows its customers, and serves them well, the customers generally respond by returning and purchasing more. This raises revenues and profits. Likewise with suppliers: the more a business engages its suppliers, the better the suppliers can provide vital inputs. This lowers costs. How to really know your customers, or suppliers, is a central problem for businesses with millions of offline and online customers.

The Mandarin Oriental in Manhattan and other high-end hotels exemplify the use of information systems and technologies to achieve customer intimacy. These hotels use computers to keep track of guests' preferences, such as their preferred room temperature, check-in time, frequently dialed telephone numbers, and television programs, and store these data in a large data repository. Individual rooms in the hotels are networked to a central network server computer so that they can be remotely monitored or controlled. When a customer arrives at one of these hotels, the system automatically changes the room conditions, such as dimming the lights, setting the room temperature, or selecting appropriate music, based on the customer's digital profile. The hotels also analyze their customer data to identify their best customers and to develop individualized marketing campaigns based on customers' preferences.

JCPenney exemplifies the benefits of information systems-enabled supplier intimacy. Every time a dress shirt is bought at a JCPenney store in the United States, the record of the sale appears immediately on computers in Hong Kong at the TAL Apparel Ltd. supplier, a contract manufacturer that produces one in eight dress shirts sold in the United States. TAL runs the numbers through a computer model it developed and then decides how many replacement shirts to make, and in what styles, colors, and sizes. TAL then sends the shirts to each JCPenney store, bypassing completely the retailer's warehouses. In other words, JCPenney's shirt inventory is near zero, as is the cost of storing it.

Improved Decision Making

Many business managers operate in an information fog bank, never really having the right information at the right time to make an informed decision. Instead, managers rely on forecasts, best guesses, and luck. The result is over- or underproduction of goods and services, misallocation of resources, and poor response times. These poor outcomes raise costs and lose customers. In the past decade, information systems and technologies have made it possible for managers to use real-time data from the marketplace when making decisions.

For instance, Verizon Corporation, one of the largest telecommunication companies in the United States, uses a Web-based digital dashboard to provide managers with precise real-time information on customer complaints, network performance for each locality served, and line outages or storm-damaged lines. Using this information, managers can immediately allocate repair resources to affected areas, inform consumers of repair efforts, and restore service fast.

Competitive Advantage

When firms achieve one or more of these business objectives—operational excellence; new products, services, and business models; customer/supplier intimacy; and improved decision making—chances are they have already achieved a competitive advantage. Doing things better than your competitors, charging less for superior products, and responding to customers and suppliers in real time all add up to higher sales and higher profits that your competitors cannot match. Apple Inc., Walmart, and UPS, described later in this chapter, are industry leaders because they know how to use information systems for this purpose.

Survival

Business firms also invest in information systems and technologies because they are necessities of doing business. Sometimes these "necessities" are driven by industry-level changes. For instance, after Citibank introduced the first automated teller machines (ATMs) in the New York region in 1977 to attract customers through higher service levels, its competitors rushed to provide ATMs to their customers to keep up with Citibank. Today, virtually all banks in the United States have regional ATMs and link to national and international ATM networks, such as CIRRUS. Providing ATM services to retail banking customers is simply a requirement of being in and surviving in the retail banking business.

There are many federal and state statutes and regulations that create a legal duty for companies and their employees to retain records, including digital records. For instance, the Toxic Substances Control Act (1976), which regulates the exposure of U.S. workers to more than 75,000 toxic chemicals, requires firms to retain records on employee exposure for 30 years. The Sarbanes-Oxley Act (2002), which was intended to improve the accountability of public firms and their auditors, requires certified public accounting firms that audit public companies to retain audit working papers and records, including all e-mails, for five years. The Dodd-Frank Wall Street Reform and Consumer Protection Act (2010) which was intended to strengthen regulation of the banking industry requires firms to retain all records for ten years. Many other pieces of federal and state legislation in health care, financial services, education, and privacy protection impose significant information retention and reporting requirements on U.S. businesses. Firms turn to information systems and technologies to provide the capability to respond to these challenges.

1.2 WHAT IS AN INFORMATION SYSTEM? HOW DOES IT WORK? WHAT ARE ITS MANAGEMENT, ORGANIZATION, AND TECHNOLOGY COMPONENTS AND WHY ARE COMPLEMENTARY ASSETS ESSENTIAL FOR ENSURING THAT INFORMATION SYSTEMS PROVIDE GENUINE VALUE FOR AN ORGANIZATION?

So far we've used *information systems* and *technologies* informally without defining the terms. **Information technology (IT)** consists of all the hardware and software that a firm needs to use in order to achieve its business objectives. This includes not only computer machines, storage devices, and handheld mobile devices, but also software, such as the Windows or Linux operating systems, the Microsoft Office desktop productivity suite, and the many thousands of computer programs that can be found in a typical large firm. "Information systems" are more complex and can be best understood by looking at them from both a technology and a business perspective.

WHAT IS AN INFORMATION SYSTEM?

An **information system** can be defined technically as a set of interrelated components that collect (or retrieve), process, store, and distribute information to support decision making and control in an organization. In addition to supporting decision making, coordination, and control, information systems may also help managers and workers analyze problems, visualize complex subjects, and create new products.

Information systems contain information about significant people, places, and things within the organization or in the environment surrounding it. By **information** we mean data that have been shaped into a form that is meaningful and useful to human beings. **Data**, in contrast, are streams of raw facts representing events occurring in organizations or the physical environment before they have been organized and arranged into a form that people can understand and use.

A brief example contrasting information and data may prove useful. Supermarket checkout counters scan millions of pieces of data from bar codes, which describe each product. Such pieces of data can be totaled and analyzed to provide meaningful information, such as the total number of bottles of dish detergent sold at a particular store, which brands of dish detergent were selling the most rapidly at that store or sales territory, or the total amount spent on that brand of dish detergent at that store or sales region (see Figure 1.3).

Three activities in an information system produce the information that organizations need to make decisions, control operations, analyze problems, and create new products or services. These activities are input, processing, and output (see Figure 1.4). **Input** captures or collects raw data from within the organization or from its external environment. **Processing** converts this raw input into a meaningful form. **Output** transfers the processed

FIGURE 1.3   DATA AND INFORMATION

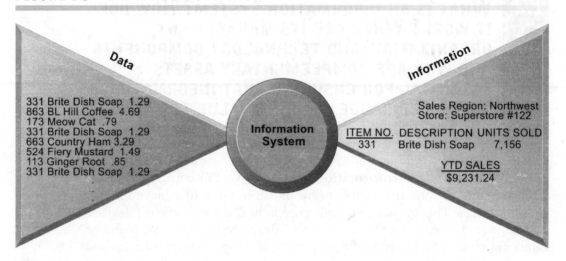

Raw data from a supermarket checkout counter can be processed and organized to produce meaningful information, such as the total unit sales of dish detergent or the total sales revenue from dish detergent for a specific store or sales territory.

FIGURE 1.4   FUNCTIONS OF AN INFORMATION SYSTEM

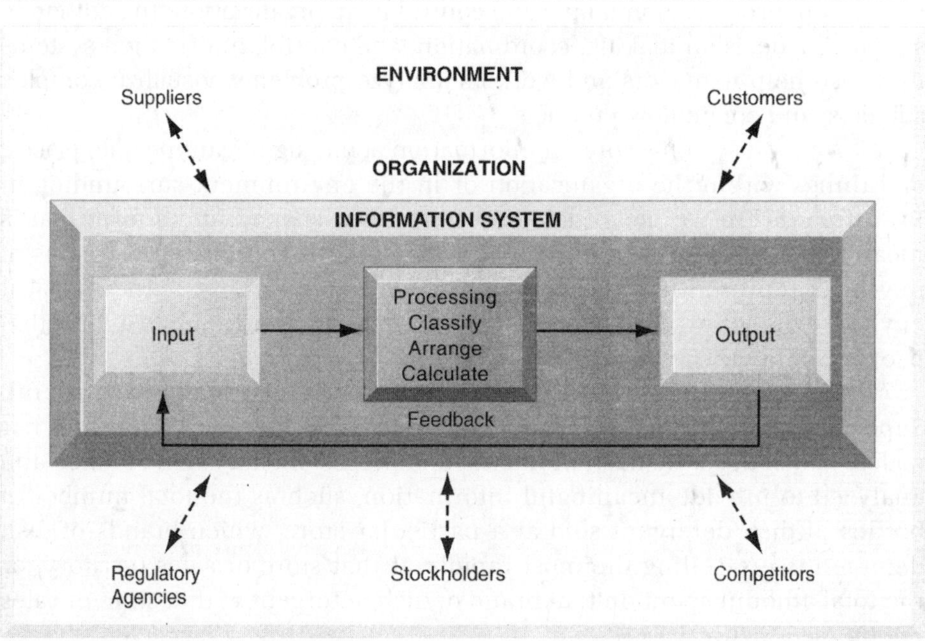

An information system contains information about an organization and its surrounding environment. Three basic activities—input, processing, and output—produce the information organizations need. Feedback is output returned to appropriate people or activities in the organization to evaluate and refine the input. Environmental actors, such as customers, suppliers, competitors, stockholders, and regulatory agencies, interact with the organization and its information systems.

information to the people who will use it or to the activities for which it will be used. Information systems also require **feedback**, which is output that is returned to appropriate members of the organization to help them evaluate or correct the input stage.

In the San Francisco Giants system for selling tickets, the raw input consists of order data for tickets, such as the purchaser's name, address, credit card number, number of tickets ordered, and the date of the game for which the ticket is being purchased. Another input would be the ticket price, which would fluctuate based on computer analysis of how much could optimally be charged for a ticket for a particular game. Computers store these data and process them to calculate order totals, to track ticket purchases, and to send requests for payment to credit card companies. The output consists of tickets to print out, receipts for orders, and reports on online ticket orders. The system provides meaningful information, such as the number of tickets sold for a particular game or at a particular price, the total number of tickets sold each year, and frequent customers.

Although computer-based information systems use computer technology to process raw data into meaningful information, there is a sharp distinction between a computer and a computer program on the one hand, and an information system on the other. Electronic computers and related software programs are the technical foundation, the tools and materials, of modern information systems. Computers provide the equipment for storing and processing information. Computer programs, or software, are sets of operating instructions that direct and control computer processing. Knowing how computers and computer programs work is important in designing solutions to organizational problems, but computers are only part of an information system.

A house is an appropriate analogy. Houses are built with hammers, nails, and wood, but these do not make a house. The architecture, design, setting, landscaping, and all of the decisions that lead to the creation of these features are part of the house and are crucial for solving the problem of putting a roof over one's head. Computers and programs are the hammers, nails, and lumber of computer-based information systems, but alone they cannot produce the information a particular organization needs. To understand information systems, you must understand the problems they are designed to solve, their architectural and design elements, and the organizational processes that lead to these solutions.

DIMENSIONS OF INFORMATION SYSTEMS

To fully understand information systems, you must understand the broader organization, management, and information technology dimensions of systems (see Figure 1.5) and their power to provide solutions to challenges and problems in the business environment. We refer to this broader understanding of information systems, which encompasses an understanding of the management and organizational dimensions of systems as well as the technical dimensions of systems, as **information systems literacy**. **Computer literacy**, in contrast, focuses primarily on knowledge of information technology.

FIGURE 1.5   INFORMATION SYSTEMS ARE MORE THAN COMPUTERS

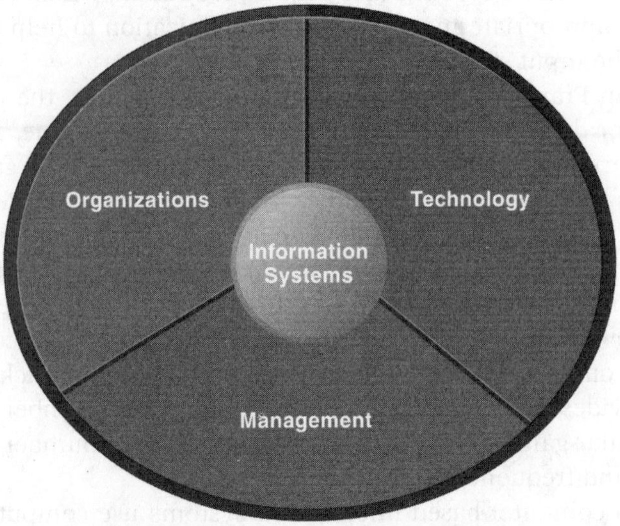

Using information systems effectively requires an understanding of the organization, management, and information technology shaping the systems. An information system creates value for the firm as an organizational and management solution to challenges posed by the environment.

The field of **management information systems (MIS)** tries to achieve this broader information systems literacy. MIS deals with behavioral issues as well as technical issues surrounding the development, use, and impact of information systems used by managers and employees in the firm.

Let's examine each of the dimensions of information systems—organizations, management, and information technology.

Organizations

Information systems are an integral part of organizations. Indeed, for some companies, such as credit reporting firms, there would be no business without an information system. The key elements of an organization are its people, structure, business processes, politics, and culture. We introduce these components of organizations here and describe them in greater detail in Chapters 2 and 3.

Organizations have a structure that is composed of different levels and specialties. Their structures reveal a clear-cut division of labor. Authority and responsibility in a business firm are organized as a hierarchy, or a pyramid structure. The upper levels of the hierarchy consist of managerial, professional, and technical employees, whereas the lower levels consist of operational personnel.

Senior management makes long-range strategic decisions about products and services as well as ensures financial performance of the firm. **Middle management** carries out the programs and plans of senior management, and **operational management** is responsible for monitoring the daily activities of the business. **Knowledge workers**, such as engineers, scientists, or architects, design products or services and create new knowledge

FIGURE 1.6 LEVELS IN A FIRM

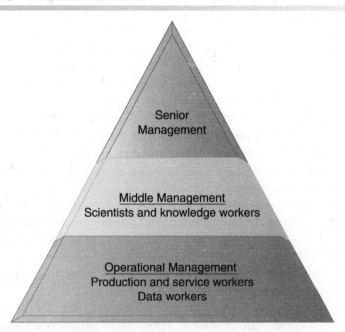

Business organizations are hierarchies consisting of three principal levels: senior management, middle management, and operational management. Information systems serve each of these levels. Scientists and knowledge workers often work with middle management.

for the firm, whereas **data workers**, such as secretaries or clerks, assist with scheduling and communications at all levels of the firm. **Production or service workers** actually produce the product and deliver the service (see Figure 1.6).

Experts are employed and trained for different business functions. The major **business functions**, or specialized tasks performed by business organizations, consist of sales and marketing, manufacturing and production, finance and accounting, and human resources (see Table 1.2). Chapter 2 provides more detail on these business functions and the ways in which they are supported by information systems.

An organization coordinates work through its hierarchy and through its **business processes**, which are logically related tasks and behaviors for

TABLE 1.2 MAJOR BUSINESS FUNCTIONS

FUNCTION	PURPOSE
Sales and marketing	Selling the organization's products and services
Manufacturing and production	Producing and delivering products and services
Finance and accounting	Managing the organization's financial assets and maintaining the organization's financial records
Human resources	Attracting, developing, and maintaining the organization's labor force; maintaining employee records

accomplishing work. Developing a new product, fulfilling an order, and hiring a new employee are examples of business processes.

Most organizations' business processes include formal rules that have been developed over a long time for accomplishing tasks. These rules guide employees in a variety of procedures, from writing an invoice to responding to customer complaints. Some of these business processes have been written down, but others are informal work practices, such as a requirement to return telephone calls from coworkers or customers, that are not formally documented. Information systems automate many business processes. For instance, how a customer receives credit or how a customer is billed is often determined by an information system that incorporates a set of formal business processes.

Each organization has a unique **culture**, or fundamental set of assumptions, values, and ways of doing things, that has been accepted by most of its members. You can see organizational culture at work by looking around your university or college. Some bedrock assumptions of university life are that professors know more than students, the reasons students attend college is to learn, and that classes follow a regular schedule.

Parts of an organization's culture can always be found embedded in its information systems. For instance, UPS's first priority is customer service, which is an aspect of its organizational culture that can be found in the company's package tracking systems, which we describe later in this section.

Different levels and specialties in an organization create different interests and points of view. These views often conflict over how the company should be run and how resources and rewards should be distributed. Conflict is the basis for organizational politics. Information systems come out of this cauldron of differing perspectives, conflicts, compromises, and agreements that are a natural part of all organizations. In Chapter 3, we examine these features of organizations and their role in the development of information systems in greater detail.

Management

Management's job is to make sense out of the many situations faced by organizations, make decisions, and formulate action plans to solve organizational problems. Managers perceive business challenges in the environment; they set the organizational strategy for responding to those challenges; and they allocate the human and financial resources to coordinate the work and achieve success. Throughout, they must exercise responsible leadership. The business information systems described in this book reflect the hopes, dreams, and realities of real-world managers.

But managers must do more than manage what already exists. They must also create new products and services and even re-create the organization from time to time. A substantial part of management responsibility is creative work driven by new knowledge and information. Information technology can play a powerful role in helping managers design and deliver new products and services and redirecting and redesigning their organizations. Chapter 12 treats management decision making in detail.

Information Technology

Information technology is one of many tools managers use to cope with change. **Computer hardware** is the physical equipment used for input, processing, and output activities in an information system. It consists of the following: computers of various sizes and shapes (including mobile handheld devices); various input, output, and storage devices; and telecommunications devices that link computers together.

Computer software consists of the detailed, preprogrammed instructions that control and coordinate the computer hardware components in an information system. Chapter 5 describes the contemporary software and hardware platforms used by firms today in greater detail.

Data management technology consists of the software governing the organization of data on physical storage media. More detail on data organization and access methods can be found in Chapter 6.

Networking and telecommunications technology, consisting of both physical devices and software, links the various pieces of hardware and transfers data from one physical location to another. Computers and communications equipment can be connected in networks for sharing voice, data, images, sound, and video. A **network** links two or more computers to share data or resources, such as a printer.

The world's largest and most widely used network is the **Internet**. The Internet is a global "network of networks" that uses universal standards (described in Chapter 7) to connect millions of different networks with nearly 3 billion users in over 230 countries around the world.

The Internet has created a new "universal" technology platform on which to build new products, services, strategies, and business models. This same technology platform has internal uses, providing the connectivity to link different systems and networks within the firm. Internal corporate networks based on Internet technology are called **intranets**. Private intranets extended to authorized users outside the organization are called **extranets**, and firms use such networks to coordinate their activities with other firms for making purchases, collaborating on design, and other interorganizational work. For most business firms today, using Internet technology is both a business necessity and a competitive advantage.

The **World Wide Web** is a service provided by the Internet that uses universally accepted standards for storing, retrieving, formatting, and displaying information in a page format on the Internet. Web pages contain text, graphics, animations, sound, and video and are linked to other Web pages. By clicking on highlighted words or buttons on a Web page, you can link to related pages to find additional information and links to other locations on the Web. The Web can serve as the foundation for new kinds of information systems such as UPS's Web-based package tracking system described in the following Interactive Session.

All of these technologies, along with the people required to run and manage them, represent resources that can be shared throughout the organization and constitute the firm's **information technology (IT) infrastructure**. The IT infrastructure provides the foundation, or *platform*, on which the firm can build its specific information systems. Each organization must carefully design and manage its IT infrastructure so that it has the set of technology services it needs for the work it wants to accomplish with information systems. Chapters 5 through 8 of this book examine each major technology component of information technology infrastructure and show how they all work together to create the technology platform for the organization.

The Interactive Session on Technology describes some of the typical technologies used in computer-based information systems today. UPS invests heavily in information systems technology to make its business more efficient and customer oriented. It uses an array of information technologies, including bar code scanning systems, wireless networks, large mainframe computers, handheld computers, the Internet, and many different pieces of software for tracking packages, calculating fees, maintaining customer accounts, and managing logistics.

Let's identify the organization, management, and technology elements in the UPS package tracking system we have just described. The organization element anchors the package tracking system in UPS's sales and production functions (the main product of UPS is a service—package delivery). It specifies the required procedures for identifying packages with both sender and recipient information, taking inventory, tracking the packages en route, and providing package status reports for UPS customers and customer service representatives.

The system must also provide information to satisfy the needs of managers and workers. UPS drivers need to be trained in both package pickup and delivery procedures and in how to use the package tracking system so that they can work efficiently and effectively. UPS customers may need some training to use UPS in-house package tracking software or the UPS Web site.

UPS's management is responsible for monitoring service levels and costs and for promoting the company's strategy of combining low cost and superior service. Management decided to use computer systems to increase the

Using a handheld computer called a Delivery Information Acquisition Device (DIAD), UPS drivers automatically capture customers' signatures along with pickup, delivery, and time card information. UPS information systems use these data to track packages while they are being transported.

© Bill Aron/PhotoEdit

INTERACTIVE SESSION: TECHNOLOGY

UPS COMPETES GLOBALLY WITH INFORMATION TECHNOLOGY

United Parcel Service (UPS) started out in 1907 in a closet-sized basement office. Jim Casey and Claude Ryan—two teenagers from Seattle with two bicycles and one phone—promised the "best service and lowest rates." UPS has used this formula successfully for more than a century to become the world's largest ground and air package-delivery company. It's a global enterprise with nearly 400,000 employees, 96,000 vehicles, and the world's ninth largest airline.

Today UPS delivers 16.3 million packages and documents each day in the United States and more than 220 other countries and territories. The firm has been able to maintain leadership in small-package delivery services despite stiff competition from FedEx and Airborne Express by investing heavily in advanced information technology. UPS spends more than $1 billion each year to maintain a high level of customer service while keeping costs low and streamlining its overall operations.

It all starts with the scannable bar-coded label attached to a package, which contains detailed information about the sender, the destination, and when the package should arrive. Customers can download and print their own labels using special software provided by UPS or by accessing the UPS Web site. Before the package is even picked up, information from the "smart" label is transmitted to one of UPS's computer centers in Mahwah, New Jersey, or Alpharetta, Georgia and sent to the distribution center nearest its final destination.

Dispatchers at this center download the label data and use special software to create the most efficient delivery route for each driver that considers traffic, weather conditions, and the location of each stop. In 2009, UPS began installing sensors in its delivery vehicles that can capture the truck's speed and location, the number of times it's placed in reverse and whether the driver's seat belt is buckled. At the end of each day, these data are uploaded to a UPS central computer and analyzed. By combining GPS information and data from fuel-efficiency sensors installed on more than 46,000 vehicles in

2011, UPS reduced fuel consumption by 8.4 million gallons and cut 85 million miles off its routes. UPS estimates that saving only one daily mile driven per driver saves the company $30 million.

The first thing a UPS driver picks up each day is a handheld computer called a Delivery Information Acquisition Device (DIAD), which can access a wireless cell phone network. As soon as the driver logs on, his or her day's route is downloaded onto the handheld. The DIAD also automatically captures customers' signatures along with pickup and delivery information. Package tracking information is then transmitted to UPS's computer network for storage and processing. From there, the information can be accessed worldwide to provide proof of delivery to customers or to respond to customer queries. It usually takes less than 60 seconds from the time a driver presses "complete" on a the DIAD for the new information to be available on the Web.

Through its automated package tracking system, UPS can monitor and even re-route packages throughout the delivery process. At various points along the route from sender to receiver, bar code devices scan shipping information on the package label and feed data about the progress of the package into the central computer. Customer service representatives are able to check the status of any package from desktop computers linked to the central computers and respond immediately to inquiries from customers. UPS customers can also access this information from the company's Web site using their own computers or mobile phones. UPS now has mobile apps and a mobile Web site for iPhone, BlackBerry, and Android smartphone users.

Anyone with a package to ship can access the UPS Web site to track packages, check delivery routes, calculate shipping rates, determine time in transit, print labels, and schedule a pickup. The data collected at the UPS Web site are transmitted to the UPS central computer and then back to the customer after processing. UPS also provides tools that enable customers, such Cisco Systems, to embed UPS functions, such as tracking and cost calculations, into their own Web sites so that they can track shipments without visiting the UPS site.

A Web-based Post Sales Order Management System (OMS) manages global service orders and inventory for critical parts fulfillment. The system enables high-tech electronics, aerospace, medical equipment, and other companies anywhere in the world that ship critical parts to quickly assess their critical parts inventory, determine the most optimal routing strategy to meet customer needs, place orders online, and track parts from the warehouse to the end user. An automated e-mail or fax feature keeps customers informed of each shipping milestone and can provide notification of any changes to flight schedules for commercial airlines carrying their parts.

UPS is now leveraging its decades of expertise managing its own global delivery network to manage logistics and supply chain activities for other companies. It created a UPS Supply Chain Solutions division that provides a complete bundle of standardized services to subscribing companies at a fraction of what it would cost to build their own systems and infrastructure. These services include supply-chain design and management, freight forwarding, customs brokerage, mail services, multimodal transportation, and financial services, in addition to logistics services.

For example, UPS handles logistics for Lighting Science Group, the world's leading maker of advanced light products such as energy-efficient light-emitting diode (LED) lamps and custom design lighting systems. The company has manufacturing operations in Satellite Beach, Florida and China. UPS conducted a warehouse/distribution analysis to shape the manufacturer's distribution strategy, in which finished goods from China are brought to a UPS warehouse in Fort Worth, Texas, for distribution. The UPS warehouse repackages finished goods,

handles returns and conducts daily cycle counts as well as annual inventory. Lighting Science uses UPS Trade Management Services and UPS Customs Brokerage to help manage import and export compliance to ensure timely, reliable delivery and reduce customs delays. UPS also helps Lighting Science reduce customer inventory and improve order fulfillment.

UPS manages logistics and international shipping for Celaris, the world's largest wireless accessory vendor, selling mobile phone cases, headphones, screen protectors, and chargers. Cellaris has nearly 1,000 franchises in the United States, Canada and the United Kingdom. The company's supply chain is complex, with products developed in Georgia, manufactured at more than 25 locations in Asia and 10 locations in the U.S., warehoused in a Georgia distribution center, and shipped to franchisees and customers worldwide. UPS redesigned Celaris's inbound/outbound supply chain and introduced new services to create a more efficient shipping model. UPS Buyer Consolidation for International Air Freight reduces complexity in dealing with multiple international manufacturing sources. UPS Worldwide Express Freight guarantees on-time service for critical freight pallet shipments and UPS Customs Brokerage enables single-source clearance for multiple transportation modes. These changes have saved Celaris more than 5,000 hours and $500,000 annually, and the supply chain redesign alone has saved more than 15 percent on shipments.

Sources: "A Good Call Becomes a Thriving Business," UPS Compass, February 2014;"High-Tech Manufacturer Masters Logistics, UPS Compass, January 2014; www.ups.com, accessed April 17, 2014; Steve Rosenbush and Michael Totty, "How Big Data Is Transforming Business," *The Wall Street Journal*, March 10, 2013; Thomas H. Davenport, "Analytics That Tell You What to Do," *The Wall Street Journal*, April 3, 2013; Elana Varon, "How UPS Trains Front-Line Workers to Use Predictive Analytics," DataInformed, January 31, 2013; and Jennifer Levitz and Timothy W. Martin, "UPS, Other Big Shippers, Carve Health Care Niches," *The Wall Street Journal*, June 27, 2012.

CASE STUDY QUESTIONS

1. What are the inputs, processing, and outputs of UPS's package tracking system?

2. What technologies are used by UPS? How are these technologies related to UPS's business strategy?

3. What strategic business objectives do UPS's information systems address?

4. What would happen if UPS's information systems were not available?

ease of sending a package using UPS and of checking its delivery status, thereby reducing delivery costs and increasing sales revenues.

The technology supporting this system consists of handheld computers, bar code scanners, desktop computers, wired and wireless communications networks, UPS's data center, storage technology for the package delivery data, UPS in-house package tracking software, and software to access the World Wide Web. The result is an information system solution to the business challenge of providing a high level of service with low prices in the face of mounting competition.

IT ISN'T JUST TECHNOLOGY: A BUSINESS PERSPECTIVE ON INFORMATION SYSTEMS

Managers and business firms invest in information technology and systems because they provide real economic value to the business. The decision to build or maintain an information system assumes that the returns on this investment will be superior to other investments in buildings, machines, or other assets. These superior returns will be expressed as increases in productivity, as increases in revenues (which will increase the firm's stock market value), or perhaps as superior long-term strategic positioning of the firm in certain markets (which produce superior revenues in the future).

We can see that from a business perspective, an information system is an important instrument for creating value for the firm. Information systems enable the firm to increase its revenue or decrease its costs by providing information that helps managers make better decisions or that improves the execution of business processes. For example, the information system for analyzing supermarket checkout data illustrated in Figure 1.3 can increase firm profitability by helping managers make better decisions as to which products to stock and promote in retail supermarkets.

Every business has an information value chain, illustrated in Figure 1.7, in which raw information is systematically acquired and then transformed through various stages that add value to that information. The value of an information system to a business, as well as the decision to invest in any new information system, is, in large part, determined by the extent to which the system will lead to better management decisions, more efficient business processes, and higher firm profitability. Although there are other reasons why systems are built, their primary purpose is to contribute to corporate value.

From a business perspective, information systems are part of a series of value-adding activities for acquiring, transforming, and distributing information that managers can use to improve decision making, enhance organizational performance, and, ultimately, increase firm profitability.

The business perspective calls attention to the organizational and managerial nature of information systems. An information system represents an organizational and management solution, based on information technology, to a challenge or problem posed by the environment. Every chapter in this book begins with a short case study that illustrates this concept. A diagram at the beginning of each chapter illustrates the relationship between a business challenge and resulting management and organizational decisions

FIGURE 1.7   THE BUSINESS INFORMATION VALUE CHAIN

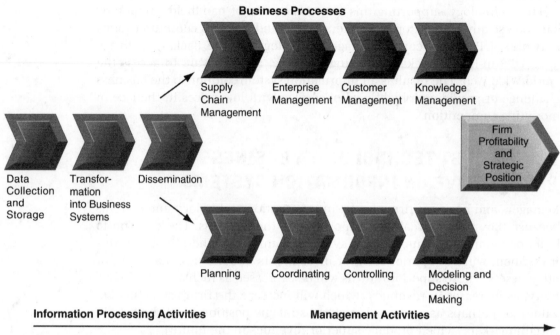

From a business perspective, information systems are part of a series of value-adding activities for acquiring, transforming, and distributing information that managers can use to improve decision making, enhance organizational performance, and, ultimately, increase firm profitability.

to use IT as a solution to challenges generated by the business environment. You can use this diagram as a starting point for analyzing any information system or information system problem you encounter.

Review the diagram at the beginning of this chapter. The diagram shows how the San Francisco Giants' systems solved the business problem presented by the need to generate revenue in a highly competitive industry. These systems provide a solution that takes advantage of opportunities provided by new digital technology and the Internet. They opened up new channels for selling tickets and interacting with customers, optimized ticket pricing, and used new tools to analyze player performance. These systems were essential in improving the Giants's overall business performance. The diagram also illustrates how management, technology, and organizational elements work together to create the systems.

COMPLEMENTARY ASSETS: ORGANIZATIONAL CAPITAL AND THE RIGHT BUSINESS MODEL

Awareness of the organizational and managerial dimensions of information systems can help us understand why some firms achieve better results from their information systems than others. Studies of returns from information

FIGURE 1.8   VARIATION IN RETURNS ON INFORMATION TECHNOLOGY
INVESTMENT

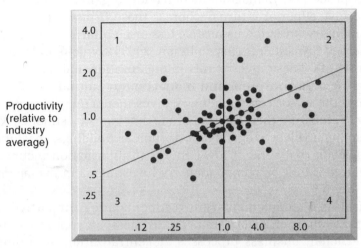

IT Capital Stock (relative to industry average)

Although, on average, investments in information technology produce returns far above those
returned by other investments, there is considerable variation across firms.

Source: Based on Brynjolfsson and Hitt (2000).

technology investments show that there is considerable variation in the
returns firms receive (see Figure 1.8). Some firms invest a great deal and
receive a great deal (quadrant 2); others invest an equal amount and receive
few returns (quadrant 4). Still other firms invest little and receive much
(quadrant 1), whereas others invest little and receive little (quadrant 3).
This suggests that investing in information technology does not by itself
guarantee good returns. What accounts for this variation among firms?

The answer lies in the concept of complementary assets. Information
technology investments alone cannot make organizations and managers
more effective unless they are accompanied by supportive values, structures,
and behavior patterns in the organization and other complementary assets.
Business firms need to change how they do business before they can really
reap the advantages of new information technologies.

Some firms fail to adopt the right business model that suits the new
technology, or seek to preserve an old business model that is doomed by new
technology. For instance, recording label companies refused to change their
old business model, which was based on physical music stores for distribution rather than adopt a new online distribution model. As a result, online
legal music sales are dominated not by record companies but by a technology company called Apple Computer.

Complementary assets are those assets required to derive value from
a primary investment (Teece, 1988). For instance, to realize value from
automobiles requires substantial complementary investments in highways,
roads, gasoline stations, repair facilities, and a legal regulatory structure to
set standards and control drivers.

Research indicates that firms that support their technology investments with investments in complementary assets, such as new business models, new business processes, management behavior, organizational culture, or training, receive superior returns, whereas those firms failing to make these complementary investments receive less or no returns on their information technology investments (Brynjolfsson, 2003; Brynjolfsson and Hitt, 2000; Laudon, 1974). These investments in organization and management are also known as **organizational and management capital**.

Table 1.3 lists the major complementary investments that firms need to make to realize value from their information technology investments. Some of this investment involves tangible assets, such as buildings, machinery, and tools. However, the value of investments in information technology depends to a large extent on complementary investments in management and organization.

Key organizational complementary investments are a supportive business culture that values efficiency and effectiveness, an appropriate business model, efficient business processes, decentralization of authority, highly distributed decision rights, and a strong information system (IS) development team.

Important managerial complementary assets are strong senior management support for change, incentive systems that monitor and reward individual innovation, an emphasis on teamwork and collaboration, training programs, and a management culture that values flexibility and knowledge.

Important social investments (not made by the firm but by the society at large, other firms, governments, and other key market actors) are the Internet

TABLE 1.3 COMPLEMENTARY SOCIAL, MANAGERIAL, AND ORGANIZATIONAL ASSETS REQUIRED TO OPTIMIZE RETURNS FROM INFORMATION TECHNOLOGY INVESTMENTS

Organizational assets	Supportive organizational culture that values efficiency and effectiveness
	Appropriate business model
	Efficient business processes
	Decentralized authority
	Distributed decision-making rights
	Strong IS development team
Managerial assets	Strong senior management support for technology investment and change
	Incentives for management innovation
	Teamwork and collaborative work environments
	Training programs to enhance management decision skills
	Management culture that values flexibility and knowledge-based decision making.
Social assets	The Internet and telecommunications infrastructure
	IT-enriched educational programs raising labor force computer literacy
	Standards (both government and private sector)
	Laws and regulations creating fair, stable market environments
	Technology and service firms in adjacent markets to assist implementation

and the supporting Internet culture, educational systems, network and computing standards, regulations and laws, and the presence of technology and service firms.

Throughout the book we emphasize a framework of analysis that considers technology, management, and organizational assets and their interactions. Perhaps the single most important theme in the book, reflected in case studies and exercises, is that managers need to consider the broader organization and management dimensions of information systems to understand current problems as well as to derive substantial above-average returns from their information technology investments. As you will see throughout the text, firms that can address these related dimensions of the IT investment are, on average, richly rewarded.

1.3 WHAT ACADEMIC DISCIPLINES ARE USED TO STUDY INFORMATION SYSTEMS AND HOW DOES EACH CONTRIBUTE TO AN UNDERSTANDING OF INFORMATION SYSTEMS?

The study of information systems is a multidisciplinary field. No single theory or perspective dominates. Figure 1.9 illustrates the major disciplines that contribute problems, issues, and solutions in the study of information systems. In general, the field can be divided into technical and behavioral approaches.

FIGURE 1.9   CONTEMPORARY APPROACHES TO INFORMATION SYSTEMS

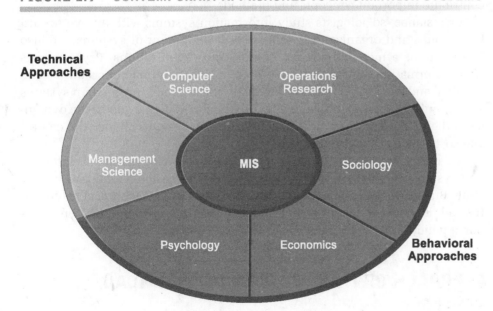

The study of information systems deals with issues and insights contributed from technical and behavioral disciplines.

Information systems are sociotechnical systems. Though they are composed of machines, devices, and "hard" physical technology, they require substantial social, organizational, and intellectual investments to make them work properly.

TECHNICAL APPROACH

The technical approach to information systems emphasizes mathematically based models to study information systems, as well as the physical technology and formal capabilities of these systems. The disciplines that contribute to the technical approach are computer science, management science, and operations research.

Computer science is concerned with establishing theories of computability, methods of computation, and methods of efficient data storage and access. Management science emphasizes the development of models for decision-making and management practices. Operations research focuses on mathematical techniques for optimizing selected parameters of organizations, such as transportation, inventory control, and transaction costs.

BEHAVIORAL APPROACH

An important part of the information systems field is concerned with behavioral issues that arise in the development and long-term maintenance of information systems. Issues such as strategic business integration, design, implementation, utilization, and management cannot be explored usefully with the models used in the technical approach. Other behavioral disciplines contribute important concepts and methods.

For instance, sociologists study information systems with an eye toward how groups and organizations shape the development of systems and also how systems affect individuals, groups, and organizations. Psychologists study information systems with an interest in how human decision makers perceive and use formal information. Economists study information systems with an interest in understanding the production of digital goods, the dynamics of digital markets, and how new information systems change the control and cost structures within the firm.

The behavioral approach does not ignore technology. Indeed, information systems technology is often the stimulus for a behavioral problem or issue. But the focus of this approach is generally not on technical solutions. Instead, it concentrates on changes in attitudes, management and organizational policy, and behavior.

APPROACH OF THIS TEXT: SOCIOTECHNICAL SYSTEMS

Throughout this book you will find a rich story with four main actors: suppliers of hardware and software (the technologists); business firms making investments and seeking to obtain value from the technology; managers and employees seeking to achieve business value (and other goals); and the contemporary legal, social, and cultural context (the firm's environment). Together these actors produce what we call *management information systems*.

The study of management information systems (MIS) arose to focus on the use of computer-based information systems in business firms and government agencies. MIS combines the work of computer science, management science, and operations research with a practical orientation toward developing system solutions to real-world problems and managing information technology resources. It is also concerned with behavioral issues surrounding the development, use, and impact of information systems, which are typically discussed in the fields of sociology, economics, and psychology.

Our experience as academics and practitioners leads us to believe that no single approach effectively captures the reality of information systems. The successes and failures of information are rarely all technical or all behavioral. Our best advice to students is to understand the perspectives of many disciplines. Indeed, the challenge and excitement of the information systems field is that it requires an appreciation and tolerance of many different approaches.

The view we adopt in this book is best characterized as the **sociotechnical view** of systems. In this view, optimal organizational performance is achieved by jointly optimizing both the social and technical systems used in production.

Adopting a sociotechnical systems perspective helps to avoid a purely technological approach to information systems. For instance, the fact that information technology is rapidly declining in cost and growing in power does not necessarily or easily translate into productivity enhancement or bottom-line profits. The fact that a firm has recently installed an enterprise-wide financial reporting system does not necessarily mean that it will be used, or used effectively. Likewise, the fact that a firm has recently introduced new business procedures and processes does not necessarily mean employees will be more productive in the absence of investments in new information systems to enable those processes.

In this book, we stress the need to optimize the firm's performance as a whole. Both the technical and behavioral components need attention. This means that technology must be changed and designed in such a way as to fit organizational and individual needs. Sometimes, the technology may have to be "de-optimized" to accomplish this fit. For instance, mobile phone users adapt this technology to their personal needs, and as a result manufacturers quickly seek to adjust the technology to conform with user expectations. Organizations and individuals must also be changed through training, learning, and planned organizational change to allow the technology to operate and prosper. Figure 1.10 illustrates this process of mutual adjustment in a sociotechnical system.

FIGURE 1.10 A SOCIOTECHNICAL PERSPECTIVE ON INFORMATION SYSTEMS

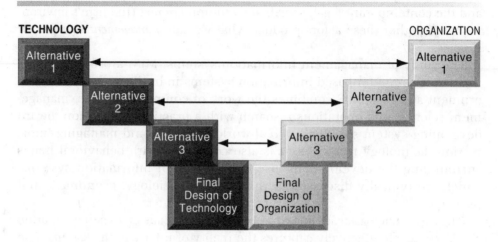

In a sociotechnical perspective, the performance of a system is optimized when both the technology and the organization mutually adjust to one another until a satisfactory fit is obtained.

Review Summary

1. *How are information systems transforming business, and why are they essential for running and managing a business today?*

   E-mail, online conferencing, smartphones, and tablet computers have become essential tools for conducting business. Information systems are the foundation of fast-paced supply chains. The Internet allows many businesses to buy, sell, advertise, and solicit customer feedback online. Organizations are trying to become more competitive and efficient by digitally enabling their core business processes and evolving into digital firms. The Internet has stimulated globalization by dramatically reducing the costs of producing, buying, and selling goods on a global scale. New information system trends include the emerging mobile digital platform, online software as a service, and cloud computing.

   Information systems are a foundation for conducting business today. In many industries, survival and the ability to achieve strategic business goals are difficult without extensive use of information technology. Businesses today use information systems to achieve six major objectives: operational excellence; new products, services, and business models; customer/supplier intimacy; improved decision making; competitive advantage; and day-to-day survival.

2. *What is an information system? How does it work? What are its management, organization, and technology components and why are complementary assets essential for ensuring that information systems provide genuine value for organizations?*

   From a technical perspective, an information system collects, stores, and disseminates information from an organization's environment and internal operations to support organizational functions and decision making, communication, coordination, control, analysis, and visualization. Information systems transform raw data into useful information through three basic activities: input, processing, and output.

From a business perspective, an information system provides a solution to a problem or challenge facing a firm and represents a combination of management, organization, and technology elements. The management dimension of information systems involves issues such as leadership, strategy, and management behavior. The technology dimension consists of computer hardware, software, data management technology, and networking/telecommunications technology (including the Internet). The organization dimension of information systems involves issues such as the organization's hierarchy, functional specialties, business processes, culture, and political interest groups.

In order to obtain meaningful value from information systems, organizations must support their technology investments with appropriate complementary investments in organizations and management. These complementary assets include new business models and business processes, supportive organizational culture and management behavior, appropriate technology standards, regulations, and laws. New information technology investments are unlikely to produce high returns unless businesses make the appropriate managerial and organizational changes to support the technology.

3. *What academic disciplines are used to study information systems and how does each contribute to an understanding of information systems?*

The study of information systems deals with issues and insights contributed from technical and behavioral disciplines. The disciplines that contribute to the technical approach focusing on formal models and capabilities of systems are computer science, management science, and operations research. The disciplines contributing to the behavioral approach focusing on the design, implementation, management, and business impact of systems are psychology, sociology, and economics. A sociotechnical view of systems considers both technical and social features of systems and solutions that represent the best fit between them.

Key Terms

Business functions, 21
Business model, 15
Business processes, 21
Complementary assets, 29
Computer hardware, 23
Computer literacy, 19
Computer software, 23
Culture, 22
Data, 17
Data management technology, 23
Data workers, 21
Digital firm, 12
Extranets, 23
Feedback, 18
Information, 17
Information system, 17
Information systems literacy, 19
Information technology (IT), 17

Information technology (IT) infrastructure, 23
Input, 17
Internet, 23
Intranets, 23
Knowledge workers, 20
Management information systems (MIS), 20
Middle management, 20
Network, 23
Networking and telecommunications technology, 23
Operational management, 20
Organizational and management capital, 30
Output, 17
Processing, 17
Production or service workers, 21
Senior management, 20
Sociotechnical view, 33
World Wide Web, 23

Review Questions

1-1 How are information systems transforming business, and why are they so essential for running and managing a business today?

- Describe how information systems have changed the way businesses operate and their products and services.
- Identify three major new information system trends.
- Describe the characteristics of a digital firm.
- Describe the challenges and opportunities of globalization in a "flattened" world.
- List and describe six reasons why information systems are so important for business today.

1-2 What is an information system? How does it work? What are its management, organization, and technology components and why are complementary assets essential for ensuring that information systems provide genuine value for organizations?

- Define an information system and describe the activities it performs.
- List and describe the organizational, management, and technology dimensions of information systems.

- Distinguish between data and information and between information systems literacy and computer literacy.
- Explain how the Internet and the World Wide Web are related to the other technology components of information systems.
- Define complementary assets and describe their relationship to information technology.
- Describe the complementary social, managerial, and organizational assets required to optimize returns from information technology investments.

1-3 What academic disciplines are used to study information systems and how does each contribute to an understanding of information systems?

- List and describe each discipline that contributes to a technical approach to information systems.
- List and describe each discipline that contributes to a behavioral approach to information systems.
- Describe the sociotechnical perspective on information systems.

Discussion Questions

1-4 Information systems are too important to be left to computer specialists. Do you agree? Why or why not?

1-5 If you were setting up the Web site for another Major League Baseball team, what

management, organization, and technology issues might you encounter?

1-6 What are some of the organizational, managerial, and social complementary assets that help make UPS's information systems so successful?

Hands-On MIS Projects

The projects in this section give you hands-on experience in analyzing financial reporting and inventory management problems, using data management software to improve management decision making about increasing sales, and using Internet software for researching job requirements.

Management Decision Problems

1-7   Snyders of Hanover, which sells about 80 million bags of pretzels, snack chips, and organic snack items each year, had its financial department use spreadsheets and manual processes for much of its data gathering and reporting. Hanover's financial analyst would spend the entire final week of every month collecting spreadsheets from the heads of more than 50 departments worldwide. She would then consolidate and re-enter all the data into another spreadsheet, which would serve as the company's monthly profit-and-loss statement. If a department needed to update its data after submitting the spreadsheet to the main office, the analyst had to return the original spreadsheet, then wait for the department to re-submit its data before finally submitting the updated data in the consolidated document. Assess the impact of this situation on business performance and management decision making.

1-8   Dollar General Corporation operates deep-discount stores offering housewares, cleaning supplies, clothing, health and beauty aids, and packaged food, with most items selling for $1. Its business model calls for keeping costs as low as possible. The company has no automated method for keeping track of inventory at each store. Managers know approximately how many cases of a particular product the store is supposed to receive when a delivery truck arrives, but the stores lack technology for scanning the cases or verifying the item count inside the cases. Merchandise losses from theft or other mishaps have been rising and now represent over 3 percent of total sales. What decisions have to be made before investing in an information system solution?

Improving Decision Making: Using the Internet to Locate Jobs Requiring Information Systems Knowledge

Software skills: Internet-based software
Business skills: Job searching

1-9   Visit a job-posting Web site such as Monster.com. Spend some time at the site examining jobs for accounting, finance, sales, marketing, and human resources. Find two or three descriptions of jobs that require some information systems knowledge. What information systems knowledge do these jobs require? What do you need to do to prepare for these jobs? Write a one- to two-page report summarizing your findings.

The Domino's PULSE™ System: Reading the Pulse of the Customer
CASE STUDY

Domino's is an international pizza-delivery franchise, headquartered in Ann Arbour in the United States. Founded in 1960, Domino's Pizza has more than 10,000 corporate and franchise stores in 70 countries across the world. Domino's was sold to Bain Capital in 1998 and went public in 2004. The company started operations in India in 1996. It subsequently changed its name to Jubiliant FoodWorks Limited in 2009. Due to the sluggish growth of the U.S. economy, the company started spreading its operations aggressively to other nations. More than half of Domino's revenues come from its overseas businesses. It sells more pizzas in India than anywhere else outside the U.S. With four lakh pizzas every day, and more than 12 crore pizzas every year, Domino's sells nearly twice the number of burgers McDonald's sells in India.

Owing to an aggressive expansion of operations and growing order counts from customers, the information system employed by Domino's plays an important role in increasing the operating efficiencies of the pizza chain. It provides the management with accurate information at any given point of time. Right from the time a customer places an order to when the management wants to track sales, the information system supplies the data in real time.

Domino's PULSE™ point-of-sale (PoS) system is a graphical user-interface and touch-screen based computerized information system that manages ordering, inventory, and reporting at Domino's Pizza. It has been implemented in over 50% of the international stores. More than one-third of the stores' orders originate from online sources; so to efficiently manage orders, the firm decided to roll out its new PoS system at all its domestic stores.

The PULSE™ user-interface is kept simple: it gives information about menu, functions, and customers. A Domino's employee selects a menu item (based on the customer's choice) from a list of available items appearing as tabs on the screen. When a customer orders or calls Domino's for a pizza, the representative enquires about some basic information of the customer (such as their name and contact number and the address they are calling from), which serves as a primary input for processing the order. For returning callers, the contact number is used to identify the customer and retrieve their account details. Whenever Domino's receives a call, the customer's number flashes on the screen. Since all previous orders are saved in PULSE™, the representative knows whether the call is from a new or existing customer. The employee makes suggestions to the customer based on their order history.

Once an order is placed, be it via phone, online, or at the counter, it automatically gets transferred into a centralized computer and the main servers. This enables the management to plan their operations effectively. When a manager sees that a particular customer has not ordered for some time, he or she personally calls the customer with a special offer to encourage them to come back.

Domino's has also successfully deployed Voice over IP (VoIP). Using this facility, the pizza chain has been able to allocate a particular number to a specific region or geographic area. When a customer calls the pizza chain, VoIP automatically detects the location of the caller and intelligently routes the call to their nearest store location. This way, the customer does not need to memorize more than one number for different store locations. For the firm too, this system eliminates the need to maintain multiple analog lines for each number, thereby saving costs. Since VoIP transmits voice calls over the Internet by converting voice into packet data, there is a significant reduction in telecommunication expenses for the company.

Additionally Domino's maintains hosting agents or virtual call centers along with its VoIP services. When the incoming load at the store is at its peak, such as during weekends or holidays, the calls are routed to these agents who professionally take orders and transmit them to the nearest pizza chain, where they are processed and delivered.

Domino's PULSE™ even manages the refund process in case a customer is not satisfied with the product, the wrong order is delivered, or the delivery is not made within the stipulated time.

Considering the volume of orders received by Domino's, a back-up server has been installed at each store to increase the speed of processing of the orders. The operating system has also been upgraded from Windows XP to Windows Server 2008 R2, which has a Hyper-V virtualization technology built into it. This has not only increased the performance of the PoS system, but also lowered the IT costs.

To provide additional comfort to its online customers, Domino's Pizza launched a new initiative: a mobile phone application for both Android and iOS devices. This application allows the user to browse through all products on the menu and also access their promotional coupons. Besides this, the app lets the consumer design their own pizza. The interface of the app is user-friendly—it displays the order at the top of the screen while the user is navigating through other content. The payment and delivery options can also be selected by the user. The app fetches the account details whenever the user logs into the application. The success of this app is also due to the fact that Domino's focuses strongly on SMS marketing. The user who receives a lucrative offer via SMS now does not have to call or visit the Domino's website to redeem it. The user can redeem the offer by ordering using the mobile app.

Due its large presence over multiple geographical areas, internal communication among the employees within the chain was a key challenge for Domino's. The solution to this was provided by eConnect, a sub-system within PULSE™. Through eConnect, a branch manager can contact any of the other branches or even the headquarters. For evaluating the performance of the stores, managers can generate reports from PULSE™. Each store prepares a monthly report using this system, which helps determine the consolidated performance of the store. Some of the items which the report contains are:

- Net sales of the present month, net sales for this month last year, net sales of the last month, and expected sales

- Growth rate and achievement over budget for the month
- Orders delivered

These reports help compare the past sales for different months with the current month. This can be used to make future projections and check the growth or decline in sales for each branch. These reports are then forwarded to the senior management with the help of the 'push' facility within PULSE™. In a similar manner, any data can be accessed from the information system using the 'pull' feature. Reports of daily services, inventory, and even the guidelines from superiors are issued via the push–pull feature.

No firm can run without having an efficient evaluation and tracking system in place. In order to keep an eye on the sales of a Domino's store, its manager analyzes the store sales every week. The manager assesses the order frequencies and also identifies the areas from where new orders are coming. On the basis of the data collected, the manager divides the areas into three main sectors discussed below:

1. **Yellow:** The localities from where new customers have started ordering pizzas are categorized as yellow. These are 5 to 10% of total orders. In order to encourage these customers to order more frequently, the manager initiates distribution of pamphlets in these localities, that contain a few of the basic, inexpensive pizzas from Domino's.
2. **Green:** The localities from where the orders are coming at a steady rate are categorized as green. These are 10% to 30% of the total orders. In order to increase the orders in this segment, the manager orders distribution of pamphlets containing medium-range pizzas.
3. **Red:** The localities from where the store receives the maximum orders are categorized as red. These are 60% of the total orders. The order frequency in this segment is higher than that of any other area, and so the manager orders distribution of pamphlets containing the store's specialized range of pizzas. The most costly items are promoted in these areas.

PULSE™ also aids in inventory management. The details of the inventory at each branch are regularly prepared in a worksheet. Each item of raw material which is used to make the finished products is described in this sheet. The used quantity of each item is compared against available quantity and ideal usage. Then variance is calculated to identify whether products are being optimally utilized. This helps conduct wastage analysis at each branch, and the reports are then collated at the head office to see the comparative wastage at different branches.

These are some of the ways in which the information system at Domino's Pizza has been able to provide a competitive edge to the chain. It has ensured real-time data processing, efficient communication, consistent reporting for decision making, and effective management of store operations. In a nutshell, it has guaranteed customer satisfaction.

Sources: Domino's PULSE™ point-of-sale system" (2009). Retrieved from http://www.wikinvest.com/stock/ Domino's_Pizza_(DPZ)/Dominos_Pulse_Point-of-sale_System; "Nortel Enables Advanced Communications for Smaller Companies, Branch Offices; Domino's Pizza, Others Lower Costs, Improve Customer Service with Nortel BCM 50.",, The Free Library (2014). Retrieved from http://www.the-freelibrary.comNortel + Enables + Advanced + Communications + for + Smaller + Companies, + Branch...-a0132342682; "Domino's Pizza and Breakaway rollout new Pulse POS system" (2003). Retrieved from http://www.pizzamarketplace. com/article/112033/Domino-s-Pizza-and-Breakaway-rollout-new-Pulse-POS-system; Phi, Hoang, "Domino's Pizza tailoring to local tastes", The Saigon Times (2012). Retrieved from http://english.thesaigontimes.vn/Home/interviews/busi-nesstalk/26936/; "Domino's Pizza and Breakaway Complete Corporate Rollout of New POS System" (2003). Retrieved from http://www.prnewswire.com/news-releases/dominos-pizza-and-breakaway-complete-corporate-rollout-of-new-pos-system-74186392.html; Alfs, Lizzy, "What's next for Domino's Pizza? CEO Patrick Doyle outlines some goals", The Ann Arbor News (2013). Retrieved from http://www.annarbor. com/business-review/whats-next-for-dominos-pizza-ceo-patrick-doyle-outlines-some-goals/; "Domino's Android App". Retrieved from http://www.dominospizza.co.nz/corporate/ android-app; "Dominos Pizza, Inc.'s Annual Report Persuant to Section 13 or 15(d) of the Securities Exchange Act of 1934", United States Securities and Exchange Commission (2013). Retrieved from http://www.sec.gov/Archives/ edgar/data/1286681/000119312513081957/d466015d10k.htm; Bhushan, Ratna,"India emerges as Domino's biggest market outside US", The Economic Times (2014). Retrieved from http://articles.economictimes.indiatimes.com/2014-12-01/ news/56614530_1_pizza-india-ajay-kaul-jubilant-foodworks.

CASE STUDY QUESTIONS

1-10 How does Domino's PULSE™ system help manage customers' orders? Is there a system in place to identify the new customers?

1-11 How does PULSE™ help the manager to segregate the areas of customer orders and use appropriate targeting strategies?

1-12 As a senior manager, discuss how you could conduct wastage analysis in Domino's stores through PULSE™.

1-13 Discuss the eConnect and reporting feature of the Domino's PULSE™ system.

1-14 How does VoIP help Domino's serve its customers in an efficient manner?

1-15 Share your experience of unique customer service at Domino's and try to link that service with the features of the PULSE™ system.

Chapter 1 References

Brynjolfsson, Erik and Lorin M. Hitt. "Beyond Computation: Information Technology, Organizational Transformation, and Business Performance." Journal of Economic Perspectives 14, No. 4 (2000).

Brynjolfsson, Erik. "VII Pillars of IT Productivity." Optimize (May 2005).

Bureau of Economic Analysis. *National Income and Product Accounts.*www.bea.gov, accessed August 19, 2014.

Carr, Nicholas. "IT Doesn't Matter." *Harvard Business Review* (May 2003).

Chae, Ho-Chang, Chang E. Koh, and Victor Prybutok. "Information Technology Capability and Firm Performance: Contradictory Findings and Their Possible Causes." *MIS Quarterly* 38, No. 1 (March 2014).

Dedrick, Jason, Vijay Gurbaxani, and Kenneth L. Kraemer. "Information Technology and Economic Performance: A Critical Review of the Empirical Evidence." Center for Research on Information Technology and Organizations, University of California, Irvine (December 2001).

Domaintools.com, accessed September 28, 2014.

eMarketer. "US Ad Spending Forecast 2014." (March 2014).

eMarketer. "US Internet Users Complete Forecast." (March 2014).

FedEx Corporation. "SEC Form 10-K For the Fiscal Year Ended 2014."

Friedman, Thomas. *The World is Flat.* New York: Picador (2007).

Garretson, Rob. "IT Still Matters." *CIO Insight* 81 (May 2007).

Hughes, Alan and Michael S. Scott Morton. "The Transforming Power of Complementary Assets." *MIT Sloan Management Review* 47. No. 4 (Summer 2006).

Lamb, Roberta, Steve Sawyer, and Rob Kling. "A Social Informatics Perspective of Socio-Technical Networks." http://lamb.cba.hawaii.edu/pubs (2004).

Laudon, Kenneth C. *Computers and Bureaucratic Reform.* New York: Wiley (1974).

Lev, Baruch. "Intangibles: Management, Measurement, and Reporting." The Brookings Institution Press (2001).

Nevo, Saggi and Michael R. Wade. "The Formation and Value of IT-Enabled Resources: Antecedents and Consequences of Synergistic Relationships." *MIS Quarterly* 34, No. 1 (March 2010).

Otim, Samual, Dow, Kevin E. , Grover, Varun and Wong, Jeffrey A. "The Impact of Information Technology Investments on Downside Risk of the Firm: Alternative Measurement of the Business Value of IT." *Journal of Management Information Systems* 29, No. 1 (Summer 2012).

Pew Internet and American Life Project. "What Internet Users Do Online." (May 2013)

Ross, Jeanne W. And Peter Weill. "Four Questions Every CEO Should Ask About IT." *Wall Street Journal* (April 25, 2011).

Sampler, Jeffrey L. and Michael J. Earl. "What's Your Information Footprint?" *MIT Sloan Management Review* (Winter 2014).

Teece David. *Economic Performance and Theory of the Firm*: The Selected Papers of David Teece. London: Edward Elgar Publishing (1998).

U.S. Bureau of Labor Statistics. *Occupational Outlook Handbook*, 2014–2015. (April 15, 2014).

U.S. Census."Statistical Abstract of the United States 2013."U.S. Department of Commerce (2013).

Weill, Peter and Jeanne Ross. *IT Savvy: What Top Executives Must Know to Go from Pain to Gain.* Boston: Harvard Business School Press (2009).

Wurmser, Yory. "US Retail Ecommerce: 2014 Trends and Forecast," eMarketer (April 29, 2014).

Global E-business and Collaboration

CHAPTER 2

LEARNING OBJECTIVES

After reading this chapter, you will be able to answer the following questions:

1. What are business processes? How are they related to information systems?

2. How do systems serve the different management groups in a business and how do systems that link the enterprise improve organizational performance?

3. Why are systems for collaboration and social business so important and what technologies do they use?

4. What is the role of the information systems function in a business?

CHAPTER CASES

Azure Medical System: Integrating
    Departments Using Enterprise System
HDFC Banking on Business Intelligence
    and Analytics Technology

Is Social Business Working Out?
Ranbaxy: Taking the ERP Pill

AZURE MEDICAL SYSTEM: INTEGRATING DEPARTMENTS USING ENTERPRISE SYSTEM

Azure Medical Systems is the leading manufacturer of X-ray field equipment in north India and the second-largest producer of high-end X-ray machines after Meditronics (Phillips). It has a manufacturing facility in Punjab and Baddi (Himachal Pradesh), with its corporate offices in Chandigarh, and 29 sales and services centers across India. The company has an annual turnover of about ₹ 200 crore with a well-established market in Asia, South America, the Arabic countries, and South Africa. Azure has a total workforce of nearly 1,000 employees, most of whom are in the marketing and services departments. Azure lays a lot of emphasis on forecasting, planning to locate potential markets, and innovating products.

At the start of the manufacturing cycle, the production planning and control (PPC) department first makes a list of materials required for manufacturing a specified equipment, checks what is available in-house, and places an order for the rest of the material. The PPC department then generates a bill of material (BOM) and releases the orders to the store, and the production, purchase, vendor development, quality, and logistics departments. In case of special orders, which are made to the customer's specifications, the process is slightly altered. Information of the order is given to the PPC unit and the in-house R&D department is consulted for viability, timelines, and costing.

© Cseke Timea/Shutterstock

Earlier, the various departments coordinated over e-mails, and the hard copies of all the decisions were filed. This resulted in a duplication of data and drawings, and it took hours to locate a specific BOM. To solve these issues, the company has now developed an Oracle-based enterprise system which runs all applications for the different functional departments. The system keeps a dump of all the BOMs, indents, purchase orders, gate receiving slips (GRS), bills, quality reports, vendor reports, suggestion forms, codes, and vendor and drawing numbers. All this data can be accessed using an employee ID.

All the reports within a period of six months can be directly accessed through a special permission. Once an order is confirmed, the concerned departments give their feedback to the PPC division with the time period required to process the order. If there is any deviation from the actual, expected time, the company has processes in place to overcome the gaps in scheduling, both at the customer and manufacturer ends. Using a uniform tracking system, all departments can plan their work to achieve one common goal of delivering the product to the customer.

The PPC department uses the enterprise system to integrate the various departments so that they can work with one another better. Earlier, to create an indent, a hard copy was required to be generated and personally approved by the various authorized personnel. But now, an executive simply needs to put in the name or code of the item into the enterprise system, and its various specifications, cost, vendors, and inventory status can be fetched at a moment's notice. Departments can now order the required raw material from a centralized store and make indents. If the store does not have adequate quantities of the required material, it knows exactly when to release purchase orders to procure those materials from outside.

The store is the major user of the enterprise system, with thousands of items in its listing. Materials are categorized into semi-finished and finished products. The company outsources its pre-paint assemblies and assembles the semi-finished materials inside the plant. The finished products include every item, from screws to finished assemblies. The store keeps a record of all these items and assigns a unique code to each. Whenever a new product is added to the system, a BOM is raised for it and circulated among all the departments. As the company is ISO-certified, every new revision of the BOM and the drawings is highlighted and re-circulated for approval. Moreover, dynamic conditions and stiff competition demand regular modification in the designs and constant re-engineering of the product. This calls for a constant change in specifications and costs. The enterprise system takes care of this without sweat: all the store manager needs to do is make modification, and the changes are communicated to every functional department that has access to the BOM.

Sources: Ackermanns & Helden, v., 2002. *Critical success factors concerning ERP systems implementation*. s.l.:s.n; Al-Mashari, M., Zairi, M. & Al-Mudimigh, A., 2010. ERP Implementation: An Integrated Methodology. *European Center for best practice management*; Bancroft, N., Seip, H. & Sprengel, A., n.d. *Implementing SAP R/3: How to introduce a large system into a large organization*. S.l.: Manning Publication Co., USA1998; Berry, B., 2008. *Aligning Enterprise Architecture and ERP*. Oregon: s.n; Chang, S. -I., 2004. ERP *Life* *cycle Implementation, Management and Support: Implications for Practice and Research.* Hawaii, 37th Hawaii International Conference on System Sciences; Davenport, T., 1998. *Putting the Enterprise into the Enterprise System.* S.l.: Harvard Business Review; Davenport, T. H., 2000. *Mission Critical: Realizing the Promise of Enterprise Systems.* 1st Ed. S.l.: Harvard Business Press; Gibson, N. & Holland, C. a. L. B., 1999. A Case Study of a fast Track SAP R/3 Implementation at Guilbert. *Electronic Markets,* Issue June, pp. 190–193; Ginzberg, M., 1981. Early Diagnosis of MIS Implementation Failure: Promising Results and Unanswered Questions. *Management Science,* 27(4), pp. 459–476; Gupta, A., 2000. Enterprise Resource Planning: the emerging organizational value systems. *Industrial Management and data systems,* 100(3), pp. 114–118; Holland, C. & Light, B., 1999. A Critical Success Factors Model for ERP implementation. *IEEE Software,* May/ June, pp. 30–35; *How CISCO IT upgraded Its ERP Purchasing Module* (1992-2007) Cisco System, Inc.; Idorn, N., 2008. *A business process management approach to ERP implementation. A study of ERP implementation in the light of third wave of Process Management.* s.l.:s.n; Jarrar, Y., Al-Mudimmigh, A. & Zairi, M., 2000. ERP implementation critical success factors–the role and impact of business process management. *Management of Innovation and Technology,* Volume I, pp. 122-127; Johansson, B. & Sudzina, F., 2009. How factors affecting selection of implementation approach influence ERP system implementation costs. *17th European Conference on Information Systems;* Klaus, H., Rosemann, M. & Gable, G., 2000. What is ERP?. *Information Systems Frontiers,* II(2), pp. 141–162; Koen, H. & Noordveld, P., n.d. *BPM based ERP Implementation.* s.l.:s.n; Mabert, V., Soni, A. & Venkataraman, M., 2003. The impact of organizational size on ERP implementation in the U.S. manufacturing sector. *Omega,* 20(2), pp. 235–246; Mandal, P. & Gunasekaran, A., 2003. Issues in implementing ERP: A Case Study. *European Journal of Operational Research,* Volume 146, pp. 274–283; Martin, M., 1998. An ERP Strategy. *Fortune,* pp. 149–151; Prouty, K., 2011. *ERP much better off with than without (Analyst Insight),* s.l.: Aberdeen Group; Sadagopan, S., 1999. ERP: *A Managerial Perspective.* s.l.:Tata McGraw Hill Education Private Limited; Sage, 2011. *White paper on ERP - Building on the Basics,* s.l.: Sage; Seranmadevi, R. & Natarajan, M. L., 2009. Extended Enterprise Application Software - An Indian Perspective - "Zeal to Zenith". *Journal of Computer Applications,* II(3); Sheikh, K., 2001. An Introduction to ERP: Arcitecture, Implementation and Cases. In: *Manufacturing Resource Planning (MRP II) with introduction to ERP, SCM and CRM.* New Delhi: Tata McGraw Hill, pp. 494–537; Sumner, M., 1999. Critical Success Factors in *Enterprise Wide Information Management Systems Projects.* s.l., AMICS; Wagle, D., 1998. The case for ERP systems. *The McKniseys Quarterly (2),* pp. 130–138; Welti, N., 1999. *Successful SAP R/3 Implementation: Practical Management of ERP projects.* USA: Addison Wesley Longman Limited; Yusuf, Y., Gunasekaran, A. & Abthorpe, M. S., 2004. Enterprise Information System Project Implementation: A Case Study of ERP in Rolls Royce. *International Journal of Production Economics,* Volume 87, pp. 251-266.

The experience of Azure Medical Systems illustrates how much organizations these days rely on information system to improve their performance and remain competitive. It also shows how much system supporting collaboration and coordination between departments can make a difference in improving the efficiency of operations at a manufacturing plant.

The chapter-opening diagram calls for attention to important points raised by this case and this chapter. Azure is a leading manufacturer of X-ray field equipments with a clear focus on forecasting, accurate planning, and innovating, but it was hampered by outdated processes for managing information that prevented various departments from working efficiently and effectively. Hence, the company decided to move away from the conventional email system to enterprise system through which various departments could coordinate their activities. The Oracle-based enterprise system ran all the applications for different departments, and as a result of which Azure is able to solve problems posed by conventional email system. The enterprise system

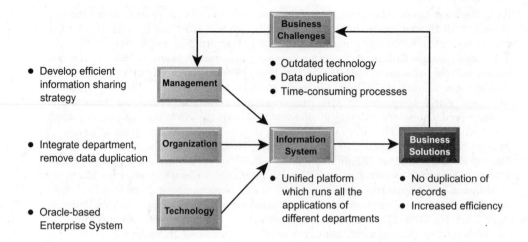

helped Azure Medical Systems integrate all the key activities of the manufacturing cycle. Apart from managing the key operations of the PPC department, the enterprise system also helped Azure to efficiently manage the items in the store department. With this system, a store manager at Azure can now communicate all the changes in costing and specifications to every functional department because of the fact that every department is seamlessly integrated applying enterprise system.

2.1 WHAT ARE BUSINESS PROCESSES? HOW ARE THEY RELATED TO INFORMATION SYSTEMS?

In order to operate, businesses must deal with many different pieces of information about suppliers, customers, employees, invoices, and payments, and of course their products and services. They must organize work activities that use this information to operate efficiently and enhance the overall performance of the firm. Information systems make it possible for firms to manage all their information, make better decisions, and improve the execution of their business processes.

BUSINESS PROCESSES

Business processes, which we introduced in Chapter 1, refer to the manner in which work is organized, coordinated, and focused to produce a valuable product or service. Business processes are the collection of activities required to produce a product or service. These activities are supported by flows of material, information, and knowledge among the participants in business processes. Business processes also refer to the unique ways in which organizations coordinate work, information, and knowledge, and the ways in which management chooses to coordinate work.

To a large extent, the performance of a business firm depends on how well its business processes are designed and coordinated. A company's business

TABLE 2.1 EXAMPLES OF FUNCTIONAL BUSINESS PROCESSES

FUNCTIONAL AREA	BUSINESS PROCESS
Manufacturing and production	Assembling the product Checking for quality Producing bills of materials
Sales and marketing	Identifying customers Making customers aware of the product Selling the product
Finance and accounting	Paying creditors Creating financial statements Managing cash accounts
Human resources	Hiring employees Evaluating employees' job performance Enrolling employees in benefits plans

processes can be a source of competitive strength if they enable the company to innovate or to execute better than its rivals. Business processes can also be liabilities if they are based on outdated ways of working that impede organizational responsiveness and efficiency. The chapter-opening case describing Kluwer's improvements in knowledge-sharing processes clearly illustrates these points, as do many of the other cases in this text.

Every business can be seen as a collection of business processes, some of which are part of larger encompassing processes. For instance, uses of mentoring, wikis, blogs, and videos are all part of the overall knowledge management process. Many business processes are tied to a specific functional area. For example, the sales and marketing function is responsible for identifying customers, and the human resources function is responsible for hiring employees. Table 2.1 describes some typical business processes for each of the functional areas of business.

Other business processes cross many different functional areas and require coordination across departments. For instance, consider the seemingly simple business process of fulfilling a customer order (see Figure 2.1). Initially, the sales department receives a sales order. The order passes first to accounting to ensure the customer can pay for the order either by a credit verification or request for immediate payment prior to shipping. Once the customer credit is established, the production department pulls the product from inventory or produces the product. Then the product is shipped (and this may require working with a logistics firm, such as UPS or FedEx). A bill or invoice is generated by the accounting department, and a notice is sent to the customer indicating that the product has shipped. The sales department is notified of the shipment and prepares to support the customer by answering calls or fulfilling warranty claims.

What at first appears to be a simple process, fulfilling an order, turns out to be a very complicated series of business processes that require the close coordination of major functional groups in a firm. Moreover, to efficiently perform all these steps in the order fulfillment process requires a great deal

FIGURE 2.1   THE ORDER FULFILLMENT PROCESS

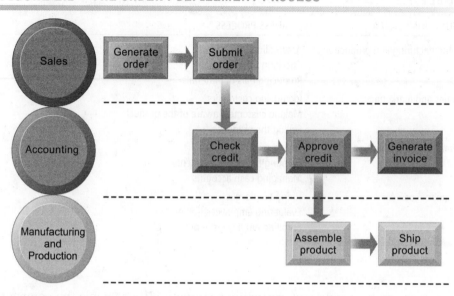

Fulfilling a customer order involves a complex set of steps that requires the close coordination of the sales, accounting, and manufacturing functions.

of information. The required information must flow rapidly both within the firm from one decision maker to another; with business partners, such as delivery firms; and with the customer. Computer-based information systems make this possible.

HOW INFORMATION TECHNOLOGY IMPROVES BUSINESS PROCESSES

Exactly how do information systems improve business processes? Information systems automate many steps in business processes that were formerly performed manually, such as checking a client's credit, or generating an invoice and shipping order. But today, information technology can do much more. New technology can actually change the flow of information, making it possible for many more people to access and share information, replacing sequential steps with tasks that can be performed simultaneously, and eliminating delays in decision making. New information technology frequently changes the way a business works and supports entirely new business models. Downloading a Kindle e-book from Amazon, buying a computer online at Best Buy, and downloading a music track from iTunes are entirely new business processes based on new business models that would be inconceivable without today's information technology.

That's why it's so important to pay close attention to business processes, both in your information systems course and in your future career. By analyzing business processes, you can achieve a very clear understanding of how a business actually works. Moreover, by conducting a business process analysis, you will also begin to understand how to change the business by improving its processes to make it more efficient or effective. Throughout this book, we examine business processes with a view to understanding how they might be improved by using information technology to achieve greater efficiency, innovation, and customer service.

2.2 HOW DO SYSTEMS SERVE THE DIFFERENT MANAGEMENT GROUPS IN A BUSINESS AND HOW DO SYSTEMS THAT LINK THE ENTERPRISE IMPROVE ORGANIZATIONAL PERFORMANCE?

Now that you understand business processes, it is time to look more closely at how information systems support the business processes of a firm. Because there are different interests, specialties, and levels in an organization, there are different kinds of systems. No single system can provide all the information an organization needs.

A typical business organization has systems supporting processes for each of the major business functions—sales and marketing, manufacturing and production, finance and accounting, and human resources. You can find examples of systems for each of these business functions in the Learning Tracks for this chapter. Functional systems that operate independently of each other are becoming a thing of the past because they cannot easily share information to support cross-functional business processes. Many have been replaced with large-scale cross-functional systems that integrate the activities of related business processes and organizational units. We describe these integrated cross-functional applications later in this section.

A typical firm also has different systems supporting the decision-making needs of each of the main management groups we described in Chapter 1. Operational management, middle management, and senior management each use systems to support the decisions they must make to run the company. Let's look at these systems and the types of decisions they support.

SYSTEMS FOR DIFFERENT MANAGEMENT GROUPS

A business firm has systems to support different groups or levels of management. These systems include transaction processing systems and systems for business intelligence.

Transaction Processing Systems

Operational managers need systems that keep track of the elementary activities and transactions of the organization, such as sales, receipts, cash deposits, payroll, credit decisions, and the flow of materials in a factory. **Transaction processing systems (TPS)** provide this kind of information. A transaction processing system is a computerized system that performs and records the daily routine transactions necessary to conduct business, such as sales order entry, hotel reservations, payroll, employee record keeping, and shipping.

The principal purpose of systems at this level is to answer routine questions and to track the flow of transactions through the organization. How many parts are in inventory? What happened to Mr. Smith's payment? To answer these kinds of questions, information generally must be easily available, current, and accurate.

At the operational level, tasks, resources, and goals are predefined and highly structured. The decision to grant credit to a customer, for instance, is made by a lower-level supervisor according to predefined criteria. All that must be determined is whether the customer meets the criteria.

Figure 2.2 illustrates a TPS for payroll processing. A payroll system keeps track of money paid to employees. An employee time sheet with the employee's name, social security number, and number of hours worked per week represents a single transaction for this system. Once this transaction is input into the system, it updates the system's master file (or database—see Chapter 6) that permanently maintains employee information for the organization. The data in the system are combined in different ways to create reports of interest to management and government agencies and to send paychecks to employees.

Managers need TPS to monitor the status of internal operations and the firm's relations with the external environment. TPS are also major producers of information for the other systems and business functions. For example, the payroll system illustrated in Figure 2.2, along with other accounting TPS,

FIGURE 2.2   A PAYROLL TPS

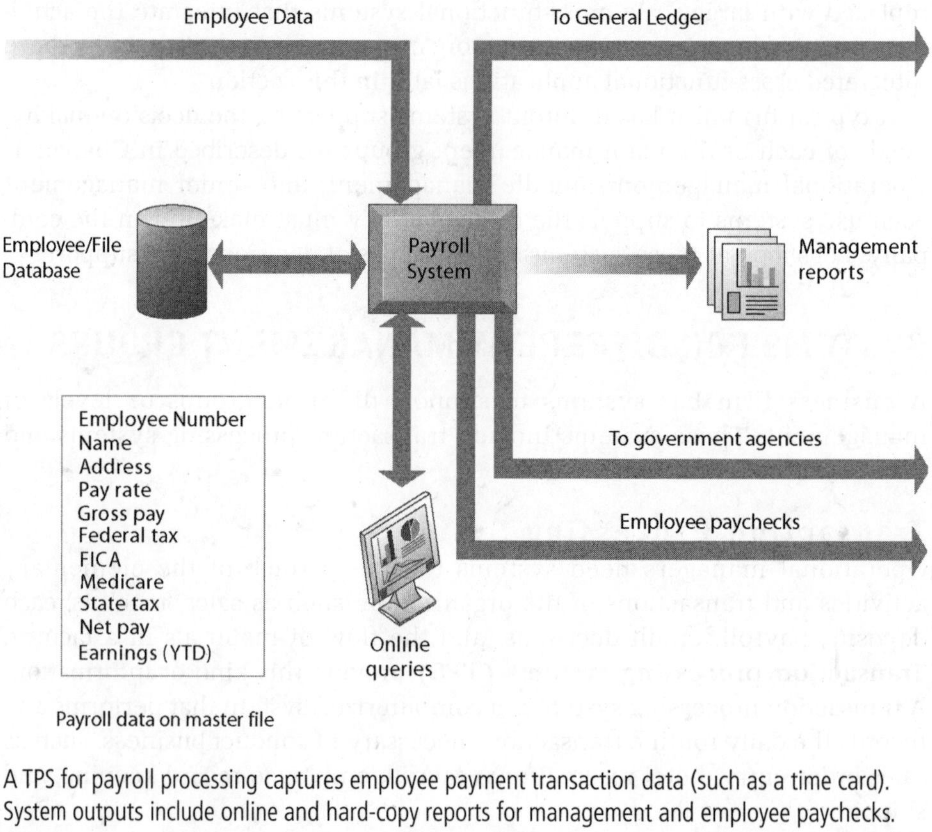

A TPS for payroll processing captures employee payment transaction data (such as a time card). System outputs include online and hard-copy reports for management and employee paychecks.

supplies data to the company's general ledger system, which is responsible for maintaining records of the firm's income and expenses and for producing reports such as income statements and balance sheets. It also supplies employee payment history data for insurance, pension, and other benefits calculations to the firm's human resources function, and employee payment data to government agencies such as the U.S. Internal Revenue Service and Social Security Administration.

Transaction processing systems are often so central to a business that TPS failure for a few hours can lead to a firm's demise and perhaps that of other firms linked to it. Imagine what would happen to UPS if its package tracking system was not working! What would the airlines do without their computerized reservation systems?

Systems for Business Intelligence

Firms also have business intelligence systems that focus on delivering information to support management decision making. **Business intelligence** is a contemporary term for data and software tools for organizing, analyzing, and providing access to data to help managers and other enterprise users make more informed decisions. Business intelligence addresses the decision-making needs of all levels of management. This section provides a brief introduction to business intelligence. You'll learn more about this topic in Chapters 6 and 12.

Business intelligence systems for middle management help with monitoring, controlling, decision-making, and administrative activities. In Chapter 1, we defined management information systems as the study of information systems in business and management. The term **management information systems (MIS)** also designates a specific category of information systems serving middle management. MIS provide middle managers with reports on the organization's current performance. This information is used to monitor and control the business and predict future performance.

MIS summarize and report on the company's basic operations using data supplied by transaction processing systems. The basic transaction data from TPS are compressed and usually presented in reports that are produced on a regular schedule. Today, many of these reports are delivered online. Figure 2.3 shows how a typical MIS transforms transaction-level data from inventory, production, and accounting into MIS files that are used to provide managers with reports. Figure 2.4 shows a sample report from this system.

MIS typically provide answers to routine questions that have been specified in advance and have a predefined procedure for answering them. For instance, MIS reports might list the total pounds of lettuce used this quarter by a fast-food chain or, as illustrated in Figure 2.4, compare total annual sales figures for specific products to planned targets. These systems generally are not flexible and have little analytical capability. Most MIS use simple routines, such as summaries and comparisons, as opposed to sophisticated mathematical models or statistical techniques.

As the organization grows, it becomes important to segregate the working of the organization on specific functional aspects. Every organization, depending on the product it manufactures or service it renders, will have some or all of the following functional areas: marketing, finance, production

FIGURE 2.3 HOW MANAGEMENT INFORMATION SYSTEMS OBTAIN THEIR DATA FROM THE ORGANIZATION'S TPS

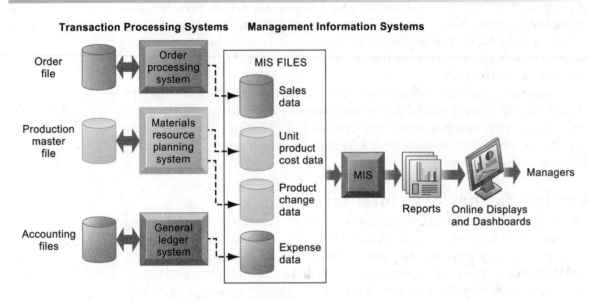

In the system illustrated by this diagram, three TPS supply summarized transaction data to the MIS reporting system at the end of the time period. Managers gain access to the organizational data through the MIS, which provides them with the appropriate reports.

and inventory, and human resources. These departments are required to work in close coordination with one another to achieve the firm's common objectives. Each functional area is managed by an independent manager. The functional managers work in highly dynamic and competitive environment. Earlier, the scope of each of these departments used to be narrower, but it has increased tremendously over the years, so much so that it is not possible

FIGURE 2.4 SAMPLE MIS REPORT

Consolidated Consumer Products Corporation Sales by Product and Sales Region: 2015

PRODUCT CODE	PRODUCT DESCRIPTION	SALES REGION	ACTUAL SALES	PLANNED	ACTUAL versus PLANNED
4469	Carpet Cleaner	Northeast	4,066,700	4,800,000	0.85
		South	3,778,112	3,750,000	1.01
		Midwest	4,867,001	4,600,000	1.06
		West	4,003,440	4,400,000	0.91
	TOTAL		16,715,253	17,550,000	0.95
5674	Room Freshener	Northeast	3,676,700	3,900,000	0.94
		South	5,608,112	4,700,000	1.19
		Midwest	4,711,001	4,200,000	1.12
		West	4,563,440	4,900,000	0.93
	TOTAL		18,559,253	17,700,000	1.05

This report, showing summarized annual sales data, was produced by the MIS in Figure 2.3.

for the managers to take care of all the tasks manually. Since each functional area performs a specific, demarcated task, their information needs are also differ. It is not possible to use a common information system across the entire organization. Some of the function-specific information systems used to help managers take prompt decisions are discussed here.

Marketing Information System

The role of this type of information system is to help the manager identify key customers. It can be used to generate reports based on time, region, and so on. If a customer is identified as a potential souce of revenue, their loyalty can be appreciated in the form of personalized after-sales service, discounts, new offerings, or prioritizing their orders. Customer satisfaction is key to the success of businesses today, and so it becomes important to identify the target market accurately. Marketing information systems help with this segmentation, so that the appropriate marketing activities can be targeted at the relevant segment. Very few firms today produce products for the mass market. Most businesses with similar offerings try to differentiate themselves through the experience they create for customers.

Marketing information system processes data such as sales figures, past trends, and government policies to get the useful information that can be utilized by managers for taking decisions. For example, when you buy an item from a retail store, your billing data is fed into the system. Managers can take a look at the consolidated statements of such data and draw conclusions about the products that are in demand. If a discount scheme was offered, managers can understand the impact that had on sales. Similarly, the performance of sales team in the store can also be evaluated based on data from the marketing imformation system.

Human Resource Information System

Human resource information systems (HRIS) aids HR managers perform different activities related to the human resources of their oragnizations. An HRIS uses information technology to perform various HR processes, so as to eliminate the complexity of performance of those tasks manually. This system also allows HR managers take better and timely decisions. A typical HRIS will have the following modules to manage all the activities carried out by any HR department:

- **Payroll module:** Several components need to be taken into consideration while computing the salary payout of employees. These might be tax deductions, provident fund contributions, leave and attendance data, previous tax reports, incentive (if any), among others. The HRIS helps manage the payment process by gathering data on all these components. The system draws data from other modules such as the performance appraisal module, attendance module, and so on, which are integrated to generate the net payable amount. The payment module is also linked to a financial management information system for the clearance of funds.

- **Time and attendance modules:** The HRIS gathers data related to time and work. It logs the numbers of hours each employee works every day, thereby keeping tab on the efficiency levels of employees. This information can be used to analyze the efficiency at the workplace on a given work day or calculate the average time required to perform a task.

- **Benefits administration module:** A major component of compensation is benefits. Some of the benefits offered to employees such as insurance or medical claims vary with the employees' job category. An HRIS can link this information to work out which benefit can be availed by which employee in a particular job band.

- **HR management module:** This module covers several HR tasks related to on-boadring and off-boarding of employees. It contains basic demographic data of employees, such as their personal details, addresses, mode of selection, training programs participated in, capabilities and achievements, skills, compensation planning records, among others. The HRIS aids in the performace of HR tasks such as recruitment, selection, compensation, training, promotion, and superannuation.

- **Training module:** Evolution of concepts such as "learning organizations", in which firms learn from their previous performance and continually adapt themselves to the changing environment, have led to the development of learning management systems. The training module is used to administer and track employee training and development. This system contains details regarding the educational qualifications of the employees and offers appropriate courses to develop skills. It also recommends the most appropriate mode of learning: CDs, books, e-learning courses, and so on. The HRIS also helps managers budget for training and keep track of the training undertaken by each of their team members.

- **Employee self-service module:** This module allows employees to access data on their salary, deductions, leaves, and attendance. It reduces the need for employees to continually approach the HR department to avail such data.

Financial Management Information System

The financial management information system (FMIS) finds extensive application in managing the financial matters of an organization. The finance department of a firm handles functions related to capital structuring, budgeting, appraisal, and control of funds. A firm usually avails finance from two main sources: equity and debt. An FIMS allows managers to evaluate the sources of funds that would be best suited for the firm, those that bear the least risk, and those that reaps the most gain. The FMIS can also be used to decide how much money should be raised from equity and how much from debt. Such a system has wide application in banks. It helps manage all the important daily transactional data from withdrawals to demand draft creation. It also processs this data and converts it into useful information and helpsstore the information securely.

Production Management Information System

Production management is concerned with the planning and control of all those activities that transform input into output, by adding some value to the former to make the latter. The production department of an organization deals with the following activities:

- **Production planning:** This includes activities such as routing, scheduling, and loading.

- **Production control:** This function helps maintain quality of the products by keeping a close eye on activities such as ordering, follow-ups, and inventory control.

- **Product design:** This function deals with all the activities that give shape to the product.

- **Product development:** This function deals with activities that help create product according to a pre-decided design. The product development team undertakes tasks such as standardization, specialization, simplification, and diversification.

- **Plant location and layout:** These help organizations build plants in places where production can be carried out without hassles. The layout teams allow the organization to achieve optimum utilization of space by arranging machinery and workstations in such a way that they do not hinder the free movement of workers and materials.

The production management information system helps a firm accomplish all these objectives. In a highly dynamic business environment, with complex production processes, volumes of data are massive. This system stores and manages this data and guides the manager in achieving effective control of production activities. For example, the inventory control system, which is a part of the production management information system, makes it easy to manage inventory automatically.

Other types of business intelligence systems support more non-routine decision making. **Decision-support systems (DSS)** focus on problems that are unique and rapidly changing, for which the procedure for arriving at a solution may not be fully predefined in advance. They try to answer questions such as these: What would be the impact on production schedules if we were to double sales in the month of December? What would happen to our return on investment if a factory schedule were delayed for six months?

Although DSS use internal information from TPS and MIS, they often bring in information from external sources, such as current stock prices or product prices of competitors. These systems are employed by "super-user" managers and business analysts who want to use sophisticated analytics and models to analyze data.

An interesting, small, but powerful DSS is the voyage-estimating system of a large global shipping company that transports bulk cargoes of coal, oil, ores, and finished products. The firm owns some vessels, charters others, and bids for shipping contracts in the open market to carry general cargo. A voyage-estimating system calculates financial and technical voyage details. Financial calculations include ship/time costs (fuel, labor, capital), freight rates for various types of cargo, and port expenses. Technical details include a myriad of factors, such as ship cargo capacity, speed, port distances, fuel and water consumption, and loading patterns (location of cargo for different ports).

The system can answer questions such as the following: Given a customer delivery schedule and an offered freight rate, which vessel should be assigned

INTERACTIVE SESSION: TECHNOLOGY

HDFC BANKING ON BUSINESS INTELLIGENCE AND ANALYTICS TECHNOLOGY

The Housing Development Finance Corporation Limited (HDFC) was among the first financial bodies to receive an in-principle approval from the Reserve Bank of India (RBI) to set up a bank in the private sector. This was part of RBI's liberalization plan for the Indian banking industry in 1994. The bank was incorporated in August 1994 as HDFC Bank Limited, with its registered offices in Mumbai. HDFC Bank commenced operations as a scheduled commercial bank in January 1995. It was the first bank in the country to adopt new-age technology in its banking operations. More than 65% of its current customers conduct banking transactions through online direct channels.

HDFC partnered with the Statistical Analysis System (SAS) Institute to apply business intelligence and analytics technology in order to take vital decisions in the diverse areas of banking. As a first step, it integrated its CRM solution with the SAS analytics suite. In this manner, SAS analytics could be deployed on the entire customer database. This gave HDFC a greater insight into customer behavior and encouraged the bank to cross-sell. For example, bank executives were easily able to figure out if a customer had an active account or just a salary account. Besides, they could also determine if the customer used the HDFC account as a primary account.

Since the SAS analytics suite was implemented on top of the bank's data warehouse, it offered the bank a consolidated, 360-degree view of its customers—relating to all the customer interactions with the bank, be it for the credit card facility, fixed deposits, or asset accounts. The analytics allowed for the segmentation of customers and the identification of "imperia customers". These were customers who ranked high in the bank's value chain because of the high profit margins they represented. The bank's executives could aggressively target these customers, who were said to bring in great profits at comparatively lower costs to the bank.

The SAS tool also provided suggestions for the kind of products that should be sold to specific customers. Based on the customer's pro-file, behavior, and lifecycle, SAS identified the products that the customer was most likely to find viable or attractive. Based on advanced statistical models, a solution for customer acquisition, customer retention, and value management was generated. This reduced the turnaround time and increased the response rate for each marketing campaign. More than 70% of HDFC's credit cards have been sold to customers with existing savings or salary accounts with the bank. This has proven the effectiveness of the SAS model, which has been able to utilize customer data and assign buying and spending propensities to each customer.

The SAS tool has also enabled the bank to identify suspicious activities in banking transactions such as large cash deposit, sudden withdrawals in otherwise dormant accounts, movement of money into multiple accounts (called "layering"), or opening several accounts within a short period of time. All this is part of the anti-money laundering (AML) regulations. Similarly, the bank is also KYC-complaint. The SAS application cleanses customer data and classifies each profile into good or bad. This way, when a customer opens an account with the bank, the SAS analytics tool can identify the bad profiles with ease. The identification of suspicious activity by the SAS tool is so comprehensive and reliable that these records are valuable even to the Financial Intelligence Unit.

HDFC has implemented fast-track retail loan (home, car, or personal) processing for amounts of less than five lakh rupees. Customers can track the status of their loan application online within minutes of applying (the same process took 24 hours earlier). Given that HDFC processes eight to ten thousand loan applications in a span of eight hours, a speedy credit approval process has proved to be a blessing and has been made possible due to the robust and dependable technology offered by SAS. When a customer applies for a loan online, the SAS analytics tool verifies the customer's identity. Analytical models are then run on top of the customer's data to generate certain metrics, such as the application score and propensity to default. Loan approvers have all the information they need to make their decision within minutes. The customers can also determine the loan amount and tenure of repayment that they are eligible for based on their current income, among other factors.

For wholesale credit approval, a slightly different approach is followed. Using the specific analytical models developed for each segment of wholesale credit (such as those for large corporates, SME-manufacturing, SME-services, and so on) risks for each segment are assessed. These might be individual risk, business risk, management risk, and financial risk. Based on the output from each of the four categories, the weighted aggregate is computed and the application is rated on a scale of 1 to 10, where 1 is the best score and 10, the worst.

Using the SAS application, HDFC can identify the debt exposure of each customer. Each month, HDFC rejects up to 2% of the loan applications because of the applicant's record of defaulting repayment. This way, the bank has been able to reduce its losses by nearly 1%.

The bank rightly credits its power of effective decision making to the success of the SAS tool. HDFC has ambitious plans for the future. It aims to inculcate analytics in its strategic decisions as well. The bank is also working on using analytics to measure channel efficiency and allocate resources. Since customers can now be reached through a variety of channels such as phones, e-mail, social networks, and so on, this analysis will help examine the different parameters of costs, usage, or efficiency for each channel. It will be useful in identifying the best channel through which a customer can be reached. Also it will allow the bank to determine how much should be spent on each channel to optimize profits.

Sources: "Improve cross-selling capabilities". Retrieved from http://www.sas.com/en_us/customers/hdfc.html; "HDFC Bank signs Analytics Service Agreement", *Money Control*. Retrieved from http://www.moneycontrol.com/news/business/hdfc-bank-signs-analytics-service-agreement_188236.html; Shah, Aatash, "Banking on Big Data analytics" (2014). Retrieved from http://www.edvancer.in/banking-on-big-data-analytics/; "Credit Risk", *WikiInvest*. Retrieved from http://www.wikinvest.com/stock/HDFC_Bank_LTD_Ads_(HDB)/Credit_Risk; "HDFC Bank uses SAS analytics to streamline cross-selling" (2010). Retrieved from https://www.youtube.com/watch?v = Py5evoyYgyw.

CASE STUDY QUESTIONS

1. What are the benefits of integrating the SAS analytics suite with the HDFC Bank's CRM?

2. How do SAS analytics ensure that HDFC Bank is compliant with the anti-money laundering (AML) regulations?

3. Discuss the use of SAS analytics in loan processing at the HDFC Bank.

4. What do you understand by debt exposure and the role of analytics in determining it?

5. What is the future of analytics at the HDFC Bank?

at what rate to maximize profits? What is the optimal speed at which a particular vessel can optimize its profit and still meet its delivery schedule? What is the optimal loading pattern for a ship bound for the U.S. West Coast from Malaysia? Figure 2.5 illustrates the DSS built for this company. The system operates on a powerful desktop personal computer, providing a system of menus that makes it easy for users to enter data or obtain information.

The voyage-estimating DSS we have just described draws heavily on models. Other business intelligence systems are more data-driven, focusing instead on extracting useful information from massive quantities of data. For example, large ski resort companies such as Intrawest and Vail Resorts collect and store large amounts of customer data from call centers, lodging and

FIGURE 2.5   VOYAGE-ESTIMATING DECISION-SUPPORT SYSTEM

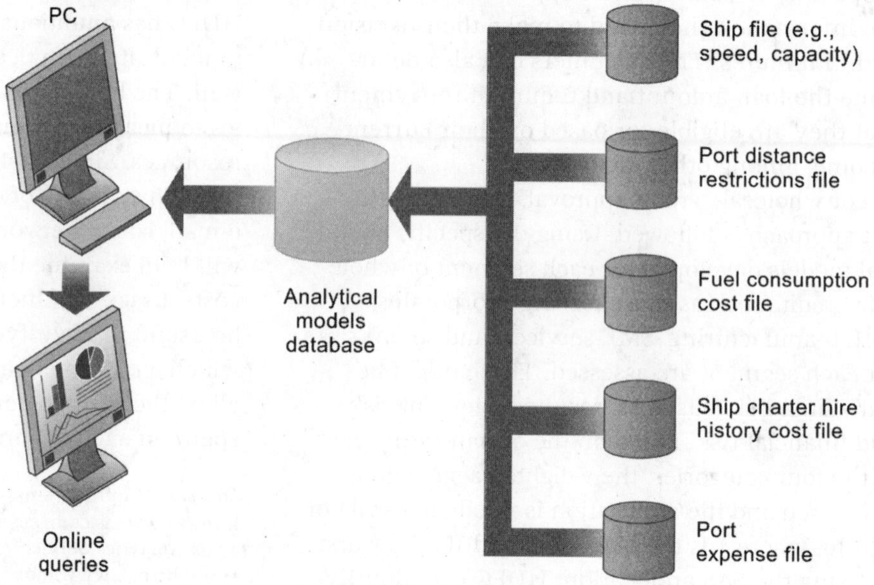

This DSS operates on a powerful PC. It is used daily by managers who must develop bids on shipping contracts.

dining reservations, ski schools, and ski equipment rental stores. They use special software to analyze these data to determine the value, revenue potential, and loyalty of each customer to help managers make better decisions about how to target their marketing programs.

Business intelligence systems also address the decision-making needs of senior management. Senior managers need systems that focus on strategic issues and long-term trends, both in the firm and in the external environment. They are concerned with questions such as: What will employment levels be in five years? What are the long-term industry cost trends? What products should we be making in five years?

Executive support systems (ESS) help senior management make these decisions. They address non-routine decisions requiring judgment, evaluation, and insight because there is no agreed-on procedure for arriving at a solution. ESS present graphs and data from many sources through an interface that is easy for senior managers to use. Often the information is delivered to senior executives through a **portal**, which uses a Web interface to present integrated personalized business content.

ESS are designed to incorporate data about external events, such as new tax laws or competitors, but they also draw summarized information from internal MIS and DSS. They filter, compress, and track critical data, displaying the data of greatest importance to senior managers. Increasingly, such systems include business intelligence analytics for analyzing trends, forecasting, and "drilling down" to data at greater levels of detail.

For example, the CEO of Leiner Health Products, the largest manufacturer of private-label vitamins and supplements in the United States, has

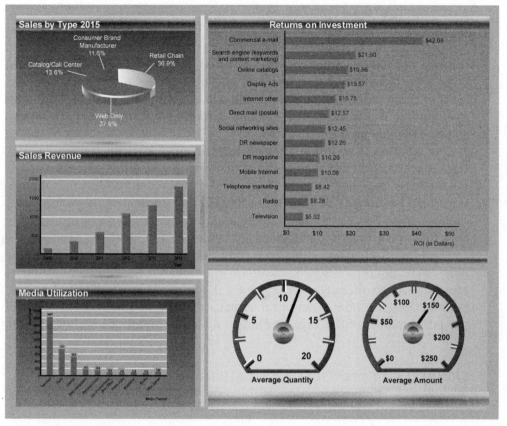

A digital dashboard delivers comprehensive and accurate information for decision making often using a single screen. The graphical overview of key performance indicators helps managers quickly spot areas that need attention.

an ESS that provides on his desktop a minute-to-minute view of the firm's financial performance as measured by working capital, accounts receivable, accounts payable, cash flow, and inventory. The information is presented in the form of a **digital dashboard**, which displays on a single screen graphs and charts of key performance indicators for managing a company. Digital dashboards are becoming an increasingly popular tool for management decision makers.

Contemporary business intelligence and analytics technology have promoted data-driven management, where decision makers rely heavily on analytical tools and data at their fingertips to guide their work. Data captured at the factory or sales floor level are immediately available for high-level or detailed views in executive dashboards and reports. It's real-time management.

SYSTEMS FOR LINKING THE ENTERPRISE

Reviewing all the different types of systems we have just described, you might wonder how a business can manage all the information in these different systems. You might also wonder how costly it is to maintain so many different systems. And you might wonder how all these different systems can share information and how managers and employees are able to coordinate their work. In fact, these are all important questions for businesses today.

Enterprise Applications

Getting all the different kinds of systems in a company to work together has proven a major challenge. Typically, corporations are put together both through normal "organic" growth and through acquisition of smaller firms. Over a period of time, corporations end up with a collection of systems, most of them older, and face the challenge of getting them all to "talk" with one another and work together as one corporate system. There are several solutions to this problem.

One solution is to implement **enterprise applications**, which are systems that span functional areas, focus on executing business processes across the business firm, and include all levels of management. Enterprise applications help businesses become more flexible and productive by coordinating their business processes more closely and integrating groups of processes so they focus on efficient management of resources and customer service.

There are four major enterprise applications: enterprise systems, supply chain management systems, customer relationship management systems, and knowledge management systems. Each of these enterprise applications integrates a related set of functions and business processes to enhance the performance of the organization as a whole. Figure 2.6 shows that the

FIGURE 2.6   ENTERPRISE APPLICATION ARCHITECTURE

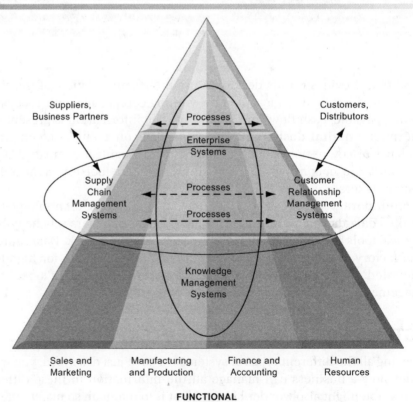

Enterprise applications automate processes that span multiple business functions and organizational levels and may extend outside the organization.

architecture for these enterprise applications encompasses processes spanning the entire organization and, in some cases, extending beyond the organization to customers, suppliers, and other key business partners.

Enterprise Systems Firms use **enterprise systems**, also known as enterprise resource planning (ERP) systems, to integrate business processes in manufacturing and production, finance and accounting, sales and marketing, and human resources into a single software system. Information that was previously fragmented in many different systems is stored in a single comprehensive data repository where it can be used by many different parts of the business.

For example, when a customer places an order, the order data flow automatically to other parts of the company that are affected by them. The order transaction triggers the warehouse to pick the ordered products and schedule shipment. The warehouse informs the factory to replenish whatever has been depleted. The accounting department is notified to send the customer an invoice. Customer service representatives track the progress of the order through every step to inform customers about the status of their orders. Managers are able to use firmwide information to make more precise and timely decisions about daily operations and longer-term planning.

Supply Chain Management Systems Firms use **supply chain management (SCM) systems** to help manage relationships with their suppliers. These systems help suppliers, purchasing firms, distributors, and logistics companies share information about orders, production, inventory levels, and delivery of products and services so they can source, produce, and deliver goods and services efficiently. The ultimate objective is to get the right amount of their products from their source to their point of consumption in the least amount of time and at the lowest cost. These systems increase firm profitability by lowering the costs of moving and making products and by enabling managers to make better decisions about how to organize and schedule sourcing, production, and distribution.

Supply chain management systems are one type of **interorganizational system** because they automate the flow of information across organizational boundaries. You will find examples of other types of interorganizational information systems throughout this text because such systems make it possible for firms to link electronically to customers and to outsource their work to other companies.

Customer Relationship Management Systems Firms use **customer relationship management (CRM) systems** to help manage their relationships with their customers. CRM systems provide information to coordinate all of the business processes that deal with customers in sales, marketing, and service to optimize revenue, customer satisfaction, and customer retention. This information helps firms identify, attract, and retain the most profitable customers; provide better service to existing customers; and increase sales.

Knowledge Management Systems Some firms perform better than others because they have better knowledge about how to create, produce, and deliver products and services. This firm knowledge is unique, difficult to imitate, and can be leveraged into long-term strategic benefits. **Knowledge management systems (KMS)** enable organizations to better manage processes for capturing and applying knowledge and expertise. These systems collect all relevant knowledge and experience in the firm, and make it available wherever and whenever it is needed to improve business processes and management decisions. They also link the firm to external sources of knowledge.

We examine enterprise systems and systems for supply chain management and customer relationship management in greater detail in Chapter 9. We discuss collaboration systems that support knowledge management in this chapter and cover other types of knowledge management applications in Chapter 11.

Intranets and Extranets

Enterprise applications create deep-seated changes in the way the firm conducts its business, offering many opportunities to integrate important business data into a single system. They are often costly and difficult to implement. Intranets and extranets deserve mention here as alternative tools for increasing integration and expediting the flow of information within the firm, and with customers and suppliers.

Intranets are simply internal company Web sites that are accessible only by employees. The term "intranet" refers to an internal network, in contrast to the Internet, which is a public network linking organizations and other external networks. Intranets use the same technologies and techniques as the larger Internet, and they often are simply a private access area in a larger company Web site. Likewise with extranets. Extranets are company Web sites that are accessible to authorized vendors and suppliers, and are often used to coordinate the movement of supplies to the firm's production apparatus.

For example, Six Flags, which operates 19 theme parks throughout North America, maintains an intranet for its 2,500 full-time employees that provides company-related news and information on each park's day-to-day operations, including weather forecasts, performance schedules, and details about groups and celebrities visiting the parks. The company also uses an extranet to broadcast information about schedule changes and park events to its 30,000 seasonal employees. We describe the technology for intranets and extranets in more detail in Chapter 7.

E-BUSINESS, E-COMMERCE, AND E-GOVERNMENT

The systems and technologies we have just described are transforming firms' relationships with customers, employees, suppliers, and logistic partners into digital relationships using networks and the Internet. So much business is now enabled by or based upon digital networks that we use the terms "electronic business" and "electronic commerce" frequently throughout this text.

Electronic business, or **e-business**, refers to the use of digital technology and the Internet to execute the major business processes in the enterprise. E-business includes activities for the internal management of the firm and for coordination with suppliers and other business partners. It also includes **electronic commerce**, or **e-commerce**.

E-commerce is the part of e-business that deals with the buying and selling of goods and services over the Internet. It also encompasses activities supporting those market transactions, such as advertising, marketing, customer support, security, delivery, and payment.

The technologies associated with e-business have also brought about similar changes in the public sector. Governments on all levels are using Internet technology to deliver information and services to citizens, employees, and businesses with which they work. **E-government** refers to the application of the Internet and networking technologies to digitally enable government and public sector agencies' relationships with citizens, businesses, and other arms of government.

In addition to improving delivery of government services, e-government makes government operations more efficient and also empowers citizens by giving them easier access to information and the ability to network electronically with other citizens. For example, citizens in some states can renew their driver's licenses or apply for unemployment benefits online, and the Internet has become a powerful tool for instantly mobilizing interest groups for political action and fund-raising.

2.3 WHY ARE SYSTEMS FOR COLLABORATION AND SOCIAL BUSINESS SO IMPORTANT AND WHAT TECHNOLOGIES DO THEY USE?

With all these systems and information, you might wonder how is it possible to make sense of them? How do people working in firms pull it all together, work towards common goals, and coordinate plans and actions? Information systems can't make decisions, hire or fire people, sign contracts, agree on deals, or adjust the price of goods to the marketplace. In addition to the types of systems we have just described, businesses need special systems to support collaboration and teamwork.

WHAT IS COLLABORATION?

Collaboration is working with others to achieve shared and explicit goals. Collaboration focuses on task or mission accomplishment and usually takes place in a business, or other organization, and between businesses. You collaborate with a colleague in Tokyo having expertise on a topic about which you know nothing. You collaborate with many colleagues in publishing a company blog. If you're in a law firm, you collaborate with accountants in an accounting firm in servicing the needs of a client with tax problems.

Collaboration can be short-lived, lasting a few minutes, or longer term, depending on the nature of the task and the relationship among participants. Collaboration can be one-to-one or many-to-many.

Employees may collaborate in informal groups that are not a formal part of the business firm's organizational structure or they may be organized into formal teams. **Teams** have a specific mission that someone in the business assigned to them. Team members need to collaborate on the accomplishment of specific tasks and collectively achieve the team mission. The team mission might be to "win the game," or "increase online sales by 10 percent." Teams are often short-lived, depending on the problems they tackle and the length of time needed to find a solution and accomplish the mission.

Collaboration and teamwork are more important today than ever for a variety of reasons.

- *Changing nature of work.* The nature of work has changed from factory manufacturing and pre-computer office work where each stage in the production process occurred independently of one another, and was coordinated by supervisors. Work was organized into silos. Within a silo, work passed from one machine tool station to another, from one desktop to another, until the finished product was completed. Today, jobs require much closer coordination and interaction among the parties involved in producing the service or product. A recent report from the consulting firm McKinsey & Company argued that 41 percent of the U.S. labor force is now composed of jobs where interaction (talking, e-mailing, presenting, and persuading) is the primary value-adding activity. Even in factories, workers today often work in production groups, or pods.

- *Growth of professional work.* "Interaction" jobs tend to be professional jobs in the service sector that require close coordination and collaboration. Professional jobs require substantial education, and the sharing of information and opinions to get work done. Each actor on the job brings specialized expertise to the problem, and all the actors need to take one another into account in order to accomplish the job.

- *Changing organization of the firm.* For most of the industrial age, managers organized work in a hierarchical fashion. Orders came down the hierarchy, and responses moved back up the hierarchy. Today, work is organized into groups and teams, and the members are expected to develop their own methods for accomplishing the task. Senior managers observe and measure results, but are much less likely to issue detailed orders or operating procedures. In part, this is because expertise and decision-making power have been pushed down in organizations.

- *Changing scope of the firm.* The work of the firm has changed from a single location to multiple locations—offices or factories throughout a region, a nation, or even around the globe. For instance, Henry Ford developed the first mass-production automobile plant at a single Dearborn, Michigan factory. In 2014, Ford employed 180,000 people at around 965 plants and facilities worldwide. With this kind of global presence, the need for close coordination of design, production, marketing, distribution, and service obviously takes on new importance and scale. Large global companies need to have teams working on a global basis.

- *Emphasis on innovation.* Although we tend to attribute innovations in business and science to great individuals, these great individuals are most likely working with a team of brilliant colleagues. Think of Bill Gates and Steve Jobs (founders of Microsoft and Apple), both of whom are highly regarded innovators, and both of whom built strong collaborative teams to nurture and support innovation in their firms. Their initial innovations derived from close collaboration with colleagues and partners. Innovation, in other words, is a group and social process, and most innovations derive from collaboration among individuals in a lab, a business, or government agencies. Strong collaborative practices and technologies are believed to increase the rate and quality of innovation.

- *Changing culture of work and business.* Most research on collaboration supports the notion that diverse teams produce better outputs, faster, than individuals working on their own. Popular notions of the crowd ("crowdsourcing," and the "wisdom of crowds") also provide cultural support for collaboration and teamwork.

WHAT IS SOCIAL BUSINESS?

Many firms today enhance collaboration by embracing **social business**—the use of social networking platforms, including Facebook, Twitter, and internal corporate social tools—to engage their employees, customers, and suppliers. These tools enable workers to set up profiles, form groups, and "follow" each other's status updates. The goal of social business is to deepen interactions with groups inside and outside the firm to expedite and enhance information-sharing, innovation, and decision making.

A key word in social business is "conversations." Customers, suppliers, employees, managers, and even oversight agencies continually have conversations about firms, often without the knowledge of the firm or its key actors (employees and managers).

Supporters of social business argue that, if firms could tune into these conversations, they would strengthen their bonds with consumers, suppliers, and employees, increasing their emotional involvement in the firm.

All of this requires a great deal of information transparency. People need to share opinions and facts with others quite directly, without intervention from executives or others. Employees get to know directly what customers and other employees think; suppliers will learn very directly the opinions of supply chain partners; and even managers presumably will learn more directly from their employees how well they are doing. Nearly everyone involved in the creation of value will know much more about everyone else.

If such an environment could be created, it is likely to drive operational efficiencies, spur innovation, and accelerate decision making. If product designers can learn directly about how their products are doing in the market in real time, based on consumer feedback, they can speed up the redesign process. If employees can use social connections inside and outside the company to capture new knowledge and insights, they will be able to work more efficiently and solve more business problems.

Table 2.2 describes important applications of social business inside and outside the firm. This chapter focuses on enterprise social business—its internal corporate uses. Chapters 7 and 10 describe social business applications relating to customers and suppliers outside the company.

TABLE 2.2 APPLICATIONS OF SOCIAL BUSINESS

SOCIAL BUSINESS APPLICATION	DESCRIPTION
Social networks	Connect through personal and business profiles
Crowdsourcing	Harness collective knowledge to generate new ideas and solutions
Shared workspaces	Coordinate projects and tasks; co-create content
Blogs and wikis	Publish and rapidly access knowledge; discuss opinions and experiences
Social commerce	Share opinions about purchasing or purchase on social platforms
File sharing	Upload, share, and comment on photos, videos, audio, text documents
Social marketing	Use social media to interact with customers; derive customer insights
Communities	Discuss topics in open forums; share expertise

BUSINESS BENEFITS OF COLLABORATION AND SOCIAL BUSINESS

Although many articles and books have been written about collaboration, nearly all of the research on this topic is anecdotal. Nevertheless, there is a general belief among both business and academic communities that the more a business firm is "collaborative," the more successful it will be, and that collaboration within and among firms is more essential than in the past. A recent global survey of business and information systems managers found that investments in collaboration technology produced organizational improvements that returned over four times the amount of the investment, with the greatest benefits for sales, marketing, and research and development functions (Frost and White, 2009). Another study of the value of collaboration also found that the overall economic benefit of collaboration was significant: for every word seen by an employee in e-mails from others, $70 of additional revenue was generated (Aral, Brynjolfsson, and Van Alstyne, 2007). McKinsey & Company consultants predict that social technologies used within and across enterprises could potentially raise the productivity of interaction workers by 20 to 25 percent (McKinsey, 2012).

Table 2.3 summarizes some of the benefits of collaboration and social business that have been identified. Figure 2.7 graphically illustrates how collaboration is believed to impact business performance.

BUILDING A COLLABORATIVE CULTURE AND BUSINESS PROCESSES

Collaboration won't take place spontaneously in a business firm, especially if there is no supportive culture or business processes. Business firms, especially large firms, had a reputation in the past for being "command and

TABLE 2.3 BUSINESS BENEFITS OF COLLABORATION AND SOCIAL BUSINESS

BENEFIT	RATIONALE
Productivity	People interacting and working together can capture expert knowledge and solve problems more rapidly than the same number of people working in isolation from one another. There will be fewer errors.
Quality	People working collaboratively can communicate errors, and corrective actions faster than if they work in isolation. Collaborative and take social technologies help reduce time delays in design and production.
Innovation	People working collaboratively can come up with more innovative ideas for products, services, and administration than the same number working in isolation from one another. Advantages to diversity and the "wisdom of crowds."
Customer service	People working together using collaboration and social tools can solve customer complaints and issues faster and more effectively than if they were working in isolation from one another.
Financial performance (profitability, sales, and sales growth)	As a result of all of the above, collaborative firms have superior sales, sales growth, and financial performance.

control" organizations where the top leaders thought up all the really important matters, and then ordered lower-level employees to execute senior management plans. The job of middle management supposedly was to pass messages back and forth, up and down the hierarchy.

FIGURE 2.7 REQUIREMENTS FOR COLLABORATION

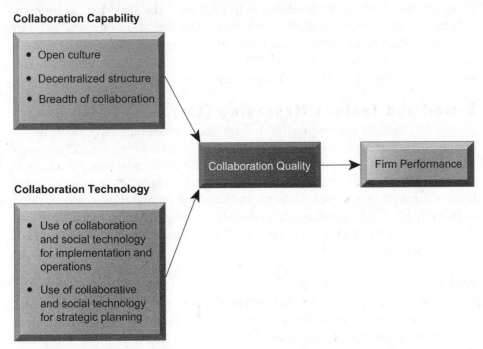

Successful collaboration requires an appropriate organizational structure and culture, along with appropriate collaboration technology.

Command and control firms required lower-level employees to carry out orders without asking too many questions, with no responsibility to improve processes, and with no rewards for teamwork or team performance. If your work group needed help from another work group, that was something for the bosses to figure out. You never communicated horizontally, always vertically, so management could control the process. Together, the expectations of management and employees formed a culture, a set of assumptions about common goals and how people should behave. Many business firms still operate this way.

A collaborative business culture and business processes are very different. Senior managers are responsible for achieving results, but rely on teams of employees to achieve and implement the results. Policies, products, designs, processes, and systems are much more dependent on teams at all levels of the organization to devise, to create, and to build. Teams are rewarded for their performance, and individuals are rewarded for their performance in a team. The function of middle managers is to build the teams, coordinate their work, and monitor their performance. The business culture and business processes are more "social." In a collaborative culture, senior management establishes collaboration and teamwork as vital to the organization, and it actually implements collaboration for the senior ranks of the business as well.

TOOLS AND TECHNOLOGIES FOR COLLABORATION AND SOCIAL BUSINESS

A collaborative, team-oriented culture won't produce benefits without information systems in place to enable collaboration and social business. Currently there are hundreds of tools designed to deal with the fact that, in order to succeed in our jobs, we are all much more dependent on one another, our fellow employees, customers, suppliers and managers. Some of these tools are expensive, but others are available online for free (or with premium versions for a modest fee). Let's look more closely at some of these tools.

E-mail and Instant Messaging (IM)

E-mail and instant messaging (including text messaging) have been major communication and collaboration tools for interaction jobs. Their software operates on computers, cell phones, and other wireless devices and includes features for sharing files as well as transmitting messages. Many instant messaging systems allow users to engage in real-time conversations with multiple participants simultaneously. In recent years, e-mail use has declined, with messaging and social media becoming preferred channels of communication.

Wikis

Wikis are a type of Web site that makes it easy for users to contribute and edit text content and graphics without any knowledge of Web page development or programming techniques. The most well-known wiki is Wikipedia, the largest collaboratively edited reference project in the world. It relies on volunteers, makes no money and accepts no advertising.

Wikis are very useful tools for storing and sharing corporate knowledge and insights. Enterprise software vendor SAP AG has a wiki that acts as a base of information for people outside the company, such as customers and software developers who build programs that interact with SAP software. In the past, those people asked and sometimes answered questions in an informal way on SAP online forums, but that was an inefficient system, with people asking and answering the same questions over and over.

Virtual Worlds

Virtual worlds, such as Second Life, are online 3-D environments populated by "residents" who have built graphical representations of themselves known as avatars. Companies like IBM, Cisco, and Intel Corporations use the online world for meetings, interviews, guest speaker events, and employee training. Real-world people represented by avatars meet, interact, and exchange ideas at these virtual locations using gestures, chat box conversations, and voice communication.

Collaboration and Social Business Platforms

There are now suites of software products providing multi-function platforms for collaboration and social business among teams of employees who work together from many different locations. The most widely used are Internet-based audio conferencing and video conferencing systems, cloud collaboration services such as Google's online tools and cyberlockers, corporate collaboration systems such as Microsoft SharePoint, and enterprise social networking tools such as Salesforce Chatter, Microsoft's Yammer, Jive, and IBM Connections.

Virtual Meeting Systems In an effort to reduce travel expenses, many companies, both large and small, are adopting videoconferencing and Web conferencing technologies. Companies such as Heinz, General Electric, and Pepsico are using virtual meeting systems for product briefings, training courses, strategy sessions, and even inspirational chats.

A videoconference allows individuals at two or more locations to communicate simultaneously through two-way video and audio transmissions. High-end videoconferencing systems feature **telepresence** technology, an integrated audio and visual environment which allows a person to give the appearance of being present at a location other than his or her true physical location. Free or low-cost Internet-based systems such as Skype group videoconferencing, Google + Hangouts, Zoom, and ooVoo are of lower quality, but still useful for smaller companies. Apple's FaceTime is useful for one-to-one videoconferencing.

Companies of all sizes are finding Web-based online meeting tools such as Cisco WebEx, Microsoft Lync, and Adobe Connect especially helpful for training and sales presentations. These products enable participants to share documents and presentations in conjunction with audioconferencing and live video via Webcam.

Cloud Collaboration Services: Google Tools and Cyberlockers Google offers many online tools and services, and some are suitable for collaboration. They include Google Drive, Google Docs, Google Apps, Google Sites, and Google +. Most are free of charge.

Google Drive is a file storage and synchronization service for cloud storage, file sharing and collaborative editing. Google Drive is an example of a cloud-based **cyberlocker**. Cyberlockers are online file-sharing services that allow users to upload files to secure online storage sites from which the files can be shared with others. Microsoft OneDrive and Dropbox are other leading cyberlocker services. They feature both free and paid services, depending on the amount of storage space and administration required. Users are able to synchronize their files stored online with their local PCs and other kinds of devices, with options for making the files private or public and for sharing them with designated contacts.

Google Drive and Microsoft OneDrive are integrated with tools for document creation and sharing. OneDrive provides online storage for Microsoft Office documents and other files and works with Microsoft Office apps, both installed and on the Web. It can share to Facebook as well. Google Drive is integrated with Google Docs, a suite of productivity applications that offer collaborative editing on documents, spreadsheets, and presentations. Google's cloud-based productivity suite for businesses (word processing, spreadsheets, presentations, calendars, and mail) called Google Apps for Business also works with Google Drive.

Google Sites allows users to quickly create online team-oriented sites where multiple people can collaborate and share files. Google + is Google's effort to make these tools and other products and services it offers more "social" for both consumer and business use. Google + users can create a profile as well as "Circles," for organizing people into specific groups for sharing and collaborating. "Hangouts" enable people to engage in group video chat, with a maximum of 10 people participating at any point in time.

Microsoft SharePoint Microsoft SharePoint is a browser-based collaboration and document management platform, combined with a powerful search engine that is installed on corporate servers. SharePoint has a Web-based interface and close integration with everyday tools such as Microsoft Office desktop software products. SharePoint software makes it possible for employees to share their documents and collaborate on projects using Office documents as the foundation.

SharePoint can be used to host internal Web sites that organize and store information in one central workspace to enable teams to coordinate work activities, collaborate on and publish documents, maintain task lists, implement workflows, and share information via wikis and blogs. Users are able to control versions of documents and document security. Because SharePoint stores and organizes information in one place, users can find relevant information quickly and efficiently while working together closely on tasks, projects, and documents. Enterprise search tools help locate people, expertise, and content. SharePoint now features social tools.

The Fair Work Ombudsman (FWO) is an independent statutory office of the Australian federal government that provides advice and related services to employers and employees on workplace relations and entitlements. FWO has around 800 full time staff in offices in all Australian capital cities and 18 regional locations. FWO had been overwhelmed with the details of project management and compliance, with staff having to draw information from many different systems and piece it together manually. FWO implemented Microsoft Sharepoint Server to create a single organization-wide secure and reliable platform for managing and reporting on Projects, Programs, and Portfolios that would also facilitate collaboration. The Sharepoint system captures all project types undertaken by FWO; supports built-in user roles, views and security; provides storage and access to data, including project documentation; and automates workflows, including approvals, alerts and communication (Microsoft, 2014).

IBM Notes IBM Notes (formerly Lotus Notes)is a collaborative software system with capabilities for sharing calendars, e-mail, messaging, collective writing and editing, shared database access, and electronic meetings. Notes software installed on desktop or laptop computers obtains applications stored on an IBM Domino server. Notes is Web-enabled, and offers an application development environment so that users can build custom applications to suit their unique needs. Notes has also added capabilities for blogs, microblogs, wikis, RSS aggregators, help desk systems, voice and video conferencing, and online meetings. A related IBM product called Quickr provides more specialized tools for teamwork (team spaces, content libraries, discussion forums, wikis) and is able to access information from Notes.

IBM Notes promises high levels of security and reliability, and the ability to retain control over sensitive corporate information. Finncontainers, a Helsinki, Finland logistics company specializing in the sale, rental, and transportation of new and used shipping containers, selected Notes as a dependable collaboration platform on which to build a strong network of partners, suppliers and customers. The company did not want to miss sales opportunities if its e-mail system went down suddenly. (IBM, 2013).

Enterprise Social Networking Tools The tools we have just described include capabilities for supporting social business, but there are also more specialized social tools for this purpose, such as Salesforce Chatter, Microsoft's Yammer, Jive, and IBM Connections. Enterprise social networking tools create business value by connecting the members of an organization through profiles, updates, and notifications, similar to Facebook features, but tailored to internal corporate uses. Table 2.4 provides more detail about these internal social capabilities.

Although companies have benefited from enterprise social networking, internal social networking has not caught on as quickly as consumer uses of Facebook, Twitter, and other public social networking products. The Interactive Session on Management addresses this topic.

Checklist for Managers: Evaluating and Selecting Collaboration and Social Software Tools

With so many collaboration and social business tools and services available, how do you choose the right collaboration technology for your firm? To answer this question, you need a framework for understanding just what problems these tools are designed to solve. One framework that has been helpful for us to talk about collaboration tools is the time/space collaboration and social tool matrix developed in the early 1990s by a number of collaborative work scholars (Figure 2.8).

The time/space matrix focuses on two dimensions of the collaboration problem: time and space. For instance, you need to collaborate with people

TABLE 2.4 ENTERPRISE SOCIAL NETWORKING SOFTWARE CAPABILITIES

SOCIAL SOFTWARE CAPABILITY	DESCRIPTION
Profiles	Ability to set up member profiles describing who individuals are, educational background, interests. Includes work-related associations and expertise (skills, projects, teams).
Content Sharing	Share, store, and manage content including documents, presentations, images, and videos.
Feeds and Notifications	Real-time information streams, status updates, and announcements from designated individuals and groups.
Groups and Team Workspaces	Establish groups to share information, collaborate on documents, and work on projects, with the ability to set up private and public groups and to archive conversations to preserve team knowledge.
Tagging and Social Bookmarking	Indicate preferences for specific pieces of content, similar to the Facebook "like" button. Tagging lets people add keywords to identify content they like.
Permissions and Privacy	Ability to make sure private information stays within the right circles, as determined by the nature of relationships. In enterprise social networks, there is a need to establish who in the company has permission to see what information.

FIGURE 2.8   THE TIME/SPACE COLLABORATION AND SOCIAL TOOL MATRIX

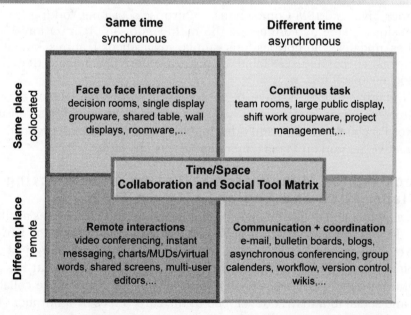

Collaboration and social technologies can be classified in terms of whether they support interactions at the same or different time or place, and whether these interactions are remote or colocated.

INTERACTIVE SESSION: MANAGEMENT

IS SOCIAL BUSINESS WORKING OUT?

Social networking has never been more popular, with social tools accounting for 20 percent of all online activity, according to ComScore. Many of today's employees are already well versed in the basics of public social networking using tools such as Facebook, Twitter, and Instagram. Larry Ellison, head of the giant software firm Oracle, even went so far as to declare that social networking should be the backbone of business applications and that Facebook is a good model for how users should interact with software. But when it comes to actually using social tools for internal business purposes, the results have been mixed.

Information Week's 2013 Social Networking in the Enterprise Survey found that only 18 percent of respondents believed their internal social networking programs were successful. The Information Week survey cited lackluster adoption as a major obstacle to success. As with many technology upgrades, companies that have tried to deploy internal social networks have found that employees are used to doing business in a certain way, and overcoming that organizational inertia can prove difficult. IT leaders hoping to switch to a more social, collaborative office culture usually find that most employees still prefer to use e-mail, for example. The employees may feel too time-pressed to learn a new software tool.

Employees who are used to collaborating and doing business in more traditional ways need an incentive to use social software. Most companies are not providing that incentive: only 22 percent of social software users believe the technology to be necessary to their jobs. You might join Facebook because all your friends are on it, but in the workplace, ease of use and increased job efficiency are more important than peer pressure in driving adoption.

IT organizations need to take charge to ensure that the internal and external social networking efforts of the company are providing genuine value to the business. Content on the networks needs to be relevant, up-to-date, and easy to access; users need to be able to connect to people that have the information they need and that would otherwise be out of reach or difficult to reach. Social business tools should be appropriate for the tasks on hand and the organization's business processes, and users need to understand how and why to use them.

In the summer of 2009, the NASA's Goddard Space Flight Center launched a custom-built enterprise social network called Spacebook to help small teams collaborate without e-mailing larger groups. Spacebook featured user profiles, group workspaces (wikis, file sharing, discussion forums, groups), and social bookmarks. Very few users adopted it, and Spacebook was decommissioned on June 1, 2012. According to Kevin Jones, a consulting social and organizational strategist at NASA's Marshall and Goddard Space Flight Centers, Spacebook failed because it didn't focus enough on people. It had been designed and developed without taking into consideration the organization's culture and politics. No one knew how Spacebook would help them do their jobs, as opposed to an existing method of collaboration such as e-mail.

Despite the pitfalls associated with launching an internal social network, there are companies using these networks successfully. For example, Red Robin, a chain of 355 restaurants with over 20,000 employees, uses social networking to give its frontline employees who interact with customers a greater voice in the company. Chris Laping, Red Robin's CIO and senior vice-president of business transformation believed that engaging these workers would also increase employee loyalty.

Red Robin decided to try out Yammer, which is referred to as a "Facebook for business." Yammer lets people create conversations, perform status updates, upload and share files, and set up workgroups for small project teams. The social collaboration software would allow Red Robin to get out a message and receive immediate feedback, so that the company could rapidly make modifications. For example, when Red Robin introduced its new Tavern Burger product line in April, 2012, it was able to refine the recipes and operational procedures in restaurants in about four weeks. The process would have taken 6 to 18 months in the past. Guests reported their feedback to servers in the restaurants, who relayed this information to their managers. Then all the managers got together right away on Yammer.

Red Robin used a viral approach to drive adoption. In the first month, 20 to 25 employees started using it and invited others. Membership spread quickly and Red Robin wound up with two Yammer networks: "Yummversity" is a network for training employees, while "Yummer" is a network for restaurant managers, regional managers, and corporate office members to exchange information and respond to questions from the field staff. Yummer provides a voice for the company's front-line workers. In the past they would pass information up the corporate management chain, but rarely received feedback about what was done with the information.

Yummer also provided the foundation for the company's "Blueprint Project" designed to identify the best employee idea for cutting expenses without negatively impacting the customer experience. Thousands of people contributed ideas to compete for a $1000 prize. The winning entry was from a Seattle location manager who proposed replacing disposable child beverage cups with reusable ones. This seemingly small change produced a six-figure savings for the company.

Sources: David Lavenda, "How Red Robin Transformed Its Business with Yammer," Fast Company, February 6, 2014; James Niccolai, "Ellison: Facebook the New Model for Business Applications," IDG News Service, January 30, 2014; Margaret Jones, "Top Four Social Collaboration Software Fails," SearchConsumerization.com, accessed February 3, 2014; Michael Healey, "Why Enterprise Social Networking Falls Short," *Information Week*, March 4, 2013; Debra Donston-Miller, "10 Ways to Foster Effective Social Employees," *Information Week*, March 6, 2013; Jacob Morgan, "How to Market Collaboration to Employees," *Information Week*, March 21, 2013; " www.nasa.gov, accessed February 20, 2014; and Justin Kern, "Enterprises 'Like' Social Networks, Don't 'Love' Results," Information Management, February 28, 2012.

CASE STUDY QUESTIONS

1. Identify the management, organization, and technology factors responsible for impeding adoption of internal corporate social networks.

2. Compare the experiences for implementing internal social networks of the two

   organizations. Why was one more successful than the other? What role did management play in this process?

3. Should all companies implement internal enterprise social networks? Why or why not?

in different time zones and you cannot all meet at the same time. Midnight in New York is noon in Bombay, so this makes it difficult to have a videoconference (the people in New York are too tired). Time is clearly an obstacle to collaboration on a global scale.

Place (location) also inhibits collaboration in large global or even national and regional firms. Assembling people for a physical meeting is made difficult by the physical dispersion of distributed firms (firms with more than one location), the cost of travel, and the time limitations of managers.

The collaboration and social technologies we have just described are ways of overcoming the limitations of time and space. Using this time/space framework will help you to choose the most appropriate collaboration and teamwork tools for your firm. Note that some tools are applicable in more than one time/place scenario. For example, Internet collaboration suites such as Lotus Notes have capabilities for both synchronous (instant messaging, electronic meeting tools) and asynchronous (e-mail, wikis, document editing) interactions.

Here's a "to-do" list to get started. If you follow these six steps, you should be led to investing in the correct collaboration software for your firm at a price you can afford, and within your risk tolerance.

1. What are the collaboration challenges facing the firm in terms of time and space? Locate your firm in the time/space matrix. Your firm can occupy more than one cell in the matrix. Different collaboration tools will be needed for each situation.

2. Within each cell of the matrix where your firm faces challenges, exactly what kinds of solutions are available? Make a list of vendor products.

3. Analyze each of the products in terms of their cost and benefits to your firm. Be sure to include the costs of training in your cost estimates, and the costs of involving the information systems department, if needed.

4. Identify the risks to security and vulnerability involved with each of the products. Is your firm willing to put proprietary information into the hands of external service providers over the Internet? Is your firm willing to risk its important operations to systems controlled by other firms? What are the financial risks facing your vendors? Will they be here in three to five years? What would be the cost of making a switch to another vendor in the event the vendor firm fails?

5. Seek the help of potential users to identify implementation and training issues. Some of these tools are easier to use than others.

6. Make your selection of candidate tools, and invite the vendors to make presentations.

2.4   WHAT IS THE ROLE OF THE INFORMATION SYSTEMS FUNCTION IN A BUSINESS?

We've seen that businesses need information systems to operate today and that they use many different kinds of systems. But who is responsible for running these systems? Who is responsible for making sure the hardware, software, and other technologies used by these systems are running properly and are up to date? End users manage their systems from a business standpoint, but managing the technology requires a special information systems function.

In all but the smallest of firms, the **information systems department** is the formal organizational unit responsible for information technology services. The information systems department is responsible for maintaining the hardware, software, data storage, and networks that comprise the firm's IT infrastructure. We describe IT infrastructure in detail in Chapter 5.

THE INFORMATION SYSTEMS DEPARTMENT

The information systems department consists of specialists, such as programmers, systems analysts, project leaders, and information systems managers. **Programmers** are highly trained technical specialists who write the software instructions for computers. **Systems analysts** constitute the principal liaisons between the information systems groups and the rest of the organization. It is the systems analyst's job to translate business problems and requirements into information requirements and systems. **Information systems managers** are leaders of teams of programmers and analysts, project managers, physical facility managers, telecommunications managers, or database specialists. They are also managers of computer operations and data entry staff. Also, external specialists, such as hardware vendors and manufacturers, software firms, and consultants, frequently participate in the day-to-day operations and long-term planning of information systems.

In many companies, the information systems department is headed by a **chief information officer (CIO)**. The CIO is a senior manager who oversees the use of information technology in the firm. Today's CIOs are expected to have a strong business background as well as information systems expertise and to play a leadership role in integrating technology into the firm's business strategy. Large firms today also have positions for a chief security officer, chief knowledge officer, and chief privacy officer, all of whom work closely with the CIO.

The **chief security officer (CSO)** is in charge of information systems security for the firm and is responsible for enforcing the firm's information security policy (see Chapter 8). (Sometimes this position is called the chief information security officer [CISO] where information systems security is separated from physical security.) The CSO is responsible for educating and training users and information systems specialists about security, keeping management aware of security threats and breakdowns, and maintaining the tools and policies chosen to implement security.

Information systems security and the need to safeguard personal data have become so important that corporations collecting vast quantities of personal data have established positions for a **chief privacy officer (CPO)**. The CPO is responsible for ensuring that the company complies with existing data privacy laws.

The **chief knowledge officer (CKO)** is responsible for the firm's knowledge management program. The CKO helps design programs and systems to find new sources of knowledge or to make better use of existing knowledge in organizational and management processes.

The **chief data officer (CDO)** is responsible for enterprise-wide governance and utilization of information to maximize the value the organization can realize from its data. The CDO ensures that the firm is collecting the appropriate data to serve its needs, deploying appropriate technologies for analyzing the data and using the results to support business decisions. This position arose to deal with the massive amounts of data organizations are now generating and collecting (see Chapter 6).

End users are representatives of departments outside of the information systems group for whom applications are developed. These users are playing an increasingly large role in the design and development of information systems.

In the early years of computing, the information systems group was composed mostly of programmers who performed highly specialized but limited technical functions. Today, a growing proportion of staff members are systems analysts and network specialists, with the information systems department acting as a powerful change agent in the organization. The information systems department suggests new business strategies and new information-based products and services, and coordinates both the development of the technology and the planned changes in the organization.

In the next five years, employment growth in IS/MIS jobs will be about 50 percent greater than the average job growth in other fields. Out of 114 occupations, MIS is ranked 15th in terms of salaries. While all IS occupations show above-average growth, the fastest growing occupations are computer support specialists (30%), systems analysts (21%), software engineers and programmers (20%), and information systems managers (17%) (Bureau of Labor Statistics, 2012). With businesses and government agencies increasingly relying on the Internet for computing and communication resources, system and network security management positions are especially in demand. See the Learning Track for this chapter titled "Occupational and Career Outlook for Information Systems Majors 2012–2018" for more details on IS job opportunities.

ORGANIZING THE INFORMATION SYSTEMS FUNCTION

There are many types of business firms, and there are many ways in which the IT function is organized within the firm. A very small company will not have a formal information systems group. It might have one employee who is responsible for keeping its networks and applications running, or it might use consultants for these services. Larger companies will have a separate information systems department, which may be organized along several different lines, depending on the nature and interests of the firm. Our Learning Track describes alternative ways of organizing the information systems function within the business.

The question of how the information systems department should be organized is part of the larger issue of IT governance. **IT governance** includes the strategy and policies for using information technology within an organization. It specifies the decision rights and framework for accountability to ensure that the use of information technology supports the organization's strategies and objectives. How much should the information systems function be centralized? What decisions must be made to ensure effective management and use of information technology, including the return on IT investments? Who should make these decisions? How will these decisions be made and monitored? Firms with superior IT governance will have clearly thought out the answers (Weill and Ross, 2004).

Review Summary

1. **What are business processes? How are they related to information systems?**

    A business process is a logically related set of activities that defines how specific business tasks are performed, and it represents a unique way in which an organization coordinates work, information, and knowledge. Managers need to pay attention to business processes because they determine how well the organization can execute its business, and they may be a source of strategic advantage. There are business processes specific to each of the major business functions, but many business processes are cross-functional. Information systems automate parts of business processes, and they can help organizations redesign and streamline these processes.

2. **How do systems serve the different management groups in a business and how do systems that link the enterprise improve organizational performance?**

    Systems serving operational management are transaction processing systems (TPS), such as payroll or order processing, that track the flow of the daily routine transactions necessary to conduct business. Management information systems (MIS) produce reports serving middle management by condensing information from TPS, and these are not highly analytical. Decision-support systems (DSS) support management decisions that are unique and rapidly changing using advanced analytical models. All of these types of systems provide business intelligence that helps managers and enterprise employees make more informed decisions. These systems for business intelligence serve multiple levels of management, and include executive support systems (ESS) for senior management that provide data in the form of graphs, charts, and dashboards delivered via portals using many sources of internal and external information.

    Enterprise applications are designed to coordinate multiple functions and business processes. Enterprise systems integrate the key internal business processes of a firm into a single software system to improve coordination and decision making. Supply chain management systems help the firm manage its relationship with suppliers to optimize the planning, sourcing, manufacturing, and delivery of products and services. Customer relationship management (CRM) systems coordinate the business processes surrounding the firm's customers. Knowledge management systems enable firms to optimize the creation, sharing, and distribution of knowledge. Intranets and extranets are private corporate networks based on Internet technology that assemble information from disparate systems. Extranets make portions of private corporate intranets available to outsiders.

3. **Why are systems for collaboration and social business so important and what technologies do they use?**

    Collaboration is working with others to achieve shared and explicit goals. Social business is the use of internal and external social networking platforms to engage employees, customers, and suppliers, and it can enhance collaborative work. Collaboration and social business have become increasingly important in business because of globalization, the decentralization of decision making, and growth in jobs where interaction is the primary value-adding activity. Collaboration and social business enhance innovation, productivity, quality, and customer service. Tools for collaboration and social business include e-mail and instant messaging, wikis, virtual meeting systems, virtual worlds, cloud-based cyberlockers and online services such as those of Google and Microsoft, corporate collaboration systems such as Microsoft Sharepoint, and enterprise social networking tools such as Chatter, Yammer, Jive, and IBM Connections.

4. *What is the role of the information systems function in a business?*

The information systems department is the formal organizational unit responsible for information technology services. It is responsible for maintaining the hardware, software, data storage, and networks that comprise the firm's IT infrastructure. The department consists of specialists, such as programmers, systems analysts, project leaders, and information systems managers, and is often headed by a CIO.

Key Terms

Business intelligence, 51
Chief data officer (CDO), 76
Chief information officer (CIO), 76
Chief knowledge officer (CKO), 76
Chief privacy officer (CPO), 76
Chief security officer (CSO), 76
Collaboration, 76
Customer relationship management (CRM) systems, 61
Cyberlockers, 69
Decision-support systems (DSS), 55
Digital dashboard, 59
Electronic business (e-business), 62
Electronic commerce (e-commerce), 62
E-government, 63
End users, 76
Enterprise applications, 60

Enterprise systems, 61
Executive support systems (ESS), 58
Information systems department, 75
Information systems managers, 75
Interorganizational system, 61
IT governance, 77
Knowledge management systems (KMS), 61
Management information systems (MIS), 51
Portal, 58
Programmers, 75
Social business, 65
Supply chain management (SCM) systems, 61
Systems analysts, 75
Teams, 63
Telepresence, 69
Transaction processing systems (TPS), 49

Review Questions

2-1 What are business processes? How are they related to information systems?

- Define business processes and describe the role they play in organizations.

- Describe the relationship between information systems and business processes.

2-2 How do systems serve the different management groups and how do systems that link the enterprise improve organizational performance?

- Describe the characteristics of transaction processing systems (TPS) and the roles they play in a business and how do systems that link the enterprise improve organizational performance?

- Describe the characteristics of management information systems (MIS) and explain how MIS differ from TPS and from DSS.

- Describe the characteristics of decision-support systems (DSS) and how they benefit businesses.

- Describe the characteristics of executive support systems (ESS) and explain how these systems differ from DSS.

- Explain how enterprise applications improve organizational performance.

- Define enterprise systems, supply chain management systems, customer relationship management systems, and knowledge management systems and describe their business benefits.

- Explain how intranets and extranets help firms integrate information and business processes.

2-3 Why are systems for collaboration and social business so important and what technologies do they use?

- Define collaboration and social business, and explain why they have become so important in business today.
- List and describe the business benefits of collaboration and social business.
- Describe a supportive organizational culture and business processes for collaboration.
- List and describe the various types of collaboration and social business tools.

2-4 What is the role of the information systems function in a business?

- Describe how the information systems function supports a business.
- Compare the roles played by programmers, systems analysts, information systems managers, the chief information officer (CIO), chief security officer (CSO), chief data officer (CDO), and chief knowledge officer (CKO).

Discussion Questions

2-5 How could information systems be used to support the order fulfillment process illustrated in Figure 2.1? What are the most important pieces of information these systems should capture? Explain your answer.

2-6 Identify the steps that are performed in the process of selecting and checking out a book from your college library and the information that flows among these activi-

ties. Diagram the process. Are there any ways this process could be changed to improve the performance of your library or your school? Diagram the improved process.

2-7 Use the Time/Space Collaboration and Social Tool Matrix to classify the collaboration and social technologies used by Kluwer..

Hands-On MIS Projects

The projects in this section give you hands-on experience analyzing opportunities to improve business processes with new information system applications, using a spreadsheet to improve decision making about suppliers, and using Internet software to plan efficient transportation routes.

Management Decision Problems

2-8 Don's Lumber Company on the Hudson River features a large selection of materials for flooring, decks, moldings, windows, siding, and roofing. The prices of lumber and other building materials are constantly changing. When a customer inquires about the price on pre-finished wood flooring, sales representatives consult a manual price sheet and then call the supplier for the most recent price. The supplier in turn uses a manual price sheet, which has been updated each day. Often, the supplier must call back Don's sales reps because the company does not have the newest pricing information immediately on hand. Assess the business impact of this situation, describe how this process could be improved with information technology, and identify the decisions that would have to be made to implement a solution.

2-9 Henry's Hardware is a small family business in Sacramento, California. The owners, Henry and Kathleen, must use every square foot of store space as profitably as possible. They have never kept detailed inventory or sales records. As soon as a shipment of goods arrives, the items are immediately placed on store shelves. Invoices from suppliers are only kept for tax purposes. When an item is sold, the item number and price are rung up at the cash register. The owners use their own judgment in identifying items that need to be reordered. What is the business impact of this situation? How could information systems help Henry and Kathleen run their business? What data should these systems capture? What decisions could the systems improve?

Ranbaxy: Taking the ERP Pill
CASE STUDY

Ranbaxy Laboratories Ltd started its operations in 1961. It is one of the leading pharmaceutical companies in India, and also has significant presence the world over. Before the implementation of the ERP package, SAP, Ranbaxy used legacy systems to run its various operations. Tally was used by the finance department, while the inventory and product planning departments used MRP-I and MRP-II for material requirement planning and to schedule the inventory processes and activities of various departments. MRP-II also focused on the processes related to product planning, inventory management, and manufacturing. There were several issues with these legacy systems, the major problem being that of disconnection among all of them. Tally, the accounting software, was used by the finance teams only. It had no link to the processes followed by the other departments. As a result, it was difficult for managers to avail a streamlined flow of information. The MRP systems kept stock at Ranbaxy at a very rudimentary level, leading to frequent ordering of materials.

In order to integrate the processes of various departments, Ranbaxy decided to implement the SAP ERP package. Since Ranbaxy is a manufacturing organization and works in a competitive market, it is important that it increases organizational efficiency, controls its inventory levels through proper planning, reduces cost, increases profits, and streamlines its business flow. With SAP, the information generated by these departments is more accurate and available in real time. Each project manager is responsible for the exact planning, forecasting, and budgeting for a particular project. All the other departments work according to the plan for the project, or products and services. All functional departments have the clearest understanding of the operations to be performed, right from procurement to finance, project management, and sales.

SAP divides a single process into smaller subprocesses. For example, the process for stocking the store is further divided into generation of item codes, assigning item codes to the appropriate location, defining the stock levels, receipt and delivery of materials, and so on. Keeping track of every subprocess is important, especially since coordination between so many different departments may cause delays if proper tracking systems are not in place. The activity or department that slows down performance is identified early, and appropriate decisions are taken in order to enhance the efficiency of that department.

Maintaining the quality of the medicines and heatlhcare products is of utmost importance at Ranbaxy. SAP focuses on each process involved in the manufacturing of medicines, and identifies the processes that are responsible for defects. Through this information, the management takes effective decisions to overcome problems, thereby ensuring the quality of medicines. SAP has also helped reduce various kinds of costs. It has enhanced organizational productivity. Over time, labor costs have been minimized. Ranbaxy now also uses standard processes to raise purchase orders. Unlike the MRP systems that placed orders haphazardly, the orders in SAP are placed in accordance with the min–max plan of the inventory department. This has reduced the ordering and transportation costs of the company to a great extent. SAP has also integrated the various suppliers or vendors. Communication among different departments and the vendors has improved vastly.

Information is the backbone of an organization. Accurate, timely information helps the management take decisions at the right time. SAP provides timely information related to inventory, project planning, project costs, sales, and production.

The processes followed at Ranbaxy after the implementation of the SAP ERP are as follows:

1. Project planning and forecasting: The SAP helps managers plan the manufacturing process effectively. It lets them know the exact quantity of the medicines to be manufactured along with the date of exhaustion of stock.

2. Raising indent: Whenever there is a need to procure material for manufacturing, the manager raises an indent using SAP. The indent contains the exact purpose for which the material is requisitioned and the location at which it is needed. This indent is forwarded to the store manager for approval, after which the procurement teams go ahead with the purchase of the material.

3. RFQ (request for quotation): This module of SAP sends requests for quotations to the various approved suppliers. The procurement department compares these quotations and selects the best supplier after taking into consideration cost, quality, time, shipment, and other relevant factors.

4. Creation of purchase orders (POs): Once the quotation is finalized, the purchase department generates a PO for the approved indent. This PO contains the terms and conditions laid out by the legal department. A copy of this PO is forwarded to the finance department through the notification summary feature in the SAP for approval.

5. Receiving and delivering material: The ordered material is finally received, inspected, and delivered to the store. The store generates a receipt in the SAP to acknowledge the successful delivery of material.

6. Manufacturing requests: The material needed by the manufacturing personnel is issued through a move-order request. After obtaining the necessary approvals for the move, the material is issued to the requester.

7. Invoice creation: Finally, the SAP generates invoices for the finance department and records the entries into the GL (general ledger).

This is how SAP has been successfully implemented to achieve integration among all the functional departments at Ranbaxy and increase the efficiency of the business processes.

Sources: Aladwani, A.M., "Change management strategies for successful ERP implementation", *Business Process Management Journal*, Vol. 7, No. 3, pp. 266–75 (2001); Atkinson, H., "ERP software requires good planning", *Journal of Commerce*, p. 14 (1999); Burns, M., "ERPs: a buyers' market", *CAmagazine*, Vol. 132, No. 7, pp. 37–45 (1999); "Keebler sharpens demand planning processes with my SAP", *Business Wire* (2001); Caldwell, B., "GTE goes solo on SAP R/3", *Information Week*, No. 685, p. 150 (1998); Campbell, S., "Merisel gets powered by SAP ERP", *Computer Reseller News*, p. 66 (1999); Collett, S., "Rayovac charges into SAP with a big bang", *ComputerWorld*, p. 56 (1999); Collett, S., "SAP gets stuck in the spin cycle", *Computer World*, p. 1 (1999); Davenport, T., "Mission Critical—Realizing the Promise of Enterprise Systems", *Harvard Business School Publishing*, Boston, MA (2000); Dong, L., "Modeling top management influence on ES implementation", *Business Process Management Journal*, Vol. 7 No. 3, pp. 243–50 (2001); Geishecker, L., "ERP vs best of breed", *Strategic Management*, pp. 63–66 (1999); Huang, Z. and P. Palvia, "ERP implementation issues in advanced and developing countries", *Business Process Management Journal*, Vol. 7, No. 3, pp. 276–84 (2001).

CASE STUDY QUESTIONS

2-10 Discuss the flow of information before the implementation of the ERP system at Ranbaxy.

2-11 Discuss how the SAP has helped Ranbaxy overcome its previous problems.

2-12 Discuss the process flow after the implementation of the SAP ERP system.

Chapter 2 References

Aral, Sinan; Erik Brynjolfsson; and Marshall Van Alstyne, "Productivity Effects of Information Diffusion in Networks," MIT Center for Digital Business (July 2007).

Banker, Rajiv D., Nan Hu, Paul A. Pavlou, and Jerry Luftman. "CIO Reporting Structure, Strategic Positioning, and Firm Performance ." MIS Quarterly 35. No. 2 (June 2011).

Bernoff, Josh and Charlene Li. "Harnessing the Power of Social Applications." *MIT Sloan Management Review* (Spring 2008).

Bughin, Jacques, Angela Hung Byers, and Michael Chui. "How Social Technologies Are Extending the Organization." McKinsey Quarterly (November 2011).

Bureau of Labor Statistics. "Occupational Outlook Handbook 2012-2013 Edition." Bureau of Labor Statistics (July 2012).

Forrester Consulting, "Total Economic Impact of IBM Social Collaboration Tools" (September 2010).

Forrester Research. "Social Business: Delivering Critical Business Value" (April 2012).

Karen A. Frenkel. "How the CIO's Role Will Change by 2018." *CIO Insight* (January 31, 2014).

Dwoskin, Elizabeth. "Big Data's High-Priests of Algorithms." *Wall Street Journal* (August 8, 2014).

Frost & White. "Meetings Around the World II: Charting the Course of Advanced Collaboration." (October 14, 2009).

Greengard, Samuel. "Collaboration: At the Center of Effective Business." *Baseline* (January 24, 2014).

_____. "The Social Business Gets Results." Baseline (June 19, 2014).

Guillemette, Manon G. and Guy Pare."Toward a New Theory of the Contribution of the IT Function in Organizations." *MIS Quarterly* 36, No. 2 (June 2012).

IBM. "Finncontainers Grows into a Nimble, Efficient Enterprise." (June 27, 2013).

Johnson, Bradford, James Manyika, and Lareina Yee. "The Next Revolution in Interactions," *McKinsey Quarterly* No. 4 (2005).

Kane, Gerald C., Doug Palmer, Anh Nguyen Phillips and David Kiron. "Finding the Value in Social Business. *MIT Sloan Management Review*, 55, No. 3 (Spring 2014).

Kiron, David, Doug Palmer, Anh Nguyen Phillips and Nina Kruschwitz. "What Managers Really Think About Social Business." *MIT Sloan Management Review* 53, No. 4 (Summer 2012).

Kolfschoten, Gwendolyn L. , Niederman, Fred, Briggs, Robert O. and Vreede, Gert-Jan De. "Facilitation Roles and Responsibilities for Sustained Collaboration Support in Organizations." Journal of Management Information Systems 28, No. 4 (Spring 2012).

Li, Charlene. "Making the Business Case for Enterprise Social Networks." Altimeter Group (February 22, 2012).

Malone, Thomas M., Kevin Crowston, Jintae Lee, and Brian Pentland. "Tools for Inventing Organizations: Toward a Handbook of Organizational Processes." *Management Science* 45, No. 3 (March 1999).

McKinsey Global Institute. "The Social Economy: Unlocking Value and Productivity Through Social Technologies." McKinsey & Company (July 2012).

Microsoft Corporation. "Fair Work OmbudsmanAustralian Government Body Increases Compliance through LOB Connection." (February 2, 2014).

Poltrock, Steven and Mark Handel. "Models of Collaboration as the Foundation for Collaboration Technologies." *Journal of Management Information Systems* 27, No. 1 (Summer 2010).

Saunders, Carol, A. F. Rutkowski, Michiel van Genuchten, Doug Vogel, and Julio Molina Orrego. "Virtual Space and Place: Theory and Test." MIS Quarterly 35, No. 4 (December 2011).

Siebdrat, Frank, Martin Hoegl, and Holger Ernst. "How to Manage Virtual Teams." *MIT Sloan Management Review* 50, No. 4 (Summer 2009).

Tallon, Paul P. , Ronald V.Ramirez, and James E. Short . "The Information Artifact in IT Governance: Toward a Theory of Information Governance." *Journal of Management Information Systems* 30, No. 3 (Winter 2014).

Violino, Bob. "What Is Driving the Need for Chief Data Officers?" *Information Management* (February 3, 2014).

Weill, Peter and Jeanne W. Ross. *IT Governance*. Boston: Harvard Business School Press (2004).

Information Systems, Organizations, and Strategy

CHAPTER 3

LEARNING OBJECTIVES

After reading this chapter, you will be able to answer the following questions:

1. Which features of organizations do managers need to know about to build and use information systems successfully?

2. What is the impact of information systems on organizations?

3. How do Porter's competitive forces model, the value chain model, synergies, core competencies, and network economics help companies develop competitive strategies using information systems?

4. What are the challenges posed by strategic information systems and how should they be addressed?

CHAPTER CASES

AIRASIA: SAVING ON OPERATIONAL COSTS THROUGH EFFECTIVE INFORMATION SYSTEMS

AirAsia India is a leading Indo-Malaysian low-cost ailrine. It was launched in 1996 and now has a fleet of 72 aircrafts, flies to 61 domestic and international destinations over 108 routes, and operates about 400 flights daily. AirAsia India was launched in 2013 as a joint venture between AirAsia Berhad, Tata Sons, and Telestra Tradeplace. In India, it currently operates in seven destinations. AirAsia's success can be traced back to the time when Tim Fernandes purchased the company, became the CEO, and restructured the organization. At a time when every other airline was offering tickets at comparable prices with the same facilities, Tim came up with the concept of a no-frills, hassle-free, low-cost airline. Although the concept had already been implemented in SouthwestAirlines in the U.S., applying the same strategy in India was a challenge. Since Indian customers are generally price-sensitive, Tim saw a huge potential in offering low-cost services here. "Being an unproven model, the low-cost, long-haul business is rather risky ... When we first started, many people thought it was a crazy idea to offer low fares as it was not economically viable. Especially with an airline with high acquisitions like us, we were expected to fail. However, with strong persistence and right strategies we persevered and we are now the leading and largest low-cost carrier in Asia," says Tim.

© Gts. Shutterstock

Airlines face several challanges while trying to provide services at low costs. When reducing the price, the quality of service cannot be compromised, and this is especially true for airlines where passenger safety is of utmost importance. AirAsia implemented the low-cost carrier strategy in two different ways. It first amended the basic facilities provided to passengers and then reduced the operational expenses of the company. AirAsia brought about a no-frills service policy, by which it meant that no free meals would be provided on board flights. This helped the company reduce both the number of employees required to cater to and serve passengers and the turnaround time needed to clear the airplane for the next destination. While the airlines that provided meals on board took about an hour to leave the airport, AirAsia took only 30 minutes. This helped AirAsia fly 20 to 30 per cent more flights than its competitors. The airline started flying economy class passengers exclusively, which helped them seat 20% more people on a single flight.

To save on the operational costs, AirAsia implemented effective information systems in the following manner:

1. **Yield management system:** Ticketing and routes are two of the most important aspects of the airlines business. An yield management system helps sell tickets at the most appropriate price and optimally manage the routes. AirAsia has managed to sell the same type of seats on the same route at different prices because of its yield management system. The system charges passengers based on the time of the reservations. Passengers who reserve tickets in advance are charged less for the same seat as compared to a passenger who reserves a seat closer to the date of flying. This helped AirAsia reap maximum profit from tickets and also motivate passengers to book in advance. The system of advance booking has helped AirAsia know the occupancy status of flights. Moreover, it has enabled the company to figure out the routes on which the demand is high.

2. **Customer reservation system:** AirAsia discontinued the conventional system of booking tickets through travel agents, thereby reducing the airline's total expenses by 11 to 15 per cent. AirAsia implemented its own customer reservation system, a Web-enabled online reservation suite provided by Navitaine Open Skies Technology. This system allows passenger book tickets directly, without using the services of travel agents. By doing so, AirAsia also saved on the cost of printing paper tickets, since the system provided the customer with the option to print tickets at their end. This whole process has helped AirAsia reduce its operational expenses by 40 to 45 per cent.

3. **Operators management software:** As the operations of AirAsia grew exponentially, the company implemented an airline operators management software, Merlot.aero, to forecast, organize, and report on the airline and crew activities. AirAsia can now easily manage the crew requirement. Crew members can intimate the management about their absence from duty using their personal mobile phones, and the software automatically helps find the best possible replacement for the absent employee. The software also provides the schedule and other necessary flight information to all the concerned parties. This keeps

AirAsia connected to all the important stakeholders. Finally, this software helps manage critical activities such as flight scheduling, network planning, aircraft portal and maintenance, and crew payroll management, among others.

Sources: Alexander, Keith L. (2004). The Economics of Low Cost Carriers – All the Numbers Add Down for the Nation's Low-Cost Carriers. Washington Post, Feb 29, 2004; Economist, The (2004). Low Cost Airlines – Turbulent Skies. Economist Print Edition – July 89, 2004; http://www.economist.com/business/displaystory.cfm?story_id = 2897525; Hecker, JayEtta Z. (2004, June 3). COMMERCIAL AVIATION – Despite Industry Turmoil, Low-Cost Airlines are Growing and Profitable; United States General Accounting Office – Testimony Before the Subcommittee on Aviation, Committee on Transportation and Infrastructure, House of Representatives;Kong, Ying & Le Dressay, Andre (2003); Spinning off low cost cariers – when does it make sense? Journal of the Academy of Business and Economics, April 2003; Schneiderbauer, Dieter & Fainsilber, Olivier (2004). Impact of low cost airlines – Summary of Mercer Study; Mercer Management Company; John Carney: "The man who bought AirAsia for 50 CENTS when it had just two aircraft and turned it into a hugely successful budget airline... now it's his 'worst nightmare'", December 29, 2014; accessed on December 2, 2015 (http://www.dailymail.co.uk/news/article-2889449/Meet-multi-millionaire-bought-AirAsia-50-cents-thirteen-years-ago-just-two-aircraft-turned-hugely-successful-budget-airline.html); AirAsia: AirAsia wins Airline Strategy Award 2008; Accessed on December 2, 2015 (https://www.facebook.com/notes/airasia/airasia-wins-airline-strategy-award-2008/19413023741); "AirAsia is best Asian low-cost airline"; accessed on December 2, 2015 (http://www.eturbonews.com/5559/airasia-best-asian-low-cost-airline); http://www.academia.edu/9150463/Air_asia_marketing_strategies

The AirAsia case illustrates some of the ways through which information systems help businesses compete as well as the challenges of finding the right business strategy and how to use technology in that strategy.

The airline industry is an extremely crowded playing field with large number of players operating and vying for the same customers. Even though AirAsia is an established player in the industry, it has many competitors, and it is searching for a way to use the information system that will work with its particular business model. The chapter-opening diagram calls attention to important points raised by this case and this chapter. AirAsia has been a

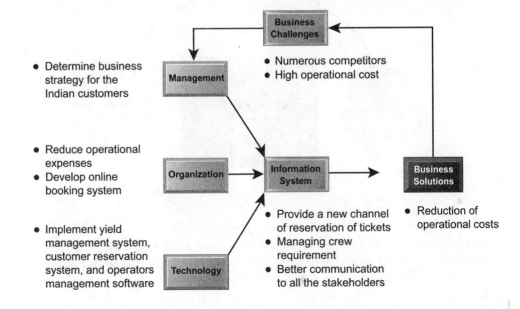

leading airline player which operates more than 400 flights everyday. The present business model is being challenged by the fact that many players in the market are offering tickets at comparable prices with the same facilities. Tim Fernaedes, CEO of AirAsia, thought of a new business model of having a no-frills and low-cost airline service especially for the Indian customers. Accordingly new strategy was implemented in which apart from reducing the basic facilities offered to the customers, information system was also implemented in order to curtail the operational costs.

Here are some questions to think about: What role does technology play in AirAsia's success. Assess the contribution of the systems described in the case study.

3.1 WHICH FEATURES OF ORGANIZATIONS DO MANAGERS NEED TO KNOW ABOUT TO BUILD AND USE INFORMATION SYSTEMS SUCCESSFULLY?

Information systems and organizations influence one another. Information systems are built by managers to serve the interests of the business firm. At the same time, the organization must be aware of and open to the influences of information systems to benefit from new technologies.

The interaction between information technology and organizations is complex and is influenced by many mediating factors, including the organization's structure, business processes, politics, culture, surrounding environment, and management decisions (see Figure 3.1). You will need to understand

FIGURE 3.1 THE TWO-WAY RELATIONSHIP BETWEEN ORGANIZATIONS AND INFORMATION TECHNOLOGY

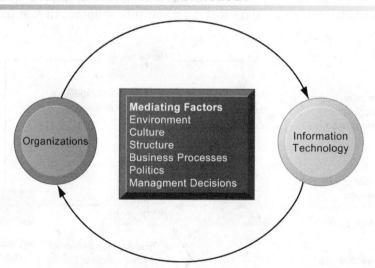

This complex two-way relationship is mediated by many factors, not the least of which are the decisions made—or not made—by managers. Other factors mediating the relationship include the organizational culture, structure, politics, business processes, and environment.

how information systems can change social and work life in your firm. You will not be able to design new systems successfully or understand existing systems without understanding your own business organization.

As a manager, you will be the one to decide which systems will be built, what they will do, and how they will be implemented. You may not be able to anticipate all of the consequences of these decisions. Some of the changes that occur in business firms because of new information technology (IT) investments cannot be foreseen and have results that may or may not meet your expectations. Who would have imagined fifteen years ago, for instance, that e-mail and instant messaging would become a dominant form of business communication and that many managers would be inundated with more than 200 e-mail messages each day?

WHAT IS AN ORGANIZATION?

An **organization** is a stable, formal social structure that takes resources from the environment and processes them to produce outputs. This technical definition focuses on three elements of an organization. Capital and labor are primary production factors provided by the environment. The organization (the firm) transforms these inputs into products and services in a production function. The products and services are consumed by environments in return for supply inputs (see Figure 3.2).

An organization is more stable than an informal group (such as a group of friends that meets every Friday for lunch) in terms of longevity and routineness. Organizations are formal legal entities with internal rules and procedures that must abide by laws. Organizations are also social structures because they are a collection of social elements, much as a machine has a structure—a particular arrangement of valves, cams, shafts, and other parts.

This definition of organizations is powerful and simple, but it is not very descriptive or even predictive of real-world organizations. A more realistic behavioral definition of an organization is a collection of rights, privileges,

FIGURE 3.2   THE TECHNICAL MICROECONOMIC DEFINITION OF THE ORGANIZATION

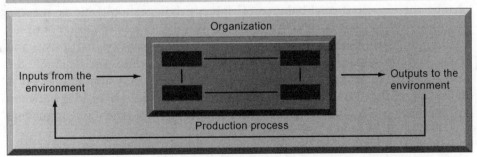

In the microeconomic definition of organizations, capital and labor (the primary production factors provided by the environment) are transformed by the firm through the production process into products and services (outputs to the environment). The products and services are consumed by the environment, which supplies additional capital and labor as inputs in the feedback loop.

FIGURE 3.3   THE BEHAVIORAL VIEW OF ORGANIZATIONS

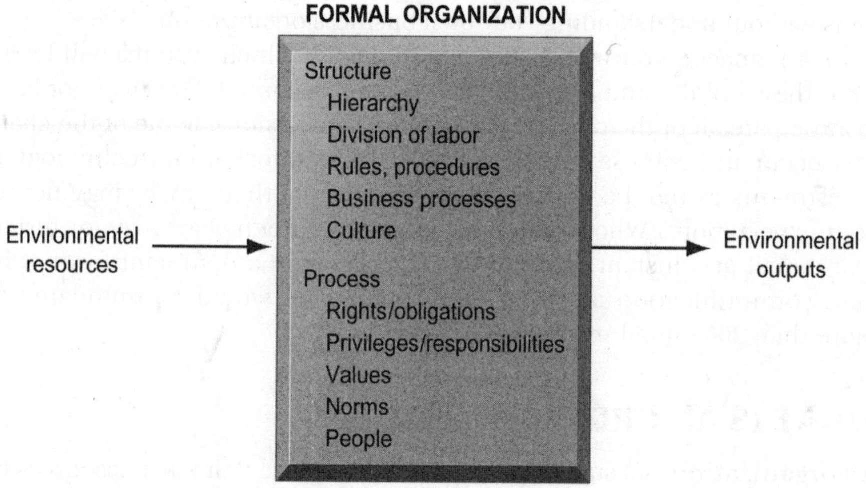

FORMAL ORGANIZATION

Environmental
resources

Structure
   Hierarchy
   Division of labor
   Rules, procedures
   Business processes
   Culture
Process
   Rights/obligations
   Privileges/responsibilities
   Values
   Norms
   People

Environmental
outputs

The behavioral view of organizations emphasizes group relationships, values, and structures.

obligations, and responsibilities delicately balanced over a period of time through conflict and conflict resolution (see Figure 3.3).

In this behavioral view of the firm, people who work in organizations develop customary ways of working; they gain attachments to existing relationships; and they make arrangements with subordinates and superiors about how work will be done, the amount of work that will be done, and under what conditions work will be done. Most of these arrangements and feelings are not discussed in any formal rulebook.

How do these definitions of organizations relate to information systems technology? A technical view of organizations encourages us to focus on how inputs are combined to create outputs when technology changes are introduced into the company. The firm is seen as infinitely malleable, with capital and labor substituting for each other quite easily. But the more realistic behavioral definition of an organization suggests that building new information systems, or rebuilding old ones, involves much more than a technical rearrangement of machines or workers—that some information systems change the organizational balance of rights, privileges, obligations, responsibilities, and feelings that have been established over a long period of time.

Changing these elements can take a long time, be very disruptive, and requires more resources to support training and learning. For instance, the length of time required to implement a new information system effectively is much longer than usually anticipated simply because there is a lag between implementing a technical system and teaching employees and managers how to use the system.

Technological change requires changes in who owns and controls information, who has the right to access and update that information, and who makes decisions about whom, when, and how. This more complex view forces us to look at the way work is designed and the procedures used to achieve outputs.

The technical and behavioral definitions of organizations are not contradictory. Indeed, they complement each other: The technical definition tells us how thousands of firms in competitive markets combine capital, labor, and information technology, whereas the behavioral model takes us inside the individual firm to see how that technology affects the organization's inner workings. Section 3.2 describes how each of these definitions of organizations can help explain the relationships between information systems and organizations.

FEATURES OF ORGANIZATIONS

All modern organizations share certain characteristics. They are bureaucracies with clear-cut divisions of labor and specialization. Organizations arrange specialists in a hierarchy of authority in which everyone is accountable to someone and authority is limited to specific actions governed by abstract rules or procedures. These rules create a system of impartial and universal decision making. Organizations try to hire and promote employees on the basis of technical qualifications and professionalism (not personal connections). The organization is devoted to the principle of efficiency: maximizing output using limited inputs. Other features of organizations include their business processes, organizational culture, organizational politics, surrounding environments, structure, goals, constituencies, and leadership styles. All of these features affect the kinds of information systems used by organizations.

Routines and Business Processes

All organizations, including business firms, become very efficient over time because individuals in the firm develop **routines** for producing goods and services. Routines—sometimes called *standard operating procedures*—are precise rules, procedures, and practices that have been developed to cope with virtually all expected situations. As employees learn these routines, they become highly productive and efficient, and the firm is able to reduce its costs over time as efficiency increases. For instance, when you visit a doctor's office, receptionists have a well-developed set of routines for gathering basic information from you; nurses have a different set of routines for preparing you for an interview with a doctor; and the doctor has a well-developed set of routines for diagnosing you. *Business processes*, which we introduced in Chapters 1 and 2, are collections of such routines. A business firm, in turn, is a collection of business processes (Figure 3.4).

Organizational Politics

People in organizations occupy different positions with different specialties, concerns, and perspectives. As a result, they naturally have divergent viewpoints about how resources, rewards, and punishments should be distributed. These differences matter to both managers and employees, and they result in political struggle for resources, competition, and conflict within every organization. Political resistance is one of the great difficulties of bringing about organizational change—especially the development

FIGURE 3.4   ROUTINES, BUSINESS PROCESSES, AND FIRMS

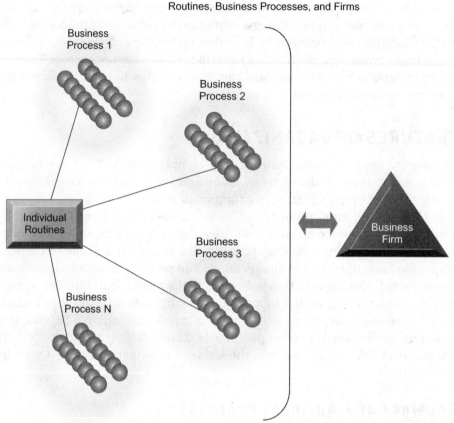

Routines, Business Processes, and Firms

All organizations are composed of individual routines and behaviors, a collection of which make up a business process. A collection of business processes make up the business firm. New information system applications require that individual routines and business processes change to achieve high levels of organizational performance.

of new information systems. Virtually all large information systems investments by a firm that bring about significant changes in strategy, business objectives, business processes, and procedures become politically charged events. Managers who know how to work with the politics of an organization will be more successful than less-skilled managers in implementing new information systems. Throughout this book, you will find many examples where internal politics defeated the best-laid plans for an information system.

Organizational Culture

All organizations have bedrock, unassailable, unquestioned (by the members) assumptions that define their goals and products. Organizational culture encompasses this set of assumptions about what products the organization should produce, how it should produce them, where, and for whom. Generally, these cultural assumptions are taken totally for granted and are rarely publicly announced or discussed. Business processes—the actual way business firms produce value—are usually ensconced in the organization's culture.

You can see organizational culture at work by looking around your university or college. Some bedrock assumptions of university life are that professors know more than students, the reason students attend college is to learn, and classes follow a regular schedule. Organizational culture is a powerful unifying force that restrains political conflict and promotes common understanding, agreement on procedures, and common practices. If we all share the same basic cultural assumptions, agreement on other matters is more likely.

At the same time, organizational culture is a powerful restraint on change, especially technological change. Most organizations will do almost anything to avoid making changes in basic assumptions. Any technological change that threatens commonly held cultural assumptions usually meets a great deal of resistance. However, there are times when the only sensible way for a firm to move forward is to employ a new technology that directly opposes an existing organizational culture. When this occurs, the technology is often stalled while the culture slowly adjusts.

Organizational Environments

Organizations reside in environments from which they draw resources and to which they supply goods and services. Organizations and environments have a reciprocal relationship. On the one hand, organizations are open to, and dependent on, the social and physical environment that surrounds them. Without financial and human resources—people willing to work reliably and consistently for a set wage or revenue from customers—organizations could not exist. Organizations must respond to legislative and other requirements imposed by government, as well as the actions of customers and competitors. On the other hand, organizations can influence their environments. For example, business firms form alliances with other businesses to influence the political process; they advertise to influence customer acceptance of their products.

Figure 3.5 illustrates the role of information systems in helping organizations perceive changes in their environments and also in helping organizations act on their environments. Information systems are key instruments for *environmental scanning*, helping managers identify external changes that might require an organizational response.

Environments generally change much faster than organizations. New technologies, new products, and changing public tastes and values (many of which result in new government regulations) put strains on any organization's culture, politics, and people. Most organizations are unable to adapt to a rapidly changing environment. Inertia built into an organization's standard operating procedures, the political conflict raised by changes to the existing order, and the threat to closely held cultural values inhibit organizations from making significant changes. Young firms typically lack resources to sustain even short periods of troubled times. It is not surprising that only 10 percent of the Fortune 500 companies in 1919 still exist today.

FIGURE 3.5 ENVIRONMENTS AND ORGANIZATIONS HAVE A RECIPROCAL RELATIONSHIP

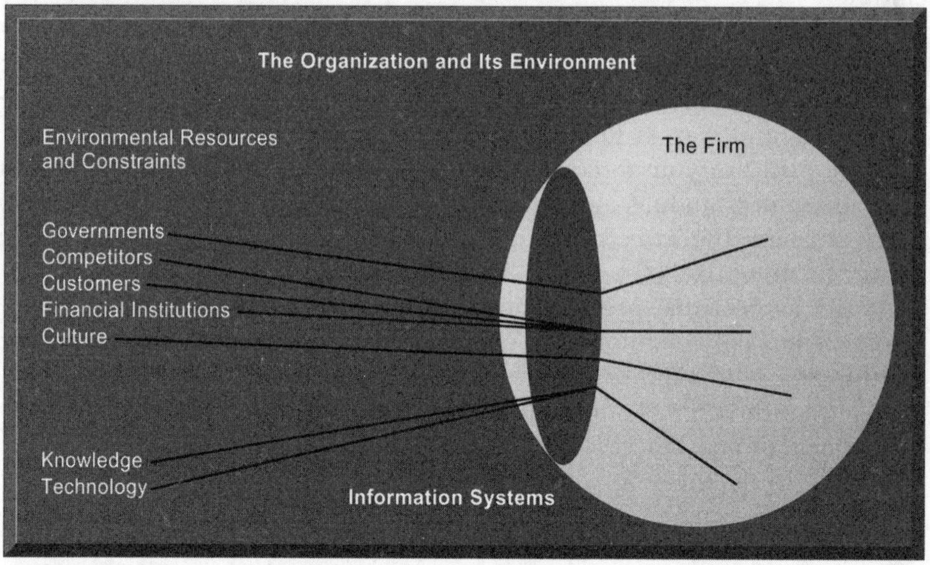

Environments shape what organizations can do, but organizations can influence their environments and decide to change environments altogether. Information technology plays a critical role in helping organizations perceive environmental change and in helping organizations act on their environment.

Disruptive Technologies: Riding the Wave. Sometimes a technology and resulting business innovation comes along to radically change the business landscape and environment. These innovations are loosely called "disruptive." (Christensen, 2003). What makes a technology disruptive? In some cases, **disruptive technologies** are substitute products that perform as well as or better (often much better) than anything currently produced. The car substituted for the horse-drawn carriage; the word processor for typewriters; the Apple iPod for portable CD players; digital photography for process film photography.

In these cases, entire industries were put out of business. In other cases, disruptive technologies simply extend the market, usually with less functionality and much less cost, than existing products. Eventually they turn into low-cost competitors for whatever was sold before. Disk drives are an example: Small hard disk drives used in PCs extended the market for disk drives by offering cheap digital storage for small files. Eventually, small PC hard disk drives became the largest segment of the disk drive marketplace.

Some firms are able to create these technologies and ride the wave to profits; others learn quickly and adapt their business; still others are obliterated because their products, services, and business models become obsolete. They may be very efficient at doing what no longer needs to be done! There are also cases where no firms benefit, and all the gains go to consumers (firms fail to capture any profits). Table 3.1 describes just a few disruptive technologies from the past.

TABLE 3.1 DISRUPTIVE TECHNOLOGIES: WINNERS AND LOSERS

TECHNOLOGY	DESCRIPTION	WINNERS AND LOSERS
Microprocessor chips (1971)	Thousands and eventually millions of transistors on a silicon chip	Microprocessor firms win (Intel, Texas Instruments) while transistor firms (GE) decline.
Personal computers (1975)	Small, inexpensive, but fully functional desktop computers	PC manufacturers (HP, Apple, IBM), and chip manufacturers prosper (Intel), while mainframe (IBM) and minicomputer (DEC) firms lose.
Digital photography (1975)	Using CCD (charge-coupled device) image sensor chips to record images	CCD manufacturers and traditional camera companies win, manufacturers of film products lose.
World Wide Web (1989)	A global database of digital files and "pages" instantly available	Owners of online content, news benefit while traditional publishers (newspapers, magazines, and broadcast television) lose.
Internet music, video, TV services (1998)	Repositories of downloadable music, video, TV broadcasts on the Web	Owners of Internet platforms, telecommunications providers owning Internet backbone (ATT, Verizon), local Internet service providers win, while content owners and physical retailers lose (Tower Records, Blockbuster).
PageRank algorithm	A method for ranking Web pages in terms of their popularity to supplement Web search by key terms	Google is the winner (they own the patent), while traditional key word search engines (Alta Vista) lose.
Software as Web service	Using the Internet to provide remote access to online software	Online software services companies (Salesforce.com) win, while traditional "boxed" software companies (Microsoft, SAP, Oracle) lose.

Disruptive technologies are tricky. Firms that invent disruptive technologies as "first movers" do not always benefit if they lack the resources to exploit the technology or fail to see the opportunity. The MITS Altair 8800 is widely regarded as the first PC, but its inventors did not take advantage of their first mover status. Second movers, so-called "fast followers" such as IBM and Microsoft, reaped the rewards. Citibank's ATMs revolutionized retail banking, but they were copied by other banks. Now all banks use ATMs, with the benefits going mostly to the consumers.

Organizational Structure

All organizations have a structure or shape. Mintzberg's classification, described in Table 3.2, identifies five basic kinds of organizational structure (Mintzberg, 1979).

The kind of information systems you find in a business firm—and the nature of problems with these systems—often reflects the type of organizational structure. For instance, in a professional bureaucracy such as a hospital, it is not unusual to find parallel patient record systems operated by the administration, another by doctors, and another by other professional staff such as nurses and social workers. In small entrepreneurial firms, you will often find poorly designed systems developed in a rush that often quickly outgrow their usefulness. In huge multidivisional firms operating in hundreds of locations, you will often find there is not a single integrating information system, but instead each locale or each division has its set of information systems.

TABLE 3.2 ORGANIZATIONAL STRUCTURES

ORGANIZATIONAL TYPE	DESCRIPTION	EXAMPLES
Entrepreneurial structure	Young, small firm in a fast-changing environment. It has a simple structure and is managed by an entrepreneur serving as its single chief executive officer.	Small start-up business
Machine bureaucracy	Large bureaucracy existing in a slowly changing environment, producing standard products. It is dominated by a centralized management team and centralized decision making.	Midsize manufacturing firm
Divisionalized bureaucracy	Combination of multiple machine bureaucracies, each producing a different product or service, all topped by one central headquarters.	Fortune 500 firms, such as General Motors
Professional bureaucracy	Knowledge-based organization where goods and services depend on the expertise and knowledge of professionals. Dominated by department heads with weak centralized authority.	Law firms, school systems, hospitals
Adhocracy	Task force organization that must respond to rapidly changing environments. Consists of large groups of specialists organized into short-lived multidisciplinary teams and has weak central management.	Consulting firms, such as the Rand Corporation

Other Organizational Features

Organizations have goals and use different means to achieve them. Some organizations have coercive goals (e.g., prisons); others have utilitarian goals (e.g., businesses). Still others have normative goals (universities, religious groups). Organizations also serve different groups or have different constituencies, some primarily benefiting their members, others benefiting clients, stockholders, or the public. The nature of leadership differs greatly from one organization to another—some organizations may be more democratic or authoritarian than others. Another way organizations differ is by the tasks they perform and the technology they use. Some organizations perform primarily routine tasks that can be reduced to formal rules that require little judgment (such as manufacturing auto parts), whereas others (such as consulting firms) work primarily with nonroutine tasks.

3.2 WHAT IS THE IMPACT OF INFORMATION SYSTEMS ON ORGANIZATIONS?

Information systems have become integral, online, interactive tools deeply involved in the minute-to-minute operations and decision making of large organizations. Over the last decade, information systems have fundamentally altered the economics of organizations and greatly increased the possibilities for organizing work. Theories and concepts from economics and sociology help us understand the changes brought about by IT.

ECONOMIC IMPACTS

From the point of view of economics, IT changes both the relative costs of capital and the costs of information. Information systems technology can be viewed as a factor of production that can be substituted for traditional capital and labor. As the cost of information technology decreases, it is substituted for labor, which historically has been a rising cost. Hence, information technology should result in a decline in the number of middle managers and clerical workers as information technology substitutes for their labor.

As the cost of information technology decreases, it also substitutes for other forms of capital such as buildings and machinery, which remain relatively expensive. Hence, over time we should expect managers to increase their investments in IT because of its declining cost relative to other capital investments.

IT also affects the cost and quality of information and changes the economics of information. Information technology helps firms contract in size because it can reduce transaction costs—the costs incurred when a firm buys on the marketplace what it cannot make itself. According to **transaction cost theory**, firms and individuals seek to economize on transaction costs, much as they do on production costs. Using markets is expensive because of costs such as locating and communicating with distant suppliers, monitoring contract compliance, buying insurance, obtaining information on products, and so forth (Coase, 1937; Williamson, 1985). Traditionally, firms have tried to reduce transaction costs through vertical integration, by getting bigger, hiring more employees, and buying their own suppliers and distributors, as both General Motors and Ford used to do.

Information technology, especially the use of networks, can help firms lower the cost of market participation (transaction costs), making it worthwhile for firms to contract with external suppliers instead of using internal sources. As a result, firms can shrink in size (numbers of employees) because it is far less expensive to outsource work to a competitive marketplace rather than hire employees.

For instance, by using computer links to external suppliers, auto makers such as Chrysler, Toyota, and Honda can achieve economies by obtaining more than 70 percent of their parts from the outside. Information systems make it possible for companies such as Cisco Systems and Dell Inc. to outsource their production to contract manufacturers such as Flextronics instead of making their products themselves.

As transaction costs decrease, firm size (the number of employees) should shrink because it becomes easier and cheaper for the firm to contract for the purchase of goods and services in the marketplace rather than to make the product or offer the service itself. Firm size can stay constant or contract even as the company increases its revenues. For example, when Eastman Chemical Company split off from Kodak in 1994, it had $3.3 billion in revenue and 24,000 full-time employees. In 2013, it generated over $9.3 billion in revenue with only 14,000 employees.

Information technology also can reduce internal management costs. According to **agency theory**, the firm is viewed as a "nexus of contracts" among self-interested individuals rather than as a unified, profit-maximizing entity (Jensen and Meckling, 1976). A principal (owner) employs "agents" (employees) to perform work on his or her behalf. However, agents need constant supervision and management; otherwise, they will tend to pursue their own interests rather than those of the owners. As firms grow in size and scope, agency costs or coordination costs rise because owners must expend more and more effort supervising and managing employees.

Information technology, by reducing the costs of acquiring and analyzing information, permits organizations to reduce agency costs because it becomes easier for managers to oversee a greater number of employees. By reducing overall management costs, information technology enables firms to increase revenues while shrinking the number of middle managers and clerical workers. We have seen examples in earlier chapters where information technology expanded the power and scope of small organizations by enabling them to perform coordinating activities such as processing orders or keeping track of inventory with very few clerks and managers.

Because IT reduces both agency and transaction costs for firms, we should expect firm size to shrink over time as more capital is invested in IT. Firms should have fewer managers, and we expect to see revenue per employee increase over time.

ORGANIZATIONAL AND BEHAVIORAL IMPACTS

Theories based in the sociology of complex organizations also provide some understanding about how and why firms change with the implementation of new IT applications.

IT Flattens Organizations

Large, bureaucratic organizations, which primarily developed before the computer age, are often inefficient, slow to change, and less competitive than newly created organizations. Some of these large organizations have downsized, reducing the number of employees and the number of levels in their organizational hierarchies.

Behavioral researchers have theorized that information technology facilitates flattening of hierarchies by broadening the distribution of information to empower lower-level employees and increase management efficiency (see Figure 3.6). IT pushes decision-making rights lower in the organization because lower-level employees receive the information they need to make decisions without supervision. (This empowerment is also possible because of higher educational levels among the workforce, which give employees the capabilities to make intelligent decisions.) Because managers now receive so much more accurate information on time, they become much faster at making decisions, so fewer managers are required. Management costs decline as a percentage of revenues, and the hierarchy becomes much more efficient.

These changes mean that the management span of control has also been broadened, enabling high-level managers to manage and control more workers spread over greater distances. Many companies have eliminated thousands of middle managers as a result of these changes.

FIGURE 3.6   FLATTENING ORGANIZATIONS

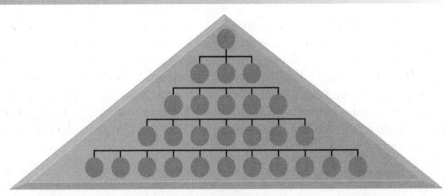

A traditional hierarchical organization with many levels of management

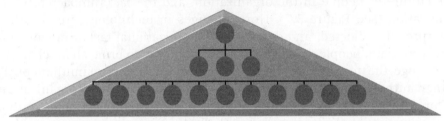

An organization that has been "flattened" by removing layers of management

Information systems can reduce the number of levels in an organization by providing managers with information to supervise larger numbers of workers and by giving lower-level employees more decision-making authority.

Postindustrial Organizations

Postindustrial theories based more on history and sociology than economics also support the notion that IT should flatten hierarchies. In postindustrial societies, authority increasingly relies on knowledge and competence, and not merely on formal positions. Hence, the shape of organizations flattens because professional workers tend to be self-managing, and decision making should become more decentralized as knowledge and information become more widespread throughout the firm (Drucker, 1988).

Information technology may encourage task force-networked organizations in which groups of professionals come together—face to face or electronically—for short periods of time to accomplish a specific task (e.g., designing a new automobile); once the task is accomplished, the individuals join other task forces. The global consulting service Accenture is an example. Many of its 293,000 employees move from location to location to work on projects at client locations in more than 56 different countries.

Who makes sure that self-managed teams do not head off in the wrong direction? Who decides which person works on which team and for how long? How can managers evaluate the performance of someone who is constantly rotating from team to team? How do people know where their careers are headed? New approaches for evaluating, organizing, and informing workers are required, and not all companies can make virtual work effective.

Understanding Organizational Resistance to Change

Information systems inevitably become bound up in organizational politics because they influence access to a key resource—namely, information. Information systems can affect who does what to whom, when, where, and how in an organization. Many new information systems require changes in personal, individual routines that can be painful for those involved and require retraining and additional effort that may or may not be compensated. Because information systems potentially change an organization's structure, culture, business processes, and strategy, there is often considerable resistance to them when they are introduced.

There are several ways to visualize organizational resistance. Research on organizational resistance to innovation suggests that four factors are paramount: the nature of the IT innovation, the organization's structure, the culture of people in the organization, and the tasks impacted by the innovation (see Figure 3.7). Here, changes in technology are absorbed, interpreted, deflected, and defeated by organizational task arrangements, structures, and people. In this model, the only way to bring about change is to change the technology, tasks, structure, and people simultaneously. Other authors have spoken about the need to "unfreeze" organizations before introducing an innovation, quickly implementing it, and "refreezing" or institutionalizing the change (Kolb, 1970).

Because organizational resistance to change is so powerful, many information technology investments flounder and do not increase productivity.

FIGURE 3.7   ORGANIZATIONAL RESISTANCE TO INFORMATION SYSTEM INNOVATIONS

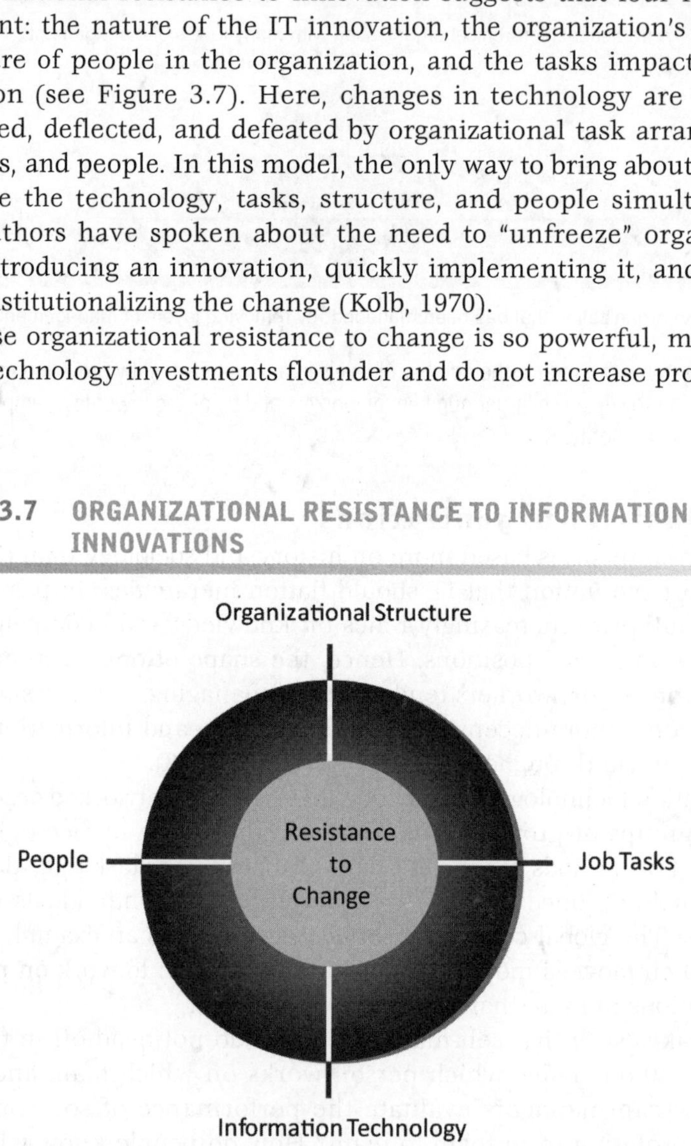

Implementing information systems has consequences for task arrangements, structures, and people. According to this model, to implement change, all four components must be changed simultaneously.

Indeed, research on project implementation failures demonstrates that the most common reason for failure of large projects to reach their objectives is not the failure of the technology, but organizational and political resistance to change. Chapter 14 treats this issue in detail. Therefore, as a manager involved in future IT investments, your ability to work with people and organizations is just as important as your technical awareness and knowledge.

THE INTERNET AND ORGANIZATIONS

The Internet, especially the World Wide Web, has an important impact on the relationships between many firms and external entities, and even on the organization of business processes inside a firm. The Internet increases the accessibility, storage, and distribution of information and knowledge for organizations. In essence, the Internet is capable of dramatically lowering the transaction and agency costs facing most organizations. For instance, brokerage firms and banks in New York can now deliver their internal operating procedures manuals to their employees at distant locations by posting them on the corporate Web site, saving millions of dollars in distribution costs. A global sales force can receive nearly instant product price information updates using the Web or instructions from management sent by e-mail or text messaging on smartphones or mobile laptops. Vendors of some large retailers can access retailers' internal Web sites directly to find up-to-the-minute sales information and to initiate replenishment orders instantly.

Businesses are rapidly rebuilding some of their key business processes based on Internet technology and making this technology a key component of their IT infrastructures. If prior networking is any guide, one result will be simpler business processes, fewer employees, and much flatter organizations than in the past.

IMPLICATIONS FOR THE DESIGN AND UNDERSTANDING OF INFORMATION SYSTEMS

To deliver genuine benefits, information systems must be built with a clear understanding of the organization in which they will be used. In our experience, the central organizational factors to consider when planning a new system are the following:

- The environment in which the organization must function
- The structure of the organization: hierarchy, specialization, routines, and business processes
- The organization's culture and politics
- The type of organization and its style of leadership
- The principal interest groups affected by the system and the attitudes of workers who will be using the system
- The kinds of tasks, decisions, and business processes that the information system is designed to assist

3.3   HOW DO PORTER'S COMPETITIVE FORCES MODEL, THE VALUE CHAIN MODEL, SYNERGIES, CORE COMPETENCIES, AND NETWORK ECONOMICS HELP COMPANIES DEVELOP COMPETITIVE STRATEGIES USING INFORMATION SYSTEMS?

In almost every industry you examine, you will find some firms do better than most others. There's almost always a stand-out firm. In the automotive industry, Toyota is considered a superior performer. In pure online retail, Amazon is the leader; in off-line retail, Walmart, the largest retailer on earth, is the leader. In online music, Apple's iTunes is considered the leader with more than 60 percent of the downloaded music market and in the related industry of digital music players, the iPod is the leader. In Web search, Google is considered the leader.

Firms that "do better" than others are said to have a competitive advantage over others: They either have access to special resources that others do not, or they are able to use commonly available resources more efficiently—usually because of superior knowledge and information assets. In any event, they do better in terms of revenue growth, profitability, or productivity growth (efficiency), all of which ultimately in the long run translate into higher stock market valuations than their competitors.

But why do some firms do better than others and how do they achieve competitive advantage? How can you analyze a business and identify its strategic advantages? How can you develop a strategic advantage for your own business? And how do information systems contribute to strategic advantages? One answer to that question is Michael Porter's competitive forces model.

PORTER'S COMPETITIVE FORCES MODEL

Arguably, the most widely used model for understanding competitive advantage is Michael Porter's **competitive forces model** (see Figure 3.8). This model provides a general view of the firm, its competitors, and the firm's environment. Earlier in this chapter, we described the importance of a firm's environment and the dependence of firms on environments. Porter's model is all about the firm's general business environment. In this model, five competitive forces shape the fate of the firm.

Traditional Players

There are certain companies that have been in the market for a long duration. These conventional market players pose stiff competition to other organizations. For example, in the soft drink market, Coca-Cola and Pepsi can be considered the traditional competitors.

New Market Entrants

As the economy grows, not only do the traditional players get stronger, but the new players also get an opportunity to enter the market. With

FIGURE 3.8   PORTER'S COMPETITIVE FORCES MODEL

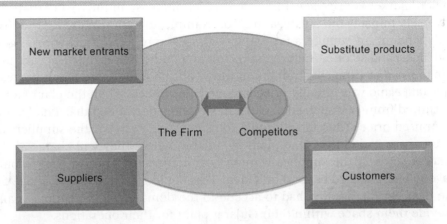

In Porter's competitive forces model, the strategic position of the firm and its strategies are determined not only by competition with its traditional direct competitors but also by four other forces in the industry's environment: new market entrants, substitute products, customers, and suppliers.

relaxed government norms, it is very easy in the present times for a new organization to start a business. The new entrants have a distinct advantage. They can consult the historical records on the existing players, analyze their weaknesses, and plug those mistakes. They are able to enter the market with innovative and improved products or services. For example, when Kinetic came to India, Bajaj was a leader in the two-wheeler market. Kinetic figured out that there was a need for a gearless scooter that could be started easily and effortlessly, and this is how it captured the market.

Substitute Products and Services

With rapid advancement in technology, the life-cycle of products and even services is becoming shorter. Constant innovation and upgradation can lead to the manufacturing of substitute products and new improved ways of rendering services. These substitute products and services are the greatest threat to an established organization. For example, BSNL was a major player in landline telephony. But with the widespread use of cell phones, providers such as Spice and Airtel have taken away a major portion of BSNL's market share.

Customers

With so many options available in the market, the customer has become a major competitive force. Organizations cannot take the loyalty of the customer for granted. The customer is always looking for better options. Organization, therefore, cannot afford to be complacent. They need to pay attention to retaining their customers by being sensitive to their changing demands.

Suppliers

Organizations depend on their suppliers to provide them with right quantity of products at the right price and at the right time. Any delay in this chain can affect the delivery schedule of products or services. Moreover, as the Indian market is price-sensitive, any sudden increase in the cost of material adversely impacts the organization. For example, to manufacture a car, a firm is dependent on suppliers for window glasses, tyres, electrical wires, lights and locks, and so on. A failure to procure any of the pieces, however minute, due to price or time constraints can throw off the entire production process. The Tata Nano was initially priced at one lakh rupees. When the plant had to be shifted from West Bengal to Gujarat, suppliers demanded that Tata Motors pay raised prices (due to additional transportation costs) or the suppliers be given space inside the Nano plant in Gujarat, where they will charge at the existing rates. If the supplies were to cost higher, the price of Nano would have to be increased beyond one lakh. This could lead to a loss of image for the firm. So Tata Motors had to accede to the demands of the suppliers and provide them space within their Gujarat plant for their operations.

STRATEGIES FORMULATED BY INFORMATION SYSTEMS

Organizations are always facing competitive forces. To counter these forces, companies adopt some of the following information-systems-enabled strategies:

Low-cost Leadership

The organizations need to reduce their operational costs so as to deliver the product or service at the most optimum price. Information systems play an important role in managing the operational cost of an organization. For example, Shoppers Stop's uses the J.D. Armstrong (JDA) information system to reduce its operational expenses. JDA has various modules, such as the merchandize management module that helps Shoppers Stop formulate purchase orders and decide on the margins at which they buy items from the vendors. The warehouse management module enables Shoppers Stop to manage stored items in the warehouse. This module also provides aid in transporting the right quantity of item from the warehouse to a particular store. The auto-replenishment module helps the company manage stocks. This module automatically orders replenishment as the stock reaches the minimum level. It is very important to forecast properly so that the organization doesn't end up ordering products for which there will be no demand in the future. The Arthur planning module of the JDA helps accomplish this task.

Product Differentiation

Companies constantly strive to provide their customers with products or services that are different from those available in the market. This creates a positive attitude towards the brand in the eyes of the consumer. For example, e-Commerce sites in India provide the cash-on-delivery (COD) facility to customers because a certain section of the Indian population is not comfortable purchasing products online using credit cards or internet banking. The Punjab State Power Corporation Limited (PSPCL), the sole power-generation and distribution company in Punjab, introduced the facility that would enable subscribers to be their electricity bills online. Customers who would earlier have to wait in long queues, now simply needed to log into the PSPCL website to instantly pay the bill.

Table 3.3 lists a number of companies that have developed IT-based products and services that other firms have found difficult to copy, or at least a long time to copy.

Focus on Niche Markets

Information systems help organizations record the buying behaviour and demands of the customers. This information enables companies to serve customers in an efficient manner. For example, organizations often offer loyalty cards to customers, so that when the customer make purchases, that information gets recorded in the central database of the organization and also on the magnetic chip on the loyalty card. Organizations give points for each purchase that can be accumulated and redeemed at a later date. This is how organizations reward loyal customers. The Fresh and Ground Stores of Café Coffee Day offer loyalty cards to customers. The customer collects points for every purchase made using the card. For example, for a purchase of 100g of coffee or tea, the customer gets five points, for a purchase of 250g, the customer gets 15 points, and so on.

Strengthen Customer and Supplier Intimacy

Companies have found it to their advantage to encourage relations between customers and suppliers. e-Commerce companies like Flipkart allow customers to rate the suppliers. Since the companies keep track of all purchases made by the customer, and also of all the items viewed by the customer on their website, they can make suggestions to customers based on that data. Organizations make deliberate efforts to involve suppliers in key decisions so that the suppliers feel a sense of belonging towards the organization. For example, companies like Fiat and Volkswagen have a dedicated Internet portal which provides a platform for communication between the suppliers and members of the organization. Fiat shares all the important information relating to technology, requirement, planning, quality, and compliance standards with the suppliers using this portal. Similarly suppliers also use this portal to communicate with organization regarding any queries concerning contracts and bids. Volkswagen uses its platform to request for quotations from suppliers, who can also give feedback to the Volkswagen engineers working on product development.

TABLE 3.3 IT-ENABLED NEW PRODUCTS AND SERVICES PROVIDING COMPETITIVE ADVANTAGE

Amazon: One-click shopping	Amazon holds a patent on one-click shopping that it licenses to other online retailers.
Online music: Apple iPod and iTunes	The iPod is an integrated handheld player backed up with an online library of over 13 million songs.
Golf club customization: Ping	Customers can select from more than 1 million different golf club options; a build-to-order system ships their customized clubs within 48 hours.
Online person-to-person payment: PayPal	PayPal enables the transfer of money between individual bank accounts and between bank accounts and credit card accounts.

INTERACTIVE SESSION: TECHNOLOGY

SECURING FLIPKART

Flipkart is one of the leading eCommerce companies in India. Located in Bangalore, it started its operation in 2007 by selling books online. Gradually, it widened its array of offerings to include a host of other products including electronics and lifestyle goods. In order to manage its growing business, Flipkart also had to increase the number of delivery partners. Prompt delivery of the products has never been more important than in the context of online retail.

The logistical challenge of such a business is huge. Every single order must be delivered, without fail. It is this realization that led Flipkart to develop an online logistics application called eKart, which is a part of W.S. Retail Services Private Limited, the business-to-customer wing of Flipkart. With the help of this information system, delivery executives can get vital information on their mobile devices. Since a large part of Flipkart's operations involve movement of goods, the relevance of a mobile application cannot be overstated. However, organizations need to be cautious when deploying sensitive business data to employees and other trade partners over mobile applications. Flipkart realized that in order to manage the flow of information to so many people in their delivery channels, it would need to come up with an effective way of monitoring the devices on which delivery information was shared. Vendors like XenMobile, Mobilerin, AirWatch, and Fiberlink came up with solutions to Flipkart's challenges. After an extensive analysis of all these applications, Flipkart decided to go with the Fiberlink MaaS360 mobile data management (MDM) solution. Fiberlink offered a competitive advantage to Flipkart and demonstrated an ability to work towards helping Flipkart achieve its goals.

MaaS360, an IBM company, is a leader in mobile management and security solutions for organizations. The solutions developed by MaaS360 help organizations securely manage and integrate mobile technology to their businesses. In 2013, MaaS360 won the SIIA CODiE award for the best mobile device application for enterprises.

As more and more organizations are following the bring your own device (BYOD) policy, concerns about mobile data confidentiality are increasing. The MDM solution developed by MaaS360 addresses this issue. This application, which is available for all the major operating systems (Android, Windows, and iOS), registers the official devices and authenticates them using a unique password. The administrator can then track the device, receive alerts, and if necessary, even lock the device remotely or reset its password. The homepage of MDM provides an interactive dashboard showing all the devices, users, documents, applications, and location of the device.

MaaS360's AppSecurity feature enables organizations to share and manage confidential information. It even sets a time-out for a single sign-on session on a particular application. It provides a threat management facility that allows administrators detect applications with malware and uninstall those applications remotely. MaaS360 Secure Mail allows only authorized users to access confidential email. Organizations can restrict the forwarding, copying, pasting, and screen capture options in such emails.

A large host of features such as these makes MaaS360 a good choice for a mobile data management application for Flipkart. The eCommerce company operates in more than a dozen delivery hubs across India. Using MaaS360's MDM solution, it can seed all the devices at one centralized location, thus eliminating the need for decentralized IT teams at each of the delivery hubs. This centralization of devices has helped Flipkart save costs. Delivery executives get the information of where to deliver the parcels on their official mobile devices. In addition, MaaS360 enables Flipkart to track the physical location of the delivery executives and ensure that they follow the recommended routes, which helps save both time and cost. MaaS360 also ensures that all the devices get remote updates from Flipkart's in-house logistics program application, so that everyone is using the latest version of the application. All these features of MDM technology have enabled Flipkart to be a leading provider of online retail services in India.

Sources: MaaS360. Retrieved from http://www.maas360.com/; "Raising Efficiency While Reducing Administrative Burdens for Flipkart". Retrieved from http://content.maas360.com/www/content/cs/cs_maas360_mdm_flipkart.pdf; Nair, Radhika P., "Flipkart to throw open its logistics arm 'eKart' to deliver packages of competitors", The Economic Times (2014). Retrieved from http://articles.economictimes.indiatimes.com/2014-02-13/news/47305247_1_logistics-arm-payzippy-sachin-bansal.

CASE STUDY QUESTIONS

1. Do you think Flipkart was in need of MDM technology? How is it adding value to the firm?
2. How are the employees benefiting from this technology? How is the management benefiting from the deployment of this technology?
3. Discuss the key features of MDM as provided by IBM's MaaS360.
4. Do you think the technology provides any competitive edge to Flipkart?

KEY APPLICATIONS OF STRATEGIC INFORMATION SYSTEMS

There is no clear-cut distinction between management information systems and strategic information systems. But when the information systems help organizations gain competitive advantage, it is said to be using the strategic information system. This competitive advantage can be provided in the following ways:

Competitive Advantage in Selling

Strategic information systems assist organizations with innovating new models of the product or service. They also help customers find product details online, and enable them to make payments over the Internet using debit cards, credit cards and electronic fund transfers (EFT). The sales teams can remain connected to the central database and know the current status of the available products. The organizations can forecast trends by analyzing the past and current trends using strategic information systems. They can develop electronic kiosks where the customer can get information regarding the products.

Reducing Costs

Organizations use strategic information systems to reduce costs and increase revenue. Retail stores use such systems to manage inventory. For example, Walmart uses the Retail Link software to connect each store to the central warehouse. Each time a product is sold, the information is electronically sent to the central database. This helps replenish inventory as soon as the stock reaches the minimum level. Strategic information systems also help organizations charge the optimum price for the product. For example, airlines use a yield management system to determine pricing of tickets so that it generates the maximum possible revenue.

Production Differentiation and Customization

Organizations create products according to customer needs. Some of the apparel manufacturing companies have started using body scanners to know the right size of clothing for customers. This is done so that the customer need not try different sizes to get the right fit. PEPSU Road Transport Corporation (PRTC) is another organization that has been using information systems strategically. PRTC used to suffer large losses due to its manual ticketing system. PRTC decided to implement hand-held machines (HHM). Now, the conductor simply needs to enter the route in the portable HHM and the receipt gets automatically generated for the customer. Information regarding the sale of tickets on a particular route is periodically transferred to a database using a USB port. This helps managers take prompt corrective actions to curtail losses.

Maintenance

Organizations use strategic information systems to provide after-sales services. In case of car manufacturers, the information system checks the date on which a vehicle is due for a service, and automatically sends a message or mail to the customer. The customer can provide their preferred time for the service online so that a visit can be scheduled.

Value Chain

The set of activities that enhance the value of the product or service for the customer are said to be part of the value chain. Information systems aid organizations to increase customer satisfaction, which automatically increases the credibility of the brand. Some of the important activities in the value chain that help enhance it are as follows:

a. *Inbound logistics:* This includes all the activities that manage the supply of raw materials and semi-finished materials. Information systems help the organization have better coordination with suppliers.

b. *Operational activities:* Information systems are instrumental in allowing for customer-integrated manufacturing (CIM) processes. Here, production is taken care of by using advanced robotics, which are controlled by specialized information systems. Organizations can also efficiently manage the product

TABLE 3.4 FOUR BASIC COMPETITIVE STRATEGIES

STRATEGY	DESCRIPTION	EXAMPLE
Low-cost leadership	Use information systems to produce products and services at a lower price than competitors while enhancing quality and level of service	Shoppers Stop, Walmart
Product differentiation	Use information systems to differentiate products, and enable new services and products	PSPCL, Google, eBay, Apple, Lands' End
Focus on market niche	Use information systems to enable a focused strategy on a single market niche; specialize	Café Coffee Day, Hilton Hotels, Harrah's
Customer and supplier intimacy	Use information systems to develop strong ties and loyalty with customers and suppliers	Volkswagen, Chrysler Corporation, Amazon

development using the concept of the concurrent engineering, where product design and manufacturing are conducted concurrently to save time and money.

c. Outbound activities: These are activities that help the finished product or service reach the customer. For example, ATM machines help banks disburse cash at any time. With the help of information systems, the customer accounts are kept updated whenever the customer withdraws or deposits cash through an ATM. The system also automatically sends text messages to customers in case of any debit or credit of cash.

THE INTERNET'S IMPACT ON COMPETITIVE ADVANTAGE

Because of the Internet, the traditional competitive forces are still at work, but competitive rivalry has become much more intense (Porter, 2001). Internet technology is based on universal standards that any company can use, making it easy for rivals to compete on price alone and for new competitors to enter the market. Because information is available to everyone, the Internet raises the bargaining power of customers, who can quickly find the lowest-cost provider on the Web. Profits have been dampened. Table 3.5 summarizes some of the potentially negative impacts of the Internet on business firms identified by Porter.

The Internet has nearly destroyed some industries and has severely threatened more. For instance, the printed encyclopedia industry and the travel agency industry have been nearly decimated by the availability of substitutes over the Internet. Likewise, the Internet has had a significant impact on the retail, music, book, retail brokerage, software, telecommunications, and newspaper industries.

However, the Internet has also created entirely new markets, formed the basis for thousands of new products, services, and business models, and provided new opportunities for building brands with very large and loyal

TABLE 3.5 IMPACT OF THE INTERNET ON COMPETITIVE FORCES AND INDUSTRY STRUCTURE

COMPETITIVE FORCE	IMPACT OF THE INTERNET
Substitute products or services	Enables new substitutes to emerge with new approaches to meeting needs and performing functions
Customers' bargaining power	Availability of global price and product information shifts bargaining power to customers
Suppliers' bargaining power	Procurement over the Internet tends to raise bargaining power over suppliers; suppliers can also benefit from reduced barriers to entry and from the elimination of distributors and other intermediaries standing between them and their users
Threat of new entrants	Internet reduces barriers to entry, such as the need for a sales force, access to channels, and physical assets; it provides a technology for driving business processes that makes other things easier to do
Positioning and rivalry among existing competitors	Widens the geographic market, increasing the number of competitors, and reducing differences among competitors; makes it more difficult to sustain operational advantages; puts pressure to compete on price

INTERACTIVE SESSION: ORGANIZATIONS

IDENTIFYING MARKET NICHES IN THE AGE OF BIG DATA

With the amount of data available to companies doubling every year, new sources of data, and innovations in data collection, possibilities for marketers to identify market niches and finely tune campaigns are boundless. In the e-book market, for example, three reading subscription service startups—Scribd, Oyster, and Entitle—aim to turn a profit by discovering exactly what makes readers tick.

A flat monthly fee gives users unlimited access to a broad selection of titles from these companies' digital libraries. Like Barnes and Noble and Amazon, the newcomers will collect an assortment of data from their customers' digital reading devices (e-readers, tablets, smartphones), including whether a book is completed, if pages are skimmed or skipped, and which genres are most often finished. These subscription services intend to disseminate what they have learned. The idea is that writers can use it to better tailor their work to their readership, and book editors can use it to choose which manuscripts to publish.

When customers sign up with these services, they are informed that some of their data will be collected and used but assured that their identities will be protected. Large independent publisher Smash words is enthusiastic about the value of such data to the authors who use its platform to self-publish and distribute their work. Many contemporary authors have already explored the feedback opportunities available through their own Web sites, social networking sites, and Goodreads, a user-populated database of books, annotations, and reviews now owned by Amazon. The subscription services will take this type of market research to a more quantifiable level.

Preliminary data analysis has already revealed that as the length of a mystery novel increases so does the likelihood that a reader will skip to the end to discover the resolution. Business books are less likely to be finished than biographies, most readers complete just a single chapter of a yoga book, and some of the quickest reading is recorded for romance novels, with erotica leading the pack. Shorter chapters entice readers on e-readers, tablets, and smartphones to finish a book 25 percent more often than books with long chapters.

But does book completion translate to book sales? And how will this knowledge impact the creative process? Will quality be negatively impacted to satisfy reader preferences? Before any of these questions can be answered, authors will need access to comprehensive data. And that depends on the large publishing houses signing deals with the subscription services. After nearly two decades of market disruptions spearheaded by Amazon, publishers are not flocking to supply titles. So far, only Harper Collins has signed with Oyster and Scribd, while Random House, Penguin, and Simon & Schuster remain on the sidelines.

In the airline industry, nearly all carriers collect passenger data, but some are aggressively pursuing data mining to personalize the flying experience. Previously unlinked data sets can now be consolidated to build comprehensive customer profiles. Cabin crews equipped with tablets or smartphones can identify the top five customers on the plane, passengers with special diets or allergies, seat preferences, newlyweds embarking on their honeymoon, and customers whose luggage was misplaced or who experienced flight delays on their previous flights. In-flight browsing history and Facebook likes are even used to fashion relevant marketing pitches.

This "captive audience" aspect of air travel in conjunction with the sheer volume of information airlines collect presents a unique opportunity to marketers. Allegiant Travel company has already been able to sell show tickets, car rentals, and helicopter tours to Las Vegas travelers. United Airlines' revamp of its Web site, kiosks, and mobile app, along with its data integration initiative, have enabled it to target flyers predisposed to upgrading to an economy plus seat.

Not all customers are pleased. A user on Delta's FlyerTalk forum complained that a link from the new DL.com Web site led to a personal profile that included a lot more than her miles accumulated and home airport. Annual income, home value, and the age ranges of her children were included along with expected data such as amount spent on airfare, hotel preference, and type of credit card. The resulting negative publicity prompted Delta to apologize, but it defended its use of demographic data and data not covered under its privacy policy. Credit-card partner American Express had supplied some data, as allowed under the policy. Global information services group Experian supplied the rest, unbeknownst to consumers.

These data-driven marketing approaches are not flawless. Even customers who accept the inevitability of profiling are miffed when they receive unsuitable offers based on faulty personal information. A Qantas survey of frequent fliers found that most customers want a line drawn between data collection to facilitate useful offers and data collection that is too intrusive. British Airways crossed the line with its "Know Me" program. Google Image searches were used to identify VIP customers as they entered the airport and first class lounge. The practice has since been discontinued. Customers can opt out of British Airways personalization services—but not its data collection. Upon request, a note is added to the customer profile, which nonetheless continues to grow. None of the carriers currently allow customers to opt out of their data programs.

As car companies explore their Big Data opportunities, customer privacy will become an issue for them as well. Ford Motor Company began exploring how integrating databases and using complex algorithms could lead to increased sales three years ago when it developed a program for its dealerships to more closely match car lot inventory to buyer demand. Using buying trends, local and national vehicle supply, and current car lot inventory, Ford devised a program to make purchasing recommendations to dealers. Not only did

vehicle turnover rate improve, but net price—the price a consumer pays minus the manufacturer subsidy—rose, fueling an upturn in Ford's profits.

But Ford is thinking even bigger. Performance monitoring using vehicle Internet connections to collect fuel economy, mechanical failure, and other safety and performance metrics could soon be used to improve product engineering. What's more, onboard connections can be used to message drivers about potential breakdown issues, perhaps heading off an expensive recall. Since Ford estimates that by 2016, up to a third of all its consumer communication will occur inside vehicles, possibilities abound. Leased vehicle usage data could inform end-of-lease marketing pitches; driving pattern, schedule, and driving maneuver data could suggest routes most compatible to a driver's habits; car location data could be sent to traffic management systems to control stop lights; data from networked cars could alert other drivers to hazardous conditions and traffic jams, and current car value and payment data can advise drivers of their optimal trade-in date.

It's not hard to foresee the privacy issues that could come into play as drivers realize that not only their location, but their every movement inside their vehicle is being tracked. There are implications for law enforcement—traffic tickets and accident blame attribution. Balancing privacy dilemmas with convenience, security, and expediency of transactions will be the challenge going forward for all companies as they explore emerging big data analysis capabilities.

Sources: Tim Winship, "Big Brother Unmasked as ... Delta Air Lines," smartertravel.com, January 28, 2013; Jack Nicas, "When Is Your Birthday? The Flight Attendant Knows," *Wall Street Journal*, November 7, 2013 and "How Airlines Mine Personal Data In-Flight," *Wall Street Journal*, November 8, 2013; David Streitfeld, "As New Services Track Habits, the E-Books Are Reading You," *New York Times*, December 24, 2013; Ian Sherr and Mike Ramsey, "Drive into the Future," *Wall Street Journal*, March 7, 2013.

CASE STUDY QUESTIONS

1. Describe the kinds of data being analyzed by the companies in this case.

2. How is this fine-grained data analysis improving operations and decision making in the companies described in this case? What business strategies are being supported?

3. Are there any disadvantages to mining customer data? Explain your answer.

4. How do you feel about airlines mining your in-flight data? Is this any different from companies mining your credit card purchases or Web surfing?

customer bases. Amazon, eBay, iTunes, YouTube, Facebook, Travelocity, and Google are examples. In this sense, the Internet is "transforming" entire industries, forcing firms to change how they do business.

For most forms of media, the Internet has posed a threat to business models and profitability. Growth in book sales other than textbooks and professional publications has been sluggish, as new forms of entertainment continue to compete for consumers' time. Newspapers and magazines have been hit even harder, as their readerships diminish, their advertisers shrink, and more people get their news for free online. The television and film industries have been forced to deal with pirates who are robbing them of some of their profits, as well as with online services streaming videos and TV shows.

THE BUSINESS VALUE CHAIN MODEL

Although the Porter model is very helpful for identifying competitive forces and suggesting generic strategies, it is not very specific about what exactly to do, and it does not provide a methodology to follow for achieving competitive advantages. If your goal is to achieve operational excellence, where do you start? Here's where the business value chain model is helpful.

The **value chain model** highlights specific activities in the business where competitive strategies can best be applied (Porter, 1985) and where information systems are most likely to have a strategic impact. This model identifies specific, critical leverage points where a firm can use information technology most effectively to enhance its competitive position. The value chain model views the firm as a series or chain of basic activities that add a margin of value to a firm's products or services. These activities can be categorized as either primary activities or support activities (see Figure 3.9).

Primary activities are most directly related to the production and distribution of the firm's products and services, which create value for the customer. Primary activities include inbound logistics, operations, outbound logistics, sales and marketing, and service. Inbound logistics includes receiving and storing materials for distribution to production. Operations transforms inputs into finished products. Outbound logistics entails storing and distributing finished products. Sales and marketing includes promoting and selling the firm's products. The service activity includes maintenance and repair of the firm's goods and services.

Support activities make the delivery of the primary activities possible and consist of organization infrastructure (administration and management), human resources (employee recruiting, hiring, and training), technology (improving products and the production process), and procurement (purchasing input).

Now you can ask at each stage of the value chain, "How can we use information systems to improve operational efficiency, and improve customer and supplier intimacy?" This will force you to critically examine how you perform value-adding activities at each stage and how the business processes might be improved. You can also begin to ask how information systems can be used to improve the relationship with customers and with suppliers

FIGURE 3.9 THE VALUE CHAIN MODEL

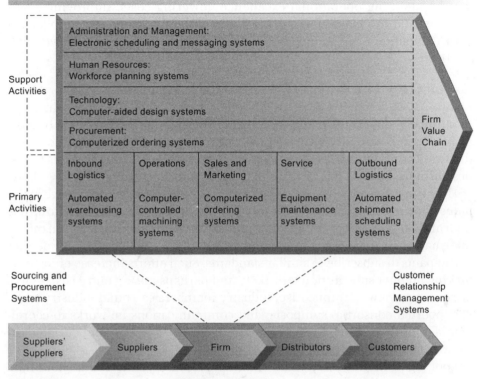

This figure provides examples of systems for both primary and support activities of a firm and of its value partners that can add a margin of value to a firm's products or services.

who lie outside the firm's value chain but belong to the firm's extended value chain where they are absolutely critical to your success. Here, supply chain management systems that coordinate the flow of resources into your firm, and customer relationship management systems that coordinate your sales and support employees with customers, are two of the most common system applications that result from a business value chain analysis. We discuss these enterprise applications in detail later in Chapter 9.

Using the business value chain model will also cause you to consider benchmarking your business processes against your competitors or others in related industries, and identifying industry best practices. **Benchmarking** involves comparing the efficiency and effectiveness of your business processes against strict standards and then measuring performance against those standards. Industry **best practices** are usually identified by consulting companies, research organizations, government agencies, and industry associations as the most successful solutions or problem-solving methods for consistently and effectively achieving a business objective.

Once you have analyzed the various stages in the value chain at your business, you can come up with candidate applications of information systems. Then, once you have a list of candidate applications, you can decide which to develop first. By making improvements in your own business value chain that your competitors might miss, you can achieve competitive advantage by attaining operational excellence, lowering costs, improving profit margins, and forging a closer relationship with customers and suppliers. If your competitors are making similar improvements, then at least you will not be at a competitive disadvantage—the worst of all cases!

Extending the Value Chain: The Value Web

Figure 3.9 shows that a firm's value chain is linked to the value chains of its suppliers, distributors, and customers. After all, the performance of most firms depends not only on what goes on inside a firm but also on how well the firm coordinates with direct and indirect suppliers, delivery firms (logistics partners, such as FedEx or UPS), and, of course, customers.

How can information systems be used to achieve strategic advantage at the industry level? By working with other firms, industry participants can use information technology to develop industry-wide standards for exchanging information or business transactions electronically, which force all market participants to subscribe to similar standards. Such efforts increase efficiency, making product substitution less likely and perhaps raising entry costs—thus discouraging new entrants. Also, industry members can build industry-wide, IT-supported consortia, symposia, and communications networks to coordinate activities concerning government agencies, foreign competition, and competing industries.

Looking at the industry value chain encourages you to think about how to use information systems to link up more efficiently with your suppliers, strategic partners, and customers. Strategic advantage derives from your ability to relate your value chain to the value chains of other partners in the process. For instance, if you are Amazon.com, you want to build systems that:

- Make it easy for suppliers to display goods and open stores on the Amazon site
- Make it easy for customers to pay for goods
- Develop systems that coordinate the shipment of goods to customers
- Develop shipment tracking systems for customers

Internet technology has made it possible to create highly synchronized industry value chains called value webs. A **value web** is a collection of independent firms that use information technology to coordinate their value chains to produce a product or service for a market collectively. It is more customer driven and operates in a less linear fashion than the traditional value chain.

Figure 3.10 shows that this value web synchronizes the business processes of customers, suppliers, and trading partners among different companies in an industry or in related industries. These value webs are flexible and adaptive to changes in supply and demand. Relationships can be bundled or unbundled in response to changing market conditions. Firms will accelerate time to market and to customers by optimizing their value web relationships to make quick decisions on who can deliver the required products or services at the right price and location.

FIGURE 3.10 THE VALUE WEB

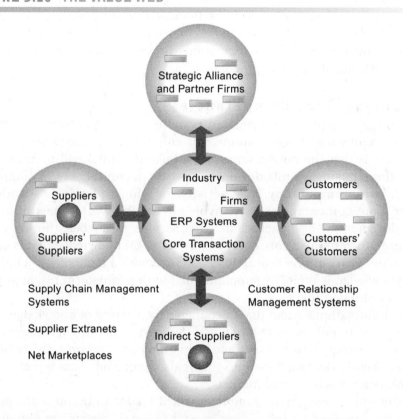

The value web is a networked system that can synchronize the value chains of business partners within an industry to respond rapidly to changes in supply and demand.

SYNERGIES, CORE COMPETENCIES, AND NETWORK-BASED STRATEGIES

A large corporation is typically a collection of businesses. Often, the firm is organized financially as a collection of strategic business units and the returns to the firm are directly tied to the performance of all the strategic business units. Information systems can improve the overall performance of these business units by promoting synergies and core competencies.

Synergies

The idea of synergies is that when the output of some units can be used as inputs to other units, or two organizations pool markets and expertise, these relationships lower costs and generate profits. Recent bank and financial firm mergers, such as the merger of JPMorgan Chase and Bank of New York as well as Bank of America and Countrywide Financial Corporation occurred precisely for this purpose.

One use of information technology in these synergy situations is to tie together the operations of disparate business units so that they can act as a whole. For example, acquiring Countrywide Financial enabled Bank of

America to extend its mortgage lending business and to tap into a large pool of new customers who might be interested in its credit card, consumer banking, and other financial products. Information systems would help the merged companies consolidate operations, lower retailing costs, and increase cross-marketing of financial products.

Enhancing Core Competencies

Yet another way to use information systems for competitive advantage is to think about ways that systems can enhance core competencies. The argument is that the performance of all business units will increase insofar as these business units develop, or create, a central core of competencies. A **core competency** is an activity for which a firm is a world-class leader. Core competencies may involve being the world's best miniature parts designer, the best package delivery service, or the best thin-film manufacturer. In general, a core competency relies on knowledge that is gained over many years of practical field experience with a technology. This practical knowledge is typically supplemented with a long-term research effort and committed employees.

Any information system that encourages the sharing of knowledge across business units enhances competency. Such systems might encourage or enhance existing competencies and help employees become aware of new external knowledge; such systems might also help a business leverage existing competencies to related markets.

For example, Procter & Gamble, a world leader in brand management and consumer product innovation, uses a series of systems to enhance its core competencies. An intranet called InnovationNet helps people working on similar problems share ideas and expertise. InnovationNet connects those working in research and development (R&D), engineering, purchasing, marketing, legal affairs, and business information systems around the world, using a portal to provide browser-based access to documents, reports, charts, videos, and other data from various sources. It includes a directory of subject matter experts who can be tapped to give advice or collaborate on problem solving and product development, and links to outside research scientists and entrepreneurs who are searching for new, innovative products worldwide.

Network-Based Strategies

The availability of Internet and networking technology have inspired strategies that take advantage of firms' abilities to create networks or network with each other. Network-based strategies include the use of network economics, a virtual company model, and business ecosystems.

Network Economics. Business models based on a network may help firms strategically by taking advantage of **network economics**. In traditional economics—the economics of factories and agriculture—production experiences diminishing returns. The more any given resource is applied to production, the lower the marginal gain in output, until a point is reached where the additional inputs produce no additional outputs. This is the law of diminishing returns, and it is the foundation for most of modern economics.

In some situations, the law of diminishing returns does not work. For instance, in a network, the marginal costs of adding another participant are about zero, whereas the marginal gain is much larger. The larger the number of subscribers in a telephone system or the Internet, the greater the value to all participants because each user can interact with more people. It is not much more expensive to operate a television station with 1,000 subscribers than with 10 million subscribers. The value of a community of people grows with size, whereas the cost of adding new members is inconsequential.

From this network economics perspective, information technology can be strategically useful. Internet sites can be used by firms to build communities of users—like-minded customers who want to share their experiences. This builds customer loyalty and enjoyment, and builds unique ties to customers. EBay, the giant online auction site, and iVillage, an online community for women, are examples. Both businesses are based on networks of millions of users, and both companies have used the Web and Internet communication tools to build communities. The more people offering products on eBay, the more valuable the eBay site is to everyone because more products are listed, and more competition among suppliers lowers prices. Network economics also provides strategic benefits to commercial software vendors. The value of their software and complementary software products increases as more people use them, and there is a larger installed base to justify continued use of the product and vendor support.

Virtual Company Model. Another network-based strategy uses the model of a virtual company to create a competitive business. A **virtual company**, also known as a virtual organization, uses networks to link people, assets, and ideas, enabling it to ally with other companies to create and distribute products and services without being limited by traditional organizational boundaries or physical locations. One company can use the capabilities of another company without being physically tied to that company. The virtual company model is useful when a company finds it cheaper to acquire products, services, or capabilities from an external vendor or when it needs to move quickly to exploit new market opportunities and lacks the time and resources to respond on its own.

Fashion companies, such as GUESS, Ann Taylor, Levi Strauss, and Reebok, enlist Hong Kong-based Li & Fung to manage production and shipment of their garments. Li & Fung handles product development, raw material sourcing, production planning, quality assurance, and shipping. Li & Fung does not own any fabric, factories, or machines, outsourcing all of its work to a network of more than 15,000 suppliers in 40 countries all over the world. Customers place orders to Li & Fung over its private extranet. Li & Fung then sends instructions to appropriate raw material suppliers and factories where the clothing is produced. The Li & Fung extranet tracks the entire production process for each order. Working as a virtual company keeps Li & Fung flexible and adaptable so that it can design and produce the products ordered by its clients in short order to keep pace with rapidly changing fashion trends.

FIGURE 3.11 AN ECOSYSTEM STRATEGIC MODEL

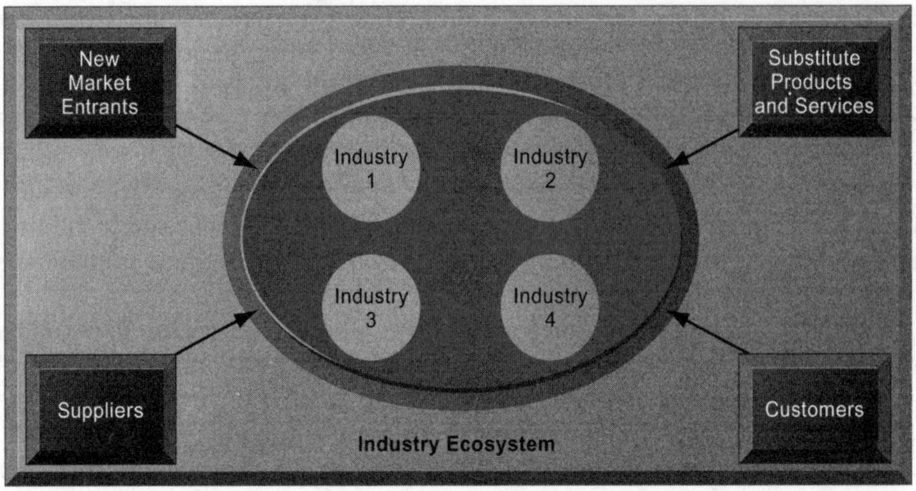

The digital firm era requires a more dynamic view of the boundaries among industries, firms, customers, and suppliers, with competition occurring among industry sets in a business ecosystem. In the ecosystem model, multiple industries work together to deliver value to the customer. IT plays an important role in enabling a dense network of interactions among the participating firms.

Business Ecosystems: Keystone and Niche Firms. The Internet and the emergence of digital firms call for some modification of the industry competitive forces model. The traditional Porter model assumes a relatively static industry environment; relatively clear-cut industry boundaries; and a relatively stable set of suppliers, substitutes, and customers, with the focus on industry players in a market environment. Instead of participating in a single industry, some of today's firms are much more aware that they participate in industry sets—collections of industries that provide related services and products (see Figure 3.11). **Business ecosystem** is another term for these loosely coupled but interdependent networks of suppliers, distributors, outsourcing firms, transportation service firms, and technology manufacturers (Iansiti and Levien, 2004).

The concept of a business ecosystem builds on the idea of the value web described earlier, the main difference being that cooperation takes place across many industries rather than many firms. For instance, both Microsoft and Walmart provide platforms composed of information systems, technologies, and services that thousands of other firms in different industries use to enhance their own capabilities. Microsoft has estimated that more than 40,000 firms use its Windows platform to deliver their own products, support Microsoft products, and extend the value of Microsoft's own firm. Walmart's order entry and inventory management system is a platform used by thousands of suppliers to obtain real-time access to customer demand, track shipments, and control inventories.

Business ecosystems can be characterized as having one or a few keystone firms that dominate the ecosystem and create the platforms used by other niche firms. Keystone firms in the Microsoft ecosystem include Microsoft and technology producers such as Intel and IBM. Niche firms include thousands of software application firms, software developers, service firms, networking firms, and consulting firms that both support and rely on the Microsoft products.

Information technology plays a powerful role in establishing business ecosystems. Obviously, many firms use information systems to develop into keystone firms by building IT-based platforms that other firms can use. In the digital firm era, we can expect greater emphasis on the use of IT to build industry ecosystems because the costs of participating in such ecosystems will fall and the benefits to all firms will increase rapidly as the platform grows.

Individual firms should consider how their information systems will enable them to become profitable niche players in larger ecosystems created by keystone firms. For instance, in making decisions about which products to build or which services to offer, a firm should consider the existing business ecosystems related to these products and how it might use IT to enable participation in these larger ecosystems.

A powerful, current example of a rapidly expanding ecosystem is the mobile Internet platform. In this ecosystem there are four industries: device makers (Apple iPhone, Samsung Galaxy, Motorola, LG, and others), wireless telecommunication firms (AT&T, Verizon, T-Mobile, Sprint, and others), independent software applications providers (generally small firms selling games, applications, and ring tones), and Internet service providers (who participate as providers of Internet service to the mobile platform).

Each of these industries has its own history, interests, and driving forces. But these elements come together in a sometimes cooperative, and sometimes competitive, new industry we refer to as the mobile digital platform ecosystem. More than other firms, Apple has managed to combine these industries into a system. It is Apple's mission to sell physical devices (iPhones) that are nearly as powerful as today's personal computers. These devices work only with a high-speed broadband network supplied by the wireless phone carriers. In order to attract a large customer base, the iPhone had to be more than just a cell phone. Apple differentiated this product by making it a "smart phone," one capable of running over one million different, useful applications. Apple could not develop all these applications itself. Instead it relies on generally small, independent software developers to provide these applications, which can be purchased at the iTunes store. In the background is the Internet service provider industry, which makes money whenever iPhone users connect to the Internet.

3.4 WHAT ARE THE CHALLENGES POSED BY STRATEGIC INFORMATION SYSTEMS AND HOW SHOULD THEY BE ADDRESSED?

Strategic information systems often change the organization as well as its products, services, and operating procedures, driving the organization into new behavioral patterns. Successfully using information systems to achieve a competitive advantage is challenging and requires precise coordination of technology, organizations, and management.

SUSTAINING COMPETITIVE ADVANTAGE

The competitive advantages that strategic systems confer do not necessarily last long enough to ensure long-term profitability. Because competitors can retaliate and copy strategic systems, competitive advantage is not always sustainable. Markets, customer expectations, and technology change; globalization has made these changes even more rapid and unpredictable. The Internet can make competitive advantage disappear very quickly because virtually all companies can use this technology. Classic strategic systems, such as American Airlines's SABRE computerized reservation system, Citibank's ATM system, and FedEx's package tracking system, benefited by being the first in their industries. Then rival systems emerged. Amazon was an e-commerce leader but now faces competition from eBay, Yahoo, and Google. Information systems alone cannot provide an enduring business advantage. Systems originally intended to be strategic frequently become tools for survival, required by every firm to stay in business, or they may inhibit organizations from making the strategic changes essential for future success.

ALIGNING IT WITH BUSINESS OBJECTIVES

The research on IT and business performance has found that (a) the more successfully a firm can align information technology with its business goals, the more profitable it will be, and (b) only one-quarter of firms achieve alignment of IT with the business. About half of a business firm's profits can be explained by alignment of IT with business (Luftman, 2003).

Most businesses get it wrong: Information technology takes on a life of its own and does not serve management and shareholder interests very well. Instead of business people taking an active role in shaping IT to the enterprise, they ignore it, claim not to understand IT, and tolerate failure in the IT area as just a nuisance to work around. Such firms pay a hefty price in poor performance. Successful firms and managers understand what IT can do and how it works, take an active role in shaping its use, and measure its impact on revenues and profits.

Management Checklist: Performing a Strategic Systems Analysis

To align IT with the business and use information systems effectively for competitive advantage, managers need to perform a strategic systems analysis. To identify the types of systems that provide a strategic advantage to their firms, managers should ask the following questions:

1. What is the structure of the industry in which the firm is located?

   • What are some of the competitive forces at work in the industry? Are there new entrants to the industry? What is the relative power of suppliers, customers, and substitute products and services over prices?

- Is the basis of competition quality, price, or brand?
- What are the direction and nature of change within the industry? From where are the momentum and change coming?
- How is the industry currently using information technology? Is the organization behind or ahead of the industry in its application of information systems?

2. What are the business, firm, and industry value chains for this particular firm?

- How is the company creating value for the customer—through lower prices and transaction costs or higher quality? Are there any places in the value chain where the business could create more value for the customer and additional profit for the company?
- Does the firm understand and manage its business processes using the best practices available? Is it taking maximum advantage of supply chain management, customer relationship management, and enterprise systems?
- Does the firm leverage its core competencies?
- Is the industry supply chain and customer base changing in ways that benefit or harm the firm?
- Can the firm benefit from strategic partnerships and value webs?
- Where in the value chain will information systems provide the greatest value to the firm?

3. Have we aligned IT with our business strategy and goals?

- Have we correctly articulated our business strategy and goals?
- Is IT improving the right business processes and activities to promote this strategy?
- Are we using the right metrics to measure progress toward those goals?

MANAGING STRATEGIC TRANSITIONS

Adopting the kinds of strategic systems described in this chapter generally requires changes in business goals, relationships with customers and suppliers, and business processes. These sociotechnical changes, affecting both social and technical elements of the organization, can be considered **strategic transitions**—a movement between levels of sociotechnical systems.

Such changes often entail blurring of organizational boundaries, both external and internal. Suppliers and customers must become intimately linked and may share each other's responsibilities. Managers will need to devise new business processes for coordinating their firms' activities with those of customers, suppliers, and other organizations. The organizational change requirements surrounding new information systems are so important that they merit attention throughout this text. Chapter 14 examines organizational change issues in more detail.

Review Summary

1. *Which features of organizations do managers need to know about to build and use information systems successfully?*

   All modern organizations are hierarchical, specialized, and impartial, using explicit routines to maximize efficiency. All organizations have their own cultures and politics arising from differences in interest groups, and they are affected by their surrounding environment. Organizations differ in goals, groups served, social roles, leadership styles, incentives, types of tasks performed, and type of structure. These features help explain differences in organizations' use of information systems. Information systems and the organizations in which they are used interact with and influence each other.

2. *What is the impact of information systems on organizations?*

   The introduction of a new information system will affect organizational structure, goals, work design, values, competition between interest groups, decision making, and day-to-day behavior. At the same time, information systems must be designed to serve the needs of important organizational groups and will be shaped by the organization's structure, business processes, goals, culture, politics, and management. Information technology can reduce transaction and agency costs, and such changes have been accentuated in organizations using the Internet. New systems disrupt established patterns of work and power relationships, so there is often considerable resistance to them when they are introduced.

3. *How do Porter's competitive forces model, the value chain model, synergies, core competencies, and network economics help companies develop competitive strategies using information systems?*

   In Porter's competitive forces model, the strategic position of the firm, and its strategies, are determined by competition with its traditional direct competitors, but they are also greatly affected by new market entrants, substitute products and services, suppliers, and customers. Information systems help companies compete by maintaining low costs, differentiating products or services, focusing on market niche, strengthening ties with customers and suppliers, and increasing barriers to market entry with high levels of operational excellence.

   The value chain model highlights specific activities in the business where competitive strategies and information systems will have the greatest impact. The model views the firm as a series of primary and support activities that add value to a firm's products or services. Primary activities are directly related to production and distribution, whereas support activities make the delivery of primary activities possible. A firm's value chain can be linked to the value chains of its suppliers, distributors, and customers. A value web consists of information systems that enhance competitiveness at the industry level by promoting the use of standards and industry-wide consortia, and by enabling businesses to work more efficiently with their value partners.

   Because firms consist of multiple business units, information systems achieve additional efficiencies or enhance services by tying together the operations of disparate business units. Information systems help businesses leverage their core competencies by promoting the sharing of knowledge across business units. Information systems facilitate business models based on large networks of users or subscribers that take advantage of network economics. A virtual company strategy uses networks to link to other firms so that a company can use the capabilities of other companies to build, market, and distribute products and services. In business ecosystems, multiple industries work together to deliver value to the customer. Information systems support a dense network of interactions among the participating firms.

4. *What are the challenges posed by strategic information systems and how should they be addressed?*

   Implementing strategic systems often requires extensive organizational change and a transition from one sociotechnical level to another. Such changes are called strategic transitions and are often difficult and painful to achieve. Moreover, not all strategic systems are profitable, and they can be expensive to build. Many strategic information systems are easily copied by other firms so that strategic advantage is not always sustainable.

Key Terms

Review Questions

3-1   Which features of organizations do managers need to know about to build and use information systems successfully?

- Define an organization and compare the technical definition of organizations with the behavioral definition.

- Identify and describe the features of organizations that help explain differences in organizations' use of information systems.

3-2   What is the impact of information systems on organizations?

- Describe the major economic theories that help explain how information systems affect organizations.

- Describe the major behavioral theories that help explain how information systems affect organizations.

- Explain why there is considerable organizational resistance to the introduction of information systems.

- Describe the impact of the Internet and disruptive technologies on organizations.

3-3   How do Porter's competitive forces model, the value chain model, synergies, core competencies, and network economics help companies develop competitive strategies using information systems?

- Define Porter's competitive forces model and explain how it works.

- Describe what the competitive forces model explains about competitive advantage.

- List and describe four competitive strategies enabled by information systems that firms can pursue.

- Describe how information systems can support each of these competitive strategies and give examples.

- Explain why aligning IT with business objectives is essential for strategic use of systems.

- Define and describe the value chain model.

- Explain how the value chain model can be used to identify opportunities for information systems.

- Define the value web and show how it is related to the value chain.

- Explain how the value web helps businesses identify opportunities for strategic information systems.

- Describe how the Internet has changed competitive forces and competitive advantage.

- Explain how information systems promote synergies and core competencies.

- Describe how promoting synergies and core competencies enhances competitive advantage.

- Explain how businesses benefit by using network economics.

- Define and describe a virtual company and the benefits of pursuing a virtual company strategy.

3-4   What are the challenges posed by strategic information systems and how should they be addressed?

- List and describe the management challenges posed by strategic information systems.

- Explain how to perform a strategic systems analysis.

Discussion Questions

3-5 It has been said that there is no such thing as a sustainable strategic advantage. Do you agree? Why or why not?

3-6 It has been said that the advantage that leading-edge retailers such as Dell and Walmart have over their competition isn't technology; it's their management. Do you agree? Why or why not?

3-7 What are some of the issues to consider in determining whether the Internet would provide your business with a competitive advantage?

Hands-On MIS Projects

The projects in this section give you hands-on experience identifying information systems to support a business strategy and to solve a customer retention problem, using a database to improve decision making about business strategy, and using Web tools to configure and price an automobile.

Management Decision Problems

3-8 Macy's, Inc., through its subsidiaries, operates approximately 840 department stores in the United States. Its retail stores sell a range of merchandise, including apparel, home furnishings, and housewares. Senior management has decided that Macy's needs to tailor merchandise more to local tastes, and that the colors, sizes, brands, and styles of clothing and other merchandise should be based on the sales patterns in each individual Macy's store. How could information systems help Macy's management implement this new strategy? What pieces of data should these systems collect to help management make merchandising decisions that support this strategy?

3-9 Despite aggressive campaigns to attract customers with lower mobile phone prices, T-Mobile has been losing large numbers of its most lucrative two-year contract subscribers. Management wants to know why so many customers are leaving T-Mobile and what can be done to entice them back. Are customers deserting because of poor customer service, uneven network coverage, wireless service charges, or competition from carriers with Apple iPhone service? How can the company use information systems to help find the answer? What management decisions could be made using information from these systems?

Improving Decision Making: Using Web Tools to Configure and Price an Automobile

Software skills: Internet-based software
Business skills: Researching product information and pricing

3-10 In this exercise, you will use software at car Web sites to find product information about a car of your choice and use that information to make an important purchase decision. You will also evaluate two of these sites as selling tools.

You are interested in purchasing a new Ford Escape (or some other car of your choice). Go to the Web site of CarsDirect (www.carsdirect.com) and begin your investigation. Locate the Ford Escape. Research the various Escape models, choose one you prefer in terms of price, features, and safety ratings. Locate and read at least two reviews. Surf the Web site of the manufacturer, in this case Ford (www.ford.com). Compare the information available on Ford's Web site with that of CarsDirect for the Ford Escape. Try to locate the lowest price for the car you want in a local dealer's inventory. Suggest improvements for CarsDirect.com and Ford.com.

Who's The World's Top Retailer? Walmart and Amazon Duke It Out
CASE STUDY

Walmart is the world's largest and most successful retailer, with $476 billion in fiscal 2014 sales and nearly 11,000 stores world-wide, including over 4,000 in the United States. Walmart has 2 million employees, and ranks Number 1 on the Fortune 500 list of companies. Walmart had such a large and powerful selling machine that it really didn't have any serious competitors. No other retailer came close—until now. Today Walmart's greatest threat is no other than Amazon.com, often called the "Walmart of the Web." Amazon sells not only books but just about everything else people want to buy— DVDs, video and music streaming downloads, software, video games, electronics, apparel, furniture, food, toys, and jewelry. The company also produces consumer electronics—notably the Amazon Kindle e-book reader. No other online retailer can match Amazon's breadth of selection, low prices, and fast, reliable shipping.

For many years, Amazon has been the leader in online retail and is now the world's largest e-commerce retailer. It, too, has a very large and powerful selling machine, although it has primarily focused on selling through the Internet. But if Amazon has its way, that's about to change, because it dearly wants to move in on Walmart's turf.

Walmart was founded as a traditional, off-line, physical store in 1962, and that's still what it does best. But it is being forced to compete in e-commerce, whether it likes it or not. Six or seven years ago, only one-fourth of all Walmart customers shopped at Amazon.com, according to data from researcher Kantar Retail. Today, however, half of Walmart customers say they've shopped at both retailers. Online competition from Amazon has become too tough to ignore.

Why is this happening to Walmart? There are two trends that threaten its dominance. First, Walmart's traditional customers—who are primarily bargain hunters making less than $50,000 per year—are becoming more comfortable using technology. More affluent customers who started shopping at Walmart during the recession are returning to Amazon as their finances improve. Amazon has started stocking merchandise categories that Walmart traditionally sold, such as vacuum bags, diapers,and apparel, and its revenue is growing much faster than Walmart's.In 2013, Amazon had sales of nearly $67 billion, compared to online sales of about $9 billion for Walmart.

If more people want to do even some of their shopping online, Amazon has some clear cut advantages. Amazon has created a recognizable and highly successful brand in online retailing. The company has developed extensive warehousing facilities and an extremely efficient distribution network specifically designed for Web shopping. Its premium shipping service, Amazon Prime, provides fast "free" two-day shipping at an affordable fixed annual subscription price ($99 per year), often considered to be a weak point for online retailers. According to the *Wall Street Journal*, Amazon's shipping costs are lower than Walmart's, ranging from $3 to $4 per package, while Walmart's online shipping can run $5–$7 per parcel. Walmart's massive supply chain needs to support more than 4,000 physical stores worldwide, which Amazon doesn't have to worry about. Shipping costs can make a big difference for a store like Walmart where popular purchases tend to be low-cost items like $10 packs of underwear. It makes no sense for Walmart to create a duplicate supply chain for e-commerce.

However, Walmart is no pushover. It is an even larger and more recognizable brand than Amazon. Consumers associate Walmart with the lowest price, which Walmart has the flexibility to offer on any given item because of its size. The company can lose money selling a hot product at extremely low margins and expect to make money on the strength of the large quantities of other items it sells. Walmart also has a significant physical presence, with stores all across the United States, and its stores provide the instant gratification of shopping, buying an item, and taking it home immediately, as opposed to waiting when ordering from Amazon. Two-thirds of the U.S. population is within five miles of a Walmart store, according to company management.

Walmart has steadily increased its investment in its online business, spending more than $300 million to acquire five tech firms, including Small Society, One Riot, Kosmix, and Grabble, while hiring more than 300 engineers and code writers. Other recent acquisitions include Torbit, OneOps, Tasty Labs, and Inkiru, that will help give Walmart more expertise in things like improving the product recommendations for Web visitors to Walmart.com, using smartphones as a marketing channel, and personalizing the shopping experience. Walmart has been steadily adding new applications to its mobile and online shopping channels, and is expanding its integration with social networks such as Pinterest

The company's technology team is working on an application called Endless Aisle, which would allow shoppers to immediately order from Walmart.com using their smartphones if an item is out of stock. A Pay With Cash program enables the 25 percent of Walmart customers who don't have credit cards or bank accounts to order their products online and then pay for them in cash at their nearest Walmart store. Walmart's online and digital development division @WalmartLabs acquired the recipe technology startup Yumprint in order to expand its online grocery delivery services. Management hopes that Yumprint will help Walmart customers more easily make shopping lists from recipes they find in Yumprint before they shop. The company also hired former eBay executive Jamie Iannone to manage the integration of Sam's Club's Website with Walmart's global e-commerce unit.

Walmart's Sam's Club has been testing a new subscription service called My Subscriptions that allows its 47 million members to order over 700 items, including baby, beauty, and office supplies in order to compete with Amazon's Subscribe & Save program. Online customers will not need to pay shipping fees for these subscription items. Sam's Club used to be unaffected by competitors like Amazon among shoppers of fresh food,

groceries, and basic products that were either not sold on Amazon, or were more expensive online. Now 35-40 million households enrolled in Amazon Prime, and many Sam's Club members tend to belong to Amazon Prime as well. Sam's Club is starting to feel the pressure. Amazon is looking into starting a new business called "Pantry," which would allow customers to purchase goods like toilet paper and cleaning supplies in bigger bundles for cheaper shipping costs.

Walmart is also trying to improve links between its store inventory, Web site, and mobile phone apps so that more customers can order online and pick up their purchases at stores. Shoppers can order items online and pick them up from lockers in local stores without waiting in line. (Walmart already offers in-store pick up of online orders.) Walmart's lockers are similar to Amazon's recent deal with Staples and 7-Eleven to do the same. The idea is to be able to offer Walmart products anywhere a consumer prefers to shop, whether that's online, in stores, or on the phone.

The company is re-thinking its in-store experience to draw more people into its stores. More than half of Walmart customers own smartphones. Walmart has designed its mobile app to maximize Walmart's advantage over Amazon: its physical locations. About 140 million people visit a Walmart store each week. The company started testing the app's in-store mode, which detects when a customer is in a physical store. When the mode is activated, customers can check their wish lists, locate items of interest in the store, and see local promotions. The app's "Scan & Go" feature lets customers scan items as they shop so they can move quickly through self-checkout. Shoppers can add items to their lists using voice or by scanning bar codes.

The Walmart Web site uses software to monitor prices at competing retailers in real time and lower its online prices if necessary. The company is also doubling inventory sold from third-party retailers in its online marketplace and tracking patterns in search and social media data to help it select more trendy products. This strikes directly at Amazon's third party marketplace which accounts for a significant revenue stream for Amazon. Additionally, Walmart is expanding its online offerings to include upscale items like $146 Nike sunglasses and wine refrigerators costing more than $2,500 to attract customers who never set foot in a Walmart store.

Amazon is working on expanding its selection of goods to be as exhaustive as Walmart's. Amazon has allowed third-party sellers to sell goods through its Web site for a number of years, and it has dramatically expanded product selection via acquisitions such as its 2009 purchase of online shoe shopping site Zappos.com to give Amazon an edge in footwear.

On June 18, 2014, Amazon announced its own Fire Phone to provide a better mobile platform for selling its products and services online. Amazon's smartphone has four cameras that can track faces to show images that appear to have depth similar to a hologram. Users are able to scroll through Web or book pages just by tilting the device or to quickly navigate menus, access shortcuts, and view notifications. Mayday is a 24-hour customer support service for users of Amazon's devices, offering one-tap access to Amazon customer service agents who can talk to phone users via video chat, and take over the screen on their devices to show them exactly how to do something. Firefly is a tool that automatically recognizes through the camera over 100 million items, including merchandise, music, or television shows, then offers a way to buy them through Amazon's online store. For example, a user could point the phone at a pair of running shoes and then order them immediately from Amazon.com.

Amazon continues to build more fulfillment centers closer to urban centers and expand its same-day delivery services, and it has a supply chain optimized for online commerce that Walmart just can't match. But Walmart has thousands of stores, in almost every neighborhood that Amazon won't ever be able to match. The winner of this epic struggle will be which company leverages its advantage better. Walmart's technology initiative looks promising, but it still hasn't succeeded in getting its local stores to be anything more than local stores. Still up in the air is the question of the relationship of online selling to Walmart's overall business model. Should Walmart try to best Amazon as the world's dominant e-commerce site? Or would it be better off using online selling to boost revenue for all of Walmart. Would more companywide profits be generated by having a modest online site and using technology to boost store profits?

Sources: Shelly Banjo, "Wal-Mart Looks to Grow by Embracing Smaller Stores, "Wall Street Journal, July 8, 2014; Greg Bensinger, "Amazon Unveils 'Fire Phone' Smartphone," *Wall Street Journal*, June 18, 2014 and "Amazon Raises Prime Subscription Price To $99 A Year," *Wall Street Journal*, March 13, 2014; Anna Rose Welch, "Walmart, Sam's Club Amp Up Online Shopping Experiences, "Integrated Solutions for Retailers, February 28, 2014; Donna Tam, "Walmart: Amazon image recognition a 'shiny object'," CNET, February 6, 2014; Brian O'Keefe, "Walmart Plans to Be an Online Juggernaut," Fortune, July 23, 2013; Claire Cain Miller and Stephanie Clifford, "To Catch Up, Walmart Moves to Amazon Turf," *New York Times*, October 19, 2013; Claire Cain Miller, "Wall-Mart Introduces Lockers as It Battles Amazon in E-Commerce," *New York Times*, March 27, 2013; Evan Schuman, "Amazon's Supply Chain Kicking the SKUs Out of Walmart's," StorefrontBacktalk, June 19, 2013; and David Welch, "Walmart Is Worried About Amazon," *Business Week*, March 29, 2012.

CASE STUDY QUESTIONS

3-11 Analyze Walmart and Amazon.com using the competitive forces and value chain models.

3-12 Compare Walmart and Amazon's business models and business strategies.

3-13 What role does information technology play in each of these businesses? How is it helping them refine their business strategies?

3-14 Will Walmart be successful against Amazon.com? Explain your answer.

Chapter 3 References

Attewell, Paul, and James Rule. "Computing and Organizations: What We Know and What We Don't Know." *Communications of the ACM* 27, No. 12 (December 1984).

Bresnahan, Timohy F., Erik Brynjolfsson, and Lorin M. Hitt, "Information Technology, Workplace Organization, and the Demand for Skilled Labor." *Quarterly Journal of Economics* 117 (February 2002).

Cash, J. I., and Benn R. Konsynski. "IS Redraws Competitive Boundaries." *Harvard Business Review* (March–April 1985).

Ceccagnoli, Marco, Chris Forman, Peng Huang, and D. J. Wu. "Cocreationof Value in a Platform Ecosystem: The Case of Enterprise Software. *MIS Quarterly* 36, No. 1 (March 2012).

Chen, Daniel Q., Martin Mocker, David S. Preston, and Alexander Teubner. "Information Systems Strategy: Reconceptualization, Measurement, and Implications." *MIS Quarterly* 34, No. 2 (June 2010).

Christensen, Clayton M. *The Innovator's Dilemma: The Revolutionary Book That Will Change the Way You Do Business,* New York: HarperCollins (2003)

Christensen, Clayton. "The Past and Future of Competitive Advantage." *Sloan Management Review* 42, No. 2 (Winter 2001).

Clemons, Eric K. "Evaluation of Strategic Investments in Information Technology." *Communications of the ACM* (January 1991).

Clemons, Eric. "The Power of Patterns and Pattern Recognition When Developing Information-Based Strategy. *Journal of Management Information Systems* 27, No. 1 (Summer 2010).

Coase, Ronald H. "The Nature of the Firm."(1937) in Putterman, Louis and Randall Kroszner. *The Economic Nature of the Firm: A Reader,* Cambridge University Press, 1995.

Drucker, Peter. "The Coming of the New Organization." *Harvard Business Review* (January–February 1988).

Freeman, John, Glenn R. Carroll, and Michael T. Hannan. "The Liability of Newness: Age Dependence in Organizational Death Rates." *American Sociological Review* 48 (1983).

Goh, Kim Huat and Kauffman, Robert J." Firm Strategy and the Internet in U.S. Commercial Banking." *Journal of Management Information Systems* 30, No. 2 (Fall 2013).

Gurbaxani, V., and S. Whang, "The Impact of Information Systems on Organizations and Markets." *Communications of the ACM* 34, No. 1 (Jan. 1991).

Heinz, Theo-Wagner, Daniel Beimborn, and Tim Weitzel." How Social Capital Among Information Technology and Business Units Drives Operational Alignment and IT Business." *Journal of Management Information Systems* 31 No. 1 (Summer 2014).

Hitt, Lorin M. "Information Technology and Firm Boundaries: Evidence from Panel Data." *Information Systems Research* 10, No. 2 (June 1999).

Hitt, Lorin M., and Erik Brynjolfsson. "Information Technology and Internal Firm Organization: An Exploratory Analysis." *Journal of Management Information Systems* 14, No. 2 (Fall 1997).

Iansiti, Marco, and Roy Levien. "Strategy as Ecology." *Harvard Business Review* (March 2004).

Iyer, Bala and Thomas H. Davenport. "Reverse Engineering Google's Innovation Machine." *Harvard Business Review* (April 2008).

Jensen, M. C., and W. H. Meckling. "Specific and General Knowledge and Organizational Science." *In Contract Economics,* edited by L. Wetin and J. Wijkander. Oxford: Basil Blackwell (1992).

Jensen, Michael C., and William H. Meckling. "Theory of the Firm: Managerial Behavior, Agency Costs, and Ownership Structure." *Journal of Financial Economics* 3 (1976).

Kauffman, Robert J. and Yu-Ming Wang. "The Network Externalities Hypothesis and Competitive Network Growth." *Journal of Organizational Computing and Electronic Commerce* 12, No. 1 (2002).

Kettinger, William J., Varun Grover, Subashish Guhan, and Albert H. Segors. "Strategic Information Systems Revisited: A Study in Sustainability and Performance." *MIS Quarterly* 18, No. 1 (March 1994).

King, J. L., V. Gurbaxani, K. L. Kraemer, F. W. McFarlan, K. S. Raman, and C. S. Yap. "Institutional Factors in Information Technology Innovation." *Information Systems Research* 5, No. 2 (June 1994).

Kling, Rob. "Social Analyses of Computing: Theoretical Perspectives in Recent Empirical Research." *Computing Survey* 12, No. 1 (March 1980).

Kolb, D. A., and A. L. Frohman. "An Organization Development Approach to Consulting." *Sloan Management Review* 12, No. 1 (Fall 1970).

Kraemer, Kenneth, John King, Debora Dunkle, and Joe Lane. *Managing Information Systems.* Los Angeles: Jossey-Bass (1989).

Lamb, Roberta and Rob Kling. "Reconceptualizing Users as Social Actors in Information Systems Research." *MIS Quarterly* 27, No. 2 (June 2003).

Laudon, Kenneth C. "A General Model of the Relationship Between Information Technology and Organizations." Center for Research on Information Systems, New York University. Working paper, National Science Foundation (1989).

———. "Environmental and Institutional Models of Systems Development." *Communications of the ACM* 28, No. 7 (July 1985).

———. *Dossier Society: Value Choices in the Design of National Information Systems.* New York: Columbia University Press (1986).

Laudon, Kenneth C. and Kenneth L. Marr, "Information Technology and Occupational Structure." (April 1995).

Leavitt, Harold J. "Applying Organizational Change in Industry: Structural, Technological, and Humanistic Approaches." In *Handbook of Organizations,* edited by James G. March. Chicago: Rand McNally (1965).

Leavitt, Harold J., and Thomas L. Whisler. "Management in the 1980s." *Harvard Business Review* (November–December 1958).

Ling Xue, Gautam Ray, and VallabhSambamurthy. "Efficiency or Innovation: How Do Industry Environments Moderate the Effects of Firms' IT Asset Portfolios ." *MIS Quarterly* 36, No. 2 (June 2012).

Luftman, Jerry. Competing in the Information Age: Align in the Sand. Oxford University Press USA 2 edition (August 6, 2003).

Malone, Thomas W., JoAnne Yates, and Robert I. Benjamin. "Electronic Markets and Electronic Hierarchies." *Communications of the ACM* (June 1987).

March, James G., and Herbert A. Simon. *Organizations*. New York: Wiley (1958).

Markus, M. L. "Power, Politics, and MIS Implementation." *Communications of the ACM* 26, No. 6 (June 1983).

McAfee, Andrew and Erik Brynjolfsson. "Investing in the IT That Makes a Competitive Difference." *Harvard Business Review* (July/August 2008).

McFarlan, F. Warren. "Information Technology Changes the Way You Compete." *Harvard Business Review* (May–June 1984).

McLaren, Tim S., Milena M. Head, Yufei Yuan, and Yolande E. Chan. "A Multilevel Model for Measuring Fit Between a Firm's Competitive Strategies and Information Systems Capabilities." *MIS Quarterly* 35, No. 4 (December 2011).

Mintzberg, Henry. "Managerial Work: Analysis from Observation." Management Science 18 (October 1971).

Piccoli, Gabriele, and Blake Ives. "Review: IT-Dependent Strategic Initiatives and Sustained Competitive Advantage: A Review and Synthesis of the Literature." *MIS Quarterly* 29, No. 4 (December 2005).

Porter, Michael E. "The Five Competitive Forces that Shape Strategy." *Harvard Business Review* (January 2008).

Porter, Michael E. and Scott Stern. "Location Matters." *Sloan Management Review* 42, No. 4 (Summer 2001).

Porter, Michael. *Competitive Advantage*. New York: Free Press (1985).

_____. *Competitive Strategy*. New York: Free Press (1980).

_____ "Strategy and the Internet." *Harvard Business Review* (March 2001).

Robey, Daniel and Marie-Claude Boudreau. "Accounting for the Contradictory Organizational Consequences of Information Technology: Theoretical Directions and Methodological Implications." *Information Systems Research* 10, No. 42 (June 1999).

Shapiro, Carl, and Hal R. Varian. *Information Rules*. Boston, MA: Harvard Business School Press (1999).

Starbuck, William H. "Organizations as Action Generators." American Sociological Review 48 (1983).

Tallon, Paul P. "Value Chain Linkages and the Spillover Effects of Strategic Information Technology Alignment: A Process-Level View." *Journal of Management Information Systems* 28, No. 3 (Winter 2014).

Tushman, Michael L., and Philip Anderson. "Technological Discontinuities and Organizational Environments." *Administrative Science Quarterly* 31 (September 1986).

Weber, Max. *The Theory of Social and Economic Organization*. Translated by Talcott Parsons. New York: Free Press (1947).

Williamson, Oliver E. *The Economic Institutions of Capitalism*. New York: Free Press, (1985).

Ethical and Social Issues in Information Systems

CHAPTER 4

LEARNING OBJECTIVES

After reading this chapter, you will be able to answer the following questions:

1. What ethical, social, and political issues are raised by information systems?

2. What specific principles for conduct can be used to guide ethical decisions?

3. Why do contemporary information systems technology and the Internet pose challenges to the protection of individual privacy and intellectual property?

4. How have information systems affected laws for establishing accountability, liability, and the quality of everyday life?

CHAPTER CASES

Content Pirates Sail the Web
Ethical Issues of Google Earth

Big Data Gets Personal: Behavioral
 Targeting
Facebook: It's About the Money

CONTENT PIRATES SAIL THE WEB

More than 11 million HBO subscribers watched each episode of *Game of Thrones* in 2012, but another 3.7 to 4.2 million were able to watch the same shows without paying a cent. They were watching pirated versions of each episode that were made available by companies specializing in distributing digital content for free without paying the owners and creators of that content for using it. Television shows, music, movies, and videogames have all been plundered this way.

Such "content pirates" have sailed the World Wide Web since its earliest days, but today they are bolder, faster and better equipped than ever. The antipiracy and security firm Irdeto detected 14 billion instances of pirated online content in 2012, up from 5.4 billion instances in 2009.

Pirated content threatens television industry profits, much of which comes from subscription fees on cable channels like HBO and USA. Viewers watching pirated versions of shows are less likely to pay for cable subscriptions or to buy movies or rent them from services such as Netflix. According to one estimate, pirated content costs the U.S. economy $58 billion a year, including theft of content, lost entertainment jobs and taxes lost to federal and state governments.

© Eldeiv/Shutterstock

The explosion in pirated TV shows and movies has been made possible by faster Internet speeds. Longer videos can be downloaded within minutes from peer-to-peer networks and online cyberlockers. A great deal of illegal content, including live sports, is also available through instant streaming. Online ad networks also help finance piracy by placing ads on sites that traffic in unauthorized content. A summer 2012 study commissioned in part by Google found that 86 percent of peer-to-peer sharing sites depend on advertising for income.

One of the biggest content pirate sites is The Pirate Bay, based in Sweden, which offers free access to millions of copyrighted songs and thousands of copyrighted movies. The Pirate Bay uses BitTorrent file-sharing technology, which breaks up large computer files into small pieces so they can zip across the Web. In April 2014, The Pirate Bay had over 6.5 million registered users and was the 87th most trafficked site in the world. There have been many legal efforts to shut it down, but The Pirate Bay finds ways to keep going.

What can be done to stop this pirating? Google adjusted its search algorithm to obscure search results for sites with pirated content. NBCUniversal uses armies of automated "crawlers" to scour the Web for unauthorized videos and also applies "content recognition" technology to its programming, which it then passes on to video sites like YouTube to help block illegal uploads. NBC sends out digital snapshots of its shows to YouTube and other video sites to prevent users from putting up copyrighted shows. The five major Internet service providers, including NBC's parent company, Comcast, initiated an alert system which notifies users suspected of piracy and results in progressive penalties, including slowed Web access in some cases. Digital content owners are taking much harder stance with advertising networks and payment platforms supporting piracy to encourage them to close down ad-funded pirate sites.

New products and services have made pirated content less attractive. High-quality content now can be streamed for a small fee to both tethered and mobile devices. Apple's iTunes made buying individual songs inexpensive and easy, while new subscription-based services such as Spotify and Rhapsody have attracted 20 million paying subscribers. Netflix and other video services offer access to movies and television shows at low prices. Right now content pirates are still sailing, but new and better ways to listen to music and view videos may eventually put them out of business.

Sources: Jack Marshall, "More Ad Dollars Flow to Pirated Video," *Wall Street Journal*, May 7, 2014; Adam Nightingale, "Will 2014 Be the Year of IPTV Streaming Piracy? RapidTVNews.com, accessed April 11, 2014; www.alexa.com, accessed April 10, 2014; Christopher S. Stuart, "As TV Pirates Run Rampant, TV Studios Dial Up Pursuit," *The Wall Street Journal*, March 3, 2013; "Pirate Bay Sails to the Caribbean," I4U News, May 2, 2013; and L. Gordon Crovitz, "A Six-Strike Rule for Internet Privacy," *The Wall Street Journal*, March 3, 2013.

The prevalence and brazen activities of "content pirates" described in the chapter-opening case show that technology can be a double-edged sword. It can be the source of many benefits, including the ability to share and transmit legitimate photos, music, videos, and information over the Internet at high speeds. But, at the same time, digital technology creates new opportunities for breaking the law or taking benefits away from others,

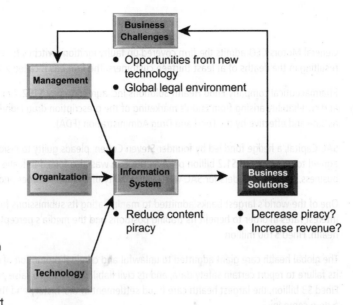

- Design anti-piracy strategy
- Monitor sales and pirating activity

- Develop proprietary content
- Implement anti-piracy policies
- Develop inexpensive digital products

- Adjust search algorithm
- Deploy Web crawlers
- Implement content reognition technology
- Initiate Internet user alert system

including owners of valuable intellectual property, such as music, videos, and television shows that are protected by copyright law.

The chapter-opening diagram calls attention to important points raised by this case and this chapter. Content pirating has become rampant because of opportunities created by broadband communications technology and the global nature of the Internet. Various policies and technology solutions have been put in place to put a stop to content piracy, but the practice still prevails. New technology-based products and services that make online content purchase and downloads very quick and inexpensive may eventually provide a solution.

This case illustrates an ethical dilemma because it shows two sets of interests at work—the interests of people and organizations that have worked to develop intellectual property and need to be rewarded versus those of groups who fervently believe the Internet should foster the free exchange of content and ideas. As a manager, you will need to be sensitive to both the positive and negative impacts of information systems for your firm, employees and customers. You will need to learn how to resolve ethical dilemmas involving information systems.

4.1 WHAT ETHICAL, SOCIAL, AND POLITICAL ISSUES ARE RAISED BY INFORMATION SYSTEMS?

I n the past 10 years, we have witnessed, arguably, one of the most ethically challenging periods for U.S. and global business. Table 4.1 provides a small sample of recent cases demonstrating failed ethical judgment by senior and middle managers. These lapses in ethical and business judgment occurred across a broad spectrum of industries.

TABLE 4.1 RECENT EXAMPLES OF FAILED ETHICAL JUDGMENT BY SENIOR MANAGERS

General Motors Inc. (2014)	General Motors CEO admits the firm covered up faulty ignition switches for more than a decade resulting in the deaths of at least thirteen customers. The firm has recalled 2.7 million cars.
Endo Health Solutions, Inc. (2014)	Pharmaceutical company Endo Health Solutions Inc. agreed to pay $192.7 million to resolve criminal and civil liability arising from Endo's marketing of the prescription drug Lidoderm for uses not approved as safe and effective by the Food and Drug Administration (FDA).
SAC Capital (2013)	SAC Capital, a hedge fund led by founder Steven Cohen, pleads guilty to insider trading charges and agreed to pay a record $1.2 billion penalty. The firm was also forced to leave the money management business. Individual traders for SAC were found guilty of criminal charges and were sentenced to prison.
Barclays Bank PLC (2012)	One of the world's largest banks admitted to manipulating its submissions for the LIBOR benchmark interest rates in order to benefit its trading positions and the media's perception of the bank's financial health. Fined $160 million.
GlaxoSmithKline LLC (2012)	The global health care giant admitted to unlawful and criminal promotion of certain prescription drugs, its failure to report certain safety data, and its civil liability for alleged false price reporting practices. Fined $3 billion, the largest health care fraud settlement in U.S. history and the largest payment ever by a drug company.
Walmart Inc. (2012)	Walmart executives in Mexico accused of paying millions in bribes to Mexican officials in order to receive building permits. Under investigation by the Department of Justice.
Galleon Group (2011)	Founder of the Galleon Group sentenced to 11 years in prison for trading on insider information. Found guilty of paying $250 million to Wall Street banks, and in return received market information that other investors did not get.
Siemens (2009)	The world's largest engineering firm paid over $4 billion to German and U.S. authorities for a decades-long, worldwide bribery scheme approved by corporate executives to influence potential customers and governments. Payments concealed from normal reporting accounting systems.
McKinsey & Company (2011)	CEO Rajat Gupta heard on tapes leaking insider information. The former CEO of prestigious management consulting firm McKinsey & Company was found guilty in 2012 and sentenced to two years in prison.
Bank of America (2012)	Federal prosecutors accused Bank of America and its affiliate Countrywide Financial of defrauding government-backed mortgage agencies by churning out loans at a rapid pace without proper controls. Prosecutors are seeking $1 billion in penalties from the bank as compensation for the behavior that they say forced taxpayers to guarantee billions in bad loans.

In today's new legal environment, managers who violate the law and are convicted will most likely spend time in prison. U.S. federal sentencing guidelines adopted in 1987 mandate that federal judges impose stiff sentences on business executives based on the monetary value of the crime, the presence of a conspiracy to prevent discovery of the crime, the use of structured financial transactions to hide the crime, and failure to cooperate with prosecutors (U.S. Sentencing Commission, 2004).

Although business firms would, in the past, often pay for the legal defense of their employees enmeshed in civil charges and criminal investigations, firms are now encouraged to cooperate with prosecutors to reduce charges against the entire firm for obstructing investigations. These developments mean that, more than ever, as a manager or an employee, you will have to decide for yourself what constitutes proper legal and ethical conduct.

Although these major instances of failed ethical and legal judgment were not masterminded by information systems departments, information systems were instrumental in many of these frauds. In many cases, the perpetrators of these crimes artfully used financial reporting information systems to bury their decisions from public scrutiny in the vain hope they would never be caught.

We deal with the issue of control in information systems in Chapter 8. In this chapter, we will talk about the ethical dimensions of these and other actions based on the use of information systems.

Ethics refers to the principles of right and wrong that individuals, acting as free moral agents, use to make choices to guide their behaviors. Information systems raise new ethical questions for both individuals and societies because they create opportunities for intense social change, and thus threaten existing distributions of power, money, rights, and obligations. Like other technologies, such as steam engines, electricity, the telephone, and the radio, information technology can be used to achieve social progress, but it can also be used to commit crimes and threaten cherished social values. The development of information technology will produce benefits for many and costs for others.

Ethical issues in information systems have been given new urgency by the rise of the Internet and electronic commerce. Internet and digital firm technologies make it easier than ever to assemble, integrate, and distribute information, unleashing new concerns about the appropriate use of customer information, the protection of personal privacy, and the protection of intellectual property.

Other pressing ethical issues raised by information systems include establishing accountability for the consequences of information systems, setting standards to safeguard system quality that protects the safety of the individual and society, and preserving values and institutions considered essential to the quality of life in an information society. When using information systems, it is essential to ask, "What is the ethical and socially responsible course of action?"

A MODEL FOR THINKING ABOUT ETHICAL, SOCIAL, AND POLITICAL ISSUES

Ethical, social, and political issues are closely linked. The ethical dilemma you may face as a manager of information systems typically is reflected in social and political debate. One way to think about these relationships is shown in Figure 4.1. Imagine society as a more or less calm pond on a summer day, a delicate ecosystem in partial equilibrium with individuals and with social and political institutions. Individuals know how to act in this pond because social institutions (family, education, organizations) have developed well-honed rules of behavior, and these are supported by laws developed in the political sector that prescribe behavior and promise sanctions for violations. Now toss a rock into the center of the pond. What happens? Ripples, of course.

Imagine instead that the disturbing force is a powerful shock of new information technology and systems hitting a society more or less at rest.

FIGURE 4.1 THE RELATIONSHIP BETWEEN ETHICAL, SOCIAL, AND POLITICAL ISSUES IN AN INFORMATION SOCIETY

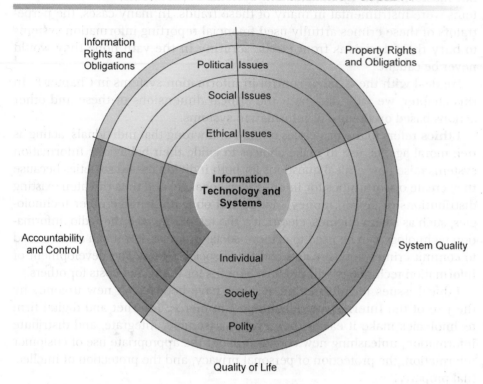

The introduction of new information technology has a ripple effect, raising new ethical, social, and political issues that must be dealt with on the individual, social, and political levels. These issues have five moral dimensions: information rights and obligations, property rights and obligations, system quality, quality of life, and accountability and control.

Suddenly, individual actors are confronted with new situations often not covered by the old rules. Social institutions cannot respond overnight to these ripples—it may take years to develop etiquette, expectations, social responsibility, politically correct attitudes, or approved rules. Political institutions also require time before developing new laws and often require the demonstration of real harm before they act. In the meantime, you may have to act. You may be forced to act in a legal gray area.

We can use this model to illustrate the dynamics that connect ethical, social, and political issues. This model is also useful for identifying the main moral dimensions of the information society, which cut across various levels of action—individual, social, and political.

FIVE MORAL DIMENSIONS OF THE INFORMATION AGE

The major ethical, social, and political issues raised by information systems include the following moral dimensions:

- *Information rights and obligations.* What **information rights** do individuals and organizations possess with respect to themselves? What can they protect?

- *Property rights and obligations.* How will traditional intellectual property rights be protected in a digital society in which tracing and accounting for ownership are difficult and ignoring such property rights is so easy?

- *Accountability and control.* Who can and will be held accountable and liable for the harm done to individual and collective information and property rights?

- *System quality.* What standards of data and system quality should we demand to protect individual rights and the safety of society?

- *Quality of life.* What values should be preserved in an information- and knowledge-based society? Which institutions should we protect from violation? Which cultural values and practices are supported by the new information technology?

We explore these moral dimensions in detail in Section 4.3.

KEY TECHNOLOGY TRENDS THAT RAISE ETHICAL ISSUES

Ethical issues long preceded information technology. Nevertheless, information technology has heightened ethical concerns, taxed existing social arrangements, and made some laws obsolete or severely crippled. There are five key technological trends responsible for these ethical stresses and they are summarized in Table 4.2.

The doubling of computing power every 18 months has made it possible for most organizations to use information systems for their core production processes. As a result, our dependence on systems and our vulnerability to system errors and poor data quality have increased. Social rules and laws have not yet adjusted to this dependence. Standards for ensuring the accuracy and reliability of information systems (see Chapter 8) are not universally accepted or enforced.

Advances in data storage techniques and rapidly declining storage costs have been responsible for the multiplying databases on individuals—employees, customers, and potential customers—maintained by private and public organizations. These advances in data storage have made the

TABLE 4.2 TECHNOLOGY TRENDS THAT RAISE ETHICAL ISSUES

TREND	IMPACT
Computing power doubles every 18 months	More organizations depend on computer systems for critical operations.
Data storage costs rapidly decline	Organizations can easily maintain detailed databases on individuals.
Data analysis advances	Companies can analyze vast quantities of data gathered on individuals to develop detailed profiles of individual behavior.
Networking advances	The cost of moving data and making it accessible from anywhere falls exponentially .
Mobile device growth Impact	Individual cell phones may be tracked without user consent or knowledge.

routine violation of individual privacy both cheap and effective. Enormous data storage systems for terabytes and petabytes of data are now available on-site or as online services for firms of all sizes to use in identifying customers.

Advances in data analysis techniques for large pools of data are another technological trend that heightens ethical concerns because companies and government agencies are able to find out highly detailed personal information about individuals. With contemporary data management tools (see Chapter 6), companies can assemble and combine the myriad pieces of information about you stored on computers much more easily than in the past.

Think of all the ways you generate computer information about yourself—credit card purchases, telephone calls, magazine subscriptions, video rentals, mail-order purchases, banking records, local, state, and federal government records (including court and police records), and visits to Web sites. Put together and mined properly, this information could reveal not only your credit information but also your driving habits, your tastes, your associations, what you read and watch, and your political interests.

Companies with products to sell purchase relevant information from these sources to help them more finely target their marketing campaigns. Chapters 6 and 11 describe how companies can analyze large pools of data from multiple sources to rapidly identify buying patterns of customers and suggest individual responses. The use of computers to combine data from multiple sources and create electronic dossiers of detailed information on individuals is called **profiling**.

For example, several thousand of the most popular Web sites allow DoubleClick (owned by Google), an Internet advertising broker, to track the activities of their visitors in exchange for revenue from advertisements based on visitor information DoubleClick gathers. DoubleClick uses this information to create a profile of each online visitor, adding more detail to the profile as the visitor accesses an associated DoubleClick site. Over time, DoubleClick can create a detailed dossier of a person's spending and computing habits on the Web that is sold to companies to help them target their Web ads more precisely. The top 50 Web sites in the United States contain on average over 100 tracking programs installed by advertising firms to track your online behavior.

ChoicePoint gathers data from police, criminal, and motor vehicle records, credit and employment histories, current and previous addresses, professional licenses, and insurance claims to assemble and maintain electronic dossiers on almost every adult in the United States. The company sells this personal information to businesses and government agencies. Demand for personal data is so enormous that data broker businesses such as ChoicePoint are flourishing. The two largest credit card networks, Visa Inc. and MasterCard Inc., have agreed to link credit card purchase information with consumer social network and other information to create customer profiles that could be sold to advertising firms. In 2013, Visa processed more than 45 billion transactions a year and MasterCard processed more than 23 billion transactions. Currently, this transactional information is not linked with consumer Internet activities.

FIGURE 4.2 NONOBVIOUS RELATIONSHIP AWARENESS (NORA)

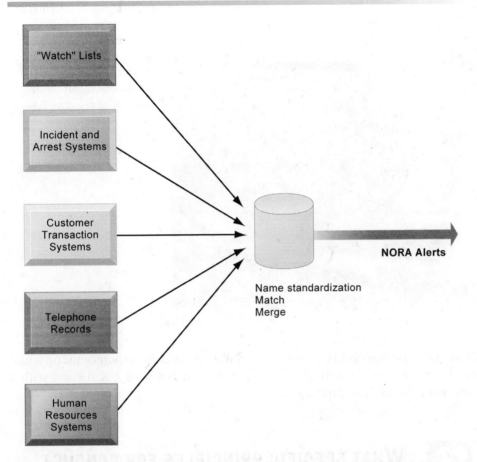

NORA technology can take information about people from disparate sources and find obscure, nonobvious relationships. It might discover, for example, that an applicant for a job at a casino shares a telephone number with a known criminal and issue an alert to the hiring manager.

A new data analysis technology called **nonobvious relationship aware-ness (NORA)** has given both the government and the private sector even more powerful profiling capabilities. NORA can take information about people from many disparate sources, such as employment applications, telephone records, customer listings, and "wanted" lists, and correlate relationships to find obscure hidden connections that might help identify criminals or terrorists (see Figure 4.2).

NORA technology scans data and extracts information as the data are being generated so that it could, for example, instantly discover a man at an airline ticket counter who shares a phone number with a known terrorist before that person boards an airplane. The technology is considered a valuable tool for homeland security but does have privacy implications because it can provide such a detailed picture of the activities and associations of a single individual.

Finally, advances in networking, including the Internet, promise to greatly reduce the costs of moving and accessing large quantities of data

Credit card purchases can make personal information available to market researchers, telemarketers, and direct mail companies. Advances in information technology facilitate the invasion of privacy.

and open the possibility of mining large pools of data remotely using small desktop machines, permitting an invasion of privacy on a scale and with a precision heretofore unimaginable.

4.2 WHAT SPECIFIC PRINCIPLES FOR CONDUCT CAN BE USED TO GUIDE ETHICAL DECISIONS?

Ethics is a concern of humans who have freedom of choice. Ethics is about individual choice: When faced with alternative courses of action, what is the correct moral choice? What are the main features of ethical choice?

BASIC CONCEPTS: RESPONSIBILITY, ACCOUNTABILITY, AND LIABILITY

Ethical choices are decisions made by individuals who are responsible for the consequences of their actions. **Responsibility** is a key element of ethical action. Responsibility means that you accept the potential costs, duties, and obligations for the decisions you make. **Accountability** is a feature of systems and social institutions: It means that mechanisms are in place to determine who took responsible action, and who is responsible. Systems and institutions in which it is impossible to find out who took what action are inherently incapable of ethical analysis or ethical action. **Liability** extends the concept of responsibility further to the area of laws. Liability is a feature of political systems in which a body of laws is in place that permits individuals to recover the damages done to them by other actors, systems, or

INTERACTIVE SESSION: MANAGEMENT

ETHICAL ISSUES OF GOOGLE EARTH

Google Earth provides free satellite models of the earth. Originally developed by Keyhole Inc., a company funded by the Central Intelligence Agency (CIA), it was acquired by Google in 2004 and relaunched as Google Earth in 2005. Initially, Google Earth just provided locations of buildings and other structures, but gradually it widened its services to provide street maps in form of its Google Street View feature. In 2007, Google even started offering real-time traffic data. With such features, Google Earth has been able to uncover a variety of crimes such as:

- Catching thieves by identifying the images of the miscreants on Street View.
- Detecting other illegal activities, such as the Marijuana plantations in Oregon in 2013, which was grown three times beyond its permissible limits, or the detection of illegal logging of the rain forests in the Philippines.
- Finding tax evaders by using Google Earth to determine the true size of the properties of homeowners, as done by the Greek government in recent times.
- Spotting stolen or illegally dumped vehicles.
- Detecting drug-dealing gangs and identifying the areas in which they operate.

Although the advantages of Google Earth are many, it has not been without its share of ethical controversies. Some of the developing countries are concerned about the surveillance modes used by Google Earth. In such countries, where IT laws are less stringent, the threat of global terrorism has compounded. In 2005, when Google Earth started showing different places of the earth as full-color photographs, it was considered to be a boon for developing countries like India, which has severe traffic problems. This service could help users in these countries locate their destination easily and reduce traffic chaos. It could also give users two-dimensional images of far-flung areas, making them more accessible.

South Korea was probably one of the first countries to voice concerns against Google Earth. South Korea, which was then engaged in a war with North Korea, felt that the Google Earth images compromised their territory. The Austrian Nuclear Science and Technology Organization (ANSTO) also raised concern over the sensitive information provided by Google Earth. Similarly, in 2005, the Dutch legislators, Frans Weekers and Aleing Wolfson, asked, "Should the Dutch government consider taking measures (against Google Earth) and if not, why not"? There were security concerns raised in Iraq as well, as many thought that the Al-Qaida used Google Earth as an intelligence tool in its fight against the U.S. In 2007, all these concerns reached their crescendo when it was reported that terrorists are using Google Earth to target British bases in Basra. Meanwhile, India was also uneasy about the imaging conducted by Google Earth. In 2007, Indian President A.P.J. Abdul Kalam held a meeting with police officials to express concerns about the high-resolution images of the country's strategic sites on Google Earth.

Several countries are now contemplating the idea of launching their own service similar to that provided by Google Earth. In May 2008, the Indian Space Research Organization (ISRO) announced its plan to develop Bhuvan. In this tool, it was proposed that the high-security areas would be blurred out, so as to have more control over the content being displayed on the Internet. Moreover, the Bhuvan application could only be downloaded by registered users. A beta version of Bhuvan was released in 2009, and now it supports additional features such as providing flood and forest fire alerts, information about agricultural landslides, and so on. However, Bhuvan is not as sophisticated as Google Earth and has a lot of performance issues.

Imaging the entire planet is not an easy task, and it requires advanced technology and infrastructure. The countries that have tried to develop their own solution have realized the challenges of undertaking this project. As a workaround, some countries have demanded that Google take permission from the host country regarding the images that are safe to display and those that need to be camouflaged so that sensitive areas are not made public. But the problem here is: how does a government identify sensitive locations? For example, citizens might want places such as railway stations and bus stands to be mapped, while government might think that these are sensitive areas.

There have been several calls to ban Google Earth over the years. However, in this age of global information sharing, there have been debates as to whether that would be the right thing to do. Advocates such as Amit Karkhanis have filed a petition before the Mumbai High Court to ban Google Earth on the grounds that it is helping terrorists navigate their way to Mumbai via sea. However, such individuals have little legal evidence to substantiate their allegations. The satellites used for mapping do not cause noise, light, or air pollution, and hence, it is difficult to prove that the imaging causes any nuisance.

Apart from the apparent danger to national security posed by Google Earth, there has been some objection to Google mapping people's houses. Many argue that it is an invasion of privacy. There have also been accusations against Google for stealing personal information like name, address, passwords, and medical information from unsecured Wi-Fi networks.

The U.S. courts, however, have ruled that capturing the aerial view of someone's property does not amount to a trespass against that person: "We have said that the airspace is a public highway. Yet it is obvious that if the landowner is to have full enjoyment of the land, he must have exclusive control of the immediate reaches of the enveloping atmosphere. Otherwise buildings could not be erected, trees could not be planted, and even fences could not be run ... The landowner owns at least as much of the space above the ground as he can occupy or use in connection with the land."

Acknowledging the concerns raised by various governments, and especially the Indian government, Google Earth issued an official statement, which says, "Google has been talking and will continue to talk to the Indian government about any security concerns it may have regarding Google Earth. We are pleased to have initiated dialogue with the Indian government, the discussions have been substantive and constructive, but no agreements have been made ... We have committed to continue the dialogue." In the end, it is the openness or conservatism of individual governments that will determine to what extent its people are allowed to enjoy the benefits of a service like Google Earth.

Sources: Zhu, Yueqin, Jiantong Zhang and Liqiu Meng, "Ethical Concerns for Online Geoinformation Services". Retrieved from http://icaci.org/files/documents/ICC_proceedings/ ICC2009/html/nonref/22_3.pdf. http://www.spatial.maine. edu/~onsrud/GSDIArchive/gis_ethics.pdf. Doyle, Jack, "How Google lied over street spies: Watchdog relaunches inquiry into search engine's data trawl", *The Daily Mail* (2012). Retrieved from http://www.dailymail.co.uk/news/article-2158307/Google-facing-new-privacy-probe-Street-View-cars-data-theft-alleged-misled-watchdog.html. Strachan, Lindsey A., "Re-mapping Privacy Law: How the Google Maps Scandal Requires Tort Law Reform", *Richmond Journal of Law and Technology*, Vol. 15, Issue 4 (2011). Retrieved from http://jolt.richmond.edu/v17i4/article14. pdf. Banerjee, Debadyuti, "'Is My Laptop A Viable Tool To Invade Your Privacy?'—Such and Other Critical Legal Issues Generated By Google Earth", *Journal of International Commercial Law and Technology*, Vol. 5, Issue 4 (2010). Retrieved from http://www.jiclt. com/index.php/jiclt/article/viewFile/120/118. *Google Earth.* Retrieved from http://www.google.com/earth/explore/show-case/historical.html. Sui, Daniel and Michael Goodchild, "The convergence of GIS and social media: challenges for GIScience", *International Journal of Geographical Information Science* (2011). Retrieved from http://www.geog.ucsb.edu/~good/papers/516. pdf. *Bhuvan.* Retrieved from http://www.bhuvan.nrsc.gov.in/ bhuvan_links.php#. Saxena, Anupam, "India's 'Google Earth' Bhuvan Upgraded: Disaster Services, Tourism Info, High Res", *Medianama* (2013). Retrieved from http://www.medianama. com/2013/01/223-bhuvan-new-datasets/. *National Remote Sensing Centre: Indian Space Research Organisation.* Retrieved from http://nrsc.gov.in/. "10 Crimes Caught On Google Earth", Yahoo! News. Retrieved on https://screen.yahoo.com/top-viral-videos/10-crimes-caught-google-earth-172002790.html

CASE STUDY QUESTIONS

1. Discuss the features of Google Earth and the benefits it offers.

2. What are the ethical concerns raised by the different countries against Google Earth? Do you think they are justified?

3. What are the various methods adopted to contemplate the ethical issues raised by Google Earth?

4. Do you think Google's response to such concerns is appropriate?

organizations. **Due process** is a related feature of law-governed societies and is a process in which laws are known and understood, and there is an ability to appeal to higher authorities to ensure that the laws are applied correctly.

These basic concepts form the underpinning of an ethical analysis of information systems and those who manage them. First, information technologies are filtered through social institutions, organizations, and individuals. Systems do not have impacts by themselves. Whatever information system impacts exist are products of institutional, organizational, and individual actions and behaviors. Second, responsibility for the consequences of technology falls clearly on the institutions, organizations, and individual managers who choose to use the technology. Using information technology in a socially responsible manner means that you can and will be held accountable for the consequences of your actions. Third, in an ethical, political society, individuals and others can recover damages done to them through a set of laws characterized by due process.

ETHICAL ANALYSIS

When confronted with a situation that seems to present ethical issues, how should you analyze it? The following five-step process should help:

1. *Identify and describe the facts clearly.* Find out who did what to whom, and where, when, and how. In many instances, you will be surprised at the errors in the initially reported facts, and often you will find that simply getting the facts straight helps define the solution. It also helps to get the opposing parties involved in an ethical dilemma to agree on the facts.

2. *Define the conflict or dilemma and identify the higher-order values involved.* Ethical, social, and political issues always reference higher values. The parties to a dispute all claim to be pursuing higher values (e.g., freedom, privacy, protection of property, and the free enterprise system). Typically, an ethical issue involves a dilemma: two diametrically opposed courses of action that support worthwhile values. For example, the chapter-opening case study illustrates two competing values: the need to improve access to digital content and the need to respect the property rights of the owners of that content.

3. *Identify the stakeholders.* Every ethical, social, and political issue has stakeholders: players in the game who have an interest in the outcome, who have invested in the situation, and usually who have vocal opinions. Find out the identity of these groups and what they want. This will be useful later when designing a solution.

4. *Identify the options that you can reasonably take.* You may find that none of the options satisfy all the interests involved, but that some options do a better job than others. Sometimes arriving at a good or ethical solution may not always be a balancing of consequences to stakeholders.

5. *Identify the potential consequences of your options.* Some options may be ethically correct but disastrous from other points of view. Other options may work in one instance but not in other similar instances. Always ask yourself, "What if I choose this option consistently over time?"

CANDIDATE ETHICAL PRINCIPLES

Once your analysis is complete, what ethical principles or rules should you use to make a decision? What higher-order values should inform your judgment? Although you are the only one who can decide which among many ethical principles you will follow, and how you will prioritize them, it is helpful to consider some ethical principles with deep roots in many cultures that have survived throughout recorded history:

1. Do unto others as you would have them do unto you (the **Golden Rule**). Putting yourself into the place of others, and thinking of yourself as the object of the decision, can help you think about fairness in decision making.

2. If an action is not right for everyone to take, it is not right for anyone (**Immanuel Kant's Categorical Imperative**). Ask yourself, "If everyone did this, could the organization, or society, survive?"

3. If an action cannot be taken repeatedly, it is not right to take at all. This is the slippery-slope rule: An action may bring about a small change now that is acceptable, but if it is repeated, it would bring unacceptable changes in the long run. In the vernacular, it might be stated as "once started down a slippery path, you may not be able to stop."

4. Take the action that achieves the higher or greater value (**Utilitarian Principle**). This rule assumes you can prioritize values in a rank order and understand the consequences of various courses of action.

5. Take the action that produces the least harm or the least potential cost (**Risk Aversion Principle**). Some actions have extremely high failure costs of very low probability (e.g., building a nuclear generating facility in an urban area) or extremely high failure costs of moderate probability (speeding and automobile accidents). Avoid these high-failure-cost actions, paying greater attention to high-failure-cost potential of moderate to high probability.

6. Assume that virtually all tangible and intangible objects are owned by someone else unless there is a specific declaration otherwise. (This is the **ethical "no free lunch" rule**.) If something someone else has created is useful to you, it has value, and you should assume the creator wants compensation for this work.

Actions that do not easily pass these rules deserve close attention and a great deal of caution. The appearance of unethical behavior may do as much harm to you and your company as actual unethical behavior.

PROFESSIONAL CODES OF CONDUCT

When groups of people claim to be professionals, they take on special rights and obligations because of their special claims to knowledge, wisdom, and respect. Professional codes of conduct are promulgated by associations of professionals, such as the American Medical Association (AMA), the American Bar Association (ABA), the Association of Information Technology Professionals (AITP), and the Association for Computing Machinery (ACM). These professional groups take responsibility for the partial regulation of their professions by determining entrance qualifications and competence. Codes of ethics are promises by professions to regulate themselves in the general interest of society. For example, avoiding harm to others, honoring property rights (including intellectual property), and respecting privacy are among the General Moral Imperatives of the ACM's Code of Ethics and Professional Conduct.

SOME REAL-WORLD ETHICAL DILEMMAS

Information systems have created new ethical dilemmas in which one set of interests is pitted against another. For example, many of the large telephone companies in the United States are using information technology to reduce the sizes of their workforces. Voice recognition software reduces the need for human operators by enabling computers to recognize a customer's responses to a series of computerized questions. Many companies monitor what their employees are doing on the Internet to prevent them from wasting company resources on non-business activities. Facebook monitors its subscribers and then sells the information to advertisers and app developers (see the chapter-ending case study).

In each instance, you can find competing values at work, with groups lined up on either side of a debate. A company may argue, for example, that it has a right to use information systems to increase productivity and reduce the size of its workforce to lower costs and stay in business. Employees displaced by information systems may argue that employers have some responsibility for their welfare. Business owners might feel obligated to monitor employee e-mail and Internet use to minimize drains on productivity. Employees might believe they should be able to use the Internet for short personal tasks in place of the telephone. A close analysis of the facts can sometimes produce compromised solutions that give each side "half a loaf." Try to apply some of the principles of ethical analysis described to each of these cases. What is the right thing to do?

4.3

WHY DO CONTEMPORARY INFORMATION SYSTEMS TECHNOLOGY AND THE INTERNET POSE CHALLENGES TO THE PROTECTION OF INDIVIDUAL PRIVACY AND INTELLECTUAL PROPERTY?

In this section, we take a closer look at the five moral dimensions of information systems first described in Figure 4.1. In each dimension, we identify the ethical, social, and political levels of analysis and use real-world examples to illustrate the values involved, the stakeholders, and the options chosen.

INFORMATION RIGHTS: PRIVACY AND FREEDOM IN THE INTERNET AGE

Privacy is the claim of individuals to be left alone, free from surveillance or interference from other individuals or organizations, including the state. Claims to privacy are also involved at the workplace: Millions of employees are subject to electronic and other forms of high-tech surveillance. Information technology and systems threaten individual claims to privacy by making the invasion of privacy cheap, profitable, and effective.

The claim to privacy is protected in the U.S., Canadian, and German constitutions in a variety of different ways and in other countries through various statutes. In the United States, the claim to privacy is protected primarily by the First Amendment guarantees of freedom of speech and association, the Fourth Amendment protections against unreasonable search and seizure of one's personal documents or home, and the guarantee of due process.

Table 4.3 describes the major U.S. federal statutes that set forth the conditions for handling information about individuals in such areas as credit reporting, education, financial records, newspaper records, and electronic communications. The Privacy Act of 1974 has been the most important of these laws, regulating the federal government's collection, use, and disclosure of information. At present, most U.S. federal privacy laws apply only to the federal government and regulate very few areas of the private sector.

Most American and European privacy law is based on a regime called **Fair Information Practices (FIP)** first set forth in a report written in 1973 by a federal government advisory committee and updated most recently in 2010 to take into account new privacy-invading technology (FTC, 2010; U.S. Department of Health, Education, and Welfare, 1973). FIP is a set of principles governing the collection and use of information about individuals. FIP principles are based on the notion of a mutuality of interest between the

TABLE 4.3 FEDERAL PRIVACY LAWS IN THE UNITED STATES

GENERAL FEDERAL PRIVACY LAWS	PRIVACY LAWS AFFECTING PRIVATE INSTITUTIONS
Freedom of Information Act of 1966 as Amended (5 USC 552)	Fair Credit Reporting Act of 1970
Privacy Act of 1974 as Amended (5 USC 552a)	Family Educational Rights and Privacy Act of 1974
Electronic Communications Privacy Act of 1986	Right to Financial Privacy Act of 1978
Computer Matching and Privacy Protection Act of 1988	Privacy Protection Act of 1980
Computer Security Act of 1987	Cable Communications Policy Act of 1984
Federal Managers Financial Integrity Act of 1982	Electronic Communications Privacy Act of 1986
Driver's Privacy Protection Act of 1994	Video Privacy Protection Act of 1988
E-Government Act of 2002	The Health Insurance Portability and Accountability Act of 1996 (HIPAA)
	Children's Online Privacy Protection Act (COPPA) of 1998
	Financial Modernization Act (Gramm-Leach-Bliley Act) of 1999

TABLE 4.4 FEDERAL TRADE COMMISSION FAIR INFORMATION PRACTICE PRINCIPLES

1.	Notice/awareness (core principle). Web sites must disclose their information practices before collecting data. Includes identification of collector; uses of data; other recipients of data; nature of collection (active/inactive); voluntary or required status; consequences of refusal; and steps taken to protect confidentiality, integrity, and quality of the data.
2.	Choice/consent (core principle). There must be a choice regime in place allowing consumers to choose how their information will be used for secondary purposes other than supporting the transaction, including internal use and transfer to third parties.
3.	Access/participation. Consumers should be able to review and contest the accuracy and completeness of data collected about them in a timely, inexpensive process.
4.	Security. Data collectors must take responsible steps to assure that consumer information is accurate and secure from unauthorized use.
5.	Enforcement. There must be in place a mechanism to enforce FIP principles. This can involve self-regulation, legislation giving consumers legal remedies for violations, or federal statutes and regulations.

record holder and the individual. The individual has an interest in engaging in a transaction, and the record keeper—usually a business or government agency—requires information about the individual to support the transaction. Once information is gathered, the individual maintains an interest in the record, and the record may not be used to support other activities without the individual's consent. In 1998, the FTC restated and extended the original FIP to provide guidelines for protecting online privacy. Table 4.4 describes the FTC's Fair Information Practice principles.

The FTC's FIP principles are being used as guidelines to drive changes in privacy legislation. In July 1998, the U.S. Congress passed the Children's Online Privacy Protection Act (COPPA), requiring Web sites to obtain parental permission before collecting information on children under the age of 13. The FTC has recommended additional legislation to protect online consumer privacy in advertising networks that collect records of consumer Web activity to develop detailed profiles, which are then used by other companies to target online ads. In 2010, the FTC added three practices to its framework for privacy. Firms should adopt "privacy by design," building products and services that protect privacy. Firms should increase the transparency of their data practices. And firms should require consumer consent and provide clear options to opt out of data collection schemes (FTC, 2010). Other proposed Internet privacy legislation focuses on protecting the online use of personal identification numbers, such as social security numbers; protecting personal information collected on the Internet that deals with individuals not covered by COPPA; and limiting the use of data mining for homeland security.

Beginning in 2009 and continuing through 2012, the FTC extended its FIP doctrine to address the issue of behavioral targeting. The FTC held hearings to discuss its program for voluntary industry principles for regulating behavioral targeting. The online advertising trade group Network Advertising Initiative (discussed later in this section), published its own self-regulatory principles that largely agreed with the FTC. Nevertheless, the government, privacy groups, and the online ad industry are still at loggerheads over two issues. Privacy advocates want both an opt-in policy at all sites and a national Do Not Track list. The industry opposes these moves and continues to insist on an opt-out capability being the only way to avoid tracking. In May 2011, Senator Jay D. Rockefeller (D-WV), Chairman of the Senate Commerce Subcommittee on Consumer Protection, Product Safety, and Insurance, held hearings to discuss consumer privacy concerns and to explore the possible role of the federal government in protecting consumers in the mobile marketplace. Rockefeller supports the Do-Not-Track Online Act of 2011 (reintroduced in 2013), which requires firms to notify consumers they are being tracked and allows consumers to opt out of the tracking (U.S. Senate, 2011). Nevertheless, there is an emerging consensus among all parties that greater transparency and user control (especially making opting out of tracking the default option) is required to deal with behavioral tracking. While there are many studies of privacy issues at the federal level, there has been no significant legislation in recent years.

Privacy protections have also been added to recent laws deregulating financial services and safeguarding the maintenance and transmission of health information about individuals. The Gramm-Leach-Bliley Act of 1999, which repeals earlier restrictions on affiliations among banks, securities firms, and insurance companies, includes some privacy protection for consumers of financial services. All financial institutions are required to disclose their policies and practices for protecting the privacy of nonpublic personal information and to allow customers to opt out of information-sharing arrangements with nonaffiliated third parties.

The Health Insurance Portability and Accountability Act (HIPAA) of 1996, which took effect on April 14, 2003, includes privacy protection for medical records. The law gives patients access to their personal medical records maintained by health care providers, hospitals, and health insurers, and the right to authorize how protected information about themselves can be used or disclosed. Doctors, hospitals, and other health care providers must limit the disclosure of personal information about patients to the minimum amount necessary to achieve a given purpose.

The European Directive on Data Protection

In Europe, privacy protection is much more stringent than in the United States. Unlike the United States, European countries do not allow businesses to use personally identifiable information without consumers' prior consent. On October 25, 1998, the European Commission's Directive on Data Protection went into effect, broadening privacy protection in the European Union (EU) nations. The directive requires companies to inform people when they collect information about them and disclose how it will be stored and used. Customers must provide their **informed consent** before any company can legally use data about them, and they have the right to access that information, correct it, and request that no further data be collected. Informed consent can be defined as consent given with knowledge of all the facts needed to make a rational decision. EU member nations must translate these principles into their own laws and cannot transfer personal data to countries, such as the United States, that do not have similar privacy protection regulations. In 2009, the European Parliament passed new rules governing the use of third-party cookies for behavioral tracking purposes. These new rules were implemented in May 2011 and require that Web site visitors must give explicit consent to be tracked by cookies. Web sites will be required to have highly visible warnings on their pages if third-party cookies are being used (European Parliament, 2009).

In January 2012, the E.U. issued significant proposed changes to its data protection rules, the first overhaul since 1995 (European Commission, 2012). The new rules would apply to all companies providing services in Europe, and require Internet companies like Amazon, Facebook, Apple, Google, and others to obtain explicit consent from consumers about the use of their personal data, delete information at the user's request (based on the "right to be forgotten"), and retain information only as long as absolutely necessary. In 2014 the European Union is considering significant changes in privacy policies by extending greater control to users of the Internet. While the privacy policies of United States firms are largely voluntary, in Europe privacy policies are mandated, and more consistent across jurisdictions. Among the changes being discussed are a requirement that firms inform users before collecting data, and every time they collect data, and how it will be used. Users would have to give consent to any data collection. Other proposals call for users to have a "right of access" to personal data, and the "right to be forgotten."

Working with the European Commission, the U.S. Department of Commerce developed a safe harbor framework for U.S. firms. A **safe harbor** is a private, self-regulating policy and enforcement mechanism that meets the objectives of government regulators and legislation but does not involve government regulation or enforcement. U.S. businesses would be allowed to use personal data from EU countries if they develop privacy protection policies that meet EU standards. Enforcement would occur in the United States using self-policing, regulation, and government enforcement of fair trade statutes.

Internet Challenges to Privacy

Internet technology has posed new challenges for the protection of individual privacy. Information sent over this vast network of networks may pass through many different computer systems before it reaches its final destination. Each of these systems is capable of monitoring, capturing, and storing communications that pass through it.

Web sites track searches that have been conducted, the Web sites and Web pages visited, the online content a person has accessed, and what items that person has inspected or purchased over the Web. This monitoring and tracking of Web site visitors occurs in the background without the visitor's knowledge. It is conducted not just by individual Web sites but by advertising networks such as Microsoft Advertising, Yahoo, and Google's DoubleClick that are capable of tracking personal browsing behavior across thousands of Web sites. Both Web site publishers and the advertising industry defend tracking of individuals across the Web because doing so allows more relevant ads to be targeted to users, and it pays for the cost of publishing Web sites. In this sense, it's like broadcast television: advertiser-supported content that is free to the user. The commercial demand for this personal information is virtually insatiable. However, these practices also impinge on individual privacy, as discussed in the Interactive Session on Technology.

Cookies are small text files deposited on a computer hard drive when a user visits Web sites. Cookies identify the visitor's Web browser software and track visits to the Web site. When the visitor returns to a site that has stored a cookie, the Web site software will search the visitor's computer, find the cookie, and know what that person has done in the past. It may also update the cookie, depending on the activity during the visit. In this way, the site can customize its content for each visitor's interests. For example, if you purchase a book on Amazon.com and return later from the same browser, the site will welcome you by name and recommend other books of interest based on your past purchases. DoubleClick, described earlier in this chapter, uses cookies to build its dossiers with details of online purchases and to examine the behavior of Web site visitors. Figure 4.3 illustrates how cookies work.

Web sites using cookie technology cannot directly obtain visitors' names and addresses. However, if a person has registered at a site, that information can be combined with cookie data to identify the visitor. Web site owners can also combine the data they have gathered from cookies and other Web site monitoring tools with personal data from other sources, such as offline data collected from surveys or paper catalog purchases, to develop very detailed profiles of their visitors.

FIGURE 4.3   HOW COOKIES IDENTIFY WEB VISITORS

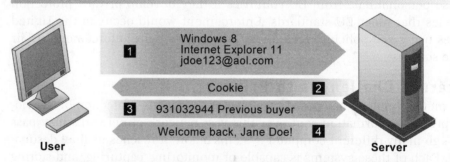

1. The Web server reads the user's Web browser and determines the operating system, browser name, version number, Internet address, and other information.
2. The server transmits a tiny text file with user identification information called a cookie, which the user's browser receives and stores on the user's computer hard drive.
3. When the user returns to the Web site, the server requests the contents of any cookie it deposited previously in the user's computer.
4. The Web server reads the cookie, identifies the visitor, and calls up data on the user.

Cookies are written by a Web site on a visitor's hard drive. When the visitor returns to that Web site, the Web server requests the ID number from the cookie and uses it to access the data stored by that server on that visitor. The Web site can then use these data to display personalized information.

INTERACTIVE SESSION: TECHNOLOGY

BIG DATA GETS PERSONAL: BEHAVIORAL TARGETING

Ever get the feeling somebody is trailing you on the Web, watching your every click? Do you wonder why you start seeing display ads and pop-ups just after you've been searching the Web for a car, a dress, or cosmetic product? Well, you're right: your behavior is being tracked, and you are being targeted on the Web as you move from site to site in order to expose you to certain "targeted" ads. It's Big Data's dark side.

Individual Web sites and companies whose business is identifying and tracking Internet users for advertisers and marketers are collecting data on your every online move. Google, which handles more than 3.5 billion Web searches each day, knows more about you than your mother does. Many of the tracking tools gather incredibly personal information such as age, gender, race, income, marital status, health concerns (health topics you search on), TV shows and movies viewed, magazines and newspapers read, and books purchased. A $31 billion dollar online ad industry is driving this intense data collection. Facebook, which maintains detailed data on over 1 billion users, employs its Like button to follow users around the Web even if you log off. Its social networking site is one giant tracking system that remembers what you like, what your friends like, and whatever you reveal on your Wall. (See the chapter-ending case study.) Plus, Google's social networking tool, knows about your friendships on Gmail, the places you go on maps, and how you spend your time on the more than two million websites in Google's ad network. It is able to gather this information even though relatively few people use Plus for their social network.

While tracking firms claim the information they gather is anonymous, this is true in name only. Scholars have shown that with just a few pieces of information, such as age, gender, zip code, and marital status, specific individuals can be easily identified. Moreover, tracking firms combine their online data with data they purchase from offline firms who track retail store purchases of virtually all Americans. Here, personal names and other identifiers are used.

Use of real identities across the Web is going mainstream at a rapid clip. A Wall Street Journal examination of nearly 1,000 top Websites found that 75% now include code from social networks, such as Facebook's "Like" or Twitter's "Tweet" buttons. Such code can match people's identities with their Web-browsing activities on an unprecedented scale and can even track a user's arrival on a page if the button is never clicked.

In separate research, the Journal examined what happens when people logged in to roughly 70 popular Websites that request a login and found that more than a quarter of the time, the sites passed along a user's real name, email address or other personal details to third-party companies.

Online advertising titans like Google, Microsoft, and Yahoo are all looking for ways to monetize their huge collections of online behavioral data. While search engine marketing is arguably the most effective form of advertising in history, untargeted banner display ad marketing is highly inefficient because it displays ads to everyone regardless of their interests. As a result, these firms cannot charge much for display ads. However, by tracking the online movements of 245 million U.S. Internet users, they can develop a very clear picture of who you are, and use that information to show you ads that might be of interest to you. This would make the marketing process more efficient, and more profitable for all the parties involved.

You're also being tracked closely when you use your mobile phone to access the Internet, visit your Facebook page, get Twitter feeds, watch video, and listen to music. The mobile Web is working hard to keep track of your whereabouts, locations, habits, and friends in the hope of selling you even more products and services.

New technologies found on smartphones can identify where you are located within a few yards. Performing routine actions using your smart phone makes it possible to locate you throughout the day, to report this information to corporate databases, retain and analyze the information, and then sell it to advertisers. Most of the popular apps report your location. Law enforcement agencies certainly have an interest in knowing the whereabouts of criminals and suspects. There are, of course, many times when you would like to report your location either automatically or on your command. If you were injured, for instance, you might like your cell phone to be able to automatically report your location to authorities, or, if you were in a restaurant, you might want to notify your friends where you are and what you are doing. But what about occasions when you don't want anyone to know where you are, least of all advertisers and marketers?

Location data gathered from cell phones has extraordinary commercial value because advertising companies can send you highly targeted advertisements, coupons, and flash bargains, based on where you are located. This technology is the foundation for many location-based services, which include smartphone maps and charts, shopping apps, and social apps that you can use to let your friends know where you are and what you are doing. Revenues from the global location-based services market are projected to reach reach $10.3 billion in 2015, according to Gartner.

Both Apple's iPhone and Google's Android phones collect personal, private location data, and both firms are building massive databases that can pinpoint your location. Advertising firms pay Apple and Google for that information and for distributing their mobile ads, and they are becoming increasingly important sources of revenue. In 2012, Google earned $2.2 billion from its mobile ads. Smartphone apps that provide location-based services are also sources of personal, private location information based on the smartphone GPS capability.

Expect those eyes to follow your movements even more in the future as behavioral targeting becomes even more precise. New software is being developed to help advertisers track users across devices by establishing cross-screen identities. That means that companies will be able to serve ads to your mobile phone based on what they learned about you from surfing the Web on your PC.

Sources: Claire Cain Miller, "The Plus in Google Plus? It's Mostly for Google," *New York Times*, February 14, 2014; Elizabeth Dwoskin, "Internet Users Tap Tech Tools That Protect Them From Prying Eyes," *Wall Street Journal*, March 23, 2014; Claire Cain Miller and Somni Sengupta, "Selling Secrets of Phone Users to Advertisers," *New York Times*, October 5, 2013; Natasha Singer, "Their Apps Track You, Will Congress Track Them?" *The New York Times*, January 5, 2013; Spencer E. Ante, "Online Ads Can Now Follow Your Home," *The Wall Street Journal*, April 29, 2013; Jennifer Valentino-Devries and Jeremy Singer, "*They Know What You're Shopping For,*" The Wall Street Journal, December 7 , 2013.

CASE STUDY QUESTIONS

1. Why is behavioral tracking such an important ethical dilemma today? Identify the stakeholders and interest groups in favor of and opposed to behavioral tracking.

2. How do businesses benefit from behavioral tracking? Do people benefit? Explain your answer.

3. What would happen if there were no behavioral tracking on the Internet?

There are now even more subtle and surreptitious tools for surveillance of Internet users. So-called "super cookies" or Flash cookies cannot be easily deleted and can be installed whenever a person clicks on a Flash video. These so-called "Local Shared Object" files are used by Flash to play videos and are put on the user's computer without their consent. Marketers use Web beacons as another tool to monitor online behavior. **Web beacons**, also called *Web bugs* (or simply "tracking files"), are tiny software programs that keep a record of users' online clickstream and report this data back to whomever owns the tracking file invisibly embedded in e-mail messages and

Web pages that are designed to monitor the behavior of the user visiting a Web site or sending e-mail. Web beacons are placed on popular Web sites by third-party firms who pay the Web sites a fee for access to their audience. So how common is Web tracking? In a path-breaking series of articles in the *Wall Street Journal* in 2010 and 2011, researchers examined the tracking files on 50 of the most popular U.S Web sites. What they found revealed a very widespread surveillance system. On the 50 sites, they discovered 3,180 tracking files installed on visitor computers. Only one site, Wikipedia, had no tracking files. Some popular sites such as Dictionary.com, MSN, and Comcast, installed more than 100 tracking files! Two-thirds of the tracking files came from 131 companies whose primary business is identifying and tracking Internet users to create consumer profiles that can be sold to advertising firms looking for specific types of customers. The biggest trackers were Google, Microsoft, and Quantcast, all of whom are in the business of selling ads to advertising firms and marketers. A follow-up study in 2012 found the situation had worsened: tracking on the 50 most popular sites had risen nearly five fold! The cause: growth of online ad auctions where advertisers buy the data about users' Web browsing behavior.

Other **spyware** can secretly install itself on an Internet user's computer by piggybacking on larger applications. Once installed, the spyware calls out to Web sites to send banner ads and other unsolicited material to the user, and it can report the user's movements on the Internet to other computers. More information is available about intrusive software in Chapter 8.

Nearly 80 percent of global Internet users use Google Search and other Google services, making Google the world's largest collector of online user data. Whatever Google does with its data has an enormous impact on online privacy. Most experts believe that Google possesses the largest collection of personal information in the world—more data on more people than any government agency. The nearest competitor is Facebook.

After Google acquired the advertising network DoubleClick in 2007, Google has been using behavioral targeting to help it display more relevant ads based on users' search activities and to target individuals as they move from one site to another in order to show them display or banner ads. Google allows tracking software on its search pages, and using DoubleClick, it is able to track users across the Internet. One of its programs enables advertisers to target ads based on the search histories of Google users, along with any other information the user submits to Google such as age, demographics, region, and other Web activities (such as blogging). Google's AdSense program enables Google to help advertisers select keywords and design ads for various market segments based on search histories, such as helping a clothing Web site create and test ads targeted at teenage females. A recent study found that 88 percent of 400,000 Web sites had at least one Google tracking bug.

Google has also been scanning the contents of messages received by users of its free Web-based e-mail service called Gmail. Ads that users see when they read their e-mail are related to the subjects of these messages. Profiles are developed on individual users based on the content in their e-mail. Google now displays targeted ads on YouTube and on Google mobile applications, and its DoubleClick ad network serves up targeted banner ads.

The United States has allowed businesses to gather transaction information generated in the marketplace and then use that information for other marketing purposes without obtaining the informed consent of the individual whose information is being used. An **opt-out** model of informed consent permits the collection of personal information until the consumer specifically requests that the data not be collected. Privacy advocates would like to see wider use of an **opt-in** model of informed consent in which a business is prohibited from collecting any personal information unless the consumer specifically takes action to approve information collection and use. Here, the default option is no collection of user information.

The online industry has preferred self-regulation to privacy legislation for protecting consumers. The online advertising industry formed the Online Privacy Alliance to encourage self-regulation to develop a set of privacy guidelines for its members. The group promotes the use of online seals, such as that of TRUSTe, certifying Web sites adhering to certain privacy principles. Members of the advertising network industry, including Google's DoubleClick, have created an additional industry association called the Network Advertising Initiative (NAI) to develop its own privacy policies to help consumers opt out of advertising network programs and provide consumers redress from abuses.

Individual firms like Microsoft, Mozilla Foundation, Yahoo, and Google have recently adopted policies on their own in an effort to address public concern about tracking people online. Microsoft's Internet Explorer 10 Web browser was shipped with the opt-out option as the default in 2013. Other browsers have opt out options but users need to turn them on, and most users fail to do this. AOL established an opt-out policy that allows users of its site to not be tracked. Yahoo follows NAI guidelines and also allows opt-out for tracking and Web beacons (Web bugs). Google has reduced retention time for tracking data.

In general, most Internet businesses do little to protect the privacy of their customers, and consumers do not do as much as they should to protect themselves. For commercial Web sites that depend on advertising to support themselves, most revenue derives from selling customer information. Of the companies that do post privacy polices on their Web sites, about half do not monitor their sites to ensure they adhere to these policies. The vast majority of online customers claim they are concerned about online privacy, but less than half read the privacy statements on Web sites. In general, Web site privacy policies require a law degree to understand and are ambiguous about key terms (Laudon and Traver, 2015). In 2014 what firms like Facebook and Google call a "Privacy Policy" is in fact a "Data Use Policy." The concept of privacy is associated with consumer rights, which firms do not wish to recognize. A Data Use Policy simply tells customers how the information will be used without any mention of rights.

In one of the more insightful studies of consumer attitudes towards Internet privacy, a group of Berkeley students conducted surveys of online users, and of complaints filed with the FTC involving privacy issues. Here are some of their results: people feel they have no control over the information collected about them, and they don't know who to complain to. Web sites collect all this information, but do not let users have access, the Web site policies are unclear, and they share data with "affiliates" but never identify who the affiliates are and how many there are. Web bug trackers are ubiquitous and users are not informed of trackers on the pages they visit. The results of this study and others suggest that consumers are not saying "Take my privacy, I don't care, send me the service for free." They are saying "We want access to the information, we want some controls on what can be collected, what is done with the information, the ability to opt out of the entire tracking enterprise, and some clarity on what the policies really are, and we don't want those policies changed without our participation and permission." (The full report is available at knowprivacy.org.)

Technical Solutions

In addition to legislation, there are a few technologies that can protect user privacy during interactions with Web sites. Many of these tools are used for encrypting e-mail, for making e-mail or surfing activities appear anonymous, for preventing client computers from accepting cookies, or for detecting and eliminating spyware. For the most part, technical solutions have failed to protect users from being tracked as they move from one site to another.

Because of growing public criticism of behavioral tracking, targeting of ads, and the failure of industry to self-regulate, attention has shifted to browsers. Many browsers have Do Not Track options. For users who have selected the Do Not Track browser option, their browser will send a request to Web sites requesting the user's behavior not be tracked. But Web sites are not obligated to honor their visitors' requests not to be tracked. There is no online advertising industry agreement on how to respond to Do Not Track requests, and currently no legislation requiring Web sites to stop tracking.

PROPERTY RIGHTS: INTELLECTUAL PROPERTY

Contemporary information systems have severely challenged existing laws and social practices that protect private **intellectual property**. Intellectual property is considered to be intangible property created by individuals or corporations. Information technology has made it difficult to protect intellectual property because computerized information can be so easily copied or distributed on networks. Intellectual property is subject to a variety of protections under three different legal traditions: trade secrets, copyright, and patent law.

Trade Secrets

Any intellectual work product—a formula, device, pattern, or compilation of data—used for a business purpose can be classified as a **trade secret**, provided it is not based on information in the public domain. Protections for trade secrets vary from state to state. In general, trade secret laws grant a monopoly on the ideas behind a work product, but it can be a very tenuous monopoly.

Software that contains novel or unique elements, procedures, or compilations can be included as a trade secret. Trade secret law protects the actual ideas in a work product, not only their manifestation. To make this claim, the creator or owner must take care to bind employees and customers with nondisclosure agreements and to prevent the secret from falling into the public domain.

The limitation of trade secret protection is that, although virtually all software programs of any complexity contain unique elements of some sort, it is difficult to prevent the ideas in the work from falling into the public domain when the software is widely distributed.

Copyright

Copyright is a statutory grant that protects creators of intellectual property from having their work copied by others for any purpose during the life of the author plus an additional 70 years after the author's death. For corporate-owned works, copyright protection lasts for 95 years after their initial creation. Congress has extended copyright protection to books, periodicals, lectures, dramas, musical compositions, maps, drawings, artwork of any kind, and motion pictures. The intent behind copyright laws has been to encourage creativity and authorship by ensuring that creative people receive the financial and other benefits of their work. Most industrial nations have their own copyright laws, and there are several international conventions and bilateral agreements through which nations coordinate and enforce their laws.

In the mid-1960s, the Copyright Office began registering software programs, and in 1980, Congress passed the Computer Software Copyright Act, which clearly provides protection for software program code and for copies of the original sold in commerce, and sets forth the rights of the purchaser to use the software while the creator retains legal title.

Copyright protects against copying of entire programs or their parts. Damages and relief are readily obtained for infringement. The drawback to copyright protection is that the underlying ideas behind a work are not protected, only their manifestation in a work. A competitor can use your software, understand how it works, and build new software that follows the same concepts without infringing on a copyright.

"Look and feel" copyright infringement lawsuits are precisely about the distinction between an idea and its expression. For instance, in the early 1990s, Apple Computer sued Microsoft Corporation and Hewlett-Packard for infringement of the expression of Apple's Macintosh interface, claiming that the defendants copied the expression of overlapping windows. The defendants countered that the idea of overlapping windows can be expressed only in a single way and, therefore, was not protectable under the merger doctrine of copyright law. When ideas and their expression merge, the expression cannot be copyrighted.

In general, courts appear to be following the reasoning of a 1989 case—*Brown Bag Software v. Symantec Corp*—in which the court dissected the elements of software alleged to be infringing. The court found that similar concept, function, general functional features (e.g., drop-down menus), and colors are not protectable by copyright law (*Brown Bag Software v. Symantec Corp.*, 1992).

Patents

A **patent** grants the owner an exclusive monopoly on the ideas behind an invention for 20 years. The congressional intent behind patent law was to ensure that inventors of new machines, devices, or methods receive the full financial and other rewards of their labor and yet make widespread use of the invention possible by providing detailed diagrams for those wishing to use the idea under license from the patent's owner. The granting of a patent is determined by the United States Patent and Trademark Office and relies on court rulings.

The key concepts in patent law are originality, novelty, and invention. The Patent Office did not accept applications for software patents routinely until a 1981 Supreme Court decision that held that computer programs could be a part of a patentable process. Since that time, hundreds of patents have been granted and thousands await consideration.

The strength of patent protection is that it grants a monopoly on the underlying concepts and ideas of software. The difficulty is passing stringent criteria of nonobviousness (e.g., the work must reflect some special understanding and contribution), originality, and novelty, as well as years of waiting to receive protection.

In what some call the patent trial of the century, in 2011, Apple sued Samsung for violating its patents for iPhones, iPads, and iPods. On August 24, 2012, a California jury in federal district court delivered a decisive victory to Apple and a stunning defeat to Samsung. The jury awarded Apple $1 billion in damages. The decision established criteria for determining just how close a competitor can come to an industry-leading and standard-setting product like Apple's iPhone before it violates the design and utility patents of the leading firm. The same court ruled that Samsung could not sell its new tablet computer (Galaxy 10.1) in the United States. In a later patent dispute, Samsung won an infringement case against Apple. In June 2013, the United States International Trade Commission issued a ban for a handful of older iPhone and iPad devices because they violated Samsun patents from years ago. In 2014 Apple sued Samsung again, claiming infringement of five patents. The patents cover hardware and software techniques for handling photos, videos, and lists used on the popular Galaxy 5. Apple is seeking $2 billion in damages.

To make matters more complicated, Apple has been one of Samsung's largest customers for flash memory processors, graphic chips, solid-state drives and display parts that are used in Apple's iPhones, iPads, iPod Touch devices, and MacBooks. The Samsung and Apple patent cases are indicative of the complex relationships among the leading computer firms.

Challenges to Intellectual Property Rights

Contemporary information technologies, especially software, pose severe challenges to existing intellectual property regimes and, therefore, create significant ethical, social, and political issues. Digital media differ from books, periodicals, and other media in terms of ease of replication; ease of transmission; ease of alteration; difficulty in classifying a software work as a program, book, or even music; compactness—making theft easy; and difficulties in establishing uniqueness.

The proliferation of electronic networks, including the Internet, has made it even more difficult to protect intellectual property. Before widespread use of networks, copies of software, books, magazine articles, or films had to be stored on physical media, such as paper, computer disks, or videotape, creating some hurdles to distribution. Using networks, information can be more widely reproduced and distributed. The Ninth Annual Global Software Piracy Study conducted by International Data Corporation and the Business Software Alliance reported that the rate of global software piracy climbed to 42 percent in 2013, representing $73 billion in global losses from software piracy. Worldwide, for every $100 worth of legitimate software sold that year, an additional $75 worth was obtained illegally (Business Software Alliance, 2014).

The Internet was designed to transmit information freely around the world, including copyrighted information. With the World Wide Web in particular, you can easily copy and distribute virtually anything to thousands and even millions of people around the world, even if they are using different types of computer systems. Information can be illicitly copied from one place and distributed through other systems and networks even though these parties do not willingly participate in the infringement.

Individuals have been illegally copying and distributing digitized music files on the Internet for several decades. File-sharing services such as Napster, and later Grokster, Kazaa, and Morpheus, Megaupload, The Pirate Bay, sprung up to help users locate and swap digital music and video files, including those protected by copyright. Illegal file sharing became so widespread that it threatened the viability of the music recording industry and, at one point, consumed 20 percent of Internet bandwidth. The recording industry won several legal battles for shutting these services down, but it has not been able to halt illegal file sharing entirely. The motion picture and cable television industries are waging similar battles, as described in the chapter-opening case study. Several European nations have worked with U.S. authorities to shut down illegal sharing sites, with mixed results. In France, illegal downloaders can lose access to the Internet for a year or more.

As legitimate online music stores like the iTunes Store expanded, and more recently as Internet radio services like Pandora expanded, some forms of illegal file sharing have declined. Technology has radically altered the prospects for intellectual property protection from theft, at least for music, videos, and television shows (less so for software). The Apple iTunes Store legitimated paying for music and entertainment, and created a closed environment where music and videos could not be easily copied and widely distributed unless played on Apple devices. Amazon's Kindle also protects the rights of publishers and writers because its books cannot be copied to the Internet and distributed. Streaming of Internet radio, on services such as Pandora and Spotify, and Hollywood movies (at sites such as Hulu and Netflix) also inhibits piracy because the streams cannot be easily recorded on separate devices and videos can be downloaded so easily. Moreover, the large Web distributors like Apple, Google, and Amazon do not want to encourage piracy in music or videos simply because they need these properties to earn revenue.

The Digital Millennium Copyright Act (DMCA) of 1998 also provides some copyright protection. The DMCA implemented a World Intellectual

Property Organization Treaty that makes it illegal to circumvent technology-based protections of copyrighted materials. Internet service providers (ISPs) are required to take down sites of copyright infringers they are hosting once the ISPs are notified of the problem. Microsoft and other major software and information content firms are represented by the Software and Information Industry Association (SIIA), which lobbies for new laws and enforcement of existing laws to protect intellectual property around the world. The SIIA runs an antipiracy hotline for individuals to report piracy activities, offers educational programs to help organizations combat software piracy, and has published guidelines for employee use of software.

4.4   HOW HAVE INFORMATION SYSTEMS AFFECTED LAWS FOR ESTABLISHING ACCOUNTABILITY, LIABILITY, AND THE QUALITY OF EVERYDAY LIFE?

Along with privacy and property laws, new information technologies are challenging existing liability laws and social practices for holding individuals and institutions accountable. If a person is injured by a machine controlled, in part, by software, who should be held accountable and, therefore, held liable? Should a social network site like Facebook or Twitter be held liable and accountable for the posting of pornographic material or racial insults, or should they be held harmless against any liability for what users post (as is true of common carriers, such as the telephone system)? What about the Internet? If you outsource your information processing, to the Cloud, and the Cloud provider fails to provide adequate service, what can you do? Cloud providers often claim the software you are using is the problem, not the Cloud servers. Some real-world examples may shed light on these questions.

COMPUTER-RELATED LIABILITY PROBLEMS

In the final days of the 2013 holiday shopping season, Target, one of the largest U.S. retailers, confirmed publicly that credit and debit card information for 40 million of its customers had been compromised. A few weeks later, the company said additional personal information, like email and mailing addresses, from some 70 to 110 million customers, had been exposed as well. In the meantime, security analysts noticed a huge spike in the number of credit card numbers for sale on hacker Web sites. Target's sales took an immediate hit from which it has still not recovered. The company claims that east European hackers entered their point of sale systems by using brute force techniques to crack their security. Federal officials believe that six other large retailers also were hacked by the same group, including Nieman Marcus. Later in 2014, Target's senior technology officer resigned from Target. Target says it has spent over $60 million to strengthen its systems. It has paid an even greater price through the loss of sales and trust. (You can find out more about Target's hacking problems in the Chapter 8 Interactive Session on Management.)

Who is liable for any economic harm caused to individuals or businesses that had their credit cards compromised? Is Target responisble for allowing the breach to occur despite efforts it did make to secure the information? Or is this just a cost of doing business in a credit card world where customers and businesses have insurance policies to protect them against losses? Customers, for instance, have a maximum liability of $50 for credit card theft under federal banking law.

This case reveals the difficulties faced by information systems executives who ultimately are responsible for any harm done by systems they have selected and installed. Beyond IT managers, insofar as computer software is part of a machine, and the machine injures someone physically or economically, the producer of the software and the operator can be held liable for damages. Insofar as the software acts like a book, storing and displaying information, courts have been reluctant to hold authors, publishers, and booksellers liable for contents (the exception being instances of fraud or defamation), and hence courts have been wary of holding software authors liable for software.

In general, it is very difficult (if not impossible) to hold software producers liable for their software products that are considered to be like books, regardless of the physical or economic harm that results. Historically, print publishers of books and periodicals have not been held liable because of fears that liability claims would interfere with First Amendment rights guaranteeing freedom of expression. And the kind of harm caused by software failures is rarely fatal and typically inconveniences users but does not physically harm them (the exception being medical devices).

What about software as a service? ATM machines are a service provided to bank customers. Should this service fail, customers will be inconvenienced and perhaps harmed economically if they cannot access their funds in a timely manner. Should liability protections be extended to software publishers and operators of defective financial, accounting, simulation, or marketing systems?

Software is very different from books. Software users may develop expectations of infallibility about software; software is less easily inspected than a book, and it is more difficult to compare with other software products for quality; software claims to perform a task rather than describe a task, as a book does; and people come to depend on services essentially based on software. Given the centrality of software to everyday life, the chances are excellent that liability law will extend its reach to include software even when the software merely provides an information service.

Telephone systems have not been held liable for the messages transmitted because they are regulated common carriers. In return for their right to provide telephone service, they must provide access to all, at reasonable rates, and achieve acceptable reliability. But broadcasters and cable television stations are subject to a wide variety of federal and local constraints on content and facilities. In the United States, with few exceptions, Web sites are not held liable for content posted on their sites regardless if it was placed their by the Web site owners or users.

SYSTEM QUALITY: DATA QUALITY AND SYSTEM ERRORS

White Christmas turned into a black out for millions of Netflix customers, and social network users, on December 25th, 2012. The blackout was caused by the failure of Amazon's cloud computing service, which provides storage and computing power for all kinds of Web sites and services, including Netflix. The loss of service lasted for a day. Amazon blamed it on "Elastic Load Balancing," a software program that balances the loads on all its cloud servers to prevent overload. Amazon's cloud computing services have had several subsequent outages, although not as long-lasting as the Christmas Eve outage. Outages at cloud computing services are rare, but are recurring. These outages have called into question the reliability and quality of cloud services. Are these outages acceptable?

The debate over liability and accountability for unintentional consequences of system use raises a related but independent moral dimension: What is an acceptable, technologically feasible level of system quality? At what point should system managers say, "Stop testing, we've done all we can to perfect this software. Ship it!" Individuals and organizations may be held responsible for avoidable and foreseeable consequences, which they have a duty to perceive and correct. The gray area is that some system errors are foreseeable and correctable only at very great expense, an expense so great that pursuing this level of perfection is not feasible economically—no one could afford the product.

For example, although software companies try to debug their products before releasing them to the marketplace, they knowingly ship buggy products because the time and cost of fixing all minor errors would prevent these products from ever being released. What if the product was not offered on the marketplace, would social welfare as a whole not advance and perhaps even decline? Carrying this further, just what is the responsibility of a producer of computer services—should it withdraw the product that can never be perfect, warn the user, or forget about the risk (let the buyer beware)?

Three principal sources of poor system performance are (1) software bugs and errors, (2) hardware or facility failures caused by natural or other causes, and (3) poor input data quality. A Chapter 8 Learning Track discusses why zero defects in software code of any complexity cannot be achieved and why the seriousness of remaining bugs cannot be estimated. Hence, there is a technological barrier to perfect software, and users must be aware of the potential for catastrophic failure. The software industry has not yet arrived at testing standards for producing software of acceptable but imperfect performance.

Although software bugs and facility catastrophes are likely to be widely reported in the press, by far the most common source of business system failure is data quality. Few companies routinely measure the quality of their data, but individual organizations report data error rates ranging from 0.5 to 30 percent.

QUALITY OF LIFE: EQUITY, ACCESS, AND BOUNDARIES

The negative social costs of introducing information technologies and systems are beginning to mount along with the power of the technology. Many of these negative social consequences are not violations of individual rights or property crimes. Nevertheless, these negative consequences can be extremely harmful to individuals, societies, and political institutions. Computers and information technologies potentially can destroy valuable elements of our culture and society even while they bring us benefits. If there is a balance of good and bad consequences of using information systems, who do we hold responsible for the bad consequences? Next, we briefly examine some of the negative social consequences of systems, considering individual, social, and political responses.

Balancing Power: Center Versus Periphery

An early fear of the computer age was that huge, centralized mainframe computers would centralize power in the nation's capital, resulting in a Big Brother society, as was suggested in George Orwell's novel 1984. The shift toward highly decentralized client-server computing, coupled with an ideology of empowerment of Twitter and social media users, and the decentralization of decision making to lower organizational levels, up until recently reduced the fears of power centralization in government institutions. Yet much of the empowerment described in popular business magazines is trivial. Lower-level employees may be empowered to make minor decisions, but the key policy decisions may be as centralized as in the past. At the same time, corporate Internet behemoths like Google, Apple, Yahoo, Amazon, and Microsoft have come to dominate the collection and analysis of personal private information of all citizens. Since the terrorist attacks against the United States on September 11, 2001, the federal government has greatly expanded its use of this private sector information, as well as other forms of digital communication, in pursuit of national security. In this sense, power has become more centralized into the hands of a few private oligopolies and large government agencies.

Rapidity of Change: Reduced Response Time to Competition

Information systems have helped to create much more efficient national and international markets. Today's more efficient global marketplace has reduced the normal social buffers that permitted businesses many years to adjust to competition. Time-based competition has an ugly side: The business you work for may not have enough time to respond to global competitors and may be wiped out in a year, along with your job. We stand the risk of developing a "just-in-time society" with "just-in-time jobs" and "just-in-time" workplaces, families, and vacations.

Maintaining Boundaries: Family, Work, and Leisure

Parts of this book were produced on trains and planes, as well as on vacations and during what otherwise might have been "family" time. The danger to ubiquitous computing, telecommuting, nomad computing, mobile computing, and the "do anything anywhere" computing environment is that it is actually coming true. The traditional boundaries that separate work from family and just plain leisure have been weakened.

Although authors have traditionally worked just about anywhere, the advent of information systems, coupled with the growth of knowledge-work occupations, means that more and more people are working when traditionally they would have been playing or communicating with family and friends. The work umbrella now extends far beyond the eight-hour day into commuting time, vacation time, and leisure time. The explosive growth and use of smart phones has only heightened the sense of many employees that they are never "away from work."

Even leisure time spent on the computer threatens these close social relationships. Extensive Internet and cell phone use, even for entertainment or recreational purposes, takes people away from their family and friends. Among middle school and teenage children, it can lead to harmful anti-social behavior, such as the recent upsurge in cyberbullying.

Weakening these institutions poses clear-cut risks. Family and friends historically have provided powerful support mechanisms for individuals, and they act as balance points in a society by preserving private life, providing a place for people to collect their thoughts, allowing people to think in ways contrary to their employer, and dream.

Dependence and Vulnerability

Today, our businesses, governments, schools, and private associations, such as churches, are incredibly dependent on information systems and are, therefore, highly vulnerable if these systems fail. Secondary schools, for instance, increasingly use and rely on educational software. Test results are often stored off campus. If these systems were to shut down, there is no backup educational structure or content that can make up for the loss of the system. With systems now as ubiquitous as the telephone system, it is startling to remember that there are no regulatory or standard-setting forces in place that are similar to telephone, electrical, radio, television, or other public utility technologies. The absence of standards and the criticality of some system applications will probably call forth demands for national standards and perhaps regulatory oversight.

Computer Crime and Abuse

New technologies, including computers, create new opportunities for committing crime by creating new valuable items to steal, new ways to steal them, and new ways to harm others. **Computer crime** is the commission of illegal acts through the use of a computer or against a computer system. Computers or computer systems can be the object of the crime (destroying a company's computer center or a company's computer files), as well as the instrument of a crime (stealing computer lists by illegally gaining access to a computer

Although some people enjoy the convenience of working at home, the "do anything anywhere" computing environment can blur the traditional boundaries between work and family time.

© Monkey Business Images/Shutterstock

system using a home computer). Simply accessing a computer system without authorization or with intent to do harm, even by accident, is now a federal crime. How common is computer crime? One source of information is the Internet Crime Complaint Center ("IC3"), a partnership between the National White Collar Crime Center and the Federal Bureau of Investigation. The IC3 data is useful for gauging the types of e-commerce crimes most likely to be reported by consumers. In 2012, the IC3 processed about 290,000 Internet crime complaints, the second-highest number in its 11-year history. Over half the complainants reported a financial loss, with the total reported amount at $525 million. The average amount of loss for those who reported a financial loss was more than $4,573. The most common complaints were for scams involving the FBI, identity theft, and advance fee fraud (National White Collar Crime Center and the Federal Bureau of Investigation, 2013). The Computer Security Institute's annual *Computer Crime and Security Survey* is another source of information. In 2011, its most recent report, the survey was based on the responses of 351 security practitioners in U.S. corporations, government agencies, financial institutions, medical institutions, and universities. The survey reported that 46 percent of responding organizations experienced a computer security incident within the past year. The most common type of attack experienced was a malware infection (67%), followed by phishing fraud (39%), laptop and mobile hardware theft (34%), attacks by botnets (29%), and insider abuse (25%). The true cost of all computer crime is estimated to be in the billions of dollars. On average, the cost to a firm of a single computer crime averages about $8.9 million (Ponemon Institute, 2012).

Computer abuse is the commission of acts involving a computer that may not be illegal but that are considered unethical. The popularity of the Internet and e-mail has turned one form of computer abuse—spamming—into a serious problem for both individuals and businesses. Originally, **Spam** is junk e-mail sent by an organization or individual to a mass audience of Internet users who have expressed no interest in the product or service being marketed. But as cell phone use has mushroomed, spam was certain to follow. Identity and financial theft cyber criminals are turning their attention to smart phones as users check mail, do online banking, pay bills, and reveal personal information. Cell phone spam usually comes in the form of SMS text messages, but increasingly users are receiving spam in their Facebook Newsfeed and messaging service as well. Verizon estimates that it blocks about 200 million spam messages a month using its filters and security checks. Spammers tend to market pornography, fraudulent deals and services, outright scams, and other products not widely approved in most civilized societies. Some countries have passed laws to outlaw spamming or to restrict its use. In the United States, it is still legal if it does not involve fraud and the sender and subject of the e-mail are properly identified.

Spamming has mushroomed because it costs only a few cents to send thousands of messages advertising wares to Internet users. The percentage of all e-mail that is spam was estimated at around 66 percent in 2014 (Symantec, 2014). Most spam originates from bot networks, which consist of thousands of captured PCs that can initiate and relay spam messages. Spam volume has declined somewhat since authorities took down the Rustock botnet in 2011. Spam is seasonally cyclical, and varies monthly due to the impact of new technologies (both supportive and discouraging of spammers), new prosecutions, and seasonal demand for products and services. Spam costs for businesses are very high (estimated at over $50 billion per year) because of the computing and network resources consumed by billions of unwanted e-mail messages and the time required to deal with them.

Internet service providers and individuals can combat spam by using spam filtering software to block suspicious e-mail before it enters a recipient's e-mail inbox. However, spam filters may block legitimate messages. Spammers know how to skirt around filters by continually changing their e-mail accounts, by incorporating spam messages in images, by embedding spam in e-mail attachments and electronic greeting cards, and by using other people's computers that have been hijacked by botnets (see Chapter 8). Many spam messages are sent from one country while another country hosts the spam Web site.

Spamming is more tightly regulated in Europe than in the United States. In 2002, the European Parliament passed a ban on unsolicited commercial messaging. Electronic marketing can be targeted only to people who have given prior consent.

The U.S. CAN-SPAM Act of 2003, which went into effect in 2004, does not outlaw spamming but does ban deceptive e-mail practices by requiring commercial e-mail messages to display accurate subject lines, identify the true senders, and offer recipients an easy way to remove their names from e-mail lists. It also prohibits the use of fake return addresses. A few people have been prosecuted under the law, but it has had a negligible impact on spamming in large part because of the Internet's exceptionally poor security and the use of offshore servers and botnets. In 2008, Robert Soloway, the so-called Seattle "Spam King," was sentenced to 47 months in prison for sending over 90 million spam messages in just three months off two servers. In 2011, the so-called Facebook "Spam King," Sanford Wallace, was indicted for sending over 27 million spam messages to Facebook users. He is facing a 40-year sentence because of prior spamming convictions. In 2014 most large scale spamming has moved offshore to Russia and Eastern Europe where hackers control global botnets capable of generating billions of spam messages. The largest spam network in 2013 was the Russian network Festi based in St. Petersburg. Festi is best known as the spam generator behind the global Viagra-spam industry which stretches from Russia to Indian pharmaceutical firms selling counterfeit Viagra. The spam industry in Russia generates an estimated $60 million for criminal groups (Kramer, 2013).

Employment: Trickle-Down Technology and Reengineering Job Loss

Reengineering work is typically hailed in the information systems community as a major benefit of new information technology. It is much less frequently noted that redesigning business processes has caused millions of mid-level factory managers, and clerical workers to lose their jobs. One economist has raised the possibility that we will create a society run by a small "high tech elite of corporate professionals . . . in a nation of the permanently unemployed" (Rifkin, 1993). In 2011, some economists have sounded new alarms about information and computer technology threatening middle-class, white-collar jobs (in addition to blue-collar factory jobs). Erik Brynjolfsson and Andrew P. McAfee argue that the pace of automation has picked up in recent years because of a combination of technologies including robotics, numerically controlled machines, computerized inventory control, pattern recognition, voice recognition, and online commerce. One result is that machines can now do a great many jobs heretofore reserved for humans including tech support, call center work, X-ray examiners, and even legal document review (Brynjolfsson and McAfee, 2011). These views contrast with earlier assessments by economists that both labor and capital would receive stable shares of income, and that new technologies created as many or more new jobs as they destroyed old ones. But there is no guarantee this will happen in the future, and the income wealth share of labor may continue to fall relative to capital, resulting in a loss of high paying jobs and further declines in wages.

Other economists are much more sanguine about the potential job losses. They believe relieving bright, educated workers from reengineered jobs will result in these workers moving to better jobs in fast-growth industries. Missing from this equation are unskilled, blue-collar workers and older, less well-educated middle managers. It is not clear that these groups can be retrained easily for high-quality (high-paying) jobs.

Equity and Access: Increasing Racial and Social Class Cleavages

Does everyone have an equal opportunity to participate in the digital age? Will the social, economic, and cultural gaps that exist in the United States and other societies be reduced by information systems technology? Or will the cleavages be increased, permitting the better off to become even more better off relative to others?

These questions have not yet been fully answered because the impact of systems technology on various groups in society has not been thoroughly studied. What is known is that information, knowledge, computers, and access to these resources through educational institutions and public libraries are inequitably distributed along ethnic and social class lines, as are many other information resources. Several studies have found that poor and minority groups in the United States are less likely to have computers or online Internet access even though computer ownership and Internet access have soared in the past five years. Although the gap is narrowing, higher-income families in each ethnic group are still more likely to have home computers and Internet access than lower-income families in the same group.

A similar **digital divide** exists in U.S. schools, with schools in high-poverty areas less likely to have computers, high-quality educational technology programs, or Internet access availability for their students. Left uncorrected, the digital divide could lead to a society of information haves, computer literate and skilled, versus a large group of information have-nots, computer illiterate and unskilled. Public interest groups want to narrow this digital divide by making digital information services—including the Internet—available to virtually everyone, just as basic telephone service is now.

Health Risks: RSI, CVS, and Technostress

A common occupational disease today is **repetitive stress injury (RSI)**. RSI occurs when muscle groups are forced through repetitive actions often with high-impact loads (such as tennis) or tens of thousands of repetitions under low-impact loads (such as working at a computer keyboard). The incidence of repetitive stress syndrome is estimated to be 3% to 6% of the workforce (LeBlanc and Cestia, 2011).

The single largest source of RSI is computer keyboards. The most common kind of computer-related RSI is **carpal tunnel syndrome (CTS)**, in which pressure on the median nerve through the wrist's bony structure, called a carpal tunnel, produces pain. The pressure is caused by constant repetition of keystrokes: in a single shift, a word processor may perform 23,000 keystrokes. Symptoms of carpal tunnel syndrome include numbness, shooting pain, inability to grasp objects, and tingling. Millions of workers have been diagnosed with carpal tunnel syndrome.

RSI is avoidable. Designing workstations for a neutral wrist position (using a wrist rest to support the wrist), proper monitor stands, and footrests all contribute to proper posture and reduced RSI. Ergonomically correct keyboards are also an option. These measures should be supported by frequent rest breaks and rotation of employees to different jobs.

RSI is not the only occupational illness computers cause. Back and neck pain, leg stress, and foot pain also result from poor ergonomic designs of workstations. **Computer vision syndrome (CVS)** refers to any eyestrain condition related to display screen use in desktop computers, laptops,

Repetitive stress injury (RSI) is the leading occupational disease today. The single largest cause of RSI is computer keyboard work.

© Donna Cuic/Shuttertock

e-readers, smartphones, and handheld video games. CVS affects about 90 percent of people who spend three hours or more per day at a computer (Beck, 2010). Its symptoms, which are usually temporary, include headaches, blurred vision, and dry and irritated eyes.

The newest computer-related malady is **technostress**, which is stress induced by computer and cell phone use. Its symptoms include aggravation, hostility toward humans, impatience, and fatigue. According to experts, humans working continuously with computers come to expect other humans and human institutions to behave like computers, providing instant responses, attentiveness, and an absence of emotion. Technostress is thought to be related to high levels of job turnover in the computer industry, high levels of early retirement from computer-intense occupations, and elevated levels of drug and alcohol abuse.

The incidence of technostress is not known but is thought to be in the millions and growing in the United States. Computer-related jobs now top the list of stressful occupations based on health statistics in several industrialized countries.

In addition to these maladies, computer technology may be harming our cognitive functions or at least changing how we think and solve problems. Although the Internet has made it much easier for people to access, create, and use information, some experts believe that it is also preventing people from focusing and thinking clearly.

The computer has become a part of our lives—personally as well as socially, culturally, and politically. It is unlikely that the issues and our choices will become easier as information technology continues to transform our world. The growth of the Internet and the information economy suggests that all the ethical and social issues we have described will be heightened further as we move into the first digital century.

Review Summary

1. *What ethical, social, and political issues are raised by information systems?*

   Information technology is introducing changes for which laws and rules of acceptable conduct have not yet been developed. Increasing computing power, storage, and networking capabilities—including the Internet—expand the reach of individual and organizational actions and magnify their impacts. The ease and anonymity with which information is now communicated, copied, and manipulated in online environments pose new challenges to the protection of privacy and intellectual property. The main ethical, social, and political issues raised by information systems center around information rights and obligations, property rights and obligations, accountability and control, system quality, and quality of life.

2. *What specific principles for conduct can be used to guide ethical decisions?*

   Six ethical principles for judging conduct include the Golden Rule, Immanuel Kant's Categorical Imperative, Descartes' rule of change, the Utilitarian Principle, the Risk Aversion Principle, and the ethical "no free lunch" rule. These principles should be used in conjunction with an ethical analysis.

3. *Why do contemporary information systems technology and the Internet pose challenges to the protection of individual privacy and intellectual property?*

   Contemporary data storage and data analysis technology enables companies to easily gather personal data about individuals from many different sources and analyze these data to create detailed electronic profiles about individuals and their behaviors. Data flowing over the Internet can be monitored at many points. Cookies and other Web monitoring tools closely track the activities of Web site visitors. Not all Web sites have strong privacy protection policies, and they do not always allow for informed consent regarding the use of personal information. Traditional copyright laws are insufficient to protect against software piracy because digital material can be copied so easily and transmitted to many different locations simultaneously over the Internet.

4. *How have information systems affected laws for establishing accountability, liability, and the quality of everyday life?*

   New information technologies are challenging existing liability laws and social practices for holding individuals and institutions accountable for harm done to others. Although computer systems have been sources of efficiency and wealth, they have some negative impacts. Computer errors can cause serious harm to individuals and organizations. Poor data quality is also responsible for disruptions and losses for businesses. Jobs can be lost when computers replace workers or tasks become unnecessary in reengineered business processes. The ability to own and use a computer may be exacerbating socioeconomic disparities among different racial groups and social classes. Widespread use of computers increases opportunities for computer crime and computer abuse. Computers can also create health problems, such as repetitive stress injury, computer vision syndrome, and technostress.

Key Terms

Accountability, 140
Carpal tunnel syndrome (CTS), 167
Computer abuse, 164
Computer crime, 163
Computer vision syndrome (CVS), 167
Cookies, 150
Copyright, 156
Digital divide, 167
Digital Millennium Copyright Act (DMCA), 158
Due process, 143

Ethical "no free lunch" rule, 144
Ethics, 135
Fair Information Practices (FIP), 146
Golden Rule, 144
Immanuel Kant's Categorical Imperative, 144
Information rights, 136
Informed consent, 148
Intellectual property, 155
Liability, 140
Nonobvious relationship awareness (NORA), 140

Review Questions

4-1 What ethical, social, and political issues are raised by information systems?

- Explain how ethical, social, and political issues are connected and give some examples.
- List and describe the key technological trends that heighten ethical concerns.
- Differentiate between responsibility, accountability, and liability.

4-2 What specific principles for conduct can be used to guide ethical decisions?

- List and describe the five steps in an ethical analysis.
- Identify and describe six ethical principles.

4-3 Why do contemporary information systems technology and the Internet pose challenges to the protection of individual privacy and intellectual property?

- Define privacy and fair information practices.
- Explain how the Internet challenges the protection of individual privacy and intellectual property.

- Explain how informed consent, legislation, industry self-regulation, and technology tools help protect the individual privacy of Internet users.
- List and define the three different regimes that protect intellectual property rights.

4-4 How have information systems affected laws for establishing accountability, liability, and the quality of everyday life?

- Explain why it is so difficult to hold software services liable for failure or injury.
- List and describe the principal causes of system quality problems.
- Name and describe four quality of life impacts of computers and information systems.
- Define and describe technostress and repetitive stress injury (RSI) and explain their relationship to information technology.

Discussion Questions

4-5 Should producers of software-based services, such as ATMs, be held liable for economic injuries suffered when their systems fail?

4-6 Should companies be responsible for unemployment caused by their information systems? Why or why not?

4-7 Discuss the pros and cons of allowing companies to amass personal data for behavioral targeting.

Hands-On MIS Projects

The projects in this section give you hands-on experience in analyzing the privacy implications of using online data brokers, developing a corporate policy for employee Web usage, using blog creation tools to create a simple blog, and using Internet newsgroups for market research.

Management Decision Problems

4-8 InfoFree's Web site is linked to massive databases that consolidate personal data on millions of people and. Users can purchase marketing lists of consumers broken down by location, age, income level, home value, and interests. One could use this capability to obtain a list, for example, of everyone in Peekskill, New York, making $150,000 or more per year. Do data brokers such as InfoFree raise privacy issues? Why or why not? If your name and other personal information were in this database, what limitations on access would you want in order to preserve your privacy? Consider the following data users: government agencies, your employer, private business firms, other individuals.

Achieving Operational Excellence: Creating a Simple Blog

Software skills: Blog creation
Business skills: Blog and Web page design

4-9 In this project, you'll learn how to build a simple blog of your own design using the online blog creation software available at Blogger.com. Pick a sport, hobby, or topic of interest as the theme for your blog. Name the blog, give it a title, and choose a template for the blog. Post at least four entries to the blog, adding a label for each posting. Edit your posts, if necessary. Upload an image, such as a photo from your hard drive or the Web to your blog. Add capabilities for other registered users, such as team members, to comment on your blog. Briefly describe how your blog could be useful to a company selling products or services related to the theme of your blog. List the tools available to Blogger that would make your blog more useful for business and describe the business uses of each. Save your blog and show it to your instructor.

Improving Decision Making: Analyzing Web Browser Privacy

Software Skills: Web browser software
Business Skills: Analyzing Web browser privacy protection features

4-10 This project will help develop your Internet skills for using the privacy protection features of leading Web browser software.

Examine the privacy protection features and settings for two leading Web browsers, such as Internet Explorer, Mozilla Firefox or Google Chrome. Make a table comparing the features of two of these browsers in terms of functions provided and ease of use.

- How do these privacy protection features protect individuals?
- How do these privacy protection features impact what businesses can do on the Internet?
- Which does the best job of protecting privacy. Why?

Facebook Privacy: There Is No Privacy
CASE STUDY

Over the course of less than a decade, Facebook has morphed from a small, niche networking site for mostly Ivy League college students into a publicly traded company with a market worth of $148 billion in 2014 (up from $59 billion in 2013). Facebook boasts that it is free to join and always will be, so where's the money coming from to service 1 billion worldwide subscribers? Just like its fellow tech titan and rival Google, Facebook's revenue comes almost entirely from advertising. Facebook does not have a diverse array of hot new gadgets, a countrywide network of brick-and-mortar retail outlets, or a full inventory of software for sale; instead, it has your personal information, and the information of hundreds of millions of others with Facebook accounts.

Advertisers have long understood the value of Facebook's unprecedented trove of personal information. They can serve ads using highly specific details, like relationship status, location, employment status, favorite books, movies, or TV shows, and a host of other categories. For example, an Atlanta woman who posts that she has become engaged might be offered an ad for a wedding photographer on her Facebook page. When advertisements are served to finely targeted subsets of users, the response is much more successful than traditional types of.advertising. A growing number of companies both big and small have taken notice: In 2014, Facebook generated $7.8 billion in revenue, 88 percent of which ($7 billion) was from selling ads, and the remainder from selling games, and virtual goods. Facebook's ad revenues in 2012 grew by 63 percent over the previous year, driven mostly by adding new users. Existing users are not clicking on more ads.

That was good news for Facebook, which launched its IPO (initial public stock offering) in May 2012, and is expected to continue to increase its revenue in coming years. But is it good news for you, the Facebook user? More than ever, companies like Facebook and Google, which made approximately $55 billion in advertising revenue

in 2013, are using your online activity to develop a frighteningly accurate picture of your life. Facebook's goal is to serve advertisements that are more relevant to you than anywhere else on the Web, but the personal information they gather about you both with and without your consent can also be used against you in other ways.

Facebook has a diverse array of compelling and useful features. Facebook's partnership with the Department of Labor helps to connect job seekers and employers; Facebook has helped families find lost pets after natural disasters, such as when tornadoes hit the Midwest in 2012; Facebook allows active-duty soldiers to stay in touch with their families; it gives smaller companies a chance to further their e-commerce efforts and larger companies a chance to solidify their brands; and, perhaps most obviously, Facebook allows you to more easily keep in touch with your friends. These are the reasons why so many people are on Facebook.

However, Facebook's goal is to get its users to share as much data as possible, because the more Facebook knows about you, the more accurately it can serve relevant advertisements to you. Facebook CEO Mark Zuckerberg often says that people want the world to be more open and connected. It's unclear whether that is truly the case, but it is certainly true that Facebook wants the world to be more open and connected, because it stands to make more money in that world. Critics of Facebook are concerned that the existence of a repository of personal data of the size that Facebook has amassed requires protections and privacy controls that extend far beyond those that Facebook currently offers.

Facebook wanting to make more money is not a bad thing, but the company has a checkered past of privacy violations and missteps that raise doubts about whether it should be responsible for the personal data of hundreds of millions of people. There are no laws in the United States that give consumers the right to know what data companies like Facebook have compiled. You can challenge information in credit reports, but you can't even see what data Facebook has gathered about you, let alone try to change it. It's different in Europe: you can request Facebook to turn over a report of all the information it has about you. More than ever, your every move, every click, on social networks is being used by outside entities to assess your interests, and behavior, and then pitch you an ad based on this knowledge. Law enforcement agencies use social networks to gather evidence on tax evaders, and other criminals; employers use social networks to make decisions about prospective candidates for jobs; and data aggregators are gathering as much information about you as they can sell to the highest bidder.

In a recent study, Consumer Reports found that of 150 million Americans on Facebook everyday, at least 4.8 million are willingly sharing information that could be used against them in some way. That includes plans to travel on a particular day, which burglars could use to time robberies, or Liking a page about a particular health condition or treatment, which insurers could use to deny coverage. Thirteen million users have never adjusted Facebook's privacy controls, which allow friends using Facebook applications to unwittingly transfer your data to a third party without your knowledge. Credit card companies and other similar organizations have begun engaging in "weblining", taken from the phrase redlining, by altering their treatment of you based on the actions of other people with profiles similar to yours.

Ninety-three percent of people polled believe that Internet companies should be forced to ask for permission before using your personal information, and 72 percent want the ability to opt out of online tracking. Why, then, do so many people share sensitive details of their life on Facebook? Often it's because users do not realize that their data are being collected and transmitted in this way. A Facebook user's friends are not notified if information about them is collected by that user's applications. Many of Facebook's features and services are enabled by default when they are launched without notifying users. And a study by Siegel + Gale found that Facebook's privacy policy is more difficult to comprehend than government

notices or typical bank credit card agreements, which are notoriously dense. Next time you visit Facebook, click on Privacy Settings, and see if you can understand your options.

Facebook's value and growth potential is determined by how effectively it can leverage the personal data it aggregated about its users to attract advertisers. Facebook also stands to gain from managing and avoiding the privacy concerns raised by its users and government regulators. For Facebook users that value the privacy of their personal data, this situation appears grim. But there are some signs that Facebook might become more responsible with its data collection processes, whether by its own volition or because it is forced to do so. As a publicly traded company, Facebook now invites more scrutiny from investors and regulators because, unlike in the past, their balance sheets, assets, and financial reporting documents are readily available.

In August 2012, Facebook settled a lawsuit with the FTC in which they were barred from misrepresenting the privacy or security of users' personal information. Facebook was charged with deceiving its users by telling them they could keep their information on Facebook private, but then repeatedly allowing it to be shared and made public. Facebook agreed to obtain user consent before making any change to that user's privacy preferences, and to submit to bi-annual privacy audits by an independent firm for the next 20 years. Privacy advocate groups like the Electronic Privacy Information Center (EPIC) want Facebook to restore its more robust privacy settings from 2009, as well as to offer complete access to all data it keeps about its users. Facebook has also come under fire from EPIC for collecting information about users who are not even logged into Facebook or may not even have accounts on Facebook. Facebook keeps track of activity on other sites that have Like buttons or "recommendations" widgets, and records the time of your visit and your IP address when you visit a site with those features, regardless of whether or not you click on them.

While U.S. Facebook users have little recourse to access data that Facebook has collected on them, users from other countries have made inroads in this regard. An Austrian law student was able to get a full copy of his personal information from Facebook's Dublin office, due to the more stringent consumer privacy protections in Ireland. The full document was 1,222 pages long and covered three years of activity on the site, including deleted Wall posts and messages with sensitive personal information and deleted e-mail addresses. In Europe, 40,000 Facebook users have already requested their data, and European law requires that Facebook respond to these requests within 40 days.

It isn't just text-based data that Facebook is stockpiling, either. Facebook is also compiling a biometric database of unprecedented size. The company stores more than 60 billion photos on its servers and that number grows by 250 million each day. A recent feature launched by Facebook called Tag Suggest scans photographs using facial recognition technology. When Tag Suggest was launched, it was enabled for many users without opting in. This database has value to law enforcement and other organizations looking to compile profiles of users for use in advertising. EPIC also has demanded that Facebook stop creating facial recognition profiles without user consent.

In 2012, as part of the settlement of another class-action lawsuit, Facebook agreed to allow users to opt in to its Sponsored Stories service, which serves advertisements in the user's News Feed that highlight products and businesses that your Facebook friends are using. This allowed users to control which of their actions on Facebook generate advertisements that their friends will see. Sponsored Stories are one of the most effective forms of advertising on Facebook because they don't seem like advertisements at all to most users. Facebook had previously argued that users were giving "implied consent" every time they clicked a Like button on a page. Despite this earlier settlement, in January 2014, Facebook closed down its Sponsored Stories feature entirely, after many lawsuits, attempted settlements, and criticism from privacy groups, the FTC, and annoyed parents whose children's photos were being used throughout Facebook to sell products. In August 2013, Facebook had agreed to a settlement in a class action lawsuit brought by parents of teenagers caught up in the Facebook information machine. Every time their

children liked a product on Facebook, their photos were used to promote the product not just to their friends, but to everyone on Facebook who potentially might be interested. The legal settlement only enraged privacy advocates and Congress, leading to Facebook's abandonment of Sponsored Stories.

While Facebook has shut down one of its more egregious privacy-invading features, the company's Data Use policies make it very clear that, as a condition of using the service, users grant the company wide latitude in using their information in advertising. This includes a person's name, photo, comments, and other information. Facebook's existing policies make clear that users are required to grant the company wide permission to use their personal information in advertising as a condition of using the service. This includes "social advertising" where your personal information is broadcast to your friends, and indeed, the entire Facebook service if the company sees fit. While users can limit some uses, an advanced degree in Facebook data features is required.

Despite consumer protests and government scrutiny, Facebook continues to challenge its customers' sense of control over their personal information. In January 2013, Facebook launched its Graph Search program, a social network search engine intended to rival Google but based on a totally different approach. Rather than scour the Internet for information related to a user's search term, Graph Search responds to user queries with information produced by all Facebook users on their personal pages, and their friends personal pages. For instance, Graph Search, without consent of the user, allows any Facebook user to type in your name, and click the link "Photos of..." which appears underneath the search bar. Complete strangers can find pictures of you. The person searched may not be able to control who sees personal photos: it depends on the privacy settings of other users with whom the photos were shared. If you shared your photos with friends who had less strict privacy settings, then those lesser settings determine who will have access to your photos. Graph Search results in new pages being created that contain the search results. These pages present Facebook with additional opportunities to sell ads, and to monetize the activities and information of its users.

The future of Facebook as a private corporation, and its stock price, will depend on its ability to monetize its most valuable asset: personal, private information.

Sources: Elizabeth Dwoskin, "Facebook to Shut Down Ad Program," Wall Street Journal, January 9, 2014; Vindu Goelfeb, "Facebook Deal on Privacy Is Under Attack," *New York Times*, February 14, 2014; Vindu Goel and Edward Wyatt, "Facebook Privacy Change Is Subject of F.T.C. Inquiry," *New York Times*. September 11, 2013; Sarah Perez, "Facebook Graph Search Didn't Break Your Privacy Settings, It Only Feels Like That," TechCrunch, February 4, 2013; Claire Cain Miller, "Tech Companies Concede to Surveillance Program," *New York Times*, June 7, 2013; "SEC Form 10K for the Fiscal Year Ending December 31, 2013," Facebook, March 31, 2014; "Selling You on Facebook," Julia Angwin and Jeremy Singer-Vine, *The Wall Street Journal*, April 7, 2012; Consumer Reports, "Facebook and Your Privacy," May 3, 2012; "Facebook Is Using You," Lori Andrews, *The New York Times*, Feb. 4, 2012; "Personal Data's Value? Facebook Set to Find Out," Somini Sengupta and Evelyn M. Rusli, *The New York Times*, Jan. 31, 2012; "Facebook, Eye on Privacy Laws, Offers More Disclosure to Users," Kevin J O'Brien, *The New York Times*, April 13, 2012; "To Settle Lawsuit, Facebook Alters Policy for Its 'Like' Button," Somini Sengupta, *The New York Times*, June 21, 2012.

CASE STUDY QUESTIONS

4-11 Perform an ethical analysis of Facebook. What is the ethical dilemma presented by this case?

4-12 What is the relationship of privacy to Facebook's business model?

4-13 Describe the weaknesses of Facebook's privacy policies and features. What management, organization, and technology factors have contributed to those weaknesses?

4-14 Will Facebook be able to have a successful business model without invading privacy? Explain your answer. Are there any measures Facebook could take to make this possible?

Chapter 4 References

Angwin, Julia. "Online Tracking Ramps Up." *Wall Street Journal* (June 17, 2012).

Ante, Spencer E. "Online Ads Can Follow You Home." *Wall Street Journal* (April 29, 2013).

Austen, Ian. "With Apologies, Officials Say Blackberry Service is Restored." *New York Times* (October 13, 2011).

Belanger, France and Robert E. Crossler. "Privacy in the Digital Age: A Review of Information Privacy Research in Information Systems." *MIS Quarterly* 35, No. 4 (December 2011).

Bertolucci, Jeff. "Big Data Firm Chronicles Your Online, Offline Lives." *Information Week* (May 7, 2013).

Bilski v. Kappos, 561 US, (2010).

Brown Bag Software vs. Symantec Corp. 960 F2D 1465 (Ninth Circuit, 1992).

Brynjolfsson, Erik and Andrew McAfee. *Race Against the Machine*. Digital Frontier Press (2011).

Business Software Alliance, "Shadow Market: 2011 BSA Global Software Piracy Study," Ninth edition (May 2012).

Computer Security Institute. "CSI Computer Crime and Security Survey 2012." (2012).

Culnan, Mary J. and Cynthia Clark Williams. "How Ethics Can Enhance Organizational Privacy." *MIS Quarterly* 33, No. 4 (December 2009).

European Parliament. "Directive 2009/136/EC of the European Parliament and of the Council of November 25, 2009." European Parliament (2009).

Fowler, Geoffrey A. "Tech Giants Agree to Deal on Privacy Policies for Apps." *Wall Street Journal* (February 23, 2012).

Federal Trade Commission. "Protecting Consumer Privacy In an Era of Rapid Change." Washington D.C. (2012).

Frank, Adam. "Big Data and Its Big Problems." NPR (September 18, 2012).

Goldfarb, Avi, and Catherine Tucker. "Why Managing Consumer Privacy Can Be an Opportunity." *MIT Sloan Management Review* 54, No. 3 (Spring 2013).

Hsieh, J.J. Po-An, Arun Rai, and Mark Keil. "Understanding Digital Inequality: Comparing Continued Use Behavioral Models of the Socio-Economically Advantaged and Disadvantaged." *MIS Quarterly* 32, No. 1 (March 2008).

Laudon, Kenneth C. and Carol Guercio Traver. *E-Commerce: Business, Technology, Society 9th Edition*. Upper Saddle River, NJ: Prentice-Hall (2013).

Laudon, Kenneth C. *Dossier Society: Value Choices in the Design of National Information Systems*. New York: Columbia University Press (1986b).

Leblanc, KE, and W. Cestia . "Carpal Tunnel Syndrome." American Family Physician, 83(8), 2011.

Lee, Dong-Joo, Jae-Hyeon Ahn, and Youngsok Bang. "Managing Consumer Privacy Concerns in Personalization: A Strategic Analysis of Privacy Protection." *MIS Quarterly* 35, No. 2 (June 2011).

National White Collar Crime Center and the Federal Bureau of Investigation. "Internet Crime Complaint Center 2012 Internet Crime Report. (2013).

Ponemon Institute. "2012 Cost of Cyber Crime Study: United States." October 2012.

Rifkin, Jeremy. "Watch Out for Trickle-Down Technology." *New York Times* (March 16, 1993).

Robinson, Francis. "EU Unveils Web-Privacy Rules." *Wall Street Journal* (January 26, 2012).

Singer, Natasha. "When the Privacy Button Is Already Pressed." New York Times (September 15, 2012).

Smith, H. Jeff. "The Shareholders vs. Stakeholders Debate." *MIS Sloan Management Review* 44, No. 4 (Summer 2003).

Symantec. "2014 Internet Security Threat Report, Volume 19" (August 2014).

United States Department of Health, Education, and Welfare. Records, Computers, and the Rights of Citizens. Cambridge: MIT Press (1973).

U.S. Senate. "Do-Not-Track Online Act of 2011." Senate 913 (May 9, 2011).

U.S. Sentencing Commission. "Sentencing Commission Toughens Requirements for Corporate Compliance Programs." (April 13, 2004).

PART TWO

Information Technology Infrastructure

Part Two provides the technical foundation for understanding information systems by examining hardware, software, database, and networking technologies along with tools and techniques for security and control. This part answers questions such as: What technologies do businesses today need to accomplish their work? What do I need to know about these technologies to make sure they enhance the performance of the firm? How are these technologies likely to change in the future? What technologies and procedures are required to ensure that systems are reliable and secure?

IT Infrastructure and Emerging Technologies

CHAPTER 5

LEARNING OBJECTIVES

After reading this chapter, you will be able to answer the following questions:

1. What is IT infrastructure and what are the stages and drivers of IT infrastructure evolution?

2. What are the components of IT infrastructure?

3. What are the current trends in computer hardware platforms?

4. What are the current trends in computer software platforms?

5. What are the challenges of managing IT infrastructure and management solutions?

CHAPTER CASES

Portugal Telecom Offers IT Infrastructure for Sale

Establishing Global Classrooms through WebEx

Wipro on the Cloud

The Pleasures and Pitfalls of BYOD

PORTUGAL TELECOM OFFERS IT INFRASTRUCTURE FOR SALE

Portugal Telecom SGPS SA (Portugal Telecom, also known as PT) is a Portugal-based holding company providing telecommunications and information technology services in Portugal, Brazil, Angola, Macao, and Namibia. The company serves more than 100 million business and residential customers worldwide and generates 58 percent of its revenue outside Portugal. The global telecommunications industry is unusually fast-changing and competitive, due to the end of state-owned or monopoly enterprises and the emergence of new services, including mobile phones, the Internet, and digital television.

PT today provides a range of telecommunications and multimedia services, including fixed line and mobile telephone services; television (TV) distribution; Internet Service Provider (ISP) services; and data transmission. These services are delivered primarily over digital networks and are very information-technology intensive. Portugal Telecom has been able to leverage its technology expertise to provide information technology (IT) systems and services to other companies of all sizes.

Portugal Telecom's newest data center is in the mountain city of Covilhã, Portugal, where it can take advantage of "free cooling" from Covilhã's often-chilly mountain air 99 percent of the time, thereby reducing energy usage. The Covilhã center opened in September 2013, and combines progressive architecture, sustainability and leading-edge information technology. The entire project, once complete, will fea-

© Nmedia/Shutterstock

ture four block-like data center structures spanning 75,500 square meters, equivalent to about 800,000 square feet. The PT facility is built to have minimum impact on the environment and features a rain water collection system (which forms a moat around the data center building) and a garden with more than 600 trees. Large numbers of solar panels around the facility are an additional source of clean energy.

The center boasts a power usage effectiveness (PUE) rating of just 1.25, compared to an industry average of 1.88, making it among the most energy-efficient data centers in the world. (PUE is a metric for determining the energy efficiency of a data center and is calculated by dividing the total amount of power consumed by a data center by the amount of power used to run the computer infrastructure within it. The closer PUE approaches 1.0, the greater the overall energy efficiency.) When completely built out, the Covilhã data center will be the largest in the country and one of the largest in the world, capable of hosting 56,000 servers. The Covilhã data center is expected to achieve an annual availability of 99.98 percent.

PT management estimates that just one-sixth of the Covilhã data center's eventual capacity will be required for domestic needs. The rest will provide cloud-based applications and services to other countries, including Brazil and African nations, enabling the company to expand its services across the globe. The Covilhã data center and six other domestic data centers run cloud-based information technology services for other companies known as SmartCloudPT. These cloud services include cloud storage and file synchronization services, infrastructure as a service (IaaS), platform as a service (PaaS), and software as a service (SaaS). Companies who subscribe to SmartCloudPT pay only for the services they actually use. PT and Oracle are now working on incorporating Oracle software applications into SmartCloudPT. Customers need only to register at the SmartCloud PT Web site and log in to purchase the available services that they need, which are billed in the customers' PT invoice, together with other PT services.

PT claims the benefits of its cloud services include having the information protected in the country's largest data center network, the speed and reliability that customers' businesses need, access to PT's cutting-edge technology, and having certified security, advantages that only PT can provide. And because of its energy savings, PT estimates it can price its services 34 percent lower than the average price for premium data centers in Europe. For PT, green computing is good for business.

Sources: SAP AG, "Newsbyte: Portugal Telecom Brings Customers Streamlined Operations and Increased Agility via Cloud Services for SAP® Business One Cloud Powered by SAP HANA® Available Worldwide," February 24, 2014; www.telecom.pt/InternetResource/ PTSIte/UK, accessed March 12, 2014; Archana Venkatraman, "Portugal Telecom Opens Modular Datacentre to Boost Cloud Offering," ComputerWeekly.com, September 24, 2013; Fred Sandesmark, "Core Strengths," Profit Magazine, November 2013; and Rich Miller, "Portugal Telecom's High-Concept Green Data Center,"datacenterknowledge.com, November 11, 2013.

The experience of Portugal Telecom illustrates the importance of information technology infrastructure in running a business today. The right technology at the right price will improve organizational performance.

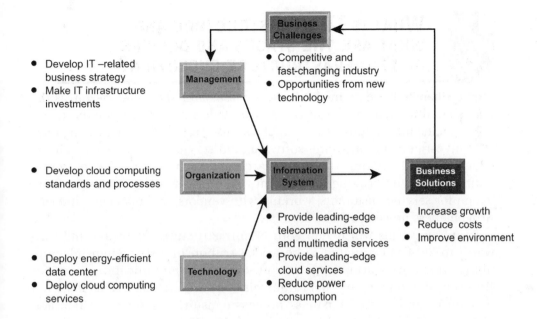

- Develop IT –related business strategy
- Make IT infrastructure investments

Business Challenges
- Competitive and fast-changing industry
- Opportunities from new technology

Management

- Develop cloud computing standards and processes

Organization

Information System

Business Solutions
- Increase growth
- Reduce costs
- Improve environment

- Provide leading-edge telecommunications and multimedia services
- Provide leading-edge cloud services
- Reduce power consumption

- Deploy energy-efficient data center
- Deploy cloud computing services

Technology

Because of the need to prevail in a highly competitive industry requiring leading-edge information technology, PT had world-class expertise in computer hardware, software, and networking technology that enabled it to run its business effectively. The company was then able to leverage its IT investment to sell some of its computing resources and expertise as on-line "cloud" services to other companies. This helped other companies achieve cost savings or acquire information technology resources that they were unable to manage on their own to make their businesses more competitive and efficient.

The chapter-opening case diagram calls attention to important points raised by this case and this chapter. Telecommunications services today are largely computer-based. As a leading telecommunications provider, Portugal Telecom had huge investments in hardware, software, and networking technology and a vast pool of internal IT experts. The company could then sell this expertise and its excess computing capacity as a service to other companies in need of such resources. These services appealed to small, medium-sized businesses and even larger enterprises that were saddled with outdated or inappropriate information technology that prevented them from operating as efficiently and effectively as they could have.

PT created a global data center network for itself and its business customers on several continents. These data centers provide subscribing companies with cloud computing services featuring leading-edge information technologies at very affordable prices. PT's cloud services are easy to purchase and to use, the services are always available, and they include a high level of security protection. The solution is also serving important social goals: lower energy consumption and carbon emissions through more energy-efficient computing.

Here are some questions to think about: How does information technology help Portugal Telecom solve its own business problems? How does PT use technology to help other companies solve their business problems?

5.1   WHAT IS IT INFRASTRUCTURE AND WHAT ARE THE STAGES AND DRIVERS OF IT INFRASTRUCTURE EVOLUTION?

In Chapter 1, we defined *information technology (IT) infrastructure* as the shared technology resources that provide the platform for the firm's specific information system applications. An IT infrastructure includes investment in hardware, software, and services—such as consulting, education, and training—that are shared across the entire firm or across entire business units in the firm. A firm's IT infrastructure provides the foundation for serving customers, working with vendors, and managing internal firm business processes (see Figure 5.1).

Supplying firms worldwide with IT infrastructure (hardware and software) in 2014 is estimated to be a $3.8 trillion industry when telecommunications, networking equipment, and telecommunications services (Internet, telephone, and data transmission) are included. This does not include IT and related business process consulting services, which add another $400 billion. Investments in infrastructure account for between 25 and 50 percent of information technology expenditures in large firms, led by financial services firms where IT investment is well over half of all capital investment.

FIGURE 5.1   CONNECTION BETWEEN THE FIRM, IT INFRASTRUCTURE, AND BUSINESS CAPABILITIES

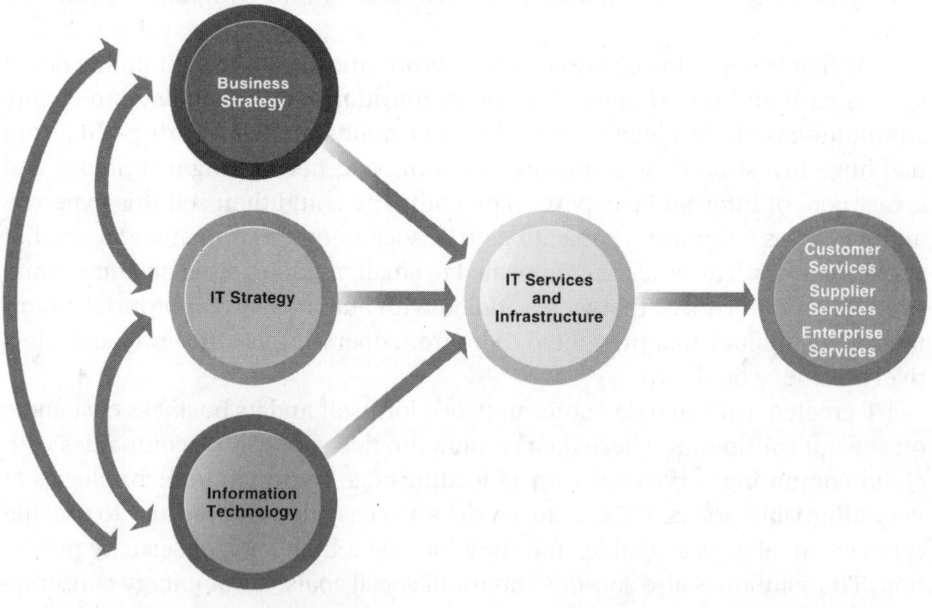

The services a firm is capable of providing to its customers, suppliers, and employees are a direct function of its IT infrastructure. Ideally, this infrastructure should support the firm's business and information systems strategy. New information technologies have a powerful impact on business and IT strategies, as well as the services that can be provided to customers.

DEFINING IT INFRASTRUCTURE

An IT infrastructure consists of a set of physical devices and software applications that are required to operate the entire enterprise. But an IT infrastructure is also a set of firmwide services budgeted by management and comprising both human and technical capabilities. These services include the following:

- Computing platforms used to provide computing services that connect employees, customers, and suppliers into a coherent digital environment, including large mainframes, midrange computers, desktop and laptop computers, and mobile handheld and remote cloud computing services.
- Telecommunications services that provide data, voice, and video connectivity to employees, customers, and suppliers
- Data management services that store and manage corporate data and provide capabilities for analyzing the data
- Application software services, including online software services, that provide enterprise-wide capabilities such as enterprise resource planning, customer relationship management, supply chain management, and knowledge management systems that are shared by all business units
- Physical facilities management services that develop and manage the physical installations required for computing, telecommunications, and data management services
- IT management services that plan and develop the infrastructure, coordinate with the business units for IT services, manage accounting for the IT expenditure, and provide project management services
- IT standards services that provide the firm and its business units with policies that determine which information technology will be used, when, and how
- IT education services that provide training in system use to employees and offer managers training in how to plan for and manage IT investments
- IT research and development services that provide the firm with research on potential future IT projects and investments that could help the firm differentiate itself in the marketplace

This "service platform" perspective makes it easier to understand the business value provided by infrastructure investments. For instance, the real business value of a fully loaded personal computer operating at 3.4 gigahertz that costs about $1,000 and a high-speed Internet connection is hard to understand without knowing who will use it and how it will be used. When we look at the services provided by these tools, however, their value becomes more apparent: The new PC makes it possible for a high-cost employee making $100,000 a year to connect to all the company's major systems and the public Internet. The high-speed Internet service saves this employee about one hour per day in reduced wait time for Internet information. Without this PC and Internet connection, the value of this one employee to the firm might be cut in half.

EVOLUTION OF IT INFRASTRUCTURE

The IT infrastructure in organizations today is an outgrowth of over 50 years of evolution in computing platforms. There have been five stages in this evolution, each representing a different configuration of computing power and infrastructure elements (see Figure 5.2). The five eras are general-purpose mainframe and minicomputer computing, personal computers, client/server networks, enterprise computing, and cloud and mobile computing.

Technologies that characterize one era may also be used in another time period for other purposes. For example, some companies still run traditional mainframe systems or use mainframe computers as massive servers supporting large Web sites and corporate enterprise applications.

General-Purpose Mainframe and Minicomputer Era: (1959 to Present)

The introduction of the IBM 1401 and 7090 transistorized machines in 1959 marked the beginning of widespread commercial use of **mainframe** computers. In 1965, the mainframe computer truly came into its own with the introduction of the IBM 360 series. The 360 was the first commercial computer with a powerful operating system that could provide time sharing, multitasking, and virtual memory in more advanced models. IBM has dominated mainframe computing from this point on. Mainframe computers became powerful enough to support thousands of online remote terminals connected to the centralized mainframe using proprietary communication protocols and proprietary data lines.

The mainframe era was a period of highly centralized computing under the control of professional programmers and systems operators (usually in a corporate data center), with most elements of infrastructure provided by a single vendor, the manufacturer of the hardware and the software.

This pattern began to change with the introduction of **minicomputers** produced by Digital Equipment Corporation (DEC) in 1965. DEC minicomputers (PDP-11 and later the VAX machines) offered powerful machines at far lower prices than IBM mainframes, making possible decentralized computing, customized to the specific needs of individual departments or business units rather than time sharing on a single huge mainframe. In recent years, the minicomputer has evolved into a midrange computer or midrange server and is part of a network.

Personal Computer Era: (1981 to Present)

Although the first truly personal computers (PCs) appeared in the 1970s (the Xerox Alto, the MITS Altair 8800, and the Apple I and II, to name a few), these machines had only limited distribution to computer enthusiasts. The appearance of the IBM PC in 1981 is usually considered the beginning of the PC era because this machine was the first to be widely adopted by American

FIGURE 5.2   ERAS IN IT INFRASTRUCTURE EVOLUTION

Stages in IT Infrastructure Evolution

Mainframe/
Minicomputer
(1959–present)

Personal
Computer
(1981–present)

Client/Server
(1983–present)

Enterprise
Computing
1992–present)

Enterprise
Server

Internet

Cloud
Computing
(2000–present)

- Hardware
- Software
- Services

THE INTERNET

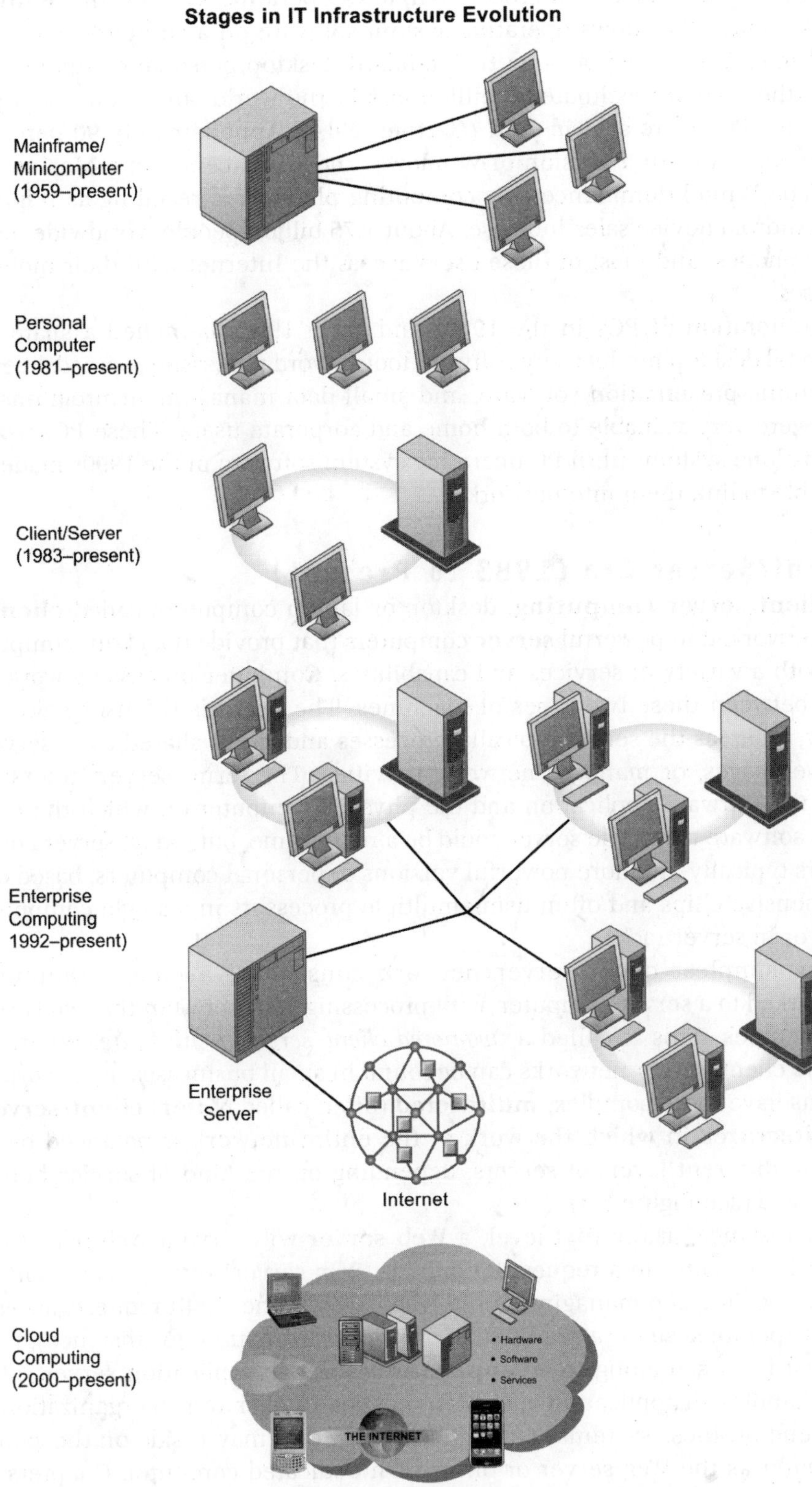

Illustrated here are the typical computing configurations characterizing each of the five eras
of IT infrastructure evolution.

businesses. At first using the DOS operating system, a text-based command language, and later the Microsoft Windows operating system, the **Wintel PC** computer (Windows operating system software on a computer with an Intel microprocessor) became the standard desktop personal computer. In 2014, there are an estimated 2 billion PCs in the world, and about 276 million new PCs were sold in 2014 (Gartner, 2014). Approximately 90 percent are thought to run a version of Windows, and 10 percent run a Macintosh OS. The Wintel dominance as a computing platform is receding as iPhone and Android device sales increase. About 1.75 billion people worldwide own smartphones, and most of these users access the Internet with their mobile devices.

Proliferation of PCs in the 1980s and early 1990s launched a spate of personal desktop productivity software tools—word processors, spreadsheets, electronic presentation software, and small data management programs—that were very valuable to both home and corporate users. These PCs were stand-alone systems until PC operating system software in the 1990s made it possible to link them into networks.

Client/Server Era (1983 to Present)

In **client/server computing**, desktop or laptop computers called **clients** are networked to powerful **server** computers that provide the client computers with a variety of services and capabilities. Computer processing work is split between these two types of machines. The client is the user point of entry, whereas the server typically processes and stores shared data, serves up Web pages, or manages network activities. The term "server" refers to both the software application and the physical computer on which the network software runs. The server could be a mainframe, but today, server computers typically are more powerful versions of personal computers, based on inexpensive chips and often using multiple processors in a single computer box., or in server racks.

The simplest client/server network consists of a client computer networked to a server computer, with processing split between the two types of machines. This is called a *two-tiered client/server architecture*. Whereas simple client/server networks can be found in small businesses, most corporations have more complex, **multitiered** (often called **N-tier**) **client/server architectures** in which the work of the entire network is balanced over several different levels of servers, depending on the kind of service being requested (see Figure 5.3).

For instance, at the first level, a **Web server** will serve a Web page to a client in response to a request for service. Web server software is responsible for locating and managing stored Web pages. If the client requests access to a corporate system (a product list or price information, for instance), the request is passed along to an **application server**. Application server software handles all application operations between a user and an organization's back-end business systems. The application server may reside on the same computer as the Web server or on its own dedicated computer. Chapters 6 and 7 provide more detail on other pieces of software that are used in multitiered client/server architectures for e-commerce and e-business.

FIGURE 5.3 A MULTITIERED CLIENT/SERVER NETWORK (N-TIER)

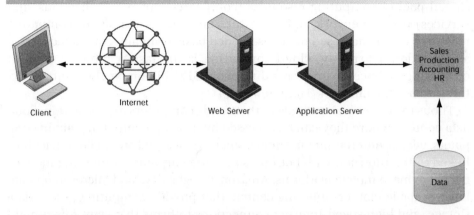

In a multitiered client/server network, client requests for service are handled by different levels of servers.

Client/server computing enables businesses to distribute computing work across a series of smaller, inexpensive machines that cost much less than centralized mainframe systems. The result is an explosion in computing power and applications throughout the firm.

Novell NetWare was the leading technology for client/server networking at the beginning of the client/server era. Today, Microsoft is the market leader with its **Windows** operating systems (Windows Server, Windows 8, Windows 7, and Windows Vista).

Enterprise Computing Era (1992 to Present)

In the early 1990s, firms turned to networking standards and software tools that could integrate disparate networks and applications throughout the firm into an enterprise-wide infrastructure. As the Internet developed into a trusted communications environment after 1995, business firms began seriously using the *Transmission Control Protocol/Internet Protocol (TCP/IP)* networking standard to tie their disparate networks together. We discuss TCP/IP in detail in Chapter 7.

The resulting IT infrastructure links different pieces of computer hardware and smaller networks into an enterprise-wide network so that information can flow freely across the organization and between the firm and other organizations. It can link different types of computer hardware, including mainframes, servers, PCs, and mobile devices, and it includes public infrastructures such as the telephone system, the Internet, and public network services. The enterprise infrastructure also requires software to link disparate applications and enable data to flow freely among different parts of the business, such as enterprise applications (see Chapters 2 and 9) and Web services (discussed in Section 5.4).

Cloud and Mobile Computing Era (2000 to Present)

The growing bandwidth power of the Internet has pushed the client/server model one step further, towards what is called the "Cloud Computing Model."

Cloud computing refers to a model of computing that provides access to a shared pool of computing resources (computers, storage, applications, and services) over a network, often the Internet. These "clouds" of computing resources can be accessed on an as-needed basis from any connected device and location. Currently, cloud computing is the fastest growing form of computing, with companies spending about $175 billion on cloud infrastructure and services in 2014 (Hamilton, 2014).

Thousands or even hundreds of thousands computers are located in cloud data centers, where they can be accessed by desktop computers, laptop computers, tablets, entertainment centers, smartphones, and other client machines linked to the Internet, with both personal and corporate computing increasingly moving to mobile platforms. Amazon, Google, IBM, and Microsoft operate huge, scalable cloud computing centers that provide computing power, data storage, and high-speed Internet connections to firms that want to maintain their IT infrastructures remotely.Firms such as Google, Microsoft, SAP, Oracle, and Salesforce.com sell software applications as services delivered over the Internet.

We discuss cloud and mobile computing in more detail in Section 5.3. The Learning Tracks include a table titled Comparing Stages in IT Infrastructure Evolution, which compares each era on the infrastructure dimensions introduced.

TECHNOLOGY DRIVERS OF INFRASTRUCTURE EVOLUTION

The changes in IT infrastructure we have just described have resulted from developments in computer processing, memory chips, storage devices, telecommunications and networking hardware and software, and software design that have exponentially increased computing power while exponentially reducing costs. Let's look at the most important developments.

Moore's Law and Microprocessing Power

In 1965, Gordon Moore, the director of Fairchild Semiconductor's Research and Development Laboratories, an early manufacturer of integrated circuits, wrote in *Electronics* magazine that since the first microprocessor chip was introduced in 1959, the number of components on a chip with the smallest manufacturing costs per component (generally transistors) had doubled each year. This assertion became the foundation of **Moore's Law**. Moore later reduced the rate of growth to a doubling every two years.

This law would later be interpreted in multiple ways. There are at least three variations of Moore's Law, none of which Moore ever stated: (1) the power of microprocessors doubles every 18 months; (2) computing power doubles every 18 months; and (3) the price of computing falls by half every 18 months.

Figure 5.4 illustrates the relationship between number of transistors on a microprocessor and millions of instructions per second (MIPS), a common measure of processor power. Figure 5.5 shows the exponential decline in the cost of transistors and rise in computing power. For instance, in 2014, you

FIGURE 5.4   MOORE'S LAW AND MICROPROCESSOR PERFORMANCE

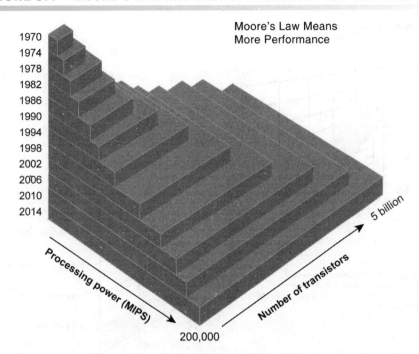

Packing over 5 billion transistors into a tiny microprocessor has exponentially increased processing power. Processing power has increased to over 200,000 MIPS (2.6 billion instructions per second).

Source: Authors' estimate.

can buy an Intel i7 quad-core processor chip with 2.5 billion transistors for about one ten-millionth of a dollar per transistor.

Exponential growth in the number of transistors and the power of processors coupled with an exponential decline in computing costs is likely to continue. Chip manufacturers continue to miniaturize components. Today's transistors should no longer be compared to the size of a human hair but rather to the size of a virus.

By using nanotechnology, chip manufacturers can even shrink the size of transistors down to the width of several atoms. **Nanotechnology** uses individual atoms and molecules to create computer chips and other devices that are thousands of times smaller than current technologies permit. Chip manufacturers are trying to develop a manufacturing process to produce nanotube processors economically (Figure 5.6). Stanford University scientists have built a nanotube computer.

The Law of Mass Digital Storage

A second technology driver of IT infrastructure change is the Law of Mass Digital Storage. The amount of digital information is roughly doubling every year (Gantz and Reinsel, 2011; Lyman and Varian, 2003). Fortunately, the cost of storing digital information is falling at an exponential rate of 100 percent a year. Figure 5.7 shows that the number of megabytes that can be stored on magnetic media for $1 from 1950 to the present roughly doubled every 15 months. In 2014, a 500 gigabyte hard disk drive sells at retail for about $60.

FIGURE 5.5   FALLING COST OF CHIPS

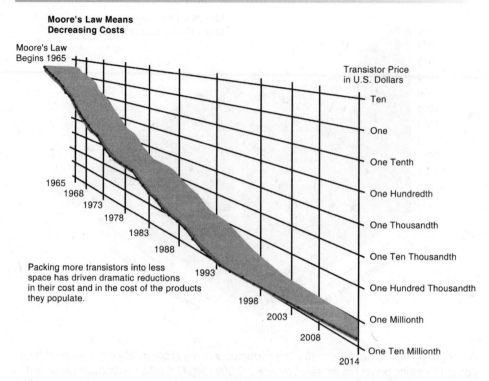

Moore's Law Means Decreasing Costs

Moore's Law Begins 1965

Transistor Price in U.S. Dollars

Ten
One
One Tenth
One Hundredth
One Thousandth
One Ten Thousandth
One Hundred Thousandth
One Millionth
One Ten Millionth

1965
1968
1973
1978
1983
1988
1993
1998
2003
2008
2014

Packing more transistors into less space has driven dramatic reductions in their cost and in the cost of the products they populate.

Packing more transistors into less space has driven down transistor costs dramatically as well as the cost of the products in which they are used.

Source: Authors' estimate.

FIGURE 5.6   EXAMPLE OF NANOTUBES

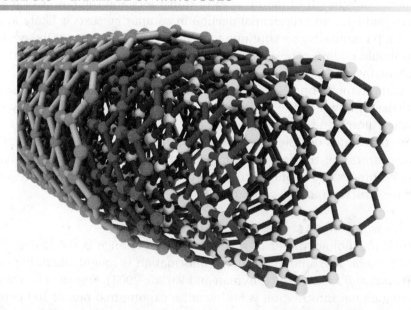

Nanotubes are tiny tubes about 10,000 times thinner than a human hair. They consist of rolled-up sheets of carbon hexagons and have the potential uses as minuscule wires or in ultrasmall electronic devices and are very powerful conductors of electrical current. © Tyler Boyes/Shutterstock.

FIGURE 5.7 THE AMOUNT OF STORAGE PER DOLLAR RISES
EXPONENTIALLY, 1950–2014

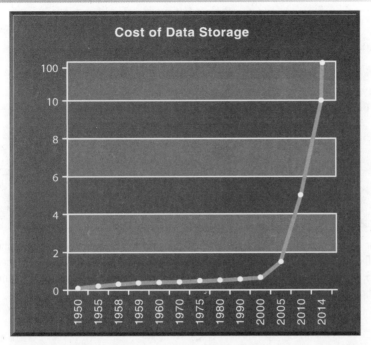

Since the first magnetic storage device was used in 1955, the amount of storage a dollar buys
has risen exponentially, doubling the amount of digital storage for each dollar expended every
15 months on average. Cloud storage services provide 100 gigabytes of storage for about $1.00

Source: Authors' estimates.

Metcalfe's Law and Network Economics

Moore's Law and the Law of Mass Storage help us understand why computing resources are now so readily available. But why do people want more
computing and storage power? The economics of networks and the growth of
the Internet provide some answers.

Robert Metcalfe—inventor of Ethernet local area network technology—
claimed in 1970 that the value or power of a network grows exponentially
as a function of the number of network members. Metcalfe and others point
to the *increasing returns to scale* that network members receive as more and
more people join the network. As the number of members in a network grows
linearly, the value of the entire system grows exponentially and continues to
grow forever as members increase. Demand for information technology has
been driven by the social and business value of digital networks, which rapidly
multiply the number of actual and potential links among network members.

Declining Communications Costs and the Internet

A fourth technology driver transforming IT infrastructure is the rapid
decline in the costs of communication and the exponential growth in
the size of the Internet. There are over 3 billion Internet users worldwide (Internetlivestats.com, 2014). Figure 5.8 illustrates the exponentially
declining cost of communication both over the Internet and over telephone

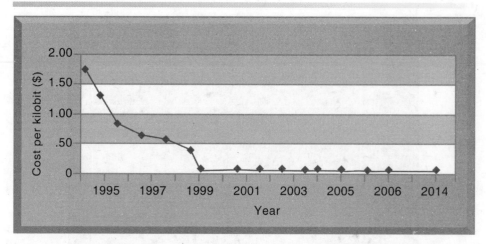

FIGURE 5.8 EXPONENTIAL DECLINES IN INTERNET COMMUNICATIONS COSTS

One reason for the growth in the Internet population is the rapid decline in Internet connection and overall communication costs. The cost per kilobit of Internet access has fallen exponentially since 1995. Digital subscriber line (DSL) and cable modems now deliver a kilobit of communication for a retail price of less than one penny.

Source: Authors.

networks (which increasingly are based on the Internet). As communication costs fall toward a very small number and approach 0, utilization of communication and computing facilities explode.

To take advantage of the business value associated with the Internet, firms must greatly expand their Internet connections, including wireless connectivity, and greatly expand the power of their client/server networks, desktop clients, and mobile computing devices. There is every reason to believe these trends will continue.

Standards and Network Effects

Today's enterprise infrastructure and Internet computing would be impossible—both now and in the future—without agreements among manufacturers and widespread consumer acceptance of **technology standards**. Technology standards are specifications that establish the compatibility of products and the ability to communicate in a network (Stango, 2004).

Technology standards unleash powerful economies of scale and result in price declines as manufacturers focus on the products built to a single standard. Without these economies of scale, computing of any sort would be far more expensive than is currently the case. Table 5.1 describes important standards that have shaped IT infrastructure.

Beginning in the 1990s, corporations started moving toward standard computing and communications platforms. The Wintel PC with the Windows operating system and Microsoft Office desktop productivity applications became the standard desktop and mobile client computing platform. (It now shares the spotlight with other standards, such as Apple's iOS and Macintosh operating systems and the Android operating system.) Widespread adoption

TABLE 5.1 SOME IMPORTANT STANDARDS IN COMPUTING

STANDARD	SIGNIFICANCE
American Standard Code for Information Interchange (ASCII) (1958)	Made it possible for computer machines from different manufacturers to exchange data; later used as the universal language linking input and output devices such as keyboards and mice to computers. Adopted by the American National Standards Institute in 1963.
Common Business Oriented Language (COBOL) (1959)	An easy-to-use software language that greatly expanded the ability of programmers to write business-related programs and reduced the cost of software. Sponsored by the Defense Department in 1959.
Unix (1969–1975)	A powerful multitasking, multiuser, portable operating system initially developed at Bell Labs (1969) and later released for use by others (1975). It operates on a wide variety of computers from different manufacturers. Adopted by Sun, IBM, HP, and others in the 1980s, it became the most widely used enterprise-level operating system.
Transmission Control Protocol/Internet Protocol (TCP/IP) (1974)	Suite of communications protocols and a common addressing scheme that enables millions of computers to connect together in one giant global network (the Internet). Later, it was used as the default networking protocol suite for local area networks and intranets. Developed in the early 1970s for the U.S. Department of Defense.
Ethernet (1973)	A network standard for connecting desktop computers into local area networks that enabled the widespread adoption of client/server computing and local area networks, and further stimulated the adoption of personal computers.
IBM/Microsoft/Intel Personal Computer (1981)	The standard Wintel design for personal desktop computing based on standard Intel processors and other standard devices, Microsoft DOS, and later Windows software. The emergence of this standard, low-cost product laid the foundation for a 25-year period of explosive growth in computing throughout all organizations around the globe. Today, more than 1 billion PCs power business and government activities every day.
World Wide Web (1989–1993)	Standards for storing, retrieving, formatting, and displaying information as a worldwide web of electronic pages incorporating text, graphics, audio, and video enables creation of a global repository of billions of Web pages.

of Unix-Linux as the enterprise server operating system of choice made possible the replacement of proprietary and expensive mainframe infrastructures. In telecommunications, the Ethernet standard enabled PCs to connect together in small local area networks (LANs; see Chapter 7), and the TCP/IP standard enabled these LANs to be connected into firmwide networks, and ultimately, to the Internet.

5.2 WHAT ARE THE COMPONENTS OF IT INFRASTRUCTURE?

IT infrastructure today is composed of seven major components. Figure 5.9 illustrates these infrastructure components and the major vendors within each component category. These components constitute investments that must be coordinated with one another to provide the firm with a coherent infrastructure.

In the past, technology vendors supplying these components were often in competition with one another, offering purchasing firms a mixture of

FIGURE 5.9   THE IT INFRASTRUCTURE ECOSYSTEM

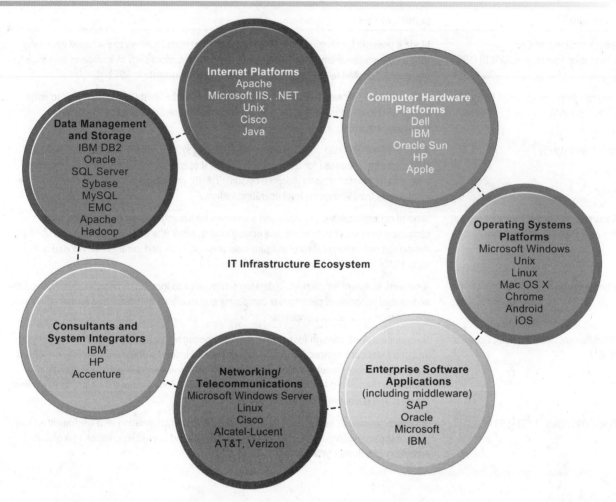

IT Infrastructure Ecosystem

There are seven major components that must be coordinated to provide the firm with a coherent IT infrastructure. Listed here are major technologies and suppliers for each component.

incompatible, proprietary, partial solutions. But increasingly the vendor firms have been forced by large customers to cooperate in strategic partnerships with one another. For instance, a hardware and services provider such as IBM cooperates with all the major enterprise software providers, has strategic relationships with system integrators, and promises to work with whichever database products its client firms wish to use (even though it sells its own database management software called DB2).

COMPUTER HARDWARE PLATFORMS

Firms worldwide are expected to spend $669 billion on computer hardware devices in 2014, including mainframes, servers, PCs, tablets, and smartphones. You can think of all these computers and their processors as the computer hardware platform for corporate (and personal) computing worldwide.

There are approximately 2 billion PCs in the world today, 2,000 government data centers, and an estimated 8,000 corporate data centers and cloud computing centers. Nearly all their computing takes place using microprocessor "chips" manufactured or designed by Intel Corporation, and to a lesser extent, AMD Corporation. Intel and AMD processors are often referred to as "i86" processors because the original IBM PCs used an Intel 8086 processor, and all the Intel (and AMD) chips that followed are downward compatible with this processor. (For instance, you should be able to run a software application designed ten years ago on a new PC computer you bought yesterday.) Without this commonality in i86 processors, it is unlikely that today's installed base of 2 billion PCs would exist.

The computer platform has changed dramatically in the last decade, with the introduction of mobile computing devices, from the iPod in 2001, to the iPhone in 2007, and the iPad in 2010. Worldwide, 1.7 billion people use smartphones. You can think of these devices as a second computer hardware platform, one that is consumer device-driven.

The computers with Intel microprocessors in the first computer hardware platform use complex instruction set computing (CISC), with several thousand native instructions built into the chip. This requires a considerable number of transistors per processor, consumes power, and generates heat. Mobile devices in the second computer hardware platform are not required to perform as many tasks as computers in the first computer hardware platform. They are able to use reduced instruction set computing (RISC), which contains a smaller set of instructions, consumes less power, and generates less heat. Apple and Samsung consumer devices use microprocessors designed by ARM Holdings, Inc., a British firm. RISC processors for mobile devices are manufactured by a wide range of firms, including Apple, Texas Instruments, Samsung, and Qualcomm.

The server market, which includes infrastructures ranging from a few computers to large data centers with over 10,000 individual computers, uses mostly Intel and AMD processors in the form of blade servers on racks. **Blade servers** are computers consisting of a circuit board with processors, memory and network connections that are stored in racks. They take up less space than traditional box-based PC servers. Secondary storage is provided by a hard drive in each blade server, but more commonly by external mass-storage devices. Some specialized servers use Sun SPARC or IBM microprocessors specifically designed for server use.

Mainframes have not disappeared. Mainframes continue to be used to reliably and securely handle huge volumes of transactions, for analyzing very large quantities of data, and for handling large workloads in cloud computing centers. The mainframe is still the digital workhorse for banking and telecommunications networks that are often running software programs that are older and require a specific hardware platform. However, the number of providers has dwindled to one:IBM. IBM has also repurposed its mainframe systems so they can be used as giant servers for massive enterprise networks and corporate Web sites. A single IBM mainframe can run up to 17,000 instances of Linux or Windows Server software and is capable of replacing thousands of smaller blade servers (see the discussion of virtualization in Section 5.3).

OPERATING SYSTEM PLATFORMS

Microsoft Windows Server comprises about 35 percent of the server operating system market, with 65 percent of corporate servers using some form of the **Unix** operating system or **Linux**, an inexpensive and robust open source relative of Unix. Microsoft Windows Server is capable of providing enterprise-wide operating system and network services, and appeals to organizations seeking Windows-based IT infrastructures.

Unix and Linux are scalable, reliable, and much less expensive than mainframe operating systems. They can also run on many different types of processors. The major providers of Unix operating systems are IBM, HP, and Sun, each with slightly different and partially incompatible versions.

At the client level, 90 percent of PCs use some form of the Microsoft Windows **operating system** (such as Windows 8, Windows 7, or Windows Vista) to manage the resources and activities of the computer. However, there is now a much greater variety of operating systems than in the past, with new operating systems for computing on handheld mobile digital devices or cloud-connected computers.

Google's **Chrome OS** provides a lightweight operating system for cloud computing using a Web-connected computer. Programs are not stored on the user's computer but are used over the Internet and accessed through the Chrome Web browser. User data reside on servers across the Internet. **Android** is an open source operating system for mobile devices such as smartphones and tablet computers developed by the Open Handset Alliance led by Google. It has become the most popular smartphone platform worldwide, competing with iOS, Apple's mobile operating system for the iPhone, iPad, and iPod Touch.

Conventional client operating system software is designed around the mouse and keyboard, but increasingly becoming more natural and intuitive by using touch technology. **iOS**, the operating system for the phenomenally popular Apple iPad, iPhone, and iPod Touch, features a **multitouch** interface, where users employ one or more fingers to manipulate objects on a screen without a mouse or keyboard. Microsoft's **Windows 8,** which runs on tablets as well as PCs, has a user interface optimized for touch, but also works with a mouse and keyboard. Multitouch capabilities are also available on some Android devices.

ENTERPRISE SOFTWARE APPLICATIONS

Firms worldwide are expected to spend about $320 billion in 2014 on software for enterprise applications that are treated as components of IT infrastructure. We introduced the various types of enterprise applications in Chapter 2, and Chapter 9 provides a more detailed discussion of each.

The largest providers of enterprise application software are SAP and Oracle (which acquired PeopleSoft). Also included in this category is middleware software supplied by vendors such as IBM and Oracle for achieving firmwide integration by linking the firm's existing application systems. Microsoft is attempting to move into the lower ends of this market by focusing on small and medium-sized businesses that have not yet implemented enterprise applications.

DATA MANAGEMENT AND STORAGE

Enterprise database management software is responsible for organizing and managing the firm's data so that they can be efficiently accessed and used. Chapter 6 describes this software in detail. The leading database software providers are IBM (DB2), Oracle, Microsoft (SQL Server), and Sybase (Adaptive Server Enterprise), which supply more than 90 percent of the U.S. database software marketplace. MySQL is a Linux open source relational database product now owned by Oracle Corporation, and Apache Hadoop is an open source software framework for managing massive data sets (see Chapter 6).

The physical data storage market is dominated by EMC Corporation for large-scale systems, and a small number of PC hard disk manufacturers led by Seagate and Western Digital.

Digital information is doubling every two years and the market for digital data storage devices has been growing at more than 15 percent annually over the last five years. In addition to traditional disk arrays and tape libraries, large firms are turning to network-based storage technologies. **Storage area networks (SANs)** connect multiple storage devices on a separate high-speed network dedicated to storage. The SAN creates a large central pool of storage that can be rapidly accessed and shared by multiple servers.

NETWORKING/TELECOMMUNICATIONS PLATFORMS

Companies worldwide are expected to spend $1.65 trillion for telecommunications services in 2014 (Gartner, 2014). Chapter 7 is devoted to an in-depth description of the enterprise networking environment, including the Internet. Windows Server is predominantly used as a local area network operating system, followed by Linux and Unix. Large, enterprise wide area networks use some variant of Unix. Most local area networks, as well as wide area enterprise networks, use the TCP/IP protocol suite as a standard (see Chapter 7).

The leading networking hardware providers are Cisco, Alcatel-Lucent, and Juniper Networks. Telecommunications platforms are typically provided by telecommunications/telephone services companies that offer voice and data connectivity, wide area networking, wireless services, and Internet access. Leading telecommunications service vendors include AT&T and Verizon. This market is exploding with new providers of cellular wireless, high-speed Internet, and Internet telephone services.

INTERNET PLATFORMS

Internet platforms overlap with, and must relate to, the firm's general networking infrastructure and hardware and software platforms. They include hardware, software, and management services to support a firm's

Web site, including Web hosting services, routers, and cabling or wireless equipment. A **Web hosting service** maintains a large Web server, or series of servers, and provides fee-paying subscribers with space to maintain their Web sites.

The Internet revolution created a veritable explosion in server computers, with many firms collecting thousands of small servers to run their Internet operations. Since then there has been a steady push toward server consolidation, reducing the number of server computers by increasing the size and power of each and by using software tools that make it possible to run more applications on a single server. The Internet hardware server market has become increasingly concentrated in the hands of IBM, Dell, Sun (Oracle), and HP, as prices have fallen dramatically.

The major Web software application development tools and suites are supplied by Microsoft (Microsoft Visual Studio and the Microsoft .NET family of development tools), Oracle-Sun (Sun's Java is the most widely used tool for developing interactive Web applications on both the server and client sides), and a host of independent software developers, including Adobe (Creative Suite) and Real Networks (media software). Chapter 7 describes the components of the firm's Internet platform in greater detail.

CONSULTING AND SYSTEM INTEGRATION SERVICES

Today, even a large firm does not have the staff, the skills, the budget, or the necessary experience to deploy and maintain its entire IT infrastructure. Implementing a new infrastructure requires (as noted in Chapters 3 and 14) significant changes in business processes and procedures, training and education, and software integration. Leading consulting firms providing this expertise include Accenture, IBM Global Services, HP, Infosys, and Wipro Technologies.

Software integration means ensuring the new infrastructure works with the firm's older, so-called legacy systems and ensuring the new elements of the infrastructure work with one another. **Legacy systems** are generally older transaction processing systems created for mainframe computers that continue to be used to avoid the high cost of replacing or redesigning them. Replacing these systems is cost prohibitive and generally not necessary if these older systems can be integrated into a contemporary infrastructure.

5.3 WHAT ARE THE CURRENT TRENDS IN COMPUTER HARDWARE PLATFORMS?

The exploding power of computer hardware and networking technology has dramatically changed how businesses organize their computing power, putting more of this power on networks and mobile handheld devices. We look at seven hardware trends: the mobile digital platform, consumerization of IT, quantum computing, virtualization, cloud computing, green computing, and high-performance/power-saving processors.

THE MOBILE DIGITAL PLATFORM

Chapter 1 pointed out that new mobile digital computing platforms have emerged as alternatives to PCs and larger computers. Smartphones such as the iPhone, Android, and BlackBerry smartphones have taken on many functions of PCs, including transmission of data, surfing the Web, transmitting e-mail and instant messages, displaying digital content, and exchanging data with internal corporate systems. The new mobile platform also includes small, lightweight netbooks optimized for wireless communication and Internet access, **tablet computers** such as the iPad, and digital e-book readers such as Amazon's Kindle with Web access capabilities.

Smartphones and tablet computers are becoming an important means of accessing the Internet. These devices are increasingly used for business computing as well as for consumer applications. For example, senior executives at General Motors are using smartphone applications that drill down into vehicle sales information, financial performance, manufacturing metrics, and project management status.

Wearable computing devices are a recent addition to the mobile digital platform. These include smartwatches, smart glasses, smart badges, and activity trackers. Wearable computing technology is still in its infancy, but it already has business uses, as described in the Interactive Session on Technology.

CONSUMERIZATION OF IT AND BYOD

The popularity, ease of use, and rich array of useful applications for smartphones and tablet computers have created a groundswell of interest in allowing employees to use their personal mobile devices in the workplace, a phenomenon popularly called *"bring your own device"* (BYOD). BYOD is one aspect of the **consumerization of IT**, in which new information technology that first emerges in the consumer market spreads into business organizations. Consumerization of IT includes not only mobile personal devices but also business uses of software services that originated in the consumer marketplace as well, such as Google and Yahoo search, Gmail, Google Apps, Dropbox (see Chapter 2), and even Facebook and Twitter.

Consumerization of IT is forcing businesses, especially large enterprises, to rethink the way they obtain and manage information technology equipment and services. Historically, at least in large firms, the IT department was responsible for selecting and managing the information technology and applications used by the firm and its employees. It furnished employees with desktops or laptops that were able to access corporate systems securely. The IT department maintained control over the firm's hardware and software to ensure that the business was being protected and that information systems served the purposes of the firm and its management. Today, employees and business departments are playing a much larger role in technology selection, in many cases demanding that employees be able to use their own personal computers, smartphones, and tablets to access the corporate network. It is more difficult for the firm to manage and control

INTERACTIVE SESSION: TECHNOLOGY

ESTABLISHING GLOBAL CLASSROOMS THROUGH WEBEX

Synopsys Electronics Education and Research (Seer) Akademi, an academic initiative of the Worldwide University Program of Nasdaq-listed Synopsys Inc, offers undergraduate and postgraduate degrees in VLSI (very large-scale integration) and embedded systems across rural India. The start-up was pioneered by California-based entrepreneur, Srikanth Jadcherla, who worked as an executive at Synopsys, an electronic design automation company. He is now the chairman and CEO of Seer Akademi. The institute deploys a non-traditional architecture of education, which is pending for a patent. This unique model of imparting education combines classroom curriculum conducted by local and online faculty, skill-based learning, and practical application of learning in state-of-the-art labs. The theory to practice ratio is 35 to 65, unlike any other course offered in India.

Since the institute targets rural students, providing quality and research-oriented education regardless of location with a lack of qualified facilitators is a key challenge. In addition, poor research in electronics in India and the time required for students to travel from remote rural locations to attend classes also pose problem for the institute. Although India has the largest population in the world under the age of 14 that is waiting to be organized into a potential soucrce of electronics expertise, these challenges inhibit their growth. One feasible solution that Jadcherla could think of was Web-conferencing.

Web-conferencing enables real-time face-to-face conversations through a Web browser at any place, and at any time. It requires wireless devices with internet connectivity, an audio connection, and an optional webcam. However, rural areas have limited bandwidth and students are not well-versed in the concept of collaborative online learning. Therefore, it was imperative that the solution offered not only a robust and reliable platform, but was also easy to use. Jadcherla evaluated several available products and decided to go with Cisco's WebEx technology. WebEx has been designed to minimize the amount of data transmitted over the network and works well in areas with low bandwidth or areas prone to network congestion. WebEx's use of internet data varies with the type of files shared. For example, if students view slides over the network, no or very little network traffic is generated, compared to video conferencing. Its several easy-to-use features include online collaboration tools such as discussion forums, document sharing, calendar, and so on. It allows for the creation of virtual teams and online sharing of content.

Using this technology, Seer Akademi has been able to setup global classrooms through which students in rural India can collaborate with professors located across the world. Instructors can share their desktops imparting real-time lectures on chip design and electronic processes from remote locations. WebEx provides tools for facilitators to mark-up documents as they are shared and take notes. Compared to the interactive whiteboard technology, the WebEx interface is far more superior in terms of ease of use. It also costs a lot less than other similar technology. WebEx is compatible with a range of mobile devices. "In 2009, the remote town of Nandyal was completely cut off from the rest of the world due to flooding, but the students there did not want to miss class. So a group of them gathered around an Apple iPhone and attended the WebEx session that way," says Jadcherla.

From offering certification courses, Seer Akademi has now moved to full-time degree programmes in microelectronics. Students who graduate from this institute are deemed skilled to get a higher degree in their field or placed in leading firms as well as innovative start-ups such as Broadcom, Synopsys, AMD, Blaze, and so on.

With the success of its pedagogy-laden engineering education, Jadcherla hopes that the model will be followed in engineering colleges across the world and expects his institute to grow 14 times in the coming years. According to the estimates of the India Electronics and Semiconductor Association, by 2020, the country will face around 2.8 million shortage of manpower in electronics. Jadcherla has, therefore, entered into joint ventures with other groups to set up advanced electronics labs and incubation centers. Besides, he also hopes to build a microelectronics laboratory that will give students hands-on experience with real-world electronics engineering technologies.

Currently the institute operates from offices in Hyderabad and Bangalore and has eight regional centers. It is looking forward to expand to places like Vietnam, Malaysia, Dubai, and other South Asian and Middle Eastern countries.

Sources: Benefits of WebEx, WebEx.com, accessed on December 21, 2015 (http://www.webex.co.in/overview/web-conferencing.html); http://www.cisco.com/c/dam/en/us/products/collateral/conferencing/seer_akademi_case_study.pdf; Mobile Meetings, WebEx.com, accessed on December 21, 2015 (http://www.webex.co.in/overview/mobile-meetings.html)

CASE STUDY QUESTIONS

1. Discuss how Srikanth Jadcherla's vision of spreading engineering education to rural India has materialized by the application of technology?

2. Identify the features of Cisco's WebEx technology.

3. Discuss the challenges faced by Jadcherla before the implementation of Web conferencing. How did Cisco help him overcome these challenges?

these consumer technologies, and make sure they serve the needs of the business. The chapter-ending case study explores some of these management challenges created by BYOD and IT consumerization.

QUANTUM COMPUTING

Quantum computing is an emerging technology with the potential to dramatically boost computer processing power to find answers to problems that would take conventional computers many years to solve. **Quantum computing** uses the principles of quantum physics to represent data and perform operations on these data. A quantum computer would gain enormous processing power through the ability to be in many different states at once, allowing it to perform multiple operations simultaneously and solve some scientific and business problems millions of times faster than can be done today. Researchers at IBM, MIT, and the Los Alamos National Laboratory have been working on quantum computing, and the aerospace firm Lockheed Martin has purchased a quantum computer for commercial use.

VIRTUALIZATION

Virtualization is the process of presenting a set of computing resources (such as computing power or data storage) so that they can all be accessed in ways that are not restricted by physical configuration or geographic location. Virtualization enables a single physical resource (such as a server or a storage device) to appear to the user as multiple logical resources. For example, a server or mainframe can be configured to run many instances of an operating system (or different operating systems) so that it acts like many different machines. Each virtual server "looks" like a real physical server to software programs, and multiple virtual servers can run in parallel on a single machine. Virtualization also enables multiple physical resources (such as storage devices or servers) to appear as a single logical resource, as would be the case with storage area networks. VMware is the leading virtualization software vendor for Windows and Linux servers.

Server virtualization is a common method of reducing technology costs by providing the ability to host multiple systems on a single physical machine. Most servers run at just 15-20 percent of capacity, and virtualization can boost utilization server utilization rates to 70 percent or higher. Higher utilization rates translate into fewer computers required to process the same amount of work, reduced data center space to house machines, and lower energy usage. Virtualization also facilitates centralization and consolidation of hardware administration. It is now possible for companies and individuals to perform all of their computing work using a virtualized IT infrastructure in a remote location, as is the case with cloud computing.

CLOUD COMPUTING

Cloud computing is a model of computing in which computer processing, storage, software, and other services are provided as a pool of virtualized resources over a network, primarily the Internet. These "clouds" of computing resources can be accessed on an as-needed basis from any connected device and location. Figure 5.10 illustrates the cloud computing concept.

The U.S. National Institute of Standards and Technology (NIST) defines cloud computing as having the following essential characteristics (Mell and Grance, 2009):

- **On-demand self-service:** Consumers can obtain computing capabilities such as server time or network storage as needed automatically on their own.

- **Ubiquitous network access:** Cloud resources can be accessed using standard network and Internet devices, including mobile platforms.

- **Location-independent resource pooling:** Computing resources are pooled to serve multiple users, with different virtual resources dynamically assigned according to user demand. The user generally does not know where the computing resources are located.

- **Rapid elasticity:** Computing resources can be rapidly provisioned, increased, or decreased to meet changing user demand.

- **Measured service:** Charges for cloud resources are based on amount of resources actually used.

Cloud computing consists of three different types of services:

- **Infrastructure as a Service (IaaS):** Customers use processing, storage, networking, and other computing resources from cloud service providers to run their information systems. For example, Amazon uses the spare capacity of its IT infrastructure to provide a broadly based cloud environment selling IT infrastructure services. These include its Simple Storage Service (S3) for storing customers' data and its Elastic

FIGURE 5.10 CLOUD COMPUTING PLATFORM

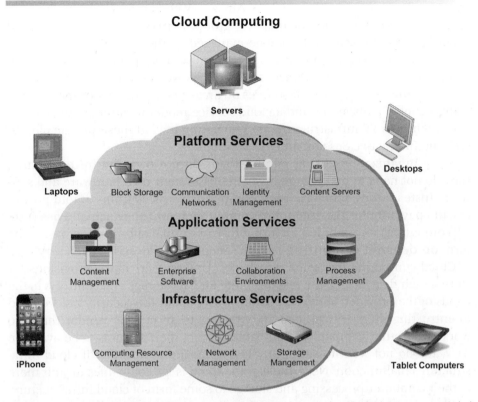

In cloud computing, hardware and software capabilities are a pool of virtualized resources provided over a network, often the Internet. Businesses and employees have access to applications and IT infrastructure anywhere, at any time, and on any device.

Compute Cloud (EC2) service for running their applications. Users pay only for the amount of computing and storage capacity they actually use. (See the Interactive Session on Organizations).

- **Platform as a Service (PaaS):** Customers use infrastructure and programming tools supported by the cloud service provider to develop their own applications. For example, IBM offers a Smart Business Application Development & Test service for software development and testing on the IBM Cloud. Another example is Salesforce.com's Force.com, which allows developers to build applications that are hosted on its servers as a service.

- **Software as a Service (SaaS):** Customers use software hosted by the vendor on the vendor's cloud infrastructure and delivered over a network. Leading examples are Google Apps, which provides common business applications online and Salesforce.com, which also leases customer relationship management and related software services over the Internet. Both charge users an annual subscription fee, although Google provides a free version of some of its business productivity tools. Users access these applications from a Web browser, and the data and software are maintained on the providers' remote servers.

A cloud can be private or public. A **public cloud** is owned and maintained by a cloud service provider, such as Amazon Web Services, and made available to the general public or industry group. A **private cloud** is operated solely for an organization. It may be managed by the organization or a third party and may exist on premise or off premise. Like public clouds, private clouds are able to allocate storage, computing power, or other resources seamlessly to provide computing resources on an as-needed basis. Companies that want flexible IT resources and a cloud service model while retaining control over their own IT infrastructure are gravitating toward these private clouds. (See the Interactive Session on Organizations.)

Since organizations using public clouds do not own the infrastructure, they do not have to make large investments in their own hardware and software. Instead, they purchase their computing services from remote providers and pay only for the amount of computing power they actually use (utility computing) or are billed on a monthly or annual subscription basis. The term **on-demand computing** has also been used to describe such services.

Cloud computing has some drawbacks. Unless users make provisions for storing their data locally, the responsibility for data storage and control is in the hands of the provider. Some companies worry about the security risks related to entrusting their critical data and systems to an outside vendor that also works with other companies. Companies expect their systems to be available 24/7 and do not want to suffer any loss of business capability if cloud infrastructures malfunction. Nevertheless, the trend is for companies to shift more of their computer processing and storage to some form of cloud infrastructure.

Cloud computing is more immediately appealing to small and medium-sized businesses that lack resources to purchase and own their own hardware and software. However, large corporations have huge investments in complex proprietary systems supporting unique business processes, some of which give them strategic advantages. The cost savings from switching to cloud services are not always easy to determine for large companies that already have their own IT infrastructures in place. Corporate data centers typically work with an IT budget that accounts for a mix of operational and capital expenses. Pricing for cloud services is usually based on a per-hour or other per-use charge. Even if a company can approximate the hardware and software costs to run a specific computing task on premises, it still needs to figure in how much of the firm's network management, storage management, system administration, electricity, and real estate costs should be allocated to a single on-premises IT service. An information systems department may not have the right information to analyze those factors on a service-by-service basis.

Large firms are most likely to adopt a **hybrid cloud** computing model where they use their own infrastructure for their most essential core activities and adopt public cloud computing for less-critical systems or for additional processing capacity during peak business periods. Cloud computing will gradually shift firms from having a fixed infrastructure capacity toward a more flexible infrastructure, some of it owned by the firm, and some of it rented from giant computer centers owned by computer hardware vendors. You can find out more about cloud computing in the Learning Tracks for this chapter.

INTERACTIVE SESSION: ORGANIZATIONS

WIPRO ON THE CLOUD

Wipro Limited is a global information technology, consulting, and outsourcing company with over 1.5 lakh employees serving clients in more than 175 cities across the world. To enhance the value for its enterprise for customers, Wipro is continuously looking for ways to use technology more effectively. Building solutions that can take advantage of cloud platforms, be delivered over the Internet, and hosted in a separate data center is one such initiative. Cloud platforms play an important role in B2B selling. They help integrate customers and their partners to enterprises across organizational boundaries in a cost-effective manner.

The tool that Wipro uses to achieve these objectives is called Windows Azure. It is an Internet cloud services platform hosted in the Microsoft data centers. The advantage of using this technology is that customers can deploy their applications on a dynamically scalable platform and pay as per usage. This helps the firm reduce costs for its clients and add new revenue streams for its own operations. The features supported by this platform are wide-ranging and many. Windows Azure offers binary large object (BLOB) storage, where large amounts of unstructured data such as text or binary can be stored and accessed from anywhere in the world. It also has the capacity to offer a relational database, billing facility, and a pay-as-you-go pricing model.

Wipro has tested the application in quite a few B2B firms. The leading oil and gas company, Shell, was one of the first to see an implementation of Windows Azure for a B2B operation. There were two primary channels at Shell that customers used to buy fuel and lubricants. Large B2B customers used electronic data interchange (EDI), while the small- and medium-sized customers used a Web-based application to place orders, view order status, and obtain their account information or order history. Wipro decided to move these processes to Windows Azure. Figure 5.11 depicts the application design.

When a customer places an order, the order processing service routes it to a queue in Windows Azure storage. The platform then pushes the order to the on-premise Microsoft BizTalk Server 2006 R2 application. The function of the BizTalk Server is to enable communication between the business processes through adapters, which aid in integrating the different software systems of these processes. The Biztalk Server integrates with the SAP system that processes orders and generates invoices. At the same time, the order is stored in Windows Azure as BLOB. Customer invoices generated from SAP are also stored in and accessible through BLOB.

Wipro is now actively exploring the capabilities of Windows Azure for use in other industries. For example, it is building an insurance hub that will integrate more than 30,000 active auto insurance agents in the United States. The hub will facilitate in obtaining insurance rate comparisons and quotes from multiple insurance providers. To complement this, Wipro is developing a virtual service center that will help insurance providers offer online services to agents and customers without having to maintain their own field infrastructure and applications. This portal also makes use of the federated authentication feature, which is a characteristic of Windows Azure. A merged active directory is created to support multiple authentications. This directory is linked to insurance providers' database, which in turn enables the authentication of customers, agencies, and insurance providers.

Using Windows Azure, Wipro has been able to provide its enterprise customers with cost-effective solutions that scale dynamically to meet demand. The availability of Windows Azure data centers around the world help eliminate network performance differences. This localized service also helps ensure that all geographical locations have the same high availability of service and are easier to regulate. Wipro plans to evaluate cloud capabilities for its internal applications as well and apply them where necessary.

Sources: "Wipro & Microsoft presents 'Cloud Power with Windows Azure'" (2012). Retrieved from www.youtube.com/watch?v=0oSe-Z3-djo; "About Wipro". Retrieved from http://www.wipro.com/about-wipro/., http://www.microsoft.com/india/casestudies/microsoft-azure/wipro-limited/it-services-company-reduces-costs-expands-opportunities-with-new-cloud-platform/4000006700; "Wipro productizes EIM offering—demos cloud to Shell" (2010). Retrieved from http://www.oilit.com/2journal/2article/1005_15.htm

FIGURE 5.11   THE APPLICATION DESIGN OF WINDOWS AZURE

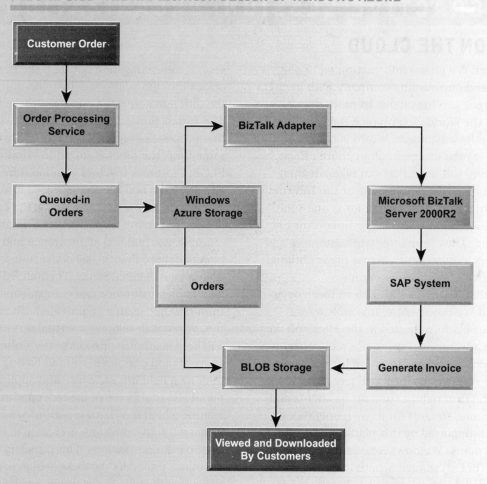

CASE STUDY QUESTIONS

1. Discuss the features of Windows Azure as a cloud service.

2. Discuss the application of Azure in B2B scenarios.

3. How can cloud computing be applied to an insurance hub?

4. How can the cloud be used to build solutions that bring global consistency?

GREEN COMPUTING

By curbing hardware proliferation and power consumption, virtualization has become one of the principal technologies for promoting green computing. **Green computing** or **green IT**, refers to practices and technologies for designing, manufacturing, using, and disposing of computers, servers, and associated devices such as monitors, printers, storage devices, and networking and communications systems to minimize impact on the environment.

Reducing computer power consumption has been a very high "green" priority. Information technology is responsible for about 2 percent of total U.S. power demand and is believed to contribute about 2 percent of the world's greenhouse gases. A corporate data center can easily consume more than 100 times more power than a standard office building. All this additional power consumption has a negative impact on the environment and corporate operating costs. The chapter-opening case on Portugal Telecom illustrates some of the technologies and data center design considerations for green computing and the business and environmental benefits of cutting power consumption in the data center.

HIGH-PERFORMANCE AND POWER-SAVING PROCESSORS

Another way to reduce power requirements and hardware sprawl is to use more efficient and power-saving processors. Contemporary microprocessors now feature multiple processor cores (which perform the reading and execution of computer instructions) on a single chip. A **multicore processor** is an integrated circuit to which two or more processor cores have been attached for enhanced performance, reduced power consumption, and more efficient simultaneous processing of multiple tasks. This technology enables two or more processing engines with reduced power requirements and heat dissipation to perform tasks faster than a resource-hungry chip with a single processing core. Today you'll find PCs with dual-core, quad-core, six-core, and eight core processors and servers with 16-core processors.

Intel and other chip manufacturers have developed microprocessors that minimize power consumption, which is essential for prolonging battery life in small mobile digital devices. You will now find highly power-efficient microprocessors, such as the A6 and A7 processors used in the Apple iPhone and iPad, and Intel's Atom processor for netbooks and mobile Internet devices. The Apple micrprocessors have about one-fiftieth the power consumption of a laptop dual-core processor. Intel recently unveiled a line of ultrasmall low-power microprocessors called Quark that can be used in wearable devices, skin patches, or even swallowed to gather medical data.

WHAT ARE THE CURRENT TRENDS IN COMPUTER SOFTWARE PLATFORMS?

There are four major themes in contemporary software platform evolution:

- Linux and open source software
- Java, HTML, and HTML5
- Web services and service-oriented architecture
- Software outsourcing and cloud services

LINUX AND OPEN SOURCE SOFTWARE

Open source software is software produced by a community of several hundred thousand programmers around the world. According to the leading open source professional association, OpenSource.org, open source software is free and can be modified by users. Works derived from the original code must also be free, and the software can be redistributed by the user without additional licensing. Open source software is by definition not restricted to any specific operating system or hardware technology, although most open source software is currently based on a Linux or Unix operating system.

The open source movement has been evolving for more than 30 years and has demonstrated that it can produce commercially acceptable, high-quality software. Popular open source software tools include the Linux operating system, the Apache HTTP Web server, the Mozilla Firefox Web browser, and the Apache OpenOffice desktop productivity suite. Google's Android mobile operating system and Chrome Web browser are based on open source tools. You can find out more out more about the Open Source Definition from the Open Source Initiative and the history of open source software at the Learning Tracks for this chapter.

Linux

Perhaps the most well-known open source software is Linux, an operating system related to Unix. Linux was created by the Finnish programmer Linus Torvalds and first posted on the Internet in August 1991. Linux applications are embedded in cell phones, smartphones, tablet computers and consumer electronics. Linux is available in free versions downloadable from the Internet or in low-cost commercial versions that include tools and support from vendors such as Red Hat.

Although Linux is not used in many desktop systems, it is a leading operating system on servers, mainframe computers, and supercomputers. Linux has become the operating system of choice in the high performance computing market, powering 97 percent of the world's fastest computers. IBM, HP, Intel, Dell, and Oracle have made Linux a central part of their offerings to corporations. The popular Android operating system for mobile devices has a Linux foundation.

The rise of open source software, particularly Linux and the applications it supports, has profound implications for corporate software platforms: cost reduction, reliability and resilience, and integration, because Linux works on all the major hardware platforms from mainframes to servers to clients.

SOFTWARE FOR THE WEB: JAVA, HTML, AND HTML5

Java is an operating system-independent, processor-independent, object-oriented programming language that has become the leading interactive environment for the Web. Java was created by James Gosling and the Green Team at Sun Microsystems in 1992. In November 13, 2006, Sun released much of Java as open source software under the terms of the GNU General Public License (GPL), completing the process on May 8, 2007.

The Java platform has migrated into cell phones, smartphones, automobiles, music players, game machines, and into set-top cable television systems serving interactive content and pay-per-view services. Java software is designed to run on any computer or computing device, regardless of the specific microprocessor or operating system the device uses. Java is the most popular development platform for mobile devices running the Android operating system. For each of the computing environments in which Java is used, Sun created a Java Virtual Machine that interprets Java programming code for that machine. In this manner, the code is written once and can be used on any machine for which there exists a Java Virtual Machine.

Java developers can create small applet programs that can be embedded in Web pages and downloaded to run on a Web browser. A **Web browser** is an easy-to-use software tool with a graphical user interface for displaying Web pages and for accessing the Web and other Internet resources. Microsoft's Internet Explorer, Mozilla Firefox, and Google Chrome browser are examples. At the enterprise level, Java is being used for more complex e-commerce and e-business applications that require communication with an organization's back-end transaction processing systems.

HTML and HTML5

HTML (Hypertext Markup Language) is a page description language for specifying how text, graphics, video, and sound are placed on a Web page and for creating dynamic links to other Web pages and objects. Using these links, a user need only point at a highlighted keyword or graphic, click on it, and immediately be transported to another document.

HTML was originally designed to create and link static documents composed largely of text. Today, however, the Web is much more social and interactive, and many Web pages have multimedia elements—images, audio, and video. Third-party plug-in applications like Flash, Silverlight, and Java have been required to integrate these rich media with Web pages. However, these add-ons require additional programming and put strains on computer processing. The next evolution of HTML, called **HTML5**, solves this problem by making it possible to embed images, audio, video, and other elements directly into a document without processor-intensive add-ons. HTML5 makes it easier for Web pages to function across different display devices, including mobile devices as well as desktops, and it will support the storage of data offline for apps that run over the Web. Other popular programming tools for Web applications include Ruby and Python. Ruby is an object-oriented programming language known for speed and ease of use in building Web applications and Python (praised for its clarity) is being used for building cloud computing applications. Major Web sites such as Google, Facebook, Amazon, and Twitter use Python and Ruby as well as Java.

WEB SERVICES AND SERVICE-ORIENTED ARCHITECTURE

Web services refer to a set of loosely coupled software components that exchange information with each other using universal Web communication standards and languages. They can exchange information between two different systems regardless of the operating systems or programming languages on which the systems are based. They can be used to build open

TABLE 5.2 EXAMPLES OF XML

PLAIN ENGLISH	XML
Subcompact	<AUTOMOBILETYPE="Subcompact">
4 passenger	<PASSENGERUNIT="PASS">4</PASSENGER>
$16,800	<PRICE CURRENCY="USD">$16,800</PRICE>

standard Web-based applications linking systems of two different organizations, and they can also be used to create applications that link disparate systems within a single company. Web services are not tied to any one operating system or programming language, and different applications can use them to communicate with each other in a standard way without time-consuming custom coding.

The foundation technology for Web services is **XML**, which stands for **Extensible Markup Language**. This language was developed in 1996 by the World Wide Web Consortium (W3C, the international body that oversees the development of the Web) as a more powerful and flexible markup language than hypertext markup language (HTML) for Web pages. Whereas HTML is limited to describing how data should be presented in the form of Web pages, XML can perform presentation, communication, and storage of data. In XML, a number is not simply a number; the XML tag specifies whether the number represents a price, a date, or a ZIP code. Table 5.2 illustrates some sample XML statements.

By tagging selected elements of the content of documents for their meanings, XML makes it possible for computers to manipulate and interpret their data automatically and perform operations on the data without human intervention. Web browsers and computer programs, such as order processing or enterprise resource planning (ERP) software, can follow programmed rules for applying and displaying the data. XML provides a standard format for data exchange, enabling Web services to pass data from one process to another.

Web services communicate through XML messages over standard Web protocols. Companies discover and locate Web services through a directory much as they would locate services in the Yellow Pages of a telephone book. Using Web protocols, a software application can connect freely to other applications without custom programming for each different application with which it wants to communicate. Everyone shares the same standards.

The collection of Web services that are used to build a firm's software systems constitutes what is known as a service-oriented architecture. A **service-oriented architecture (SOA)** is set of self-contained services that communicate with each other to create a working software application. Business tasks are accomplished by executing a series of these services. Software developers reuse these services in other combinations to assemble other applications as needed.

Virtually all major software vendors provide tools and entire platforms for building and integrating software applications using Web services. IBM includes Web service tools in its WebSphere e-business software platform, and Microsoft has incorporated Web services tools in its Microsoft .NET platform.

Dollar Rent A Car's systems use Web services for its online booking system with Southwest Airlines' Web site. Although both companies' systems are based on different technology platforms, a person booking a flight on Southwest.com can reserve a car from Dollar without leaving the airline's Web site. Instead of struggling to get Dollar's reservation system to share data with Southwest's information systems, Dollar used Microsoft .NET Web services technology as an intermediary. Reservations from Southwest are translated into Web services protocols, which are then translated into formats that can be understood by Dollar's computers.

Other car rental companies have linked their information systems to airline companies' Web sites before. But without Web services, these connections had to be built one at a time. Web services provide a standard way for Dollar's computers to "talk" to other companies' information systems without having to build special links to each one. Dollar is now expanding its use of Web services to link directly to the systems of a small tour operator and a large travel reservation system as well as a wireless Web site for cell phones and smartphones. It does not have to write new software code for each new partner's information systems or each new wireless device (see Figure 5.12).

FIGURE 5.12 HOW DOLLAR RENT A CAR USES WEB SERVICES

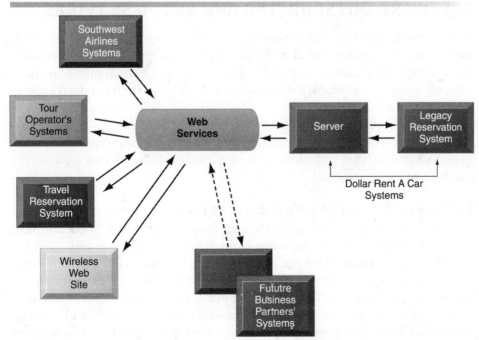

Dollar Rent A Car uses Web services to provide a standard intermediate layer of software to "talk" to other companies' information systems. Dollar Rent A Car can use this set of Web services to link to other companies' information systems without having to build a separate link to each firm's systems.

FIGURE 5.13 CHANGING SOURCES OF FIRM SOFTWARE

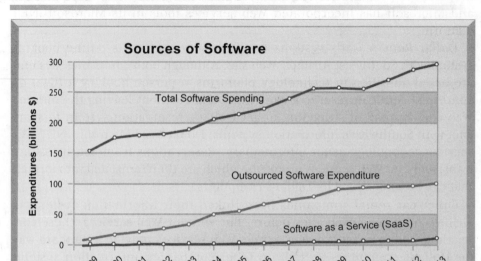

In 2014, U.S. firms will spend over $279 billion on software. About 35 percent of that will originate outside the firm, either from enterprise software vendors selling firmwide applications or individual application service providers leasing or selling software modules. Another 4 percent ($11 billion) will be provided by SaaS vendors as an online cloud-based service.

Sources: BEA National Income and Product Accounts, 2014; authors' estimates.

SOFTWARE OUTSOURCING AND CLOUD SERVICES

Today, many business firms continue to operate legacy systems that continue to meet a business need and that would be extremely costly to replace. But they will purchase or rent most of their new software applications from external sources. Figure 5.13 illustrates the rapid growth in external sources of software for U.S. firms.

There are three external sources for software: software packages from a commercial software vendor, outsourcing custom application development to an external vendor, (which may or may not be offshore), and cloud-based software services and tools.

Software Packages and Enterprise Software

We have already described software packages for enterprise applications as one of the major types of software components in contemporary IT infrastructures. A **software package** is a prewritten commercially available set of software programs that eliminates the need for a firm to write its own software programs for certain functions, such as payroll processing or order handling.

Enterprise application software vendors such as SAP and Oracle-PeopleSoft have developed powerful software packages that can support the primary business processes of a firm worldwide from warehousing, customer relationship management, and supply chain management, to finance and human resources. These large-scale enterprise software systems provide a single, integrated, worldwide software system for firms at a cost much less than they would pay if they developed it themselves. Chapter 9 discusses enterprise systems in detail.

Software Outsourcing

Software **outsourcing** enables a firm to contract custom software development or maintenance of existing legacy programs to outside firms, which often operate offshore in low-wage areas of the world. According to industry analysts, spending on global IT outsourcing services was approximately $440 billion in 2014 (Kanaracus, 2014).

For example, Cemex, Mexico's largest cement manufacturer, signed a 10-year $1 billion outsourcing deal with IBM in July 2012. Under the deal, IBM responsibilities include application development and maintenance as well as IT infrastructure management at Cemex company headquarters in Monterrey, Mexico, and around the globe. IBM will take over and run Cemex's finance, accounting, and human resources systems (McDougall, 2012).

Offshore software outsourcing firms have primarily provided lower-level maintenance, data entry, and call center operations, although more sophisticated and experienced offshore firms, particularly in India, have been hired for new-program development. However, as wages offshore rise, and the costs of managing offshore projects are factored in (see Chapter 13), some work that would have been sent offshore is returning to domestic companies.

Cloud-Based Software Services and Tools

In the past, software such as Microsoft Word or Adobe Illustrator came in a box and was designed to operate on a single machine. Today, you're more likely to download the software from the vendor's Web site, or to use the software as a cloud service delivered over the Internet.

Cloud-based software and the data it uses are hosted on powerful servers in massive data centers, and can be accessed with an Internet connection and standard Web browser. In addition to free or low-cost tools for individuals and small businesses provided by Google or Yahoo, enterprise software and other complex business functions are available as services from the major commercial software vendors. Instead of buying and installing software programs, subscribing companies rent the same functions from these services, with users paying either on a subscription or per-transaction basis. Services for delivering and providing access to software remotely as a Web-based service are now referred to as **software as a service (SaaS)**. A leading example is Salesforce. com, which provides on-demand software services for customer relationship management.

In order to manage their relationship with an outsourcer or technology service provider, firms need a contract that includes a **service level agreement (SLA)**. The SLA is a formal contract between customers and their service providers that defines the specific responsibilities of the service provider and the level of service expected by the customer. SLAs typically specify the nature and level of services provided, criteria for performance measurement, support options, provisions for security and disaster recovery, hardware and software ownership and upgrades, customer support, billing, and conditions for terminating the agreement. We provide a Learning Track on this topic.

Mashups and Apps

The software you use for both personal and business tasks may consist of large self-contained programs, or it may be composed of interchangeable components that integrate freely with other applications on the Internet. Individual users and entire companies mix and match these software components to create their own customized applications and to share information with others. The resulting software applications are called **mashups**. The idea is to take different sources and produce a new work that is "greater than" the sum of its parts. You have performed a mashup if you've ever personalized your Facebook profile or your blog with a capability to display videos or slide shows.

Web mashups combine the capabilities of two or more online applications to create a kind of hybrid that provides more customer value than the original sources alone. For instance, ZipRealty uses Google Maps and data provided by online real estate database Zillow.com to display a complete list of multiple listing service (MLS) real estate listings for any zip code specified by the user. Amazon uses mashup technologies to aggregate product descriptions with partner sites and user profiles.

Apps are small specialized software programs that run on the Internet, on your computer, or on your mobile phone or tablet and are generally delivered over the Internet. Google refers to its online services as apps, including the Google Apps suite of desktop productivity tools. But when we talk about apps today, most of the attention goes to the apps that have been developed for the mobile digital platform. It is these apps that turn smartphones and other mobile handheld devices into general-purpose computing tools.

Some downloaded apps do not access the Web but many do, providing faster access to Web content than traditional Web browsers. They provide a non-browser pathway for users to experience the Web and perform a number of tasks, ranging from reading the newspaper to shopping, searching, and buying. Because so many people are now accessing the Internet from their mobile devices, some say that apps are "the new browsers." Apps are also starting to influence the design and function of traditional Web sites as consumers are attracted to the look and feel of apps and their speed of operation.

Many apps are free or purchased for a small charge, much less than conventional software, which further adds to their appeal. There are already over 1 million apps for the Apple iPhone and iPad platform and a similar number that run on devices using Google's Android operating system. The success of these mobile platforms depends in large part on the quantity and the quality of the apps they provide. Apps tie the customer to a specific hardware platform: As the user adds more and more apps to his or her mobile phone, the cost of switching to a competing mobile platform rises.

At the moment, the most commonly downloaded apps are games, news and weather, maps/navigation, social networking, music, and video/movies. But there are also serious apps for business users that make it possible to create and edit documents, connect to corporate systems, schedule and participate in meetings, track shipments, and dictate voice messages (see the Chapter 1 Interactive Session on Management). There are also a huge number of e-commerce apps for researching and buying goods and services online.

5.5 WHAT ARE THE CHALLENGES OF MANAGING IT INFRASTRUCTURE AND MANAGEMENT SOLUTIONS?

Creating and managing a coherent IT infrastructure raises multiple challenges: dealing with platform and technology change (including cloud and mobile computing), management and governance, and making wise infrastructure investments.

DEALING WITH PLATFORM AND INFRASTRUCTURE CHANGE

As firms grow, they often quickly outgrow their infrastructure. As firms shrink, they can get stuck with excessive infrastructure purchased in better times. How can a firm remain flexible when most of the investments in IT infrastructure are fixed-cost purchases and licenses? How well does the infrastructure scale? **Scalability** refers to the ability of a computer, product, or system to expand to serve a large number of users without breaking down. New applications, mergers and acquisitions, and changes in business volume all impact computer workload and must be considered when planning hardware capacity.

Firms using mobile computing and cloud computing platforms will require new policies and procedures for managing these platforms. They will need to inventory all of their mobile devices in business use and develop policies and tools for tracking, updating, and securing them and for controlling the data and applications that run on them. Firms using cloud computing and SaaS will need to fashion new contractual arrangements with remote vendors to make sure that the hardware and software for critical applications are always available when needed and that they meet corporate standards for information security. It is up to business management to determine acceptable levels of computer response time and availability for the firm's mission-critical systems to maintain the level of business performance they expect.

MANAGEMENT AND GOVERNANCE

A long-standing issue among information system managers and CEOs has been the question of who will control and manage the firm's IT infrastructure. Chapter 2 introduced the concept of IT governance and described some issues it addresses. Other important questions about IT governance are: Should departments and divisions have the responsibility of making their own information technology decisions or should IT infrastructure be centrally controlled and managed? What is the relationship between central information systems management and business unit information systems management? How will infrastructure costs be allocated among business units? Each organization will need to arrive at answers based on its own needs.

MAKING WISE INFRASTRUCTURE INVESTMENTS

IT infrastructure is a major investment for the firm. If too much is spent on infrastructure, it lies idle and constitutes a drag on the firm's financial performance. If too little is spent, important business services cannot be delivered and the firm's competitors (who spent just the right amount) will outperform the under-investing firm. How much should the firm spend on infrastructure? This question is not easy to answer.

A related question is whether a firm should purchase and maintain its own IT infrastructure components or rent them from external suppliers, including those offering cloud services. The decision either to purchase your own IT assets or rent them from external providers is typically called the *rent-versus-buy* decision.

Cloud computing may be a low-cost way to increase scalability and flexibility, but firms should evaluate this option carefully in light of security requirements and impact on business processes and workflows. In some instances, the cost of renting software adds up to more than purchasing and maintaining an application in-house. Yet there may be benefits to using cloud services, if this allows the company to focus on core business issues instead of technology challenges.

Total Cost of Ownership of Technology Assets

The actual cost of owning technology resources includes the original cost of acquiring and installing hardware and software, as well as ongoing administration costs for hardware and software upgrades, maintenance, technical support, training, and even utility and real estate costs for running and housing the technology. The **total cost of ownership (TCO)** model can be used to analyze these direct and indirect costs to help firms determine the actual cost of specific technology implementations. Table 5.3 describes the most important TCO components to consider in a TCO analysis.

When all these cost components are considered, the TCO for a PC might run up to three times the original purchase price of the equipment. Although the purchase price of a wireless handheld for a corporate employee may run several hundred dollars, the TCO for each device is much higher, ranging from $1,000 to $3,000, according to various consultant estimates. Gains in productivity and efficiency from equipping employees with mobile computing devices must be balanced against increased costs from integrating these devices into the firm's IT infrastructure and from providing technical support. Other cost components include fees for wireless airtime, end-user training, help desk support, and software for special applications. Costs are higher if the mobile devices run many different applications or need to be integrated into back-end systems such as enterprise applications.

Hardware and software acquisition costs account for only about 20 percent of TCO, so managers must pay close attention to administration costs to understand the full cost of the firm's hardware and software. It is possible to reduce some of these administration costs through better management. Many large firms are saddled with redundant, incompatible hardware and software because their departments and divisions have been allowed to make their own technology purchases.

In addition to switching to cloud services, these firms could reduce their TCO through greater centralization and standardization of their hardware and software resources. Companies could reduce the size of the information systems staff required to support their infrastructure if the firm minimizes the number of different computer models and pieces of software that employees are allowed to use. In a centralized infrastructure, systems can

TABLE 5.3 TOTAL COST OF OWNERSHIP (TCO) COST COMPONENTS

INFRASTRUCTURE COMPONENT	COST COMPONENTS
Hardware acquisition	Purchase price of computer hardware equipment, including computers, terminals, storage, and printers
Software acquisition	Purchase or license of software for each user
Installation	Cost to install computers and software
Training	Cost to provide training for information systems specialists and end users
Support	Cost to provide ongoing technical support, help desks, and so forth
Maintenance	Cost to upgrade the hardware and software
Infrastructure	Cost to acquire, maintain, and support related infrastructure, such as networks and specialized equipment (including storage backup units)
Downtime	Cost of lost productivity if hardware or software failures cause the system to be unavailable for processing and user tasks
Space and energy	Real estate and utility costs for housing and providing power for the technology

be administered from a central location and troubleshooting can be performed from that location.

Competitive Forces Model for IT Infrastructure Investment

Figure 5.14 illustrates a competitive forces model you can use to address the question of how much your firm should spend on IT infrastructure.

Market demand for your firm's services. Make an inventory of the services you currently provide to customers, suppliers, and employees. Survey each group, or hold focus groups to find out if the services you currently offer are meeting the needs of each group. For example, are customers complaining of slow responses to their queries about price and availability? Are employees complaining about the difficulty of finding the right information for their jobs? Are suppliers complaining about the difficulties of discovering your production requirements?

Your firm's business strategy. Analyze your firm's five-year business strategy and try to assess what new services and capabilities will be required to achieve strategic goals.

Your firm's IT strategy, infrastructure, and cost. Examine your firm's information technology plans for the next five years and assess its alignment with the firm's business plans. Determine the total IT infrastructure costs. You will want to perform a TCO analysis. If your firm has no IT strategy, you will need to devise one that takes into account the firm's five-year strategic plan.

Information technology assessment. Is your firm behind the technology curve or at the bleeding edge of information technology? Both situations are to be avoided. It is usually not desirable to spend resources on advanced technologies that are still experimental, often expensive, and sometimes unreliable. You want to spend on technologies for which standards have been established and IT vendors are competing on cost, not

FIGURE 5.14 COMPETITIVE FORCES MODEL FOR IT INFRASTRUCTURE

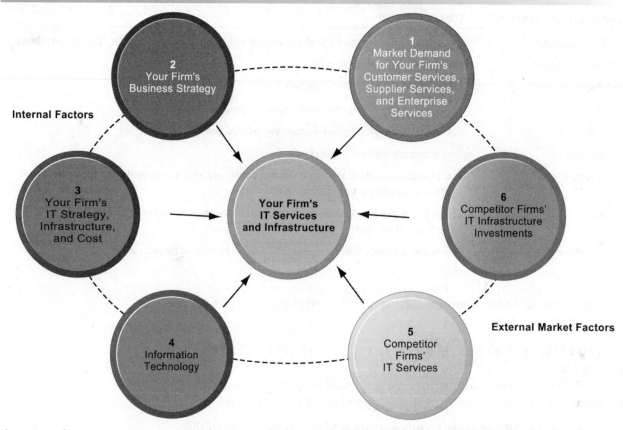

There are six factors you can use to answer the question, "How much should our firm spend on IT infrastructure?"

design, and where there are multiple suppliers. However, you do not want to put off investment in new technologies or allow competitors to develop new business models and capabilities based on the new technologies.

Competitor firm services. Try to assess what technology services competitors offer to customers, suppliers, and employees. Establish quantitative and qualitative measures to compare them to those of your firm. If your firm's service levels fall short, your company is at a competitive disadvantage. Look for ways your firm can excel at service levels.

Competitor firm IT infrastructure investments. Benchmark your expenditures for IT infrastructure against your competitors. Many companies are quite public about their innovative expenditures on IT. If competing firms try to keep IT expenditures secret, you may be able to find IT investment information in public companies' SEC Form 10-K annual reports to the federal government when those expenditures impact a firm's financial results.

Your firm does not necessarily need to spend as much as, or more than, your competitors. Perhaps it has discovered much less-expensive ways of providing services, and this can lead to a cost advantage. Alternatively, your firm may be spending far less than competitors and experiencing commensurate poor performance and losing market share.

Review Summary

1. *What is IT infrastructure and what are the stages and drivers of IT infrastructure evolution?*

   IT infrastructure is the shared technology resources that provide the platform for the firm's specific information system applications. IT infrastructure includes hardware, software, and services that are shared across the entire firm.

   The five stages of IT infrastructure evolution are: the mainframe era, the personal computer era, the client/server era, the enterprise computing era, and the cloud and mobile computing era. Moore's Law deals with the exponential increase in processing power and decline in the cost of computer technology, stating that every 18 months the power of microprocessors doubles and the price of computing falls in half. The Law of Mass Digital Storage deals with the exponential decrease in the cost of storing data, stating that the number of kilobytes of data that can be stored on magnetic media for $1 roughly doubles every 15 months. Metcalfe's Law states that a network's value to participants grows exponentially as the network takes on more members. The rapid decline in costs of communication and growing agreement in the technology industry to use computing and communications standards is also driving an explosion of computer use.

2. *What are the components of IT infrastructure?*

   Major IT infrastructure components include computer hardware platforms, operating system platforms, enterprise software platforms, networking and telecommunications platforms, database management software, Internet platforms, and consulting services and systems integrators.

3. *What are the current trends in computer hardware platforms?*

   Increasingly, computing is taking place on a mobile digital platform. Quantum computing is an emerging technology that could dramatically boost processing power through the ability to be in more than one state at the same time. Consumerization of IT is the business use of information technology that originated in the consumer market. Virtualization organizes computing resources so that their use is not restricted by physical configuration or geographic location. In cloud computing, firms and individuals obtain computing power and software as services over a network, including the Internet, rather than purchasing and installing the hardware and software on their own computers. A multicore processor is a microprocessor to which two or more processing cores have been attached for enhanced performance. Green computing includes practices and technologies for producing, using, and disposing of information technology hardware to minimize negative impact on the environment.

4. *What are the current trends in computer software platforms?*

   Open source software is produced and maintained by a global community of programmers and is often downloadable for free. Linux is a powerful, resilient open source operating system that can run on multiple hardware platforms and is used widely to run Web servers. Java is an operating-system– and hardware-independent programming language that is the leading interactive programming environment for the Web. HTML5 makes it possible to embed images, audio, and video directly into a Web document without add-on programs. Web services are loosely coupled software components based on open Web standards that work with any application software and operating system. They can be used as components of Web-based applications linking the systems of two different organizations or to link disparate systems of a single company. Companies are purchasing their new software applications from outside sources, including software packages, by outsourcing custom application development to an external vendor (that may be offshore), or by renting online software services (SaaS). Mashups combine two different software services to create new software applications and services. Apps are small pieces of software that run on the Internet, on a computer, or on a mobile phone and are generally delivered over the Internet.

5. *What are the challenges of managing IT infrastructure and management solutions?*

   Major challenges include dealing with platform and infrastructure change, infrastructure management and governance, and making wise infrastructure investments. Solution guidelines include using a competitive forces model to determine how much to spend on IT infrastructure and where to make strategic infrastructure investments, and establishing the total cost of ownership (TCO) of information technology assets. The total cost of owning technology resources includes not only the original cost of computer hardware and software but also costs for hardware and software upgrades, maintenance, technical support, and training.

Key Terms

Review Questions

5-1 What is IT infrastructure and what are the stages and drivers of IT infrastructure evolution?

- Define IT infrastructure from both a technology and a services perspective.
- List each of the eras in IT infrastructure evolution and describe its distinguishing characteristics.
- Define and describe the following: Web server, application server, multitiered client/server architecture.
- Describe Moore's Law and the Law of Mass Digital Storage.
- Describe how network economics, declining communications costs, and technology standards affect IT infrastructure.

5-2 What are the components of IT infrastructure?

- List and describe the components of IT infrastructure that firms need to manage.

5-3 What are the current trends in computer hardware platforms?

- Describe the evolving mobile platform, consumerization of IT, and cloud computing.

- Explain how businesses can benefit from virtualization, green computing, and multicore processors.

5-4 What are the current trends in computer software platforms?

- Define and describe open source software and Linux and explain their business benefits.
- Define Java and HTML5 and explain why they are important.
- Define and describe Web services and the role played by XML.
- Name and describe the three external sources for software.
- Define and describe software mashups and apps.

5-5 What are the challenges of managing IT infrastructure and management solutions?

- Name and describe the management challenges posed by IT infrastructure.
- Explain how using a competitive forces model and calculating the TCO of technology assets help firms make good infrastructure investments.

Discussion Questions

5-6 Why is selecting computer hardware and software for the organization an important management decision? What management, organization, and technology issues should be considered when selecting computer hardware and software?

5-7 Should organizations use software service providers for all their software needs? Why or why not? What management, organization, and technology factors should be considered when making this decision?

5-8 What are the advantages and disadvantages of cloud computing?

Hands-On MIS Projects

The projects in this section give you hands-on experience in developing solutions for managing IT infrastructures and IT outsourcing, using spreadsheet software to evaluate alternative desktop systems, and using Web research to budget for a sales conference.

Management Decision Problems

5-9 The University of Pittsburgh Medical Center (UPMC) relies on information systems to operate 19 hospitals, a network of other care sites, and international and commercial ventures. Demand for additional servers and storage technology was growing by 20 percent each year. UPMC was setting up a separate server for every application, and its servers and other computers were running a number of different operating systems, including several versions of Unix and Windows. UPMC had to manage technologies from many different vendors, including Hewlett-Packard (HP), Sun Microsystems, Microsoft, and IBM. Assess the impact of this situation on business performance. What factors and management decisions must be considered when developing a solution to this problem?

5-10 Qantas Airways, Australia's leading airline, faces cost pressures from high fuel prices and lower levels of global airline traffic. To remain competitive, the airline must find ways to keep costs low while providing a high level of customer service. Qantas had a 30-year-old data center. Management had to decide whether to replace its IT infrastructure with newer technology or outsource it. What factors should be considered by Qantas management when deciding whether to outsource? If Qantas decides to outsource, list and describe points that should be addressed in a service level agreement.

Improving Decision Making: Using Web Research to Budget for a Sales Conference

Software skills: Internet-based software
Business skills: Researching transportation and lodging costs

5-11 The Foremost Composite Materials Company is planning a two-day sales conference for October 19–20, starting with a reception on the evening of October 18. The conference consists of all-day meetings that the entire sales force, numbering 120 sales representatives and their 16 managers, must attend. Each sales representative requires his or her own room, and the company needs two common meeting rooms, one large enough to hold the entire sales force plus a few visitors (200) and the other able to hold half the force. Management has set a budget of $175,000 for the representatives' room rentals. The company would like to hold the conference in either Miami or Marco Island, Florida, at a Hilton- or Marriott-owned hotel.

Use the Hilton and Marriott Web sites to select a hotel in whichever of these cities that would enable the company to hold its sales conference within its budget and meet its sales conference requirements. Then locate flights arriving the afternoon prior to the conference. Your attendees will be coming from Los Angeles (54), San Francisco (32), Seattle (22), Chicago (19), and Pittsburgh (14). Determine costs of each airline ticket from these cities. When you are finished, create a budget for the conference. The budget will include the cost of each airline ticket, the room cost, and $70 per attendee per day for food.

The Pleasures and Pitfalls of BYOD
CASE STUDY

Just about everyone who has a smartphone wants to be able to bring it to work and use it on the job. And why not? Employees using their own smartphones would allow companies to enjoy all of the same benefits of a mobile workforce without spending their own money to purchase these devices. Smaller companies are able to go mobile without making large investments in devices and mobile services. One IBM-sponsored study by Forrester Consulting found that a BYOD program using mobile enterprise services from IBM achieved a 108 percent return on investment and payback within one month. "Anywhere/anytime" access to computing tools increased workplace productivity and raised effective employee work time by 45–60 minutes per week. According to Gartner Inc., by 2017, 50 percent of employers will require employees to supply their own mobile devices for the workplace. BYOD is becoming the "new normal."

But...wait a minute. Nearly three out of five enterprises believe that BYOD represents a growing problem for their organizations, according to a survey of 162 enterprises conducted by Osterman Research on behalf of Dell Inc. Although BYOD can improve employee job satisfaction and productivity, it also can cause a number of problems if not managed properly: support for personally owned devices is more difficult than it is for company-supplied devices, the cost of managing mobile devices can increase, and protecting corporate data and networks becomes more difficult. Research conducted by the Aberdeen Group found that on average, an enterprise with 1,000 mobile devices spends an extra $170,000 per year when it allows BYOD. So it's not that simple.

BYOD requires a significant portion of corporate IT resources dedicated to managing and maintaining a large number of devices within the organization. In the past, companies tried to limit business smartphone use to a single platform. This made it easier to keep track of each mobile device and to roll out software upgrades or fixes, because all employees were using the same devices, or at the very least, the same operating system. The most popular employer-issued smartphone used to be Research in Motion's BlackBerry, because it was considered the "most secure" mobile platform available. (BlackBerry mobile devices access corporate e-mail and data using a proprietary software and networking platform that is company-controlled and protected from outsiders.)

Today, the mobile digital landscape is much more complicated, with a variety of devices and operating systems on the market that do not have well-developed tools for administration and security. Android has over 79 percent of the worldwide smartphone market, but it is more difficult to use for corporate work than Apple mobile devices using the iOS operating system. IOS is considered a closed system and runs only on a limited number of different Apple mobile devices. In contrast, Android's fragmentation makes it more difficult and costly for corporate IT to manage. As of July 2013, there were at least 11,868 different Android-based devices were available from more than 1,700 different brands, according to a report by OpenSignal, which researches wireless networks and devices. Android's huge consumer market share attracts many hackers. Android is also vulnerable because it has an open-source architectureand comes in multiple versions.

If employees are allowed to work with more than one type of mobile device and operating system, companies need an effective way to keep track of all the devices employees are using. To access company information, the company's networks must be configured to receive connections from that device. When employees make changes to their personal phone, such as switching cellular carriers, changing their phone number, or buying a new mobile device altogether, companies will need to quickly and flexibly ensure that their employees are still able to remain productive. Firms need an efficient inventory management system that keeps track of which devices employees are using, where the device is located, whether it is being used, and what software it is equipped with. For unprepared companies, keeping track of who gets access to what data could be a nightmare.

With the large variety of phones and operating systems available, providing adequate technical support for every employee could be difficult. When employees are not able to access critical data or encounter other problems with their mobile devices, they will need assistance from the information systems department. Companies that rely on desktop computers tend to have many of the same computers with the same specs and operating systems, making tech support that much easier. Mobility introduces a new layer of variety and complexity to tech support that companies need to be prepared to handle.

There are significant concerns with securing company information accessed with mobile devices. If a device is stolen or compromised, companies need ways to ensure that sensitive or confidential information isn't freely available to anyone. Mobility puts assets and data at greater risk than if they were only located within company walls and on company machines. Companies often use technologies that allow them to wipe data from devices remotely, or encrypt data so that if it is stolen, it cannot be used. You'll find a detailed discussion of mobile security issues in Chapter 8.

IBM's CIO Jeanette Horan believes that BYOD may cause as many problems as it solves. BYOD was not saving IBM any money and had actually created new challenges for the IT department because employees' devices are full of software that IBM doesn't control. IBM provides secure BlackBerrys for about 40,000 of its 400,000 workers while allowing 80,000 more employees to use their own smartphones or tablets to access IBM networks.

The IBM IT department found it had no grasp of which apps and services employees were using on their personal devices, and employees themselves were "blissfully unaware" of the security risks posed by popular apps. IBM decided to ban the use of such popular services as the Dropbox cloud-based cyberlocker, fearing that employees would put IBM-sensitive information in their personal Dropbox accounts, forward internal email to public Web mail services, or use their smartphones as mobile Wi-Fi hotspots. According to research by the International Data Company (IDC), 20 percent of corporate employees using personal cloud storage services admitted to using them to store enterprise data, so this is becoming a serious problem.

IBM will not allow an employee to access its corporate networks with his or her personal device unless it secures the device. The IT department configures the device so that its memory can be erased remotely if it is lost or stolen. The IT group also disables public file-transfer programs like Apple's iCloud; instead, employees use an IBM-hosted version called MyMobileHub. IBM even turns off Siri, the voice-activated personal assistant, on employees' iPhones because the spoken queries are uploaded to Apple servers.

Each employee's device is treated differently, depending on the model and the job responsibilities of the person using it. Some people are only allowed to receive IBM e-mail, calendars, and contacts on their portable devices, while others can access internal IBM applications and files (see Chapter 8). IBM equips the mobile devices of the latter category of employees with additional software, such as programs that encrypt information as it travels to and from corporate networks.

One company that has successfully implemented BYOD is Intel Corporation, the giant semiconductor company. About 70 percent of the 39,000 devices registered on its network are personal devices. Intel approached in BYOD in a positive manner, trying to find ways to make it work rather than to defeat it. Diane Bryant, then Intel's CIO, didn't want to be dependent on a single mobile vendor or device.

Intel hammered out a BYOD strategy and created an end-user service-level agreement that clarified that end users were voluntarily using BYOD rather than being mandated by Intel. The company developed different policies, rules, and access limits for each type of device-smartphone, tablet, or laptop—with multiple levels of controls in place. Intel maintains a list of approved devices. If a device does not meet its requirements, it is blocked from the network. Intel's BYOD program today offers 40 proprietary applications, including travel tools to help schedule a flight and conference room finders. The company has an internal "app store" and uses a variety of software and security tools, including mobile device management (MDM) software and mobile app management (MAM) software.

Intel's goal for BYOD is not to save money but to make employees happier and more productive. Employees like being able to use their own device and apps alongside specialized Intel apps. On average, Intel workers report that bringing their own devices saves them about 57 minutes per day, which amounts to 5 million hours annually company-wide.

Canadian Tire decided not to allow BYOD at all and issued new BlackBarry Q10 and Z10 smartphones to its 3,000 corporate employees. (Canadian Tire is one of Canada's largest companies, with an online e-commerce store and 1,200 retail outlets selling automotive, sports, leisure, home products, and apparel; petroleum outlets; and financial services.) The company felt that for its purposes, the bring-your-own-device model was not sufficiently secure. Canadian Tire's chief technology officer (CTO) Eugene Roman worries that an email could sent a virus into the company's core infrastructure. At present, Canadian Tire's management thinks BYOD is interesting but is not yet ready for the company's mainstream business applications.

In order to successfully deploy mobile devices, companies need to carefully examine their business processes and determine whether or not mobility makes sense for them. Not every firm will benefit from mobility to the same degree. Without a clear idea of how exactly mobile devices fit into the long term plans for the firm, companies will end up wasting their money on unnecessary devices and programs.

Sources: Dennis McCafferty, "Surprising Facts About Mobility and BYOD," Baseline, January 29, 2014; Beatrice Piquer-Durand, "BYOD and BYOA: Dangers and Complications," Techradar Pro, March 24, 2014; Tam Harbert, "Android Invades the Enterprise," Computerworld BYOD Consumerization of IT," November 2013; Forrester Consulting, "The Total Economic Impact of IBM Managed Mobility for BYOD," May 2013; Fred Donovan, "The Growing BYOD Problem," FierceMobileIT, February 13, 2013; Brian Bergstein, "IBM Faces the Perils of 'Bring Your Own Device'," MIT Technology Review, May 21, 2013; and Matt Hamblen, "Canadian Tire forgoes BYOD, Issues BlackBerries to Workers," Computerworld, May 20, 2013.

CASE STUDY QUESTIONS

5-12 What are the advantages and disadvantages of allowing employees to use their personal smartphones for work?

5-13 What management, organization, and technology factors should be addressed when deciding whether to allow employees to use their personal smartphones for work?

5-14 Compare the BYOD experiences of IBM and Intel. Why did BYOD at Intel work so well?

5-15 Allowing employees use their own smartphones for work will save the company money. Do you agree? Why or why not?

Chapter 5 References

Andersson, Henrik, James Kaplan, and Brent Smolinski. "Capturing Value from IT Infrastructure Innovation." McKinsey Quarterly (October 2012).

Babcock, Charles. "Cloud's Thorniest Question: Does It Pay Off?" Information Week (June 4, 2012).

Benlian , Alexander, Marios Koufaris and Thomas Hess. "Service Quality in Software-as-a-Service: Developing the SaaS-Qual Measure and Examining Its Role in Usage Continuance." Journal of Management Information Systems, 28, No. 3 (Winter 2012).

Carr, Nicholas. *The Big Switch.* New York: Norton (2008).

Clark, Don. "Intel Unveils Tiny Quark Chips for Wearable Devices." *Wall Street Journal* (September 10, 2013).

Choi, Jae, Derek L. Nazareth, and Hemant K. Jain. "Implementing Service-Oriented Architecture in Organizations." *Journal of Management Information Systems* 26, No. 4 (Spring 2010).

David, Julie Smith, David Schuff, and Robert St. Louis. "Managing Your IT Total Cost of Ownership." *Communications of the ACM* 45, No. 1 (January 2002).

EMarketer. "Smartphone Users Worldwide Will Total 1.75 Billion in 2014." (Jan 16, 2014).

Evangelista, Michelle. "The Total Impact of IBM Managed Mobility for BYOD." IBM (2013).

Fitzgerald, Brian. "The Transformation of Open Source Software." *MIS Quarterly* 30, No. 3 (September 2006).

Gartner, Inc. "Gartner Says Worldwide IT Spending on Pace to Reach $3.8 Trillion in 2014." (January 6, 2014).

Gartner, Inc. "Gartner Says Worldwide Traditional PC, Tablet, Ultramobile and Mobile Phone Shipments to Grow 4.2 Percent in 2014." (July 7, 2014).

Grossman, Lev. "Quantum Leap." *Time* (February 17, 2014).

Hagel III, John and John Seeley Brown. "Your Next IT Strategy." *Harvard Business Review* (October, 2001).

Hamilton, David. "Enterprise Cloud IT Spending to Grow 20% in 2014, Reaching $174.2B: IHS Research." The Whir.com (February 19, 2014).

Hamilton, David. "Smartphone Users Worldwide Will Total 1.75 Billion in 2014". TheWhir.com (February 19, 2014).

Hardy, Quentin. "The Era of Cloud Computing." *New York Times* (June 11, 2014).

"Internet Users." Internetlivestats.com (April 1, 2014).

Kanaracus, Chris. "Global IT Spending Outlook 'Better but Subpar' for 2014, Forrester Says." *CIO* (January 2, 2014).

Kauffman, Robert J. and Julianna Tsai. "The Unified Procurement Strategy for Enterprise Software: A Test of the 'Move to the Middle' Hypothesis." *Journal of Management Information Systems* 26, No. 2 (Fall 2009).

King, John. "Centralized vs. Decentralized Computing: Organizational Considerations and Management Options." *Computing Surveys* (October 1984).

Lyman, Peter and Hal R. Varian. "How Much Information 2003?" University of California at Berkeley School of Information Management and Systems (2003).

McAfee, Andrew. "What Every CEO Needs to Know about the Cloud." Harvard Business Review (November 2011).

McCafferty, Dennis. "Eight Interesting Facts About Java." *CIO Insight* (June 16, 2014).

Mell, Peter and Tim Grance. "The NIST Definition of Cloud Computing" Version 15. NIST (October 17, 2009).

Moore, Gordon. "Cramming More Components Onto Integrated Circuits," *Electronics* 38, Number 8 (April 19, 1965).

Mueller, Benjamin, Goetz Viering, Christine Legner, and Gerold Riempp. "Understanding the Economic Potential of Service-Oriented Architecture." *Journal of Management Information Systems* 26, No. 4 (Spring 2010).

Schuff, David and Robert St. Louis. "Centralization vs. Decentralization of Application Software." *Communications of the ACM* 44, No. 6 (June 2001).

Stango, Victor. "The Economics of Standards Wars." *Review of Network Economics* 3, Issue 1 (March 2004).

Susarla, Anjana, Anitesh Barua, and Andrew B. Whinston. "A Transaction Cost Perspective of the 'Software as a Service' Business Model. " *Journal of Management Information Systems* 26, No. 2 (Fall 2009).

Taft, Darryl K. "Application Development: Java Death Debunked: 10 Reasons Why It's Still Hot." eWeek (February 22, 2012).

Torode, Christine, Linda Tucci and Karen Goulart. "Managing the Next-Generation Data Center." *Modern Infrastructure CIO Edition* (January 2013).

Weill, Peter, and Marianne Broadbent. *Leveraging the New Infrastructure.* Cambridge, MA: Harvard Business School Press (1998).

Weitzel, Tim. *Economics of Standards in Information Networks.* Springer (2004).

Foundations of Business Intelligence: Databases and Information Management

CHAPTER 6

LEARNING OBJECTIVES

After reading this chapter, you will be able to answer the following questions:

1. What are the problems of managing data resources in a traditional file environment?

2. What are the major capabilities of database management systems (DBMS) and why is a relational DBMS so powerful?

3. What are the principal tools and technologies for accessing information from databases to improve business performance and decision making?

4. Why are information policy, data administration, and data quality assurance essential for managing the firm's data resources?

CHAPTER CASES

Better Data Management Helps the Toronto Globe and Mail Reach Its Customers

Driving ARI Fleet Management with Real-Time Analytics

The Gym Database

Does Big Data Bring Big Rewards?

BETTER DATA MANAGEMENT HELPS THE TORONTO GLOBE AND MAIL REACH ITS CUSTOMERS

Have you ever received a new subscription offer from a newspaper or magazine to which you already subscribed? In addition to being an annoyance, sending a superfluous offer to customers increases marketing costs. So why is this happening? The answer is probably because of poor data management. The newspaper most likely was unable to match its existing subscriber list, which it maintained in one place, with another file containing its list of marketing prospects.

The Globe and Mail, based in Toronto, Canada, was one of those publications that had these problems. In print for 167 years, it is Canada's largest newspaper, with a cumulative six-day readership of nearly 3.3 million. The paper has a very ambitious marketing program, viewing every Canadian household that does not already subscribe as a prospect. But it has had trouble housing and managing the data on these prospects.

Running a major newspaper requires managing huge amounts of data, including circulation data, advertising revenue data, marketing prospect and "do not contact" data, and data on logistics and deliveries. Add to that the data required to run any business, including finance and human resources data.

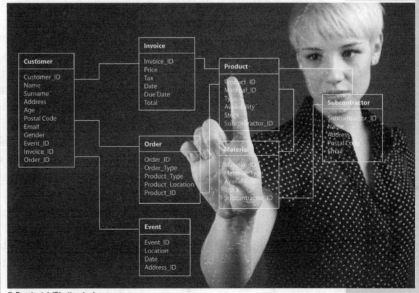

© Semisatch/Shutterstock

227

For many years The Globe and Mail housed much of its data in a mainframe system where the data were not easy to access and analyze. If users needed any information, they had to extract the data from the mainframe and bring it to one of a number of local databases for analysis, including those maintained in Microsoft Access, Foxbase Pro, and Microsoft Excel. This practice created numerous pockets of data maintained in isolated databases for specific purposes but no central repository where the most up-to-date data could be accessed from a single place. With data scattered in so many different systems throughout the company, it was very difficult to cross-reference subscribers with prospects when developing the mailing list for a marketing campaign. There were also security issues: The Globe and Mail collects and stores customer payment information, and housing this confidential data in multiple places makes it more difficult to ensure that proper data security controls are in place.

In 2002, the newspaper began addressing these problems by implementing a SAP enterprise system with a SAP NetWeaver BW data warehouse that would contain all of the company's data from its various data sources in a single location where the data could be easily accessed and analyzed by business users.

The first data to populate the data warehouse was advertising sales data, which is a major source of revenue. In 2007, The Globe and Mail added circulation data to the warehouse, including delivery data details such as how much time is left on a customer's subscription and data on marketing prospects from third-party sources. Data on prospects were added to the warehouse as well.

With all these data in a single place, the paper can easily match prospect and customer data to avoid targeting existing customers with subscription promotions. It can also match the data to "do not contact" and delivery area data to determine if a newspaper can be delivered or whether a customer should be targeted with a promotion for a digital subscription.

Despite the obvious benefits of the new data warehouse, not all of The Globe and Mail's business users immediately came on board. People who were used to extracting data from the mainframe system and manipulating it in their own local databases or file continued to do the same thing after the data warehouse went live. They did not understand the concept of a data warehouse or the need to work towards enterprise-wide data management. The Globe and Mail's management decided to tackle this new problem by educating its users, especially its marketing professionals, with the value of having all the organization's data in a data warehouse and the tools available for accessing and analyzing these data.

The Globe and Mail's new data analysis capabilities produced savings from efficiencies and streamlined processes that paid for the investment in one year. Marketing campaigns that previously took two weeks to complete now only take one day. The newspaper can determine its saturation rates in a given area to guide its marketing plans. And there are fewer complaints from subscribers and potential subscribers about being contacted unnecessarily.

To capitalize further on data management and analytics, The Globe and Mail turned to the cloud. A key business goal for the company was to beef up

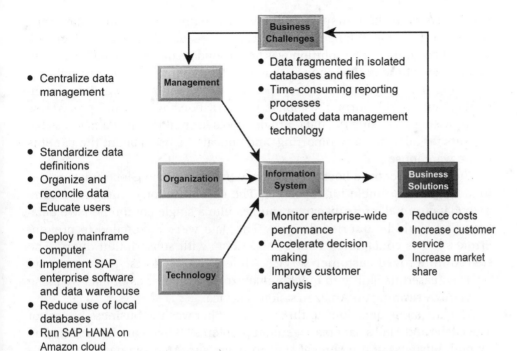

- Centralize data management

- Standardize data definitions
- Organize and reconcile data
- Educate users

- Deploy mainframe computer
- Implement SAP enterprise software and data warehouse
- Reduce use of local databases
- Run SAP HANA on Amazon cloud

Business Challenges

Management
- Data fragmented in isolated databases and files
- Time-consuming reporting processes
- Outdated data management technology

Organization

Information System
- Monitor enterprise-wide performance
- Accelerate decision making
- Improve customer analysis

Technology

Business Solutions
- Reduce costs
- Increase customer service
- Increase market share

online content and increase the paper's digital subscriber base. The Globe and Mail devoted more resources to digital online content, with different subscription rates for online-only customers and print customers. To aggressively court digital subscribers, The Globe and Mail had to mine its clickstream data logging user actions on the Web to target potential digital subscribers based not only on their specific interests but also their interests on a particular day. The volume of data was too large to be handled by the company's conventional Oracle database. The solution was to use SAP HANA ONE in-memory computing software running on the Amazon Web Services cloud computing platform, which accelerates data analysis and processing by storing data in the computer's main memory (RAM) rather than on external storage devices. This cloud solution lets The Globe and Mail pay for only what capabilities it uses on an hourly basis.

Sources: www.theglobeandmail.com, accessed March 1, 2014; "The Globe and Mail Uses SAP HANA in the Cloud to row Its Digital Audience," SAP Insider Profiles, April 1, 2013; and David Hannon, "Spread the News," SAP Insider Profiles, October-December 2012.

The experience of The Globe and Mail illustrates the importance of data management. Business performance depends on what a firm can or cannot do with its data. The Globe and Mail was a large and thriving business, but both operational efficiency and management decision making were hampered by fragmented data stored in multiple systems that were difficult to access. How businesses store, organize, and manage their data has an enormous impact on organizational effectiveness.

The chapter-opening diagram calls attention to important points raised by this case and this chapter. The Globe and Mail's business users were maintaining their own local databases because the company's data were so difficult to access in the newspaper's traditional mainframe system. Marketing campaigns took much longer than necessary because the required data took so long to assemble. The solution was to consolidate organizational data in an enterprise-wide data warehouse that provided a single source of data for reporting and analysis. The newspaper had to reorganize its data into a standard company-wide format, establish rules, responsibilities, and procedures for accessing and using the data, provide tools for making the data accessible to users for querying and reporting, and educate its users about the benefits of the warehouse.

The data warehouse boosted efficiency by making the Globe's data easier to locate and assemble for reporting. The data warehouse integrated company data from all of its disparate sources into a single comprehensive database that could be queried directly. The data were reconciled to prevent errors such as contacting existing subscribers with subscription offers. The solution improved customer service while reducing costs. The Globe and Mail increased its ability to quickly analyze vast quantities of data by using SAP HANA running on Amazon's cloud service.

Here are some questions to think about: What was the business impact of The Globe and Mail's data management problems? What work had to be done by both business and technical staff to make sure that the data warehouse produced the results envisioned by management?

6.1 WHAT ARE THE PROBLEMS OF MANAGING DATA RESOURCES IN A TRADITIONAL FILE ENVIRONMENT?

An effective information system provides users with accurate, timely, and relevant information. Accurate information is free of errors. Information is timely when it is available to decision makers when it is needed. Information is relevant when it is useful and appropriate for the types of work and decisions that require it.

You might be surprised to learn that many businesses don't have timely, accurate, or relevant information because the data in their information systems have been poorly organized and maintained. That's why data management is so essential. To understand the problem, let's look at how information systems arrange data in computer files and traditional methods of file management.

FILE ORGANIZATION TERMS AND CONCEPTS

A computer system organizes data in a hierarchy that starts with bits and bytes and progresses to fields, records, files, and databases (see Figure 6.1). A **bit** represents the smallest unit of data a computer can handle. A group of bits, called a **byte**, represents a single character, which can be a letter, a number, or another symbol. A grouping of characters into a word, a group of words, or a complete number (such as a person's name or age) is called a

FIGURE 6.1   THE DATA HIERARCHY

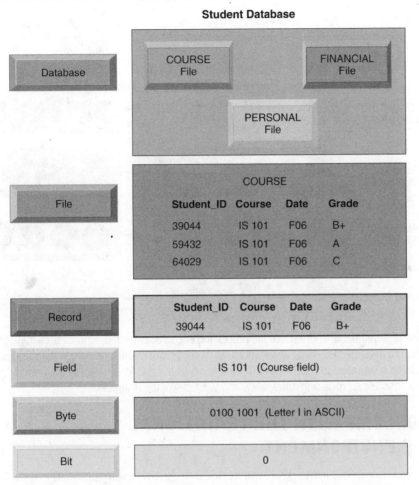

A computer system organizes data in a hierarchy that starts with the bit, which represents either a 0 or a 1. Bits can be grouped to form a byte to represent one character, number, or symbol. Bytes can be grouped to form a field, and related fields can be grouped to form a record. Related records can be collected to form a file, and related files can be organized into a database.

field. A group of related fields, such as the student's name, the course taken, the date, and the grade, comprises a **record**; a group of records of the same type is called a **file**.

For example, the records in Figure 6.1 could constitute a student course file. A group of related files makes up a database. The student course file illustrated in Figure 6.1 could be grouped with files on students' personal histories and financial backgrounds to create a student database.

A record describes an entity. An **entity** is a person, place, thing, or event on which we store and maintain information. Each characteristic or quality describing a particular entity is called an **attribute**. For example, Student_ID, Course, Date, and Grade are attributes of the entity COURSE. The specific values that these attributes can have are found in the fields of the record describing the entity COURSE.

FIGURE 6.2 TRADITIONAL FILE PROCESSING

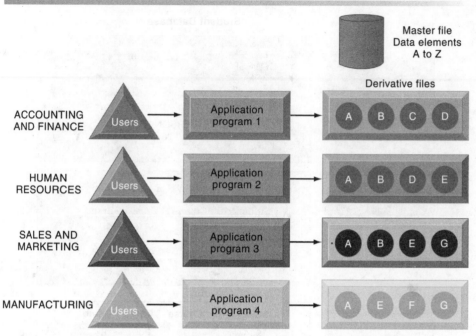

The use of a traditional approach to file processing encourages each functional area in a corporation to develop specialized applications. Each application requires a unique data file that is likely to be a subset of the master file. These subsets of the master file lead to data redundancy and inconsistency, processing inflexibility, and wasted storage resources.

PROBLEMS WITH THE TRADITIONAL FILE ENVIRONMENT

In most organizations, systems tended to grow independently without a company-wide plan. Accounting, finance, manufacturing, human resources, and sales and marketing all developed their own systems and data files. Figure 6.2 illustrates the traditional approach to information processing.

Each application, of course, required its own files and its own computer program to operate. For example, the human resources functional area might have a personnel master file, a payroll file, a medical insurance file, a pension file, a mailing list file, and so forth until tens, perhaps hundreds, of files and programs existed. In the company as a whole, this process led to multiple master files created, maintained, and operated by separate divisions or departments. As this process goes on for 5 or 10 years, the organization is saddled with hundreds of programs and applications that are very difficult to maintain and manage. The resulting problems are data redundancy and inconsistency, program-data dependence, inflexibility, poor data security, and an inability to share data among applications.

Data Redundancy and Inconsistency

Data redundancy is the presence of duplicate data in multiple data files so that the same data are stored in more than one place or location. Data redundancy occurs when different groups in an organization independently collect the same piece of data and store it independently of each other. Data redundancy wastes storage resources and also leads to **data inconsistency**, where the same attribute may have different values. For example, in instances of the entity COURSE illustrated in Figure 6.1, the Date may be updated in some systems but not in others. The same attribute, Student_ID, may also have different names in different systems throughout the organization. Some systems might use Student_ID and others might use ID, for example.

Additional confusion might result from using different coding systems to represent values for an attribute. For instance, the sales, inventory, and manufacturing systems of a clothing retailer might use different codes to represent clothing size. One system might represent clothing size as "extra large," whereas another might use the code "XL" for the same purpose. The resulting confusion would make it difficult for companies to create customer relationship management, supply chain management, or enterprise systems that integrate data from different sources.

Program-Data Dependence

Program-data dependence refers to the coupling of data stored in files and the specific programs required to update and maintain those files such that changes in programs require changes to the data. Every traditional computer program has to describe the location and nature of the data with which it works. In a traditional file environment, any change in a software program could require a change in the data accessed by that program. One program might be modified from a five-digit to a nine-digit zip code. If the original data file were changed from five-digit to nine-digit zip codes, then other programs that required the five-digit zip code would no longer work properly. Such changes could cost millions of dollars to implement properly.

Lack of Flexibility

A traditional file system can deliver routine scheduled reports after extensive programming efforts, but it cannot deliver ad hoc reports or respond to unanticipated information requirements in a timely fashion. The information required by ad hoc requests is somewhere in the system but may be too expensive to retrieve. Several programmers might have to work for weeks to put together the required data items in a new file.

Poor Security

Because there is little control or management of data, access to and dissemination of information may be out of control. Management may have no way of knowing who is accessing or even making changes to the organization's data.

Lack of Data Sharing and Availability

Because pieces of information in different files and different parts of the organization cannot be related to one another, it is virtually impossible for information to be shared or accessed in a timely manner. Information cannot flow freely across different functional areas or different parts of the organization. If users find different values of the same piece of information in two different systems, they may not want to use these systems because they cannot trust the accuracy of their data.

6.2   WHAT ARE THE MAJOR CAPABILITIES OF DATABASE MANAGEMENT SYSTEMS (DBMS) AND WHY IS A RELATIONAL DBMS SO POWERFUL?

Database technology cuts through many of the problems of traditional file organization. A more rigorous definition of a **database** is a collection of data organized to serve many applications efficiently by centralizing the data and controlling redundant data. Rather than storing data in separate files for each application, data appears to users as being stored in only one location. A single database services multiple applications. For example, instead of a corporation storing employee data in separate information systems and separate files for personnel, payroll, and benefits, the corporation could create a single common human resources database.

DATABASE MANAGEMENT SYSTEMS

A **database management system (DBMS)** is software that permits an organization to centralize data, manage them efficiently, and provide access to the stored data by application programs. The DBMS acts as an interface between application programs and the physical data files. When the application program calls for a data item, such as gross pay, the DBMS finds this item in the database and presents it to the application program. Using traditional data files, the programmer would have to specify the size and format of each data element used in the program and then tell the computer where they were located.

The DBMS relieves the programmer or end user from the task of understanding where and how the data are actually stored by separating the logical and physical views of the data. The *logical view* presents data as they would be perceived by end users or business specialists, whereas the *physical view* shows how data are actually organized and structured on physical storage media.

The database management software makes the physical database available for different logical views required by users. For example, for the human resources database illustrated in Figure 6.3, a benefits specialist might require a view consisting of the employee's name, social security number, and health insurance coverage. A payroll department member might need data such as the employee's name, social security number, gross pay, and net pay. The data for all these views are stored in a single database, where they can be more easily managed by the organization.

How a DBMS Solves the Problems of the Traditional File Environment

A DBMS reduces data redundancy and inconsistency by minimizing isolated files in which the same data are repeated. The DBMS may not enable the

FIGURE 6.3   HUMAN RESOURCES DATABASE WITH MULTIPLE VIEWS

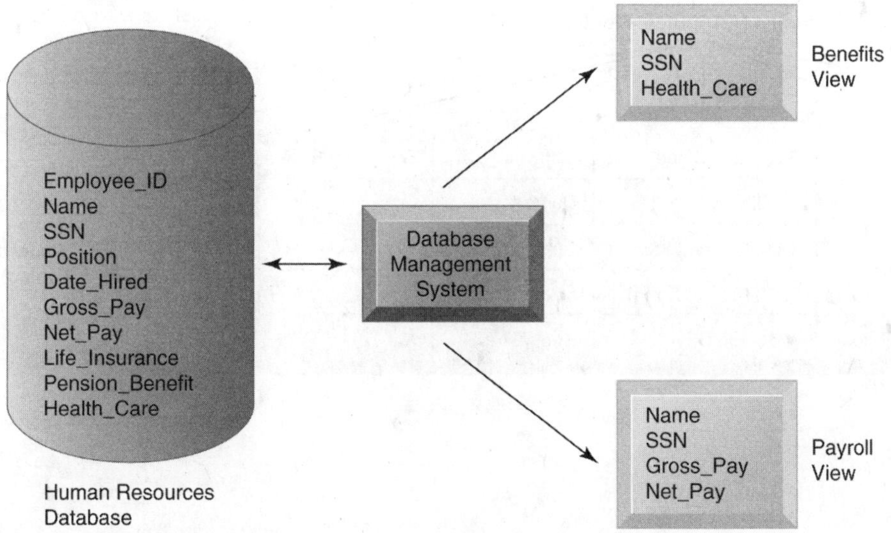

A single human resources database provides many different views of data, depending on the information requirements of the user. Illustrated here are two possible views, one of interest to a benefits specialist and one of interest to a member of the company's payroll department.

organization to eliminate data redundancy entirely, but it can help control redundancy. Even if the organization maintains some redundant data, using a DBMS eliminates data inconsistency because the DBMS can help the organization ensure that every occurrence of redundant data has the same values. The DBMS uncouples programs and data, enabling data to stand on their own. The description of the data used by the program does not have to be specified in detail each time a different program is written. Access and availability of information will be increased and program development and maintenance costs reduced because users and programmers can perform ad hoc queries of the database for many simple applications without having to write complicated programs. The DBMS enables the organization to centrally manage data, their use, and security. Data-sharing throughout the organization is easier because the data are presented to users as being in a single location rather than fragmented in many different systems and files.

Relational DBMS

Contemporary DBMS use different database models to keep track of entities, attributes, and relationships. The most popular type of DBMS today for PCs as well as for larger computers and mainframes is the **relational DBMS**. Relational databases represent data as two-dimensional tables (called relations). Tables may be referred to as files. Each table contains data on an entity and its attributes. Microsoft Access is a relational DBMS for desktop systems, whereas DB2, Oracle Database, and Microsoft SQL Server are relational DBMS for large mainframes and midrange computers. MySQL is a popular open source DBMS.

Let's look at how a relational database organizes data about suppliers and parts (see Figure 6.4). The database has a separate table for the entity

FIGURE 6.4   RELATIONAL DATABASE TABLES

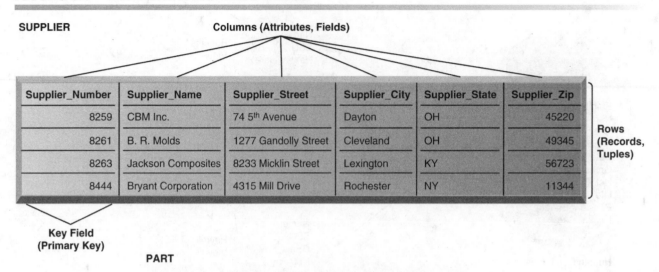

A relational database organizes data in the form of two-dimensional tables. Illustrated here are tables for the entities SUPPLIER and PART showing how they represent each entity and its attributes. Supplier_Number is a primary key for the SUPPLIER table and a foreign key for the PART table.

SUPPLIER and a table for the entity PART. Each table consists of a grid of columns and rows of data. Each individual element of data for each entity is stored as a separate field, and each field represents an attribute for that entity. Fields in a relational database are also called columns. For the entity SUPPLIER, the supplier identification number, name, street, city, state, and zip code are stored as separate fields within the SUPPLIER table and each field represents an attribute for the entity SUPPLIER.

The actual information about a single supplier that resides in a table is called a row. Rows are commonly referred to as records, or in very technical terms, as **tuples**. Data for the entity PART have their own separate table.

The field for Supplier_Number in the SUPPLIER table uniquely identifies each record so that the record can be retrieved, updated, or sorted. It is called a **key field**. Each table in a relational database has one field that is designated as its **primary key**. This key field is the unique identifier for all the information in any row of the table and this primary key cannot be duplicated. Supplier_Number is the primary key for the SUPPLIER table and Part_Number is the primary key for the PART table. Note that Supplier_Number appears in both the SUPPLIER and PART tables. In the SUPPLIER table, Supplier_Number is the primary key. When the field Supplier_Number appears in the PART table, it is called a **foreign key** and is essentially a lookup field to look up data about the supplier of a specific part.

Operations of a Relational DBMS

Relational database tables can be combined easily to deliver data required by users, provided that any two tables share a common data element. Suppose we wanted to find in this database the names of suppliers who could provide us with part number 137 or part number 150. We would need information from two tables: the SUPPLIER table and the PART table. Note that these two files have a shared data element: Supplier_Number.

In a relational database, three basic operations, as shown in Figure 6.5, are used to develop useful sets of data: select, join, and project. The *select* operation creates a subset consisting of all records in the file that meet stated criteria. Select creates, in other words, a subset of rows that meet certain criteria. In our example, we want to select records (rows) from the PART table where the Part_Number equals 137 or 150. The *join* operation combines relational tables to provide the user with more information than is available in individual tables. In our example, we want to join the now-shortened PART table (only parts 137 or 150 will be presented) and the SUPPLIER table into a single new table.

The *project* operation creates a subset consisting of columns in a table, permitting the user to create new tables that contain only the information required. In our example, we want to extract from the new table only the following columns: Part_Number, Part_Name, Supplier_Number, and Supplier_Name.

Non-Relational Databases and Databases in the Cloud

For over 30 years, relational database technology has been the gold standard. Cloud computing, unprecedented data volumes, massive workloads for Web services, and the need to store new types of data require database alternatives to the traditional relational model of organizing data in the form of tables, columns, and rows. Companies are turning to "*NoSQL*" non-relational database technologies for this purpose. **Non-relational database management systems** use a more flexible data model and are designed for managing large data sets across many distributed machines and for easily scaling up or down. They are useful for accelerating simple queries against large volumes of structured and unstructured data, including Web, social media, graphics, and other forms of data that are difficult to analyze with traditional SQL-based tools.

There are several different kinds of NoSQL databases, each with its own technical features and behavior. Oracle NoSQL Database is one example, as is Amazon's SimpleDB, one of the Amazon Web Services that run in the

FIGURE 6.5 THE THREE BASIC OPERATIONS OF A RELATIONAL DBMS

PART

Part_Number	Part_Name	Unit_Price	Supplier_Number
137	Door latch	22.00	8259
145	Side mirror	12.00	8444
150	Door molding	6.00	8263
152	Door lock	31.00	8259
155	Compressor	54.00	8261
178	Door handle	10.00	8259

Select Part_Number = 137 or 150

SUPPLIER

Supplier_Number	Supplier_Name	Supplier_Street	Supplier_City	Supplier_State	Supplier_Zip
8259	CBM Inc.	74 5th Avenue	Dayton	OH	45220
8261	B. R. Molds	1277 Gandolly Street	Cleveland	OH	49345
8263	Jackson Components	8233 Micklin Street	Lexington	KY	56723
8444	Bryant Corporation	4315 Mill Drive	Rochester	NY	11344

Join by Supplier_Number

Part_Number	Part_Name	Supplier_Number	Supplier_Name
137	Door latch	8259	CBM Inc.
150	Door molding	8263	Jackson Components

Project selected columns

The select, join, and project operations enable data from two different tables to be combined and only selected attributes to be displayed.

cloud. SimpleDB provides a simple Web services interface to create and store multiple data sets, query data easily, and return the results. There is no need to pre-define a formal database structure or change that definition if new data are added later. For example, MetLife decided to employ the MongoDB open source NoSQL database to quickly integrate disparate data and deliver a consolidated view of the customer. MetLife's database brings together data from more than 70 separate administrative systems, claims systems and other data sources, including semi-structured and unstructured data, such as images of health records and death certificates. The NoSQLdatabase is able to ingest structured, semi-structured and unstructured information without requiring tedious, expensive and time-consuming database-mapping (Henschen, 2013).

Amazon and other cloud computing vendors provide relational database services as well. Amazon Relational Database Service (Amazon RDS) offers MySQL, SQL Server, or Oracle Database as database engines. Pricing is based on usage. Oracle has its own database cloud service using its relational Oracle Database and Microsoft SQL Azure Database is a cloud-based relational database service based on Microsoft's SQL Server DBMS. Cloud-based data management services have special appeal for Web-focused start-ups or small to medium-sized businesses seeking database capabilities at a lower price than in-house database products.

In addition to public cloud-based data management services, companies now have the option of using databases in private clouds. For example, Sabre Holdings, the world's largest software as a service (SaaS) provider for the aviation industry, has a private database cloud that supports more than 100 projects and 700 users. A consolidated database spanning a pool of standardized servers running Oracle Database provides database services for multiple applications.

CAPABILITIES OF DATABASE MANAGEMENT SYSTEMS

A DBMS includes capabilities and tools for organizing, managing, and accessing the data in the database. The most important are its data definition language, data dictionary, and data manipulation language.

DBMS have a **data definition** capability to specify the structure of the content of the database. It would be used to create database tables and to define the characteristics of the fields in each table. This information about the database would be documented in a data dictionary. A **data dictionary** is an automated or manual file that stores definitions of data elements and their characteristics.

Microsoft Access has a rudimentary data dictionary capability that displays information about the name, description, size, type, format, and other properties of each field in a table (see Figure 6.6). Data dictionaries for large corporate databases may capture additional information, such as usage, ownership (who in the organization is responsible for maintaining the data), authorization, security, and the individuals, business functions, programs, and reports that use each data element.

FIGURE 6.6 ACCESS DATA DICTIONARY FEATURES

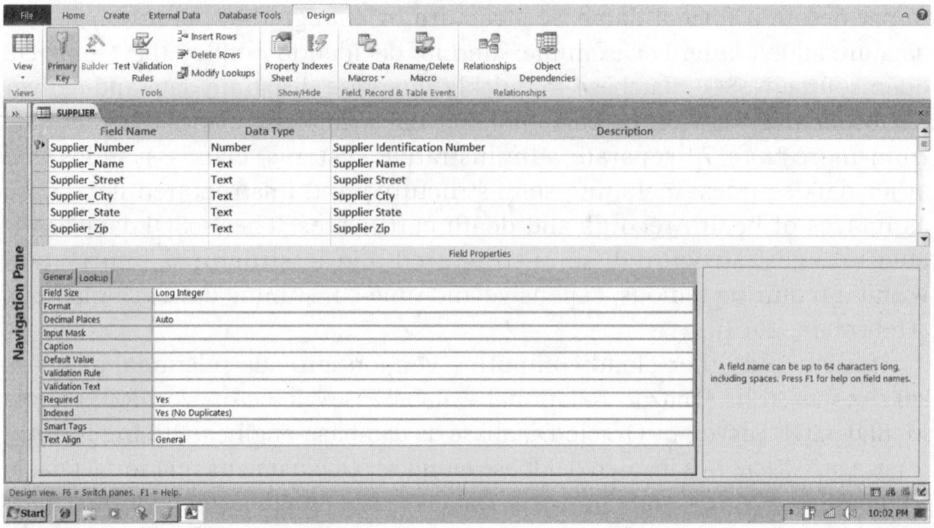

Microsoft Access has a rudimentary data dictionary capability that displays information about the size, format, and other characteristics of each field in a database. Displayed here is the information maintained in the SUPPLIER table. The small key icon to the left of Supplier_Number indicates that it is a key field.

Querying and Reporting

DBMS includes tools for accessing and manipulating information in databases. Most DBMS have a specialized language called a **data manipulation language** that is used to add, change, delete, and retrieve the data in the database. This language contains commands that permit end users and programming specialists to extract data from the database to satisfy information requests and develop applications. The most prominent data manipulation language today is **Structured Query Language**, or **SQL**. Figure 6.7 illustrates the SQL query that would produce the new resultant table in Figure 6.5. You can find out more about how to perform SQL queries in our Learning Tracks for this chapter.

Users of DBMS for large and midrange computers, such as DB2, Oracle, or SQL Server, would employ SQL to retrieve information they needed from the database. Microsoft Access also uses SQL, but it provides its own set of user-friendly tools for querying databases and for organizing data from databases into more polished reports.

FIGURE 6.7 EXAMPLE OF AN SQL QUERY

```
SELECT PART.Part_Number, PART.Part_Name, SUPPLIER.Supplier_Number,
SUPPLIER.Supplier_Name
FROM PART, SUPPLIER
WHERE PART.Supplier_Number = SUPPLIER.Supplier_Number AND
Part_Number = 137 OR Part_Number = 150;
```

Illustrated here are the SQL statements for a query to select suppliers for parts 137 or 150. They produce a list with the same results as Figure 6.5.

FIGURE 6.8   AN ACCESS QUERY

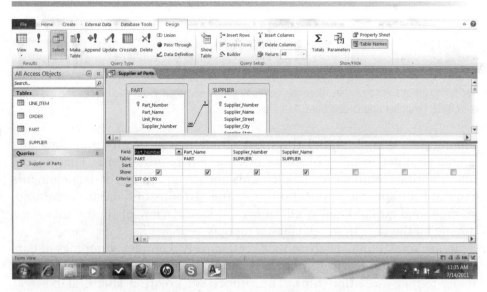

Illustrated here is how the query in Figure 6.7 would be constructed using Microsoft Access query-building tools. It shows the tables, fields, and selection criteria used for the query.

In Microsoft Access, you will find features that enable users to create queries by identifying the tables and fields they want and the results, and then selecting the rows from the database that meet particular criteria. These actions in turn are translated into SQL commands. Figure 6.8 illustrates how the same query as the SQL query to select parts and suppliers would be constructed using the Microsoft query-building tools.

Microsoft Access and other DBMS include capabilities for report generation so that the data of interest can be displayed in a more structured and polished format than would be possible just by querying. Crystal Reports is a popular report generator for large corporate DBMS, although it can also be used with Access. Access also has capabilities for developing desktop system applications. These include tools for creating data entry screens, reports, and developing the logic for processing transactions.

DESIGNING DATABASES

To create a database, you must understand the relationships among the data, the type of data that will be maintained in the database, how the data will be used, and how the organization will need to change to manage data from a company-wide perspective. The database requires both a conceptual design and a physical design. The conceptual, or logical, design of a database is an abstract model of the database from a business perspective, whereas the physical design shows how the database is actually arranged on direct-access storage devices.

Normalization and Entity-Relationship Diagrams

The conceptual database design describes how the data elements in the database are to be grouped. The design process identifies relationships

FIGURE 6.9   AN UNNORMALIZED RELATION FOR ORDER

ORDER (Before Normalization)

An unnormalized relation contains repeating groups. For example, there can be many parts and suppliers for each order. There is only a one-to-one correspondence between Order_Number and Order_Date.

among data elements and the most efficient way of grouping data elements together to meet business information requirements. The process also identifies redundant data elements and the groupings of data elements required for specific application programs. Groups of data are organized, refined, and streamlined until an overall logical view of the relationships among all the data in the database emerges.

To use a relational database model effectively, complex groupings of data must be streamlined to minimize redundant data elements and awkward many-to-many relationships. The process of creating small, stable, yet flexible and adaptive data structures from complex groups of data is called **normalization**. Figures 6.9 and 6.10 illustrate this process.

In the particular business modeled here, an order can have more than one part but each part is provided by only one supplier. If we build a relation called ORDER with all the fields included here, we would have to repeat the name and address of the supplier for every part on the order, even though the order is for parts from a single supplier. This relationship contains what are called repeating data groups because there can be many parts on a single order to a given supplier. A more efficient way to arrange the data is to break down ORDER into smaller relations, each of which describes a single entity. If we go step by step and normalize the relation ORDER, we emerge with the relations illustrated in Figure 6.10. You can find out more about normalization, entity-relationship diagramming, and database design in the Learning Tracks for this chapter.

FIGURE 6.10   NORMALIZED TABLES CREATED FROM ORDER

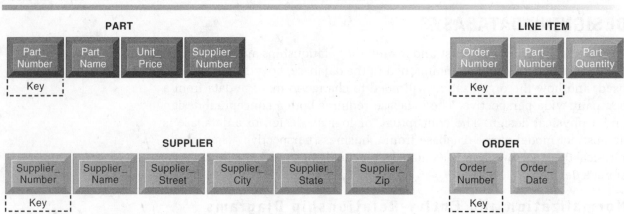

After normalization, the original relation ORDER has been broken down into four smaller relations. The relation ORDER is left with only two attributes and the relation LINE_ITEM has a combined, or concatenated, key consisting of Order_Number and Part_Number.

FIGURE 6.11 AN ENTITY-RELATIONSHIP DIAGRAM

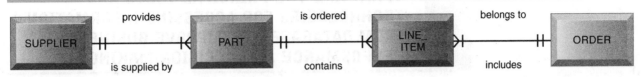

This diagram shows the relationships between the entities SUPPLIER, PART, LINE_ITEM, and ORDER that might be used to model the database in Figure 6.10.

Relational database systems try to enforce **referential integrity** rules to ensure that relationships between coupled tables remain consistent. When one table has a foreign key that points to another table, you may not add a record to the table with the foreign key unless there is a corresponding record in the linked table. In the database we examined earlier in this chapter, the foreign key Supplier_Number links the PART table to the SUPPLIER table. We may not add a new record to the PART table for a part with Supplier_Number 8266 unless there is a corresponding record in the SUPPLIER table for Supplier_ Number 8266. We must also delete the corresponding record in the PART table if we delete the record in the SUPPLIER table for Supplier_Number 8266. In other words, we shouldn't have parts from nonexistent suppliers!

Database designers document their data model with an **entity-relation-ship diagram**, illustrated in Figure 6.11. This diagram illustrates the relationship between the entities SUPPLIER, PART, LINE_ITEM, and ORDER. The boxes represent entities. The lines connecting the boxes represent relationships. A line connecting two entities that ends in two short marks designates a one-to-one relationship. A line connecting two entities that ends with a crow's foot topped by a short mark indicates a one-to-many relationship. Figure 6.11 shows that one ORDER can contain many LINE_ITEMs. (A PART can be ordered many times and appear many times as a line item in a single order.) Each PART can have only one SUPPLIER, but many PARTs can be provided by the same SUPPLIER.

It can't be emphasized enough: If the business doesn't get its data model right, the system won't be able to serve the business well. The company's systems will not be as effective as they could be because they'll have to work with data that may be inaccurate, incomplete, or difficult to retrieve. Understanding the organization's data and how they should be represented in a database is perhaps the most important lesson you can learn from this course.

For example, Famous Footwear, a shoe store chain with more than 800 locations in 49 states, could not achieve its goal of having "the right style of shoe in the right store for sale at the right price" because its database was not properly designed for rapidly adjusting store inventory. The company had an Oracle relational database running on a midrange computer, but the database was designed primarily for producing standard reports for management rather than for reacting to marketplace changes. Management could not obtain precise data on specific items in inventory in each of its stores. The company had to work around this problem by building a new database where the sales and inventory data could be better organized for analysis and inventory management.

6.3   WHAT ARE THE PRINCIPAL TOOLS AND TECHNOLOGIES FOR ACCESSING INFORMATION FROM DATABASES TO IMPROVE BUSINESS PERFORMANCE AND DECISION MAKING?

Businesses use their databases to keep track of basic transactions, such as paying suppliers, processing orders, keeping track of customers, and paying employees. But they also need databases to provide information that will help the company run the business more efficiently, and help managers and employees make better decisions. If a company wants to know which product is the most popular or who is its most profitable customer, the answer lies in the data.

THE CHALLENGE OF BIG DATA

Most data collected by organizations used to be transaction data that could easily fit into rows and columns of relational database management systems. We are now witnessing an explosion of data from Web traffic, e-mail messages, and social media content (tweets, status messages), as well as machine-generated data from sensors (used in smart meters, manufacturing sensors, and electrical meters) or from electronic trading systems. These data may be unstructured or semi-structured and thus not suitable for relational database products that organize data in the form of columns and rows. We now use the term **big data** to describe these datasets with volumes so huge that they are beyond the ability of typical DBMS to capture, store, and analyze.

Big data doesn't refer to any specific quantity, but usually refers to data in the petabyte and exabyte range—in other words, billions to trillions of records, all from different sources. Big data are produced in much larger quantities and much more rapidly than traditional data. For example, a single jet engine is capable of generating 10 terabytes of data in just 30 minutes, and there are more than 25,000 airline flights each day. Even though "tweets" are limited to 140 characters each, Twitter generates over 8 terabytes of data daily. According to the International Data Center (IDC) technology research firm, data are more than doubling every two years, so the amount of data available to organizations is skyrocketing.

Businesses are interested in big data because they can reveal more patterns and interesting anomalies than smaller data sets, with the potential to provide new insights into customer behavior, weather patterns, financial market activity, or other phenomena. However, to derive business value from these data, organizations need new technologies and tools capable of managing and analyzing non-traditional data along with their traditional enterprise data.

BUSINESS INTELLIGENCE INFRASTRUCTURE

Suppose you wanted concise, reliable information about current operations, trends, and changes across the entire company. If you worked in a large company, the data you need might have to be pieced together from separate systems, such as sales, manufacturing, and accounting, and even from external sources, such as demographic or competitor data. Increasingly, you might need to use big data. A contemporary infrastructure for business intelligence has an array of tools for obtaining useful information from all the different types of data used by businesses today, including semi-structured and unstructured big data in vast quantities. These capabilities include data warehouses and data marts, Hadoop, in-memory computing, and analytical platforms. Some of these capabilities are available as cloud services.

Data Warehouses and Data Marts

The traditional tool for analyzing corporate data for the past two decades has been the data warehouse. A **data warehouse** is a database that stores current and historical data of potential interest to decision makers throughout the company. The data originate in many core operational transaction systems, such as systems for sales, customer accounts, and manufacturing, and may include data from Web site transactions. The data warehouse extracts current and historical data from multiple operational systems inside the organization. These data are combined with data from external sources and transformed by correcting inaccurate and incomplete data and restructuring the data for management reporting and analysis before being loaded into the data warehouse.

The data warehouse makes the data available for anyone to access as needed, but it cannot be altered. A data warehouse system also provides a range of ad hoc and standardized query tools, analytical tools, and graphical reporting facilities .

Companies often build enterprise-wide data warehouses, where a central data warehouse serves the entire organization, or they create smaller, decentralized warehouses called data marts. A **data mart** is a subset of a data warehouse in which a summarized or highly focused portion of the organization's data is placed in a separate database for a specific population of users. For example, a company might develop marketing and sales data marts to deal with customer information. Bookseller Barnes & Noble used to maintain a series of data marts—one for point-of-sale data in retail stores, another for college bookstore sales, and a third for online sales.

Hadoop

Relational DBMS and data warehouse products are not well-suited for organizing and analyzing big data or data that do not easily fit into columns and rows used in their data models. For handling unstructured and semi-structured data in vast quantities, as well as structured data, organizations are using **Hadoop**. Hadoop is an open source software framework managed by the Apache Software Foundation that enables distributed parallel processing of huge amounts of data across inexpensive computers. It breaks a big data problem down into sub-problems, distributes them among up to thousands of inexpensive computer processing nodes, and then combines the result into a smaller data set that is easier to analyze. You've probably used Hadoop to find the best airfare on the Internet, get directions to a restaurant, do a search on Google, or connect with a friend on Facebook.

Hadoop consists of several key services: the Hadoop Distributed File System (HDFS) for data storage and MapReduce for high-performance parallel data processing. HDFS links together the file systems on the numerous nodes in a Hadoop cluster to turn them into one big file system. Hadoop's MapReduce was inspired by Google's MapReduce system for breaking down processing of huge datasets and assigning work to the various nodes in a cluster. HBase, Hadoop's non-relational database, provides rapid access to the data stored on HDFS and a transactional platform for running high-scale real-time applications.

Hadoop can process large quantities of any kind of data, including structured transactional data, loosely structured data such as Facebook and Twitter feeds, complex data such as Web server log files, and unstructured audio and video data. Hadoop runs on a cluster of inexpensive servers, and processors can be added or removed as needed. Companies use Hadoop for analyzing very large volumes of data as well as for a staging area for unstructured and semi-structured data before they are loaded into a data warehouse. Facebook stores much of its data on its massive Hadoop cluster, which holds an estimated 100 petabytes, about 10,000 times more information than the Library of Congress. Yahoo uses Hadoop to track user behavior so it can modify its home page to fit their interests. Life sciences research firm NextBio uses Hadoop and HBase to process data for pharmaceutical companies conducting genomic research. Top database vendors such as IBM, Hewlett-Packard, Oracle, and Microsoft have their own Hadoop software distributions. Other vendors offer tools for moving data into and out of Hadoop or for analyzing data within Hadoop.

In-Memory Computing

Another way of facilitating big data analysis is to use **in-memory computing**, which relies primarily on a computer's main memory (RAM) for data storage. (Conventional DBMS use disk storage systems.) Users access data stored in system primary memory, thereby eliminating bottlenecks from retrieving and reading data in a traditional, disk-based database and dramatically shortening query response times. In-memory processing makes it possible for very large sets of data, amounting to the size of a data mart or small data warehouse, to reside entirely in memory. Complex business calculations that used to take hours or days are able to be completed within seconds, and this can even be accomplished on handheld devices. (See the Interactive Session on Technology.)

The previous chapter describes some of the advances in contemporary computer hardware technology that make in-memory processing possible, such as powerful high-speed processors, multicore processing, and falling computer memory prices. These technologies help companies optimize the use of memory and accelerate processing performance while lowering costs.

Leading commercial products for in-memory computing include SAP's High Performance Analytics Appliance (HANA) and Oracle Exalytics. Each provides a set of integrated software components, including in-memory database software and specialized analytics software, that run on hardware optimized for in-memory computing work.

INTERACTIVE SESSION: TECHNOLOGY

DRIVING ARI FLEET MANAGEMENT WITH REAL-TIME ANALYTICS

Automotive Resources International, better known as ARI, is the world's largest privately-held company for vehicle fleet management services. ARI is headquartered in Mt. Laurel, New Jersey, and has 2,500 employees and offices across North America, Europe, the UK, and Hong Kong. The company manages more than 1,000,000 vehicles in the U.S., Canada, Mexico, Puerto Rico, and Europe.

Businesses that need vehicles for shipments (trucks, vans, cars, ships, and rail cars) may choose to manage their own fleet of vehicles or they may outsource fleet management to companies such as ARI which specialize in these services. ARI manages the entire life cycle and operation of a fleet of vehicles for its customers, from up-front specification and acquisition to resale, including financing, maintenance, fuel management, and risk management services such as driver safety training and accident management. ARI also maintains six call centers in North America that operate 24/7, 365 days a year to support customers' fleet operations by providing assistance regarding repairs, breakdowns, accident response, preventive maintenance, and other driver needs. These call centers handle about 3.5 million calls per year from customers, drivers, and suppliers who expect access to real-time actionable information.

Providing this information has become increasingly challenging. Operating a single large commercial vehicle fleet generates high volumes of complex data, such as data on fuel consumption, maintenance, licensing, and compliance. A fuel transaction, for example, requires data on state taxes paid, fuel grade, total sale, amount sold, and time and place of purchase. A simple brake job and preventive maintenance checkup generates dozens of records for each component that is serviced. Each part and service performed on a vehicle is tracked using American Trucking Association codes. ARI collects and analyzes over 14,000 pieces of data per vehicle. Then multiply the data by hundreds of fleets, some with up to 10,000 vehicles, all operating simultaneously throughout the globe,

and you'll have an idea of the enormous volume of data ARI needs to manage, both for itself and for its customers.

ARI provided its customers with detailed information about their fleet operations, but the type of information it could deliver was very limited. For example, ARI could generate detailed reports on line-item expenditures, vehicle purchases, maintenance records, and other operational information presented as simple spreadsheets, charts, or graphs, but it was not possible to analyze all the data to spot trends and make recommendations. ARI was able to analyze data customer by customer, but it was not able to aggregate data across its entire customer base. For instance, if ARI was managing a pharmaceutical company's vehicle fleet, its information systems could not benchmark that fleet's performance against others in the industry. That type of problem required too much manual work and time, and still didn't deliver the level of insight management thought was possible.

What's more, in order to create reports, ARI had to go through internal subject matter experts in various aspects of fleet operations, who were called "reporting power users." Every request for information was passed to these power users. A request for a report would take 5 days to fill. If the report was unsatisfactory, it would go back to the report writer to make changes. ARI's process for analyzing its data was extremely drawn out.

In mid-2011, ARI implemented SAP BusinessObjects Explorer to give customers the enhanced ability to access data and run their own reports. SAP BusinessObjects Explorer is a business intelligence tool that enables business users to view, sort and analyze business intelligence data. Users search through data sources using an iTunes-like interface. They do not have to create queries to search the data and results are shown with a chart that indicates the best information match. The graphical representation of results changes as the user asks further questions of the data.

In early 2012, ARI integrated SAP BusinessObjects Explorer with HANA, SAP's in-memory computing platform that is deployable as an on-premise appliance (hardware and software) or in the cloud. HANA is optimized for performing real-time analytics and handling very high volumes of operational and transactional data in real time. HANA's in-memory analytics queries data stored in random access memory (RAM) instead of on a hard disk or flash storage.

Things started happening quickly after that. When ARI's controller wanted an impact analysis of the company's top 10 customers, SAP HANA produced the result in 3 to 3 ½ seconds. In ARI's old systems environment, this task would have been assigned to a power user versed in using reporting tools, specifications would have to be drawn up and a program designed for that specific query, a process that would have taken about 36 hours.

Using HANA, ARI is now able to quickly mine its vast data resources and generate predictions based on the results. For example, the company can produce precise figures on what it costs to operate a fleet of a certain size over a particular route across specific industries during a certain

type of weather and predict what the impact of changes in any of these variables. And it can do so nearly as easily as providing customers with a simple history of their expenditures on fuel. With such helpful information ARI provides more value to its customers.

HANA has also reduced the time required for each transaction handled by ARI's call centers—from the time a call center staffer takes a call to retrieving and delivering the requested information—by 5 percent. Since call center staff account for 40 percent of ARI's direct overhead, that time reduction translates into major cost savings.

ARI plans to make some of these real-time reporting and analytic capabilities available on mobile devices, which will enable customers to instantly approve a variety of operational procedures, such as authorizing maintenance repairs. Customers will also be able to use the mobile tools for instant insight into their fleet operations, down to a level of detail such as a specific vehicle's tire history.

Sources: "Driving 2 Million Vehicles with SAP Data," www.sap.com, accessed February 1, 2014; www.arifleet.com, accessed February 1, 2014; and "ARI Fleet Management Drives Real-Time Analytics to Customers," SAP InsiderPROFILES, April 1, 2013.

CASE STUDY QUESTIONS

1. Why was data management so problematic at ARI?

2. Describe ARI's earlier capabilities for data analysis and reporting and their impact on the business.

3. Was SAP HANA a good solution for ARI? Why or why not?

4. Describe the changes in the business as a result of adopting HANA.

Analytic Platforms

Commercial database vendors have developed specialized high-speed **analytic platforms** using both relational and non-relational technology that are optimized for analyzing large datasets. Analytic platforms such as IBM Netezza and Oracle Exadata feature preconfigured hardware-software systems that are specifically designed for query processing and analytics. For example, IBM Netezza features tightly integrated database, server, and storage components that handle complex analytic queries 10 to 100 times faster than traditional systems. Analytic platforms also include in-memory

FIGURE 6.12 CONTEMPORARY BUSINESS INTELLIGENCE INFRASTRUCTURE

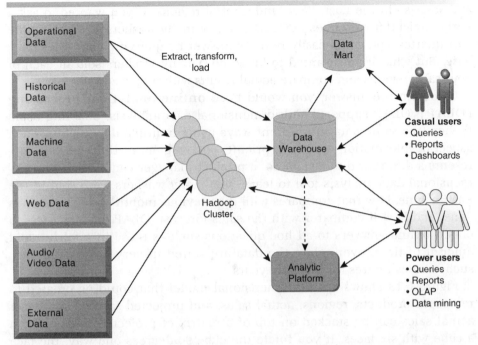

A contemporary business intelligence infrastructure features capabilities and tools to manage and analyze large quantities and different types of data from multiple sources. Easy-to-use query and reporting tools for casual business users and more sophisticated analytical toolsets for power users are included.

systems and NoSQL non-relational database management systems. Analytic platforms are now available as cloud services.

Figure 6.12 illustrates a contemporary business intelligence infrastructure using the technologies we have just described. Current and historical data are extracted from multiple operational systems along with Web data, machine-generated data, unstructured audio/visual data, and data from external sources that's been restructured and reorganized for reporting and analysis. Hadoop clusters pre-process big data for use in the data warehouse, data marts, or an analytic platform, or for direct querying by power users. Outputs include reports and dashboards as well as query results. Chapter 12 discusses the various types of BI users and BI reporting in greater detail.

ANALYTICAL TOOLS: RELATIONSHIPS, PATTERNS, TRENDS

Once data have been captured and organized using the business intelligence technologies we have just described, they are available for further analysis using software for database querying and reporting, multidimensional data analysis (OLAP), and data mining. This section will introduce you to these tools, with more detail about business intelligence analytics and applications in Chapter 12.

Online Analytical Processing (OLAP)

Suppose your company sells four different products—nuts, bolts, washers, and screws—in the East, West, and Central regions. If you wanted to ask a fairly straightforward question, such as how many washers sold during the past quarter, you could easily find the answer by querying your sales database. But what if you wanted to know how many washers sold in each of your sales regions and compare actual results with projected sales?

To obtain the answer, you would need **online analytical processing (OLAP)**. OLAP supports multidimensional data analysis, enabling users to view the same data in different ways using multiple dimensions. Each aspect of information—product, pricing, cost, region, or time period—represents a different dimension. So, a product manager could use a multidimensional data analysis tool to learn how many washers were sold in the East in June, how that compares with the previous month and the previous June, and how it compares with the sales forecast. OLAP enables users to obtain online answers to ad hoc questions such as these in a fairly rapid amount of time, even when the data are stored in very large databases, such as sales figures for multiple years.

Figure 6.13 shows a multidimensional model that could be created to represent products, regions, actual sales, and projected sales. A matrix of actual sales can be stacked on top of a matrix of projected sales to form a cube with six faces. If you rotate the cube 90 degrees one way, the face showing will be product versus actual and projected sales. If you rotate the cube 90 degrees again, you will see region versus actual and projected sales. If you rotate 180 degrees from the original view, you will see projected sales and product versus region. Cubes can be nested within cubes to build

FIGURE 6.13 MULTIDIMENSIONAL DATA MODEL

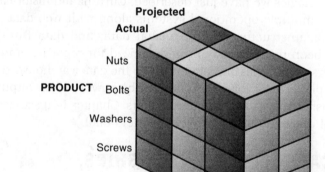

This view shows product versus region. If you rotate the cube 90 degrees, the face that will show is product versus actual and projected sales. If you rotate the cube 90 degrees again, you will see region versus actual and projected sales. Other views are possible.

complex views of data. A company would use either a specialized multidimensional database or a tool that creates multidimensional views of data in relational databases.

Data Mining

Traditional database queries answer such questions as, "How many units of product number 403 were shipped in February 2013?" OLAP, or multidimensional analysis, supports much more complex requests for information, such as, "Compare sales of product 403 relative to plan by quarter and sales region for the past two years." With OLAP and query-oriented data analysis, users need to have a good idea about the information for which they are looking.

Data mining is more discovery-driven. Data mining provides insights into corporate data that cannot be obtained with OLAP by finding hidden patterns and relationships in large databases and inferring rules from them to predict future behavior. The patterns and rules are used to guide decision making and forecast the effect of those decisions. The types of information obtainable from data mining include associations, sequences, classifications, clusters, and forecasts.

- *Associations* are occurrences linked to a single event. For instance, a study of supermarket purchasing patterns might reveal that, when corn chips are purchased, a cola drink is purchased 65 percent of the time, but when there is a promotion, cola is purchased 85 percent of the time. This information helps managers make better decisions because they have learned the profitability of a promotion.

- In *sequences*, events are linked over time. We might find, for example, that if a house is purchased, a new refrigerator will be purchased within two weeks 65 percent of the time, and an oven will be bought within one month of the home purchase 45 percent of the time.

- *Classification* recognizes patterns that describe the group to which an item belongs by examining existing items that have been classified and by inferring a set of rules. For example, businesses such as credit card or telephone companies worry about the loss of steady customers. Classification helps discover the characteristics of customers who are likely to leave and can provide a model to help managers predict who those customers are so that the managers can devise special campaigns to retain such customers.

- *Clustering* works in a manner similar to classification when no groups have yet been defined. A data mining tool can discover different groupings within data, such as finding affinity groups for bank cards or partitioning a database into groups of customers based on demographics and types of personal investments.

- Although these applications involve predictions, *forecasting* uses predictions in a different way. It uses a series of existing values to forecast what other values will be. For example, forecasting might find patterns in data to help managers estimate the future value of continuous variables, such as sales figures.

These systems perform high-level analyses of patterns or trends, but they can also drill down to provide more detail when needed. There are data mining applications for all the functional areas of business, and for government and scientific work. One popular use for data mining is to provide detailed analyses of patterns in customer data for one-to-one marketing campaigns or for identifying profitable customers.

Entertainment, formerly known as Harrah's Entertainment, is the largest gaming company in the world. It continually analyzes data about its customers gathered when people play its slot machines or use its casinos and hotels. The corporate marketing department uses this information to build a detailed gambling profile, based on a particular customer's ongoing value to the company. For instance, data mining lets Caesars know the favorite gaming experience of a regular customer at one of its riverboat casinos, along with that person's preferences for room accommodations, restaurants, and entertainment. This information guides management decisions about how to cultivate the most profitable customers, encourage those customers to spend more, and attract more customers with high revenue-generating potential. Business intelligence improved Caesars's profits so much that it became the centerpiece of the firm's business strategy.

Text Mining and Web Mining

Unstructured data, most in the form of text files, is believed to account for over 80 percent of useful organizational information and is one of the major sources of big data that firms want to analyze. E-mail, memos, call center transcripts, survey responses, legal cases, patent descriptions, and service reports are all valuable for finding patterns and trends that will help employees make better business decisions. **Text mining** tools are now available to help businesses analyze these data. These tools are able to extract key elements from unstructured big data sets, discover patterns and relationships, and summarize the information.

Businesses might turn to text mining to analyze transcripts of calls to customer service centers to identify major service and repair issues or to measure customer sentiment about their company. **Sentiment analysis** software is able to mine text comments in an e-mail message, blog, social media conversation, or survey form to detect favorable and unfavorable opinions about specific subjects.

For example, the discount broker Charles Schwab uses Attensity Analyze software to analyze hundreds of thousands of its customer interactions each month. The software analyzes Schwab's customer service notes, e-mails, survey responses, and online discussions to discover signs of dissatisfaction that might cause a customer to stop using the company's services. Attensity is able to automatically identify the various "voices" customers use to express their feedback (such as a positive, negative, or conditional voice) to pinpoint a person's intent to buy, intent to leave, or reaction to a specific product or marketing message. Schwab uses this information to take corrective actions such as stepping up direct broker communication with the customer and trying to quickly resolve the problems that are making the customer unhappy.

The Web is another rich source of unstructured big data for revealing patterns, trends, and insights into customer behavior. The discovery and analysis of useful patterns and information from the World Wide Web is called **Web mining**. Businesses might turn to Web mining to help them understand customer behavior, evaluate the effectiveness of a particular Web site, or quantify the success of a marketing campaign. For instance, marketers use the Google Trends and Google Insights for Search services, which track the popularity of various words and phrases used in Google search queries, to learn what people are interested in and what they are interested in buying.

Web mining looks for patterns in data through content mining, structure mining, and usage mining. Web content mining is the process of extracting knowledge from the content of Web pages, which may include text, image, audio, and video data. Web structure mining examines data related to the structure of a particular Web site. For example, links pointing to a document indicate the popularity of the document, while links coming out of a document indicate the richness or perhaps the variety of topics covered in the document. Web usage mining examines user interaction data recorded by a Web server whenever requests for a Web site's resources are received. The usage data records the user's behavior when the user browses or makes transactions on the Web site and collects the data in a server log. Analyzing such data can help companies determine the value of particular customers, cross marketing strategies across products, and the effectiveness of promotional campaigns.

The chapter-ending case describes organizations' experiences as they use the analytical tools and business intelligence technologies we have described to grapple with "big data" challenges.

DATABASES AND THE WEB

Have you ever tried to use the Web to place an order or view a product catalog? If so, you were probably using a Web site linked to an internal corporate database. Many companies now use the Web to make some of the information in their internal databases available to customers and business partners.

Suppose, for example, a customer with a Web browser wants to search an online retailer's database for pricing information. Figure 6.14 illustrates how that customer might access the retailer's internal database over the Web. The user accesses the retailer's Web site over the Internet using Web browser software on his or her client PC. The user's Web browser software requests data from the organization's database, using HTML commands to communicate with the Web server.

Because many back-end databases cannot interpret commands written in HTML, the Web server passes these requests for data to software that translates HTML commands into SQL so the commands can be processed by the DBMS working with the database. In a client/server environment, the DBMS resides on a dedicated computer called a **database server**. The DBMS receives the SQL requests and provides the required data. Middleware

FIGURE 6.14 LINKING INTERNAL DATABASES TO THE WEB

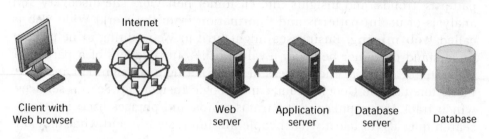

Users access an organization's internal database through the Web using their desktop PCs and Web browser software.

transfers information from the organization's internal database back to the Web server for delivery in the form of a Web page to the user.

Figure 6.14 shows that the middleware working between the Web server and the DBMS is an application server running on its own dedicated computer (see Chapter 5). The application server software handles all application operations, including transaction processing and data access, between browser-based computers and a company's back-end business applications or databases. The application server takes requests from the Web server, runs the business logic to process transactions based on those requests, and provides connectivity to the organization's back-end systems or databases. Alternatively, the software for handling these operations could be a custom program or a CGI script. A CGI script is a compact program using the *Common Gateway Interface (CGI)* specification for processing data on a Web server.

There are a number of advantages to using the Web to access an organization's internal databases. First, Web browser software is much easier to use than proprietary query tools. Second, the Web interface requires few or no changes to the internal database. It costs much less to add a Web interface in front of a legacy system than to redesign and rebuild the system to improve user access.

Accessing corporate databases through the Web is creating new efficiencies, opportunities, and business models. ThomasNet.com provides an up-to-date online directory of more than 700,000 suppliers of industrial products, such as chemicals, metals, plastics, rubber, and automotive equipment. Formerly called Thomas Register, the company used to send out huge paper catalogs with this information. Now it provides this information to users online via its Web site and has become a smaller, leaner company.

Other companies have created entirely new businesses based on access to large databases through the Web. One is the social networking service Facebook, which helps users stay connected with each other and meet new people. Facebook features "profiles" with information on more than 1.3 billion active users with information about themselves, including interests, friends, photos, and groups with which they are affiliated. Facebook maintains a massive database to house and manage all of this content. There are also many Web-enabled databases in the public sector to help consumers and citizens access helpful information.

6.4 WHY ARE INFORMATION POLICY, DATA ADMINISTRATION, AND DATA QUALITY ASSURANCE ESSENTIAL FOR MANAGING THE FIRM'S DATA RESOURCES?

Setting up a database is only a start. In order to make sure that the data for your business remain accurate, reliable, and readily available to those who need it, your business will need special policies and procedures for data management.

ESTABLISHING AN INFORMATION POLICY

Every business, large and small, needs an information policy. Your firm's data are an important resource, and you don't want people doing whatever they want with them. You need to have rules on how the data are to be organized and maintained, and who is allowed to view the data or change them.

An **information policy** specifies the organization's rules for sharing, disseminating, acquiring, standardizing, classifying, and inventorying information. Information policy lays out specific procedures and accountabilities, identifying which users and organizational units can share information, where information can be distributed, and who is responsible for updating and maintaining the information. For example, a typical information policy would specify that only selected members of the payroll and human resources department would have the right to change and view sensitive employee data, such as an employee's salary or social security number, and that these departments are responsible for making sure that such employee data are accurate.

If you are in a small business, the information policy would be established and implemented by the owners or managers. In a large organization, managing and planning for information as a corporate resource often requires a formal data administration function. **Data administration** is responsible for the specific policies and procedures through which data can be managed as an organizational resource. These responsibilities include developing information policy, planning for data, overseeing logical database design and data dictionary development, and monitoring how information systems specialists and end-user groups use data.

You may hear the term **data governance** used to describe many of these activities. Promoted by IBM, data governance deals with the policies and processes for managing the availability, usability, integrity, and security of the data employed in an enterprise, with special emphasis on promoting privacy, security, data quality, and compliance with government regulations.

A large organization will also have a database design and management group within the corporate information systems division that is responsible for defining and organizing the structure and content of the database, and maintaining the database. In close cooperation with users, the design group establishes the physical database, the logical relations among elements, and the access rules and security procedures. The functions it performs are called **database administration**.

ENSURING DATA QUALITY

A well-designed database and information policy will go a long way toward ensuring that the business has the information it needs. However, additional steps must be taken to ensure that the data in organizational databases are accurate and remain reliable.

What would happen if a customer's telephone number or account balance were incorrect? What would be the impact if the database had the wrong price for the product you sold or your sales system and inventory system showed different prices for the same product? Data that are inaccurate, untimely, or inconsistent with other sources of information lead to incorrect decisions, product recalls, and financial losses. Gartner Inc. reported that more than 25 percent of the critical data in large Fortune 1000 companies' databases is inaccurate or incomplete, including bad product codes and product descriptions, faulty inventory descriptions, erroneous financial data, incorrect supplier information, and incorrect employee data. A Sirius Decisions study on "The Impact of Bad Data on Demand Creation" found that 10 to 25 percent of customer and prospect records contain critical data errors. Correcting these errors at their source and following best practices for promoting data quality increased the productivity of the sales process and generated a 66 percent increase in revenue.

Some of these data quality problems are caused by redundant and inconsistent data produced by multiple systems feeding a data warehouse. For example, the sales ordering system and the inventory management system might both maintain data on the organization's products. However, the sales ordering system might use the term *Item Number* and the inventory system might call the same attribute *Product Number*. The sales, inventory, or manufacturing systems of a clothing retailer might use different codes to represent values for an attribute. One system might represent clothing size as "extra large," whereas the other system might use the code "XL" for the same purpose. During the design process for the warehouse database, data describing entities, such as a customer, product, or order, should be named and defined consistently for all business areas using the database.

Think of all the times you've received several pieces of the same direct mail advertising on the same day. This is very likely the result of having your name maintained multiple times in a database. Your name may have been misspelled or you used your middle initial on one occasion and not on another or the information was initially entered onto a paper form and not scanned properly into the system. Because of these inconsistencies, the database would treat you as different people! We often receive redundant mail addressed to Laudon, Lavdon, Lauden, or Landon.

If a database is properly designed and enterprise-wide data standards established, duplicate or inconsistent data elements should be minimal. Most data quality problems, however, such as misspelled names, transposed numbers, or incorrect or missing codes, stem from errors during data input. The incidence of such errors is rising as companies move their businesses to the Web and allow customers and suppliers to enter data into their Web sites that directly update internal systems.

Before a new database is in place, organizations need to identify and correct their faulty data and establish better routines for editing data once their database is in operation. Analysis of data quality often begins with a **data quality audit**, which is a structured survey of the accuracy and level of completeness of the data in an information system. Data quality audits can be performed by surveying entire data files, surveying samples from data files, or surveying end users for their perceptions of data quality.

Data cleansing, also known as *data scrubbing*, consists of activities for detecting and correcting data in a database that are incorrect, incomplete, improperly formatted, or redundant. Data cleansing not only corrects errors but also enforces consistency among different sets of data that originated in separate information systems. Specialized data-cleansing software is available to automatically survey data files, correct errors in the data, and integrate the data in a consistent company-wide format.

Data quality problems are not just business problems. They also pose serious problems for individuals, affecting their financial condition and even their jobs. For example, inaccurate or outdated data about consumers' credit histories maintained by credit bureaus can prevent creditworthy individuals from obtaining loans or lower their chances of finding or keeping a job.

The Interactive Session on Management illustrates American Water's experience with managing data as a resource. As you read this case, try to identify the policies, procedures, and technologies that were required to improve data management at this company.

INTERACTIVE SESSION: MANAGEMENT

THE GYM DATABASE

FitPro, a gymnasium and healthcare center, is a premium club spread across different locations in India. It provides differential workout routines to members including weight training, cardio-vascular routines, and aerobics and relaxation sessions. According to the current process flow, members need to schedule visits to the gym and trainers are assigned based on their availability at the time of the visit. The staff at the gym makes a manual entry in a spreadsheet against the member's name, reporting the time of the visit and the services availed. A new spreadsheet is generated daily to maintain these records. To prevent any unauthorized entry or threat to the patrons' private details, a password-based access to the computer is the only protection in place.

Due to a large number of members at the gym, the current system of recordkeeping was deemed inefficient. The management had no way of identifying the members who frequently visited the gym. Such information would be useful for the management because they could then tailor packages for tourists and communicate their offers via SMS or email. Since there was no centralized access for the members, the gym could not assign trainers to those who came in at odd hours. The members frequently complained of their inability to track the status of their health and fitness routines. Information could not be easily extracted from spreadsheets. As a result, receipts of payments could not be acknowledged on time. The gym wished to design a Web site that members could access 24/7, schedule workouts at flexible hours, and use their accounts to view their past history of sessions at the gym. The need for a central database could not be more pronounced at this stage. Hence, the gym's management hired an analyst who proposed the structure depicted in Figure 6.15.

The figure depicts the various end-users of the gym database: the employees, members, health-care professionals, equipment suppliers, and so on. To build a database, it is necessary to design tables keeping in mind the business requirements of the club. Entities, and the relationships among them, need to be determined at the outset. The analyst listed the following entities for the database design:

1. Region of operation
2. Member data
3. Employee data
4. Exercise routine
5. Program available
6. Program opted
7. Receipts
8. Payroll
9. Equipment
10. Employee schedule
11. Suppliers

Since the gym provides a variety of programs, each member's detail of the chosen program is saved as a separate entity under 'Program opted'. The employees at the gym are broadly categorized as staff (S) and trainers (T) under 'Employee type'. Figure 6.16 shows a partial view of the database for FitPro.

The relationship between the member and program opted has been depicted using the 1...* notation. This implies a one-to-many relationship. Each member is assigned a unique ID which is the primary key for the database table. This ensures that data duplicity does not occur. To identify the frequent travelers, the 'Member' entity takes two values: Y and N. If the answer is Y, information such as home country, year of visit, and so on, are recorded in a separate table. The relationship between member and tourist is depicted as 0...*, that is, it is a zero-to-many relationship. This is because not all members are tourists; but for each member who is a tourist, there can be several records for the different time periods at which they might have visited the gym.

FIGURE 6.15 PROPOSED STRUCTURE OF THE GYM'S CENTRAL DATABASE

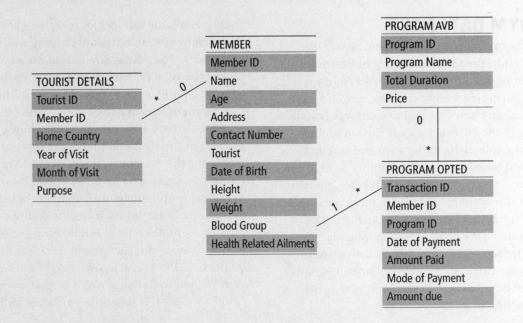

FIGURE 6.16 A PARTIAL VIEW OF THE DATABASE

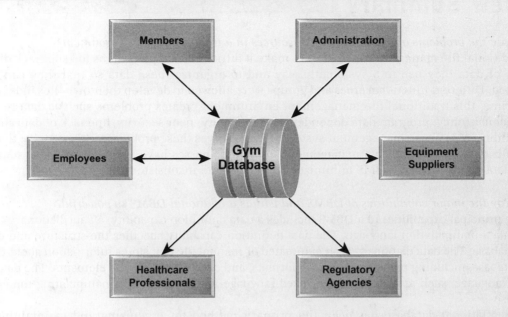

Similarly, there is a 0...* relationship between programs available and program opted. There might be programs that no member has opted for yet. The table also contains the payment details of the members, which can be used to alert the management if an account is overdue.

Using a well-designed database ensures that the records are clear of human error and data redundancy. Normalizing data entities removes information silos. The database also aids in the generation of reports for different end-users, whose levels of access can be easily controlled by the administration.

Sources: "Enterprise Manager Concepts". Retrieved from http://docs.oracle.com/cd/B19306_01/em.102/b31949/database_management.htm; Kroenke, David and Randall J. Boyle, *Using MIS*, 8/e, Prentice Hall (2015); Shah, Megha, "India's sexiest gyms", *Live Well* (2015); Retrieved from http://www.gqindia.com/live-well/fitness/indias-best-gyms. http://www.fitnessfirst.com.sg/learn-about-membership/Membership-options/; *GymMaster*. Retrieved from http://www.gymmaster.co.nz/; "Database Design Basics". Retrieved from http://office.microsoft.com/en-in/access-help/database-design-basics-HA001224247.aspx.

CASE STUDY QUESTIONS

1. Identify the relationships among the various entities of the gym database system.

2. Develop a database design by specifying primary and foreign keys for the FitPro gym.

3. What are the possible information discrepancies that can occur in the system? How can the design ensure governance?

4. Analyze the technical, organizational, scheduling, and financial feasibility by listing major operational and developmental costs of the database design.

Review Summary

1. *What are the problems of managing data resources in a traditional file environment?*

    Traditional file management techniques make it difficult for organizations to keep track of all of the pieces of data they use in a systematic way and to organize these data so that they can be easily accessed. Different functional areas and groups were allowed to develop their own files independently. Over time, this traditional file management environment creates problems such as data redundancy and inconsistency, program-data dependence, inflexibility, poor security, and lack of data sharing and availability. A database management system (DBMS) solves these problems with software that permits centralization of data and data management so that businesses have a single consistent source for all their data needs. Using a DBMS minimizes redundant and inconsistent files.

2. *What are the major capabilities of DBMS and why is a relational DBMS so powerful?*

    The principal capabilities of a DBMS includes a data definition capability, a data dictionary capability, and a data manipulation language. The data definition capability specifies the structure and content of the database. The data dictionary is an automated or manual file that stores information about the data in the database, including names, definitions, formats, and descriptions of data elements. The data manipulation language, such as SQL, is a specialized language for accessing and manipulating the data in the database.

    The relational database has been the primary method for organizing and maintaining data in information systems because it is so flexible and accessible. It organizes data in two-dimensional tables called relations with rows and columns. Each table contains data about an entity and its attributes. Each row represents a record and each column represents an attribute or field. Each table also contains a key field to uniquely identify each record for retrieval or manipulation. Relational database tables can be combined easily to deliver data required by users, provided that any two tables share a common data element. Non-relational databases are becoming popular for managing types of data that can't be handled easily by the relational data model. Both relational and non-relational database products are available as cloud computing services.

    Designing a database requires both a logical design and a physical design. The logical design models the database from a business perspective. The organization's data model should reflect its key business processes and decision-making requirements. The process of creating small, stable, flexible, and adaptive data structures from complex groups of data when designing a relational database is termed normalization. A well-designed relational database will not have many-to-many relationships, and all attributes for a specific entity will only apply to that entity. It will try to enforce referential integrity rules to ensure that relationships between coupled tables remain consistent. An entity-relationship diagram graphically depicts the relationship between entities (tables) in a relational database.

3. *What are the principal tools and technologies for accessing information from databases to improve business performance and decision making?*

    Contemporary data management technology has an array of tools for obtaining useful information from all the different types of data used by businesses today, including semi-structured and unstructured big data in vast quantities. These capabilities include data warehouses and data marts, Hadoop, in-memory computing, and analytical platforms. OLAP represents relationships among data as a multidimensional structure, which can be visualized as cubes of data and cubes within cubes of data, enabling more sophisticated data analysis. Data mining analyzes large pools of data, including the contents of data warehouses, to find patterns and rules that can be used to predict future behavior and guide decision making. Text mining tools help businesses analyze large unstructured data sets consisting of text. Web mining tools focus on analysis of useful patterns and information from the World Wide Web, examining the structure of Web sites and activities of Web site users as well as the contents of Web pages. Conventional databases can be linked via middleware to the Web or a Web interface to facilitate user access to an organization's internal data.

4. *Why are information policy, data administration, and data quality assurance essential for managing the firm's data resources?*

Developing a database environment requires policies and procedures for managing organizational data as well as a good data model and database technology. A formal information policy governs the maintenance, distribution, and use of information in the organization. In large corporations, a formal data administration function is responsible for information policy, as well as for data planning, data dictionary development, and monitoring data usage in the firm.

Data that are inaccurate, incomplete, or inconsistent create serious operational and financial problems for businesses because they may create inaccuracies in product pricing, customer accounts, and inventory data, and lead to inaccurate decisions about the actions that should be taken by the firm. Firms must take special steps to make sure they have a high level of data quality. These include using enterprise-wide data standards, databases designed to minimize inconsistent and redundant data, data quality audits, and data cleansing software.

Key Terms

Analytic platform, 248

Attribute, 231

Big data, 244

Bit, 230

Byte, 230

Data administration, 255

Data cleansing, 257

Data definition, 239

Data dictionary, 239

Data governance, 255

Data inconsistency, 233

Data manipulation language, 240

Data mart, 245

Data mining, 251

Data quality audit, 257

Data redundancy, 232

Data warehouse, 245

Database, 234

Database administration, 255

Database management system (DBMS), 234

Database server, 253

Entity, 231

Entity-relationship diagram, 243

Field, 231

File, 231

Foreign key, 239

Hadoop, 245

In-memory computing, 245

Information policy, 255

Key field, 236

Non-relational database management systems, 237

Normalization, 241

Online analytical processing (OLAP), 250

Primary key, 236

Program-data dependence, 233

Record, 231

Referential integrity, 243

Relational DBMS, 235

Sentiment analysis, 252

Structured Query Language (SQL), 000

Text mining, 252

Tuple, 236

Web mining, 253

Review Questions

6-1 What are the problems of managing data resources in a traditional file environment?

- List and describe each of the components in the data hierarchy.

- Define and explain the significance of entities, attributes, and key fields.

- List and describe the problems of the traditional file environment.

6-2 What are the major capabilities of database management systems (DBMS) and why is a relational DBMS so powerful?

- Define a database and a database management system.

- Name and briefly describe the capabilities of a DBMS.
- Define a relational DBMS and explain how it organizes data.
- List and describe the three operations of a relational DBMS.
- Explain why non-relational databases are useful.
- Define and describe normalization and referential integrity and explain how they contribute to a well-designed relational database.
- Define and describe an entity-relationship diagram and explain its role in database design.

6-3 What are the principal tools and technologies for accessing information from databases to improve business performance and decision making?

- Define big data and describe the technologies for managing and analyzing it.

- List and describe the components of a contemporary business intelligence infrastructure.
- Describe the capabilities of online analytical processing (OLAP).
- Define data mining, describing how it differs from OLAP and the types of information it provides.
- Explain how text mining and Web mining differ from conventional data mining.
- Describe how users can access information from a company's internal databases through the Web.

6-4 Why are information policy, data administration, and data quality assurance essential for managing the firm's data resources?

- Describe the roles of information policy and data administration in information management.
- Explain why data quality audits and data cleansing are essential.

Discussion Questions

6-5 It has been said there is no bad data, just bad management. Discuss the implications of this statement.

6-6 To what extent should end users be involved in the selection of a database management system and database design?

6-7 What are the consequences of an organization not having an information policy?

Hands-On MIS Projects

The projects in this section give you hands-on experience in analyzing data quality problems, establishing company-wide data standards, creating a database for inventory management, and using the Web to search online databases for overseas business resources.

Management Decision Problems

6-8 Emerson Process Management, a global supplier of measurement, analytical, and monitoring instruments and services based in Austin, Texas, had a new data warehouse designed for analyzing customer activity to improve service and marketing. However, the data warehouse was full of inaccurate and redundant data. The data in the warehouse came from numerous transaction processing systems in Europe, Asia, and other locations around the world. The team that designed the warehouse had assumed that sales groups in all these areas would enter customer names and addresses the same way. In fact, companies in different countries were using multiple ways of entering quote, billing, shipping, and other data. Assess the potential business impact of these data quality problems. What decisions have to be made and steps taken to reach a solution?

Improving Decision Making: Searching Online Databases for Overseas Business Resources

Software skills: Online databases
Business skills: Researching services for overseas operations

6-9 This project develops skills in searching Web-enabled databases with information about products and services in faraway locations.

Your company is located in Greensboro, North Carolina, and manufactures office furniture of various types. You are considering opening a facility to manufacture and sell your products in Australia. You would like to contact organizations that offer many services necessary for you to open your Australian office and manufacturing facility, including lawyers, accountants, import-export experts, and telecommunications equipment and support firm. Access the following online databases to locate companies that you would like to meet with during your upcoming trip: Australian Business Register (abr.gov.au), AustraliaTrade Now (australiatradenow.com), and the Nationwide Business Directory of Australia (www.nationwide.com.au). If necessary, use search engines such as Yahoo and Google.

- List the companies you would contact on your trip to determine whether they can help you with these and any other functions you think are vital to establishing your office.

- Rate the databases you used for accuracy of name, completeness, ease of use, and general helpfulness.

Does Big Data Bring Big Rewards?
CASE STUDY

Today's companies are dealing with an avalanche of data from social media, search, and sensors as well as from traditional sources. According to one estimate, 2.5 quintillion bytes of data per day are generated around the world. Making sense of "big data" has become one of the primary challenges for corporations of all shapes and sizes, but it also represents new opportunities. How are companies currently taking advantage of "big data?"

Green Mountain Coffee in Waterbury, Vermont, is analyzing both structured and unstructured audio and text data to learn more about customer behavior and buying patterns. The firm has 20 different brands and more than 200 different beverages, and uses Calabrio Speech Analytics to glean insights from multiple interaction channels and data streams. In the past, Green Mountain was unable to fully utilize all the data gathered when customers called into its contact center. The company wanted to know more about how many people were asking for a specific product, which products generated the most questions, and which products and categories created the most confusion. By analyzing its big data, Green Mountain was able to gather much more precise information and use it to produce materials, Web pages, and database entries to help representatives do their jobs more effectively. Management is now able to identify issues more rapidly before they create problems for customers.

AutoZone uses big data to help it adjust inventory and product prices at some of its 5,000 stores. For example, a customer walking into an AutoZone store in Waco, Texas, might find a deal on Gabriel shocks which that person would not find in most other AutoZone stores. The Mulberry, Florida AutoZone store might feature a special on a bug deflector. To target these deals at the local level, the auto parts retailer analyzes information gleaned from a variety of databases, such as the types of cars driven by people living around its

retail outlets. Software from NuoDB, which uses a cloud services model, makes it possible to quickly increase the amount of data analyzed without bringing down the system, or changing a line of code.

Benefits from analyzing big data are not limited to businesses. A number of services have emerged to analyze big data to help consumers. For example, personal devices such as the NikeFuelBand, SonySmartBand, and Jawbone UP24 enable people analyze their routines, diets, and sleeping patterns to see how they compare with others. This can lead to more-effective workouts and help people meet fitness goals. A number of online services enable consumers to check thousands of different flight and hotel options and book their own reservations, tasks previously handled by travel agents. New mobile-based services make it even easier to compare prices and pick the best travel options. For instance, a mobile app from Skyscanner Ltd. shows deals from all over the Web in one list—sorted by price, duration or airline—so travelers don't have to scour multiple sites to book within their budget. Skyscanner uses information from more than 300 airlines, travel agents and timetables and shapes the data into at-a-glance formats, with algorithms to keep pricing current and make predictions about who will have the best deal for a given market.

There are limits to using big data. A number of companies have rushed to start big data projects without first establishing a business goal for this new information. Swimming in numbers doesn't necessarily mean that the right information is being collected or that people will make smarter decisions.

Although big data is very good at detecting correlations, especially subtle correlations that an analysis of smaller data sets might miss, big data analysis doesn't necessarily indicate which correlations are meaningful. For example, examining big data might show that from 2006 to 2011 the United States murder rate was highly correlated with the market share of Internet Explorer, since both declined sharply. But that doesn't necessarily mean there is any meaningful connection between the two phenomena.

Several years ago, Google developed what it thought was a leading-edge algorithm using data it collected from Web searches to determine exactly how many people had influenza. It tried to calculate the number of people with flu in the United States by relating people's location to flu-related search queries on Google. The service has consistently overestimated flu rates, when compared to conventional data collected afterward by the US Centers for Disease Control (CDC). According to Google Flu Trends, nearly 11 percent of the U.S. population was supposed to have had influenza at the flu season's peak in mid-January 2013. However, an article in the science journal Nature stated that Google's results were twice the actual amount estimated by the U.S. Centers for Disease Control and Prevention, which had 6 percent of the population coming down with the disease. Why did this happen? Several scientists suggested that Google was "tricked" by widespread media coverage of the year's severe flu season in the U.S, which was further amplified by social media coverage. Google's algorithm only looked at numbers, not the context of the search results.

Sears Holdings, the parent company of Sears and Kmart, has been trying to use big data to get closer to its customers. Sears used to be the largest retailer in the United States, but for many years has steadily lost ground to discounters such as Walmart and Target and to competitively-priced specialty retailers such as Home Depot and Lowe's. The company has been slow to reduce operating costs, keep pace with current merchandising trends, and remodel its 2,429 stores, many of which are run-down and in undesirable locations.

Over the years, Sears had invested heavily in information technology. At one time it spent more on information technology and networking than all other non-computer firms in the United States except the Boeing Corporation. Sears used its huge customer databases of 60 million past and present Sears credit card holders to target groups such as tool buyers, appliance buyers, and gardening enthusiasts with special promotions. These efforts did not translate into competitive advantage because Sears' cost structure remained one of the highest in its industry.

The Sears company has continued to embrace new technology to revive flagging sales: online shopping, mobile apps, and an Amazon.com-like marketplace with other vendors for 18 million products, along with heavy in-store promotions. So far, these efforts have not paid off, and sales have declined since the 2005 merger with Kmart. The company posted a loss of nearly $1.4 billion for 2013.

Sears Holdings CEO Lou D'Ambrosio believes even more intensive use of technology and mining of customer data is the answer. The expectation is that deeper knowledge of customer preferences and buying patterns will make promotions, merchandising, and selling much more effective. Customers should flock to Sears stores because they will be carrying exactly what they want.

A customer loyalty program called Shop Your Way Rewards promises customers generous free deals for repeat purchases if they agree to share their personal shopping data with the company. Sears would not disclose how many customers have signed up for Shop Your Way Rewards, but loyalty-marketing firm Colloquy estimates around 50 million people are members.

Sears wanted to personalize marketing campaigns, coupons, and offers down to the individual customer, but its legacy systems were incapable of supporting that level of activity. In order to use big models on large data sets, Sears turned to Apache Hadoop and big data technology. It used to take Sears six weeks to analyze marketing campaigns for loyalty club members using a mainframe, Teradata data warehouse software, and SAS servers. Using Hadoop, the processing can be completed weekly. Certain online and mobile commerce analyses can be performed daily and targeting is much more precise, in some cases down to the individual customer. Sears's old models were able to use 10 percent of available data, but the new models are able to work with 100 percent. In the past, Sears was only able to retain data from 90 days to two years, but with Hadoop, it can keep everything, increasing its chances of finding more meaningful patterns in the data.

What's more, Hadoop processing is much less costly than conventional relational databases. A Hadoop system handling 200 terabytes of data runs about one-third the cost of a 200-terabyte relational platform. With Hadoop's massively parallel processing power, processing 2 billion records takes Sears little more than one minute longer than processing 100 million records.

Hadoop is still an immature platform, and Hadoop expertise is scarce. Sears had to learn Hadoop largely by trial and error. But it now runs critical reports on the platform, including analyses of customers, financial data, products, and supply chains. Capitalizing on its experience as a big-data innovator, Sears set up a subsidiary called MetaScale to sell big data cloud and consulting services to other companies.

Sears can point to many conceptual uses of Hadoop, but the question still lingers about whether the company is effectively using Hadoop to solve its enormous business problems. Is it truly able to offer customers personalized promotions and are they working? What is the business impact? Where are the numbers to show that big data is helping Sears become more profitable? Sears may be able to generate revenue by selling big data expertise to MetaScale customers, but will Hadoop really help turn Sears around?

Jim Sullivan, a partner at loyalty marketing firm Colloquy, notes that a good loyalty program that gives a company better intelligence about what its customers really want can be a strategic advantage, but even the best loyalty programs can't fix a fundamentally broken brand.

Sources: Laura Kolodny, "How Consumers Can Use Big Data," *Wall Street Journal*, March 23, 2014; Joseph Stromberg, "Why Google Flu Trends Can't Track the Flu (Yet), "smithsonianmag.com, March 13, 2014; Gary Marcus and Ernest Davis, "Eight (No, Nine!) Problems With Big Data," *New York Times*, April 6, 2014; Thomas H. Davenport, Big Data at Work, Harvard Business School Publishing, 2014; Samuel Greengard, "Companies Grapple With Big Data Challenges," Baseline, October 29, 2013; Rachael King and Steven Rosenbush. "Big Data Broadens Its Range." *The Wall Street Journal* (March 13, 2013; Nick Bilton, "Disruptions: Data Without a Context Tells a Misleading Story," *The New York Times*, February 24, 2013; ShiraOvide, "Big Data, Big Blunders," *The Wall Street Journal*, March 11, 2013; Mark A. Smith, "Big Data Pointless without Integration," Information Management, February 25, 2013; Frank Konkel, "Fast Failure Could Lead to Big-Data Success," Federal Computer Week, January 30, 2013; and Doug Henschen, "Why Sears Is Going All-in on Hadoop," *Information Week*, October 3, 2012.

CASE STUDY QUESTIONS

6-10 Describe the kinds of "big data" collected by the organizations described in this case.

6-11 List and describe the business intelligence technologies described in this case.

6-12 Why did the companies and services described in this case need to maintain and analyze big data? What business benefits did they obtain? How much were they helped by analyzing big data?

6-13 Identify three decisions that were improved by using big data.

6-14 Should all organizations try to analyze big data? Why or why not? What management, organization, and technology issues should be addressed before a company decides to work with big data?

Chapter 6 References

Aiken, Peter, Mark Gillenson, Xihui Zhang, and David Rafner. "Data Management and Data Administration. Assessing 25 Years of Practice." *Journal of Database Management* (July-September 2011).

Barth, Paul S. "Managing Big Data: What Every CIO Needs to Know." *CIO Insight* (January 12, 2012).

Barton, Dominic and David Court. "Making Advanced Analytics Work for You." *Harvard Business Review* (October 2012).

Baum, David. "Flying High with a Private Database Cloud." *Oracle Magazine* (November/December 2011).

Beath, Cynthia, , Irma Becerra-Fernandez, Jeanne Ross and James Short. "Finding Value in the Information Explosion." *MIT Sloan Management Review* 53, No. 4 (Summer 2012).

Bughin, Jacques, John Livingston, and Sam Marwaha. "Seizing the Potential for Big Data." The McKinsey Quarterly (October 2011).

Clifford, James, Albert Croker, and Alex Tuzhilin. "On Data Representation and Use in a Temporal Relational DBMS." *Information Systems Research* 7, No. 3 (September 1996).

Davenport, Thomas H. and D.J. Patil. "Data Scientist: The Sexiest Job of the 21st Century." *Harvard Business Review* (October 2012).

Davenport, Thomas H. Big Data at Work: *Dispelling the Myths, Uncovering the Opportunities.* Harvard Business Press (2014).

Eckerson, Wayne W. "Analytics in the Era of Big Data: Exploring a Vast New Ecosystem." TechTarget (2012).

_____. "Data Quality and the Bottom Line." The Data Warehousing Institute (2002).

Greengard, Samuel. "Big Data Unlocks Business Value." Baseline (January 2012).

Henschen, Doug. " MetLife Uses NoSQL for Customer Service Breakthrough." *Information Week* (May 13, 2013).

Hoffer, Jeffrey A., Ramesh Venkataraman, and Heikki Toppi. *Modern Database Management,* 11th ed. Upper Saddle River, NJ: Prentice-Hall (2013).

Jinesh Radadia. "Breaking the Bad Data Bottlenecks." *Information Management* (May/June 2010).

Jordan, John. "The Risks of Big Data for Companies." *Wall Street Journal* (October 20, 2013).

Kajepeeta, Sreedhar. "How Hadoop Tames Enterprises' Big Data." *Information Week* (February 2012).

Kroenke, David M. and David Auer. *Database Processing: Fundamentals, Design, and Implementation*, 13e. Upper Saddle River, NJ: Prentice-Hall (2014).

Lee, Yang W., and Diane M. Strong. "Knowing-Why about Data Processes and Data Quality." *Journal of Management Information Systems* 20, No. 3 (Winter 2004).

Lohr, Steve. "The Age of Big Data." *New York Times* (February 11, 2012).

Loveman, Gary. "Diamonds in the Datamine." *Harvard Business Review* (May 2003)

Marcus, Gary and Ernest Davis. "Eight (No, Nine!) Problems With Big Data." *New York Times* (April 6, 2014).

Martens, David and Foster Provost. "Explaining Data-Driven Document Classifications." *MIS Quarterly* 38, No. 1 (March 2014).

McAfee, Andrew and Erik Brynjolfsson. "Big Data: The Management Revolution." *Harvard Business Review* (October 2012).

McKinsey Global Institute. "Big Data: The Next Frontier for Innovation, Competition, and Productivity." McKinsey & Company (2011).

Morrison, Todd and Mark Fontecchio, "In-memory Technology Pushes Analytics Boundaries, Boosts BI Speeds," SearchBusinessAnalytics.techtarget.com, accessed May 17, 2013.

Morrow, Rich. "Apache Hadoop: The Swiss Army Knife of IT." Global Knowledge (2013).

Mulani, Narendra. "In-Memory Technology: Keeping Pace with Your Data." *Information Management (*February 27, 2013).

Redman, Thomas. *Data Driven: Profiting from Your Most Important Business Asset.* Boston: Harvard Business Press (2008).

Redman, Thomas C. "Data's Credibility Problem" *Harvard Business Review* (December 2013).

Rosenbush, Steven and Michael Totty. "How Big Data Is Transforming Business." *Wall Street Journal* (March 10, 2013).

Ross, Jeanne W., Cynthia M. Beath, and Anne Quaadgras. "You May Not Need Big Data After All." *Harvard Business Review* (December 2013).

Wallace, David J. "How Caesar's Entertainment Sustains a Data-Driven Culture." *DataInformed* (December 14, 2012).

Telecommunications, the Internet, and Wireless Technology

CHAPTER 7

LEARNING OBJECTIVES

After reading this chapter, you will be able to answer the following questions:

1. What are the principal components of telecommunications networks and key networking technologies?

2. What are the different types of networks?

3. How do the Internet and Internet technology work and how do they support communication and e-business?

4. What are the principal technologies and standards for wireless networking, communication, and Internet access?

CHAPTER CASES

Wireless Technology Makes
    Dundee Precious Metals
    Good as Gold
The Battle Over Net Neutrality

Monitoring Employees on Networks:
    Unethical or Good Business?
RFID-enabled LSmart Library
    Management System

WIRELESS TECHNOLOGY MAKES DUNDEE PRECIOUS METALS GOOD AS GOLD

Dundee Precious Metals (DPM) is a Canadian-based, international mining company engaged in the acquisition, exploration, development and mining and processing of precious metal properties. One of the company's principal assets is the Chelopech copper and gold mine east of Sofia, Bulgaria, and the company also has a gold mine in southern Armenia and a smelter in Namibia.

The price of gold and other metals has fluctuated wildly, and Dundee was looking for a way to offset lower gold prices by making its mining operations more efficient. However, mines are very complex operations, and there are special challenges with communicating and coordinating work underground.

Management decided to implement an underground wireless Wi-Fi network that allows electronic devices to exchange data wirelessly at the Chelopech mine to monitor the location of equipment, people, and ore throughout the mine's tunnels and facilities. The company deployed several hundred Cisco Systems Inc. high-speed wireless access points (in waterproof, dustproof, and crush-resistant enclosures), extended range antennas, communications boxes with industrial switches connected to 90 kilometers of fiber optic lines that snake through the mine, emergency boxes on walls for Linksys VoIP phones, protected vehicle

© TTstudio/Shutterstock

antennas that can withstand being knocked against a mine ceiling, and custom "walkie-talkie" software. Dundee was able to get access points that normally have a range of 200 meters to work at a range of 600 to 800 meters in a straight line, or 400 to 600 meters around a curve.

Another part of the solution was to use AeroScout Wi-Fi radio frequency identification (RFID) technology to track workers, equipment, and vehicles. About 1,000 AeroScout Wi-Fi RFID tags are worn by miners or mounted on vehicles and equipment, transmitting data about vehicle rock loads and mechanical status, miner locations, and the status of doors and ventilation fans over the mine's Wi-Fi network. AeroScout's Mobile View software is able to display a real-time visual representation of the location of people and items. The software can determine where loads came from, where rock should be sent, and where empty vehicles should go next. Data about any mishap or slowdown, such as a truck that made an unscheduled stop, or a miner who is behind schedule, are transmitted to Dundee's surface crew so that appropriate action can be taken.

The Mobile View interface is easy to use and provides a variety of reports and rules-based alerts. By using this wireless technology to track the location of equipment and workers underground, Dundee has been able to decrease equipment downtime and utilize resources more efficiently. Dundee also uses the data from the underground wireless network for its Dassault Systemes' Geovia mine management software and IBM mobile planning software.

Before implementing AeroScout, Dundee kept track of workers by noting who had turned in their cap lamps at the end of their shift. AeroScout has automated this process, enabling staff in the control room to quickly determine the location of miners.

It is also essential that workers driving equipment underground be able to communicate closely with the mine's control room. In the past, workers used a radio checkpoint system to relay their location. The new wireless system enables control room staff to actually see the location of machinery, so they can direct traffic more effectively, quickly identify problems, and respond more rapidly to emergencies.

Thanks to wireless technology, Dundee has been able to reduce costs and increase productivity while improving the safety of its workers. Communication costs have dropped 20 percent. According to Dundee CEO Rick Howes, the ability to use real-time data will increase the company's profit per miner by 10 to 15 percent.

Sources: www.dundeeprecious.com, accessed April 29, 2014; Eric Reguly, "Dundee's Real-Time Data Innovations Are as Good as Gold," The Globe and Mail, December 1, 2013; Howard Solomon, "How a Canadian Mining Company Put a Wi-Fi Network Underground," IT World Canada, December 3, 2013; and AeroScout, "Dundee Precious Metals Improves Safety and Operational Efficiency with AeroScout Real-time Location System, September 15, 2011.

The experience of Dundee Precious Metals illustrates some of the powerful capabilities and opportunities provided by contemporary networking technology. The company uses wireless networking, radio

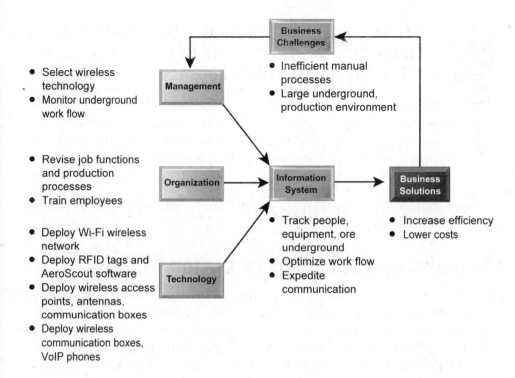

- Select wireless technology
- Monitor underground work flow

Management

Business Challenges
- Inefficient manual processes
- Large underground, production environment

- Revise job functions and production processes
- Train employees

Organization

Information System

Business Solutions

- Deploy Wi-Fi wireless network
- Deploy RFID tags and AeroScout software
- Deploy wireless access points, antennas, communication boxes
- Deploy wireless communication boxes, VoIP phones

Technology

- Track people, equipment, ore underground
- Optimize work flow
- Expedite communication

- Increase efficiency
- Lower costs

frequency identification (RFID) technology, and AeroScout MobileView software to automate tracking of workers, equipment, and ore as they move through its Chelopech underground mine.

The chapter-opening diagram calls attention to important points raised by his case and this chapter. The Dundee Precious Metals production environment in its Chelopech mine is difficult to monitor because it is underground, yet requires intensive oversight and coordination to make sure that people, materials, and equipment are available when and where they are needed underground and that work is flowing smoothly. Tracking components manually or using older radio identification methods was slow, cumbersome, and error-prone. Dundee was also under pressure to cut costs because the price of gold had dropped and precious metals typically have wild price fluctuations.

Management decided that wireless Wi-Fi technology and RFID tagging provided a solution and arranged for the deployment of a wireless Wi-Fi network throughout the entire underground Chelopech production facility. The network made it much easier to track and supervise mining activities from above ground. Dundee Precious Metals had to redesign some aspects of its production and other work processes and to train employees in the new system to take advantage of the new technology.

Here are some questions to think about: Why did wireless technology play such a key role in this solution? Describe how the new system changed the production process at the Chelopech mine.

7.1

7.1   WHAT ARE THE PRINCIPAL COMPONENTS OF TELECOMMUNICATIONS NETWORKS AND KEY NETWORKING TECHNOLOGIES?

I f you run or work in a business, you can't do without networks. You need to communicate rapidly with your customers, suppliers, and employees. Until about 1990, businesses used the postal system or telephone system with voice or fax for communication. Today, however, you and your employees use computers, e-mail, text messaging, the Internet, mobile phones, and mobile computers connected to wireless networks for this purpose. Networking and the Internet are now nearly synonymous with doing business.

NETWORKING AND COMMUNICATION TRENDS

Firms in the past used two fundamentally different types of networks: telephone networks and computer networks. Telephone networks historically handled voice communication, and computer networks handled data traffic. Telephone networks were built by telephone companies throughout the twentieth century using voice transmission technologies (hardware and software), and these companies almost always operated as regulated monopolies throughout the world. Computer networks were originally built by computer companies seeking to transmit data between computers in different locations.

Thanks to continuing telecommunications deregulation and information technology innovation, telephone and computer networks are converging into a single digital network using shared Internet-based standards and equipment. Telecommunications providers today, such as AT&T and Verizon, offer data transmission, Internet access, mobile phone service, and television programming as well as voice service. Cable companies, such as Cablevision and Comcast, offer voice service and Internet access. Computer networks have expanded to include Internet telephone and video services. Increasingly, all of these voice, video, and data communications are based on Internet technology.

Both voice and data communication networks have also become more powerful (faster), more portable (smaller and mobile), and less expensive. For instance, the typical Internet connection speed in 2000 was 56 kilobits per second, but today more than 74 percent of U.S. households have high-speed **broadband** connections provided by telephone and cable TV companies running at 1 to 15 million bits per second. The cost for this service has fallen exponentially, from 25 cents per kilobit in 2000 to a tiny fraction of a cent today.

Increasingly, voice and data communication, as well as Internet access, are taking place over broadband wireless platforms, such as mobile phones, mobile handheld devices, and PCs in wireless networks. More than half the Internet users in the United States use smartphones and tablets to access the Internet.

WHAT IS A COMPUTER NETWORK?

If you had to connect the computers for two or more employees together in the same office, you would need a computer network. Exactly what is a network? In its simplest form, a network consists of two or more connected computers. Figure 7.1 illustrates the major hardware, software, and transmission components used in a simple network: a client computer and a dedicated server computer, network interfaces, a connection medium, network operating system software, and either a hub or a switch.

Each computer on the network contains a network interface device to link the computer to the network. The connection medium for linking network components can be a telephone wire, coaxial cable, or radio signal in the case of cell phone and wireless local area networks (Wi-Fi networks).

The network operating system (NOS) routes and manages communications on the network and coordinates network resources. It can reside on every computer in the network, or it can reside primarily on a dedicated server computer for all the applications on the network. A server computer is a computer on a network that performs important network functions for client computers, such as serving up Web pages, storing data, and storing the network operating system (and hence controlling the network). Microsoft Windows Server, Linux, and Novell Open Enterprise Server are the most widely used network operating systems.

FIGURE 7.1   COMPONENTS OF A SIMPLE COMPUTER NETWORK

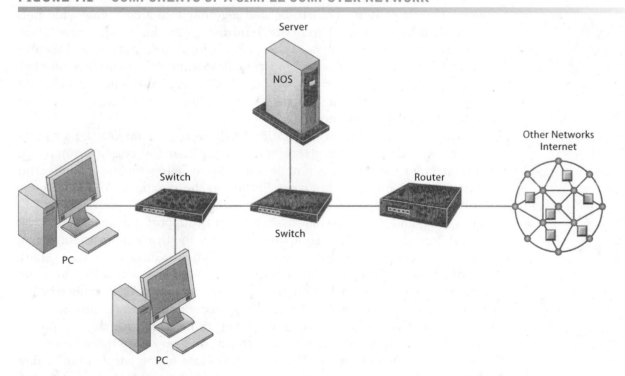

Illustrated here is a very simple computer network, consisting of computers, a network operating system (NOS) residing on a dedicated server computer, cable (wiring) connecting the devices, switches, and a router.

Most networks also contain a switch or a hub acting as a connection point between the computers. **Hubs** are very simple devices that connect network components, sending a packet of data to all other connected devices. A **switch** has more intelligence than a hub and can filter and forward data to a specified destination on the network.

What if you want to communicate with another network, such as the Internet? You would need a router. A **router** is a communications processor used to route packets of data through different networks, ensuring that the data sent gets to the correct address.

Network switches and routers have proprietary software built into their hardware for directing the movement of data on the network. This can create network bottlenecks and makes the process of configuring a network more complicated and time-consuming. **Software-defined networking (SDN)** is a new networking approach in which many of these control functions are managed by one central program, which can run on inexpensive commodity servers that are separate from the network devices themselves. This is especially helpful in a cloud computing environment with many different pieces of hardware because it allows a network administrator to manage traffic loads in a flexible and more efficient manner.

Networks in Large Companies

The network we've just described might be suitable for a small business. But what about large companies with many different locations and thousands of employees? As a firm grows, and collects hundreds of small local area networks, these networks can be tied together into a corporate-wide networking infrastructure. The network infrastructure for a large corporation consists of a large number of these small local area networks linked to other local area networks and to firmwide corporate networks. A number of powerful servers support a corporate Web site, a corporate intranet, and perhaps an extranet. Some of these servers link to other large computers supporting back-end systems.

Figure 7.2 provides an illustration of these more complex, larger scale corporate-wide networks. Here you can see that the corporate network infrastructure supports a mobile sales force using mobile phones and smartphones, mobile employees linking to the company Web site, internal company networks using mobile wireless local area networks (Wi-Fi networks), and a videoconferencing system to support managers across the world. In addition to these computer networks, the firm's infrastructure may include a separate telephone network that handles most voice data. Many firms are dispensing with their traditional telephone networks and using Internet telephones that run on their existing data networks (described later).

As you can see from this figure, a large corporate network infrastructure uses a wide variety of technologies—everything from ordinary telephone service and corporate data networks to Internet service, wireless Internet, and mobile phones. One of the major problems facing corporations today is how to integrate all the different communication networks and channels into a coherent system that enables information to flow from one part of the corporation to another, and from one system to another. As more and more

FIGURE 7.2   CORPORATE NETWORK INFRASTRUCTURE

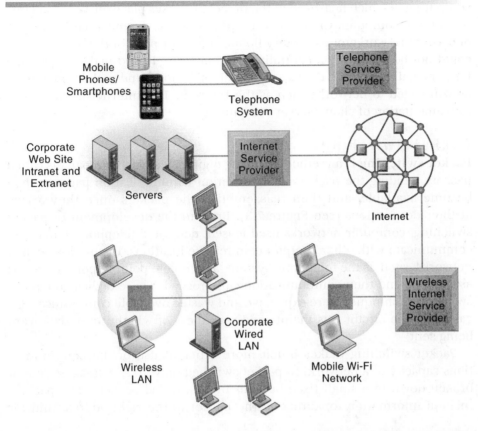

Today's corporate network infrastructure is a collection of many different networks from the public switched telephone network, to the Internet, to corporate local area networks linking workgroups, departments, or office floors.

communication networks become digital, and based on Internet technologies, it will become easier to integrate them.

KEY DIGITAL NETWORKING TECHNOLOGIES

Contemporary digital networks and the Internet are based on three key technologies: client/server computing, the use of packet switching, and the development of widely used communications standards (the most important of which is Transmission Control Protocol/Internet Protocol, or TCP/IP) for linking disparate networks and computers.

Client/Server Computing

Client/server computing, introduced in Chapter 5, is a distributed computing model in which some of the processing power is located within small, inexpensive client computers, and resides literally on desktops, laptops, or in handheld devices. These powerful clients are linked to one another through a network that is controlled by a network server computer. The server sets the rules of communication for the network and provides every client with an address so others can find it on the network.

Client/server computing has largely replaced centralized mainframe computing in which nearly all of the processing takes place on a central large mainframe computer. Client/server computing has extended computing to departments, workgroups, factory floors, and other parts of the business that could not be served by a centralized architecture. It also makes it possible for personal computing devices such as PCs, laptops, and mobile phones, to be connected to networks such as the Internet. The Internet is the largest implementation of client/server computing.

Packet Switching

Packet switching is a method of slicing digital messages into parcels called packets, sending the packets along different communication paths as they become available, and then reassembling the packets once they arrive at their destinations (see Figure 7.3). Prior to the development of packet switching, computer networks used leased, dedicated telephone circuits to communicate with other computers in remote locations. In circuit-switched networks, such as the telephone system, a complete point-to-point circuit is assembled, and then communication can proceed. These dedicated circuit-switching techniques were expensive and wasted available communications capacity—the circuit was maintained regardless of whether any data were being sent.

Packet switching makes much more efficient use of the communications capacity of a network. In packet-switched networks, messages are first broken down into small fixed bundles of data called packets. The packets include information for directing the packet to the right address and for

FIGURE 7.3   PACKET-SWITCHED NETWORKS AND PACKET COMMUNICATIONS

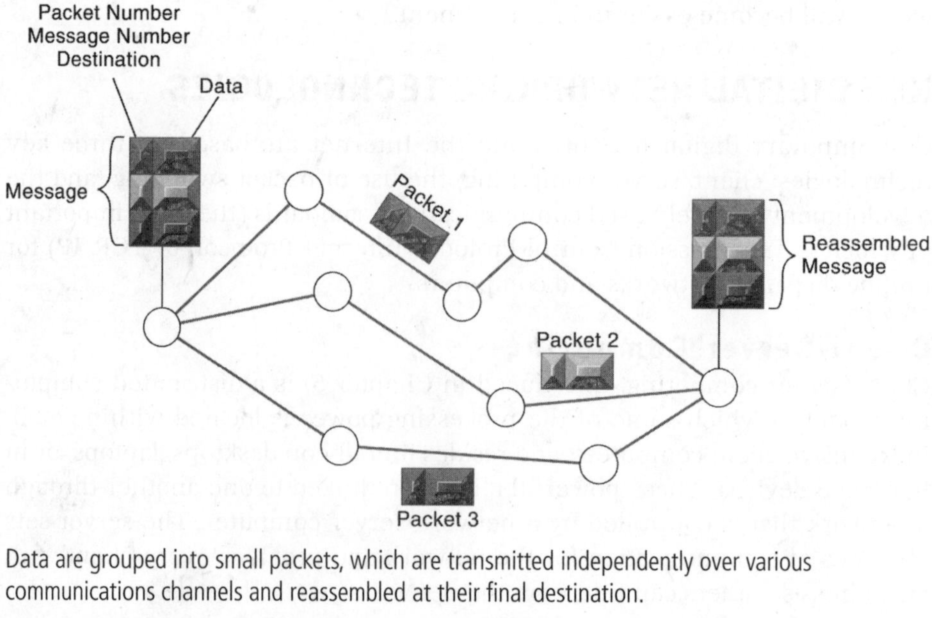

Data are grouped into small packets, which are transmitted independently over various communications channels and reassembled at their final destination.

checking transmission errors along with the data. The packets are transmitted over various communications channels using routers, each packet traveling independently. Packets of data originating at one source will be routed through many different paths and networks before being reassembled into the original message when they reach their destinations.

TCP/IP and Connectivity

In a typical telecommunications network, diverse hardware and software components need to work together to transmit information. Different components in a network communicate with each other only by adhering to a common set of rules called protocols. A **protocol** is a set of rules and procedures governing transmission of information between two points in a network.

In the past, many diverse proprietary and incompatible protocols often forced business firms to purchase computing and communications equipment from a single vendor. But today, corporate networks are increasingly using a single, common, worldwide standard called **Transmission Control Protocol/Internet Protocol (TCP/IP). TCP/IP** was developed during the early 1970s to support U.S. Department of Defense Advanced Research Projects Agency (DARPA) efforts to help scientists transmit data among different types of computers over long distances.

TCP/IP uses a suite of protocols, the main ones being TCP and IP. TCP refers to the Transmission Control Protocol, which handles the movement of data between computers. TCP establishes a connection between the computers, sequences the transfer of packets, and acknowledges the packets sent. IP refers to the Internet Protocol (IP), which is responsible for the delivery of packets and includes the disassembling and reassembling of packets during transmission. Figure 7.4 illustrates the four-layered Department of Defense reference model for TCP/IP, and the layers are described as follows:

FIGURE 7.4   THE TRANSMISSION CONTROL PROTOCOL/INTERNET PROTOCOL (TCP/IP) REFERENCE MODEL

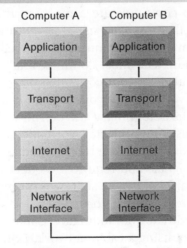

This figure illustrates the four layers of the TCP/IP reference model for communications.

1. *Application layer.*   The Application layer enables client application programs to access the other layers and defines the protocols that applications use to exchange data. One of these application protocols is the Hypertext Transfer Protocol (HTTP), which is used to transfer Web page files.

2. *Transport layer.*   The Transport layer is responsible for providing the Application layer with communication and packet services. This layer includes TCP and other protocols.

3. *Internet layer.*   The Internet layer is responsible for addressing, routing, and packaging data packets called IP datagrams. The Internet Protocol is one of the protocols used in this layer.

4. *Network Interface layer.*   At the bottom of the reference model, the Network Interface layer is responsible for placing packets on and receiving them from the network medium, which could be any networking technology.

Two computers using TCP/IP are able to communicate even if they are based on different hardware and software platforms. Data sent from one computer to the other passes downward through all four layers, starting with the sending computer's Application layer and passing through the Network Interface layer. After the data reach the recipient host computer, they travel up the layers and are reassembled into a format the receiving computer can use. If the receiving computer finds a damaged packet, it asks the sending computer to retransmit it. This process is reversed when the receiving computer responds.

7.2 WHAT ARE THE DIFFERENT TYPES OF NETWORKS?

Let's look more closely at alternative networking technologies available to businesses.

SIGNALS: DIGITAL VS. ANALOG

There are two ways to communicate a message in a network: an analog signal or a digital signal. An *analog signal* is represented by a continuous waveform that passes through a communications medium and has been used for voice communication. The most common analog devices are the telephone handset, the speaker on your computer, or your iPod earphone, all of which create analog waveforms that your ear can hear.

A *digital signal* is a discrete, binary waveform, rather than a continuous waveform. Digital signals communicate information as strings of two discrete states: one bit and zero bits, which are represented as on-off electrical pulses. Computers use digital signals and require a modem to convert these digital signals into analog signals that can be sent over (or received from) telephone lines, cable lines, or wireless media that use analog signals (see Figure 7.5). **Modem** stands for modulator-demodulator. Cable modems connect your computer to the Internet using a cable network. DSL modems connect your computer to the Internet using a telephone company's landline network.

FIGURE 7.5   FUNCTIONS OF THE MODEM

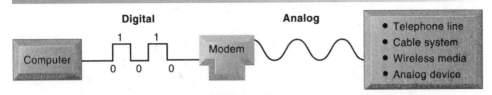

A modem is a device that translates digital signals into analog form (and vice versa) so that computers can transmit data over analog networks such as telephone and cable networks.

Wireless modems perform the same function as traditional modems, connecting your computer to a wireless network that could be a cell phone network, or a Wi-Fi network. Without modems, computers could not communicate with one another using analog networks (which include the telephone system and cable networks).

TYPES OF NETWORKS

There are many different kinds of networks and ways of classifying them. One way of looking at networks is in terms of their geographic scope (see Table 7.1).

Local Area Networks

If you work in a business that uses networking, you are probably connecting to other employees and groups via a local area network. A **local area network (LAN)** is designed to connect personal computers and other digital devices within a half-mile or 500-meter radius. LANs typically connect a few computers in a small office, all the computers in one building, or all the computers in several buildings in close proximity. LANs also are used to link to long-distance wide area networks (WANs, described later in this section) and other networks around the world using the Internet.

Review Figure 7.1, which could serve as a model for a small LAN that might be used in an office. One computer is a dedicated network file server, providing users with access to shared computing resources in the network, including software programs and data files.

The server determines who gets access to what and in which sequence. The router connects the LAN to other networks, which could be the Internet or another corporate network, so that the LAN can exchange information with networks external to it. The most common LAN operating systems are Windows, Linux, and Novell. Each of these network operating systems supports TCP/IP as its default networking protocol.

Ethernet is the dominant LAN standard at the physical network level, specifying the physical medium to carry signals between computers, access control rules, and a standardized set of bits used to carry data over the system. Originally, Ethernet supported a data transfer rate of 10 megabits per second (Mbps). Newer versions, such as Gigabit Ethernet, support a data transfer rate of 1 gigabit per second (Gbps).

TABLE 7.1 TYPES OF NETWORKS

TYPE	AREA
Local area network (LAN)	Up to 500 meters (half a mile); an office or floor of a building
Campus area network (CAN)	Up to 1,000 meters (a mile); a college campus or corporate facility
Metropolitan area network (MAN)	A city or metropolitan area
Wide area network (WAN)	A transcontinental or global area

The LAN illustrated in Figure 7.1 uses a client/server architecture where the network operating system resides primarily on a single file server, and the server provides much of the control and resources for the network. Alternatively, LANs may use a peer-to-peer architecture. A peer-to-peer network treats all processors equally and is used primarily in small networks with 10 or fewer users. The various computers on the network can exchange data by direct access and can share peripheral devices without going through a separate server.

In LANs using the Windows Server family of operating systems, the **peer-to-peer** architecture is called the *workgroup network model*, in which a small group of computers can share resources, such as files, folders, and printers, over the network without a dedicated server. The *Windows domain network model*, in contrast, uses a dedicated server to manage the computers in the network.

Larger LANs have many clients and multiple servers, with separate servers for specific services, such as storing and managing files and databases (file servers or database servers), managing printers (print servers), storing and managing e-mail (mail servers), or storing and managing Web pages (Web servers).

Metropolitan and Wide Area Networks

Wide area networks (WANs) span broad geographical distances—entire regions, states, continents, or the entire globe. The most universal and powerful WAN is the Internet. Computers connect to a WAN through public networks, such as the telephone system or private cable systems, or through leased lines or satellites. A **metropolitan area network (MAN)** is a network that spans a metropolitan area, usually a city and its major suburbs. Its geographic scope falls between a WAN and a LAN.

TRANSMISSION MEDIA AND TRANSMISSION SPEED

Networks use different kinds of physical transmission media, including twisted pair wire, coaxial cable, fiber-optic cable, and media for wireless transmission. Each has advantages and limitations. A wide range of speeds is possible for any given medium depending on the software and hardware configuration. Table 7.2 compares these media.

TABLE 7.2 PHYSICAL TRANSMISSION MEDIA

TRANSMISSION MEDIUM	DESCRIPTION	SPEED
Twisted pair wire (CAT 5)	Strands of copper wire twisted in pairs for voice and data communications. CAT 5 is the most common 10 Mbps LAN cable. Maximum recommended run of 100 meters.	10–100+ Mbps
Coaxial cable	Thickly insulated copper wire, which is capable of high-speed data transmission and less subject to interference than twisted wire. Currently used for cable TV and for networks with longer runs (more than 100 meters).	Up to 1 Gbps
Fiber-optic cable	Strands of clear glass fiber, transmitting data as pulses of light generated by lasers. Useful for high-speed transmission of large quantities of data. More expensive than other physical transmission media and harder to install; often used for network backbone.	15 Mbps to 6+ Tbps
Wireless transmission media	Based on radio signals of various frequencies and includes both terrestrial and satellite microwave systems and cellular networks. Used for long-distance, wireless communication and Internet access.	Up to 600+ Mbps

Bandwidth: Transmission Speed

The total amount of digital information that can be transmitted through any telecommunications medium is measured in bits per second (bps). One signal change, or cycle, is required to transmit one or several bits; therefore, the transmission capacity of each type of telecommunications medium is a function of its frequency. The number of cycles per second that can be sent through that medium is measured in **hertz**—one hertz is equal to one cycle of the medium.

The range of frequencies that can be accommodated on a particular telecommunications channel is called its **bandwidth**. The bandwidth is the difference between the highest and lowest frequencies that can be accommodated on a single channel. The greater the range of frequencies, the greater the bandwidth and the greater the channel's transmission capacity.

7.3 HOW DO THE INTERNET AND INTERNET TECHNOLOGY WORK AND HOW DO THEY SUPPORT COMMUNICATION AND E-BUSINESS?

We all use the Internet, and many of us can't do without it. It's become an indispensable personal and business tool. But what exactly is the Internet? How does it work, and what does Internet technology have to offer for business? Let's look at the most important Internet features.

WHAT IS THE INTERNET?

The Internet has become the world's most extensive, public communication system. It's also the world's largest implementation of client/server computing and internetworking, linking millions of individual networks all over the world. This global network of networks began in the early 1970s as a U.S. Department of Defense network to link scientists and university professors around the world.

Most homes and small businesses connect to the Internet by subscribing to an Internet service provider. **An Internet service provider (ISP)** is a commercial organization with a permanent connection to the Internet that sells temporary connections to retail subscribers. EarthLink, NetZero, AT&T, and Time Warner are ISPs. Individuals also connect to the Internet through their business firms, universities, or research centers that have designated Internet domains.

There are a variety of services for ISP Internet connections. Connecting via a traditional telephone line and modem, at a speed of 56.6 kilobits per second (Kbps), used to be the most common form of connection worldwide, but it has been largely replaced by broadband connections. Digital subscriber line, cable, satellite Internet connections, and T lines provide these broadband services.

Digital subscriber line (DSL) technologies operate over existing telephone lines to carry voice, data, and video at transmission rates ranging from 385 Kbps all the way up to 40 Mbps, depending on usage patterns and distance. **Cable Internet connections** provided by cable television vendors use digital cable coaxial lines to deliver high-speed Internet access to homes and businesses. They can provide high-speed access to the Internet of up to 50 Mbps, although most providers offer service ranging from 1 Mbps to 6 Mbps. In areas where DSL and cable services are unavailable, it is possible to access the Internet via satellite, although some satellite Internet connections have slower upload speeds than other broadband services.

T1 and T3 are international telephone standards for digital communication. They are leased, dedicated lines suitable for businesses or government agencies requiring high-speed guaranteed service levels. **T1 lines** offer guaranteed delivery at 1.54 Mbps, and T3 lines offer delivery at 45 Mbps. The Internet does not provide similar guaranteed service levels, but simply "best effort."

INTERNET ADDRESSING AND ARCHITECTURE

The Internet is based on the TCP/IP networking protocol suite described earlier in this chapter. Every computer on the Internet is assigned a unique **Internet Protocol (IP) address**, which currently is a 32-bit number represented by four strings of numbers ranging from 0 to 255 separated by periods. For instance, the IP address of www.microsoft.com is 207.46.250.119.

When a user sends a message to another user on the Internet, the message is first decomposed into packets using the TCP protocol. Each packet contains its destination address. The packets are then sent from the client to the network server and from there on to as many other servers as necessary to arrive at a specific computer with a known address. At the destination address, the packets are reassembled into the original message.

The Domain Name System

Because it would be incredibly difficult for Internet users to remember strings of 12 numbers, the **Domain Name System (DNS)** converts domain names to IP addresses. The **domain name** is the English-like name that corresponds to the unique 32-bit numeric IP address for each computer connected to the Internet. DNS servers maintain a database containing IP addresses mapped to their corresponding domain names. To access a computer on the Internet, users need only specify its domain name.

DNS has a hierarchical structure (see Figure 7.6). At the top of the DNS hierarchy is the root domain. The child domain of the root is called a top-level domain, and the child domain of a top-level domain is called a second-level domain. Top-level domains are two- and three-character names you are familiar with from surfing the Web, for example, .com, .edu, .gov, and the various country codes such as .ca for Canada or .it for Italy. Second-level domains have two parts, designating a top-level name and a second-level name—such as buy.com, nyu.edu, or amazon.ca. A host name at the bottom of the hierarchy designates a specific computer on either the Internet or a private network.

The most common domain extensions currently available and officially approved are shown in the following list. Countries also have domain names such as .uk, .au, and .fr (United Kingdom, Australia, and France, respectively), and there is a new class of "internationalized" top-level domains that use non-English characters. In the future, this list will expand to include many more types of organizations and industries.

FIGURE 7.6　THE DOMAIN NAME SYSTEM

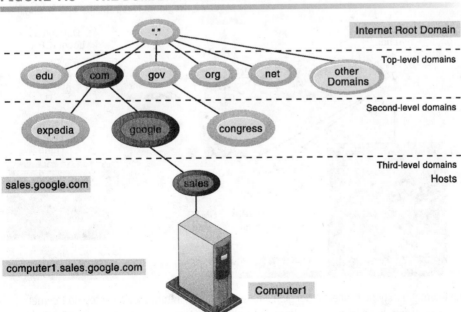

Domain Name System is a hierarchical system with a root domain, top-level domains, second-level domains, and host computers at the third level.

.com	Commercial organizations/businesses
.edu	Educational institutions
.gov	U.S. government agencies
.mil	U.S. military
.net	Network computers
.org	Nonprofit organizations and foundations
.biz	Business firms
.info	Information providers

Internet Architecture and Governance

Internet data traffic is carried over transcontinental high-speed backbone networks that generally operate in the range of 45 Mbps to 2.5 Gbps (see Figure 7.7). These trunk lines are typically owned by long-distance telephone companies (called *network service providers*) or by national governments. Local connection lines are owned by regional telephone and cable television companies in the United States that connect retail users in homes and businesses to the Internet. The regional networks lease access to ISPs, private companies, and government institutions.

FIGURE 7.7   INTERNET NETWORK ARCHITECTURE

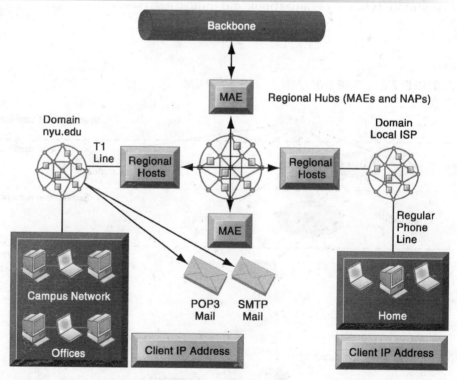

The Internet backbone connects to regional networks, which in turn provide access to Internet service providers, large firms, and government institutions. Network access points (NAPs) and metropolitan area exchanges (MAEs) are hubs where the backbone intersects regional and local networks and where backbone owners connect with one another.

Each organization pays for its own networks and its own local Internet connection services, a part of which is paid to the long-distance trunk line owners. Individual Internet users pay ISPs for using their service, and they generally pay a flat subscription fee, no matter how much or how little they use the Internet. A debate is now raging on whether this arrangement should continue or whether heavy Internet users who download large video and music files should pay more for the bandwidth they consume. The Interactive Session on Organizations explores this topic, by examining the pros and cons of net neutrality.

No one "owns" the Internet, and it has no formal management. However, worldwide Internet policies are established by a number of professional organizations and government bodies, including the Internet Architecture Board (IAB), which helps define the overall structure of the Internet; the Internet Corporation for Assigned Names and Numbers (ICANN), which assigns IP addresses; and the World Wide Web Consortium (W3C), which sets Hypertext Markup Language and other programming standards for the Web.

These organizations influence government agencies, network owners, ISPs, and software developers with the goal of keeping the Internet operating as efficiently as possible. The Internet must also conform to the laws of the sovereign nation-states in which it operates, as well as the technical infrastructures that exist within the nation-states. Although in the early years of the Internet and the Web there was very little legislative or executive interference, this situation is changing as the Internet plays a growing role in the distribution of information and knowledge, including content that some find objectionable.

ICANN was created by the Department of Commerce in 1986 to manage the domain name system, and the central core servers of the Internet domains located in the United States. Emerging nations and others have long called for the U.S. dominance of the Internet to end, and instead support a multi-national controlling agency. After the terrorist attacks on the United States on September 11, 2001, the U.S. refused to consider such a change. This opinion changed again in March 2014 when the Commerce Department announced its intention to transfer the domain name functions of the Internet over to a global, multi-stakeholder community which will be determined in 2015. Multi-stakeholder means that the leadership of the global Internet would follow the pattern of ICANN and would be composed of representatives from academia, business, governments, and public interest groups rather than a government led or an inter-governmental body. Until this body is formed, the Internet domain name system will remain under the control of the Department of Commerce. The announcement came in part as a response to widespread global hostility to U.S. control over the DNS amidst the revelations of Edward Snowden, describing how U.S. intelligence agencies used the Internet to conduct surveillance over individuals and groups around the world even though such surveillance had nothing to do with the operations of ICANN or the Department of Commerce, but instead were enabled by other technical means (NTIA, 2014; Wyatt, 2014). The hope is that the transition to a multinational body will not disrupt the orderly operation of the Internet.

INTERACTIVE SESSION: ORGANIZATIONS

THE BATTLE OVER NET NEUTRALITY

What kind of Internet user are you? Do you primarily use the Net to do a little e-mail and online banking? Or are you online all day, watching YouTube videos, downloading music files, or playing online games? Do you use your iPhone to stream TV shows and movies on a regular basis? If you're a power Internet or smart-phone user, you are consuming a great deal of bandwidth. Could hundreds of millions of people like you start to slow the Internet down?

Video streaming on Netflix accounts for 32 percent of all bandwidth use in the United States, and Google's YouTube for 19 percent of Web traffic at peak hours. If user demand overwhelms network capacity, the Internet might not come to a screeching halt, but users could face sluggish download speeds and video transmission. Heavy use of iPhones in urban areas such as New York and San Francisco has already degraded service on the AT&T wireless network. AT&T reported that 3 percent of its subscriber base accounted for 40 percent of its data traffic.

Internet service providers (ISPs) assert that network congestion is a serious problem and that expanding their networks would require passing on burdensome costs to consumers. These companies believe differential pricing methods, which include data caps and metered use—charging based on the amount of bandwidth consumed—are the fairest way to finance necessary investments in their network infrastructures. But metering Internet use is not widely accepted, because of an ongoing debate about net neutrality.

Net neutrality is the idea that Internet service providers must allow customers equal access to content and applications, regardless of the source or nature of the content. Presently, the Internet is neutral: all Internet traffic is treated equally on a first-come, first-served basis by Internet backbone owners. However, this arrangement prevents telecommunications and cable companies from charging differentiated prices based on the amount of bandwidth consumed by the content being delivered over the Internet.

The strange alliance of net neutrality advocates includes MoveOn.org; the Christian Coalition; the American Library Association; data-intensive Web businesses such as Netflix, Amazon, and Google; major consumer groups; and a host of bloggers and small businesses. Net neutrality advocates argue that differentiated pricing would impose heavy costs on heavy bandwidth users such as YouTube, Skype, and other innovative services, preventing high-bandwidth startup companies from gaining traction. Net neutrality supporters also argue that without net neutrality, ISPs that are also cable companies, such as Comcast, might block online streaming video from Netflix or Hulu in order to force customers to use the cable company's on-demand movie rental services.

Network owners believe regulation to enforce net neutrality will impede U.S. competitiveness by discouraging capital expenditure for new networks and curbing their networks' ability to cope with the exploding demand for Internet and wireless traffic. U.S. Internet service lags behind many other nations in overall speed, cost, and quality of service, adding credibility to this argument. And with enough options for Internet access, dissatisfied consumers could simply switch to providers who enforce net neutrality and allow unlimited Internet use.

The wireless industry had been largely exempted from net neutrality rules, because the government determined it was a less mature network and companies should be allowed more freedom to manage traffic. Wireless providers already have tiered plans that charge heavy bandwidth users larger service fees.

A December 2012 report by the non-profit, nonpartisan, public policy institute, New America Foundation (NAF), disputes these claims. Like personal computers, the processing capacity of the routers and switches in wired broadband networks has vastly expanded while the price has declined. Although total U.S. Internet data consumption rose 120% in 2012, the cost to transport the data decreased at a faster pace. The net cost to carriers was at worst flat and for the most part, down. The NAF report further asserts that lack of competition has enabled wired broadband carriers to charge higher rates, institute data caps, and spend less on the capital expenditures needed to upgrade and maintain their networks than they have in the past.

The courts have maintained that the Federal Communications Commission (FCC) has no authority to dictate how the Internet operates. The Communications Act of 1996 forbids the agency from managing the Internet as a "common carrier," the regulatory approach the commission took toward telephones, and the FCC itself decided not to classify broadband as a telecommunications service.

On January 14, 2014, the U.S. Court of Appeals for the District of Columbia struck down the FCC's "Open Internet" rules that required equal treatment of Internet traffic and prevented broadband providers from blocking traffic favoring certain sites or charging special fees to companies that account for the most traffic. The court said the FCC saddled broadband providers with the same sorts of obligations as traditional "common carrier" telecommunications services, such as landline phone systems, even though the commission had explicitly decided not to classify broadband as a telecommunications service.

On April 24, 2014, the FCC announced that it would propose new rules that allow companies like Disney, Google or Netflix to pay Internet service providers like Comcast and Verizon for special, faster lanes to send video and other content to their customers. Broadband providers would have to disclose how they treat all Internet traffic and on what terms they offer more rapid lanes, and would be required to act in a "commercially reasonable manner." Providers would not be allowed to block Web sites. The proposed rules would also require Internet service providers to disclose whether, in assigning faster lanes, they had favored their affiliated companies that provide content.

Nevertheless, the FCC continues to push for an open Internet. On April 30, 2014, FCC chairman Tom Wheeler announced that lack of competition has hurt consumers, and that the FCC planned to write tough new rules to enforce net neutrality.

Sources: "Should the U.S. Regulate Broadband Internet Access as a Utility?" *Wall Street Journal*, May 11, 2014; Edward Wyatt, "Stern Talk From Chief of F.C.C. on Open Net," *New York Times*, April 30, 2014 and "F.C.C., in a Shift, Backs Fast Lane for Web Traffic," *New York Times*, April 24, 2014; Amol Sharma, "Netflix, YouTube Could Feel Effects of 'Open Internet' Ruling," *Wall Street Journal*, January 14, 2014; Gautham Nagesh, "FCC to Propose New 'Net Neutrality' Rules," *Wall Street Journal*, April 23, 2014; Shira Ovide, "Moving Beyond the Net Neutrality Debate," *Wall Street Journal*, January 14, 2014; Gautham Nagesh and Amol Sharma, "Court Tosses Rules of Road for Internet," *Wall Street Journal*, January 4, 2014; UpdAlina Selyukh," S. Court to Hear Oral Arguments in Net Neutrality Case on September 9," Reuters, June 25, 2013; and Hibah Hussain, Danielle Kehl, Benjamin Lennett, and Patrick Lucey, "Capping the Nation's Broadband Future? Dwindling Competition Is Fueling the Rise of Increasingly Costly and Restrictive Internet Usage Caps," New America Foundation, December 17, 2012.

CASE STUDY QUESTIONS

1. What is net neutrality? Why has the Internet operated under net neutrality up to this point in time?

2. Who's in favor of net neutrality? Who's opposed? Why?

3. What would be the impact on individual users, businesses, and government if Internet providers switched to a tiered service model for transmission over land lines as well as wireless?

4. It has been said that net neutrality is the most important issue facing the Internet since the advent of the Internet. Discuss the implications of this statement.

5. Are you in favor of legislation enforcing network neutrality? Why or why not?

The Future Internet: IPv6 and Internet2

The Internet was not originally designed to handle the transmission of massive quantities of data and billions of users. Because of sheer Internet population growth, the world is about to run out of available IP addresses using the old addressing convention. The old addressing system is being replaced by a new version of the IP addressing schema called **IPv6** (Internet Protocol version 6), which contains 128-bit addresses (2 to the power of 128), or more than a quadrillion possible unique addresses. IPv6 is not compatible with the existing Internet addressing system, so the transition to the new standard will take years.

Internet2 is an advanced networking consortium representing over 350 U.S. universities, private businesses, and government agencies working with 66,000 institutions across the United States and international networking partners from more than 100 countries. To connect these communities, Internet2 developed a high-capacity 100 Gbps network that serves as a testbed for leading-edge technologies that may eventually migrate to the public Internet, including telemedicine, distance learning, and other advanced applications not possible with consumer-grade Internet services. The fourth generation of this network is being rolled out to provide 8.8 terabits of capacity.

INTERNET SERVICES AND COMMUNICATION TOOLS

The Internet is based on client/server technology. Individuals using the Internet control what they do through client applications on their computers, such as Web browser software. The data, including e-mail messages and Web pages, are stored on servers. A client uses the Internet to request information from a particular Web server on a distant computer, and the server sends the requested information back to the client over the Internet. Chapters 5 and 6 describe how Web servers work with application servers and database servers to access information from an organization's internal information systems applications and their associated databases. Client platforms today include not only PCs and other computers but also smartphones and tablets.

Internet Services

A client computer connecting to the Internet has access to a variety of services. These services include e-mail, chatting and instant messaging, electronic discussion groups, **Telnet**, **File Transfer Protocol (FTP)**, and the Web. Table 7.3 provides a brief description of these services.

Each Internet service is implemented by one or more software programs. All of the services may run on a single server computer, or different services may be allocated to different machines. Figure 7.8 illustrates one way that these services can be arranged in a multitiered client/server architecture.

E-mail enables messages to be exchanged from computer to computer, with capabilities for routing messages to multiple recipients, forwarding messages, and attaching text documents or multimedia files to messages.

TABLE 7.3 MAJOR INTERNET SERVICES

CAPABILITY	FUNCTIONS SUPPORTED
E-mail	Person-to-person messaging; document sharing
Chatting and instant messaging	Interactive conversations
Newsgroups	Discussion groups on electronic bulletin boards
Telnet	Logging on to one computer system and doing work on another
File Transfer Protocol (FTP)	Transferring files from computer to computer
World Wide Web	Retrieving, formatting, and displaying information (including text, audio, graphics, and video) using hypertext links

Most e-mail today is sent through the Internet. The cost of e-mail is far lower than equivalent voice, postal, or overnight delivery costs, and e-mail messages arrive anywhere in the world in a matter of seconds.

Nearly 90 percent of U.S. workplaces have employees communicating interactively using **chat** or instant messaging tools. Chatting enables two or more people who are simultaneously connected to the Internet to hold live, interactive conversations. Chat systems now support voice and video chat as well as written conversations. Many online retail businesses offer chat services on their Web sites to attract visitors, to encourage repeat purchases, and to improve customer service.

FIGURE 7.8   CLIENT/SERVER COMPUTING ON THE INTERNET

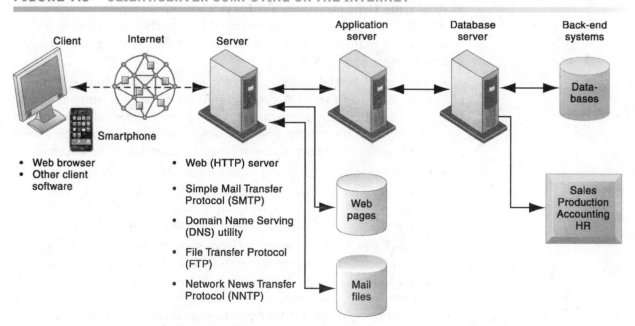

Client computers running Web browsers and other software can access an array of services on servers over the Internet. These services may all run on a single server or on multiple specialized servers.

Instant messaging is a type of chat service that enables participants to create their own private chat channels. The instant messaging system alerts the user whenever someone on his or her private list is online so that the user can initiate a chat session with other individuals. Instant messaging systems for consumers include Yahoo! Messenger, Google Talk, AOL Instant Messenger, and Facebook Chat. Companies concerned with security use proprietary communications and messaging systems such as IBM Sametime.

Newsgroups are worldwide discussion groups posted on Internet electronic bulletin boards on which people share information and ideas on a defined topic, such as radiology or rock bands. Anyone can post messages on these bulletin boards for others to read. Many thousands of groups exist that discuss almost all conceivable topics.

Organizations are applying the above mentioned Internet services in addition to some of the advanced features in the form of Groupware to facilitate official communication.

Groupware

Big organizations generally have more than one office, with employees working simultaneously from different locations. This is especially true in the case of the IT industry, where operations are spread over a number of countries. Employees situated at geographically different locations work on the same projects. Similarly in the automobile industry, various teams work from different locations for designing and manufacturing a single vehicle. Like the designing team may be in the USA and the engineering team in India. It is important that members of a team are able to communicate with one another. The Groupware technology allows for such communication. It can be divided into two categories:

- **Real-time Groupware technology:** This helps employees working at different locations communicate and share their thoughts in an interactive manner in real time. Some examples of this type of technology are:

  - *Whiteboard:* Whiteboards allow users to share information dynamically. The user can write down important notes on a whiteboard and share it with another person, who can, in turn, respond in real time. Whiteboards are mainly used in manufacturing organizations, where team members need to constantly share drawings of the designs.

  - *Chatrooms:* A user can enter a chat room and select the person to chat with. The organization can design chat rooms based on the departments and the work handled. In this technology, more than two employees can chat simultaneously and share information.

  - *GDSS:* This stands for group decision support system. GDSS helps users interact in real time using the sub-systems of DSS such as the dialogue management sub-system, the model management sub-system, and the data management sub-system. The GDSS chat room allows multiple users to communicate and take important decisions as a team. But when groups of users work simultaneously, it is very important to control the sessions. In GDSS, the group members choose a chairperson, who facilitates the session. The chairperson ensures that all participants get a chance to present their thoughts.

- **Non-real-time Groupware software:** Here, there is a disconnect between the time an employee shares the information and the time at which a response arrives. This concept is similar to sending someone a text message from your phone and waiting for their reply (or calling someone on their mobile phone and getting a response immediately). Some of the ways in which non-real-time Groupware technology is used are:

  - *E-mail*: E-mail is the most widely used type of non-real-time technology. One person sends the mail and another user reads it and responds. There is a provision to send group mails as well.

  - *Workflow system*: Documents flow within an organization based on hierarchy. A junior official often sends a report to their immediate senior. The senior, after filtration, sends the report a stage higher. This manual process is time-consuming and there are high chances of error. To overcome this, Groupware allows for the automatic hierarchical movement of an official report.

  - *Website*: Organizations create a Website to post latest information that employees can access using passwords. This restricts outside users from viewing official information. For example, the University Management School's Web site is open for all, but the teacher module can be accessed by the university staff only. Similarly, students are given a special password that allows them to download lectures and assignment from the Website. This facility is not provided to outside users.

Employee use of e-mail, instant messaging, and the Internet is supposed to increase worker productivity, but the accompanying Interactive Session on Management shows that this may not always be the case. Many company managers now believe they need to monitor and even regulate their employees' online activity. But is this ethical? Although there are some strong business reasons why companies may need to monitor their employees' e-mail and Web activities, what does this mean for employee privacy?

Voice over IP

The Internet has also become a popular platform for voice transmission and corporate networking. **Voice over IP (VoIP)** technology delivers voice information in digital form using packet switching, avoiding the tolls charged by local and long-distance telephone networks (see Figure 7.9). Calls that would ordinarily be transmitted over public telephone networks travel over the corporate network based on the Internet Protocol, or the public Internet. Voice calls can be made and received with a computer equipped with a microphone and speakers or with a VoIP-enabled telephone.

Cable firms such as Time Warner and Cablevision provide VoIP service bundled with their high-speed Internet and cable offerings. Skype offers free VoIP worldwide using a peer-to-peer network, and Google has its own free VoIP service.

INTERACTIVE SESSION: MANAGEMENT

MONITORING EMPLOYEES ON NETWORKS: UNETHICAL OR GOOD BUSINESS?

The Internet has become an extremely valuable business tool, but it's also a huge distraction for workers on the job. Employees are wasting valuable company time by surfing inappropriate Web sites (Facebook, shopping, sports, etc.), sending and receiving personal email, talking to friends via online chat, and downloading videos and music. According to IT research firm Gartner Inc., non-work-related Internet surfing results in an estimated 40% productivity loss each year for American businesses. A recent Gallup Poll found that the average employee spends over 75 minutes per day using office computers for non-business related activity. That translates into an annual loss of $6,250 per year, per employee. An average mid-size company of 500 employees could be expected to lose $3.25 million in lost productivity due to Internet misuse.

Many companies have begun monitoring employee use of e-mail and the Internet, sometimes without their knowledge. Many tools are now available for this purpose, including SONAR, Spector CNE Investigator, iSafe, OsMonitor, IMonitor, Work Examiner, Net Spy, Activity Monitor, Mobistealth, and Spytech. These products enable companies to record online searches, monitor file downloads and uploads, record keystrokes, keep tabs on emails, create transcripts of chats, or take certain screenshots of images displayed on computer screens. Instant messaging, text messaging, and social media monitoring are also increasing. Although U.S. companies have the legal right to monitor employee Internet and e-mail activity while they are at work, is such monitoring unethical, or is it simply good business?

Managers worry about the loss of time and employee productivity when employees are focusing on personal rather than company business. Too much time on personal business translates into lost revenue. Some employees may even be billing time they spend pursuing personal interests online to clients, thus overcharging them.

If personal traffic on company networks is too high, it can also clog the company's network so that legitimate business work cannot be performed. Procter & Gamble (P&G) found that on an average day, employees were listening to 4,000 hours of music on Pandora and viewing 50,000 five-minute YouTube videos. These activities involved streaming huge quantities of data, which slowed down P&G's Internet connection.

When employees use e-mail or the Web (including social networks) at employer facilities or with employer equipment, anything they do, including anything illegal, carries the company's name. Therefore, the employer can be traced and held liable. Management in many firms fear that racist, sexually explicit, or other potentially offensive material accessed or traded by their employees could result in adverse publicity and even lawsuits for the firm. An estimated 27 percent of Fortune 500 organizations have had to defend themselves against claims of sexual harassment stemming from inappropriate email. Even if the company is found not to be liable, responding to lawsuits could run up huge legal bills. Symantec's 2011 Social Media Protection Flash Poll found that the average litigation cost for companies with social media incidents ran over $650,000.

Companies also fear leakage of confidential information and trade secrets through e-mail or social networks. Another survey conducted by the American Management Association and the ePolicy Institute found that 14 percent of the employees polled admitted they had sent confidential or potentially embarrassing company e-mails to outsiders.

U.S. companies have the legal right to monitor what employees are doing with company equipment during business hours. The question is whether electronic surveillance is an appropriate tool for maintaining an efficient and positive workplace. Some companies try to ban all personal activities on corporate networks—zero tolerance. Others block employee access to specific Web sites or social sites, closely monitor e-mail messages, or limit personal time on the Web.

For example, P&G blocks Netflix and has asked employees to limit their use of Pandora. It still allows some YouTube viewing, and is not blocking access to social networking sites because staff use them for digital marketing campaigns. Ajax Boiler in Santa Ana, California, uses software from SpectorSoft Corporation that records all the Web sites employees visit, time spent at each site, and all e-mails sent. Financial services and investment firm Wedbush Securities monitors the daily e-mails, instant messaging, and social networking activity of its 1,000-plus employees. The firm's e-mail monitoring software flags certain types of messages and keywords within messages for further investigation.

A number of firms have fired employees who have stepped out of bounds. A Proofpoint survey found that one in five large U.S. companies fired an employee for violating e-mail policies in the past year. Among managers who fired employees for Internet misuse, the majority did so because the employees' e-mail contained sensitive, confidential, or embarrassing information.

No solution is problem-free, but many consultants believe companies should write corporate policies on employee e-mail, social media, and Web use. The policies should include explicit ground rules that state, by position or level,

under what circumstances employees can use company facilities for e-mail, blogging, or Web surfing. The policies should also inform employees whether these activities are monitored and explain why.

IBM now has "social computing guidelines" that cover employee activity on sites such as Facebook and Twitter. The guidelines urge employees not to conceal their identities, to remember that they are personally responsible for what they publish, and to refrain from discussing controversial topics that are not related to their IBM role.

The rules should be tailored to specific business needs and organizational cultures. For example, investment firms will need to allow many of their employees access to other investment sites. A company dependent on widespread information sharing, innovation, and independence could very well find that monitoring creates more problems than it solves.

Sources: "Should Companies Monitor Their Employees' Social Media?" *Wall Street Journal*, May 11, 2014; Rhodri Marsden, "Workplace monitoring mania may be risky business," Brisbane Times, March 30, 2014; Donna Iadipaolo, "Invading Your Privacy Is Now the Norm in the Workplace," Philly.com, April 28, 2014; "Office Slacker Stats," www.staffmonitoring.com, accessed May 1, 2014; "Office Productivity Loss," Staffmonitoring.com, accessed May 1, 2014; "Workplace Privacy and Employee Monitoring," Privacy Rights Clearinghouse, June 2013; Samuel Greengard, "How Smartphone Addiction Hurts Productivity," *CIO Insight*, March 11, 2013; Emily Glazer, "P&G Curbs Employees' Internet Use," *The Wall Street Journal*, April 4, 2012; and David L. Barron, "Social Media: Frontier for Employee Disputes," Baseline, January 19, 2012.

CASE STUDY QUESTIONS

1. Should managers monitor employee e-mail and Internet usage? Why or why not?

2. Describe an effective e-mail and Web use policy for a company.

3. Should managers inform employees that their Web behavior is being monitored? Or should managers monitor secretly? Why or why not?

Although there are up-front investments required for an IP phone system, VoIP can reduce communication and network management costs by 20 to 30 percent. For example, VoIP saves Virgin Entertainment Group $700,000 per year in long-distance bills. In addition to lowering long-distance costs and eliminating monthly fees for private lines, an IP network provides a single voice-data infrastructure for both telecommunications and computing

FIGURE 7.9   HOW VOICE OVER IP WORKS

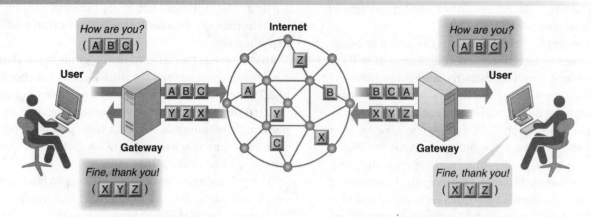

A VoIP phone call digitizes and breaks up a voice message into data packets that may travel along different routes before being reassembled at the final destination. A processor nearest the call's destination, called a gateway, arranges the packets in the proper order and directs them to the telephone number of the receiver or the IP address of the receiving computer.

services. Companies no longer have to maintain separate networks or provide support services and personnel for each different type of network.

Unified Communications

In the past, each of the firm's networks for wired and wireless data, voice communications, and videoconferencing operated independently of each other and had to be managed separately by the information systems department. Now, however, firms are able to merge disparate communications modes into a single universally accessible service using unified communications technology. **Unified communications** integrates disparate channels for voice communications, data communications, instant messaging, e-mail, and electronic conferencing into a single experience where users can seamlessly switch back and forth between different communication modes. Presence technology shows whether a person is available to receive a call. Companies will need to examine how work flows and business processes will be altered by this technology in order to gauge its value.

CenterPoint Properties, a major Chicago area industrial real estate company, used unified communications technology to create collaborative Web sites for each of its real estate deals. Each Web site provides a single point for accessing structured and unstructured data. Integrated presence technology lets team members e-mail, instant message, call, or videoconference with one click.

Virtual Private Networks

What if you had a marketing group charged with developing new products and services for your firm with members spread across the United States? You would want them to be able to e-mail each other and communicate with the home office without any chance that outsiders could intercept the communications. In the past, one answer to this problem was to work with large

FIGURE 7.10 A VIRTUAL PRIVATE NETWORK USING THE INTERNET

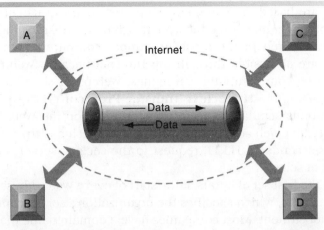

This VPN is a private network of computers linked using a secure "tunnel" connection over the Internet. It protects data transmitted over the public Internet by encoding the data and "wrapping" them within the Internet Protocol (IP). By adding a wrapper around a network message to hide its content, organizations can create a private connection that travels through the public Internet.

private networking firms who offered secure, private, dedicated networks to customers. But this was an expensive solution. A much less-expensive solution is to create a virtual private network within the public Internet.

A **virtual private network (VPN)** is a secure, encrypted, private network that has been configured within a public network to take advantage of the economies of scale and management facilities of large networks, such as the Internet (see Figure 7.10). A VPN provides your firm with secure, encrypted communications at a much lower cost than the same capabilities offered by traditional non-Internet providers who use their private networks to secure communications. VPNs also provide a network infrastructure for combining voice and data networks.

Several competing protocols are used to protect data transmitted over the public Internet, including *Point-to-Point Tunneling Protocol (PPTP)*. In a process called tunneling, packets of data are encrypted and wrapped inside IP packets. By adding this wrapper around a network message to hide its content, business firms create a private connection that travels through the public Internet.

THE WEB

The Web is the most popular Internet service. It's a system with universally accepted standards for storing, retrieving, formatting, and displaying information using a client/server architecture. Web pages are formatted using hypertext with embedded links that connect documents to one another and that also link pages to other objects, such as sound, video, or animation files. When you click a graphic and a video clip plays, you have clicked a hyperlink. A typical **Web site** is a collection of Web pages linked to a home page.

Hypertext

Web pages are based on a standard Hypertext Markup Language (HTML), which formats documents and incorporates dynamic links to other documents and pictures stored in the same or remote computers (see Chapter 5). Web pages are accessible through the Internet because Web browser software operating your computer can request Web pages stored on an Internet host server using the **Hypertext Transfer Protocol (HTTP)**. HTTP is the communications standard used to transfer pages on the Web. For example, when you type a Web address in your browser, such as http://www.sec.gov, your browser sends an HTTP request to the sec.gov server requesting the home page of sec.gov.

HTTP is the first set of letters at the start of every Web address, followed by the domain name, which specifies the organization's server computer that is storing the document. Most companies have a domain name that is the same as or closely related to their official corporate name. The directory path and document name are two more pieces of information within the Web address that help the browser track down the requested page. Together, the address is called a **uniform resource locator (URL)**. When typed into a browser, a URL tells the browser software exactly where to look for the information. For example, in the URL *http://www.megacorp.com/content/features/082610.html*, *http* names the protocol used to display Web pages, www.megacorp.com is the domain name, content/features is the directory path that identifies where on the domain Web server the page is stored, and 082610.html is the document name and the name of the format it is in (it is an HTML page).

Web Servers

A Web server is software for locating and managing stored Web pages. It locates the Web pages requested by a user on the computer where they are stored and delivers the Web pages to the user's computer. Server applications usually run on dedicated computers, although they can all reside on a single computer in small organizations.

The most common Web server in use today is Apache HTTP Server, followed by Microsoft Internet Information Services (IIS). Apache is an open source product that is free of charge and can be downloaded from the Web.

Searching for Information on the Web

No one knows for sure how many Web pages there really are. The surface Web is the part of the Web that search engines visit and about which information is recorded. For instance, Google visited an estimated 600 billion pages in 2013, and this reflects a large portion of the publicly accessible Web page population. But there is a "deep Web" that contains an estimated 1 trillion additional pages, many of them proprietary (such as the pages of the *Wall Street Journal Online*, which cannot be visited without a subscription or access code) or that are stored in protected corporate databases. Searching for information on Facebook is another matter. With an estimated 1.3 billion members, each with pages of text, photos, and media, the population of Web pages is larger than many estimates. But Facebook is a "closed" Web, and its pages are not searchable by Google or other search engines.

FIGURE 7.11 TOP WEB SEARCH ENGINES IN THE UNITED STATES

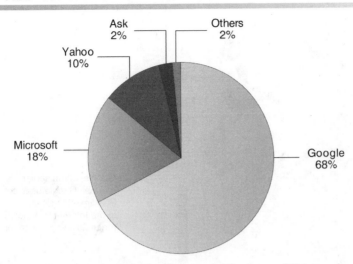

Google is the most popular search engine, handling nearly 70 percent of Web searches in the United States and around 90% in Europe.

Sources: Based on data from comScore Inc., February 2014.

Search Engines Obviously, with so many Web pages, finding specific Web pages that can help you or your business, nearly instantly, is an important problem. The question is, how can you find the one or two pages you really want and need out of billions of indexed Web pages? **Search engines** attempt to solve the problem of finding useful information on the Web nearly instantly, and, arguably, they are the "killer app" of the Internet era. Today's search engines can sift through HTML files, files of Microsoft Office applications, PDF files, as well as audio, video, and image files. There are hundreds of different search engines in the world, but the vast majority of search results are supplied by Google, Yahoo!, and Microsoft's Bing (see Figure 7.11).

Web search engines started out in the early 1990s as relatively simple software programs that roamed the nascent Web, visiting pages and gathering information about the content of each page. The first search engines were simple keyword indexes of all the pages they visited, leaving the user with lists of pages that may not have been truly relevant to their search.

In 1994, Stanford University computer science students David Filo and Jerry Yang created a hand-selected list of their favorite Web pages and called it "Yet Another Hierarchical Officious Oracle," or Yahoo. Yahoo was not initially a search engine but rather an edited selection of Web sites organized by categories the editors found useful. Currently Yahoo relies on Microsoft's Bing for search results.

In 1998, Larry Page and Sergey Brin, two other Stanford computer science students, released their first version of Google. This search engine was different: Not only did it index each Web page's words but it also ranked search results based on the relevance of each page. Page patented the idea of a page ranking system (called PageRank System), which essentially measures the popularity of a Web page by calculating the number of sites that link to that

FIGURE 7.12 HOW GOOGLE WORKS

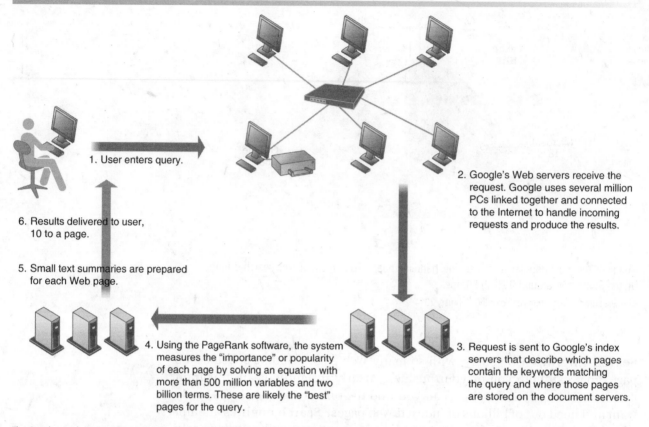

1. User enters query.

2. Google's Web servers receive the request. Google uses several million PCs linked together and connected to the Internet to handle incoming requests and produce the results.

6. Results delivered to user, 10 to a page.

5. Small text summaries are prepared for each Web page.

4. Using the PageRank software, the system measures the "importance" or popularity of each page by solving an equation with more than 500 million variables and two billion terms. These are likely the "best" pages for the query.

3. Request is sent to Google's index servers that describe which pages contain the keywords matching the query and where those pages are stored on the document servers.

The Google search engine is continuously crawling the Web, indexing the content of each page, calculating its popularity, and storing the pages so that it can respond quickly to user requests to see a page. The entire process takes about one-half second.

page as well as the number of pages to which it links. The premise is that really popular Web pages are more "relevant" to users. Brin contributed a unique Web crawler program that indexed not only keywords on a page but also combinations of words (such as authors and the titles of their articles). These two ideas became the foundation for the Google search engine. Figure 7.12 illustrates how Google works.

Mobile Search With the growth of mobile smartphones and tablet computers, and with about 167 million Americans accessing the Internet via mobile devices, the nature of e-commerce and search is changing. Mobile search from smartphones and tablets made up about 50 percent of all searches in 2014, and according to Google will expand rapidly in the next few years. Both Google and Yahoo have developed new search interfaces to make searching and shopping from smartphones more convenient. Amazon, for instance, sold over $1 billion in goods in 2013 through mobile searches of its store (Search Agency, 2013). While smartphones are widely used to shop, actual purchases typically take place on laptops or desktops, followed by tablets.

Search Engine Marketing Search engines have become major advertising platforms and shopping tools by offering what is now called **search engine**

marketing. Searching for information is one of the Web's most popular activities: 60% of American adult Internet users use a search engine at least once a day, generating about 90 billion queries a month. With this huge audience, search engines are the foundation for the most lucrative form of online marketing and advertising, search engine marketing. When users enter a search term at Google, Bing, Yahoo, or any of the other sites serviced by these search engines, they receive two types of listings: sponsored links, for which advertisers have paid to be listed (usually at the top of the search results page), and unsponsored "organic" search results. In addition, advertisers can purchase small text boxes on the side of search results pages. The paid, sponsored advertisements are the fastest growing form of Internet advertising and are powerful new marketing tools that precisely match consumer interests with advertising messages at the right moment. Search engine marketing monetizes the value of the search process. In 2014, search engine marketing is expected to generate $22.8 billion in revenue, nearly half of all online advertising ($51 billion). Google will for over 38% of all online advertising in 2014. About 97% of Google's revenue of $60 billion in 2013 came from online advertising, and 95% of the ad revenue came from search engine marketing (Google, 2014).

Because search engine marketing is so effective (it has the highest click-through rate and the highest return on ad investment), companies seek to optimize their Web sites for search engine recognition. The better optimized the page is, the higher a ranking it will achieve in search engine result listings. **Search engine optimization (SEO)** is the process of improving the quality and volume of Web traffic to a Web site by employing a series of techniques that help a Web site achieve a higher ranking with the major search engines when certain keywords and phrases are put into the search field. One technique is to make sure that the keywords used in the Web site description match the keywords likely to be used as search terms by prospective customers. For example, your Web site is more likely to be among the first ranked by search engines if it uses the keyword "lighting" rather than "lamps" if most prospective customers are searching for "lighting." It is also advantageous to link your Web site to as many other Web sites as possible because search engines evaluate such links to determine the popularity of a Web page and how it is linked to other content on the Web. Search engines can be gamed by scammers who create thousands of phony Web site pages and link them altogether, or link them to a single retailer's site in an attempt to fool Google's search engine. Firms can also pay so-called "link farms" to link to their site. Google changed its search algorithm in 2012. Codenamed "Penguin," the new algorithm examines the quality of links more carefully with the intent of down ranking sites that have a suspicious pattern of sites linking to them. Penguin is updated annually and published.

Google and other search engine firms are attempting to refine search engine algorithms to capture more of what the user intended, and more the "meaning" of a search. Google introduced Hummingbird, its new search algorithm in September 2013. Rather than evaluate each word separately in a search, Google's semantically informed Hummingbird will try to evaluate an entire sentence. So, if your search is a long sentence like "Google annual report selected financial data 2013," Hummingbird should be able to figure out that you really want the SEC Form 10k report filed with the Securities and Exchange Commission on March 31, 2014. How about "Italian restaurant Brooklyn Bridge"? This will return the name and location of a number of Italian restaurants in vicinity of the Brooklyn Bridge. Semantic search more closely follows conversational search, or search as you would ordinarily speak it to another human being. Google's predictive search is now a part of most search results. In **predictive search**, this part of the search algorithm guesses what you are looking for, and suggests search terms as you enter your search. Google searches also take advantage of Knowledge Graph, an effort of the search algorithm to anticipate what you might want to know more about as you search on a topic. Results of the knowledge graph appear on the right of the screen and contain more information about the topic or person you are searching on.

In general, search engines have been very helpful to small businesses that cannot afford large marketing campaigns. Because shoppers are looking for a specific product or service when they use search engines, they are what marketers call "hot prospects"—people who are looking for information and often intending to buy. Moreover, search engines charge only for click-throughs to a site. Merchants do not have to pay for ads that don't work, only for ads that receive a click. Consumers benefit from search engine marketing because ads for merchants appear only when consumers are looking for a specific product. There are no pop-ups, Flash animations, videos, interstitials, e-mails, or other irrelevant communications to deal with. Thus, search engine marketing saves consumers cognitive energy and reduces search costs (including the cost of transportation needed to physically search for products). One study estimated the global value of search to both merchants and consumers to be more than $800 billion, with about 65 percent of the benefit going to consumers in the form of lower search costs and lower prices (McKinsey, 2011). Google and Microsoft face challenges ahead as desktop PC search growth slows, and revenues decline because the price of search engine ads is declining slightly. The growth in mobile search does not make up for the loss of desktop search revenues because mobile ads sell for generally half as much as desktop search ads.

Social Search One problem with Google and mechanical search engines is that they are so thorough: Enter a search for "ultra computers" and in .2 seconds you will receive over 300 million reponses! Search engines are not very discriminating. **Social search** is an effort to provide fewer, more relevant, and trustworthy search results based on a person's network of social contacts. In contrast to the top search engines that use a mathematical algorithm to find pages that satisfy your query, a social search Web site would review your friends' recommendations (and their friends'), their past Web visits, and their use of "Like" buttons.

In January 2013 Facebook launched Graph Search, a social network search engine that responds to user search queries with information from the user's social network of friends and connections. Graph Search relies upon the huge amount of data on Facebook that is, or can be, linked to individuals and organizations. You might use Graph Search to search for Boston restaurants that your friends like, alumni from the University of South Carolina who like

Lady Gaga, or pictures of your friends before 2010. Google has developed Google +1 as a social layer on top of its existing search engine. Users can place a +1 next to the Web sites they found helpful, and their friends will be notified automatically. Subsequent searches by their friends would list the +1 sites recommended by friends higher up on the page. One problem with social search is that your close friends may not have intimate knowledge of topics you are exploring, or they may have tastes you don't appreciate. It's also possible your close friends don't have any knowledge about what you are searching for.

Semantic Search   Another way for search engines to become more discriminating and helpful is to make search engines that could understand what it is we are really looking for. Called "semantic search" the goal is to build a search engine that could really understand human language and behavior. For instance, in 2012 Google's search engine began delivering more than millions of links. It started to give users more facts and direct answers, and to provide more relevant links to sites based on the search engine's estimation of what the user intended, and even on the user's past search behavior. Google's search engine is trying to understand what people are most likely thinking about when they search for something. Google hopes to use its massive database of objects (people, places, things), and smart software to provide users better results than just millions of hits. For instance, do a search on "Lake Tahoe" and the search engine will return basic facts about Tahoe (altitude, average temperature, and local fish), a map, and hotel accommodations (Efrati, 2012).

Although search engines were originally designed to search text documents, the explosion of photos and videos on the Internet created a demand for searching and classifying these visual objects. Facial recognition software can create a digital version of a human face. In 2012 Facebook introduced its facial recognition software and combined it with tagging, to create a new feature called Tag Suggest. The software creates a digital facial print, similar to a finger print. Users can put their own tagged photo on their timeline, and their friend's timelines. Once a person's photo is tagged, Facebook can pick that person out of a group photo, and identify for others who is in the photo. You can also search for people on Facebook using their digital image to find and identify them.

Intelligent Agent Shopping Bots   Chapter 11 describes the capabilities of software agents with built-in intelligence that can gather or filter information and perform other tasks to assist users. **Shopping bots** use intelligent agent software for searching the Internet for shopping information. Shopping bots such as MySimon or PriceGrabber can help people interested in making a purchase filter and retrieve information about products of interest, evaluate competing products according to criteria the users have established, and negotiate with vendors for price and delivery terms. Many of these shopping agents search the Web for pricing and availability of products specified by the user and return a list of sites that sell the item along with pricing information and a purchase link.

Web 2.0

Today's Web sites don't just contain static content—they enable people to collaborate, share information, and create new services and content online. These second-generation interactive Internet-based services are referred to as **Web 2.0**. If you have shared photos over the Internet at Flickr or another photo site, pinned a photo on Pinterest, posted a video to YouTube, created a blog, or added an app to your Facebook page, you've used some of these Web 2.0 services.

Web 2.0 has four defining features: interactivity, real-time user control, social participation (sharing), and user-generated content. The technologies and services behind these features include cloud computing, software mashups and apps, blogs, RSS, wikis, and social networks.

Mashups, which we introduced in Chapter 5, are software services that enable users and system developers to mix and match content or software components to create something entirely new. For example, Yahoo's photo storage and sharing site Flickr combines photos with other information about the images provided by users and tools to make it usable within other programming environments. Web 2.0 tools and services have fueled the creation of social networks and other online communities where people can interact with one another in the manner of their choosing.

A **blog**, the popular term for a Weblog, is a personal Web site that typically contains a series of chronological entries (newest to oldest) by its author, and links to related Web pages. Blogging is a major activity for U.S. Internet users: 74 million read blogs, and 22 million write blogs or post to blogs. The blog may include a *blogroll* (a collection of links to other blogs) and *trackbacks* (a list of entries in other blogs that refer to a post on the first blog). Most blogs allow readers to post comments on the blog entries as well. The act of creating a blog is often referred to as "blogging." Blogs can be hosted by a third-party service such as Blogger.com, TypePad.com, and Xanga.com, and blogging features have been incorporated into social networks such as Facebook and collaboration platforms such as Lotus Notes. WordPress is a leading open source blogging tool and content management system. **Microblogging**, used in Twitter, is a type of blogging that features short posts of 140 characters or less.

Blog pages are usually variations on templates provided by the blogging service or software. Therefore, millions of people without HTML skills of any kind can post their own Web pages and share content with others. The totality of blog-related Web sites is often referred to as the **blogosphere**. Although blogs have become popular personal publishing tools, they also have business uses (see Chapters 2 and 10).

If you're an avid blog reader, you might use RSS to keep up with your favorite blogs without constantly checking them for updates. **RSS**, which stands for Really Simple Syndication or Rich Site Summary, pulls specified content from Web sites and feeds it automatically to users' computers. RSS reader software gathers material from the Web sites or blogs that you tell it to scan and brings new information from those sites to you. RSS readers are available through Web sites such as Google and Yahoo, and they have been incorporated into the major Web browsers and e-mail programs.

Blogs allow visitors to add comments to the original content, but they do not allow visitors to change the original posted material. **Wikis**, in contrast, are collaborative Web sites where visitors can add, delete, or modify content on the site, including the work of previous authors. Wiki comes from the Hawaiian word for "quick."

Wiki software typically provides a template that defines layout and elements common to all pages, displays user-editable software program code, and then renders the content into an HTML-based page for display in a Web browser. Some wiki software allows only basic text formatting, whereas other tools allow the use of tables, images, or even interactive elements, such as polls or games. Most wikis provide capabilities for monitoring the work of other users and correcting mistakes.

Because wikis make information sharing so easy, they have many business uses. The U.S. Department of Homeland Security's National Cyber Security Center (NCSC) deployed a wiki to facilitate collaboration among federal agencies on cybersecurity. NCSC and other agencies use the wiki for real-time information sharing on threats, attacks, and responses and as a repository for technical and standards information. Pixar Wiki is a collaborative community wiki for publicizing the work of Pixar Animation Studios. The wiki format allows anyone to create or edit an article about a Pixar film.

Social networking sites enable users to build communities of friends and professional colleagues. Members typically create a "profile," a Web page for posting photos, videos, MP3 files, and text, and then share these profiles with others on the service identified as their "friends" or contacts. Social networking sites are highly interactive, offer real-time user control, rely on user-generated content, and are broadly based on social participation and sharing of content and opinions. Leading social networking sites include Facebook, Twitter (with 1.3 billion and 270 million monthly active users respectively in 2014), and LinkedIn (for professional contacts).

For many, social networking sites are the defining Web 2.0 application, and one that has radically changed how people spend their time online; how people communicate and with whom; how business people stay in touch with customers, suppliers, and employees; how providers of goods and services learn about their customers; and how advertisers reach potential customers. The large social networking sites are also morphing into application development platforms where members can create and sell software applications to other members of the community. Facebook alone has over 1 million developers who created over 550,000 applications for gaming, video sharing, and communicating with friends and family. We talk more about business applications of social networking in Chapters 2 and 10, and you can find social networking discussions in many other chapters of this book. You can also find a more detailed discussion of Web 2.0 in our Learning Tracks.

Web 3.0 and the Future Web

Americans conducted about 19 billion searches in January 2014 (comScore, 2014). How many of these produced a meaningful result (a useful answer in the first three listings)? Arguably, fewer than half. Google, Yahoo, Microsoft, and Amazon are all trying to increase the odds of people finding meaningful answers to search engine queries. But with over 500 billion Web pages indexed, the means available for finding the information you really want are quite primitive, based on the words used on the pages, and the relative popularity of the page among people who use those same search terms. In other words, it's hit or miss.

To a large extent, the future of the Web involves developing techniques to make searching the 500 billion public Web pages more productive and meaningful for ordinary people. Web 1.0 solved the problem of obtaining access to information. Web 2.0 solved the problem of sharing that information with others and building new Web experiences. **Web 3.0** is the promise of a future Web where all this digital information, all these contacts, can be woven together into a single meaningful experience.

Sometimes this is referred to as the **Semantic Web**. "Semantic" refers to meaning. Most of the Web's content today is designed for humans to read and for computers to display, not for computer programs to analyze and manipulate. Semantic Search, described above, is a subset of a larger effort to make the Web more intelligent, more humanlike (W3C, 2012). Search engines can discover when a particular term or keyword appears in a Web document, but they do not really understand its meaning or how it relates to other information on the Web. You can check this out on Google by entering two searches. First, enter "Paris Hilton". Next, enter "Hilton in Paris". Because Google does not understand ordinary English, it has no idea that you are interested in the Hilton Hotel in Paris in the second search. Because it cannot understand the meaning of pages it has indexed, Google's search engine returns the most popular pages for those queries where "Hilton" and "Paris" appear on the pages.

First described in a 2001 *Scientific* American article, the Semantic Web is a collaborative effort led by the World Wide Web Consortium to add a layer of meaning atop the existing Web to reduce the amount of human involvement in searching for and processing Web information. For instance, the New York Times launched a semantic application called Longitude which provides a graphical interface to access the Times content. You can ask for stories about Germany in the last 24 hours, or a city in the United States, to retrieve all recent stories in the Times.

Views on the future of the Web vary, but they generally focus on ways to make the Web more "intelligent," with machine-facilitated understanding of information promoting a more intuitive and effective user experience. For instance, let's say you want to set up a party with your tennis buddies at a local restaurant Friday night after work. One problem is that you are already scheduled to go to a movie with another friend. In a Semantic Web 3.0 environment, you would be able to coordinate this change in plans with the schedules of your tennis buddies and the schedule of your movie friend, and make a reservation at the restaurant all with a single set of commands issued as text or voice to your handheld smartphone. Right now, this capability is beyond our grasp.

Work proceeds slowly on making the Web a more intelligent experience, in large part because it is difficult to make machines, including software programs, that are truly intelligent like humans. But there are other views of the future Web. Some see a 3-D Web where you can walk through pages in a 3-D environment. Others point to the idea of a pervasive Web that controls everything from a city's traffic lights and water usage, to the lights in your living room, to your car's rear view mirror, not to mention managing your calendar and appointments. This is referred to as the "Internet of Things."

The Internet of Things includes the widespread use and distribution of sensors. Firms like IBM, HP, and Oracle are exploring how to build smart machines, factories, and cities through extensive use of remote sensors and fast cloud computing. We provide more detail on this topic in the following section.

The "App Internet" is another element in the future Web. The growth of apps within the mobile platform is astounding: Over 80% of mobile minutes in the United States are generated through apps, only 20% using browsers. Apps give users direct access to content and are much faster than loading a browser and searching for content.

The **visual Web** is another part of the future Web. The "visual Web" refers to Web sites like Pinterest where pictures replace text documents, where users search on pictures, and where pictures of products replace display ads for products. Pinterest is a social networking site that provides users (as well as brands) with an online board to which they can "pin" interesting pictures. Looking for a blue dress, or black dress shirt? Google will deliver thousands of links to sites that sell these items. Pinterest will deliver a much smaller collection of magazine quality photos linked subtly to vendor Web sites. Considered the fastest growing Web site in history, Pinterest has 70 million monthly users and was the 35th most popular Web destination in 2014. The Instagram app is another example of the visual Web. Instagram is a photo and video sharing site that allows users to take pictures, enhance them, and share them with friends on other social sites like Facebook, Twitter, Tumblr, and Google+. In 2014 Instagram had 220 million monthly active users.

Other complementary trends leading toward a future Web 3.0 include more widespread use of cloud computing and software as a service (SaaS) business models, ubiquitous connectivity among mobile platforms and Internet access devices, and the transformation of the Web from a network of separate siloed applications and content into a more seamless and interoperable whole. These more modest visions of the future Web 3.0 are more likely to be realized in the near term.

7.4 WHAT ARE THE PRINCIPAL TECHNOLOGIES AND STANDARDS FOR WIRELESS NETWORKING, COMMUNICATION, AND INTERNET ACCESS?

Welcome to the wireless revolution! Cell phones, smartphones, tablets, and wireless-enabled personal computers have morphed into portable media and computing platforms that let you perform many of the computing tasks you used to do at your desk, and a whole lot more. We introduced smartphones in our discussions of the mobile digital platform in Chapters 1 and 5. **Smartphones** such as the iPhone, Android phones, and BlackBerry combine the functionality of a cell phone with that of a mobile laptop computer with Wi-Fi capability. This makes it possible to combine music, video, Internet access, and telephone service in one device. A large part of the Internet is becoming a mobile, access-anywhere, broadband service for the delivery of video, music, and Web search.

CELLULAR SYSTEMS

In 2013, over 1.8 billion cell phones were sold worldwide. In the United States, there are 365 million cell phone subscriptions, and 164 million people have smartphones. About 167 million people access the Web using their phone (eMarketer, 2014). In a few years, smartphones will be the predominant source of searches, not the desktop PC. Digital cellular service uses several competing standards. In Europe and much of the rest of the world outside the United Sates, the standard is Global System for Mobile Communications (GSM). GSM's strength is its international roaming capability. There are GSM cell phone systems in the United States, including T-Mobile and AT&T.

A competing standard in the United States is Code Division Multiple Access (CDMA), which is the system used by Verizon and Sprint. CDMA was developed by the military during World War II. It transmits over several frequencies, occupies the entire spectrum, and randomly assigns users to a range of frequencies over time, making it more efficient than GSM.

Earlier generations of cellular systems were designed primarily for voice and limited data transmission in the form of short text messages. Today wireless carriers offer 3G and 4G networks. **3G networks**, with transmission speeds ranging from 144 Kbps for mobile users in, say, a car, to more than 2 Mbps for stationary users, offer fair transmission speeds for e-mail, browsing the Web, and online shopping, but are too slow for videos. **4G networks** have much higher speeds: 100 megabits/second download, and 50 megabits upload speed, with more than enough capacity for watching high definition video on your smartphone. Long Term Evolution (LTE) and mobile Worldwide Interoperability for Microwave Access (WiMax—see the following section) are the current 4G standards.

WIRELESS COMPUTER NETWORKS AND INTERNET ACCESS

An array of technologies provide high-speed wireless access to the Internet for PCs and mobile devices. These new high-speed services have extended Internet access to numerous locations that could not be covered by traditional wired Internet services, and have made ubiquitous computing, anywhere, anytime, a reality.

Bluetooth

Bluetooth is the popular name for the 802.15 wireless networking standard, which is useful for creating small **personal area networks (PANs)**. It links up to eight devices within a 10-meter area using low-power, radio-based communication and can transmit up to 722 Kbps in the 2.4-GHz band.

Wireless phones, pagers, computers, printers, and computing devices using Bluetooth communicate with each other and even operate each other without direct user intervention (see Figure 7.13). For example, a person could

FIGURE 7.13 A BLUETOOTH NETWORK (PAN)

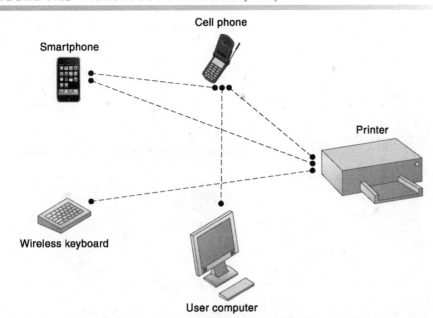

Bluetooth enables a variety of devices, including cell phones, smartphones, wireless keyboards and mice, PCs, and printers, to interact wirelessly with each other within a small 30-foot (10-meter) area. In addition to the links shown, Bluetooth can be used to network similar devices to send data from one PC to another, for example.

direct a notebook computer to send a document file wirelessly to a printer. Bluetooth connects wireless keyboards and mice to PCs or cell phones to earpieces without wires. Bluetooth has low power requirements, making it appropriate for battery-powered handheld computers or cell phones.

Although Bluetooth lends itself to personal networking, it has uses in large corporations. For example, FedEx drivers use Bluetooth to transmit the delivery data captured by their handheld PowerPad computers to cellular transmitters, which forward the data to corporate computers. Drivers no longer need to spend time docking their handheld units physically in the transmitters, and Bluetooth has saved FedEx $20 million per year.

Wi-Fi and Wireless Internet Access

The 802.11 set of standards for wireless LANs and wireless Internet access is also known as **Wi-Fi**. The first of these standards to be widely adopted was 802.11b, which can transmit up to 11 Mbps in the unlicensed 2.4-GHz band and has an effective distance of 30 to 50 meters. The 802.11g standard can transmit up to 54 Mbps in the 2.4-GHz range. 802.11n is capable of transmitting over 100 Mbps. Today's PCs and netbooks have built-in support for Wi-Fi, as do the iPhone, iPad, and other smartphones.

In most Wi-Fi communication, wireless devices communicate with a wired LAN using access points. An access point is a box consisting of a radio receiver/transmitter and antennas that links to a wired network, router, or hub. Mobile access points such as Verizon's Mobile Hotspots use the existing cellular network to create Wi-Fi connections.

FIGURE 7.14 AN 802.11 WIRELESS LAN

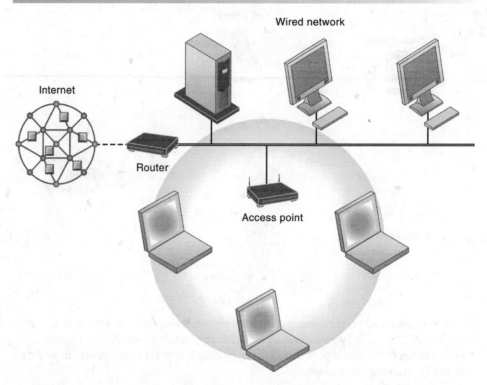

Mobile laptop computers equipped with network interface cards link to the wired LAN by communicating with the access point. The access point uses radio waves to transmit network signals from the wired network to the client adapters, which convert them into data that the mobile device can understand. The client adapter then transmits the data from the mobile device back to the access point, which forwards the data to the wired network.

Figure 7.14 illustrates an 802.11 wireless LAN that connects a small number of mobile devices to a larger wired LAN and to the Internet. Most wireless devices are client machines. The servers that the mobile client stations need to use are on the wired LAN. The access point controls the wireless stations and acts as a bridge between the main wired LAN and the wireless LAN. (A bridge connects two LANs based on different technologies.) The access point also controls the wireless stations.

The most popular use for Wi-Fi today is for high-speed wireless Internet service. In this instance, the access point plugs into an Internet connection, which could come from a cable service or DSL telephone service. Computers within range of the access point use it to link wirelessly to the Internet.

Hotspots typically consist of one or more access points providing wireless Internet access in a public place. Some hotspots are free or do not require any additional software to use; others may require activation and the establishment of a user account by providing a credit card number over the Web.

Businesses of all sizes are using Wi-Fi networks to provide low-cost wireless LANs and Internet access. Wi-Fi hotspots can be found in hotels, airport lounges, libraries, cafes, and college campuses to provide mobile access to the Internet. Dartmouth College is one of many campuses where students now use Wi-Fi for research, course work, and entertainment.

Wi-Fi technology poses several challenges, however. One is Wi-Fi's security features, which make these wireless networks vulnerable to intruders. We provide more detail about Wi-Fi security issues in Chapter 8.

Another drawback of Wi-Fi networks is susceptibility to interference from nearby systems operating in the same spectrum, such as wireless phones, microwave ovens, or other wireless LANs. However, wireless networks based on the 802.11n standard are able to solve this problem by using multiple wireless antennas in tandem to transmit and receive data and technology called *MIMO* (multiple input multiple output) to coordinate multiple simultaneous radio signals.

WiMax

A surprisingly large number of areas in the United States and throughout the world do not have access to Wi-Fi or fixed broadband connectivity. The range of Wi-Fi systems is no more than 300 feet from the base station, making it difficult for rural groups that don't have cable or DSL service to find wireless access to the Internet.

The IEEE developed a new family of standards known as WiMax to deal with these problems. **WiMax**, which stands for Worldwide Interoperability for Microwave Access, is the popular term for IEEE Standard 802.16. It has a wireless access range of up to 31 miles and transmission speed of up to 75 Mbps.

WiMax antennas are powerful enough to beam high-speed Internet connections to rooftop antennas of homes and businesses that are miles away. Cellular handsets and laptops with WiMax capabilities are appearing in the marketplace. Mobile WiMax is one of the 4G network technologies we discussed earlier in this chapter.

EVDO

EVDO stands for evolution data-optimized, or enhanced voice, data only. EVDO technology is an extension of the code division multiple access (CDMA) 2000 standard. It is a 3G communication protocol for high-speed wireless broadband connectivity. This technology uses both CDMA and TDM (time division multiplexing). Tata Photon, Reliance Interconnect Broadband, and BSNL EVDO use this technology. EVDO is to the CDMA standard what 3G is to GSM users. EVDO provides Internet speeds of up to 3.1 Mbps.

In CDMA, each user is provided a unique mathematical code, which is used to transcript the data the user wants to send. This modified message is sent across the channel with messages of several other wireless users, each having a unique code. Upon reception of the modified signal, a reversed code is applied and the original message is recovered. This is a powerful technique, which allows multiple access to the users and also secures data transmission. In EVDO, data is broken into small packets that are sent independently. This enhances the speed and security of the data. In EVDO, the forward link uses TDM, where each user is given access to the channel for a given time slot, which is modulated independently for each user. The reverse link from the mobile station to the base transceiver station uses CDMA.

The main drawback of EVDO is that it has limited coverage. The EVDO modem helps users connect to the Internet. But the user needs to subscribe to the Internet service provider. For existing CDMA users, this technology is like an upgrade, since it uses the same broadcasting frequencies as CDMA. Therefore, the cost for licensing the spectrum or building the infrastructure is negligible. This is also one of the reasons that most of the CDMA providers are now switching to EVDO.

RFID AND WIRELESS SENSOR NETWORKS

Mobile technologies are creating new efficiencies and ways of working throughout the enterprise. In addition to the wireless systems we have just described, radio frequency identification systems and wireless sensor networks are having a major impact.

Radio Frequency Identification (RFID)

Radio frequency identification (RFID) systems provide a powerful technology for tracking the movement of goods throughout the supply chain. RFID systems use tiny tags with embedded microchips containing data about an item and its location to transmit radio signals over a short distance to RFID readers. The RFID readers then pass the data over a network to a computer for processing. Unlike bar codes, RFID tags do not need line-of-sight contact to be read.

The RFID tag is electronically programmed with information that can uniquely identify an item plus other information about the item, such as its location, where and when it was made, or its status during production. Embedded in the tag is a microchip for storing the data. The rest of the tag is an antenna that transmits data to the reader.

The reader unit consists of an antenna and radio transmitter with a decoding capability attached to a stationary or handheld device. The reader emits radio waves in ranges anywhere from 1 inch to 100 feet, depending on its power output, the radio frequency employed, and surrounding environmental conditions. When a RFID tag comes within the range of the reader, the tag is activated and starts sending data. The reader captures these data, decodes them, and sends them back over a wired or wireless network to a host computer for further processing (see Figure 7.15). Both RFID tags and antennas come in a variety of shapes and sizes.

In inventory control and supply chain management, RFID systems capture and manage more detailed information about items in warehouses or in production than bar coding systems. If a large number of items are shipped together, RFID systems track each pallet, lot, or even unit item in the shipment. This technology may help companies such as Walmart improve receiving and storage operations by improving their ability to "see" exactly what stock is stored in warehouses or on retail store shelves. Dundee Precious Metals, described in the chapter-opening case, uses RFID technology to track workers, equipment, and vehicles in its underground mine.

Walmart has installed RFID readers at store receiving docks to record the arrival of pallets and cases of goods shipped with RFID tags. The RFID reader reads the tags a second time just as the cases are brought onto the sales floor

FIGURE 7.15 HOW RFID WORKS

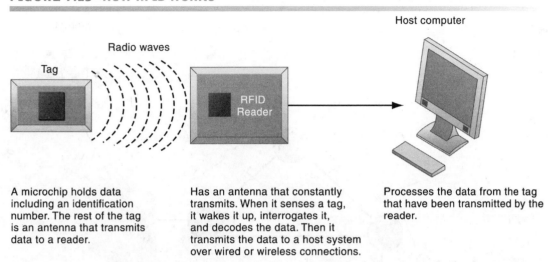

| A microchip holds data including an identification number. The rest of the tag is an antenna that transmits data to a reader. | Has an antenna that constantly transmits. When it senses a tag, it wakes it up, interrogates it, and decodes the data. Then it transmits the data to a host system over wired or wireless connections. | Processes the data from the tag that have been transmitted by the reader. |

RFID uses low-powered radio transmitters to read data stored in a tag at distances ranging from 1 inch to 100 feet. The reader captures the data from the tag and sends them over a network to a host computer for processing.

from backroom storage areas. Software combines sales data from Walmart's point-of-sale systems and the RFID data regarding the number of cases brought out to the sales floor. The program determines which items will soon be depleted and automatically generates a list of items to pick in the warehouse to replenish store shelves before they run out. This information helps Walmart reduce out-of-stock items, increase sales, and further shrink its costs.

The cost of RFID tags used to be too high for widespread use, but now it starts at around 7 cents per tag in the United States. As the price decreases, RFID is starting to become cost-effective for many applications.

In addition to installing RFID readers and tagging systems, companies may need to upgrade their hardware and software to process the massive amounts of data produced by RFID systems—transactions that could add up to tens or hundreds of terabytes.

Software is used to filter, aggregate, and prevent RFID data from overloading business networks and system applications. Applications often need to be redesigned to accept large volumes of frequently generated RFID data and to share those data with other applications. Major enterprise software vendors, including SAP and Oracle PeopleSoft, now offer RFID-ready versions of their supply chain management applications.

Wireless Sensor Networks

If your company wanted state-of-the art technology to monitor building security or detect hazardous substances in the air, it might deploy a wireless sensor network. **Wireless sensor networks (WSNs)** are networks of interconnected wireless devices that are embedded into the physical environment to provide measurements of many points over large spaces. These devices have built-in processing, storage, and radio frequency sensors and antennas. They are linked into an interconnected network that routes the data they capture to a computer for analysis.

FIGURE 7.16 A WIRELESS SENSOR NETWORK

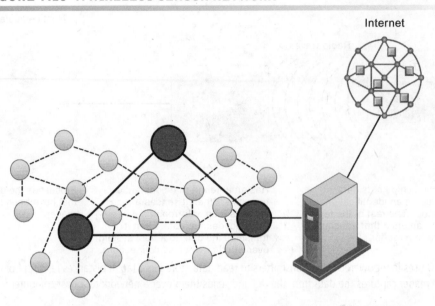

The small circles represent lower-level nodes and the larger circles represent high-end nodes. Lower-level nodes forward data to each other or to higher-level nodes, which transmit data more rapidly and speed up network performance.

These networks range from hundreds to thousands of nodes. Because wireless sensor devices are placed in the field for years at a time without any maintenance or human intervention, they must have very low power requirements and batteries capable of lasting for years.

Figure 7.16 illustrates one type of wireless sensor network, with data from individual nodes flowing across the network to a server with greater processing power. The server acts as a gateway to a network based on Internet technology.

Wireless sensor networks are valuable in areas such as monitoring environmental changes, monitoring traffic or military activity, protecting property, efficiently operating and managing machinery and vehicles, establishing security perimeters, monitoring supply chain management, or detecting chemical, biological, or radiological material.

RFID systems and wireless sensor networks are major sources of "Big Data" that organizations are starting to analyze to improve their operations and decision making. Output from these systems is fueling what is called the Industrial Internet, also known as the **Internet of Things**, in which machines such as jet engines, power plant turbines, or agricultural sensors constantly gather data and send the data over the Internet for analysis. The data might signal the need to take action, such as replacing a part that's close to wearing out, restocking a product on a store shelf, starting the watering system for a soybean field, or slowing down a turbine. Over time, more and more everyday physical objects will be connected to the Internet and will be able to identify themselves to other devices, creating networks that can sense and respond as data changes. Another example is the "smart city," described in the Chapter 12 Interactive Session on Organizations. You'll see more examples of the Internet of Things in Chapter 12.

Review Summary

1. *What are the principal components of telecommunications networks and key networking technologies?*

   A simple network consists of two or more connected computers. Basic network components include computers, network interfaces, a connection medium, network operating system software, and either a hub or a switch. The networking infrastructure for a large company includes the traditional telephone system, mobile cellular communication, wireless local area networks, videoconferencing systems, a corporate Web site, intranets, extranets, and an array of local and wide area networks, including the Internet.

   Contemporary networks have been shaped by the rise of client/server computing, the use of packet switching, and the adoption of Transmission Control Protocol/Internet Protocol (TCP/IP) as a universal communications standard for linking disparate networks and computers, including the Internet. Protocols provide a common set of rules that enable communication among diverse components in a telecommunications network.

2. *What are the different types of networks?*

   The principal physical transmission media are twisted copper telephone wire, coaxial copper cable, fiber-optic cable, and wireless transmission.

   Local area networks (LANs) connect PCs and other digital devices together within a 500-meter radius and are used today for many corporate computing tasks. Wide area networks (WANs) span broad geographical distances, ranging from several miles to continents, and are often private networks that are independently managed. Metropolitan area networks (MANs) span a single urban area.

   Digital subscriber line (DSL) technologies, cable Internet connections, and T1 lines are often used for high-capacity Internet connections.

3. *How do the Internet and Internet technology work, and how do they support communication and e-business?*

   The Internet is a worldwide network of networks that uses the client/server model of computing and the TCP/IP network reference model. Every computer on the Internet is assigned a unique numeric IP address. The Domain Name System (DNS) converts IP addresses to more user-friendly domain names. Worldwide Internet policies are established by organizations and government bodies, such as the Internet Architecture Board (IAB) and the World Wide Web Consortium (W3C).

   Major Internet services include e-mail, newsgroups, chatting, instant messaging, Telnet, FTP, and the Web. Web pages are based on Hypertext Markup Language (HTML) and can display text, graphics, video, and audio. Web site directories, search engines, and RSS technology help users locate the information they need on the Web. RSS, blogs, social networking, and wikis are features of Web 2.0.

   Firms are also starting to realize economies by using VoIP technology for voice transmission and by using virtual private networks (VPNs) as low-cost alternatives to private WANs.

4. *What are the principal technologies and standards for wireless networking, communication, and Internet access?*

   Cellular networks are evolving toward high-speed, high-bandwidth, digital packet-switched transmission. Broadband 3G networks are capable of transmitting data at speeds ranging from 144 Kbps to more than 2 Mbps. 4G networks capable of transmission speeds of 100 Mbps are starting to be rolled out.

   Major cellular standards include Code Division Multiple Access (CDMA), which is used primarily in the United States, and Global System for Mobile Communications (GSM), which is the standard in Europe and much of the rest of the world.

   Standards for wireless computer networks include Bluetooth (802.15) for small personal area networks (PANs), Wi-Fi (802.11) for local area networks (LANs), and WiMax (802.16) for metropolitan area networks (MANs).

Radio frequency identification (RFID) systems provide a powerful technology for tracking the movement of goods by using tiny tags with embedded data about an item and its location. RFID readers read the radio signals transmitted by these tags and pass the data over a network to a computer for processing. Wireless sensor networks (WSNs) are networks of interconnected wireless sensing and transmitting devices that are embedded into the physical environment to provide measurements of many points over large spaces.

Key Terms

Review Questions

7-1 What are the principal components of telecommunications networks and key networking technologies?

- Describe the features of a simple network and the network infrastructure for a large company.

- Name and describe the principal technologies and trends that have shaped contemporary telecommunications systems.

7-2 What are the different types of networks?

- Define an analog and a digital signal.

- Distinguish between a LAN, MAN, and WAN.

7-3 How do the Internet and Internet technology work, and how do they support communication and e-business?

- Define the Internet, describe how it works, and explain how it provides business value.
- Explain how the Domain Name System (DNS) and IP addressing system work.
- List and describe the principal Internet services.
- Define and describe VoIP and virtual private networks, and explain how they provide value to businesses.
- List and describe alternative ways of locating information on the Web.
- Describe how online search technologies are used for marketing.

7-4 What are the principal technologies and standards for wireless networking, communications, and Internet access?

- Define Bluetooth, Wi-Fi, WiMax, and 3G and 4G networks.
- Describe the capabilities of each and for which types of applications each is best suited.
- Define RFID, explain how it works, and describe how it provides value to businesses.
- Define WSNs, explain how they work, and describe the kinds of applications that use them.

Discussion Questions

7-5 It has been said that within the next few years, smartphones will become the single most important digital device we own. Discuss the implications of this statement.

7-6 Should all major retailing and manufacturing companies switch to RFID? Why or why not?

7-7 What are some of the issues to consider in determining whether the Internet would provide your business with a competitive advantage?

Hands-On MIS Projects

The projects in this section give you hands-on experience evaluating and selecting communications technology, using spreadsheet software to improve selection of telecommunications services, and using Web search engines for business research.

Management Decision Problems

7-8 Your company supplies ceramic floor tiles to Home Depot, Lowe's, and other home improvement stores. You have been asked to start using radio frequency identification tags on each case of tiles you ship to help your customers improve the management of your products and those of other suppliers in their warehouses. Use the Web to identify the cost of hardware, software, and networking components for an RFID system for your company. What factors should be considered? What are the key decisions that have to be made in determining whether your firm should adopt this technology?

7-9 BestMed Medical Supplies Corporation sells medical and surgical products and equipment from over 700 different manufacturers to hospitals, health clinics, and medical offices. The company employs 500 people at seven different locations in western and midwestern states, including account managers, customer service and support representatives, and warehouse staff. Employees communicate via traditional telephone voice services, e-mail, instant messaging, and cell phones. Management is inquiring about whether the company should adopt a system for unified communications. What factors should be considered? What are the key decisions that have to be made in determining whether to adopt this technology? Use the Web, if necessary, to find out more about unified communications and its costs.

Improving Decision Making: Using Spreadsheet Software to Evaluate Wireless Services

Software skills: Spreadsheet formulas, formatting
Business skills: Analyzing telecommunications services and costs

7-10 In this project, you'll use the Web to research alternative wireless services and use spreadsheet software to calculate wireless service costs for a sales force.

You would like to equip your sales force of 35, based in St. Louis, Missouri with mobile phones that have capabilities for voice transmission, text messaging, Internet access, and taking and sending photos. Use the Web to select two wireless providers that offer nationwide voice and data service as well as good service in your home area. Examine the features of the mobile handsets and wireless plans offered by each of these vendors. Assume that each of the 35 salespeople will need to spend three hours per weekday between 8 a.m. and 6 p.m. on mobile voice communication, send 30 text messages per weekday, use 1 gigabyte of data per month, and send five photos per week. Use your spreadsheet software to determine the wireless service and handset that will offer the best pricing per user over a two-year period. For the purposes of this exercise, you do not need to consider corporate discounts.

Achieving Operational Excellence: Using Web Search Engines for Business Research

Software skills: Web search tools
Business skills: Researching new technologies

7-11 This project will help develop your Internet skills in using Web search engines for business research.

Use Google and Bing to obtain information about ethanol as an alternative fuel for motor vehicles. If you wish, try some other search engines as well. Compare the volume and quality of information you find with each search tool. Which tool is the easiest to use? Which produced the best results for your research? Why?

RFID-enabled LSmart Library Management System
CASE STUDY

Radio-frequency identification (RFID) can play a key role in library management. The major advantage of using RFID is that it ensures traceability and security of a library's resources. In addition, RFID simplifies transactional processes at the library, and, as a result, cuts costs and saves time. This technology is widely used as a replacement for manual library management or barcodes. RFID tags can be embedded within a book, and unlike other forms of labeling, these tags can store information, such as author name, title, and so on. This system also speeds up the process of checking books in and out, prevents theft, and is of use in inventory management. One of the universities which has successfully set up RFID tagging as part of its library management system is Punjabi University in Patiala, India. It is one of the premier universities in north India, imparting quality education to its students. It was established in 1962 under the Punjabi University Act of 1961. The university has a vast array of resources, including books, journals, newspapers, and eBooks. The library caters to a large population of students and staff. The university's Central Library possesses over five lakh books, and subscribes to more than 300 journals and 22 newspapers. Approximately 10,000 books are added to the system every year. Over the years, as the number of books and library members increased, the library staff faced a lot of problems with the system of barcodes, which was in use since 2008. The circulation staff had to scan the barcode of the user and then the barcode of every book to complete one transaction. It meant that if a member wanted to checkout four books, the staff had to repeat the entire process four different times. Theft of resources was also a problem. To overcome these issues, in 2011 Punjabi University decided to implement the technology, LSmart, as suggested by the firm LibSys.

The whole process of implementation of LSmart was divided among two teams. The first team was given the responsibility of tagging the books on the shelves and the second team was asked to tag the books returned at the circulation counter. This process of transition was not a smooth one. The library staff lacked training. Getting regular power supply was a problem too. The power situation in Punjab, which is predominantly an agricultural state, is grim. There is always a conflict of interest of whether to provide uninterrupted supply to the agricultural or educational sector. Despite the state government's attempt to ration the power supply, there is always a scarcity. Any type of power interruption could result in the failure of the LSmart system. Punjabi University had to, therefore, purchase generators to ensure that the system kept running.

An important part of any library management system is the Online Public Access Catalogue (OPAC), which provides online access to library resources, all of which bear a unique classification number. The data is entered in the standard machine-readable Anglo-American Cataloguing Rules (AACR2) format. An index card is generated based on this information so as to enable the import or export of bibliographic data in standard exchange formats. The OPAC module supports keyword searches in many languages, and has a user-friendly interface. Since the catalogue is Web-enabled, it is easy to keep information on the availability of materials up to date.

The member management module stores profiles of all the library members, using which the books issued to and returned by the member can be tracked. In case a book is overdue, the amount of the fine is automatically recorded in the member's account. The system does not allow a member to check out books if there is a fine due.

The first step towards setting up a comprehensive RFID-enabled library system was the tagging of resources. The RFID tag is the most important aspect of the system because it contains all the information regarding a particular book in the library. The university faced several challenges at this stage. In some cases, the data entry operator made wrong entries in the system, as a result of which the system was not able to read the bibliographic details of the items at the circulation counter. In other instances, the moisture in the tags resulted in their malfunctioning. To solve these issues, the trained library staff diligently untagged all the books and then tagged them again, this time correctly. A tag contains electronically stored information that can be read from a distance of several meters. Unlike a barcode, the RFID tag does not need to be scanned in the line of sight. All the counters at the library have a touchscreen with an RFID glass sensor. Borrowers simply place books and other material on this screen, and hand over their cards to the library staff. The screen reads the RFID tags, while the card reader opens up a member's profile on the system. The staff assigns the material to the borrower in question, and issues a receipt with the date of return clearly marked. This system eliminates the need for physical recording or stamping. It also minimizes human error.

Returning books is also much easier now. Members simply drop their books into a specially designed drop-box at the library. A scanner within the box scans the RFID tag of the dropped book and marks the book as returned in the system. Member accounts are updated automatically and proof-of-return slip is issued. In case a book is overdue, the slip also displays the amount of fine that the member needs to pay.

Finally, one of the most pervasive problems in any library is that of theft. An RFID tag can be detected by the Electronic Article Surveillance (EAS) system installed at the library gates. An alarm would be triggered if any member attempts to leave with an unissued item. The EAS gates are linked to the library's surveillance station. When an offender passes through the gate, the camera takes their photograph and sends it to the surveillance station. Although this system operates independent of the library database, it is an integral part of managing the library.

The university also plans to purchase hand-held readers to help in shelf management. Since a large number of users who access the library do not put books back on shelves in the right order, shelves can become difficult to manage. Books that have been returned also have to be shelved correctly. The proposed shelf management system will

consist of a portable scanner and a base station. A solution will be designed to cover three main operations: searching for individual books, inventory checks of library stock, and locating and replacing books that have been shelved wrongly. Each book will have a shelf ID, which will be its location identification code. This information will be saved in a central database against the book's information and RFID tag. The portable scanner will fetch the information stored on a book's RFID tag, and using the shelving information stored in the database, library staff will be able move books back into their proper places. This will also help locate missing books since the portable scanner will be able to pull up the records of all the books meant to be on a specific shelf. The collected information will be compared against the library database to generate a report of missing books.

Sources: "About the Infrastructure in Punjab University", Accessed on January 5, 2016 and retrieved from http://punjabiuniversity.ac.in/pbiuniweb/pages/infrastructure.html; Khanna, Sunaina, "Impact of RFID Technology on Library Services: A Case Study of A.C. Joshi Library, Panjab University, Chandigarh", *International Journal of Digital Library Services*, Vol. 4, Issue 2 (2014). Retrieved from http://www.ijodls.in/uploads/3/6/0/3/3603729/sunaina_117-126.pdf; Anuragi, Matadeen, "RFID Technology for Libraries: An Indian Scenario", *International Journal for Research in Applied Science and Engineering Technology*, Vol. 2, Issue 2 (2014). Retrieved from http://www.ijraset.com/fileserve.php?FID = 192; Vasishta, Seema, "Roadmap for RFID Implementation in Central Library, PEC University of *Technology*", *Technology, Policy and Innovation* (2009). Retrieved from http://crl.du.ac.in/ical09/papers/index_files/ical-49_196_414_1_RV.pdf. *Libsys*. Retrieved from http://www.libsys.co.in.

CASE STUDY QUESTIONS

7-12 How can RFID technology simplify basic library processes related to the lending and returning of books?

7-13 What kind of technology does your school or university library use? Does IT play a crucial role in managing operations?

7-14 How is RFID technology helping the Central Library of Punjabi University detect and prevent the theft of books?

7-15 Discuss the various problems encountered by the Punjabi University while implementing the RFID-enabled technology in its Central Library. Also discuss how Punjabi University was able to overcome these hindrances.

Chapter 7 References

Boutin, Paul. "Search Tool on Facebook Puts Network to Work." *New York Times* (March 20, 2013).

comScore. "comScore Releases June 2014 U.S. Search Engine Rankings." (July 21, 2014).

Efrati, Amir. "Google's Search Revamp: A Step Closer to AI." *Wall Street Journal* (March 14, 2012).

eMarketer. "US Mobile Users: 2014 Complete Forecast." (Alison M McCarthy, eMarketer Report (April 2014).

Google, Inc. "SEC Form 10k for the Fiscal Year Ending December 30, 2013" Google, Inc. March 31, 2014.

Holmes, Sam and Jeffrey A. Trachtenberg. "Web Addresses Enter New Era." *Wall Street Journal* (June 21, 2011).

ICANN. "ICANN Policy Update." 10, No. 9 (September 2010).

Lahiri, Atanu, I. "The Disruptive Effect of Open Platforms on Markets for Wireless Services." *Journal of Management Information Systems* 27, No. 3 (Winter 2011).

Marin Software, Inc. "The State of Mobile Search Advertising in the US: How the Emergence of Smartphones and Tablets Changes Paid Search." Marin Software Inc. (2012).

McKinsey&Company. "The Impact of Internet Technologies: Search (July 2011).

Miller, Claire Cain. "Google, a Giant in Mobile Search, Seeks New Ways to Make It Pay," *New York Times* (April 24, 2011).

Murphy, Chris. "The Internet of Things." *Information Week* (August 13, 2012).

National Telecommunications and Information Agency. "NTIA Announces Intent to Transition Key Internet Domain Name Functions." Press Release. March 14, 2014;

Panko, Raymond R. and Julia Panko. *Business Data Networks and Telecommunications* 8e. Upper Saddle River, NJ: Prentice-Hall (2011).

SearchAgency.com. "Mobile Drives Increased Spend and Clicks on Both Google and Bing ." (July 15, 2014).

Shaw, Tony. "Innovation Web 3.0." Baseline (March/April 2011).

Simonite, Tom. "Social Indexing." Technology Review (May/June 2011).

"Software Defined Networking." Global Knowledge (2014).

SupplyChainBrain. "RFID's Role in Today's Supply Chain (November 4, 2013).

"The Internet of Things." *McKinsey Quarterly* (March 2010).

Winkler, Rolfe. "As Google Builds Out Own Content, Some Advertisers Feel Pushed Aside." *Wall Street Journal* (August 18, 2014).

Winkler, Rolfe. "Getting More than Just Words in a Google Search Result." *Wall Street Journal* (Aug. 18, 2014).

Wittman, Art. "Here Comes the Internet of Things" *Information Week* (July 22, 2013).

Worldwide Web Consortium, " Semantic Web." w3.org/standards/semanticweb (October 18, 2012).

Worthen, Ben and Cari Tuna. "Web Running Out of Addresses." *Wall Street Journal* (Feb 1, 2011).

Wyatt, Edward. "U.S. to Cede Its Oversight of Addresses on Internet." New York Times, March 14, 2014

Securing Information Systems | CHAPTER 8

LEARNING OBJECTIVES

After reading this chapter, you will be able to answer the following questions:

1. Why are information systems vulnerable to destruction, error, and abuse?

2. What is the business value of security and control?

3. What are the components of an organizational framework for security and control?

4. What are the most important tools and technologies for safeguarding information resources?

CHAPTER CASES

The 21st Century Bank Heist

SAS Helping SEBI Check Equities-trading
Malpractices

BYOD: It's Not So Safe

Securing Information: the HSBC Way

THE 21ST CENTURY BANK HEIST

One of the top ten bank heists of all time occurred in December 2012 and February 2013 when a worldwide network of cyber-criminals made away with $45 million from two digital hacking operations. The thieves targeted a company in India and a U.S.-based firm that process transactions from Visa and MasterCard prepaid debit cards. Payment processors are known to employ less stringent network security than financial institutions. Once they accessed account information, the hackers sought out prepaid debit cards issued by two Middle Eastern banks whose databases afforded another point of lax security: Rakbank (National Bank of Ras Al-Khaimah) in the United Arab Emirates and the Bank of Muscat in Oman.

Rather than accumulating numerous account numbers, the hackers eliminated the withdrawal caps on just a handful of cards. Information from just five Rakbank-issued cards generated the initial $5 million, with just twelve Bank of Muscat cards garnering the lion's share in the second strike. No individual or business bank accounts were depleted. Instead, funds were extracted from pooled reserve accounts from which prepaid debit card transactions are immediately deducted with the individual subaccounts, (the value associated with a card) reduced concurrently. Both tactics were designed to delay detection.

© Creativa/Shutterstock

Next, the hackers created new PIN (personal identification) numbers for the cards. Then, using commercially-available card encoders attached via USB ports to laptops and PCs, a network of underlings simply used the built-in software to enter the account data, clicked Write or Encode, and swiped any plastic card with a magnetic stripe they could get their hands on, including old expired credit cards and hotel key cards. With counterfeit cards in hand, crews in more than two dozen countries including Japan, Russia, Romania, Egypt, Colombia, Great Britain, Sri Lanka, Canada, and the United States began collecting the loot from ATM machines. The $45 million haul was accomplished through 36,000 bank transactions over ten hours' time.

In May 2013, seven members of the New York cell were arrested; the eighth, and purported ringleader, had been found murdered in the Dominican Republic the month before. The global mob leaders were not caught.

Magnetic stripes are an over four-decade old technology that much of the developed world has abandoned because they are so vulnerable to counterfeit replication and theft via handheld card skimmers. Other major regions of the world have been using EMV (Europay, MasterCard, and Visa) technology for nearly 20 years. Often referred to as the chip and PIN system, EMV smartcards store account information in an embedded chip, and their data encryption is stronger than that for magstripe cards. Magnetic-stripe credit cards serve the same authentication data every time they are swiped, whereas chip and PIN system cards offer a different encrypted mathematical value each time, making it harder for criminals to use stolen data for future purchases. For added security, the user must enter a PIN to verify the identity of the cardholder.

U.S. banks and merchants have balked at the expense involved in switching payment processing systems. It is not a trifling matter. Over 600 million credit cards and 520 million debit cards must be exchanged. Over 15 million POS card readers must be replaced. Over 350,000 ATM machines nationwide must all either be retrofitted or replaced. Every store, restaurant, hair salon, gas station, doctor's office, kiosk, and vending machine will be affected, as will the payment processing infrastructure at acquiring banks, where merchant accounts receive the deposits from credit card sales. Payment processors, which supply the software and tech systems to interface with the card associations (Visa, MasterCard, etc,) and process card transactions, will also be affected.

Meanwhile, in the name of global interoperability, the rest of the world had to continue issuing EMV cards with a magnetic stripe and retain magstripe infrastructure. But the U.S. switchover may finally be coming. Beginning in October 2015, and continuing through the end of 2017, if a merchant is not EMV-capable by the specified date, it will assume liability for fraudulent and disputed transactions.

Sources: Javelin Strategy & Research, "EMV IN USA: Assessment of Merchant and Card Issuer Readiness," April, 2014; Colleen Long and Martha Mendoza, "Bloodless bank heist impressed cybercrime experts," *Associated Press*, May 10, 2013; Marc Santora, "In Hours, Thieves Took $45 Million in A.T.M. Scheme, *New York Times*, May 9, 2013; Peter Svensson, Martha Mendoza, and Ezequiel Abiú López, "Global network of hackers steals $45M from ATMs," *Associated Press*, May 10, 2013; and "EMV Chip Technology, Secure Electronic Payments," *Forbes*, March, 7, 2013.

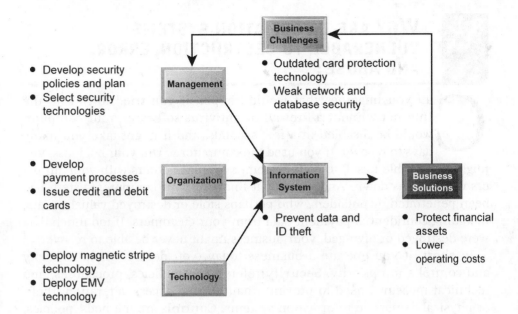

- Develop security policies and plan
- Select security technologies

Management

Business Challenges

- Outdated card protection technology
- Weak network and database security

- Develop payment processes
- Issue credit and debit cards

Organization

Information System

Business Solutions

- Prevent data and ID theft

- Protect financial assets
- Lower operating costs

- Deploy magnetic stripe technology
- Deploy EMV technology

Technology

The problems created by the bank theft of $45 million using counterfeit ATM cards illustrate some of the reasons businesses need to pay special attention to information system security. Digital ATM and credit card systems are extremely useful tools for both individuals and businesses. But from a security standpoint, as this case illustrates, they are vulnerable to hackers who were able to access supposedly protected card account data and use the data to create counterfeit cards with which to raid numerous ATM machines.

The chapter-opening diagram calls attention to important points raised by this case and this chapter. Although debit (and credit) card payment processors have some information systems security in place, the security used by some payment processors and banks was very weak. These vulnerabilities enabled criminals to break into the systems of several payment processing companies and steal debit card account information that could be used to fabricate bogus ATM cards with which to steal from two banks. The way that the banks in question processed card payments using pooled reserve accounts also helped the criminals. These banks also had weak security. Another weak link in the security chain are ATM cards themselves because the data on cards with magnetic stripe technology, including those widely used in the U.S., can be easily changed to create counterfeit cards.

EMV technology for securing cards is more secure, but is expensive to implement when payment systems in the U.S. use a different standard. Nevertheless, no matter what the expense, U.S. credit and bank cards will soon transition to EMV systems. This will not totally eliminate fraudulent uses of these cards, but it will lessen the chances of that happening.

Here are some questions to think about: What security vulnerabilities were exploited by the hackers? What management, organizational and technoloical factors contributed to these security weaknesses? What solutions are available for this problem?

8.1 WHY ARE INFORMATION SYSTEMS VULNERABLE TO DESTRUCTION, ERROR, AND ABUSE?

Can you imagine what would happen if you tried to link to the Internet without a firewall or antivirus software? Your computer would be disabled in a few seconds, and it might take you many days to recover. If you used the computer to run your business, you might not be able to sell to your customers or place orders with your suppliers while it was down. And you might find that your computer system had been penetrated by outsiders, who perhaps stole or destroyed valuable data, including confidential payment data from your customers. If too much data were destroyed or divulged, your business might never be able to recover!

In short, if you operate a business today, you need to make security and control a top priority. **Security** refers to the policies, procedures, and technical measures used to prevent unauthorized access, alteration, theft, or physical damage to information systems. **Controls** are methods, policies, and organizational procedures that ensure the safety of the organization's assets, the accuracy and reliability of its records, and operational adherence to management standards.

WHY SYSTEMS ARE VULNERABLE

When large amounts of data are stored in electronic form, they are vulnerable to many more kinds of threats than when they existed in manual form. Through communications networks, information systems in different locations are interconnected. The potential for unauthorized access, abuse, or fraud is not limited to a single location but can occur at any access point in the network. Figure 8.1 illustrates the most common threats against contemporary information systems. They can stem from technical, organizational, and environmental factors compounded by poor management decisions. In the multi-tier client/server computing environment illustrated here, vulnerabilities exist at each layer and in the communications between the layers. Users at the client layer can cause harm by introducing errors or by accessing systems without authorization. It is possible to access data flowing over networks, steal valuable data during transmission, or alter messages without authorization. Radiation may disrupt a network at various points as well. Intruders can launch denial-of-service attacks or malicious software to disrupt the operation of Web sites. Those capable of penetrating corporate systems can steal, destroy, or alter corporate data stored in databases or files.

Systems malfunction if computer hardware breaks down, is not configured properly, or is damaged by improper use or criminal acts. Errors in programming, improper installation, or unauthorized changes cause computer software to fail. Power failures, floods, fires, or other natural disasters can also disrupt computer systems.

Domestic or offshore partnering with another company adds to system vulnerability if valuable information resides on networks and computers outside the organization's control. Without strong safeguards, valuable data

FIGURE 8.1 CONTEMPORARY SECURITY CHALLENGES AND VULNERABILITIES

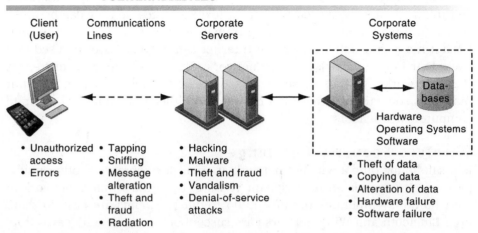

| Client (User) | Communications Lines | Corporate Servers | Corporate Systems |

- Unauthorized access
- Errors

- Tapping
- Sniffing
- Message alteration
- Theft and fraud
- Radiation

- Hacking
- Malware
- Theft and fraud
- Vandalism
- Denial-of-service attacks

Hardware
Operating Systems
Software

- Theft of data
- Copying data
- Alteration of data
- Hardware failure
- Software failure

The architecture of a Web-based application typically includes a Web client, a server, and corporate information systems linked to databases. Each of these components presents security challenges and vulnerabilities. Floods, fires, power failures, and other electrical problems can cause disruptions at any point in the network.

could be lost, destroyed, or could fall into the wrong hands, revealing important trade secrets or information that violates personal privacy.

The popularity of handheld mobile devices for business computing adds to these woes. Portability makes cell phones, smartphones, and tablet computers easy to lose or steal. Smartphones share the same security weaknesses as other Internet devices, and are vulnerable to malicious software and penetration from outsiders. Smartphones used by corporate employees often contain sensitive data such as sales figures, customer names, phone numbers, and e-mail addresses. Intruders may be able to access internal corporate systems through these devices.

Internet Vulnerabilities

Large public networks, such as the Internet, are more vulnerable than internal networks because they are virtually open to anyone. The Internet is so huge that when abuses do occur, they can have an enormously widespread impact. When the Internet becomes part of the corporate network, the organization's information systems are even more vulnerable to actions from outsiders.

Telephone service based on Internet technology (see Chapter 7) is more vulnerable than the switched voice network if it does not run over a secure private network. Most Voice over IP (VoIP) traffic over the public Internet is not encrypted, so anyone with a network can listen in on conversations. Hackers can intercept conversations or shut down voice service by flooding servers supporting VoIP with bogus traffic.

Vulnerability has also increased from widespread use of e-mail, instant messaging (IM), and peer-to-peer file-sharing programs. E-mail may contain attachments that serve as springboards for malicious software or unauthorized access to internal corporate systems. Employees may use e-mail messages to transmit valuable trade secrets, financial data, or confidential customer information to unauthorized recipients. Popular IM applications for consumers do not use a secure layer for text messages, so they can be intercepted and read by outsiders during transmission over the public Internet. Instant messaging activity over the Internet can in some cases be used as a back door to an otherwise secure network. Sharing files over peer-to-peer (P2P) networks, such as those for illegal music sharing, may also transmit malicious software or expose information on either individual or corporate computers to outsiders.

Wireless Security Challenges

Is it safe to log onto a wireless network at an airport, library, or other public location? It depends on how vigilant you are. Even the wireless network in your home is vulnerable because radio frequency bands are easy to scan. Both Bluetooth and Wi-Fi networks are susceptible to hacking by eavesdroppers. Local area networks (LANs) using the 802.11 standard can be easily penetrated by outsiders armed with laptops, wireless cards, external antennae, and hacking software. Hackers use these tools to detect unprotected networks, monitor network traffic, and, in some cases, gain access to the Internet or to corporate networks.

Wi-Fi transmission technology was designed to make it easy for stations to find and hear one another. The *service set identifiers* (SSIDs) that identify the access points in a Wi-Fi network are broadcast multiple times and can be picked up fairly easily by intruders' sniffer programs (see Figure 8.2). Wireless networks in many locations do not have basic protections against **war driving**, in which eavesdroppers drive by buildings or park outside and try to intercept wireless network traffic.

An intruder that has associated with an access point by using the correct SSID is capable of accessing other resources on the network. For example, the intruder could use the Windows operating system to determine which other users are connected to the network, access their computer hard drives, and open or copy their files.

Intruders also use the information they have gleaned to set up rogue access points on a different radio channel in physical locations close to users to force a user's radio network interface controller (NIC) to associate with the rogue access point. Once this association occurs, hackers using the rogue access point can capture the names and passwords of unsuspecting users.

MALICIOUS SOFTWARE: VIRUSES, WORMS, TROJAN HORSES, AND SPYWARE

Malicious software programs are referred to as **malware** and include a variety of threats, such as computer viruses, worms, and Trojan horses. A **computer virus** is a rogue software program that attaches itself to other software programs or data files in order to be executed, usually without user knowledge or permission. Most computer viruses deliver a "payload." The payload may be relatively benign, such as instructions to display a message or image, or it may be highly destructive—destroying programs or data,

FIGURE 8.2   WI-FI SECURITY CHALLENGES

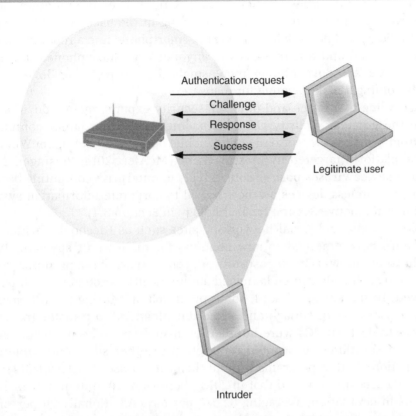

Authentication request

Challenge

Response

Success

Legitimate user

Intruder

Many Wi-Fi networks can be penetrated easily by intruders using sniffer programs to obtain an address to access the resources of a network without authorization.

clogging computer memory, reformatting a computer's hard drive, or causing programs to run improperly. Viruses typically spread from computer to computer when humans take an action, such as sending an e-mail attachment or copying an infected file.

Most recent attacks have come from **worms**, which are independent computer programs that copy themselves from one computer to other computers over a network. Unlike viruses, worms can operate on their own without attaching to other computer program files and rely less on human behavior in order to spread from computer to computer. This explains why computer worms spread much more rapidly than computer viruses. Worms destroy data and programs as well as disrupt or even halt the operation of computer networks.

Worms and viruses are often spread over the Internet from files of downloaded software, from files attached to e-mail transmissions, or from compromised e-mail messages, online ads, or instant messaging. Viruses have also invaded computerized information systems from "infected" disks or infected machines. Especially prevalent today are **drive-by downloads**, consisting of malware that comes with a downloaded file that a user intentionally or unintentionally requests.

Hackers can do to a smartphone just about anything they can do to any Internet device: request malicious files without user intervention, delete files, transmit files, install programs running in the background to monitor user actions, and potentially convert the smartphone into a robot in a botnet to send e-mail and text messages to anyone. With smartphones starting to outsell PCs, and smartphones increasingly used as payment devices, they are becoming a major avenue for malware.

According to McAfee and other IT security experts, mobile devices now pose the greatest security risks, outpacing those from larger computers. Android, which is the world's leading mobile operating system, not Windows, is the platform targeted by most hackers. (McAfee, 2014; Reisinger, 2014). Mobile device viruses pose serious threats to enterprise computing because so many wireless devices are now linked to corporate information systems (see the Interactive Session on Technology in Section 8.4).

Blogs, wikis, and social networking sites such as Facebook, Twitter, and LinkedIn have emerged as new conduits for malware or spyware. These applications allow users to post software code as part of the permissible content, and such code can be launched automatically as soon as a Web page is viewed. In the spring of 2014, some programs purporting to be Instagram "image viewers," or "image and video downloaders" to transfer Instagram photos to desktop PCs were bundled with malware. The malware caused Internet slowdown, unwanted redirection to other sites, and sometimes installation of other programs without the user's consent (Scharr, 2014).

Panda Security reported that in 2013, there were 30 million new malware strains in circulation, averaging 82,000 per day. Additionally 20 percent of all malware that has ever existed was created in that one year alone (Panda, 2014). Table 8.1 describes the characteristics of some of the most harmful worms and viruses that have appeared to date.

Over 70 percent of the infections Panda found were Trojan Horses. A **Trojan horse** is a software program that appears to be benign but then does something other than expected. The Trojan horse is not itself a virus because it does not replicate, but it is often a way for viruses or other malicious code to be introduced into a computer system. The term *Trojan horse* is based on the huge wooden horse used by the Greeks to trick the Trojans into opening the gates to their fortified city during the Trojan War. Once inside the city walls, Greek soldiers hidden in the horse revealed themselves and captured the city.

An example of a modern-day Trojan horse is the Zeus Trojan which runs on computers with the Microsoft Windows operating system. It is often used to steal login credentials for banking by surreptitiously capturing peoples' keystrokes as they use their computers. Zeus is spread mainly through drive-by downloads and phishing.

SQL injection attacks have become a major malware threat. SQL injection attacks take advantage of vulnerabilities in poorly coded Web application software to introduce malicious program code into a company's systems and networks. These vulnerabilities occur when a Web application fails to properly validate or filter data entered by a user on a Web page, which might occur when ordering something online. An attacker uses this input

TABLE 8.1 EXAMPLES OF MALICIOUS CODE

NAME	TYPE	DESCRIPTION
Conficker (aka Downadup, Downup)	Worm	First detected in November 2008 and still prevalent. Uses flaws in Windows software to take over machines and link them into a virtual computer that can be commanded remotely. Had more than 5 million computers worldwide under its control. Difficult to eradicate.
Storm	Worm/ Trojan horse	First identified in January 2007. Spreads via e-mail spam with a fake attachment. Infected up to 10 million computers, causing them to join its zombie network of computers engaged in criminal activity.
Sasser.ftp	Worm	First appeared in May 2004. Spread over the Internet by attacking random IP addresses. Causes computers to continually crash and reboot, and infected computers to search for more victims. Affected millions of computers worldwide, disrupting British Airways flight check-ins, operations of British coast guard stations, Hong Kong hospitals, Taiwan post office branches, and Australia's Westpac Bank. Sasser and its variants caused an estimated $14.8 billion to $18.6 billion in damages worldwide.
MyDoom.A	Worm	First appeared on January 26, 2004. Spreads as an e-mail attachment. Sends e-mail to addresses harvested from infected machines, forging the sender's address. At its peak, this worm lowered global Internet performance by 10 percent and Web page loading times by as much as 50 percent. Was programmed to stop spreading after February 12, 2004.
Sobig.F	Worm	First detected on August 19, 2003. Spreads via e-mail attachments and sends massive amounts of mail with forged sender information. Deactivated itself on September 10, 2003, after infecting more than 1 million PCs and doing $5 to $10 billion in damage.
ILOVEYOU	Virus	First detected on May 3, 2000. Script virus written in Visual Basic script and transmitted as an attachment to e-mail with the subject line ILOVEYOU. Overwrites music, image, and other files with a copy of itself and did an estimated $10 billion to $15 billion in damage.
Melissa	Macro virus/worm	First appeared in March 1999. Word macro script mailing infected Word file to first 50 entries in user's Microsoft Outlook address book. Infected 15 to 29 percent of all business PCs, causing $300 million to $600 million in damage.

validation error to send a rogue SQL query to the underlying database to access the database, plant malicious code, or access other systems on the network. Large Web applications have hundreds of places for inputting user data, each of which creates an opportunity for an SQL injection attack.

Malware known as **ransomware** is proliferating on both desktop and mobile devices. Ransomware tries to extort money from users by taking control of their computers or displaying annoying pop-up messages. One nasty example, CryptoLocker, encrypts an infected computer's files, forcing users to pay hundreds of dollars to regain access. You can get ransomware from donwloading an infected attachment, clicking a link inside an email or by visiting the wrong Web site.

Some types of **spyware** also act as malicious software. These small programs install themselves surreptitiously on computers to monitor user Web surfing activity and serve up advertising. Thousands of forms of spyware have been documented.

Many users find such spyware annoying, and some critics worry about its infringement on computer users' privacy. Some forms of spyware are especially nefarious. **Keyloggers** record every keystroke made on a computer to steal serial numbers for software, to launch Internet attacks, to gain access to e-mail accounts, to obtain passwords to protected computer systems, or to pick up personal information such as credit card and or bank account numbers. The Zeus Trojan described earlier uses keylogging. Other spyware programs reset Web browser home pages, redirect search requests, or slow performance by taking up too much memory.

HACKERS AND COMPUTER CRIME

A **hacker** is an individual who intends to gain unauthorized access to a computer system. Within the hacking community, the term *cracker* is typically used to denote a hacker with criminal intent, although in the public press, the terms hacker and cracker are used interchangeably. Hackers and crackers gain unauthorized access by finding weaknesses in the security protections employed by Web sites and computer systems, often taking advantage of various features of the Internet that make it an open system and easy to use.

Hacker activities have broadened beyond mere system intrusion to include theft of goods and information, as well as system damage and **cybervandalism**, the intentional disruption, defacement, or even destruction of a Web site or corporate information system. For example, a group of pro-Syrian regime hackers called the Syrian Electronic Army hacked Skype's Twitter account, blog, and Facebook page in early January 2014, publishing a fake message which read, "Don't use Microsoft emails...They are monitoring your accounts and selling the data to the governments" (Ribeiro, 2014).

Spoofing and Sniffing

Hackers attempting to hide their true identities often spoof, or misrepresent, themselves by using fake e-mail addresses or masquerading as someone else. **Spoofing** may also involve redirecting a Web link to an address different from the intended one, with the site masquerading as the intended destination. For example, if hackers redirect customers to a fake Web site that looks almost exactly like the true site, they can then collect and process orders, effectively stealing business as well as sensitive customer information from the true site. We will provide more detail on other forms of spoofing in our discussion of computer crime.

A **sniffer** is a type of eavesdropping program that monitors information traveling over a network. When used legitimately, sniffers help identify potential network trouble spots or criminal activity on networks, but when used for criminal purposes, they can be damaging and very difficult to detect. Sniffers enable hackers to steal proprietary information from anywhere on a network, including e-mail messages, company files, and confidential reports.

Denial-of-Service Attacks

In a **denial-of-service (DoS) attack**, hackers flood a network server or Web server with many thousands of false communications or requests for services to crash the network. The network receives so many queries that it cannot keep up with them and is thus unavailable to service legitimate requests. A **distributed denial-of-service (DDoS)** attack uses numerous computers to inundate and overwhelm the network from numerous launch points.

Although DoS attacks do not destroy information or access restricted areas of a company's information systems, they often cause a Web site to shut down, making it impossible for legitimate users to access the site. For example, the blogging service Typepad was subjected to a series of DDoS attacks in April 2014 which lasted five days. During that time period, the site was flooded with so much illicit traffic that it was knocked offline, preventing Typepad users from acessing their blogs and applications (Perez, 2014). For busy e-commerce sites, these attacks are costly; while the site is shut down, customers cannot make purchases. Especially vulnerable are small and midsize businesses whose networks tend to be less protected than those of large corporations.

Perpetrators of DDoS attacks often use thousands of "zombie" PCs infected with malicious software without their owners' knowledge and organized into a **botnet**. Hackers create these botnets by infecting other people's computers with bot malware that opens a back door through which an attacker can give instructions. The infected computer then becomes a slave, or zombie, serving a master computer belonging to someone else. Once hackers infect enough computers, they can use the amassed resources of the botnet to launch DDoS attacks, phishing campaigns, or unsolicited "spam" e-mail.

Ninety percent of the world's spam and 80 percent of the world's malware are delivered via botnets. For example, the Grum botnet, once the world's third-largest botnet, was reportedly responsible for 18% of worldwide spam traffic (amounting to 18 billion spam messages per day) when it was shut down on July 19, 2012. At one point Grum had infected and controlled 560,000–840,000 computers.

Computer Crime

Most hacker activities are criminal offenses, and the vulnerabilities of systems we have just described make them targets for other types of **computer crime** as well. Computer crime is defined by the U.S. Department of Justice as "any violations of criminal law that involve a knowledge of computer technology for their perpetration, investigation, or prosecution." Table 8.2 provides examples of the computer as both a target and an instrument of crime. The chapter-opening case describes one of the largest computer crime cases reported to date.

No one knows the magnitude of the computer crime problem—how many systems are invaded, how many people engage in the practice, or the total economic damage. According to the Ponemon Institute's 2013 Annual Cost of Cyber Crime Study sponsored by HP Enterprise Security, the average annualized cost of cybercrime for the organizations in the study was $11.6 million per year (Ponemon Institute, 2013). Many companies are reluctant to report computer crimes because the crimes may involve employees, or the company fears that publicizing its vulnerability will hurt its reputation. The most economically damaging kinds of computer crime are denial of service attacks, activities of malicious insiders, and Web-based attacks.

TABLE 8.2 EXAMPLES OF COMPUTER CRIME

COMPUTERS AS TARGETS OF CRIME
Breaching the confidentiality of protected computerized data
Accessing a computer system without authority
Knowingly accessing a protected computer to commit fraud
Intentionally accessing a protected computer and causing damage, negligently or deliberately
Knowingly transmitting a program, program code, or command that intentionally causes damage to a protected computer
Threatening to cause damage to a protected computer

COMPUTERS AS INSTRUMENTS OF CRIME
Theft of trade secrets
Unauthorized copying of software or copyrighted intellectual property, such as articles, books, music, and video
Schemes to defraud
Using e-mail for threats or harassment
Intentionally attempting to intercept electronic communication
Illegally accessing stored electronic communications, including e-mail and voice mail
Transmitting or possessing child pornography using a computer

Identity Theft

With the growth of the Internet and electronic commerce, identity theft has become especially troubling. **Identity theft** is a crime in which an imposter obtains key pieces of personal information, such as social security identification numbers, driver's license numbers, or credit card numbers, to impersonate someone else. The information may be used to obtain credit, merchandise, or services in the name of the victim or to provide the thief with false credentials.

Identity theft has flourished on the Internet, with credit card files a major target of Web site hackers. According to the Identity Fraud Study by Javelin Strategy & Research, identity fraud affected 13.1 million consumers in 2013. The total dolllar losses from identity theft increased to $18 billion (Javelin 2014). Moreover, e-commerce sites are wonderful sources of customer personal information—name, address, and phone number. Armed with this information, criminals are able to assume new identities and establish new credit for their own purposes.

One increasingly popular tactic is a form of spoofing called **phishing**. Phishing involves setting up fake Web sites or sending e-mail messages that look like those of legitimate businesses to ask users for confidential personal data. The e-mail message instructs recipients to update or confirm records by providing social security numbers, bank and credit card information, and other confidential data either by responding to the e-mail message, by entering the information at a bogus Web site, or by calling a telephone number. EBay, PayPal, Amazon.com, Walmart, and a variety of banks are among the top spoofed companies. In a more targeted form of phishing called *spear phishing*, messages appear to come from a trusted source, such as an individual within the recipient's own company or a friend.

Phishing techniques called evil twins and pharming are harder to detect. **Evil twins** are wireless networks that pretend to offer trustworthy Wi-Fi connections to the Internet, such as those in airport lounges, hotels, or coffee shops. The bogus network looks identical to a legitimate public network. Fraudsters try to capture passwords or credit card numbers of unwitting users who log on to the network.

Pharming redirects users to a bogus Web page, even when the individual types the correct Web page address into his or her browser. This is possible if pharming perpetrators gain access to the Internet address information stored by Internet service providers to speed up Web browsing and the ISP companies have flawed software on their servers that allows the fraudsters to hack in and change those addresses.

According to the Ponemon Institute's 2014 Cost of a Data Breach Study, the average cost of a breach to a company was $3.5 million (Ponemon, 2014). Moreover, brand damage can be significant, albeit hard to quantify. In addition to the data breaches described in the Interactive Session on Management, Table 8.3 describes other major data breaches.

The U.S. Congress addressed the threat of computer crime in 1986 with the Computer Fraud and Abuse Act, which makes it illegal to access a computer system without authorization. Most states have similar laws, and nations in Europe have comparable legislation. Congress passed the National Information Infrastructure Protection Act in 1996 to make malware distribution and hacker attacks to disable Web sites federal crimes.

TABLE 8.3 MAJOR DATA BREACHES

DATA BREACH	DESCRIPTION
EBay	Cyberattack on eBay servers during February and March 2014 compromises database containing customer names, encrypted passwords, email addresses, physical addresses, phone numbers, and birthdates. No financial data were accessed, but the information is useful for identity theft.
Heartland Payment Systems	In 2008, criminals led by Miami hacker Albert Gonzales installed spying software on the computer network of Heartland Payment Systems, a payment processor based in Princeton, NJ, and stole the numbers of as many as 100 million credit and debit cards. Gonzales was sentenced in 2010 to 20 years in federal prison, and Heartland paid about $140 million in fines and settlements.
TJX	A 2007 data breach at TJX, the retailer that owns national chains including TJ Maxx and Marshalls, cost at least $250 million. Cyber criminals took more than 45 million credit and debit card numbers, some of which were used later to buy millions of dollars in electronics from Walmart and elsewhere. Albert Gonzales, who played a major role in the Heartland hack, was linked to this cyberattack as well.
Epsilon	In March 2011, hackers stole millions of names and e-mail addresses from the Epsilon e-mail marketing firm, which handles e-mail lists for major retailers and banks like Best Buy, JPMorgan, TiVo, and Walgreens. Costs could range from $100 million to $4 billion, depending on what happens to the stolen data, with most of the costs from losing customers due to a damaged reputation.
Sony	In April 2011, hackers obtained personal information, including credit, debit, and bank account numbers, from over 100 million PlayStation Network users and Sony Online Entertainment users. The breach could cost Sony and credit card issuers up to a total of $2 billion.

INTERACTIVE SESSION: MANAGEMENT

SAS HELPING SEBI CHECK EQUITIES-TRADING MALPRACTICES

The Securities and Exchange Board of India (SEBI) regulates the securities market in India. It was formed in 1992 with the passing of the SEBI Act in the Indian parliament. Its main mandate is to protect the interest of investors and promote the development of a regulated securities markets. Since its inception, SEBI has played a key role in the development of the capital market in India by boosting confidence for both institutional and retail investors. Today, SEBI regulates the primary and secondary markets, mutual funds, brokers as well as wealth management businesses in the country.

SEBI is charged with the task of dealing with unfair trade practices and curbing illegal activities in the the securities market. It does so with guidance from the Fraudulent and Unfair Trade Practices (FUTP) regulations issued in 2013. In 2014, incidents of insider trading or front running had been reported. Front-running implies use of personal information by individuals to trade shares prior to a large order of equities. For example, in June 2014, at least 70 entities were under the scanner for insider trading in the shares of Larsen and Turbo Finance. In another incident, top executives of DLF Limited, the realty company, were banned for indulging in unfair trade practices. Considering the recent increase in such activities, SEBI has brought front-running under the ambit of the FUTP. Entities that fail to register with SEBI also come under FUTP.

Increasing regulations and scrutiny requires a robust surveillance and analytics system to detect malpractices. As a first step towards this, SEBI, with the aid of SAS, developed its own enterprise data warehouse. Every day, SEBI records more than 200 million transactions. On the whole, it collects 25GB of data per day, a figure that is likely to reach 80GB in a couple of years. The system is designed to track and analyze the collected data. Based on that, the surveillance engine generates alerts so that investigations can be conducted on a case-by-case basis. Researchers generally cull data from third-party sources, such as telephone records, print data, or other unconventional data sources. Such an analysis would have been impossible without a data warehouse. Besides, data needs to be integrated from disparate exchanges across the country. SAS utilizes its enterprise data integration server for cleansing, standardizing, and removing duplicate data, thereby building a single-entity view of market participants. The current data warehouse has 473 tables and two data marts. It collects transaction data from stock exchanges such as NSE, BSE, USE, as well as depositories such as NSDL and CDSL. The system is able to generate an average of 300 reports each day. The warehouse supports the execution of SQL queries and about five to six tables are typically scanned for each query.

Once the data is loaded from the exchanges into the warehouse in the desired format, aggregates are computed and stored in the database itself. With the help of SAS analytics, fraud can be detected on a daily, weekly, monthly, fortnightly, or quarterly basis. With the implementation of SAS, the SEBI officials are able to get hold of uniform and formatted data, ready for investigation, on the very next day. As a result, SEBI can quickly spot malpractices and act on them. The SAS analytics tool combines multiple detection methods such as business rules, predictive analytics, and entity link analytics for faster detection of fraud. The entity link analysis feature tracks associations between the different entities. This is done on the assumption that if any one entity in the linked network is found to be fraudulent, the possibility of the other linked entities being fraudulent are also high. More the number of associations, more is the likelihood of committing fraud. This tool helps uncover hidden relationships or suspicious associations among customers, market participants, and so on. Since all reports of incidents are stored in a centralized database, past cases can easily be retrived.

Another feature, the SAS scoring accelerator, enables SEBI in the parallel processing of data. The scoring accelerator executes core statistical and analytical functions within the warehouse itself, rather than moving the data to another application.

This helps prevent data inconsistency and promotes better governance of data. Since this process is automated, it requires very little human attention or intervention.

Using SAS analytics, SEBI can use analyst recommendations, blogs, and annual reports to understand the impact of social media on investor behavior. In addition to studying the behavior of market participants, it can generate the relationships between them and link them with reported frauds.

In using SAS, SEBI's main aim is to increase the conviction ratio. In 2013 and 2014, 108 new cases were taken up for investigation and 120 cases were completed. Of the 108 cases, market manipulation and price rigging accounted for 60% of the cases, insider trading, 12%, and takeover violations, 5.6%.

Going further, SEBI would like to build analytical models using the SAS Enterprise Miner to identify prevalent malpractices in the market, with special focus on insider trading, front-running, pump-and-dump, and circular trading. Pump-and-dump schemes are generally targeted at small, microcap companies. In such schemes, misleading statements about the lucrativeness of a company's shares are issued by a few miscreants. This leads to a heavy buying of the shares by investors and fraudsters alike, which leads to a consequent hike in share price. This is called pumping. Fraudsters then dump their stocks after making handsome profits, leading to a fall in share price and loss of investors' money. Circular trading is carried out among a group of traders who have prior knowledge of certain shares. The SAS Enterprise Miner conducts a predictive and descriptive modeling

of data. With the help of a user-friendly graphical interface, the mined data can be navigated. These models enable SEBI to uncover frauds in a more efficient manner. SEBI is now also trying to increase its data warehouse capacity and upgrade its analytical tools to accommodate the surge in data to twice the current load.

Sources: "Protecting investors from unscrupulous traders". Retrieved from http://www.sas.com/en_us/customers/securities-and-exchange-board-india.html; "SAS to help SEBI in probing suspicious transactions", *The Business Line* (2011). Retrieved from http://www.thehindubusinessline.com/markets/sas-to-help-sebi-in-probing-suspicious-transactions/article2388290.ece; "SEBI speeds investigations, builds confidence with SAS", *Business Wire* (2011). Retrieved from http://www.businesswire.com/news/home/20110822006092/en/Securities-Exchange-Board-India-SEBI-Speeds-Investigations#.VMdbxen9ku4; Zachariah, Reena, "Sebi to bring front-running under fraudulent and unfair trade practices regulations", *The Economic Times* (2013). Retrieved from http://articles.economictimes.indiatimes.com/2013-08-12/news/41332696_1_sebi-board-futp-securities-market-regulator-sebi; "Securities and Exchange Board of India (Prohibition of Fraudulent and Unfair Trade Practices Relating to Securities Market) Regulations, 2003". Retrieved from http://www.sebi.gov.in/acts/futpfinal.html; "Fraudulent and Unfair Trade Practices", *Money Control*. Retrieved from http://www.moneycontrol.com/news-topic/fraudulent-and-unfair-trade-practices/; Ninan, Oommen A., "SEBI bars DLF, six top executives from markets for 3 years", *The Hindu* (2014). Retrieved from http://www.thehindu.com/business/markets/sebi-bars-dlf-six-top-executives-from-markets-for-3-years/article6497041.ece; "Response to the Queries Raised by Bidders for Dwbis Capacity Augmentation". Retrieved from http://www.sebi.gov.in/cms/sebi_data/tenderdocs/1418705499261.pdf; "SEBI decides to upgrade software for fraud detection". *The Economic Times (2014). Retrieved from* http://articles.economictimes.indiatimes.com/2014-11-28/news/56540483_1_data-centres-insider-trading-market-regulator; "SEBI's Request for Proposal for Augmentation of Data Warehouse Capacity and Business Intelligence Report Capacity" (2014). Retrieved from http://www.sebi.gov.in/cms/sebi_data/tenderdocs/1416991959030.pdf.

CASE STUDY QUESTIONS

1. From your understanding of the case, discuss the role of SEBI. Also discuss the need for analytics at SEBI.

2. Why was an enterprise data warehouse (EDW) required at SEBI? List the sources of data and the different ways in which EDW is utilised at SEBI.

3. Discuss the features of SAS analytics that are used by SEBI for fraud detection and prevention.

4. Discuss the advantages of using analytics to convict fraudsters.

U.S. legislation, such as the Wiretap Act, Wire Fraud Act, Economic Espionage Act, Electronic Communications Privacy Act, E-Mail Threats and Harassment Act, and Child Pornography Act, covers computer crimes involving intercepting electronic communication, using electronic communication to defraud, stealing trade secrets, illegally accessing stored electronic communications, using e-mail for threats or harassment, and transmitting or possessing child pornography. A proposed federal Data Security and Breach Notification Act would mandate organizations that possess personal information to put in place "reasonable" security procedures to keep the data secure and to notify anyone affected by a data breach, but it has not been enacted.

Click Fraud

When you click on an ad displayed by a search engine, the advertiser typically pays a fee for each click, which is supposed to direct potential buyers to its products. **Click fraud** occurs when an individual or computer program fraudulently clicks on an online ad without any intention of learning more about the advertiser or making a purchase. Click fraud has become a serious problem at Google and other Web sites that feature pay-per-click online advertising.

Some companies hire third parties (typically from low-wage countries) to fraudulently click on a competitor's ads to weaken them by driving up their marketing costs. Click fraud can also be perpetrated with software programs doing the clicking, and botnets are often used for this purpose. Search engines such as Google attempt to monitor click fraud but have been reluctant to publicize their efforts to deal with the problem.

Global Threats: Cyberterrorism and Cyberwarfare

The cyber criminal activities we have described—launching malware, denial-of-service attacks, and phishing probes—are borderless. Attack servers for malware are now hosted in 206 countries and territories, according to the latest FireEye Advanced Threat Report. The most popular sources of malware attacks are the United States, Germany, South Korea, China, Netherlands, United Kingdom, and Russia (Karlovsky, 2014). The global nature of the Internet makes it possible for cybercriminals to operate—and to do harm—anywhere in the world.

Internet vulnerabilities have also turned individuals and even entire nation states into easy targets for politically-motivated hacking to conduct sabotage and espionage. **Cyberwarfare** is a state-sponsored activity designed to cripple and defeat another state or nation by penetrating its computers or networks for the purposes of causing damage and disruption.

In general, cyberwarfare attacks have become much more widespread, sophisticated, and potentially devastating. There are 250,000 probes trying to find their way into the U.S. Department of Defense networks every hour, and cyberattacks on U.S. federal agencies have increased 150 percent since 2008. Over the years, hackers have stolen plans for missile tracking systems, satellite navigation devices, surveillance drones, and leading-edge jet fighters.

Cyberwarfare poses a serious threat to the infrastructure of modern societies, since their major financial, health, government, and industrial institutions rely on the Internet for daily operations. Cyberwarfare also involves defending against these types of attacks. The chapter-ending case discusses this topic in greater detail.

INTERNAL THREATS: EMPLOYEES

We tend to think the security threats to a business originate outside the organization. In fact, company insiders pose serious security problems. Employees have access to privileged information, and in the presence of sloppy internal security procedures, they are often able to roam throughout an organization's systems without leaving a trace.

Studies have found that user lack of knowledge is the single greatest cause of network security breaches. Many employees forget their passwords to access computer systems or allow co-workers to use them, which compromises the system. Malicious intruders seeking system access sometimes trick employees into revealing their passwords by pretending to be legitimate members of the company in need of information. This practice is called **social engineering**.

Both end users and information systems specialists are also a major source of errors introduced into information systems. End users introduce errors by entering faulty data or by not following the proper instructions for processing data and using computer equipment. Information systems specialists may create software errors as they design and develop new software or maintain existing programs.

SOFTWARE VULNERABILITY

Software errors pose a constant threat to information systems, causing untold losses in productivity, and sometimes endangering people who use or depend on systems. Growing complexity and size of software programs, coupled with demands for timely delivery to markets, have contributed to an increase in software flaws or vulnerabilities. On April 16, 2013, American Airlines had to cancel or delay 1,950 flights due to a faulty software patch from a vendor or internal software changes that were not properly tested. A systemwide network outage downed the airline's primary systems that manage airline operations, as well as backup systems that kick in when the primary systems fail (Boulton, 2013).

A major problem with software is the presence of hidden **bugs** or program code defects. Studies have shown that it is virtually impossible to eliminate all bugs from large programs. The main source of bugs is the complexity of decision-making code. A relatively small program of several hundred lines will contain tens of decisions leading to hundreds or even thousands of different paths. Important programs within most corporations are usually much larger, containing tens of thousands or even millions of lines of code, each with many times the choices and paths of the smaller programs.

Zero defects cannot be achieved in larger programs. Complete testing simply is not possible. Fully testing programs that contain thousands of choices and millions of paths would require thousands of years. Even with rigorous testing, you would not know for sure that a piece of software was dependable until the product proved itself after much operational use.

Flaws in commercial software not only impede performance but also create security vulnerabilities that open networks to intruders. Each year security firms identify thousands of software vulnerabilities in Internet and PC software. A recent example is the Heartbleed bug, which is a flaw in OpenSSL, an open-source encryption technology that is used by an estimated two-thirds of Web servers. Hackers could exploit the bug to access visitors' personal data as well as a site's encryption keys, which can be used to collect even more "protected" data.

To correct software flaws once they are identified, the software vendor creates small pieces of software called **patches** to repair the flaws without disturbing the proper operation of the software. An example is Microsoft's Windows 7 Service Pack 1, which features security, performance, and stability updates for Windows 7. It is up to users of the software to track these vulnerabilities, test, and apply all patches. This process is called *patch management*.

Because a company's IT infrastructure is typically laden with multiple business applications, operating system installations, and other system services, maintaining patches on all devices and services used by a company is often time-consuming and costly. Malware is being created so rapidly that companies have very little time to respond between the time a vulnerability and a patch are announced and the time malicious software appears to exploit the vulnerability.

8.2 WHAT IS THE BUSINESS VALUE OF SECURITY AND CONTROL?

Many firms are reluctant to spend heavily on security because it is not directly related to sales revenue. However, protecting information systems is so critical to the operation of the business that it deserves a second look.

Companies have very valuable information assets to protect. Systems often house confidential information about individuals' taxes, financial assets, medical records, and job performance reviews. They also can contain information on corporate operations, including trade secrets, new product development plans, and marketing strategies. Government systems may store information on weapons systems, intelligence operations, and military targets. These information assets have tremendous value, and the repercussions can be devastating if they are lost, destroyed, or placed in the wrong hands. Systems that are unable to function because of security breaches, disasters, or malfunctioning technology can permanently impact a company's financial health. Some experts believe that 40 percent of all businesses will not recover from application or data losses that are not repaired within three days.

Inadequate security and control may result in serious legal liability. Businesses must protect not only their own information assets but also those of customers, employees, and business partners. Failure to do so may open the firm to costly litigation for data exposure or theft. An organization can be held liable for needless risk and harm created if the organization fails to take appropriate protective action to prevent loss of confidential information, data corruption, or breach of privacy. For example, BJ's Wholesale Club was sued by the U.S. Federal Trade Commission for allowing hackers to access its systems and steal credit and debit card data for fraudulent purchases. Banks that issued the cards with the stolen data sought $13 million from BJ's to compensate them for reimbursing card holders for the fraudulent purchases. A sound security and control framework that protects business information assets can thus produce a high return on investment. Strong security and control also increase employee productivity and lower operational costs.

LEGAL AND REGULATORY REQUIREMENTS FOR ELECTRONIC RECORDS MANAGEMENT

Recent U.S. government regulations are forcing companies to take security and control more seriously by mandating the protection of data from abuse, exposure, and unauthorized access. Firms face new legal obligations for the retention and storage of electronic records as well as for privacy protection.

If you work in the health care industry, your firm will need to comply with the Health Insurance Portability and Accountability Act (HIPAA) of 1996. **HIPAA** outlines medical security and privacy rules and procedures for simplifying the administration of health care billing and automating the transfer of health care data between health care providers, payers, and plans. It requires members of the health care industry to retain patient information for six years and ensure the confidentiality of those records. It specifies privacy, security, and electronic transaction standards for health care providers handling patient information, providing penalties for breaches of medical privacy, disclosure of patient records by e-mail, or unauthorized network access.

If you work in a firm providing financial services, your firm will need to comply with the Financial Services Modernization Act of 1999, better known as the **Gramm-Leach-Bliley Act** after its congressional sponsors. This act requires financial institutions to ensure the security and confidentiality of customer data. Data must be stored on a secure medium, and special security measures must be enforced to protect such data on storage media and during transmittal.

If you work in a publicly traded company, your company will need to comply with the Public Company Accounting Reform and Investor Protection Act of 2002, better known as the **Sarbanes-Oxley Act** after its sponsors Senator Paul Sarbanes of Maryland and Representative Michael Oxley of Ohio. This Act was designed to protect investors after the financial scandals at Enron, WorldCom, and other public companies. It imposes responsibility on companies and their management to safeguard the accuracy and integrity of financial information that is used internally and released externally. One of the Learning Tracks for this chapter discusses Sarbanes-Oxley in detail.

Sarbanes-Oxley is fundamentally about ensuring that internal controls are in place to govern the creation and documentation of information in financial statements. Because information systems are used to generate, store, and transport such data, the legislation requires firms to consider information systems security and other controls required to ensure the integrity, confidentiality, and accuracy of their data. Each system application that deals with critical financial reporting data requires controls to make sure the data are accurate. Controls to secure the corporate network, prevent unauthorized access to systems and data, and ensure data integrity and availability in the event of disaster or other disruption of service are essential as well.

ELECTRONIC EVIDENCE AND COMPUTER FORENSICS

Security, control, and electronic records management have become essential for responding to legal actions. Much of the evidence today for stock fraud, embezzlement, theft of company trade secrets, computer crime, and many civil cases is in digital form. In addition to information from printed or typewritten pages, legal cases today increasingly rely on evidence represented as digital data stored on portable storage devices, CDs, and computer hard disk drives, as well as in e-mail, instant messages, and e-commerce transactions over the Internet. E-mail is currently the most common type of electronic evidence.

In a legal action, a firm is obligated to respond to a discovery request for access to information that may be used as evidence, and the company is required by law to produce those data. The cost of responding to a discovery request can be enormous if the company has trouble assembling the required data or the data have been corrupted or destroyed. Courts now impose severe financial and even criminal penalties for improper destruction of electronic documents.

An effective electronic document retention policy ensures that electronic documents, e-mail, and other records are well organized, accessible, and neither retained too long nor discarded too soon. It also reflects an awareness of how to preserve potential evidence for computer forensics. **Computer forensics** is the scientific collection, examination, authentication, preservation, and analysis of data held on or retrieved from computer storage media in such a way that the information can be used as evidence in a court of law. It deals with the following problems:

- Recovering data from computers while preserving evidential integrity
- Securely storing and handling recovered electronic data
- Finding significant information in a large volume of electronic data
- Presenting the information to a court of law

Electronic evidence may reside on computer storage media in the form of computer files and as *ambient data*, which are not visible to the average user. An example might be a file that has been deleted on a PC hard drive. Data that a computer user may have deleted on computer storage media can be recovered through various techniques. Computer forensics experts try to recover such hidden data for presentation as evidence.

An awareness of computer forensics should be incorporated into a firm's contingency planning process. The CIO, security specialists, information systems staff, and corporate legal counsel should all work together to have a plan in place that can be executed if a legal need arises. You can find out more about computer forensics in the Learning Tracks for this chapter.

8.3 WHAT ARE THE COMPONENTS OF AN ORGANIZATIONAL FRAMEWORK FOR SECURITY AND CONTROL?

Even with the best security tools, your information systems won't be reliable and secure unless you know how and where to deploy them. You'll need to know where your company is at risk and what controls you must have in place to protect your information systems. You'll also need to develop a security policy and plans for keeping your business running if your information systems aren't operational.

INFORMATION SYSTEMS CONTROLS

Information systems controls are both manual and automated and consist of general and application controls. **General controls** govern the design, security, and use of computer programs and the security of data files in general throughout the organization's information technology infrastructure. On the whole, general controls apply to all computerized applications and consist of a combination of hardware, software, and manual procedures that create an overall control environment.

General controls include software controls, physical hardware controls, computer operations controls, data security controls, controls over implementation of system processes, and administrative controls. Table 8.4 describes the functions of each of these controls.

Application controls are specific controls unique to each computerized application, such as payroll or order processing. They include both automated and manual procedures that ensure that only authorized data

TABLE 8.4 GENERAL CONTROLS

TYPE OF GENERAL CONTROL	DESCRIPTION
Software controls	Monitor the use of system software and prevent unauthorized access of software programs, system software, and computer programs.
Hardware controls	Ensure that computer hardware is physically secure, and check for equipment malfunction. Organizations that are critically dependent on their computers also must make provisions for backup or continued operation to maintain constant service.
Computer operations controls	Oversee the work of the computer department to ensure that programmed procedures are consistently and correctly applied to the storage and processing of data. They include controls over the setup of computer processing jobs and backup and recovery procedures for processing that ends abnormally.
Data security controls	Ensure that valuable business data files on either disk or tape are not subject to unauthorized access, change, or destruction while they are in use or in storage.
Implementation controls	Audit the systems development process at various points to ensure that the process is properly controlled and managed.
Administrative controls	Formalize standards, rules, procedures, and control disciplines to ensure that the organization's general and application controls are properly executed and enforced.

are completely and accurately processed by that application. Application controls can be classified as (1) input controls, (2) processing controls, and (3) output controls.

Input controls check data for accuracy and completeness when they enter the system. There are specific input controls for input authorization, data conversion, data editing, and error handling. *Processing controls* establish that data are complete and accurate during updating. Output *controls ensure* that the results of computer processing are accurate, complete, and properly distributed. You can find more detail about application and general controls in our Learning Tracks.

RISK ASSESSMENT

Before your company commits resources to security and information systems controls, it must know which assets require protection and the extent to which these assets are vulnerable. A risk assessment helps answer these questions and determine the most cost-effective set of controls for protecting assets.

A **risk assessment** determines the level of risk to the firm if a specific activity or process is not properly controlled. Not all risks can be anticipated and measured, but most businesses will be able to acquire some understanding of the risks they face. Business managers working with information systems specialists should try to determine the value of information assets, points of vulnerability, the likely frequency of a problem, and the potential for damage. For example, if an event is likely to occur no more than once a year, with a maximum of a $1,000 loss to the organization, it is not wise to spend $20,000 on the design and maintenance of a control to protect against that event. However, if that same event could occur at least once a day, with a potential loss of more than $300,000 a year, $100,000 spent on a control might be entirely appropriate.

Table 8.5 illustrates sample results of a risk assessment for an online order processing system that processes 30,000 orders per day. The likelihood of each exposure occurring over a one-year period is expressed as a percentage. The next column shows the highest and lowest possible loss that could be expected each time the exposure occurred and an average loss calculated by adding the highest and lowest figures together and dividing by two. The expected annual loss for each exposure can be determined by multiplying the average loss by its probability of occurrence.

TABLE 8.5 ONLINE ORDER PROCESSING RISK ASSESSMENT

EXPOSURE	PROBABILITY OF OCCURRENCE (%)	LOSS RANGE/ AVERAGE ($)	EXPECTED ANNUAL LOSS ($)
Power failure	30%	$5,000–$200,000 ($102,500)	$30,750
Embezzlement	5%	$1,000–$50,000 ($25,500)	$1,275
User error	98%	$200–$40,000 ($20,100)	$19,698

This risk assessment shows that the probability of a power failure occurring in a one-year period is 30 percent. Loss of order transactions while power is down could range from $5,000 to $200,000 (averaging $102,500) for each occurrence, depending on how long processing is halted. The probability of embezzlement occurring over a yearly period is about 5 percent, with potential losses ranging from $1,000 to $50,000 (and averaging $25,500) for each occurrence. User errors have a 98 percent chance of occurring over a yearly period, with losses ranging from $200 to $40,000 (and averaging $20,100) for each occurrence.

Once the risks have been assessed, system builders will concentrate on the control points with the greatest vulnerability and potential for loss. In this case, controls should focus on ways to minimize the risk of power failures and user errors because anticipated annual losses are highest for these areas.

SECURITY POLICY

Once you've identified the main risks to your systems, your company will need to develop a security policy for protecting the company's assets. A **security policy** consists of statements ranking information risks, identifying acceptable security goals, and identifying the mechanisms for achieving these goals. What are the firm's most important information assets? Who generates and controls this information in the firm? What existing security policies are in place to protect the information? What level of risk is management willing to accept for each of these assets? Is it willing, for instance, to lose customer credit data once every 10 years? Or will it build a security system for credit card data that can withstand the once-in-a-hundred-year disaster? Management must estimate how much it will cost to achieve this level of acceptable risk.

The security policy drives other policies determining acceptable use of the firm's information resources and which members of the company have access to its information assets. An **acceptable use policy (AUP)** defines acceptable uses of the firm's information resources and computing equipment, including desktop and laptop computers, wireless devices, telephones, and the Internet. The policy should clarify company policy regarding privacy, user responsibility, and personal use of company equipment and networks. A good AUP defines unacceptable and acceptable actions for every user and specifies consequences for noncompliance. For example, security policy at Unilever, the giant multinational consumer goods company, requires every employee to use a company-specified device and employ a password or other method of identification when logging onto the corporate network.

Security policy also includes provisions for identity management. **Identity management** consists of business processes and software tools for identifying the valid users of a system and controlling their access to system resources. It includes policies for identifying and authorizing different categories of system users, specifying what systems or portions of systems each user is allowed to access, and the processes and technologies for authenticating users and protecting their identities.

FIGURE 8.3   ACCESS RULES FOR A PERSONNEL SYSTEM

SECURITY PROFILE 1

User: Personnel Dept. Clerk

Location: Division 1

Employee Identification
Codes with This Profile: 00753, 27834, 37665, 44116

Data Field Restrictions	Type of Access
All employee data for Division 1 only	Read and Update
• Medical history data	None
• Salary	None
• Pensionable earnings	None

SECURITY PROFILE 2

User: Divisional Personnel Manager

Location: Division 1

Employee Identification
Codes with This Profile: 27321

Data Field Restrictions	Type of Access
All employee data for Division 1 only	Read Only

These two examples represent two security profiles or data security patterns that might be found in a personnel system. Depending on the security profile, a user would have certain restrictions on access to various systems, locations, or data in an organization.

Figure 8.3 is one example of how an identity management system might capture the access rules for different levels of users in the human resources function. It specifies what portions of a human resource database each user is permitted to access, based on the information required to perform that person's job. The database contains sensitive personal information such as employees' salaries, benefits, and medical histories.

The access rules illustrated here are for two sets of users. One set of users consists of all employees who perform clerical functions, such as inputting employee data into the system. All individuals with this type of profile can update the system but can neither read nor update sensitive fields, such as salary, medical history, or earnings data. Another profile applies to a divisional manager, who cannot update the system but who can read all employee data fields for his or her division, including medical history and salary. We provide more detail on the technologies for user authentication later on in this chapter.

DISASTER RECOVERY PLANNING AND BUSINESS CONTINUITY PLANNING

If you run a business, you need to plan for events, such as power outages, floods, earthquakes, or terrorist attacks that will prevent your information systems and your business from operating. **Disaster recovery planning** devises plans for the restoration of computing and communications services after they have been disrupted. Disaster recovery plans focus primarily on the technical issues involved in keeping systems up and running, such as which files to back up and the maintenance of backup computer systems or disaster recovery services.

For example, MasterCard maintains a duplicate computer center in Kansas City, Missouri, to serve as an emergency backup to its primary computer center in St. Louis. Rather than build their own backup facilities, many firms contract with disaster recovery firms, such as Comdisco Disaster Recovery Services and SunGard Availability Services. These disaster recovery firms provide hot sites housing spare computers at locations around the country where subscribing firms can run their critical applications in an emergency. For example, Champion Technologies, which supplies chemicals used in oil and gas operations, is able to switch its enterprise systems from Houston to a SunGard data center in Scottsdale, Arizona, in two hours.

Business continuity planning focuses on how the company can restore business operations after a disaster strikes. The business continuity plan identifies critical business processes and determines action plans for handling mission-critical functions if systems go down. For example, Deutsche Bank, which provides investment banking and asset management services in 74 different countries, has a well-developed business continuity plan that it continually updates and refines. It maintains full-time teams in Singapore, Hong Kong, Japan, India, and Australia to coordinate plans addressing loss of facilities, personnel, or critical systems so that the company can continue to operate when a catastrophic event occurs. Deutsche Bank's plan distinguishes between processes critical for business survival and those critical to crisis support and is coordinated with the company's disaster recovery planning for its computer centers.

Business managers and information technology specialists need to work together on both types of plans to determine which systems and business processes are most critical to the company. They must conduct a business impact analysis to identify the firm's most critical systems and the impact a systems outage would have on the business. Management must determine the maximum amount of time the business can survive with its systems down and which parts of the business must be restored first.

THE ROLE OF AUDITING

How does management know that information systems security and controls are effective? To answer this question, organizations must conduct comprehensive and systematic audits. An **information systems audit** examines the firm's overall security environment as well as controls governing individual information systems. The auditor should trace the flow of sample transactions through the system and perform tests, using, if appropriate, automated audit software. The information systems audit may also examine data quality.

Security audits review technologies, procedures, documentation, training, and personnel. A thorough audit will even simulate an attack or disaster to test the response of the technology, information systems staff, and business employees.

FIGURE 8.4   SAMPLE AUDITOR'S LIST OF CONTROL WEAKNESSES

Function: Loans Location: Peoria, IL	Prepared by: J. Ericson Date: June 16, 2015		Received by: T. Benson Review date: June 28, 2015	
Nature of Weakness and Impact	Chance for Error/Abuse		Notification to Management	
	Yes/No	Justification	Report date	Management response
User accounts with missing passwords	Yes	Leaves system open to unauthorized outsiders or attackers	5/10/15	Eliminate accounts without passwords
Network configured to allow some sharing of system files	Yes	Exposes critical system files to hostile parties connected to the network	5/10/15	Ensure only required directories are shared and that they are protected with strong passwords
Software patches can update production programs without final approval from Standards and Controls group	No	All production programs require management approval; Standards and Controls group assigns such cases to a temporary production status		

This chart is a sample page from a list of control weaknesses that an auditor might find in a loan system in a local commercial bank. This form helps auditors record and evaluate control weaknesses and shows the results of discussing those weaknesses with management, as well as any corrective actions taken by management.

The audit lists and ranks all control weaknesses and estimates the probability of their occurrence. It then assesses the financial and organizational impact of each threat. Figure 8.4 is a sample auditor's listing of control weaknesses for a loan system. It includes a section for notifying management of such weaknesses and for management's response. Management is expected to devise a plan for countering significant weaknesses in controls.

8.4   WHAT ARE THE MOST IMPORTANT TOOLS AND TECHNOLOGIES FOR SAFEGUARDING INFORMATION RESOURCES?

Businesses have an array of technologies for protecting their information resources. They include tools for managing user identities, preventing unauthorized access to systems and data, ensuring system availability, and ensuring software quality.

IDENTITY MANAGEMENT AND AUTHENTICATION

Midsize and large companies have complex IT infrastructures and many different systems, each with its own set of users. Identity management software automates the process of keeping track of all these users and their system privileges, assigning each user a unique digital identity for accessing each system. It also includes tools for authenticating users, protecting user identities, and controlling access to system resources.

To gain access to a system, a user must be authorized and authenticated. **Authentication** refers to the ability to know that a person is who he or she claims to be. Authentication is often established by using **passwords** known only to authorized users. An end user uses a password to log on to a computer system and may also use passwords for accessing specific systems and files. However, users often forget passwords, share them, or choose poor passwords that are easy to guess, which compromises security. Password systems that are too rigorous hinder employee productivity. When employees must change complex passwords frequently, they often take shortcuts, such as choosing passwords that are easy to guess or keeping their passwords at their workstations in plain view. Passwords can also be "sniffed" if transmitted over a network or stolen through social engineering.

New authentication technologies, such as tokens, smart cards, and biometric authentication, overcome some of these problems. A **token** is a physical device, similar to an identification card, that is designed to prove the identity of a single user. Tokens are small gadgets that typically fit on key rings and display passcodes that change frequently. A **smart card** is a device about the size of a credit card that contains a chip formatted with access permission and other data. (Smart cards are also used in electronic payment systems.) A reader device interprets the data on the smart card and allows or denies access.

Biometric authentication uses systems that read and interpret individual human traits, such as fingerprints, irises, and voices, in order to

© Aleksey Boldin/Alamy

This smartphone has a biometric fingerprint reader for fast yet secure access to files and networks. New models of PCs and smartphones are starting to use biometric identification to authenticate users.

grant or deny access. Biometric authentication is based on the measurement of a physical or behavioral trait that makes each individual unique. It compares a person's unique characteristics, such as the fingerprints, face, or retinal image, against a stored profile of these characteristics to determine whether there are any differences between these characteristics and the stored profile. If the two profiles match, access is granted. Fingerprint and facial recognition technologies are just beginning to be used for security applications, with many PC laptops (and some smartphones) equipped with fingerprint identification devices and several models with built-in webcams and face recognition software.

The steady stream of incidents in which hackers have been able to access traditional passwords highlights the need for more secure means of authentication. **Two-factor authentication** increases security by validating users with a multi-step process. To be authenticated, a user must provide two means of identification, one of which is typically a physical token, such as a smartcard or chip-enabled bank card, and the other of which is typically data, such as a password or PIN (personal identification number). Biometric data, such as fingerprints, iris prints, or voice prints, can also be used as one of the authenticating mechanisms. A common example of two-factor authentication is a bank card: the card itself is the physical item and the PIN is the data that go with it.

FIREWALLS, INTRUSION DETECTION SYSTEMS, AND ANTIVIRUS SOFTWARE

Without protection against malware and intruders, connecting to the Internet would be very dangerous. Firewalls, intrusion detection systems, and antivirus software have become essential business tools.

Firewalls

Firewalls prevent unauthorized users from accessing private networks. A firewall is a combination of hardware and software that controls the flow of incoming and outgoing network traffic. It is generally placed between the organization's private internal networks and distrusted external networks, such as the Internet, although firewalls can also be used to protect one part of a company's network from the rest of the network (see Figure 8.5).

The firewall acts like a gatekeeper who examines each user's credentials before access is granted to a network. The firewall identifies names, IP addresses, applications, and other characteristics of incoming traffic. It checks this information against the access rules that have been programmed into the system by the network administrator. The firewall prevents unauthorized communication into and out of the network.

In large organizations, the firewall often resides on a specially designated computer separate from the rest of the network, so no incoming request directly accesses private network resources. There are a number of firewall screening technologies, including static packet filtering, stateful inspection, Network Address Translation, and application proxy filtering. They are frequently used in combination to provide firewall protection.

FIGURE 8.5   A CORPORATE FIREWALL

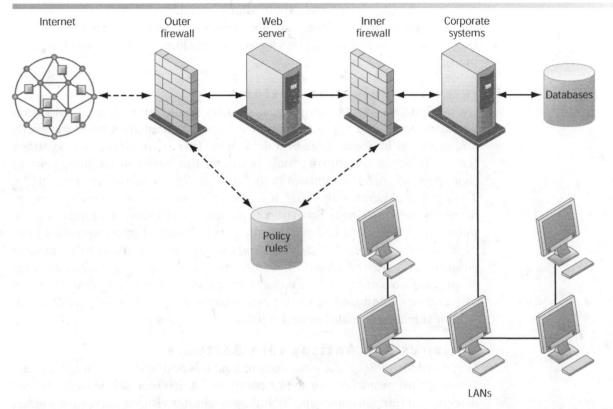

The firewall is placed between the firm's private network and the public Internet or another distrusted network to protect against unauthorized traffic.

Packet filtering examines selected fields in the headers of data packets flowing back and forth between the trusted network and the Internet, examining individual packets in isolation. This filtering technology can miss many types of attacks. *Stateful inspection* provides additional security by determining whether packets are part of an ongoing dialogue between a sender and a receiver. It sets up state tables to track information over multiple packets. Packets are accepted or rejected based on whether they are part of an approved conversation or whether they are attempting to establish a legitimate connection.

Network Address Translation (NAT) can provide another layer of protection when static packet filtering and stateful inspection are employed. NAT conceals the IP addresses of the organization's internal host computer(s) to prevent sniffer programs outside the firewall from ascertaining them and using that information to penetrate internal systems.

Application proxy filtering examines the application content of packets. A proxy server stops data packets originating outside the organization, inspects them, and passes a proxy to the other side of the firewall. If a user outside the company wants to communicate with a user inside the organization, the outside user first "talks" to the proxy application and the proxy application communicates with the firm's internal computer. Likewise, a computer user inside the organization goes through the proxy to talk with computers on the outside.

To create a good firewall, an administrator must maintain detailed internal rules identifying the people, applications, or addresses that are allowed or rejected. Firewalls can deter, but not completely prevent, network penetration by outsiders and should be viewed as one element in an overall security plan.

Intrusion Detection Systems

In addition to firewalls, commercial security vendors now provide intrusion detection tools and services to protect against suspicious network traffic and attempts to access files and databases. **Intrusion detection systems** feature full-time monitoring tools placed at the most vulnerable points or "hot spots" of corporate networks to detect and deter intruders continually. The system generates an alarm if it finds a suspicious or anomalous event. Scanning software looks for patterns indicative of known methods of computer attacks, such as bad passwords, checks to see if important files have been removed or modified, and sends warnings of vandalism or system administration errors. Monitoring software examines events as they are happening to discover security attacks in progress. The intrusion detection tool can also be customized to shut down a particularly sensitive part of a network if it receives unauthorized traffic.

Antivirus and Antispyware Software

Defensive technology plans for both individuals and businesses must include anti-malware protection for every computer. **Antivirus software** prevents, detects, and removes malware, including computer viruses, computer worms, Trojan horses, spyware, and adware. However, most antivirus software is effective only against malware already known when the software was written. To remain effective, the antivirus software must be continually updated, and even then it is not always effective. According to a report by Solutionary Security Engineering Research Team (SERT), 54 percent of malware evades anti-virus detection. Organizations need to use additional malware detection tools for better protection (Solutionary, 2013).

Unified Threat Management Systems

To help businesses reduce costs and improve manageability, security vendors have combined into a single appliance various security tools, including firewalls, virtual private networks, intrusion detection systems, and Web content filtering and antispam software. These comprehensive security management products are called **unified threat management (UTM)** systems. Although initially aimed at small and medium-sized businesses, UTM products are available for all sizes of networks. Leading UTM vendors include Blue Coat, Fortinet, and Check Point, and networking vendors such as Cisco Systems and Juniper Networks provide some UTM capabilities in their products.

SECURING WIRELESS NETWORKS

The initial security standard developed for Wi-Fi, called Wired Equivalent Privacy (WEP), is not very effective because its encryption keys are relatively easy to crack. WEP provides some margin of security, however, if users remember to enable it. Corporations can further improve Wi-Fi security by using it in conjunction with virtual private network (VPN) technology when accessing internal corporate data.

In June 2004, the Wi-Fi Alliance industry trade group finalized the 802.11i specification (also referred to as Wi-Fi Protected Access 2 or WPA2) that replaces WEP with stronger security standards. Instead of the static encryption keys used in WEP, the new standard uses much longer keys that continually change, making them harder to crack. It also employs an encrypted authentication system with a central authentication server to ensure that only authorized users access the network.

ENCRYPTION AND PUBLIC KEY INFRASTRUCTURE

Many businesses use encryption to protect digital information that they store, physically transfer, or send over the Internet. **Encryption** is the process of transforming plain text or data into cipher text that cannot be read by anyone other than the sender and the intended receiver. Data are encrypted by using a secret numerical code, called an encryption key, that transforms plain data into cipher text. The message must be decrypted by the receiver.

Two methods for encrypting network traffic on the Web are SSL and S-HTTP. **Secure Sockets Layer (SSL)** and its successor Transport Layer Security (TLS) enable client and server computers to manage encryption and decryption activities as they communicate with each other during a secure Web session. **Secure Hypertext Transfer Protocol (S-HTTP)** is another protocol used for encrypting data flowing over the Internet, but it is limited to individual messages, whereas SSL and TLS are designed to establish a secure connection between two computers.

The capability to generate secure sessions is built into Internet client browser software and servers. The client and the server negotiate what key and what level of security to use. Once a secure session is established between the client and the server, all messages in that session are encrypted.

Two methods of encryption are symmetric key encryption and public key encryption. In symmetric key encryption, the sender and receiver establish a secure Internet session by creating a single encryption key and sending it to the receiver so both the sender and receiver share the same key. The strength of the encryption key is measured by its bit length. Today, a typical key will be 128 bits long (a string of 128 binary digits).

The problem with all symmetric encryption schemes is that the key itself must be shared somehow among the senders and receivers, which exposes the key to outsiders who might just be able to intercept and decrypt the key. A more secure form of encryption called **public key encryption** uses two keys: one shared (or public) and one totally private as shown in Figure 8.6. The keys are mathematically related so that data encrypted with one key can be decrypted using only the other key. To send and receive messages, communicators first create separate pairs of private and public keys. The public key is kept in a directory and the private key must be kept secret. The sender encrypts a message with the recipient's public key. On receiving the message, the recipient uses his or her private key to decrypt it.

FIGURE 8.6 PUBLIC KEY ENCRYPTION

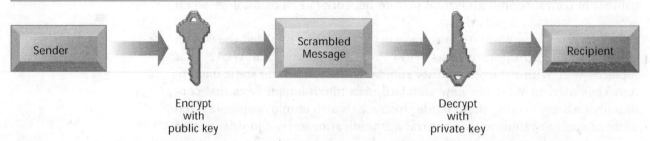

A public key encryption system can be viewed as a series of public and private keys that lock data when they are transmitted and unlock the data when they are received. The sender locates the recipient's public key in a directory and uses it to encrypt a message. The message is sent in encrypted form over the Internet or a private network. When the encrypted message arrives, the recipient uses his or her private key to decrypt the data and read the message.

Digital certificates are data files used to establish the identity of users and electronic assets for protection of online transactions (see Figure 8.7). A digital certificate system uses a trusted third party, known as a certificate authority (CA, or certification authority), to validate a user's identity. There are many CAs in the United States and around the world, including Symantec, GoDaddy, and Comodo.

The CA verifies a digital certificate user's identity offline. This information is put into a CA server, which generates an encrypted digital certificate containing owner identification information and a copy of the owner's public key. The certificate authenticates that the public key belongs to the designated

FIGURE 8.7 DIGITAL CERTIFICATES

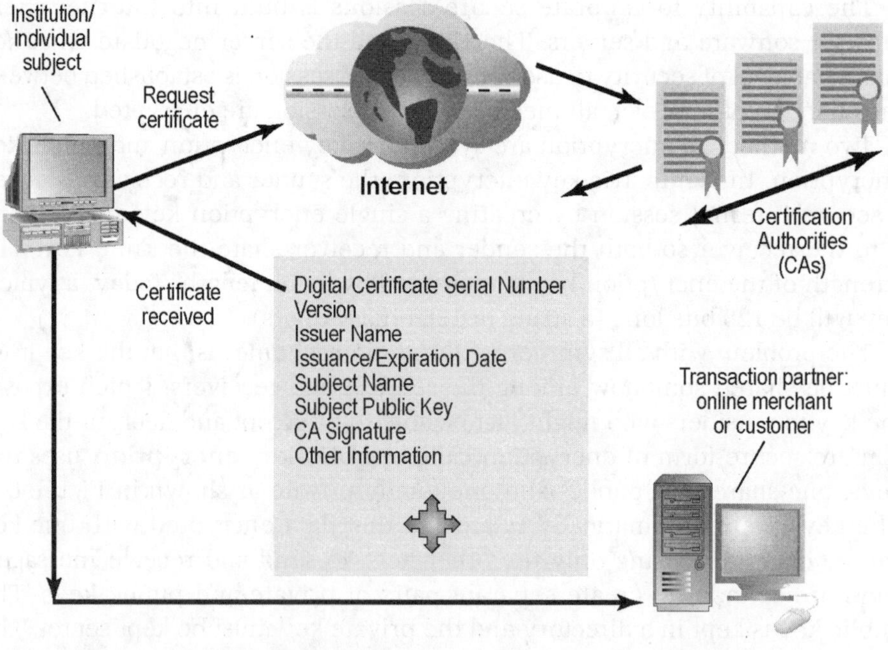

Institution/
individual
subject

Request
certificate

Internet

Certification
Authorities
(CAs)

Certificate
received

Digital Certificate Serial Number
Version
Issuer Name
Issuance/Expiration Date
Subject Name
Subject Public Key
CA Signature
Other Information

Transaction partner:
online merchant
or customer

Digital certificates help establish the identity of people or electronic assets. They protect online transactions by providing secure, encrypted, online communication.

owner. The CA makes its own public key available either in print or perhaps on the Internet. The recipient of an encrypted message uses the CA's public key to decode the digital certificate attached to the message, verifies it was issued by the CA, and then obtains the sender's public key and identification information contained in the certificate. Using this information, the recipient can send an encrypted reply. The digital certificate system would enable, for example, a credit card user and a merchant to validate that their digital certificates were issued by an authorized and trusted third party before they exchange data. **Public key infrastructure (PKI)**, the use of public key cryptography working with a CA, is now widely used in e-commerce.

ENSURING SYSTEM AVAILABILITY

As companies increasingly rely on digital networks for revenue and operations, they need to take additional steps to ensure that their systems and applications are always available. Firms such as those in the airline and financial services industries with critical applications requiring online transaction processing have traditionally used fault-tolerant computer systems for many years to ensure 100 percent availability. In **online transaction processing**, transactions entered online are immediately processed by the computer. Multitudinous changes to databases, reporting, and requests for information occur each instant.

Fault-tolerant computer systems contain redundant hardware, software, and power supply components that create an environment that provides continuous, uninterrupted service. Fault-tolerant computers use special software routines or self-checking logic built into their circuitry to detect hardware failures and automatically switch to a backup device. Parts from these computers can be removed and repaired without disruption to the computer or downtime. **Downtime** refers to periods of time in which a system is not operational.

Controlling Network Traffic: Deep Packet Inspection

Have you ever tried to use your campus network and found it was very slow? It may be because your fellow students are using the network to download music or watch YouTube. Bandwith-consuming applications such as file-sharing programs, Internet phone service, and online video are able to clog and slow down corporate networks, degrading performance. For example, Ball State University in Muncie, Indiana, found its network had slowed because a small minority of students were using P2P file-sharing programs to download movies and music.

A technology called **deep packet inspection (DPI)** helps solve this problem. DPI examines data files and sorts out low-priority online material while assigning higher priority to business-critical files. Based on the priorities established by a network's operators, it decides whether a specific data packet can continue to its destination or should be blocked or delayed while more important traffic proceeds. Using a DPI system from Allot Communications, Ball State was able to cap the amount of file-sharing traffic and assign it a much lower priority. Ball State's preferred network traffic speeded up.

Security Outsourcing

Many companies, especially small businesses, lack the resources or expertise to provide a secure high-availability computing environment on their own. They can outsource many security functions to **managed security service providers (MSSPs)** that monitor network activity and perform vulnerability testing and intrusion detection. SecureWorks, BT Managed Security Solutions Group, and Symantec are leading providers of MSSP services.

SECURITY ISSUES FOR CLOUD COMPUTING AND THE MOBILE DIGITAL PLATFORM

Although cloud computing and the emerging mobile digital platform have the potential to deliver powerful benefits, they pose new challenges to system security and reliability. We now describe some of these challenges and how they should be addressed.

Security in the Cloud

When processing takes place in the cloud, accountability and responsibility for protection of sensitive data still reside with the company owning that data. Understanding how the cloud computing provider organizes its services and manages the data is critical.

Cloud computing is highly distributed. Cloud applications reside in large remote data centers and server farms that supply business services and data management for multiple corporate clients. To save money and keep costs low, cloud computing providers often distribute work to data centers around the globe where work can be accomplished most efficiently. When you use the cloud, you may not know precisely where your data are being hosted.

The dispersed nature of cloud computing makes it difficult to track unauthorized activity. Virtually all cloud providers use encryption, such as Secure Sockets Layer, to secure the data they handle while the data are being transmitted. But if the data are stored on devices that also store other companies' data, it's important to ensure these stored data are encrypted as well.

Companies expect their systems to be running 24/7, but cloud providers haven't always been able to provide this level of service. On several occasions over the past few years, the cloud services of Amazon.com and Salesforce.com experienced outages that disrupted business operations for millions of users.

Cloud users need to confirm that regardless of where their data are stored, they are protected at a level that meets their corporate requirements. They should stipulate that the cloud provider store and process data in specific jurisdictions according to the privacy rules of those jurisdictions. Cloud clients should find how the cloud provider segregates their corporate data from those of other companies and ask for proof that encryption mechanisms are sound. It's also important to know how the cloud provider will respond if a disaster strikes, whether the provider will be able to completely restore your data, and how long this should take. Cloud users should also ask whether cloud providers will submit to external audits and security certifications. These kinds of controls can be written into the service level agreement (SLA) before signing with a cloud provider.

Securing Mobile Platforms

If mobile devices are performing many of the functions of computers, they need to be secured like desktops and laptops against malware, theft, accidental loss, unauthorized access, and hacking attempts. The Interactive Session on Technology describes these mobile vulnerabilities in greater detail and their implications for both individuals and businesses.

Mobile devices accessing corporate systems and data require special protection. Companies should make sure that their corporate security policy includes mobile devices, with additional details on how mobile devices should be supported, protected, and used. They will need mobile device management tools to authorize all devices in use; to maintain accurate inventory records on all mobile devices, users, and applications; to control updates to applications; and to lock down or erase lost or stolen devices so they can't be compromised. Data loss prevention technology can identify where critical data are saved, who is accessing the data, how data are leaving the company, and where the data are going. Firms should develop guidelines stipulating approved mobile platforms and software applications as well as the required software and procedures for remote access of corporate systems. The organization's mobile security policy should forbid employees from using unsecure, consumer-based applications for transferring and storing corporate documents and files, or sending such documents and files to oneself via e-mail without encryption.

Companies should encrypt communication whenever possible. All mobile device users should be required to use the password feature found in every smartphone. Mobile security products are available from Kaspersky, Symantec, Trend Micro, and McAfee.

Some companies insist that employees use only company-issued smartphones. BlackBerry devices are considered the most secure because they run within their own secure system. But, increasingly, companies are allowing employees to use their own devices, including iPhones, iPads, and Android phones, for work, to make employees more available and productive (see the Chapter 5 discussion of BYOD). Protective software products, such as the tools from Good Technology, are now available for segregating corporate data housed within personally owned mobile devices from the device's personal content.

ENSURING SOFTWARE QUALITY

In addition to implementing effective security and controls, organizations can improve system quality and reliability by employing software metrics and rigorous software testing. Software metrics are objective assessments of the system in the form of quantified measurements. Ongoing use of metrics allows the information systems department and end users to jointly measure the performance of the system and identify problems as they occur. Examples of software metrics include the number of transactions that can be processed in a specified unit of time, online response time, the number of payroll checks printed per hour, and the number of known bugs per hundred lines of program code. For metrics to be successful, they must be carefully designed, formal, objective, and used consistently.

INTERACTIVE SESSION: TECHNOLOGY

BYOD: IT'S NOT SO SAFE

Bring Your Own Device has become a huge trend, with nearly one-third of employees using personal devices at workplaces worldwide. This figure is expected to increase even more in the years to come. But while use of the iPhone, iPad and other mobile computing devices in the workplace is growing, so are security problems.

Whether these devices are company-assigned or employee-owned, they are opening up new avenues for accessing corporate data that need to be closely monitored and protected. Sensitive data on mobile devices travels, both physically and electronically, from the office to home and possibly other off-site locations. According to a 2012 survey of 400 technology professionals by researchers at Decisive Analytics, nearly half of companies that allow personally-owned devices to connect to the corporate network have experienced a data breach, either because of employees' unwitting mistakes or intentional wrongdoing. Quite a few security experts believe that smartphones and other mobile devices now pose one of the most serious security threats for organizations today.

One of the biggest security dangers of smartphones is that the devices could become lost. That puts all of the personal and corporate data stored on the device, as well as access to corporate data on remote servers, at risk. According to a Ponemon Institute study of 116 organizations, 62 percent of mobile devices housing data that were lost or stolen contained sensitive or confidential information. Information Week's 2014 State of Mobile Security report stated that 72 percent of responding companies said their top mobile security concern was lost or stolen devices.

Physical access to mobile devices may be a greater threat than hacking into a network because less effort is required to gain entry. Experienced attackers can easily circumvent passwords or locks on mobile devices or access encrypted data. This may include not only corporate data found on the device but also passwords residing in insecure places such as iPhone Keychain, which could grant access to corporate services such as email or the virtual private network. Moreover, many smartphone users leave their phones totally unprotected to begin with. In the Websense and the Ponemon Institute's Global Study on Mobility Risks, 59 percent of respondents reported that employees circumvented or disabled security features such as passwords and key locks. Intruders can also gain physical access to mobile devices by plugging into a device using a USB connection or SD card slot. Even leaving a device alone for a minute on a desk or chair can lead to serious theft of data in a few minutes.

Another worry today is large scale data leakage caused by use of cloud computing services. Employees are increasingly using public cloud services such as Google Drive or Dropbox for file-sharing and collaboration. For example, Mashery, a 170-employee company that helps other companies build apps, allows employees with iPhones to use Dropbox, Box, Teambox, and Google Drive to store memos, spreadsheets, and customer information . These services are vulnerable. In July 2012, Dropbox reported a loss of login names and passwords from a large number of customers, and in 2011, Chinese hackers obtained access to hundreds of U.S. government accounts on Google Gmail. There's very little a company can do to prevent employees who are allowed to use their smartphones from downloading corporate data so they can work on that data remotely.

Although deliberate hacker attacks on mobile devices have been limited in scope and impact, this situation is worsening, especially among Android devices vulnerable to rogue apps. According to McAfee, a leading computer security software firm, malware in Android mobile operating systems alone grew by 33 percent in 2013. Android is now the world's most popular operating system for mobile devices.

Security on the Android platform is much less under Google's control than Apple devices running iOS because Google has an open app model. Google does not review any Android apps (as Apple does for its apps), but instead relies on technical hurdles to limit the impact of malicious code, as well as user and security expert feedback. Google apps run in a "sandbox," where they cannot affect one another or manipulate device features without user permission. Google removes from its official Android Market any apps that break its rules against malicious activity. Google also vets the backgrounds of developers, and requires developers to register with its Checkout payment service both to encourage users to pay for apps using their service and to force developers to reveal their identities and financial information. Recent Android security enhancements include assigning varying levels of trust to each app, dictating what kind of data an app can access inside its confined domain, and providing a more robust way to store cryptographic credentials used to access sensitive information and resources. Still, from a corporate standpoint, it is almost impossible to prevent employees from downloading apps that might track critical information when people use their own devices in the workplace.

Beyond the threat of rogue apps, smartphones of all stripes are susceptible to browser-based malware that takes advantage of vulnerabilities in all browsers.

Mobile security breaches carry a hefty price tag for data loss, damage to the brand, productivity loss, and loss of customer trust. According to a 2013 study commissioned by Check Point Technologies, 52 percent of large companies reported the cost of mobile security incidents exceeded $500,000. Forty-five percent of businesses with less than 1,000 employees reported costs exceeding $100,000. These security breaches can also cause huge intangible losses to a company's reputation. The Securities and Exchange Commission requires unauthorized disclosure of confidential information, whether from unsecured devices, untrusted apps, or weak cloud security, must be publicly reported if the information could affect a company's stock price.

Sources: "*Information Week* 2014 Mobile Security Survey," March 2014; Christian Crank," Mitigating Mobile BYOD Security Risks," Baseline, March 13, 2014; John Sawyer, "Mobile Security: All About the Data," *Information Week*, April 1, 2014; "Internet Security Census 2013: A Fortinet Global Survey," www.fortinet.com, accessed March 14, 2014; Don Reisinger, "10 Mobile Security Issues that Should Worry You," *eWeek*, February 11, 2014; Dimensional Research, "The Impact of Mobile Devices on Information Security," Check Point Technologies, June 2013; October 13, 2013, Nicole Perlroth, "Bolstering a Phone's Defenses Against Breaches," *New York Times*, October 13, 2013; Dan Goodin, "Google Strengthens Android Security Muscle with SELinux Protection, Ars Technica, July 24, 2013; Karen A. Frenkel, "Best Practices of Mobile Technology Leaders," *CIO Insight*, July 24, 2013; Quentin Hardy, "Where Apps Meet Work, Secret Data Is at Risk," *New York Times*, March 3, 2013; and Ponemon Institute, "Global Study on Mobility Risks," February 2012.

CASE STUDY QUESTIONS

1. It has been said that a smartphone is a computer in your hand. Discuss the security implications of this statement.

2. What management, organizational, and technology issues must be addressed by smartphone security?

3. What problems do smartphone security weaknesses cause for businesses?

4. What steps can individuals and businesses take to make their smartphones more secure?

Early, regular, and thorough testing will contribute significantly to system quality. Many view testing as a way to prove the correctness of work they have done. In fact, we know that all sizable software is riddled with errors, and we must test to uncover these errors.

Good testing begins before a software program is even written by using a *walkthrough*—a review of a specification or design document by a small group of people carefully selected based on the skills needed for the particular objectives being tested. Once developers start writing software programs, coding walkthroughs can also be used to review program code. However, code must be tested by computer runs. When errors are discovered, the source is found and eliminated through a process called *debugging*. You can find out more about the various stages of testing required to put an information system into operation in Chapter 13. Our Learning Tracks also contain descriptions of methodologies for developing software programs that also contribute to software quality.

Review Summary

1. *Why are information systems vulnerable to destruction, error, and abuse?*

    Digital data are vulnerable to destruction, misuse, error, fraud, and hardware or software failures. The Internet is designed to be an open system and makes internal corporate systems more vulnerable to actions from outsiders. Hackers can unleash denial-of-service (DoS) attacks or penetrate corporate networks, causing serious system disruptions. Wi-Fi networks can easily be penetrated by intruders using sniffer programs to obtain an address to access the resources of the network. Computer viruses and worms can disable systems and Web sites. The dispersed nature of cloud computing makes it difficult to track unauthorized activity or to apply controls from afar. Software presents problems because software bugs may be impossible to eliminate and because software vulnerabilities can be exploited by hackers and malicious software. End users often introduce errors.

2. *What is the business value of security and control?*

    Lack of sound security and control can cause firms relying on computer systems for their core business functions to lose sales and productivity. Information assets, such as confidential employee records, trade secrets, or business plans, lose much of their value if they are revealed to outsiders or if they expose the firm to legal liability. New laws, such as HIPAA, the Sarbanes-Oxley Act, and the Gramm-Leach-Bliley Act, require companies to practice stringent electronic records management and adhere to strict standards for security, privacy, and control. Legal actions requiring electronic evidence and computer forensics also require firms to pay more attention to security and electronic records management.

3. *What are the components of an organizational framework for security and control?*

    What are the components of an organizational framework for security and control? Firms need to establish a good set of both general and application controls for their information systems. A risk assessment evaluates information assets, identifies control points and control weaknesses, and determines the most cost-effective set of controls. Firms must also develop a coherent corporate security policy and plans for continuing business operations in the event of disaster or disruption. The security policy includes policies for acceptable use and identity management. Comprehensive and systematic information systems auditing helps organizations determine the effectiveness of security and controls for their information systems.

4. *What are the most important tools and technologies for safeguarding information resources?*
   Firewalls prevent unauthorized users from accessing a private network when it is linked to the Internet. Intrusion detection systems monitor private networks from suspicious network traffic and attempts to access corporate systems. Passwords, tokens, smart cards, and biometric authentication are used to authenticate system users. Antivirus software checks computer systems for infections by viruses and worms and often eliminates the malicious software, while antispyware software combats intrusive and harmful spyware programs. Encryption, the coding and scrambling of messages, is a widely used technology for securing electronic transmissions over unprotected networks. Digital certificates combined with public key encryption provide further protection of electronic transactions by authenticating a user's identity. Companies can use fault-tolerant computer systems to make sure that their information systems are always available. Use of software metrics and rigorous software testing help improve software quality and reliability.

Key Terms

Acceptable use policy (AUP), 343
Antivirus software, 350
Application controls, 341
Authentication, 347
Biometric authentication, 347
Botnet, 331
Bugs, 337
Business continuity planning, 345
Click fraud, 336
Computer crime, 331
Computer forensics, 340
Computer virus, 326
Controls, 324
Cybervandalism, 330
Cyberwarfare, 336
Deep packet inspection (DPI), 353
Denial-of-service (DoS) attack, 330
Digital certificates, 352
Disaster recovery planning, 345
Distributed denial-of-service (DDoS) attack, 331
Downtime, 353
Drive-by download, 327
Encryption, 351
Evil twin, 333
Fault-tolerant computer systems, 353
Firewall, 348
General controls, 341
Gramm-Leach-Bliley Act, 339
Hacker, 330
HIPAA, 339
Identity management, 343

Identity theft, 332
Information systems audit, 345
Intrusion detection systems, 350
Keyloggers, 330
Malware, 326
Managed security service providers (MSSPs), 354
Online transaction processing, 353
Password, 347
Patches, 338
Pharming, 333
Phishing, 332
Public key encryption, 351
Public key infrastructure (PKI), 353
Ransomware, 329
Risk assessment, 342
Sarbanes-Oxley Act, 339
Secure Hypertext Transfer Protocol (S-HTTP), 351
Secure Sockets Layer (SSL), 351
Security, 324
Security policy, 343
Smart card, 347
Sniffer, 330
Social engineering, 339
Spoofing, 330
Spyware, 329
SQL injection attack, 328
Token, 337
Trojan horse, 328
Two-factor authentication, 348
Unified threat management (UTM), 350
War driving, 326
Worms, 327

Review Questions

8-1 Why are information systems vulnerable to destruction, error, and abuse?

- List and describe the most common threats against contemporary information systems.

- Define malware and distinguish among a virus, a worm, and a Trojan horse.

- Define a hacker and explain how hackers create security problems and damage systems.

- Define computer crime. Provide two examples of crime in which computers are targets and two examples in which computers are used as instruments of crime.
- Define identity theft and phishing and explain why identity theft is such a big problem today.
- Describe the security and system reliability problems created by employees.
- Explain how software defects affect system reliability and security.

8-2 What is the business value of security and control?
- Explain how security and control provide value for businesses.
- Describe the relationship between security and control and recent U.S. government regulatory requirements and computer forensics.

8-3 What are the components of an organizational framework for security and control?
- Define general controls and describe each type of general control.
- Define application controls and describe each type of application control.

- Describe the function of risk assessment and explain how it is conducted for information systems.
- Define and describe the following: security policy, acceptable use policy, and identity management.
- Explain how information systems auditing promotes security and control.

8-4 What are the most important tools and technologies for safeguarding information resources?
- Name and describe three authentication methods.
- Describe the roles of firewalls, intrusion detection systems, and antivirus software in promoting security.
- Explain how encryption protects information.
- Describe the role of encryption and digital certificates in a public key infrastructure.
- Distinguish between disaster recovery planning and business continuity planning.
- Identify and describe the security problems posed by cloud computing.
- Describe measures for improving software quality and reliability.

Discussion Questions

8-5 Security isn't simply a technology issue, it's a business issue. Discuss.

8-6 If you were developing a business continuity plan for your company, where would you start? What aspects of the business would the plan address?

8-7 Suppose your business had an e-commerce Web site where it sold goods and accepted credit card payments. Discuss the major security threats to this Web site and their potential impact. What can be done to minimize these threats?

Hands-On MIS Projects

The projects in this section give you hands-on experience analyzing security vulnerabilities, using spreadsheet software for risk analysis, and using Web tools to research security outsourcing services.

Management Decision Problems

8-8 Reloaded Games is an online games platform which powers leading massively multiplayer online games. The Reloaded platform serves more than 30 million users. The games can accommodate millions of players at once and are played simultaneously by people all over the world. Prepare a security analysis for this Internet-based business. What kinds of threats should it anticipate? What would be their impact on the business? What steps can it take to prevent damage to its Web sites and continuing operations?

Improving Decision Making: Evaluating Security Outsourcing Services

Software skills: Web browser and presentation software
Business skills: Evaluating business outsourcing services

8-9   This project will help develop your Internet skills in using the Web to research and evaluate security outsourcing services.

You have been asked to help your company's management decide whether to outsource security or keep the security function within the firm. Search the Web to find information to help you decide whether to outsource security and to locate security outsourcing services.

- Present a brief summary of the arguments for and against outsourcing computer security for your company.
- Select two firms that offer computer security outsourcing services, and compare them and their services.
- Prepare an electronic presentation for management summarizing your findings. Your presentation should make the case on whether or not your company should outsource computer security. If you believe your company should outsource, the presentation should identify which security outsourcing service you selected and justify your decision.

Securing Information: the HSBC Way
CASE STUDY

Hongkong and Shanghai Banking Corporation Limited (HSBC) was set up in India in the year 1853 as Mercantile Bank. It soon opened branches in London, Chennai, Singapore, and Hong Kong. In 1959, it was acquired by Shanghai Banking Corporation Limited, which laid the foundation for the HSBC group. The HSBC group develops and applies advanced technology to deliver their banking and financial services in a convenient and efficient manner. Some of the technology-driven services the bank provides include:

- ATMs
- Phone banking
- Trade and corporate banking with real-time access to a centralized information database
- Inter-city transactions through online connections among all branches
- Treasury dealing system
- Debit and credit cards
- Domestic and international VISA, MasterCard, and co-branded cards
- Internet banking
- Internet payment gateway

Even though electronic banking services are convenient from the customer's point of view, they pose transactional and operational challenges for the bank. Hackers are a major threat. They can break into confidential information and illegally transfer money. Attackers can also can utilize user information from various sources, join the dots to get a complete picture of the victim's profile, and pose as the user to perform illegal transactions on their behalf. This is called social engineering. All these risks make it important for banks to have effective policies, procedures, and controls in place to tackle these challenges. Cyber attacks and information security threats are of increasing concern in India. HSBC recognizes the importance of security in Internet transactions and has incorporated the following security measures:

- Robust authentication processes
- Protection against key-logging and denial-of-service attacks
- Two-factor authentication using security devices or smart cards to generate one-time passwords
- Encrypted sessions between the customer and the bank (SSL v3 128 bit)
- Protection of sensitive information in transit and storage to ensure confidentiality of customer data
- Industry-standard security mechanisms to protect the infrastructure
- Regular independent reviews of system security
- Robust and regularly reviewed information security policies
- Comprehensive contingency and back-up arrangements
- Round-the-clock security monitoring and centralized incident management teams
- Audit trails for administrative and transactional activities

HSBC was one of the first banks in India to introduce the two-stage authentication system to boost the security of online transactions. In addition to authenticating the user with the usual user ID and password, an additional passcode is required. This passcode is sent to a security device, which needs to be entered to complete an online transaction. This two-step verification is very useful in certain sensitive transactions like account transfers to non-registered accounts, bill payment to merchants, setting up of direct debit authorizations to designated merchants, and updating personal details.

The two-factor authentication system is also mandated by the Reserve Bank of India, the central body controlling financial activities in India. To further enhance the security of transactions, HSBC sends SMS notifications to users on completion of transactions, especially for transfers to non-registered third-party accounts and electronic bill payments. The user information is not stored on any disc or Internet-facing Web server. The Web servers are physically separated from back-office databases that hold transactional data.

Another threat that banks face is that of MitM (man in the middle) attacks. These are caused due to the downloading of malware on part of the users. MitM attackers can fraudulently conduct transactions on behalf of the user. HSBC's policy of not sending any confidential information to customers by e-mail minimizes the chances of phishing. The bank's secure portal uses the 'https' protocol to establish a secured session. HSBC uses a 128-bit secure socket layer to encrypt the information sent and received. The session is set to time out after a certain period of inactivity. All these things work together to make the electronic banking experience safe and secure for the user as well as for the bank.

Sources: Carse, David, "The Regulatory Framework of E-banking", *Hong Kong Monetary Authority* (1999). Retrieved from http://www.hkma.gov.hk/eng/key-information/speech-speakers/dcarse/speech_081099b.shtml; "Bank Profile and History". Retrieved from https://bank.hangseng.com/1/2/about-us/corporate-info/bank-profile; "Terms and Conditions". Retrieved from http://www.hangseng.com/hsb/eng/ref/bib/pdf/e_bank_tnc.pdf; "New Security Device—Frequently Asked Questions". Retrieved from http://www.hangseng.com.cn/1/PA_esf-ca-app-content/content/pws/business/pdfs/TransactionDataSigning_FAQ_HACN_Eng.pdf; "e-Banking Security". Retrieved from https://bank.hangseng.com/1/2/e-services/e-banking-security/ebanking-security; "Hong Kong tightens online banking security", *ZDNet* (2005). Retrieved from http://www.zdnet.com/hong-kong-tightens-online-banking-security-2039240308/; Zhen, Simon, "HSBC to Provide Free Security Device for Safer Online Banking", *My Bank Tracker* (2014). Retrieved from http://www.mybanktracker.com/news/2014/02/12/hsbc-provide-free-security-device-safer-online-banking/.

CASE STUDY QUESTIONS

8-10 Discuss the need for securing electronic banking at HSBC.

8-11 Discuss the two-stage verification process adopted by HSBC.

8-12 Discuss some other steps taken by HSBC to protect its electronic banking transactions.

Chapter 8 References

"Devastating Downtime: The Surprising Cost of Human Error and Unforeseen Events." Focus Research (October 2010).

Boulton, Clint."American Airlines Outage Likely Caused by Software Quality Issues." *Wall Street Journal* (April 17, 2013).

Boyle, Randall J. and Raymond R. Panko, Raymond R. Corporate *Computer Security 4/e.* Upper Saddle River NJ: Prentice-Hall (2015).

Breedon, John II. "Trojans Horses Gain Inside Track as Top Form of Malware." GCN (May 6, 2013).

Cavusoglu, Huseyin, Birendra Mishra, and Srinivasan Raghunathan. "A Model for Evaluating IT Security Investments." *Communications of the ACM* 47, No. 7 (July 2004).

Crossman, Penny. "DDoS Attacks Are Still Happening-and Getting Bigger." *Information Management* (July 29, 2014).

Dey, Debabrata, Atanu Lahiri, and Guoying Zhang. "Quality Competition and Market Segmentation in the Security Software Market. *MIS Quarterly* 38, No. 2 (June 2014).

Donohue, Brian. "Malware C&C Servers Found in 184 Countries." ThreatPost.com (August 2, 2013).

Galbreth, Michael R. and Mikhael Shor. "The Impact of Malicious Agents on the Enterprise Software Industry." *MIS Quarterly* 34, No. 3 (September 2010).

Grossman, Lev. "The Code." Time(July 21, 2014).

Hui , Kai Lung, Wendy Hui and Wei T. Yue. "Information Security Outsourcing with System Interdependency and Mandatory Security Requirement." *Journal of Management Information Systems* 29, No. 3 (Winter 2013).

Javelin Strategy & Research."2014 Identity Fraud Study." (2014).

Kaplan, James, Chris Rezek, and Kara Sprague."Protecting Information in the Cloud." *McKinsey Quarterly* (January 2013).

Karlovsky, Brian. "FireEye Names Malware's Favorite Targets, Sources." *Australian Reseller News* (March 2, 2014).

McAfee." Mobile Malware Growth Continuing in 2013." (February 21, 2013).

Osterman Research. "The Risks of Social Media and What Can Be Done to Manage Them. Commvault (June 2011).

Panda Security. "Annual Report Pandalabs 2013." (2014).

Perez, Sarah, "AY Media-Owned Blogging Platform Typepad Enters Day 5 of On-And-Off DDoS Attacks." Techcrunch. com (April 21, 2014).

Ponemon Institute. "2013 Cost of Cybercrime Study: United States (October 2013).

Ponemon Institute. "2014 Cost of Data Breach Study: United States (2014).

Reisinger, Don. "Android Security Remains a Glaring Problem: 10 Reasons Why." *eWeek* (March 2, 2014).

Ribeiro, John. "Hacker group targets Skype social media accounts," *Computer world* (January 2, 2014).

Sadeh, Norman M. "Phish Isn't Spam." *Information Week* (June 25, 2012).

Scharr, Jill. "Fake Instagram 'Image Viewers' Are Latest Malware Fad." Tom's Guide (May 8, 2014).

Schwartz, Matthew J. "Android Trojan Looks, Acts Like Windows Malware." *Information Week* (June 7, 2013).

Sengupta, Somini. "Machines that Know You without Using a Password." New York Times (September 10, 2013).

Solutionary. "Solutionary Security Engineering Research Team Unveils Annual Global Threat Intelligence Report ." (March 12, 2013).

Spears. Janine L. and Henri Barki. "User Participation in Information Systems Security Risk Management." *MIS Quarterly* 34, No. 3 (September 2010).

Stallings, William H. and Lawrie Brown. *Computer Security: Principles and Practice 3/e*. Upper Saddle River, NJ: Prentice Hall (2015).

Symantec. "State of Mobility Global Results 2013." (2013).

_____. "Symantec Internet Security Threat Report." (2014).

Temizkan , Orcun, Ram L. Kumar , Sungjune Park and Chandrasekar Subramaniam. "Patch Release Behaviors of Software Vendors in Response to Vulnerabilities: An Empirical Analysis . " *Journal of Management Information Systems* 28, No. 4 (Spring 2012).

Vance , Anthony, Paul Benjamin Lowry and Dennis Eggett. "Using Accountability to Reduce Access Policy Violations in Information Systems ." *Journal of Management Information Systems* Volume 29 Number 4 Spring 2013.

Yadron, Danny. "Companies Wrestle with the Cost of Cybersecurity." *Wall Street Journal* (February 25, 2014).

Yan Chen , K. Ram Ramamurthy and Kuang-Wei Wen." Organizations' Information Security Policy Compliance: Stick or Carrot Approach?" *Journal of Management Information Systems* 29, No. 3 (Winter 2013).

Zhao, Xia, Ling Xue and Andrew B. Whinston." Managing Interdependent Information Security Risks: Cyberinsurance, Managed Security Services, and Risk Pooling Arrangements ." *Journal of Management Information Systems* 30, No. 1 (Summer 2013).

PART THREE

Key System Applications for the Digital Age

Part Three examines the core information system applications businesses are using today to improve operational excellence and decision making. These applications include enterprise systems; systems for supply chain management, customer relationship management, and knowledge management; e-commerce applications; and business-intelligence systems. This part answers questions such as: How can enterprise applications improve business performance? How do firms use e-commerce to extend the reach of their businesses? How can systems improve decision making and help companies make better use of their knowledge assets?

Achieving Operational Excellence and Customer Intimacy: Enterprise Applications

CHAPTER 9

LEARNING OBJECTIVES

After reading this chapter, you will be able to answer the following questions:

1. How do enterprise systems help businesses achieve operational excellence?

2. How do supply chain management systems coordinate planning, production, and logistics with suppliers?

3. How do customer relationship management systems help firms achieve customer intimacy?

4. What are the challenges posed by enterprise applications and how are enterprise applications taking advantage of new technologies?

CHAPTER CASES

ACH Food Companies Transforms Its Business with Enterprise Systems

Optimizing Operations at QuarkCity: A Move Away from Legacy Systems

Scotts Miracle-Gro Cultivates Supply Chain Proficiency

CRM Tools Aid Airtel in the Efficient Handling of Customer Support Processes

Social CRM: Connecting with Customers through Social Networks

ACH FOOD COMPANIES TRANSFORMS ITS BUSINESS WITH ENTERPRISE SYSTEMS

You may not have heard of ACH Food Companies, but you can probably find their products in your pantry—Mazola, Fleischmann's, Argo Spice Islands, Karo's, and Durkee's, to name a few. ACH is headquartered in Cordova, Tennessee, has about one thousand employees, and generates about $1 billion in revenue. Until recently, ACH had done business primarily as a commercial food manufacturer for the food services and food ingredients markets. Now its primary focus is on the retail consumer and the consumer products food market. Becoming more consumer-oriented has created new opportunities for expansion, but this move required the company to become much more agile and flexible to accommodate new product launches and movement into new markets.

ACH's information systems had to change to support its new strategy and methods of doing business. ACH had been running on a series of legacy systems that were designed primarily for its old business model as a food ingredients maker. Many applications were 20 to 30 years old and had been cobbled together, with too many point-to-point interfaces. It was difficult for them to exchange data or to supply the data required for a company-wide view of firm performance. These systems also lacked the functionality required for a consumer-branded

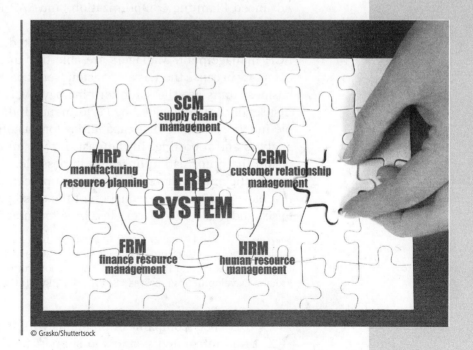

© Grasko/Shuttertsock

company that hoped to grow by acquiring more companies. ACH was not operating as efficiently as it could, nor could it move forward strategically as a consumer-branded company.

In 2007, the company began implementing SAP's Enterprise Resource Planning (ERP) system, using its software application modules for finance, order management, procure-to-pay, and business intelligence. ERP applications are integrated, and the software enforces a single set of transactional and master data. According to CIO Donnie Steward, ACH very much wanted the ability to enforce application integration across all modules, and to break down the old functional "silos" that made it difficult for business functions to coordinate in its old legacy systems. SAP had developed industry-specific ERP software for consumer food products, based on industry best practices, and this appealed to ACH as well.

At that point, the company hadn't fully transitioned to a consumer products company. So, the software required a great deal of customization to provide functionality for ACH's food ingredients and food service businesses as well as its new consumer business. Shortly after this ERP system went live, ACH decided to divest the commercial side of its business and focus solely on the consumer side. That move required the company to eliminate much of the customization work it had done to bring its old food ingredients and food service systems onto the SAP ERP platform. ACH's information systems team then focused on creating a "vanilla" ERP system where no customization was required.

In late 2009, ACH implemented additional SAP ERP functionality for product costing and quality management as well as other applications in the SAP suite—SAP Manufacturing, SAP Product Lifecycle Management, SAP Advanced Planning & Optimization, and SAP Recipe Management — with extensive business intelligence capabilities.

How have the all the new systems worked out? Very well, according to ACH management. Managers are able to make better decisions across the company because there is a consistent set of data for the entire enterprise. All business units use the same terminology. ACH has been able to develop its first set of company-wide Key Performance Indicators (KPIs) that span multiple functions and its first capabilities for customer and product profitability analysis and reporting. In the past, it took an excessive amount of time to obtain that information or it was impossible. The company operates much more efficiently: There has been a 20 percent reduction in finished goods inventory, a 25 percent reduction of the close process, from eight days down to six, and it takes 75 percent less time for internal new-product initiation.

Sources: "ACH Food Companies: Transforming from a Commercial to a Consumer-Branded Business," www.mysap.com, accessed May 26, 2014; "An ERP for Panda Bears," Inside-ERP, December 5, 2013; and Dave Hannon, "ACH Food Companies Accelerates Its Planning and Product Development Processes," SAPInsider PROFILES, July 1. 2011.

ACH Food Companies's problems with legacy systems and its need to find integrated systems to support its new consumer-products business model illustrate why companies need enterprise applications that integrate different business functions and provide consistent information

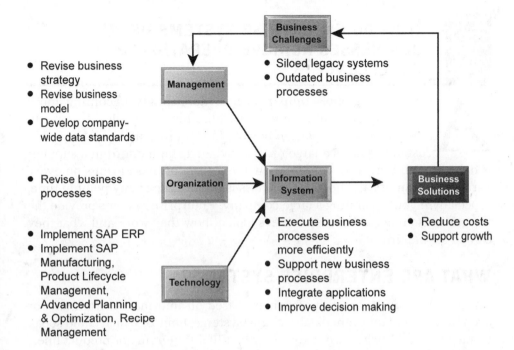

- Revise business strategy
- Revise business model
- Develop company-wide data standards

- Revise business processes

- Implement SAP ERP
- Implement SAP Manufacturing, Product Lifecycle Management, Advanced Planning & Optimization, Recipe Management

Management

Organization

Technology

Business Challenges
- Siloed legacy systems
- Outdated business processes

Information System
- Execute business processes more efficiently
- Support new business processes
- Integrate applications
- Improve decision making

Business Solutions
- Reduce costs
- Support growth

throughout the company. Enterprise resource planning (ERP) systems as well as those for supply chain management and customer relationship management can dramatically improve operational effectiveness and decision making.

The chapter-opening case calls attention to important points raised by this case and this chapter. ACH's business performance was impeded because it was saddled with a set of outdated systems designed primarily for its old business model as a commercial food-ingredients business. These systems supported outdated business processes that made it difficult for different parts of the company to work together and respond to new market opportunities. Trying to work around these systems raised costs and still left the company operating too inefficiently to pursue its new business goals.

By implementing SAP's ERP system along with related SAP applications, the company was able to implement more efficient business processes for its new business model, including forecasting, planning, profitability analysis, and new-product development. And it could support its strategic growth plan based on new acquisitions.

ACH's new systems made it possible to execute its business processes more efficiently and effectively, and also made possible new processes such as customer and product profitability analysis. However, in order to obtain these benefits from the enterprise software, ACH had to change some of its outdated business processes as well as its old legacy systems. This business process change was reflected in the company's ability to back away from customizing the enterprise software, which had been undertaken to support a business model that the company was discarding.

Here are some questions to think about: What problems did ACH Food Companies solve by implementing an ERP system? How did the new system change the way ACH ran its business?

9.1 HOW DO ENTERPRISE SYSTEMS HELP BUSINESSES ACHIEVE OPERATIONAL EXCELLENCE?

Around the globe, companies are increasingly becoming more connected, both internally and with other companies. If you run a business, you'll want to be able to react instantaneously when a customer places a large order or when a shipment from a supplier is delayed. You may also want to know the impact of these events on every part of the business and how the business is performing at any point in time, especially if you're running a large company. Enterprise systems provide the integration to make this possible. Let's look at how they work and what they can do for the firm.

WHAT ARE ENTERPRISE SYSTEMS?

Imagine that you had to run a business based on information from tens or even hundreds of different databases and systems, none of which could speak to one another? Imagine your company had 10 different major product lines, each produced in separate factories, and each with separate and incompatible sets of systems controlling production, warehousing, and distribution.

At the very least, your decision making would often be based on manual hard-copy reports, often out of date, and it would be difficult to really understand what is happening in the business as a whole. Sales personnel might not be able to tell at the time they place an order whether the ordered items are in inventory, and manufacturing could not easily use sales data to plan for new production. You now have a good idea of why firms need a special enterprise system to integrate information.

Chapter 2 introduced enterprise systems, also known as enterprise resource planning (ERP) systems, which are based on a suite of integrated software modules and a common central database. The database collects data from many different divisions and departments in a firm, and from a large number of key business processes in manufacturing and production, finance and accounting, sales and marketing, and human resources, making the data available for applications that support nearly all of an organization's internal business activities. When new information is entered by one process, the information is made immediately available to other business processes (see Figure 9.1).

If a sales representative places an order for tire rims, for example, the system verifies the customer's credit limit, schedules the shipment, identifies the best shipping route, and reserves the necessary items from inventory. If inventory stock is insufficient to fill the order, the system schedules the manufacture of more rims, ordering the needed materials and components from suppliers. Sales and production forecasts are immediately updated. General ledger and corporate cash levels are automatically updated with the revenue and cost information from the order. Users could tap into the system and find out where that particular order was at any minute. Management could obtain information at any point in time about how the business was operating. The

FIGURE 9.1   HOW ENTERPRISE SYSTEMS WORK

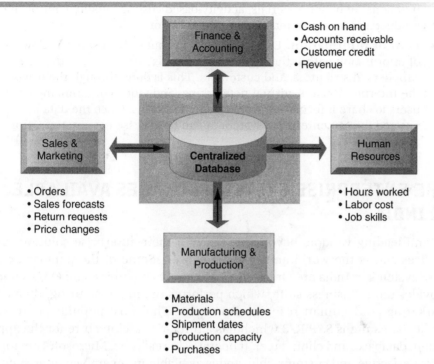

Enterprise systems feature a set of integrated software modules and a central database that enables data to be shared by many different business processes and functional areas throughout the enterprise.

system could also generate enterprise-wide data for management analyses of product cost and profitability.

CHARACTERISTICS OF AN ENTERPRISE SYSTEM

An enterprise system is characterized based on the functions it performs. Some of the properties of an enterprise system are:

- **Real-time operations:** One of the most important characteristic of enterprise systems is their ability to operate in real time. Imagine that an order has been placed by a customer through a front-end application. This order must immediately be processed by the application, an entry must be made in the database, the inventory must be deducted by the value and quantity of the order, information must be sent to the production and marketing departments, and invoice must be generated for the customer. A good enterprise system can perform all these activities seamlessly.

- **Integration of all business activities:** Enterprise systems also help plan and control the resources of the firm to achieve efficiency and profitability. This requires strategic integration of all the business functions of the firm. Business processes need to be automated and integrated so that business targets can be achieved in a timely manner. Enterprise systems provide this feature by integrating the functional areas of an organization such as accounting and finance functions (of capital budgeting, capital structure, and cash flow management) with the human resource functions (of payroll, training, and benefits), the manufacturing functions (of bill of materials, activity-based costing, quality control, and product and life-cycle management), and so on.

- **Flow of information:** Enterprise systems not only ensure the flow of information within the organization but also beyond it, to the firm's suppliers, distributors, and customers. This is done through the use of the Internet. E-mails, virtual networking, and video conferencing enable users to share information from remote locations. Once the data is entered into an enterprise system, it can be accessed at any time, from anywhere.

THE ENTERPRISE SYSTEM PACKAGES AVAILABLE IN INDIA

Several leading vendors have come up with their enterprise solutions and services across the world and in India as well. Some of the popular enterprise systems in India are Oracle, SAP, Microsoft Dynamics, and QAD. Oracle provides the E-Business suite, which performs the manufacturing, financial, marketing, and human resource functions. The most popular enterprise application suite is SAP R/3 which has a three-tier architecture for the application, database, and client layer. It operates in real time. Microsoft Dynamics is cost-effective and customizable, and is available in several versions such as Navision (NAV), Axapta (AX), Great Plains (GP), and Soloman (SL).

ENTERPRISE SOFTWARE

Enterprise software is built around thousands of predefined business processes that reflect best practices. Table 9.1 describes some of the major business processes supported by enterprise software.

Companies implementing this software would have to first select the functions of the system they wished to use and then map their business processes to the predefined business processes in the software. (One of our

TABLE 9.1 BUSINESS PROCESSES SUPPORTED BY ENTERPRISE SYSTEMS

Financial and accounting processes, including general ledger, accounts payable, accounts receivable, fixed assets, cash management and forecasting, product-cost accounting, cost-center accounting, asset accounting, tax accounting, credit management, and financial reporting

Human resources processes, including personnel administration, time accounting, payroll, personnel planning and development, benefits accounting, applicant tracking, time management, compensation, workforce planning, performance management, and travel expense reporting.

Manufacturing and production processes, including procurement, inventory management, purchasing, shipping, production planning, production scheduling, material requirements planning, quality control, distribution, transportation execution, and plant and equipment maintenance.

Sales and marketing processes, including order processing, quotations, contracts, product configuration, pricing, billing, credit checking, incentive and commission management, and sales planning.

Learning Tracks shows how SAP enterprise software handles the procurement process for a new piece of equipment.) A firm would use configuration tables provided by the software manufacturer to tailor a particular aspect of the system to the way it does business. For example, the firm could use these tables to select whether it wants to track revenue by product line, geographical unit, or distribution channel.

If the enterprise software does not support the way the organization does business, companies can rewrite some of the software to support the way their business processes work. However, enterprise software is unusually complex, and extensive customization may degrade system performance, compromising the information and process integration that are the main benefits of the system. If companies want to reap the maximum benefits from enterprise software, they must change the way they work to conform to the business processes defined by the software.

To implement a new enterprise system, Tasty Baking Company identified its existing business processes and then translated them into the business processes built into the SAP ERP software it had selected. To ensure it obtained the maximum benefits from the enterprise software, Tasty Baking Company deliberately planned for customizing less than 5 percent of the system and made very few changes to the SAP software itself. It used as many tools and features that were already built into the SAP software as it could. SAP has more than 3,000 configuration tables for its enterprise software.

Leading enterprise software vendors include SAP, Oracle, IBM, Infor Global Solutions, and Microsoft. There are versions of enterprise software packages designed for small and medium-sized businesses and on-demand versions, including software services running in the cloud (see Section 9.4).

BUSINESS VALUE OF ENTERPRISE SYSTEMS

Enterprise systems provide value both by increasing operational efficiency and by providing firmwide information to help managers make better decisions. Large companies with many operating units in different locations have used enterprise systems to enforce standard practices and data so that everyone does business the same way worldwide.

Coca-Cola, for instance, implemented a SAP enterprise system to standardize and coordinate important business processes in 200 countries. Lack of standard, company-wide business processes prevented the company from leveraging its worldwide buying power to obtain lower prices for raw materials and from reacting rapidly to market changes.

Enterprise systems help firms respond rapidly to customer requests for information or products. Because the system integrates order, manufacturing, and delivery data, manufacturing is better informed about producing only what customers have ordered, procuring exactly the right amount of components or raw materials to fill actual orders, staging production, and minimizing the time that components or finished products are in inventory.

Alcoa, the world's leading producer of aluminum and aluminum products with operations spanning 31 countries and over 200 locations, had initially been organized around lines of business, each of which had its own set of information systems. Many of these systems were redundant and inefficient. Alcoa's costs for executing requisition-to-pay and financial processes were much higher and its cycle times were longer than those of other companies in its industry. (Cycle time refers to the total elapsed time from the beginning to the end of a process.) The company could not operate as a single worldwide entity.

After implementing enterprise software from Oracle, Alcoa eliminated many redundant processes and systems. The enterprise system helped Alcoa reduce requisition-to-pay cycle time by verifying receipt of goods and automatically generating receipts for payment. Alcoa's accounts payable transaction processing dropped 89 percent. Alcoa was able to centralize financial and procurement activities, which helped the company reduce nearly 20 percent of its worldwide costs.

Enterprise systems provide much valuable information for improving management decision making. Corporate headquarters has access to up-to-the-minute data on sales, inventory, and production, and uses this information to create more accurate sales and production forecasts. Enterprise software includes analytical tools for using data captured by the system to evaluate overall organizational performance. Enterprise system data have common standardized definitions and formats that are accepted by the entire organization. Performance figures mean the same thing across the company. Enterprise systems allow senior management to easily find out at any moment how a particular organizational unit is performing, determine which products are most or least profitable, and calculate costs for the company as a whole.

For example, Alcoa's enterprise system includes functionality for global human resources management that shows correlations between investment in employee training and quality, measures the company-wide costs of delivering services to employees, and measures the effectiveness of employee recruitment, compensation, and training.

9.2 HOW DO SUPPLY CHAIN MANAGEMENT SYSTEMS COORDINATE PLANNING, PRODUCTION, AND LOGISTICS WITH SUPPLIERS?

If you manage a small firm that makes a few products or sells a few services, chances are you will have a small number of suppliers. You could coordinate your supplier orders and deliveries using a telephone and fax machine. But if you manage a firm that produces more complex products and services, then you will have hundreds of suppliers, and each of your suppliers will have its own set of suppliers. Suddenly, you are in a situation where you will need to coordinate the activities of hundreds or even thousands of other firms in order to produce your products and services. Supply chain management (SCM) systems, which we introduced in Chapter 2, are an answer to the problems of supply chain complexity and scale.

INTERACTIVE SESSION: TECHNOLOGY

OPTIMIZING OPERATIONS AT QUARKCITY: A MOVE AWAY FROM LEGACY SYSTEMS

QuarkCity India Private Limited was incorporated in October 2003 to design, study, develop, own, operate, buy, sell, or lease infrastructure projects and facilities. QuarkCity works on land acquisition, project development, and construction and management services. It recently shifted from legacy information systems to the more advanced enterprise resource planning (ERP) system. The older system involved working with Tally for accounting, Quark Commerce Software (QCMS) for purchasing, and MRP-II for material requirement planning.

The main problem with these systems was that data could not be integrated across departments in a consistent manner. For example, Tally worked independently, performing tasks related to financial transactions alone. Due to a lack of integration with any other software, flow of information was restricted. Other departments needed to manually request for information.

QCMS was a customized software only for material procurement. It could not handle service or job-order requirements, nor could it allow for the generation and approval of purchase orders. It could not record or report on returns and rejections from suppliers. Moreover, only a single unit of measurement (that is, pieces) could be used for each material. The system was not designed for multilevel approvals of purchase orders. Local taxation policies such as the excise duty or sales tax clauses were not incorporated in the purchase order formats. The purchase order, once approved, could not be amended if the need arose. There was no facility for tracking budgets against actual revenue items or capital items. Rates as well as quantities needed to be entered in absolute numbers and not in decimals.

The material requirement planning (MRP) system also had its limitations. For example, the activity codification system had no provision for checking activity codes and consumption of items. The inventory management system did not reflect the sub-stores, while the scrap management system did not codify entities properly.

In face of all these challenges posed by legacy systems, QuarkCity implemented the Oracle ERP functional suite. This helped the company avoid all issues related to data redundancy and inconsistency. Since the ERP data was centralized, updates made to any of the entries were immediately available to all the departments. Flow of information within the organization improved. For example, the purchase order requested by one department could be automatically sent to the concerned persons for approval. The inventory department could check against the same purchase order while inspecting and receiving the delivered material. The receipt of the items purchased could then be used as a basis for invoice generation and to record the transaction in the general ledger by the finance team. Moreover, the ERP could define each activity in various projects with its exact start and completion dates. This ensured that projects were completed on time, resulting in improved decision-making capabilities, productivity, and efficiency at the firm.

All the processes at QuarkCity are now managed by the ERP system, right from the procurement of materials, to their costs and consumption. Since the cost structure of each material is accurately known, it helps QuarkCity optimally utilize its resources to earn maximum profits. Besides, the ERP system tracks and controls all procurement activities, schedules production processes, and finally generates information that helps QuarkCity manage its inventory better. The ERP processes the information very quickly, which enables timely reporting of the numbers. Though the industry's standard percentage of cement and steel wastage is approximately 5%, the implementation of this system has reduced the wastage below this level. The firm's project and material management capabilities have also seen a marked improvement.

The inventory that sits in one's own warehouse just adds to the costs of the firm. Inventory levels can be reduced effectively by managing the lead time required for ordering the material. The ERP system at QuarkCity makes it possible to forecast demand of the material and help the firm in its timely purchase. Using the min/max formula for order planning, the ERP system alerts the managers when the quantity of material reaches its minimum level. With the real-estate business growing by leaps and bounds, there is need for quality work in this sector. QuarkCity has been able to successfully navigate its difficulties with legacy systems to implement a modern management information system that has ultimately allowed it to improve the quality of its business.

Sources: Appelton, E. L., "How to Survive ERP", *Datamation*, Vol. 43, No. 3, pp. 50–53 (1997); Bancroft N., *Implementing SAP R/3*, Manning Publications (1996); N. Bancroft , H. Seip and A. Sprengel, *Implementing SAP R/*, Manning Publications (1998); Bowman I., "ERP 'Coned Off' Expect Delays", *Manufacturing-Computer-Solutions*, Vol. 3, No. 1, pp. 32–33 (1997); Caldwell B., "GTE Goes Solo on SAP R/3", *Informationweek*, No. 685, p. 150 (1998); B. Hecht, "Choose the Right ERP Software", *Datamation*, Vol. 43, No. 3, pp. 50–53 (1997); Holland , Light and Gibson, "A Critical Success Factors Model for Enterprise Resource Planning Implementation", *Proceedings of the 7th European Conference on Information Systems*, pp. 273–287 (1999); McKie S., "Packaged apps for the masses", *DBMS*, Vol. 10, No. 11, pp. 64–6 and 68 (1997); Piszczalski M., "Lessons learned from Europe's SAP users", *Production*, Vol. 109, No. 1, pp. 54–56 (1997); Ross J.W., *The ERP Revolution: Surviving Versus Thriving* (1998).

CASE STUDY QUESTIONS

1. Discuss the problems associated with the three legacy systems that were earlier in use at QuarkCity.

2. Discuss how these problems were solved by the implementation of the ERP software.

3. Visit www.sap.com and study the various applications of the SAP tool for managing business organizations.

THE SUPPLY CHAIN

A firm's **supply chain** is a network of organizations and business processes for procuring raw materials, transforming these materials into intermediate and finished products, and distributing the finished products to customers. It links suppliers, manufacturing plants, distribution centers, retail outlets, and customers to supply goods and services from source through consumption. Materials, information, and payments flow through the supply chain in both directions.

Goods start out as raw materials and, as they move through the supply chain, are transformed into intermediate products (also referred to as components or parts), and finally, into finished products. The finished products are shipped to distribution centers and from there to retailers and customers. Returned items flow in the reverse direction from the buyer back to the seller.

Let's look at the supply chain for Nike sneakers as an example. Nike designs, markets, and sells sneakers, socks, athletic clothing, and accessories throughout the world. Its primary suppliers are contract manufacturers with factories in China, Thailand, Indonesia, Brazil, and other countries. These companies fashion Nike's finished products.

Nike's contract suppliers do not manufacture sneakers from scratch. They obtain components for the sneakers—the laces, eyelets, uppers, and soles—from other suppliers and then assemble them into finished sneakers. These

FIGURE 9.2   NIKE'S SUPPLY CHAIN

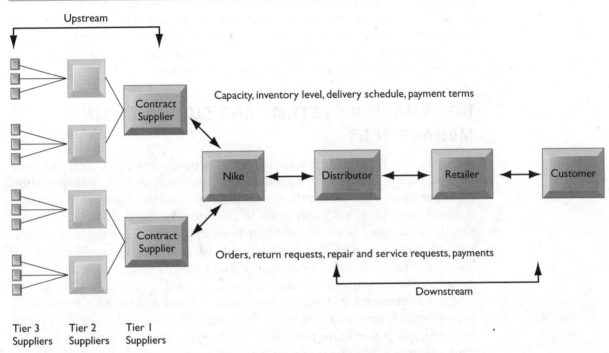

This figure illustrates the major entities in Nike's supply chain and the flow of information upstream and downstream to coordinate the activities involved in buying, making, and moving a product. Shown here is a simplified supply chain, with the upstream portion focusing only on the suppliers for sneakers and sneaker soles.

suppliers in turn have their own suppliers. For example, the suppliers of soles have suppliers for synthetic rubber, suppliers for chemicals used to melt the rubber for molding, and suppliers for the molds into which to pour the rubber. Suppliers of laces have suppliers for their thread, for dyes, and for the plastic lace tips.

Figure 9.2 provides a simplified illustration of Nike's supply chain for sneakers; it shows the flow of information and materials among suppliers, Nike, Nike's distributors, retailers, and customers. Nike's contract manufacturers are its primary suppliers. The suppliers of soles, eyelets, uppers, and laces are the secondary (Tier 2) suppliers. Suppliers to these suppliers are the tertiary (Tier 3) suppliers.

The *upstream* portion of the supply chain includes the company's suppliers, the suppliers' suppliers, and the processes for managing relationships with them. The *downstream* portion consists of the organizations and processes for distributing and delivering products to the final customers. Companies doing manufacturing, such as Nike's contract suppliers of sneakers, also manage their own *internal supply chain processes* for transforming materials, components, and services furnished by their suppliers into finished products or intermediate products (components or parts) for their customers and for managing materials and inventory.

The supply chain illustrated in Figure 9.2 has been simplified. It only shows two contract manufacturers for sneakers and only the upstream supply chain for sneaker soles. Nike has hundreds of contract manufacturers turning out finished sneakers, socks, and athletic clothing, each with its own set of suppliers. The upstream portion of Nike's supply chain would actually comprise thousands of entities. Nike also has numerous distributors and many thousands of retail stores where its shoes are sold, so the downstream portion of its supply chain is also large and complex.

INFORMATION SYSTEMS AND SUPPLY CHAIN MANAGEMENT

Inefficiencies in the supply chain, such as parts shortages, underutilized plant capacity, excessive finished goods inventory, or high transportation costs, are caused by inaccurate or untimely information. For example, manufacturers may keep too many parts in inventory because they do not know exactly when they will receive their next shipments from their suppliers. Suppliers may order too few raw materials because they do not have precise information on demand. These supply chain inefficiencies waste as much as 25 percent of a company's operating costs.

If a manufacturer had perfect information about exactly how many units of product customers wanted, when they wanted them, and when they could be produced, it would be possible to implement a highly efficient **just-in-time strategy**. Components would arrive exactly at the moment they were needed and finished goods would be shipped as they left the assembly line.

In a supply chain, however, uncertainties arise because many events cannot be foreseen—uncertain product demand, late shipments from suppliers, defective parts or raw materials, or production process breakdowns. To satisfy customers, manufacturers often deal with such uncertainties and unforeseen events by keeping more material or products in inventory than what they think they may actually need. The *safety stock* acts as a buffer for the lack of flexibility in the supply chain. Although excess inventory is expensive, low fill rates are also costly because business may be lost from canceled orders.

One recurring problem in supply chain management is the **bullwhip effect**, in which information about the demand for a product gets distorted as it passes from one entity to the next across the supply chain. A slight rise in demand for an item might cause different members in the supply chain—distributors, manufacturers, suppliers, secondary suppliers (suppliers' suppliers), and tertiary suppliers (suppliers' suppliers' suppliers)—to stockpile inventory so each has enough "just in case." These changes ripple throughout the supply chain, magnifying what started out as a small change from planned orders, creating excess inventory, production, warehousing, and shipping costs (see Figure 9.3).

For example, Procter & Gamble (P&G) found it had excessively high inventories of its Pampers disposable diapers at various points along its supply chain because of such distorted information. Although customer purchases in stores were fairly stable, orders from distributors would spike when P&G offered aggressive price promotions. Pampers and Pampers' components accumulated in warehouses along the supply chain to meet demand that

FIGURE 9.3   THE BULLWHIP EFFECT

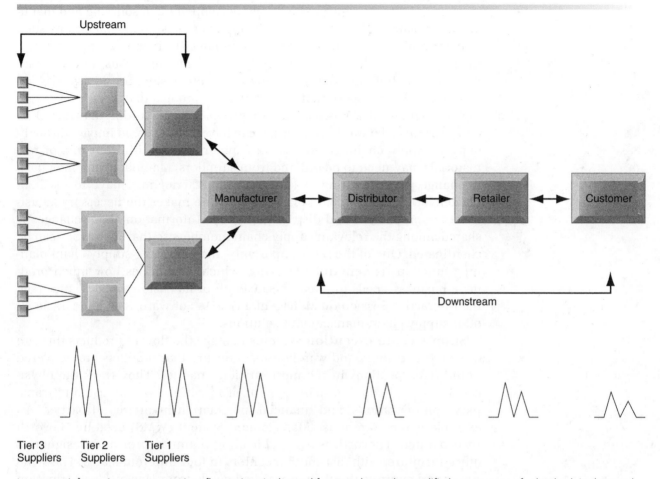

Inaccurate information can cause minor fluctuations in demand for a product to be amplified as one moves further back in the supply chain. Minor fluctuations in retail sales for a product can create excess inventory for distributors, manufacturers, and suppliers.

did not actually exist. To eliminate this problem, P&G revised its marketing, sales, and supply chain processes and used more accurate demand forecasting.

The bullwhip effect is tamed by reducing uncertainties about demand and supply when all members of the supply chain have accurate and up-to-date information. If all supply chain members share dynamic information about inventory levels, schedules, forecasts, and shipments, they have more precise knowledge about how to adjust their sourcing, manufacturing, and distribution plans. Supply chain management systems provide the kind of information that helps members of the supply chain make better purchasing and scheduling decisions.

SUPPLY CHAIN MANAGEMENT SOFTWARE

Supply chain software is classified as either software to help businesses plan their supply chains (supply chain planning) or software to help them execute the supply chain steps (supply chain execution). **Supply chain**

planning systems enable the firm to model its existing supply chain, generate demand forecasts for products, and develop optimal sourcing and manufacturing plans. Such systems help companies make better decisions such as determining how much of a specific product to manufacture in a given time period; establishing inventory levels for raw materials, intermediate products, and finished goods; determining where to store finished goods; and identifying the transportation mode to use for product delivery.

For example, if a large customer places a larger order than usual or changes that order on short notice, it can have a widespread impact throughout the supply chain. Additional raw materials or a different mix of raw materials may need to be ordered from suppliers. Manufacturing may have to change job scheduling. A transportation carrier may have to reschedule deliveries. Supply chain planning software makes the necessary adjustments to production and distribution plans. Information about changes is shared among the relevant supply chain members so that their work can be coordinated. One of the most important—and complex—supply chain planning functions is **demand planning**, which determines how much product a business needs to make to satisfy all of its customers' demands (see the Interactive Session on Management), JDA Software, SAP, and Oracle all offer supply chain management solutions.

Supply chain execution systems manage the flow of products through distribution centers and warehouses to ensure that products are delivered to the right locations in the most efficient manner. They track the physical status of goods, the management of materials, warehouse and transportation operations, and financial information involving all parties. An example is the Warehouse Management System (WMS) used by Haworth Incorporated. Haworth is a world-leading manufacturer and designer of office furniture, with distribution centers in four different states. The WMS tracks and controls the flow of finished goods from Haworth's distribution centers to its customers. Acting on shipping plans for customer orders, the WMS directs the movement of goods based on immediate conditions for space, equipment, inventory, and personnel.

GLOBAL SUPPLY CHAINS AND THE INTERNET

Before the Internet, supply chain coordination was hampered by the difficulties of making information flow smoothly among disparate internal supply chain systems for purchasing, materials management, manufacturing, and distribution. It was also difficult to share information with external supply chain partners because the systems of suppliers, distributors, or logistics providers were based on incompatible technology platforms and standards. Enterprise and supply chain management systems enhanced with Internet technology supply some of this integration.

A manager uses a Web interface to tap into suppliers' systems to determine whether inventory and production capabilities match demand for the firm's products. Business partners use Web-based supply chain management tools to collaborate online on forecasts. Sales representatives access suppliers' production schedules and logistics information to monitor customers' order status.

INTERACTIVE SESSION: MANAGEMENT

SCOTTS MIRACLE-GRO CULTIVATES SUPPLY CHAIN PROFICIENCY

When you have to make nearly all of your annual sales of 10 billion pounds of lawn fertilizer and other gardening products in a 10- to 14- week seasonal window, you realize the importance of an optimized supply chain. As the world's principal supplier of lawn and garden care products, the Scotts Miracle-Gro Company, headquartered in Marysville, Ohio, needed to optimize its entire supply chain—from shelf to supplier—in order to meet the needs of its seasonal, weather-dependent business.

When lawn care company, Scotts, and top gardening brand, Miracle-Gro, merged in 1995, a number of challenges arose. Customer lists overlapped, causing duplication of sales force efforts. Multiple supply chain designs conflicted, incompatible invoicing systems clashed, and multiple IT systems could not be coordinated to resolve the discord. The result was that despite holding the leading gardening and lawn care brands in the United States (Roundup and Ortho) in addition to the two that comprise its masthead, the Scotts Miracle-Gro Company suffered declining productivity and deteriorating customer service.

With execution during its peak-demand season suffering, the company embarked on an initiative dubbed "One Face to the Customer," that included $100 million to upgrade its IT systems. It adopted SAP's enterprise resource planning (ERP) system buttressed with supply chain and replenishment planning tools from JDA Software. The company wanted to leverage its point-of-sale (POS) data so that customer purchases would automatically trigger orders to replenish stock. The new software included tools for better demand planning, fulfillment, space and category management, production planning, collaboration, and transportation and logistics management.

These improvements, instituted between 2000 and 2005, resulted in an increase in the fill rate (the percentage of orders satisfied from stock at hand) from 92 to 99 percent, significantly decreasing the impact of stockouts on consumers. Inventory turns doubled, and average annual supply chain savings between 2 percent and 3 percent were realized.

Two key factors enabled Scotts Miracle-Gro to better respond to rapid changes in market conditions: the ability to create POS forecasts and an increased adeptness at responding to weather events.

POS forecasts at the store level are the basis for Scott's demand planning, which then incorporates promotions, media and advertising campaigns, and stockout planning. These plans are further honed by integrating safety-stock settings, on-hand quantities, and on-order quantities for each store. Scotts Miracle-Gro's supply chain is segmented by warehouse. The individualized store replenishment plans are aggregated for each warehouse so that enough product is produced to properly stock them.

Weather-related impacts are translated into plans of action for each zip code on a day-by-day and weekly basis. JDA Demand is integrated with business weather intelligence pioneer Planalytics' database of regional and seasonal weather patterns and analytical program. The improved ability to anticipate weather patterns and make sound inventory decisions also ensures that promotions are properly timed to maximize revenue increases for the company's retail partners and market share for the company.

In addition to supply chain segmentation by warehouse, Scotts Miracle-Gro also segments by product. Multiple product-centered supply chains are customized to meet the needs of its retail accounts. Scotts has over 40 production facilities as well as a number of contract manufacturers, 18 of its own distribution centers, and over 10 more third-party distribution centers. Depending on the product and the volume driving it, shipments can go to one of the distribution centers or directly to retailers. Maximizing supply chain efficiency has enhanced customer service and reduced costs, a particularly important consideration for its top three customers—Walmart, Home Depot, and Lowe's. Approximately two-thirds of Scotts Miracle-Gro's annual revenues come from these companies. Regional distribution networks complement direct shipments to these crucial customers.

For grain media and wild bird food, 26 production facilities in the United States have been strategically located close to Scotts Miracle-Gro's highest-volume purchasers. If necessary, products from the main distribution network can be shipped to one of these production points for joint delivery. For example, a shipment of a grain product can be combined with a fertilizer delivery. An assortment of supply chain possibilities is essential to the company's business model due to the abbreviated time-frame in which most shipments occur.

With the new system in place, Scotts Miracle-Gro concentrated on strengthening its collaborative practices. Supply chain managers, sales teams, and customers needed to be working together so that the 100-day peak season could be optimally supplied. A business development team in the corporate office works with business development teams for each of the big three customers as well as with a channel accounts team. Pre-season inventory planning includes previous year POS data analysis and forecasting, setting inventory targets, and creating promotional lists. Forecasts are generated both internally and externally, with consensus meetings resolving any inconsistencies. Inventory buildups and reductions are likewise determined collaboratively with calendars constructed for each customer and consensus established for system settings such as buffer stocks and minimum order quantities.

In many cases, replenishment orders are prearranged, and Scotts Miracle-Gro also reports and tracks inventory, POS data, and forecasts for its customers, particularly during the peak season. By taking charge of customer data, Scotts has improved its insight into customer needs and gained greater flexibility in meeting those needs. A channel account and JDA Marketplace Replenishment are used to place orders directly within customers' systems, even the big three. At all times, the goal is to ensure that POS and inventory targets are aligned. If Scott's JDA or POS

forecasts differ from what the customer believes is going to happen, the demand signals are reevaluated and a consensus reached. This mindset guides internal discussions as well, for example, between the sales team and the financial forecasters, so that sufficient inventory maximizes sales and excess inventory does not clog shelves when the season ends.

JDA Software solutions, including JDA Demand, JDA Fulfillment, JDA Inventory Policy Optimization, and JDA Marketplace Replenish, have enabled Scotts Miracle-Gro to develop consumer-driven demand planning that reduces new item introduction uncertainty and overcomes unrealistic forecasts by retailers. Continued attentiveness to its supply chain served both the company and its customers well during the Great Recession of 2009 and its aftermath. Retail challenges during tough economic times have been mitigated by Scotts Miracle-Gro's ability to keep costs down and improve margins. By incorporating weather-driven demand into its demand planning, strategically segmenting its supply chain, and focusing on customer collaboration programs, the company has been able to capitalize on shelf-level demand signals to improve manufacturing and distribution plans. It is now concentrating on developing commodity management tools to reduce the risk involved in its many products affected by fluctuations in commodity prices. Continuing to squeeze operating costs out of its products and distribution network will also support Scotts Miracle-Gro's exploration of emerging markets in China and Mexico, where it has already prepared the ground for a highly efficient supply chain.

Sources: Chris Petersen, "Scotts Miracle-Gro," SupplyChain World, accessed May 25, 2014; "Cultivating Shelf-Connected Success," JDA Software Case Study, 2013; "Scotts Miracle-Gro: Keeping up with peak demand," SupplyChain 24/7, April 1, 2013.

CASE STUDY QUESTIONS

1. Identify the supply chain management problems faced by Scotts Miracle-Gro. What was the business impact of not being able to manage the company's supply chain well?

2. What management, organization, and technology factors contributed to Scotts Miracle-Gro's supply chain problems?

3. How did implementing JDA Software solutions change the way Scotts Miracle-Gro ran its business?

4. How did the new supply chain systems improve management decision making? Describe two decisions that were improved by the new system solution.

Global Supply Chain Issues

More and more companies are entering international markets, outsourcing manufacturing operations, and obtaining supplies from other countries as well as selling abroad. Their supply chains extend across multiple countries and regions. There are additional complexities and challenges to managing a global supply chain.

Global supply chains typically span greater geographic distances and time differences than domestic supply chains, and have participants from a number of different countries. Performance standards may vary from region to region or from nation to nation. Supply chain management may need to reflect foreign government regulations and cultural differences.

The Internet helps companies manage many aspects of their global supply chains, including sourcing, transportation, communications, and international finance. Today's apparel industry, for example, relies heavily on outsourcing to contract manufacturers in China and other low-wage countries. Apparel companies are starting to use the Web to manage their global supply chain and production issues. (Review the discussion of Li & Fung in Chapter 3.)

In addition to contract manufacturing, globalization has encouraged outsourcing warehouse management, transportation management, and related operations to third-party logistics providers, such as UPS Supply Chain Solutions and Schneider Logistics Services. These logistics services offer Web-based software to give their customers a better view of their global supply chains. Customers are able to check a secure Web site to monitor inventory and shipments, helping them run their global supply chains more efficiently.

Demand-Driven Supply Chains: From Push to Pull Manufacturing and Efficient Customer Response

In addition to reducing costs, supply chain management systems facilitate efficient customer response, enabling the workings of the business to be driven more by customer demand. (We introduced efficient customer response systems in Chapter 3.)

Earlier supply chain management systems were driven by a push-based model (also known as build-to-stock). In a **push-based model**, production master schedules are based on forecasts or best guesses of demand for products, and products are "pushed" to customers. With new flows of information made possible by Web-based tools, supply chain management more easily follows a pull-based model. In a **pull-based model**, also known as a demand-driven or build-to-order model, actual customer orders or purchases trigger events in the supply chain. Transactions to produce and deliver only what customers have ordered move up the supply chain from retailers to distributors to manufacturers and eventually to suppliers. Only products to fulfill these orders move back down the supply chain to the retailer. Manufacturers use only actual order demand information to drive their production schedules and the procurement of components or raw materials, as illustrated in Figure 9.4. Walmart's continuous replenishment system described in Chapter 3 is an example of the pull-based model.

The Internet and Internet technology make it possible to move from sequential supply chains, where information and materials flow sequentially from

FIGURE 9.4 PUSH- VERSUS PULL-BASED SUPPLY CHAIN MODELS

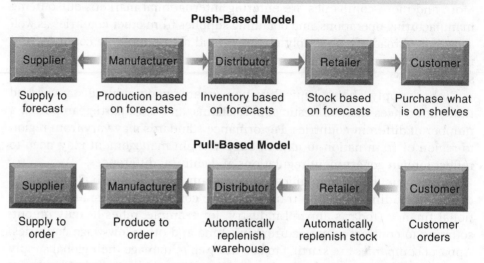

The difference between push- and pull-based models is summarized by the slogan "Make what we sell, not sell what we make."

company to company, to concurrent supply chains, where information flows in many directions simultaneously among members of a supply chain network. Complex supply networks of manufacturers, logistics suppliers, outsourced manufacturers, retailers, and distributors are able to adjust immediately to changes in schedules or orders. Ultimately, the Internet could create a "digital logistics nervous system" throughout the supply chain (see Figure 9.5).

FIGURE 9.5 THE EMERGING INTERNET-DRIVEN SUPPLY CHAIN

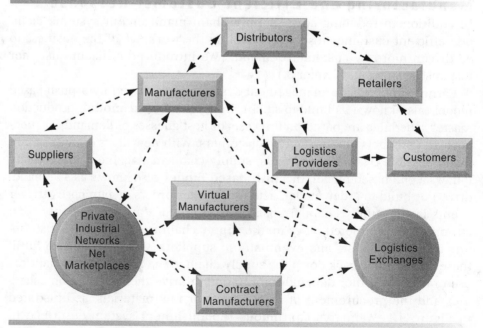

The emerging Internet-driven supply chain operates like a digital logistics nervous system. It provides multidirectional communication among firms, networks of firms, and e-marketplaces so that entire networks of supply chain partners can immediately adjust inventories, orders, and capacities.

BUSINESS VALUE OF SUPPLY CHAIN MANAGEMENT SYSTEMS

You have just seen how supply chain management systems enable firms to streamline both their internal and external supply chain processes and provide management with more accurate information about what to produce, store, and move. By implementing a networked and integrated supply chain management system, companies match supply to demand, reduce inventory levels, improve delivery service, speed product time to market, and use assets more effectively.

Total supply chain costs represent the majority of operating expenses for many businesses and in some industries approach 75 percent of the total operating budget. Reducing supply chain costs has a major impact on firm profitability.

In addition to reducing costs, supply chain management systems help increase sales. If a product is not available when a customer wants it, customers often try to purchase it from someone else. More precise control of the supply chain enhances the firm's ability to have the right product available for customer purchases at the right time.

9.3 How do CUSTOMER RELATIONSHIP MANAGEMENT SYSTEMS HELP FIRMS ACHIEVE CUSTOMER INTIMACY?

You've probably heard phrases such as "the customer is always right" or "the customer comes first." Today these words ring truer than ever. Because competitive advantage based on an innovative new product or service is often very short lived, companies are realizing that their most enduring competitive strength may be their relationships with their customers. Some say that the basis of competition has switched from who sells the most products and services to who "owns" the customer, and that customer relationships represent a firm's most valuable asset.

WHAT IS CUSTOMER RELATIONSHIP MANAGEMENT?

What kinds of information would you need to build and nurture strong, long-lasting relationships with customers? You'd want to know exactly who your customers are, how to contact them, whether they are costly to service and sell to, what kinds of products and services they are interested in, and how much money they spend on your company. If you could, you'd want to make sure you knew each of your customers well, as if you were running a small-town store. And you'd want to make your good customers feel special.

In a small business operating in a neighborhood, it is possible for business owners and managers to really know their customers on a personal, face-to-face basis. But in a large business operating on a metropolitan, regional, national, or even global basis, it is impossible to "know your customer" in this intimate way. In these kinds of businesses there are too many customers and too many different ways that customers interact with the firm (over the Web, the phone, e-mail, blogs, and in person). It becomes especially difficult to integrate information from all theses sources and to deal with the large numbers of customers.

A large business's processes for sales, service, and marketing tend to be highly compartmentalized, and these departments do not share much essential customer information. Some information on a specific customer might be stored and organized in terms of that person's account with the company. Other pieces of information about the same customer might be organized by products that were purchased. There is no way to consolidate all of this information to provide a unified view of a customer across the company.

This is where customer relationship management systems help. Customer relationship management (CRM) systems, which we introduced in Chapter 2, capture and integrate customer data from all over the organization, consolidate the data, analyze the data, and then distribute the results to various systems and customer touch points across the enterprise. A **touch point** (also known as a contact point) is a method of interaction with the customer, such as telephone, e-mail, customer service desk, conventional mail, Facebook, Twitter, Web site, wireless device, or retail store. Well-designed CRM systems provide a single enterprise view of customers that is useful for improving both sales and customer service (see Figure 9.6.)

FIGURE 9.6   CUSTOMER RELATIONSHIP MANAGEMENT (CRM)

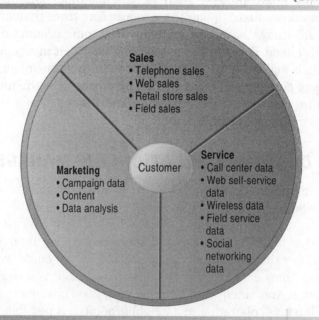

CRM systems examine customers from a multifaceted perspective. These systems use a set of integrated applications to address all aspects of the customer relationship, including customer service, sales, and marketing.

Good CRM systems provide data and analytical tools for answering questions such as these: What is the value of a particular customer to the firm over his or her lifetime? Who are our most loyal customers? It can cost six times more to sell to a new customer than to an existing customer. Who are our most profitable customers? What do these profitable customers want to buy? Firms use the answers to these questions to acquire new customers, provide better service and support to existing customers, customize their offerings more precisely to customer preferences, and provide ongoing value to retain profitable customers.

CUSTOMER RELATIONSHIP MANAGEMENT SOFTWARE

Commercial CRM software packages range from niche tools that perform limited functions, such as personalizing Web sites for specific customers, to large-scale enterprise applications that capture myriad interactions with customers, analyze them with sophisticated reporting tools, and link to other major enterprise applications, such as supply chain management and enterprise systems. The more comprehensive CRM packages contain modules for **partner relationship management (PRM)** and **employee relationship management (ERM)**.

PRM uses many of the same data, tools, and systems as customer relationship management to enhance collaboration between a company and its selling partners. If a company does not sell directly to customers but rather works through distributors or retailers, PRM helps these channels sell to customers directly. It provides a company and its selling partners with the ability to trade information and distribute leads and data about customers, integrating lead generation, pricing, promotions, order configurations, and availability. It also provides a firm with tools to assess its partners' performances so it can make sure its best partners receive the support they need to close more business.

ERM software deals with employee issues that are closely related to CRM, such as setting objectives, employee performance management, performance-based compensation, and employee training. Major CRM application software vendors include Oracle, SAP, Salesforce.com, and Microsoft Dynamics CRM.

Customer relationship management systems typically provide software and online tools for sales, customer service, and marketing. We briefly describe some of these capabilities.

Sales Force Automation (SFA)

Sales force automation modules in CRM systems help sales staff increase their productivity by focusing sales efforts on the most profitable customers, those who are good candidates for sales and services. CRM systems provide sales prospect and contact information, product information, product configuration capabilities, and sales quote generation capabilities. Such software can assemble information about a particular customer's past purchases to help the salesperson make personalized recommendations. CRM software enables sales, marketing, and delivery departments to easily share customer and prospect information. It increases each salesperson's efficiency by reducing the cost per sale as well as the cost of acquiring new customers and retaining old ones. CRM software also has capabilities for sales forecasting, territory management, and team selling.

Customer Service

Customer service modules in CRM systems provide information and tools to increase the efficiency of call centers, help desks, and customer support staff. They have capabilities for assigning and managing customer service requests.

One such capability is an appointment or advice telephone line: When a customer calls a standard phone number, the system routes the call to the correct service person, who inputs information about that customer into the system only once. Once the customer's data are in the system, any service representative can handle the customer relationship. Improved access to consistent and accurate customer information helps call centers handle more calls per day and decrease the duration of each call. Thus, call centers and customer service groups achieve greater productivity, reduced transaction time, and higher quality of service at lower cost. The customer is happier because he or she spends less time on the phone restating his or her problem to customer service representatives.

CRM systems may also include Web-based self-service capabilities: The company Web site can be set up to provide inquiring customers personalized support information as well as the option to contact customer service staff by phone for additional assistance.

Marketing

CRM systems support direct-marketing campaigns by providing capabilities for capturing prospect and customer data, for providing product and service information, for qualifying leads for targeted marketing, and for scheduling and tracking direct-marketing mailings or e-mail (see Figure 9.7). Marketing modules also include tools for analyzing marketing and customer data, identifying profitable and unprofitable customers, designing products and services to satisfy specific customer needs and interests, and identifying opportunities for cross-selling.

Cross-selling is the marketing of complementary products to customers. (For example, in financial services, a customer with a checking account might be sold a money market account or a home improvement loan.) CRM tools also help firms manage and execute marketing campaigns at all stages, from planning to determining the rate of success for each campaign.

Figure 9.8 illustrates the most important capabilities for sales, service, and marketing processes that would be found in major CRM software products. Like enterprise software, this software is business-process driven, incorporating hundreds of business processes thought to represent best practices in each of these areas. To achieve maximum benefit, companies need to revise and model their business processes to conform to the best-practice business processes in the CRM software.

Figure 9.9 illustrates how a best practice for increasing customer loyalty through customer service might be modeled by CRM software. Directly

FIGURE 9.7   HOW CRM SYSTEMS SUPPORT MARKETING

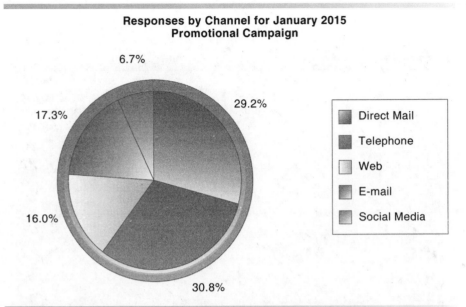

**Responses by Channel for January 2015
Promotional Campaign**

- 6.7%
- 29.2%
- 17.3%
- 16.0%
- 30.8%

Legend:
- Direct Mail
- Telephone
- Web
- E-mail
- Social Media

Customer relationship management software provides a single point for users to manage and evaluate marketing campaigns across multiple channels, including e-mail, direct mail, telephone, the Web, and social media.

servicing customers provides firms with opportunities to increase customer retention by singling out profitable long-term customers for preferential treatment. CRM software can assign each customer a score based on that person's value and loyalty to the company and provide that information to help call centers route each customer's service request to agents who can best handle that customer's needs. The system would automatically provide the service agent with a detailed profile of that customer that includes his or her score for value and loyalty. The service agent would use this information to present special offers or additional service to the customer to encourage the customer to keep transacting business with the company. You will find more information on other best-practice business processes in CRM systems in our Learning Tracks.

OPERATIONAL AND ANALYTICAL CRM

All of the applications we have just described support either the operational or analytical aspects of customer relationship management. **Operational CRM** includes customer-facing applications, such as tools for sales force automation, call center and customer service support, and marketing automation. **Analytical CRM** includes applications that analyze customer data generated by operational CRM applications to provide information for improving business performance.

Analytical CRM applications are based on data from operational CRM systems, customer touch points, and other sources that have been organized in data warehouses or analytic platforms for use in online analytical

FIGURE 9.8 CRM SOFTWARE CAPABILITIES

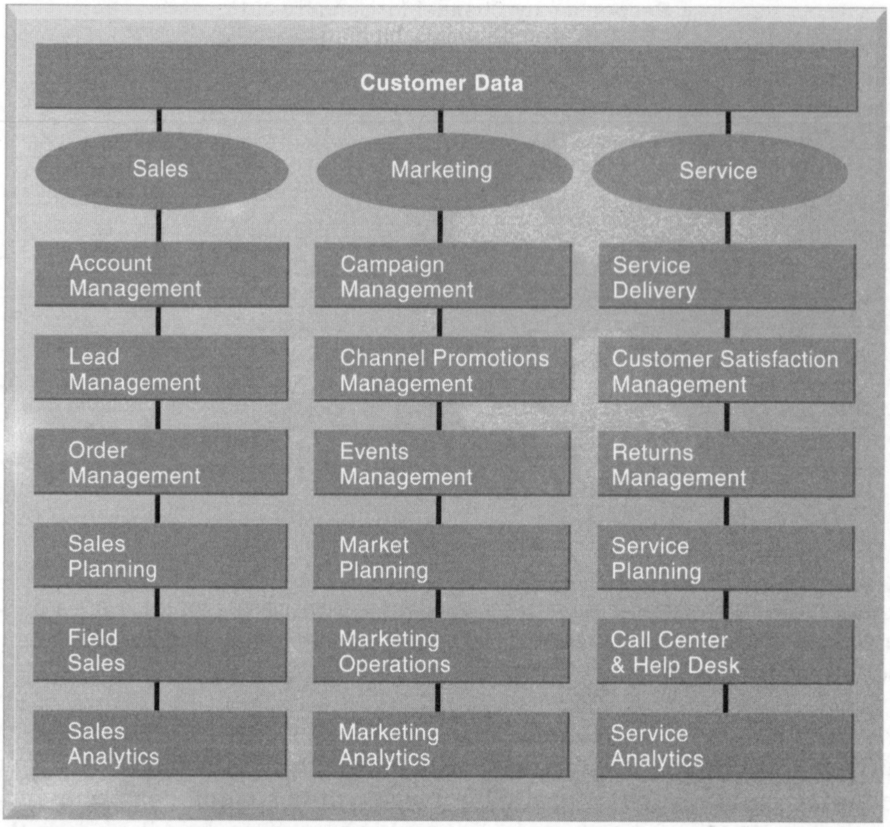

The major CRM software products support business processes in sales, service, and marketing, integrating customer information from many different sources. Included is support for both the operational and analytical aspects of CRM.

FIGURE 9.9 CUSTOMER LOYALTY MANAGEMENT PROCESS MAP

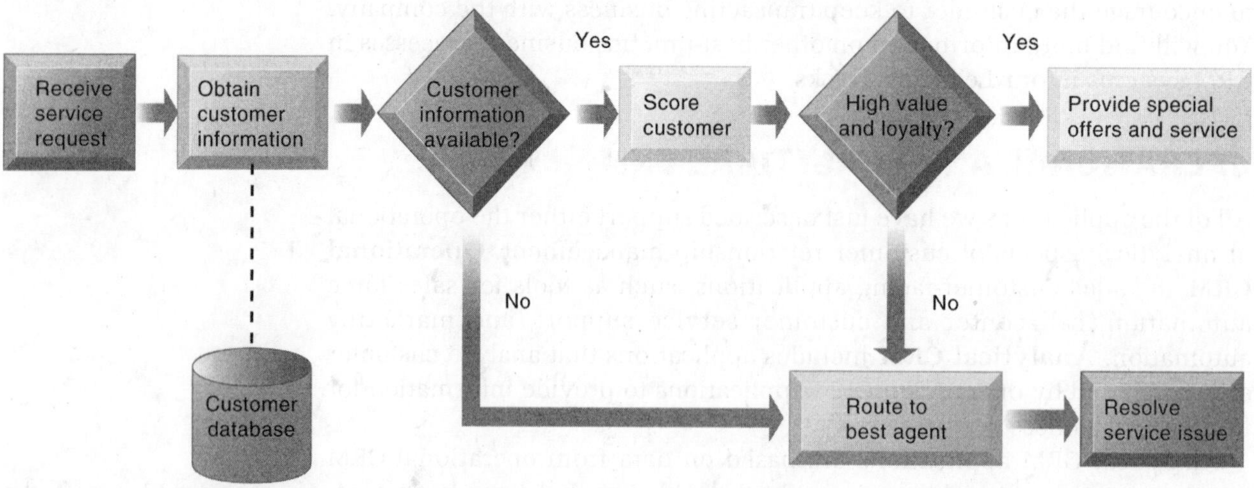

This process map shows how a best practice for promoting customer loyalty through customer service would be modeled by customer relationship management software. The CRM software helps firms identify high-value customers for preferential treatment.

FIGURE 9.10 ANALYTICAL CRM

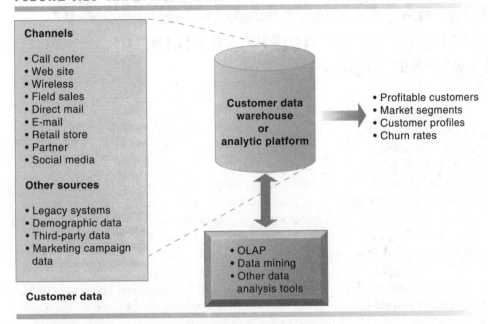

Analytical CRM uses a customer data warehouse or analytic platform and tools to analyze customer data collected from the firm's customer touch points and from other sources.

processing (OLAP), data mining, and other data analysis techniques (see Chapter 6). Customer data collected by the organization might be combined with data from other sources, such as customer lists for direct-marketing campaigns purchased from other companies or demographic data. Such data are analyzed to identify buying patterns, to create segments for targeted marketing, and to pinpoint profitable and unprofitable customers (see Figure 9.10 and the Interactive Session on Organizations).

Another important output of analytical CRM is the customer's lifetime value to the firm. **Customer lifetime value (CLTV)** is based on the relationship between the revenue produced by a specific customer, the expenses incurred in acquiring and servicing that customer, and the expected life of the relationship between the customer and the company.

BUSINESS VALUE OF CUSTOMER RELATIONSHIP MANAGEMENT SYSTEMS

Companies with effective customer relationship management systems realize many benefits, including increased customer satisfaction, reduced direct-marketing costs, more effective marketing, and lower costs for customer acquisition and retention. Information from CRM systems increases sales revenue by identifying the most profitable customers and segments for focused marketing and cross-selling.

Customer churn is reduced as sales, service, and marketing better respond to customer needs. The **churn rate** measures the number of customers who stop using or purchasing products or services from a company. It is an important indicator of the growth or decline of a firm's customer base.

INTERACTIVE SESSION: ORGANIZATIONS

CRM TOOLS AID AIRTEL IN THE EFFICIENT HANDLING OF CUSTOMER SUPPORT PROCESSES

Bharti Airtel is a leading global telecommunications company with operations in 20 countries. The firm currently operates in 22 circles in India, providing GSM services that cover 82% of the population. It also has a wide rural reach. Bharti Airtel's Convergence Project attempts to understand the evolving needs of the different customer segments. The aim is to offer converged capabilities to customers irrespective of where they are. This means that no matter which part of the country the customer is in, or what service they are subscribed to (GSM or broadband), their experience of interacting with the company should be consistent throughout.

When Airtel started its operations, all customer support processes were manual and complaint resolution stood at 40%. The subscriber base was growing at a rate of 15% to 20% at that time. Besides, there was competition from several local players. In this scenario, the inability of the firm to provide a common brand experience and centralized service to all customers, irrespective of their location, put additional pressure on the firm. There was no process in place to manage the billing operations. As a result, customer retention was low and so was the quality of service as compared to that of the competitors. Each process at Airtel (call center, direct marketing, sales, billing, and so on) had its own application, each of which functioned independently of the others. This did not allow the management to have a unified view of customer data.

To tackle this problem, Airtel conducted a gap analysis by evaluating its current technology in light of the problems it faced. Then it launched pilot program to receive suggestions and feedback from across the firm. Several processes were re-engineered and the company decided to establish a centralized system for customer relationship management (CRM). Oracle's E-Business CRM suite was adopted, which offered services in the areas of campaign management, sales management, order

entry and management, and customer service. These applications were deployed for all touch points through a variety of interaction media.

As a first step, WAN was installed at all the major locations. Extranet was established at vendor and dealer outlets. This enabled easy communication among the company, vendors, dealers, and customers. Airtel then implemented its business intelligence solution that would allow for the querying of the OLTP (transaction databases) and OLAP (data marts and warehouses) systems to meet the day-to-day reporting and analysis requirements. However, the turnaround time for these queries was quite high because of the heterogeneous nature of the databases, each having a differing underlying database schema, dependent relations, size, and technology. To address this issue of a high response time, Oracle decided to create another central database to serve as common, dedicated reporting database. It did so by implementing the Oracle Streams Replication (OSR). With the help of OSR, a replication environment (RE) was created for the various types of databases in operation at Airtel. The new database allowed for the sharing of data from the individual application-specific databases. So, any change occurring in the underlying objects in the source database would keep replicating in the destination database. The synchronized database environment now served the purpose of reporting on operational and analytical CRM queries.

Airtel also uses the CRM feature called Oracle Discoverer that allows users to retrieve reports from the synchronized dedicated database. This makes real-time data available to users. Both Airtel and Oracle discourage the use of online reporting to prevent the unnecessary loading of the CRM system. Consequently, the firm is able to achieve a unified view of its customer data across all products and services. This has enabled Airtel offer special loyalty programs and incentive schemes in a targeted manner. It utilizes data to cross-sell and up-sell relevant products and services to customers. For example, offers are made to customers based on their usage of a certain service. If a customer reaches the threshold, discounts and other perks are offered. Airtel also generates leads from the customer data for the purposes of SMS campaigns. This has not only reduced the number of calls made to the customer but also increased the number of services availed by the users.

Airtel's electronic billing service enables customers make payment from anywhere. It also provides customers with an option to customize their bills and simplify the process of payment. The CRM segregates applications from consumer complaints. This has led to an 8% faster resolution of customer faults. Besides, there has been a 3% reduction in fault re-occurrence and multiple failures. The system automatically escalates the complaint to a higher authority if it is not resolved within the set period of time. To aid in customer retention, the system automatically generates product suggestions to a leaving customer. An added advantage is that the current system is scalable, which means that it can accommodate the growing base of customers.

The Airtel CRM is divided into two kind of solutions: operational CRM and analytical CRM. The operational CRM looks after the day-to-day call center activities. The customer care cell at Airtel is divided into four departments: Hotline (handles new customers), Care Touch (deals exclusively with corporates and the executive class), Retention (handles churn and retains existing customers on the verge of leaving), and Outbound (takes care of backend processing at customer care). The analytical CRM is largely used for business development activities. For example, it is utilized by Airtel to measure the success of its products and services in the market by tracking customer acquisition costs, conversion rates, retention or churn rates, and loyalty measures. Application of the analytical CRM enables Airtel to answer several questions such as: Which are the best customers? Who are likely to leave? What can be done to retain them? What is the likelihood that the customer will churn? The answers to these questions are achieved by tracking several parameters like average bill value, payment pattern, and usage among others. A rating is then assigned to the customer between 0 and 1, where 1 indicates the highest probability of leaving. Analytics also aids in fraud detection by monitoring customer transactions.

The current CRM application at Airtel has the following modules: marketing, planning, campaign management, lead management, sales, activity management, knowledge management for FAQs and user guides, call center support, and opportunity management. In a nutshell, the CRM tool has enabled the firm develop its retention and loyalty plans, provide accurate bills, and take feedback on all services.

Sources: Retrieved from http://www.informationweek.in/informationweek/edge/276969/bharti-airtel; Dutta, Rahul, "Streams Implementation with Oracle E-Business Suite and Discoverer", *Bharti Airtel and Oracle Streams* (2009). Retrieved from http://www.oracle.com/technetwork/database/features/availability/streams-profile-bharti-130885.pdf; "Customer Relationship Magic at Airtel" (2010). Retrieved from http://www.slideshare.net/ashish1.bansal/customer-relationship-management-airtel; "Customer Relationship Management at Airtel". Retrieved from http://issuu.com/sanjaykumarguptaa/docs/customer-relationship-management-at-airtel; Mansuri, B.B., "Customer Relationship Management (CRM)—A Case Study of Airtel", *Journal of Contemporary Research in Management*, Vol. 4, No. 1 (2009). Retrieved from http://www.psgim.ac.in/journals/index.php/jcrm/article/view/51/56; Makkar, Urvashi and Harinder Kumar Makkar, *Customer Relationship Management*, McGraw-Hill Education (India) Pvt. Limited (2012).

CASE STUDY QUESTIONS

1. What were the problems faced by Airtel prior to the implementation of a CRM application?

2. What was the need for a central database at Airtel? What function has the OSR provided in Airtel's CRM tool?

3. How has the CRM application at Airtel helped in market segmentation?

4. What is the difference between the operational and analytical CRM at Airtel?

9.4 WHAT ARE THE CHALLENGES POSED BY ENTERPRISE APPLICATIONS AND HOW ARE ENTERPRISE APPLICATIONS TAKING ADVANTAGE OF NEW TECHNOLOGIES?

Many firms have implemented enterprise systems and systems for supply chain and customer relationship management because they are such powerful instruments for achieving operational excellence and enhancing decision making. But precisely because they are so powerful in changing the way the organization works, they are challenging to implement. Let's briefly examine some of these challenges, as well as new ways of obtaining value from these systems.

ENTERPRISE APPLICATION CHALLENGES

Promises of dramatic reductions in inventory costs, order-to-delivery time, more efficient customer response, and higher product and customer profitability make enterprise systems and systems for supply chain management and customer relationship management very alluring. But to obtain this value, you must clearly understand how your business has to change to use these systems effectively.

Enterprise applications involve complex pieces of software that are very expensive to purchase and implement. It might take a large Fortune 500 company several years to complete a large-scale implementation of an enterprise system or a system for SCM or CRM. According to a 2014 survey of 192 companies conducted by Panorama Consulting Solutions, the average cost of an ERP project was $2.8 million. Projects took a little over 16 months to complete, and 66 percent of the projects delivered 50 percent or less of the expected benefits (Panorama, 2014). Changes in project scope and additional customization work add to implementation delays and costs.

Enterprise applications require not only deep-seated technological changes but also fundamental changes in the way the business operates. Companies must make sweeping changes to their business processes to work with the software. Employees must accept new job functions and responsibilities. They must learn how to perform a new set of work activities and understand how the information they enter into the system can affect other parts of the company. This requires new organizational learning and should also be factored into ERP implementation costs.

Supply chain management systems require multiple organizations to share information and business processes. Each participant in the system may have to change some of its processes and the way it uses information to create a system that best serves the supply chain as a whole.

Some firms experienced enormous operating problems and losses when they first implemented enterprise applications because they didn't understand how much organizational change was required. For example, Kmart had trouble getting products to store shelves when it first implemented i2 Technologies supply chain management software. The i2 software did not work well with Kmart's promotion-driven business model, which created sharp downward spikes in demand for products. Overstock.com's order tracking system went down for a full week when the company replaced a homegrown system with an Oracle enterprise system. The company rushed to implement the software, and did not properly synchronize the Oracle software's process for recording customer refunds with its accounts receivable system. These problems contributed to a third-quarter loss of $14.5 million that year.

Enterprise applications also introduce "switching costs." Once you adopt an enterprise application from a single vendor, such as SAP, Oracle, or others, it is very costly to switch vendors, and your firm becomes dependent on the vendor to upgrade its product and maintain your installation.

Enterprise applications are based on organization-wide definitions of data. You'll need to understand exactly how your business uses its data and how the data would be organized in a customer relationship management, supply chain management, or enterprise system. CRM systems typically require some data cleansing work.

Enterprise software vendors are addressing these problems by offering pared-down versions of their software and "fast-start" programs for small and medium-sized businesses and best-practice guidelines for larger companies. Companies are also achieving more flexibility by using cloud applications for functions not addressed by the basic enterprise software so that they are not constrained by a single "do-it-all" type of system (Drobik and Rayner, 2013).

Companies adopting enterprise applications can also save time and money by keeping customizations to a minimum. For example, Kennametal, a $2 billion metal-cutting tools company in Pennsylvania, had spent $10 million over 13 years maintaining an ERP system with over 6,400 customizations. The company has now replaced it with a "plain vanilla," noncustomized version of SAP enterprise software and changed its business processes to conform to the software. ACH Food Companies, described in the chapter-opening case, moved to a "vanilla" ERP system as it simplified its business model.

NEXT-GENERATION ENTERPRISE APPLICATIONS

Today, enterprise application vendors are delivering more value by becoming more flexible, Web-enabled mobile, and capable of integration with other systems. Stand-alone enterprise systems, customer relationship management systems, and supply chain management systems are becoming a thing of the past. The major enterprise software vendors have created what they call *enterprise solutions*, *enterprise suites*, or e-business suites to make their customer relationship management, supply chain management, and enterprise systems work closely with each other, and link to systems of customers and suppliers. SAP Business Suite, Oracle E-Business Suite, and Microsoft Dynamics Suite (aimed at mid-sized companies) are examples, and they now utilize Web services and service-oriented architecture (SOA) (see Chapter 5).

SAP's next-generation enterprise applications incorporate SOA standards and are able to link SAP's own applications and Web services developed by independent software vendors. Oracle also has included SOA and business process management capabilities in its Fusion middleware products.

Businesses can use these tools to create platforms for new or improved business processes that integrate information from multiple applications.

Next-generation enterprise applications also include open source and cloud solutions, as well as more functionality available on mobile platforms. Open source products such as Compiere, Apache Open for Business (OFBiz), and Openbravo do not offer as many capabilities as large commercial enterprise software, but are attractive to companies such as small manufacturers because of their low cost.

For small- and medium-sized businesses in selected countries, SAP offers cloud-based versions of its Business One Cloud and Business ByDesign enterprise software solutions. Cloud-based enterprise systems are also offered by smaller vendors such as NetSuite and Plex Systems, but they are not as popular as cloud-based CRM products. The undisputed global market leader in cloud-based CRM systems is Salesforce.com, with over 100,000 customers. Salesforce.com delivers its service through Internet-connected computers or mobile devices and it is widely used by small, medium, and large enterprises. As cloud-based products mature, more companies will be choosing to run all or part of their enterprise applications in the cloud on an as-needed basis.

Social CRM and Business Intelligence

CRM software vendors are enhancing their products to take advantage of social networking technologies. These social enhancements help firms identify new ideas more rapidly, improve team productivity, and deepen interactions with customers (see the Chapter 10 ending case study).

Employees who interact with customers via social networking sites such as Facebook and Twitter are often able to provide customer service func-. tions much faster and at lower cost than by using telephone conversations or e-mail. Customers who are active social media users increasingly want—and expect—businesses to respond to their questions and complaints through this channel.

Social CRM tools enable a business to connect customer conversations and relationships from social networking sites to CRM processes. The leading CRM vendors now offer such tools to link data from social networks into their CRM software. SAP, Salesforce.com and Oracle CRM products now feature technology to monitor, track, and analyze social media activity in Facebook, LinkedIn, Twitter, YouTube, and other sites. Business intelligence and analytics software vendors such as SAS also have capablities for social media analytics (with several measures of customer engagement across a variety of social networks), along with campaign management tools for testing and optimizing both social and traditional Web-based campaigns.

Salesforce.com connected its system for tracking leads in the sales process with social-listening and social-media marketing tools, enabling users to tailor their social-marketing dollars to core customers and observe the resulting comments. If an ad agency wants to run a targeted Facebook or Twitter ad, these capabilities make it possible to aim the ad specifically at people in the client's lead pipeline, who are already being tracked in the CRM system. Users will be able to view tweets as they take place in real time and perhaps uncover new leads. They can also manage multiple campaigns and compare them all to figure out which ones generate the highest click-through rates and cost per click.

Business Intelligence in Enterprise Applications Enterprise application vendors have added business intelligence features to help managers obtain more meaningful information from the massive amounts of data generated by these systems. Included are tools for flexible reporting, ad hoc analysis, interactive dashboards, what-if scenario analysis, and data visualization. Rather than requiring users to leave an application and launch separate reporting and analytics tools, the vendors are starting to embed analytics within the context of the application itself. They are also offering complementary stand-alone analytics products, such as SAP BusinessObjects and Oracle Business Intelligence Enterprise Edition.

The major enterprise application vendors also offer portions of their products that work on mobile handhelds. You can find out more about this topic in our Chapter 7 Learning Track on Wireless Applications for Customer Relationship Management, Supply Chain Management, and Healthcare.

Review Summary

1. *How do enterprise systems help businesses achieve operational excellence?*

    Enterprise software is based on a suite of integrated software modules and a common central database. The database collects data from and feeds the data into numerous applications that can support nearly all of an organization's internal business activities. When new information is entered by one process, the information is made available immediately to other business processes.

    Enterprise systems support organizational centralization by enforcing uniform data standards and business processes throughout the company and a single unified technology platform. The firmwide data generated by enterprise systems helps managers evaluate organizational performance.

2. *How do supply chain management systems coordinate planning, production, and logistics with suppliers?*

    Supply chain management (SCM) systems automate the flow of information among members of the supply chain so they can use it to make better decisions about when and how much to purchase, produce, or ship. More accurate information from supply chain management systems reduces uncertainty and the impact of the bullwhip effect.

    Supply chain management software includes software for supply chain planning and for supply chain execution. Internet technology facilitates the management of global supply chains by providing the connectivity for organizations in different countries to share supply chain information. Improved communication among supply chain members also facilitates efficient customer response and movement toward a demand-driven model.

3. *How do customer relationship management systems help firms achieve customer intimacy?*

    Customer relationship management (CRM) systems integrate and automate customer-facing processes in sales, marketing, and customer service, providing an enterprise-wide view of customers. Companies can use this customer knowledge when they interact with customers to provide them with better service or to sell new products and services. These systems also identify profitable or nonprofitable customers or opportunities to reduce the churn rate.

The major customer relationship management software packages provide capabilities for both operational CRM and analytical CRM. They often include modules for managing relationships with selling partners (partner relationship management) and for employee relationship management.

4. *What are the challenges posed by enterprise applications and how are enterprise applications taking advantage of new technologies?*

Enterprise applications are difficult to implement. They require extensive organizational change, large new software investments, and careful assessment of how these systems will enhance organizational performance. Enterprise applications cannot provide value if they are implemented atop flawed processes or if firms do not know how to use these systems to measure performance improvements. Employees require training to prepare for new procedures and roles. Attention to data management is essential.

Enterprise applications are now more flexible, Web-enabled, and capable of integration with other systems, using Web services and service-oriented architecture (SOA). They also have open source and on-demand versions and are able to run in cloud infrastructures or on mobile platforms. CRM software has added social networking capabilities to enhance internal collaboration, deepen interactions with customers, and utilize data from social networking sites. Open source, mobile, and cloud versions of some of these products are becoming available.

Key Terms

Analytical CRM, 389

Bullwhip effect, 378

Churn rate, 391

Cross-selling, 388

Customer lifetime value (CLTV), 391

Demand planning, 380

Employee relationship management (ERM), 387

Enterprise software, 372

Just-in-time strategy, 378

Operational CRM, 389

Partner relationship management (PRM), 387

Pull-based model, 383

Push-based model, 383

Social CRM, 396

Supply chain, 376

Supply chain execution systems, 380

Supply chain planning systems, 379

Touch point, 386

Review Questions

9-1 How do enterprise systems help businesses achieve operational excellence?

- Define an enterprise system and explain how enterprise software works.

- Describe how enterprise systems provide value for a business.

9-2 How do supply chain management systems coordinate planning, production, and logistics with suppliers?

- Define a supply chain and identify each of its components.

- Explain how supply chain management systems help reduce the bullwhip effect and how they provide value for a business.

- Define and compare supply chain planning systems and supply chain execution systems.

- Describe the challenges of global supply chains and how Internet technology can help companies manage them better.

- Distinguish between a push-based and a pull-based model of supply chain management and explain how contemporary supply chain management systems facilitate a pull-based model.

9-3 How do customer relationship management systems help firms achieve customer intimacy?

- Define customer relationship management and explain why customer relationships are so important today.

- Describe how partner relationship management (PRM) and employee relationship management (ERM) are related to customer relationship management (CRM).

- Describe the tools and capabilities of customer relationship management software for sales, marketing, and customer service.

- Distinguish between operational and analytical CRM.

9-4 What are the challenges posed by enterprise applications and how are enterprise applications taking advantage of new technologies?

- List and describe the challenges posed by enterprise applications.

- Explain how these challenges can be addressed.

- How are enterprise applications taking advantage of SOA, Web services, open source software, and wireless technology?

- Define social CRM and explain how customer relationship management systems are using social networking.

Discussion Questions

9-5 Supply chain management is less about managing the physical movement of goods and more about managing information. Discuss the implications of this statement.

9-6 If a company wants to implement an enterprise application, it had better do its homework. Discuss the implications of this statement.

9-7 Which enterprise application should a business install first: ERP, SCM, or CRM? Explain your answer.

Hands-On MIS Projects

The projects in this section give you hands-on experience analyzing business process integration, suggesting supply chain management and customer relationship management applications, using database software to manage customer service requests, and evaluating supply chain management business services.

Management Decision Problems

9-8 Toronto-based Mercedes-Benz Canada, with a network of 55 dealers, did not know enough about its customers. Dealers provided customer data to the company on an ad hoc basis. Mercedes did not force dealers to report this information. There was no real incentive for dealers to share information with the company. How could CRM and PRM systems help solve this problem?

9-9 Office Depot sells a wide range of office supply products and services in the United States and internationally. The company tries to offer a wider range of office supplies at lower cost than other retailers by using just-in-time replenishment and tight inventory control systems. It uses information from a demand forecasting system and point-of-sale data to replenish its inventory in its 1,600 retail stores. Explain how these systems help Office Depot minimize costs and any other benefits they provide. Identify and describe other supply chain management applications that would be especially helpful to Office Depot.

Achieving Operational Excellence: Evaluating Supply Chain Management Services

Software skills: Web browser and presentation software
Business skills: Evaluating supply chain management services

9-10 In addition to carrying goods from one place to another, some trucking companies provide supply chain management services and help their customers manage their information. In this project, you'll use the Web to research and evaluate two of these business services. Investigate the Web sites of two companies, UPS Logistics and Schneider Logistics, to see how these companies' services can be used for supply chain management. Then respond to the following questions:

- What supply chain processes can each of these companies support for their clients?
- How can customers use the Web sites of each company to help them with supply chain management?
- Compare the supply chain management services provided by these companies. Which company would you select to help your firm manage its supply chain? Why?

Social CRM: Connecting with Customers through Social Networks
CASE STUDY

With the exponential increase in social media users, firms have shifted from the customer push model of branding to the customer pull model. Organizations have started to tweak their conventional customer relationship managements (CRMs) to remold them, so as to enable interaction with customers *via* the Internet. The older, conventional CRM model followed a closed relationship with customers. The company executives had one-to-one conversation with customers through the phone, e-mails, or chats. The whole focus of the conventional CRM was limited to sales or, at the most, grievance handling. But the current times call for a change in this approach. India has emerged as a leading Internet hub of the world, with an increasing number of tech-savvy young people who use new forms of social media to express themselves. Firms too have had to use social media to reach out to customers. This has led to the emergence of social CRM. Social CRM is an open CRM model that advocates real-time interaction with customers, to come up with ideas for innovation, product development and pricing, and also get instant product reviews and opportunities for word-of-mouth marketing. The social CRM model is rather complex and uncontrolled, as the customer can express their thoughts or feedback regarding a company's product or service on various social networking sites like Facebook, Twitter, LinkedIn, and so on. The social CRM enables organizations to be equipped to handle such expressions of ideas. For effective relationship-building, organizations need to capture this information and actively engage with a diverse set of customers. In addition, companies also need to create an environment where customers can interact with each other.

The use of social CRM as a marketing tool has given rise to viral marketing, brand building, market research, and effective competition analysis. For instance, when Ford launched Fiesta, instead of spending huge amounts of money on conventional forms of marketing, it invited 100 "social agents" (users who were active on social media) to try the Fiesta and share their experiences with the online community. Similarly, Proctor and Gamble (P&G) launched its Old Spice campaign ("Smell like a man, man") on YouTube, which turned out to be a huge success. Organizations are applying social CRM in product development too. P&G launched its "connect and develop" initiative to get product ideas from online users and, now, more than 35% of P&G's new products come through this initiative.

The Indian banking sector has also shifted from using conventional CRM to social CRM. According to Anand Sinha, the erstwhile deputy governor of the Reserve Bank of India (RBI) and chairman of the Institute for Development and Research in Banking Technology (IDRBT), bank communications can no longer ignore social media. New-age customers have different expectations from banks. They want to be engaged in a different manner. The noted expert in CRM, Paul Greenbag, says, "The underlying principle for social CRM's success is very different from [that of] ... traditional CRM, which was based on an internal operational approach to manage customer relationships effectively. But social CRM is based on the ability of a company to meet the personal agendas of its customers while, at the same time, meeting the objectives of its own business plan. It is aimed at customer engagement rather than customer management." The need of the hour is to listen to customers and engage with them. Users want banks to respond to their queries through online social platforms. The presence of the banks on the social media helps resolve issues before they get out of control. Social media is a rich source of information as far as understanding emerging customer trends and preferences is concerned.

To effectively utilize the full potential that social CRMs have to offer, banks need to see customers as more than just targets for selling their services to. They need to acknowledge that customers have the great power of choice and that their satisfaction is of utmost importance. Banks are, therefore, trying to find out more about each individual customer to raise awareness and spread information among them. Bank policies like KYC norms, government regulations, and credit card dos and don'ts are being communicated to customers effectively. ICICI Bank launched an interesting initiative in 2013 called Pockets. This facility was aimed at allowing fund transfers through Facebook. There are now more than 30,000 active Pockets users. Banking operations can also be carried out through Twitter hashtags. For example, account balance can be obtained by using the hashtag, #ibal. Similarly #itran and #topup are used to view recent transactions and recharge prepaid mobile phones, respectively. "Currently 90% of CRM spending is directed towards operational CRM initiatives like sales force automation, but will drop to 70% of spending by 2020. Meanwhile, spending on social CRM initiatives like customer communities and social media monitoring will grow from less than 1% to 10% by 2020," says Barney Beal, former News Director for TechTarget's Business Applications and Architecture Media Group.

Sources: Geeta Rohra and Mridul Sharma, "Social CRM—Possibilities and Challenges", White Paper of Tata Consultancy Services. Retrieved from http://www.tcs.com/SiteCollectionDocuments/White%20Papers/ConnectedMarketing_Whitepaper_Social_CRM%E2%80%93Possibilities_Challenges_0912-1.pdf; "Managed Service Providers and Cloud Service Providers". Retrieved from http://www.ibm.com/midmarket/uk/en/att/pdf/social_media_Part_Executive_Report.pdf; Camhi, Jonathan, "2014 Forecast: The Evolution of Social Media in Banking", *Information Week* (2013). Retrieved from www.banktech.com/channels/...of-social-media-in-banking/d/d-id/1296744; "Social Media Imperatives for Retail Banks", Cognizant Reports (2011). Retrieved from http://www.cognizant.com/InsightsWhitepapers/Social-Media-Imperatives-for-Retail-Banks.pdf; Ghedin, Guido, "Social Media and Banks: Best Practices from the BRIC", *Digital in the Round* (2013). Retrieved from www.digitalintheround.com/social-media-banks-brics. "Is Hashtag Banking the Next Big Thing in India?", *In.Com* (2015). Retrieved from http://www.in.com/news/business/is-hashtag-banking-the-next-big-thing-in-india-53125704-in-1.html.

DISCUSSION QUESTIONS

9-11 What do you understand by social CRM? What are the implications of using this approach?

9-12 How do banks use social CRM to reach out to customers?

9-13 Give some examples of firms that utilize social CRM as a tool? How do they use it?

Chapter 9 References

"Social and Mobile CRM Boost Productivity by 26.4 Percent." DestinationCRM (March 8, 2012).

Bozarth, Cecil and Robert B. Handfield. *Introduction to Operations and Supply Chain Management* 3e. Upper Saddle River, NJ: Prentice-Hall (2013).

Carew, Joanne. "Most Companies Failing at CRM." IT Web Business (February 14, 2013).

Cole, Brenda. "Cloud ERP Users Say Up, Up and Away." *Business Information* (February 2014).

D'Avanzo, Robert, Hans von Lewinski, and Luk N. Van Wassenhove. "The Link between Supply Chain and Financial Performance." *Supply Chain Management Review* (November 1, 2003).

Davenport, Thomas H. *Mission Critical: Realizing the Promise of Enterprise Systems.* Boston: Harvard Business School Press (2000).

Davenport, Thomas H., Leandro Dalle Mule, and John Lucke. "Know What Your Customers Want Before They Do." *Harvard Business Review* (December 2011).

Drobik, Alexander and Nigel Rayner. "Develop a Strategic Road Map for Postmodern ERP in 2013 and Beyond." Gartner Inc. (July 2013).

Essex, David. "Tomorrow's ERP Raises New Hopes, Fears." *Business Information* (February 2014).

Hitt, Lorin, D. J. Wu, and Xiaoge Zhou. "Investment in Enterprise Resource Planning: Business Impact and Productivity Measures." *Journal of Management Information Systems* 19, No. 1 (Summer 2002).

IBM Institute for Business Value. "Customer Analytics Pay Off." IBM Corporation (2011).

Kanaracus, Chris. "ERP Software Project Woes Continue to Mount, Survey Says." IT World (February 20, 2013).

Klein, Richard and Arun Rai. "Interfirm Strategic Information Flows in Logistics Supply Chain Relationships. *MIS Quarterly* 33, No. 4 (December 2009).

Laudon, Kenneth C. "The Promise and Potential of Enterprise Systems and Industrial Networks." Working paper, The Concours Group. Copyright Kenneth C. Laudon (1999).

Lee, Hau, L., V. Padmanabhan, and Seugin Whang. "The Bullwhip Effect in Supply Chains." *Sloan Management Review* (Spring 1997).

Liang, Huigang, Nilesh Sharaf, Quing Hu, and Yajiong Xue. "Assimilation of Enterprise Systems: The Effect of Institutional Pressures and the Mediating Role of Top Management." *MIS Quarterly* 31, No. 1 (March 2007).

Maklan, Stan, Simon Knox, and Joe Peppard. "When CRM Fails." *MIT Sloan Management Review* 52, No. 4 (Summer 2011).

Malik, Yogesh, Alex Niemeyer, and Brian Ruwadi. "Building the Supply Chain of the Future." *McKinsey Quarterly* (January 2011).

Mehta, Krishna. "Best Practices for Developing a Customer Lifetime Value Program." *Information Management* (July 28, 2011).

Morrison, Tod. "Custom ERP No Longer in Vogue." *Business Information* (February 2014).

Maurno, Dann Anthony. "The New Word on ERP." *CFO Magazine* (July 25, 2014).

Novet, Jordan. "New Salesforce.com Features Meld Social Media, Marketing, and CRM." Gigaom (April 23, 2013).

Oracle Corporation. "Alcoa Implements Oracle Solution 20% below Projected Cost, Eliminates 43 Legacy Systems." www.oracle.com, accessed August 21, 2005.

Panorama Consulting Solutions. "2014 ERP Report" (2014).

Rai, Arun, Paul A. Pavlou, Ghiyoung Im, and Steve Du. "Interfirm IT Capability Profiles and Communications for Cocreating Relational Value: Evidence from the Logistics Industry." *MIS Quarterly* 36, No. 1 (March 2012).

Rai, Arun, Ravi Patnayakuni, and Nainika Seth. "Firm Performance Impacts of Digitally Enabled Supply Chain Integration Capabilities." *MIS Quarterly* 30 No. 2 (June 2006).

Ranganathan, C. and Carol V. Brown. "ERP Iinvestments and the Market Value of Firms: Toward an Understanding of Influential ERP Project Variables." *Information Systems Research* 17, No. 2 (June 2006).

Sarker, Supreteek, Saonee Sarker, Arvin Sahaym, and Bjørn-Andersen. "Exploring Value Cocreation in Relationships Between an ERP Vendor and its Partners: A Revelatory Case Study." *MIS Quarterly* 36, No. 1 (March 2012).

Seldon, Peter B., Cheryl Calvert, and Song Yang. "A Multi-Project Model of Key Factors Affecting Organizational Benefits from Enterprise Systems." *MIS Quarterly* 34, No. 2 (June 2010).

Strong, Diane M. and Olga Volkoff. "Understanding Organization-Enterprise System Fit: A Path to Theorizing the Information Technology Artifact." *MIS Quarterly* 34, No. 4 (December 2010).

Sykes, Tracy Ann, Viswanath Venkatesh, and Jonathan L. Johnson." Enterprise System Implementation and Employee Job Performance: Understanding the Role of Advice Networks." *MIS Quarterly* 38, No. 1 (March 2014).

"Top 5 Reasons ERP Implementations Fail and What You Can Do About It." Ziff Davis (2013).

Wong, Christina W.Y. , Lai, Kee-Hung and Cheng, T.C.E.. "Value of Information Integration to Supply Chain Management: Roles of Internal and External Contingencies." *Journal of Management Information Systems* 28, No. 3 (Winter 2012).

E-commerce: Digital Markets, Digital Goods

CHAPTER 10

LEARNING OBJECTIVES

After reading this chapter, you will be able to answer the following questions:

1. What are the unique features of e-commerce, digital markets, and digital goods?

2. What are the principal e-commerce business and revenue models?

3. How has e-commerce transformed marketing?

4. How has e-commerce affected business-to-business transactions?

5. What is the role of m-commerce in business and what are the most important m-commerce applications?

6. What issues must be addressed when building an e-commerce presence?

CHAPTER CASES

Pinterest: How Much Is a
  Picture Worth?
Can Pandora Succeed with Freemium?
Social Media Analytics in Indian Politics

Will Mobile Technology Put Orbitz
  in the Lead?
Mobile Commerce with Airtel Money

PINTEREST: HOW MUCH IS A PICTURE WORTH?

If you love looking at pictures, you'll love Pinterest. Pinterest is a social media site launched in March 2010 that allows its users to communicate through vibrant images. You can create virtual scrapbooks of images, video, and other content that you "pin" to a virtual pin board on this Web site and also search for other visually-related content.

Many brides-to-be or women imagining their "dream wedding" have set up Pinterest boards with photos of dresses, flowers, reception dinners, and wedding locations. People pin decorating ideas for their homes or photos of an ideal vacation. Artists use Pinterest to organize inspiring images for their work. Cooks keep Pinterest recipe books. The uses are endless.

Find something you really like? In addition to "liking" and perhaps commenting on it, you can re-pin it to your own board or follow a link back to the original source. Do you see someone who shares your taste or interests? You can follow one or more of that pinner's boards and keep track of everything she or he pins. You can also share your pins and boards on Facebook and Twitter.

Pinterest is the fastest-growing site in Web history. In 2010, Pinterest had 10,000 users, then 12 million by the end of 2011, and 50 million in June 2014, with 40 million unique monthly visitors by that time. An

© Pixellover RM 2/Alamy

estimated 80 percent are women. Pinterest is now the third-largest social network in the United States, behind Facebook and Twitter, and it's also one of the "stickiest" sites on the Web. According to comScore, users spend an average of 80 minutes per session on Pinterest and almost 60 percent of users with accounts visit once or more per week.

Pinterest is becoming an important business tool for building brand image and driving traffic to a company Web site. For instance, Lands' End has several brand pages on Pinterest, one of which is Lands End Canvas, where Lands' End has pinned some of its catalog photos for Lands' End Canvas products. When you click on a photo, you get a larger version of the photo and the chance to link to the Web site (canvas.landsend.com/) where you can purchase the product and find similar ones. Whole Foods does not advertise sales using Pinterest, but instead has theme-based boards like Edible Celebrations, How Does Your Garden Grow, Super HOT Kitchens, and Sweet Tooth. These boards depict a lifestyle that can be obtained by visiting its online store. Brides magazine has nearly 80 Pinterest boards with topics like hair styles, dresses, bouquets, and wedding cakes, using Pinterest to push some of the images that are on the Brides site across the Internet and to drive traffic back to the site.

About 3 percent of referrals to retail Web sites came from Pinterest in 2013, compared to fractions of a percent from YouTube, Reddit, Google+ and other social sites. This is a long way from Facebook's 26 percent of referrals. But according to one marketing study, when Pinterest users follow an image back to its source (a referral from Pinterest) they end up purchasing on average $180 worth of goods. This reflects both the wealth of Pinterest consumers, and the high ticket prices for the goods they end up purchasing, mostly women's fashion. In comparison, Facebook users generate $80 and Twitter users $70.

The hope for marketers, and Pinterest, is that its "referral capacity" (the ability to direct users to retail Web sites where they can purchase something) will rapidly increase as its audience and intensity of use grow. Pinterest is starting to roll out paid advertising in the form of "promoted pins" from companies such as Kraft, General Mills and the Gap. For example, Kraft will be running promoted pins—mostly recipes—in four categories: dessert plays that incorporate products like Jell-O and Cool Whip; Kraft cheese brands; Philadelphia Cream Cheese; and content from Kraft Recipes. Pinterest will charge fees each time a user clicks on one of the promoted pins and is transported to the Kraft Web site. Will promoted pins generate enough revenue to turn Pinterest into a viable business?

Sources: "Pinterest Launches First Paid Ads With Kraft, Gap and Others," Advertising Age, May 12, 2014; Michael J. De La Merced, "Pinterest Launches First Paid Ads With Kraft, Gap and Others," *New York Times*, May 15, 2014; www.pinterest.com, accessed June 9, 2014; Sarah M. Mansouri, "What Is Pinterest?" EZineArticles.com, accessed August 7, 2013; Daniel Scocco, Daily Blog Tips, accessed Aug. 7, 2013; Tara Hunt, "How Pinterest Really Makes Money? Should You Care?" Inc.com, accessed September 3, 2013; Eric Fulwiler, "As Pinterest Meets With Marketers, Evolving Business Model Gets Clearer," *Advertising Age*, May 24, 2013; Saroj Kar, "Can Pinterest Build a Business Model to Justify $1 Billion Valuation?" SiliconAngle, May 25, 2013; and Kenneth C. Laudon and Carol GuercioTraver, *E-Commerce* 2014 (2014).

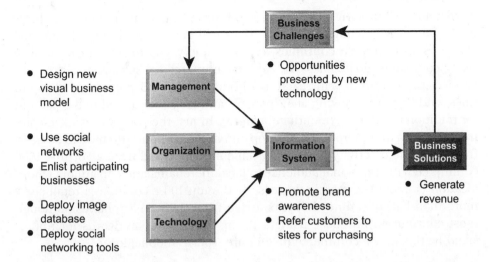

- Design new visual business model

- Use social networks
- Enlist participating businesses

- Deploy image database
- Deploy social networking tools

Pinterest exemplifies two major trends in e-commerce: It is a social networking site linking people to each other through their shared interests and fascination with images; and its social features are also used by companies for promoting goods and services. Pinterest is also an outstanding example of how e-commerce is becoming more visual, with photos and videos playing a much larger role in communicating products and ideas and more searches based on images. It's a poster child for the visual Web.

The chapter-opening diagram calls attention to important points raised by this case and this chapter. Pinterest's primary business challenge is how to wring profits from the hundreds of millions of images and social comments it stores and displays on its Web site. Pinterest's management decided to base its business on social networking tools and technology for visual display and search. Obviously Pinterest had to make a major investment in technology to support a massive database of images, tagging the images, and social networking tools for users. Many of the Pinterest photos function like display ads. The business is just starting to earn revenue through referrals to other Web sites, and it is also starting obtaining revenue from charging businesses who use its platform. Pinterest has some competition, but the real issue is whether it can generate enough revenue from companies interacting with its huge user base.

Here are some questions to think about: Why is Pinterest an expensive business to operate? Do you think its business model is viable? Why or why not? How do you feel about clicking on a Pinterest photo and being transported to a Web site for buying the item displayed in the photo?

10.1 WHAT ARE THE UNIQUE FEATURES OF E-COMMERCE, DIGITAL MARKETS, AND DIGITAL GOODS?

Bought an iTunes track lately, streamed a Netflix movie to your home TV, purchased a book at Amazon, or a diamond at Blue Nile? If so, you've engaged in e-commerce. In 2014, an estimated 196 million Americans went shopping online, and 163 million purchased something online as did millions of others worldwide. And although most purchases still take place through traditional channels, e-commerce continues to grow rapidly and to transform the way many companies do business. In 2014, e-commerce consumer sales of goods, services, and content will reach 470 billion, about 6.5 percent of all retail sales, and they are growing at 12 percent annually (compared to 3.5 percent for traditional retailers) (eMarketer, 2014a). In just the past two years, e-commerce has expanded from the desktop and home computer to mobile devices, from an isolated activity to a new social commerce, and from a Fortune 1000 commerce with a national audience to local merchants and consumers whose location is known to mobile devices. At the top 100 e-commerce retail sites, more than half of online shoppers arrive from their smartphones, although most continue to purchase using a PC or tablet. The key words for understanding this new e-commerce in 2014 are "social, mobile, local."

E-COMMERCE TODAY

E-commerce refers to the use of the Internet and the Web to transact business. More formally, e-commerce is about digitally enabled commercial transactions between and among organizations and individuals. For the most part, this means transactions that occur over the Internet and the Web. Commercial transactions involve the exchange of value (e.g., money) across organizational or individual boundaries in return for products and services.

E-commerce began in 1995 when one of the first Internet portals, Netscape.com, accepted the first ads from major corporations and popularized the idea that the Web could be used as a new medium for advertising and sales. No one envisioned at the time what would turn out to be an exponential growth curve for e-commerce retail sales, which doubled and tripled in the early years. E-commerce grew at double-digit rates until the recession of 2008–2009 when growth slowed to a crawl. In 2009, e-commerce revenues were flat (Figure 10.1), not bad considering that traditional retail sales were shrinking by 5 percent annually. In fact, e-commerce during the recession was the only stable segment in retail. Some online retailers forged ahead at a record pace: Amazon's 2009 revenues were up 25 percent over 2008 sales. Despite the continuing slow growth in 2013, the number of online buyers increased by 5 percent to 155 million, and the number of online retail transactions was up 8 percent. Amazon's sales grew to $74 billion in 2013, up an incredible 24 percent from 2012!

Mirroring the history of many technological innovations, such as the telephone, radio, and television, the very rapid growth in e-commerce in the early years created a market bubble in e-commerce stocks. Like all bubbles, the "dot-com" bubble burst (in March 2001). A large number of e-commerce companies failed during this process. Yet for many others, such as Amazon, eBay, Expedia, and Google, the results have been more positive: soaring revenues, fine-tuned business models that produce profits, and rising stock prices. By 2006, e-commerce revenues returned to solid growth, and have continued to be the fastest growing form of retail trade in the United States, Europe, and Asia.

FIGURE 10.1 THE GROWTH OF E-COMMERCE

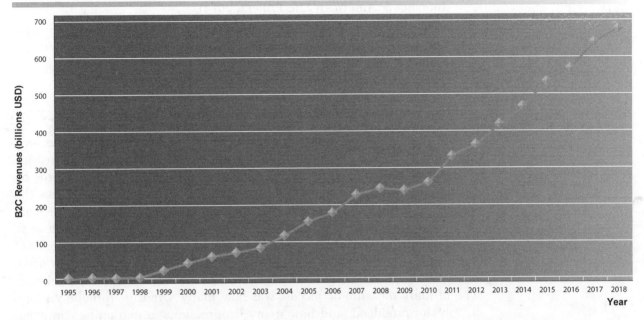

Retail e-commerce revenues grew 15–25 percent per year until the recession of 2008–2009, when they slowed measurably. In 2014, e-commerce revenues are growing again at an estimated 12 percent annually.

- Online consumer sales grew to an estimated $414 billion in 2014, an increase of more than 12 percent over 2013 (including travel services and digital downloads), with 163 million people purchasing online and an additional 39 million shopping and gathering information but not purchasing (eMarketer, 2014a).

- The number of individuals of all ages online in the United States expanded to 251 million in 2014, up from 147 million in 2004. In the world, over 2.8 billion people are now connected to the Internet. Growth in the overall Internet population has spurred growth in e-commerce (Internet World Stats, 2014).

- Approximately 90 million households have broadband access to the Internet in 2014, representing about 74 percent of all households.

- About 167 million Americans now access the Internet using a smartphone such as an iPhone, Android, or BlackBerry. Mobile e-commerce has begun a rapid growth based on apps, ringtones, downloaded entertainment, and location-based services. Mobile commerce will add up to about $84 billion in 2014 (roughly triple 2010's revenue). Amazon sold an estimated $11 billion in retail goods to mobile users in 2013. In a few years, mobile phones will be the most common Internet access device. Currently half of all mobile phone users access the Internet using their phones.

- On an average day, an estimated 212 million adult U.S. Internet users go online. About 152 million send e-mail, 152 million use a search engine, and 117 million get news. Around 124 million use a social network, 62 million do online banking, 73 million watch an online video, and 44 million look for information on Wikipedia (Pew Internet & American Life Project, 2014).

- B2B e-commerce (use of the Internet for business-to-business commerce and collaboration among business partners) expanded to more than $5.7 trillion. Table 10.1 highlights these new e-commerce developments.

THE NEW E-COMMERCE: SOCIAL, MOBILE, LOCAL

One of the biggest changes is the extent to which e-commerce has become more social, mobile, and local. Online marketing consisted largely of creating a corporate Web site, buying display ads on Yahoo, purchasing ad words on Google, and sending e-mails. The workhorse of online marketing was the display ad. It still is. But it's increasingly being replaced by video ads which are far more effective. Display ads from the very beginning of the Internet were based on television ads where brand messages were flashed before millions of users who were not expected to respond immediately, ask questions, or make observations. If the ads did not work, the solution was often to repeat the ad. The primary measure of success was how many "eyeballs" (unique visitors) a Web site produced, and how many "impressions" a marketing campaign generated. (An impression was one ad shown to one person.) Both of these measures were carry overs from the world of television, which measures marketing in terms of audience size and ad views.

From Eyeballs to Conversations

After 2007, all this changed with the rapid growth of Facebook and other social sites, the explosive growth of smartphones beginning with Apple iPhone, and the growing interest in local marketing. What's different about the new world of social-mobile-local e-commerce are the dual and related concepts of "conversations" and "engagement." Marketing in this new period is based on firms engaging in multiple online conversations with their customers, potential customers, and even critics. Your brand is being talked about on the Web and social media (that's the conversation part), and marketing your firm, building and restoring your brands, requires you to locate, identify, and participate in these conversations. Social marketing means all things social like listening, discussing, interacting, empathizing, and engaging. The emphasis in online marketing has shifted from a focus on eyeballs to a focus on participating in customer-oriented conversations. In this sense, social marketing is not simply a "new ad channel," but a collection of technology-based tools for communicating with shoppers.

In the past, firms could tightly control their brand messaging, and lead consumers down a funnel of cues that ended in a purchase. That is not true of social marketing. Consumer purchase decisions are increasingly driven by the conversations, choices, tastes, and opinions of their social network. Social marketing is all about firms participating in and shaping this social process.

From the Desktop to the Smartphone

Traditional online marketing (browser-based, search and display ads, e-mail, and games) still constitutes the majority (65 percent) of all online marketing

TABLE 10.1 THE GROWTH OF E-COMMERCE

BUSINESS TRANSFORMATION

E-commerce remains the fastest growing form of commerce when compared to physical retail stores, services, and entertainment.

Social, mobile, and local commerce have become the fastest growing forms of e-commerce.

The first wave of e-commerce transformed the business world of books, music, and air travel. In the second wave, nine new industries are facing a similar transformation scenario: marketing and advertising, telecommunications, movies, television, jewelry and luxury goods, real estate, online travel, bill payments, and software.

The breadth of e-commerce offerings grows, especially in the services economy of social networking, travel, entertainment, retail apparel, jewelry, appliances, and home furnishings.

The online demographics of shoppers broaden to match that of ordinary shoppers.

Pure e-commerce business models are refined further to achieve higher levels of profitability, whereas traditional retail brands, such as Sears, JCPenney, L.L.Bean, and Walmart, use e-commerce to retain their dominant retail positions.

Small businesses and entrepreneurs continue to flood the e-commerce marketplace, often riding on the infrastructures created by industry giants, such as Amazon, Apple, and Google, and increasingly taking advantage of cloud-based computing resources.

Mobile e-commerce begins to take off in the United States with location-based services and entertainment downloads including e-books, movies, music and television shows.

TECHNOLOGY FOUNDATIONS

Wireless Internet connections (Wi-Fi, WiMax, and 3G/4G smartphones) grow rapidly.

Powerful smartphones, and tablet computers, music, Web surfing, and entertainment as well as voice communication. Podcasting and streaming take off as mediums for distribution of video, radio, and user-generated content.

Mobile devices expand to include Apple Watch, Google Glass, and wearable computers.

The Internet broadband foundation becomes stronger in households and businesses as transmission prices fall. More than 89 million households had broadband cable or DSL access to the Internet in 2014, about 74 percent of all households in the United States (eMarketer, 2014c).

Social networking software and sites such as Facebook, Google +, Twitter, LinkedIn, and others become a major new platform for e-commerce, marketing, and advertising. Facebook hits 1.2 billion users worldwide, and 151 million in the United States (Facebook, 2014).

New Internet-based models of computing, such as smartphone apps, cloud computing, software as a service (SaaS), and Web 2.0 software greatly reduce the cost of e-commerce Web sites.

NEW BUSINESS MODELS EMERGE

More than half the Internet user population have joined an online social network, contribute to social bookmarking sites, create blogs, and share photos. Together these sites create a massive online audience as large as television that is attractive to marketers. In 2014, social networking accounts for an estimated 25 percent of online time.

The traditional advertising industry is disrupted as online advertising grows twice as fast as TV and print advertising; Google, Yahoo, and Facebook display nearly 1 trillion ads a year.

Social sharing e-commerce sites like Uber and Airbnb extend the the market creator business model to new areas.

Newspapers and other traditional media adopt online, interactive models but are losing advertising revenues to the online players despite gaining online readers. The New York Times adopts a paywall for its online edition and succeeds in capturing 850,000 subscribers. Book publishing thrives because of the growth in e-books, and the appeal of traditional books.

Online entertainment business models offering television, movies, music, and games with cooperation among the major copyright owners in Hollywood and New York and with Internet distributors like Apple, Amazon, Google, YouTube, and Facebook.

($51 billion), but it's growing much more slowly than social-mobile-local marketing. The marketing dollars are following customers and shoppers from the PC to mobile devices.

Social, mobile, and local e-commerce are connected. As mobile devices become more powerful, they are more useful for accessing Facebook and other social sites. As mobile devices become more widely adopted, they can be used by customers to find local merchants, and by merchants to alert customers in their neighborhood of special offers.

WHY E-COMMERCE IS DIFFERENT

Why has e-commerce grown so rapidly? The answer lies in the unique nature of the Internet and the Web. Simply put, the Internet and e-commerce technologies are much richer and more powerful than previous technology revolutions like radio, television, and the telephone. Table 10.2 describes the unique features of the Internet and Web as a commercial medium. Let's explore each of these unique features in more detail.

Ubiquity

In traditional commerce, a marketplace is a physical place, such as a retail store, that you visit to transact business. E-commerce is ubiquitous, meaning that it is available just about everywhere, at all times. It makes it possible to shop from your desktop, at home, at work, or even from your car, using smartphones. The result is called a **marketspace**—a marketplace extended beyond traditional boundaries and removed from a temporal and geographic location.

From a consumer point of view, ubiquity reduces **transaction costs**— the costs of participating in a market. To transact business, it is no longer necessary that you spend time or money traveling to a market, and much less mental effort is required to make a purchase.

Global Reach

E-commerce technology permits commercial transactions to cross cultural and national boundaries far more conveniently and cost effectively than is true in traditional commerce. As a result, the potential market size for e-commerce merchants is roughly equal to the size of the world's online population (estimated to be more than 2 billion).

In contrast, most traditional commerce is local or regional—it involves local merchants or national merchants with local outlets. Television, radio stations and newspapers, for instance, are primarily local and regional institutions with limited, but powerful, national networks that can attract a national audience but not easily cross national boundaries to a global audience.

Universal Standards

One strikingly unusual feature of e-commerce technologies is that the technical standards of the Internet and, therefore, the technical standards for conducting e-commerce are universal standards. They are shared by all nations around the world and enable any computer to link with any other computer regardless of the technology platform each is using. In contrast,

TABLE 10.2 EIGHT UNIQUE FEATURES OF E-COMMERCE TECHNOLOGY

E-COMMERCE TECHNOLOGY DIMENSION	BUSINESS SIGNIFICANCE
Ubiquity. Internet/Web technology is available everywhere: at work, at home, and elsewhere via desktop and mobile devices. Mobile devices extend service to local areas and merchants.	The marketplace is extended beyond traditional boundaries and is removed from a temporal and geographic location. "Marketspace" is created; shopping can take place anytime, anywhere. Customer convenience is enhanced, and shopping costs are reduced.
Global Reach. The technology reaches across national boundaries, around the earth.	Commerce is enabled across cultural and national boundaries seamlessly and without modification. The marketspace includes, potentially, billions of consumers and millions of businesses worldwide.
Universal Standards. There is one set of technology standards, namely Internet standards.	With one set of technical standards across the globe, disparate computer systems can easily communicate with each other.
Richness. Video, audio, and text messages are possible.	Video, audio, and text marketing messages are integrated into a single marketing message and consumer experience.
Interactivity. The technology works through interaction with the user.	Consumers are engaged in a dialog that dynamically adjusts the experience to the individual, and makes the consumer a co-participant in the process of delivering goods to the market.
Information Density. The technology reduces information costs and raises quality.	Information processing, storage, and communication costs drop dramatically, whereas currency, accuracy, and timeliness improve greatly. Information becomes plentiful, cheap, and more accurate.
Personalization/Customization. The technology allows personalized messages to be delivered to individuals as well as groups.	Personalization of marketing messages and customization of products and services are based on individual characteristics.
Social Technology. The technology supports content generation and social networking.	New Internet social and business models enable user content creation and distribution, and support social networks.

most traditional commerce technologies differ from one nation to the next. For instance, television and radio standards differ around the world, as does cellular telephone technology.

The universal technical standards of the Internet and e-commerce greatly lower **market entry costs**—the cost merchants must pay simply to bring their goods to market. At the same time, for consumers, universal standards reduce **search costs**—the effort required to find suitable products.

Richness

Information **richness** refers to the complexity and content of a message. Traditional markets, national sales forces, and small retail stores have great richness: They are able to provide personal, face-to-face service using aural and visual cues when making a sale. The richness of traditional markets makes them powerful selling or commercial environments. Prior to the development of the Web, there was a trade-off between richness and reach: The larger the audience reached, the less rich the message. The Web makes it possible to deliver rich messages with text, audio, and video simultaneously to large numbers of people.

Interactivity

Unlike any of the commercial technologies of the twentieth century, with the possible exception of the telephone, e-commerce technologies are interactive, meaning they allow for two-way communication between merchant and consumer. Television, for instance, cannot ask viewers any questions or enter into conversations with them, and it cannot request that customer information be entered into a form. In contrast, all of these activities are possible on an e-commerce Web site. Interactivity allows an online merchant to engage a consumer in ways similar to a face-to-face experience but on a massive, global scale.

Information Density

The Internet and the Web vastly increase **information density**—the total amount and quality of information available to all market participants, consumers, and merchants alike. E-commerce technologies reduce information collection, storage, processing, and communication costs while greatly increasing the currency, accuracy, and timeliness of information.

Information density in e-commerce markets make prices and costs more transparent. **Price transparency** refers to the ease with which consumers can find out the variety of prices in a market; **cost transparency** refers to the ability of consumers to discover the actual costs merchants pay for products.

There are advantages for merchants as well. Online merchants can discover much more about consumers than in the past. This allows merchants to segment the market into groups that are willing to pay different prices and permits the merchants to engage in **price discrimination**—selling the same goods, or nearly the same goods, to different targeted groups at different prices. For instance, an online merchant can discover a consumer's avid interest in expensive, exotic vacations and then pitch high-end vacation plans to that consumer at a premium price, knowing this person is willing to pay extra for such a vacation. At the same time, the online merchant can pitch the same vacation plan at a lower price to a more price-sensitive consumer. Information density also helps merchants differentiate their products in terms of cost, brand, and quality.

Personalization/Customization

E-commerce technologies permit **personalization**: Merchants can target their marketing messages to specific individuals by adjusting the message to a person's clickstream behavior, name, interests, and past purchases. The technology also permits **customization**—changing the delivered product or service based on a user's preferences or prior behavior. Given the interactive nature of e-commerce technology, much information about the consumer can be gathered in the marketplace at the moment of purchase. With the increase in information density, a great deal of information about the consumer's past purchases and behavior can be stored and used by online merchants.

The result is a level of personalization and customization unthinkable with traditional commerce technologies. For instance, you may be able to shape what you see on television by selecting a channel, but you cannot change the content of the channel you have chosen. In contrast, the *Wall Street Journal* Online allows you to select the type of news stories you want to see first and gives you the opportunity to be alerted when certain events happen.

Social Technology: User Content Generation and Social Networking

In contrast to previous technologies, the Internet and e-commerce technologies have evolved to be much more social by allowing users to create and share with their personal friends (and a larger worldwide community) content in the form of text, videos, music, or photos. Using these forms of communication, users are able to create new social networks and strengthen existing ones.

All previous mass media in modern history, including the printing press, use a broadcast model (one-to-many) where content is created in a central location by experts (professional writers, editors, directors, and producers) and audiences are concentrated in huge numbers to consume a standardized product. The new Internet and e-commerce empower users to create and distribute content on a large scale, and permit users to program their own content consumption. The Internet provides a unique many-to-many model of mass communications.

KEY CONCEPTS IN E-COMMERCE: DIGITAL MARKETS AND DIGITAL GOODS IN A GLOBAL MARKETPLACE

The location, timing, and revenue models of business are based in some part on the cost and distribution of information. The Internet has created a digital marketplace where millions of people all over the world are able to exchange massive amounts of information directly, instantly, and for free. As a result, the Internet has changed the way companies conduct business and increased their global reach.

The Internet reduces information asymmetry. An **information asymmetry** exists when one party in a transaction has more information that is important for the transaction than the other party. That information helps determine their relative bargaining power. In digital markets, consumers and suppliers can "see" the prices being charged for goods, and in that sense digital markets are said to be more "transparent" than traditional markets.

For example, before auto retailing sites appeared on the Web, there was a significant information asymmetry between auto dealers and customers. Only the auto dealers knew the manufacturers' prices, and it was difficult for consumers to shop around for the best price. Auto dealers' profit margins depended on this asymmetry of information. Today's consumers have access to a legion of Web sites providing competitive pricing information, and three-fourths of U.S. auto buyers use the Internet to shop around for the best deal. Thus, the Web has reduced the information asymmetry surrounding an auto purchase. The Internet has also helped businesses seeking to purchase from other businesses reduce information asymmetries and locate better prices and terms.

Digital markets are very flexible and efficient because they operate with reduced search and transaction costs, lower **menu costs** (merchants' costs of changing prices), greater price discrimination, and the ability to change prices dynamically based on market conditions. In **dynamic pricing**, the price of a product varies depending on the demand characteristics of the customer or the supply situation of the seller. For instance, online retailers from Amazon to Walmart change prices on many products based on time of day, demand for the product, and users' prior visits to their sites. Using big data analytics, some online firms can adjust prices at the individual level based on behavioral targeting parameters, such as whether the consumer is a price haggler (who will receive a lower price offer) versus a person who accepts offered prices and does not search for lower prices. Prices can also vary by zip code, with higher prices set for poor sections of a community.

These new digital markets may either reduce or increase switching costs, depending on the nature of the product or service being sold, and they may cause some extra delay in gratification. Unlike a physical market, you can't immediately consume a product such as clothing purchased over the Web (although immediate consumption is possible with digital music downloads and other digital products.)

Digital markets provide many opportunities to sell directly to the consumer, bypassing intermediaries, such as distributors or retail outlets. Eliminating intermediaries in the distribution channel can significantly lower purchase transaction costs. To pay for all the steps in a traditional distribution channel, a product may have to be priced as high as 135 percent of its original cost to manufacture.

Figure 10.2 illustrates how much savings result from eliminating each of these layers in the distribution process. By selling directly to consumers or reducing the number of intermediaries, companies are able to raise profits while charging lower prices. The removal of organizations or business process layers responsible for intermediary steps in a value chain is called **disintermediation**.

Disintermediation is affecting the market for services. Airlines and hotels operating their own reservation sites online earn more per ticket because they have eliminated travel agents as intermediaries. Table 10.3 summarizes the differences between digital markets and traditional markets.

Digital Goods

The Internet digital marketplace has greatly expanded sales of **digital goods**. Digital goods are goods that can be delivered over a digital network. Music tracks, video, Hollywood movies, software, newspapers, magazines, and books can all be expressed, stored, delivered, and sold as purely digital products. For the most part, digital goods are "intellectual property" which is defined as "works of the mind." Intellectual property is protected from misappropriation by copyright, patent, and trade secret laws (see Chapter 4).

FIGURE 10.2 THE BENEFITS OF DISINTERMEDIATION TO THE
CONSUMER

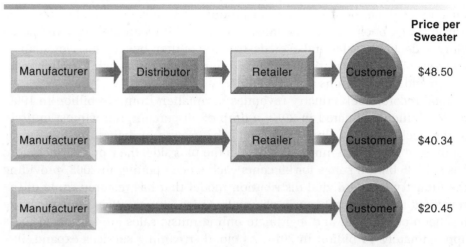

	Price per Sweater
Manufacturer → Distributor → Retailer → Customer	$48.50
Manufacturer → Retailer → Customer	$40.34
Manufacturer → Customer	$20.45

The typical distribution channel has several intermediary layers, each of which adds to the final cost
of a product, such as a sweater. Removing layers lowers the final cost to the customer.

Today, all these products are delivered as digital streams or downloads, while
their physical counterparts decline in sales.

In general, for digital goods, the marginal cost of producing another unit is
about zero (it costs nothing to make a copy of a music file). However, the cost
of producing the original first unit is relatively high—in fact, it is nearly the
total cost of the product because there are few other costs of inventory and
distribution. Costs of delivery over the Internet are very low, marketing costs
often remain the same, and pricing can be highly variable. (On the Internet,
the merchant can change prices as often as desired because of low menu costs.)

TABLE 10.3 DIGITAL MARKETS COMPARED TO TRADITIONAL MARKETS

	DIGITAL MARKETS	TRADITIONAL MARKETS
Information asymmetry	Asymmetry reduced	Asymmetry high
Search costs	Low	High
Transaction costs	Low (sometimes virtually nothing)	High (time, travel)
Delayed gratification	High (or lower in the case of a digital good)	Lower: purchase now
Menu costs	Low	High
Dynamic pricing	Low cost, instant	High cost, delayed
Price discrimination	Low cost, instant	High cost, delayed
Market segmentation	Low cost, moderate precision	High cost, less precision
Switching costs	Higher/lower (depending on product characteristics)	High
Network effects	Strong	Weaker
Disintermediation	More possible/likely	Less possible/unlikely

The impact of the Internet on the market for these kinds of digital goods is nothing short of revolutionary, and we see the results around us every day. Businesses dependent on physical products for sales—such as bookstores, music stores, book publishers, music labels, and film studios—face the possibility of declining sales and even destruction of their businesses. Newspapers and magazines subscriptions to hard copies are declining, while online readership and subscriptions are expanding.

Total record label industry revenues have fallen from $14 billion in 1999, to $7.1 billion estimated in 2013, a drop of 50 percent, due almost entirely to the decline in CD album sales, and the growth of digital music services (both legal and illegal music piracy). On the plus side, the Apple iTunes Store has sold 35 billion songs for 99 cents each since opening in 2003, providing the industry with a digital distribution model that has restored some of the revenues lost to digital music channels. Since iTunes, illegal downloading has been cut in half, and legitimate online music sales are estimated to be approximately $4 billion in 2014. As cloud streaming services expand, illegal downloading will decline further. In that sense, Apple, along with other Internet distributors, saved the record labels from extinction. In 2013, digital music sales accounted for over 64 percent of all music revenues. Yet the music labels make only about 32 cents from a single track download and only .003 cents for a streamed track (with the hope that sales of tracks or CDs will result).

Hollywood has not been similarly disrupted by digital distribution platforms, in part because it is more difficult to download high-quality, pirated copies of full-length movies. To avoid the fate of the music industry, Hollywood has struck lucrative distribution deals with Netflix, Google, Amazon, and Apple, making it convenient to download and pay for high quality movies. Content is still king. Google and Apple may own the pipes and the devices, but without compelling content, they are not very profitable. Nevertheless, these arrangements are not enough to compensate entirely for the loss in DVD sales, which fell 50 percent from 2006 to 2013, although this is changing rapidly as the online distributors like Netflix pay billions for high-quality Hollywood content. In 2014, for the first time, consumers will view more and pay more for Web-based movie downloads, rentals, and streams than for DVDs or related physical products. As with television, the demand for feature-length Hollywood movies appears to be expanding in part because of the growth of smartphones and tablets making it easier to watch movies in more locations. In addition, the surprising resurgence of music videos, led by the Web site VEVO, is attracting millions of younger viewers on smartphones and tablets. Online movies began a growth spurt in 2010 as broadband services spread throughout the country. In 2011, movie viewing doubled in a single year. In 2014, about 73 million Internet users are expected to view movies, about one-third of the adult Internet audience. While this rapid growth will not continue forever, there is little doubt that the Internet is becoming a movie distribution and television channel that rivals cable television, and someday may replace cable television entirely. Table 10.4 describes digital goods and how they differ from traditional physical goods.

TABLE 10.4   HOW THE INTERNET CHANGES THE MARKETS FOR DIGITAL GOODS

	DIGITAL GOODS	TRADITIONAL GOODS
Marginal cost/unit	Zero	Greater than zero , high
Cost of production	High (most of the cost)	Variable
Copying cost	Approximately zero	Greater than zero, high
Distributed delivery cost	Low	High
Inventory cost	Low	High
Marketing cost	Variable	Variable
Pricing	More variable (bundling, random pricing games)	Fixed, based on unit costs

10.2   WHAT ARE THE PRINCIPAL E-COMMERCE BUSINESS AND REVENUE MODELS?

E-commerce has grown from a few advertisements on early Web portals in 1995 to over 9 percent of all retail sales in 2014 (an estimated $470 billion), surpassing the mail order catalog business. E-commerce is a fascinating combination of business models and new information technologies. Let's start with a basic understanding of the types of e-commerce, and then describe e-commerce business and revenue models.

TYPES OF E-COMMERCE

There are many ways to classify electronic commerce transactions—one is by looking at the nature of the participants. The three major electronic commerce categories are business-to-consumer (B2C) e-commerce, business-to-business (B2B) e-commerce, and consumer-to-consumer (C2C) e-commerce.

- **Business-to-consumer (B2C)** electronic commerce involves retailing products and services to individual shoppers. BarnesandNoble.com, which sells books, software, and music to individual consumers, is an example of B2C e-commerce.

- **Business-to-business (B2B)** electronic commerce involves sales of goods and services among businesses. ChemConnect's Web site for buying and selling chemicals and plastics is an example of B2B e-commerce.

- **Consumer-to-consumer (C2C)** electronic commerce involves consumers selling directly to consumers. For example, eBay, the giant Web auction site, enables people to sell their goods to other consumers by auctioning their merchandise off to the highest bidder, or for a fixed price. Craigslist is the most widely used platform used by consumers to buy from and sell directly to others.

Another way of classifying electronic commerce transactions is in terms of the platforms used by participants in a transaction. Until recently, most e-commerce transactions took place using a personal computer connected to the Internet over wired networks. Several wireless mobile alternatives have emerged: smartphones, tablet computers like iPads, dedicated e-readers like the Kindle, and smartphones and small tablet computers using Wi-Fi wireless networks. The use of handheld wireless devices for purchasing goods and services from any location is termed **mobile commerce** or **m-commerce**. Both business-to-business and business-to-consumer e-commerce transactions can take place using m-commerce technology, which we discuss in detail in Section 10.3.

E-COMMERCE BUSINESS MODELS

Changes in the economics of information described earlier have created the conditions for entirely new business models to appear, while destroying older business models. Table 10.5 describes some of the most important Internet business models that have emerged. All, in one way or another, use the Internet to add extra value to existing products and services or to provide the foundation for new products and services.

TABLE 10.5 INTERNET BUSINESS MODELS

CATEGORY	DESCRIPTION	EXAMPLES
E-tailer	Sells physical products directly to consumers or to individual businesses.	Amazon RedEnvelope.com
Transaction broker	Saves users money and time by processing online sales transactions and generating a fee each time a transaction occurs.	ETrade.com Expedia
Market creator	Provides a digital environment where buyers and sellers can meet, search for products, display products, and establish prices for those products. Can serve consumers or B2B e-commerce, generating revenue from transaction fees.	eBay Priceline.com Exostar Elemica
Content provider	Creates revenue by providing digital content, such as news, music, photos, or video, over the Web. The customer may pay to access the content, or revenue may be generated by selling advertising space.	WSJ.com GettyImages.com iTunes.com Games.com
Community provider	Provides an online meeting place where people with similar interests can communicate and find useful information.	Facebook Google+ iVillage, Twitter
Portal	Provides initial point of entry to the Web along with specialized content and other services.	Yahoo Bing Google
Service provider	Provides Web 2.0 applications such as photo sharing, video sharing, and user-generated content as services. Provides other services such as online data storage and backup.	Google Apps Photobucket.com Dropbox

Portal

Portals are gateways to the Web, and are often defined as those sites which users set as their home page. Some definitions of a portal include search engines like Google and Bing even if few make these sites their home page. Portals such as Yahoo, Facebook, MSN, and AOL offer powerful Web search tools as well as an integrated package of content and services, such as news, e-mail, instant messaging, maps, calendars, shopping, music downloads, video streaming, and more, all in one place. Initially, portals were primarily "gateways" to the Internet. Today, however, the portal business model provides a destination site where users start their Web searching and linger to read news, find entertainment, meet other people, and, of course, be exposed to advertising which provides the revenues to support the portal. Portals generate revenue primarily by attracting very large audiences, charging advertisers for display ad placement (similar to traditional newspapers), collecting referral fees for steering customers to other sites, and charging for premium services. In 2014, portals (not including Google or Bing) generated an estimated $14.2 billion in display ad revenues. For comparison, search ads generated $13.8 billion, and video ads generated $4.5 billion. Although there are hundreds of portal/search engine sites, the top four portals (Yahoo, Facebook, MSN, and AOL) gather more than 95 percent of the Internet portal traffic because of their superior brand recognition (comScore, 2014a; eMarketer, 2014b).

E-tailer

Online retail stores, often called **e-tailers**, come in all sizes, from giant Amazon with 2013 revenues of more than $74.5 billion, to tiny local stores that have Web sites. An e-tailer is similar to the typical bricks-and-mortar storefront, except that customers only need to connect to the Internet to check their inventory and place an order. Altogether, online retail will generate about $304 billion in revenues for 2014. The value proposition of e-tailers is to provide convenient, low-cost shopping 24/7, offering large selections and consumer choice. Some e-tailers, such as Walmart.com or Staples.com, referred to as "bricks-and-clicks," are subsidiaries or divisions of existing physical stores and carry the same products. Others, however, operate only in the virtual world, without any ties to physical locations. Amazon, BlueNile.com, and Drugstore.com are examples of this type of e-tailer. Several other variations of e-tailers—such as online versions of direct mail catalogs, online malls, and manufacturer-direct online sales—also exist.

Content Provider

While e-commerce began as a retail product channel, it has increasingly turned into a global content channel. "Content" is defined broadly to include all forms of intellectual property. **Intellectual property** refers to all forms of human expression that can be put into a tangible medium such as text, CDs, or DVDs, or stored on any digital (or other) media, including the Web. Content providers distribute information content—such as digital video, music, photos, text, and artwork—over the Web. The value proposition of online content providers is that consumers can conveniently find a wide range of content online and purchase this content inexpensively, to be played or viewed on multiple computer devices or smartphones.

Providers do not have to be the creators of the content (although sometimes they are, like Disney.com), and are more likely to be Internet-based distributors of content produced and created by others. For example, Apple sells music tracks at its iTunes Store, but it does not create or commission new music.

The phenomenal popularity of the iTunes Store, and Apple's Internet-connected devices like the iPhone, iPod, and iPad, have enabled new forms of digital content delivery from podcasting to mobile streaming. **Podcasting** is a method of publishing audio or video broadcasts via the Internet, allowing subscribing users to download audio or video files onto their personal computers or portable music players. **Streaming** is a publishing method for music and video files that flows a continuous stream of content to a user's device without being stored locally on the device.

Estimates vary, but total online media is the fastest growing segment within e-commerce, growing at an estimated 20 percent annual rate.

Transaction Broker

Sites that process transactions for consumers normally handled in person, by phone, or by mail are transaction brokers. The largest industries using this model are financial services and travel services. The online transaction broker's primary value propositions are savings of money and time, as well as providing an extraordinary inventory of financial products and travel packages, in a single location. Online stock brokers and travel booking services charge fees that are considerably less than traditional versions of these services. Fidelity Financial Services, and Expedia, are the largest online financial and travel service firms based on a transaction broker model.

Market Creator

Market creators build a digital environment in which buyers and sellers can meet, display products, search for products, and establish prices. The value proposition of online market creators is that they provide a platform where sellers can easily display their wares and where purchasers can buy directly from sellers. Online auction markets like eBay and Priceline are good examples of the market creator business model. Another example is Amazon's Merchants platform (and similar programs at eBay) where merchants are allowed to set up stores on Amazon's Web site and sell goods at fixed prices to consumers. This is reminiscent of open air markets where the market creator operates a facility (a town square) where merchants and consumers meet. The so-called **sharing economy**, and Web sites like Uber and Airbnb, is based on the idea of a market creator building a digital platform where supply meets demand, e.g. spare auto capacity finds individuals who want transportation. Uber and Airbnb are clearly not sharing anything (sharing does not involve a transfer of cash), but the moniker is popular nevertheless. Crowdsource funding markets like Kickstarter.com and Mosaic Inc. bring together private equity investors and entrepreneurs in a funding marketplace (Cardwell, 2013). Both are examples of B2B financial market places.

Service Provider

While e-tailers sell products online, service providers offer services online. There's been an explosion in online services. Web 2.0 applications, photo sharing, and online sites for data backup and storage all use a service provider business model. Software is no longer a physical product with a CD in a box, but increasingly software as a service (SaaS) that you subscribe to online rather than purchase from a retailer, or an app that you download. Google has led the way in developing online software service applications such as Google Apps, Google Sites, Gmail, and online data storage services. Salesforce.com is a major provider of cloud-based software for customer management.

Community Provider (Social Networks)

Community providers are sites that create a digital online environment where people with similar interests can transact (buy and sell goods); share interests, photos, videos; communicate with like-minded people; receive interest-related information; and even play out fantasies by adopting online personalities called avatars. The social networking sites Facebook, Google +, Tumblr, LinkedIn, and Twitter; online communities such as iVillage; and hundreds of other smaller, niche sites such as Doostang and Sportsvite all offer users community-building tools and services. Social networking sites have been the fastest growing Web sites in recent years, often doubling their audience size in a year.

E-COMMERCE REVENUE MODELS

A firm's **revenue model** describes how the firm will earn revenue, generate profits, and produce a superior return on investment. Although there are many different e-commerce revenue models that have been developed, most companies rely on one, or some combination, of the following six revenue models: advertising, sales, subscription, free/freemium, transaction fee, and affiliate.

Advertising Revenue Model

In the **advertising revenue model**, a Web site generates revenue by attracting a large audience of visitors who can then be exposed to advertisements. The advertising model is the most widely used revenue model in e-commerce, and arguably, without advertising revenues, the Web would be a vastly different experience from what it is now. Content on the Web—everything from news to videos and opinions—is "free" to visitors because advertisers pay the production and distribution costs in return for the right to expose visitors to ads. Companies will spend an estimated $51 billion on online advertising in 2014, (in the form of a paid message on a Web site, paid search listing, video, app, game, or other online medium, such as instant messaging). About $18 billion of this will involve spending for mobile ads, the fastest growing ad platform. In the last five years, advertisers have increased online spending and cut outlays on traditional channels such as radio and newspapers. In 2014, online advertising will grow at 18 percent and constitute about 28 percent of all advertising in the United States. Television advertising has also expanded along with online advertising revenues and remains the largest advertising platform with about $68 billion in ad revenues in 2014 (eMarketer, 2014b).

Web sites with the largest viewership or that attract a highly specialized, differentiated viewership and are able to retain user attention ("stickiness") are able to charge higher advertising rates. Yahoo, for instance, derives nearly all its revenue from display ads (banner ads), and video ads, and to a lesser extent search engine text ads. Ninety-five percent of Google's revenue derives from advertising, including selling keywords (AdWord), selling ad spaces (AdSense), and selling display ad spaces to advertisers (DoubleClick). Facebook will display one-third of the trillion display ads shown on all sites in 2014. Facebook's users spend an average of over 6 hours a week on the site, far longer than any of the other portal sites.

Sales Revenue Model

In the **sales revenue model**, companies derive revenue by selling goods, information, or services to customers. Companies such as Amazon (which sells books, music, and other products), LLBean.com, and Gap.com, all have sales revenue models. Content providers make money by charging for downloads of entire files such as music tracks (iTunes Store) or books or for downloading music and/or video streams (Hulu.com TV shows). Apple has pioneered and strengthened the acceptance of micropayments. **Micropayment systems** provide content providers with a cost-effective method for processing high volumes of very small monetary transactions (anywhere from 25 cents to $5.00 per transaction). The largest micropayment system on the Web is Apple's iTunes Store, which has more than 500 million credit customers who frequently purchase individual music tracks for 99 cents. There is a Learning Track with more detail on micropayment and other e-commerce payment systems, including Bitcoin.

Subscription Revenue Model

In the **subscription revenue model**, a Web site offering content or services charges a subscription fee for access to some or all of its offerings on an ongoing basis. Content providers often use this revenue model. For instance, the online version of Consumer Reports provides access to premium content, such as detailed ratings, reviews, and recommendations, only to subscribers, who have a choice of paying a $6.95 monthly subscription fee or a $30.00 annual fee. Netflix is one of the most successful subscriber sites with more that 44 million customers by the end of 2013. The New York Times has about 1.1 million online paid subscribers, and the Wall Street Journal about 900,000 in 2014. To be successful, the subscription model requires that the content be perceived as having high added value, differentiated, and not readily available elsewhere nor easily replicated. Companies successfully offering content or services online on a subscription basis include Match.com and eHarmony (dating services), Ancestry.com and Genealogy.com (genealogy research), Microsoft's Xbox Live, and Pandora.com (music).

Free/Freemium Revenue Model

In the **free/freemium revenue model**, firms offer basic services or content for free, while charging a premium for advanced or special features. For example, Google offers free applications but charges for premium services. Pandora, the subscription radio service, offers a free service with limited play time and advertising, and a premium service with unlimited play (see the Interactive Session on Organizations). The Flickr photo-sharing service offers free basic services for sharing photos with friends and family, and also sells a $24.95 "premium" package that provides users unlimited storage, high-definition video storage and playback, and freedom from display advertising. Spotify music service also uses a fremium business model. The idea is to attract very large audiences with free services, and then to convert some of this audience to pay a subscription for premium services. One problem with this model is converting people from being "free loaders" into paying customers. "Free" can be a powerful model for losing money. None of the fremium music streaming sites have earned a profit to date. In fact they are finding the free service with ad revenue is more profitable than the paid subscriber part of their business.

Transaction Fee Revenue Model

In the **transaction fee revenue model**, a company receives a fee for enabling or executing a transaction. For example, eBay provides an online auction marketplace and receives a small transaction fee from a seller if the seller is successful in selling an item. E*Trade, an online stockbroker, receives transaction fees each time it executes a stock transaction on behalf of a customer. The transaction revenue model enjoys wide acceptance in part because the true cost of using the platform is not immediately apparent to the user.

Affiliate Revenue Model

In the **affiliate revenue model**, Web sites (called "affiliate Web sites") send visitors to other Web sites in return for a referral fee or percentage of the revenue from any resulting sales. Referral fees are also referred to as "lead generation fees." For example, MyPoints makes money by connecting companies to potential customers by offering special deals to its members. When members take advantage of an offer and make a purchase, they earn "points" they can redeem for free products and services, and MyPoints receives a referral fee. Community feedback sites such as Epinions and Yelp receive much of their revenue from steering potential customers to Web sites where they make a purchase. Amazon uses affiliates who steer business to the Amazon Web site by placing the Amazon logo on their blogs. Personal blogs often contain display ads as a part of affiliate programs. Some bloggers are paid directly by manufacturers, or receive free products, for speaking highly of products and providing links to sales channels. Commercial bloggers are in essence affiliates paid to send customers to retail sites.

10.3   HOW HAS E-COMMERCE TRANSFORMED MARKETING?

While e-commerce and the Internet have changed entire industries and enabled new business models, no industry has been more affected than marketing and marketing communications.

INTERACTIVE SESSION: ORGANIZATIONS

CAN PANDORA SUCCEED WITH FREEMIUM?

Pandora is the Internet's most successful subscription radio service. In May 2014, Pandora had 77 million registered users. Pandora accounts for over 9 percent of total U.S. radio listening hours. The music is delivered to users from a cloud server, and is not stored on user devices.

It's easy to see why Pandora is so popular. Users are able to hear only the music they like. Each user selects a genre of music based on a favorite musician or vocalist, and a computer algorithm puts together a "personal radio station" that plays the music of the selected artist plus closely related music by different artists. The algorithm uses more than 450 factors to classify songs, such as the tempo and number of vocalists. These classifications, in conjunction with other signals from users, help Pandora's algorithms select the next song to play. Users do not control what they hear.

People love Pandora, but the question is whether this popularity can be translated into profits. How can Pandora compete with other online music subscription services and online stations that have been making music available for free, sometimes without advertising? "Free" illegally downloaded music has also been a significant factor, as has been iTunes, charging 99 cents per song with no ad support. At the time of Pandora's founding (2005), iTunes was already a roaring success.

Pandora's first business model was to give away 10 hours of free music and then ask subscribers to pay $36 per month for a year once they used up their 10 free hours. Result: 100,000 people listened to their 10 hours for free and then refused to pay for the annual service. Facing financial collapse, in November 2005 Pandora introduced an ad-supported option. In 2006, Pandora added a "Buy" button to each song being played and struck deals with Amazon, iTunes, and other online retail sites. Pandora now gets an affiliate fee for directing listeners to sites where users can buy the music. In 2008, Pandora added an iPhone app to allow users to sign up from their smartphones and listen all day if they wanted. Today, 70 percent of Pandora's advertising revenue comes from mobile.

In late 2009 the company launched Pandora One, a premium service that offered no advertising, higher quality streaming music, a desktop app, and fewer usage limits. The service costs $4.99 per month. A very small percentage of Pandora listeners have opted to pay for music subscriptions, with the vast majority opting for the free service with ads. In fiscal 2013 Pandora's total revenue was $427.1 million, of which $375.2 million (88 percent) came from advertising.

Pandora has been touted as a leading example of the "freemium" revenue business model, in which a business gives away some services for free and relies on a small percentage of customers to pay for premium versions of the same service. If a market is very large, getting just 1 percent of that market to pay could be very lucrative—under certain circumstances. Although freemium is an efficient way of amassing a large group of potential customers, companies, including Pandora, have found that it challenging to convert people enjoying the free service into customers willing to pay. A freemium model works best when a business incurs very low marginal cost, approaching zero, for each free user of its services, when a business can be supported by the percentage of customers willing to pay, and when there are other revenues like advertising fees that can make up for shortfalls in subscriber revenues.

In Pandora's case, it appears that revenues will continue to come overwhelmingly from advertising, and management is not worried. For the past few years, management has considered ads as having much more revenue-generating potential than paid subscriptions and is not pushing the ad-free service. By continually refining its algorithms, Pandora is able to increase user listening hours substantially. The more time people spend with Pandora, the more opportunities there are for Pandora to deliver ads and generate ad revenue. The average Pandora user listens to 19 hours of music per month.

Pandora is now intensively mining the data collected about its users for clues about the kinds of ads most likely to engage them. Pandora collects data about listener preferences from direct feedback such as likes and dislikes (indicated by thumbs up or down on the Pandora site) and "skip this song" requests, as well as data about which device people are using to listen to Pandora music, such as mobile phones or desktop computers. Pandora uses these inputs to select songs people will want to stick around for, and listen to. Pandora has honed its algorithms so they can analyze billions more signals from users generated over billions of listening minutes per month. Pandora is also trying to figure out when people are listening in groups such as car pools and dinner parties, which might justify Pandora charging higher prices for songs heard by groups rather than single individuals.

The company is looking for correlations between users' listening habits and the kinds of ads that would appeal to these users. People's music, movie, or book choices may provide insight into their political belief, religious faith, or other personal issues. Pandora has developed a political ad-targeting system that has been used in presidential, congressional, and gubernatorial campaigns that can use users' song preferences to predict their political party of choice.

As impressive as these numbers are, Pandora (along with other streaming subscription services) is still struggling to show a profit. There are infrastructure costs and royalties to pay for content from the music labels. Pandora's royalty rates are less flexible than those of its competitor Spotify, which signed individual song royalty agreements with each record label. Pandora could be paying even higher rates when its current royalty contracts expire in 2015. About 61 percent of Pandora's revenue is currently allocated to paying royalties. Advertising can only be leveraged so far, because users who opt for free ad-supported services generally do not tolerate heavy ad loads. Apple launched its iTunes radio service for the Fall of 2013 that will compete directly with Pandora. ITunes radio has both free ad-supported options, and a subscription service for $25 per year, undercutting Pandora's annual subscription fee of $60. Can Pandora's business model succeed?

Sources: Michael Hickins, "Pandora's Improved Algorithms Yield More Listening Hours," *Wall Street Journal*, April 1, 2014; Pandora, "Pandora Announces May 2014 Audience Metrics," June 4, 2014; Natasha Singer, " Listen to Pandora, and It Listens Back," *New York Times*, January 4, 2014; Ben Sisario, "A Stream of Music, Not Revenue," *New York Times*, December 12, 2013; Glenn Peoples, "Pandora's Business Model: Is It Sustainable?" Billboard.com, August 7, 2013; Kylie Bylin, "Can Pandora Find A Business Model That Works?" Hypebot.com, accessed August 25, 2013; Paul Verna, "Internet Radio: Marketers Move In," eMarketer, February 2013; Jim Edwards, "This Crucial Detail In Spotify's Business Model Could Kill Pandora," Business Insider, July 11, 2012; and Sarah E. Needleman and Angus Loten, "When Freemium Fails," *Wall Street Journal*, August 22, 2012.

CASE STUDY QUESTIONS

1. Analyze Pandora using the value chain and competitive forces models. What competitive forces does the company have to deal with? What is its customer value proposition?

2. Explain how Pandora's "freemium" business model works. How does the company generate revenue?

3. Can Pandora succeed with its "freemium" model? Why or why not? What people, organization, and technology factors affect its success with this business model?

TABLE 10.6 ONLINE MARKETING AND ADVERTISING FORMATS (BILLIONS)

MARKETING FORMAT	2013 REVENUE	DESCRIPTION
Search engine	$22.8	Text ads targeted at precisely what the customer is looking for at the moment of shopping and purchasing. Sales oriented.
Display ads	$22.3	Banner ads (pop-ups and leave-behinds) with interactive features; increasingly behaviorally targeted to individual Web activity. Brand development and sales. Includes blog display ads.
Video	$6	Fastest-growing format, engaging and entertaining; behaviorally targeted, interactive. Branding and sales.
Classified	$2.9	Job, real estate, and services ads; interactive, rich media, and personalized to user searches. Sales and branding.
Rich media	$3.1	Animations, games, and puzzles. Interactive, targeted, and entertaining. Branding orientation.
Lead generation	$2	Marketing firms that gather sales and marketing leads online, and then sell them to online marketers for a variety of campaign types. Sales or branding orientation.
Sponsorships	$1.9	Online games, puzzles, contests, and coupon sites sponsored by firms to promote products. Sales orientation.
E-mail	$.25	Effective, targeted marketing tool with interactive and rich media potential. Sales oriented.

The Internet provides marketers with new ways of identifying and communicating with millions of potential customers at costs far lower than traditional media, including search engine marketing, data mining, recommender systems, and targeted e-mail. The Internet enables **long tail marketing**. Before the Internet, reaching a large audience was very expensive, and marketers had to focus on attracting the largest number of consumers with popular hit products, whether music, Hollywood movies, books, or cars. In contrast, the Internet allows marketers to inexpensively find potential customers for products where demand is very low. For instance, the Internet makes it possible to sell independent music profitably to very small audiences. There's always some demand for almost any product. Put a string of such long tail sales together and you have a profitable business.

The Internet also provides new ways—often instantaneous and spontaneous—to gather information from customers, adjust product offerings, and increase customer value. Table 10.6 describes the leading marketing and advertising formats used in e-commerce.

BEHAVIORAL TARGETING

Many e-commerce marketing firms use **behavioral targeting** techniques to increase the effectiveness of banners, rich media, and video ads. Behavioral targeting refers to tracking the clickstreams (history of clicking behavior) of individuals on thousands of Web sites for the purpose of understanding their interests and intentions, and exposing them to advertisements that are uniquely suited to their behavior. Proponents believe this more precise understanding of the customer leads to more efficient marketing (the firm pays for ads only to those shoppers who are most interested in their products) and larger sales and revenues. Unfortunately, behavioral targeting of millions of Web users also leads to the invasion of personal privacy without user consent. When consumers lose trust in their Web experience, they tend not to purchase anything. There is a growing backlash against the aggressive uses of personal information as consumers seek out safer havens for purchasing and messaging. SnapChat offers disappearing messages, and even Facebook has retreated by making its default for new posts to be "for friends only." (Wood, 2014).

Popular Web sites have hundreds of beacon programs on their home pages which collect data on visitors behavior, and report that behavior to their databases. There the information is often sold to data brokers, firms who collect billions of data elements on every U.S. consumer and household, frequently combining online with off-line purchase information. The data brokers in turn sell this information to advertisers who want to place ads on Web pages. A recent Federal Trade Commission report on nine data brokers found that one data broker's database had information on 1.4 billion consumer transactions and over 700 billion aggregated data elements. Another data broker had 3,000 data measures for nearly every consumer in the U.S. (FTC, 2014).

Behavioral targeting takes place at two levels: at individual Web sites or from within apps, and on various advertising networks that track users across thousands of Web sites. All Web sites collect data on visitor browser activity and store it in a database. They have tools to record the site that users visited prior to coming to the Web site, where these users go when they leave that site, the type of operating system they use, browser information, and even some location data. They also record the specific pages visited on the particular site, the time spent on each page of the site, the types of pages visited, and what the visitors purchased (see Figure 10.3). Firms analyze this information about customer interests and behavior to develop precise profiles of existing and potential customers. In addition, most major Web sites have hundreds of tracking programs on their home pages, which track your clickstream behavior across the Web by following you from site to site and re-target ads to you by showing you the same ads on different sites. The leading online advertising networks are Google's DoubleClick, Yahoo's RightMedia, and AOL's Ad Network. Ad networks represent publishers who have space to sell, and advertisers who want to market online. The lubricant of this trade is information on millions of Web shoppers, which helps advertisers target their ads to precisely the groups and individuals they desire.

This information enables firms to understand how well their Web site is working, create unique personalized Web pages that display content or ads for products or services of special interest to each user, improve the customer's experience, and create additional value through a better understanding of

FIGURE 10.3 WEB SITE VISITOR TRACKING

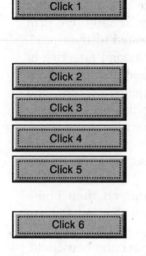

The shopper clicks on the home page. The store can tell that the shopper arrived from the Yahoo! portal at 2:30 PM (which might help determine staffing for customer service centers) and how long she lingered on the home page (which might indicate trouble navigating the site). Tracking beacons load cookies on the shopper's browser to follow her across the Web.

The shopper clicks on blouses, clicks to select a woman's white blouse, then clicks to view the same item in pink. The shopper clicks to select this item in a size 10 in pink and clicks to place it in her shopping cart. This information can help the store determine which sizes and colors are most popular. If the visitor moves to a different site, ads for pink blouses will appear from the same or different vendor.

From the shopping cart page, the shopper clicks to close the browser to leave the Web site without purchasing the blouse. This action could indicate the shopper changed her mind or that she had a problem with the Web site's checkout and payment process. Such behavior might signal that the Web site was not well designed.

E-commerce Web sites and advertising platforms like Google's DoubleClick have tools to track a shopper's every step through an online store and then across the Web as shoppers move from site to site. Close examination of customer behavior at a Web site selling women's clothing shows what the store might learn at each step and what actions it could take to increase sales.

the shopper (see Figure 10.4). By using personalization technology to modify the Web pages presented to each customer, marketers achieve some of the benefits of using individual salespeople at dramatically lower costs. For instance, General Motors will show a Chevrolet banner ad to women emphasizing safety and utility, while men will receive different ads emphasizing power and ruggedness.

What if you are a large national advertising company with many different clients trying to reach millions of consumers? What if you were a large global manufacturer trying to reach potential consumers for your products? With millions of Web sites, working with each one would be impractical. Advertising networks solve this problem by creating a network of several thousand of the most popular Web sites visited by millions of people, tracking the behavior of these users across the entire network, building profiles of each user, and then selling these profiles to advertisers. Popular Web sites download dozens of Web tracking cookies, bugs, and beacons, which report user online behavior to remote servers without the users' knowledge. Looking for young, single consumers, with college degrees, living in the Northeast, in the 18–34 age range who are interested in purchasing a European car? Not a problem. Advertising networks can identify and deliver hundreds of thousands of people who fit this profile and expose them to ads for European cars as they move from one Web site to another. Estimates vary, but behaviorally targeted ads are generally 10 times more likely to produce a consumer response than a randomly chosen banner or video ad (see Figure 10.5). So-called advertising exchanges use this same technology to auction access

FIGURE 10.4 WEB SITE PERSONALIZATION

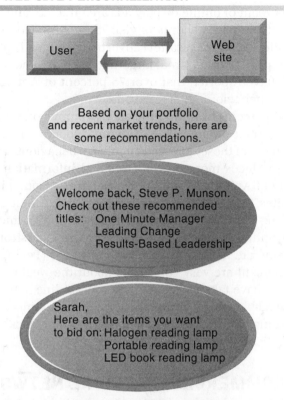

Firms can create unique personalized Web pages that display content or ads for products or services of special interest to individual users, improving the customer experience and creating additional value.

FIGURE 10.5 HOW AN ADVERTISING NETWORK SUCH AS DOUBLECLICK WORKS

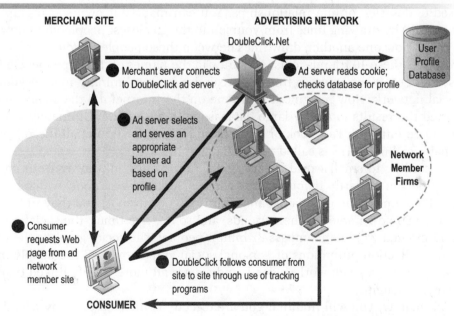

Advertising networks and their use of tracking programs have become controversial among privacy advocates because of their ability to track individual consumers across the Internet.

to people with very specific profiles to advertisers in a few milliseconds. In 2014, about 25 percent of online display ads are targeted, and the rest depend on the context of the pages shoppers visit, the estimated demographics of visitors, or so-called "blast and scatter" advertising, which is placed randomly on any available page with minimal targeting, such as time of day or season. Several surveys have reported that over 75 percent of American consumers do not approve of behaviorally targeted ads.

Two-thirds (68 percent) of Internet users disapprove of search engines and Web sites tracking their online behavior in order to aim targeted ads at them. Twenty-eight percent of those surveyed approve of behavioral targeting because they believe it produces more relevant ads and information (Pew Internet, 2012). A majority of Americans want a "Do Not Track" option in browsers that will stop Web sites from collecting information about their online behavior (Hoofnagle, et. al., 2012). According to a recent survey, Americans' privacy concerns about online invasions of privacy are growing stronger, leading to people taking concrete actions to protect themselves (Pew Research Center, 2013). Over 50 percent are very concerned about the wealth of personal data online; 86 percent have taken steps to mask their online behavior; 25 percent of Web users use ad-blocking software. Next to hackers, Americans try to avoid advertisers pursuing them while online, and 64 percent block cookies to make tracking more difficult.

SOCIAL E-COMMERCE AND SOCIAL NETWORK MARKETING

Social e-commerce is commerce based on the idea of the digital **social graph**. The digital social graph is a mapping of all significant online social relation-ships. The social graph is synonymous with the idea of a "social network" used to describe offline relationships. You can map your own social graph (network) by drawing lines from yourself to the 10 closest people you know. If they know one another, draw lines between these people. If you are ambi-tious, ask these 10 friends to list and draw in the names of the 10 people clos-est to them. What emerges from this exercise is a preliminary map of your social network. Now imagine if everyone on the Internet did the same, and posted the results to a very large database with a Web site. Ultimately, you would end up with Facebook or a site like it. The collection of all these per-sonal social networks is called "the social graph."

According to small world theory, you are only six links away from any other person on earth. If you entered your personal address book, which has, say, 100 names in it, on to a list and sent it to your friends, and they in turn entered 50 new names of their friends, and so on, five times, the social net-work created would encompass 31 billion people! The social graph is there-fore a collection of millions of personal social graphs (and all the people in them). So, it's a small world indeed, and we are all more closely linked than we ever thought.

Ultimately, you will find that you are directly connected to many friends and relatives, and indirectly connected to an even larger universe of indi-rect friends and relatives (your distant second and third cousins, and their

TABLE 10.7 FEATURES OF SOCIAL COMMERCE

SOCIAL COMMERCE FEATURE	DESCRIPTION
Newsfeed	A stream of notifications from friends, and advertisers, that social users find on their home pages.
Timelines	A stream of photos and events in the past that create a personal history for users, one that can be shared with friends.
Social sign-on	Web sites allow users to sign into their sites through their social network pages on Facebook or another social site. This allows Web sites to receive valuable social profile information from Facebook and use it in their own marketing efforts.
Collaborative shopping	Creating an environment where consumers can share their shopping experiences with one another by viewing products, chatting, or texting. Friends can chat online about brands, products, and services.
Network notification	Creating an environment where consumers can share their approval (or disapproval) of products, services, or content, or share their geo-location, perhaps a restaurant or club, with friends. Facebook's ubiquitous Like button is an example. Twitter's tweets and followers are another example.
Social search (recommendations)	Enabling an environment where consumers can ask their friends for advice on purchases of products, services, and content. While Google can help you find things, social search can help you evaluate the quality of things by listening to the evaluations of your friends, or their friends. For instance, Amazon's social recommender system can use your Facebook social profile to recommend products.

friends). Theoretically, it takes six links for any one person to find another person anywhere on earth.

If you understand the inter-connectedness of people, you will see just how important this concept is to e-commerce: The products and services you buy will influence the decisions of your friends, and their decisions will in turn influence you. If you are a marketer trying to build and strengthen a brand, the implication is clear: Take advantage of the fact that people are enmeshed in social networks, share interests and values, and communicate and influence one another. As a marketer, your target audience is not a million isolated people watching a TV show, but the social network of people who watch the show, and the viewers' personal networks. Table 10.7 describes the features of social commerce that are driving its growth.

In 2014, one of the fastest growing media for branding and marketing is social media. In 2014, companies will spend $6.7 billion using social networks like Facebook to reach millions of consumers who spend hours a day on the Facebook site. Facebook accounts for 90 percent of all social marketing in the Untied States. Expenditures for social media marketing are much smaller than television, magazines, and even newspapers, but this will change in the future. Social networks in the offline world are collections of people who voluntarily communicate with one another over an extended period of time. Online social networks, such as Facebook, LinkedIn, Twitter, Tumblr, and Google+, along with other sites with social components, are Web sites that enable users to communicate with one another, form group and individual relationships, and share interests, values, and ideas. Individuals establish online profiles with text and photos, creating an online profile of how they want others to see them, and then invite their friends to link to their profile. The network grows by word of mouth and through e-mail links. One of the most ubiquitous graphical elements on Web sites is Facebook's Like button, which allows users to tell their friends they like a product, service, or content. Facebook processes around 50 million Likes a day, or 1.5 billion a year.

While Facebook, with 137 million U.S. monthly visitors, receives most of the public attention given to social networking, the other top four social sites are also growing, but at slower rates than in the past. Facebook user growth has slowed in the United States. LinkedIn growth slowed in 2013 to 40 percent, and it has 48 million visitors a month in 2014. Twitter grew only 11 percent in 2013 to reach 37 million; the social blogging site Tumblr reached 23 million people a month; and Pinterest hit the top 50 Web sites with 26 million. MySpace, in contrast, has been shrinking for years, and attracted only 5.4 million visitors monthly. According to ComScore, about 30 percent of the total time spent online in the United States was spent on social network sites, and it is the most common online activity. (ComScore, 2014). The fastest growing smartphone applications are social network apps: nearly half of smartphone users visit social sites daily. More than 58 percent of all visits to Facebook in 2014 come from smartphones.

At **social shopping** sites like Pinterest, Kaboodle, ThisNext, and Stylehive, you can swap shopping ideas with friends. Facebook offers the Like button and Google the +1 button to let your friends know you admire something, and in some cases, purchased something online. Online communities are also ideal venues to employ viral marketing techniques. Online viral marketing is like traditional word-of-mouth marketing except that the word can spread across an online community at the speed of light, and go much further geographically than a small network of friends.

The Wisdom of Crowds

Creating sites where thousands, even millions, of people can interact offers business firms new ways to market and advertise, and to discover who likes (or hates) their products. In a phenomenon called "**the wisdom of crowds**," some argue that large numbers of people can make better decisions about a wide range of topics or products than a single person or even a small committee of experts.

Obviously this is not always the case, but it can happen in interesting ways. In marketing, the wisdom of crowds concept suggests that firms should consult with thousands of their customers first as a way of establishing a relationship with them, and second, to better understand how their products and services are used and appreciated (or rejected). Actively soliciting the comments of your customers builds trust and sends the message to your customers that you care what they are thinking, and that you need their advice.

Beyond merely soliciting advice, firms can be actively helped in solving some business problems using what is called **crowdsourcing**. For instance, in 2006, Netflix announced a contest in which it offered to pay $1 million to the person or team who comes up with a method for improving by 10 percent Netflix's prediction of what movies customers would like as measured against their actual choices. By 2009, Netflix received 44,014 entries from 5,169 teams in 186 countries. The winning team improved a key part of Netflix's business: a recommender system that recommends to its customers what new movies to order based on their personal past movie choices and the choices of millions of other customers who are like them. In 2012, BMW launched a crowdsourcing project to enlist the aid of customers in designing an urban vehicle for 2025. Kickstarter.com is arguably one of the most famous e-commerce crowdfunding sites where visitors invest in start-up companies. Other examples include Caterpillar working with customers to design better machinery, and Pepsico using Super Bowl 2013 viewers to build an online video (Boulton, 2013).

Firms can also use the wisdom of crowds in the form of prediction markets. **Prediction Markets** are established as peer-to-peer betting markets where participants make bets on specific outcomes of, say, quarterly sales of a new product, designs for new products, or political elections. The world's largest commercial prediction market is Betfair, where you bet for or against specific outcomes on football games, horse races, and whether or not the Dow Jones will go up or down in a single day. Iowa Electronic Markets (IEM) is an academic market focused on elections. You can place bets on the outcome of local and national elections. In the United States, the largest prediction market is Intrade.com, where users can buy or sell shares in predictions.

Marketing via social media is still in its early stages, and companies are experimenting in hopes of finding a winning formula. Social interactions and customer sentiment are not always easy to manage, presenting new challenges for companies eager to protect their brands. The chapter-ending case study provides specific examples of companies' social marketing efforts using Facebook and Twitter.

10.4 HOW HAS E-COMMERCE AFFECTED BUSINESS-TO-BUSINESS TRANSACTIONS?

The trade between business firms (business-to-business commerce or B2B) represents a huge marketplace. The total amount of B2B trade in the United States in 2014 is estimated to be about $13.8 trillion, with B2B e-commerce (online B2B) contributing about $5.7 trillion of that amount (U.S. Census Bureau, 2013; authors' estimates). By 2017, B2B e-commerce is expected to grow to about $7.8 trillion in the United States. The process of conducting trade among business firms is complex and requires significant human intervention, and therefore, it consumes significant resources. Some firms estimate that each corporate purchase order for support products costs them, on average, at least $100 in administrative overhead. Administrative overhead includes processing paper, approving purchase decisions, spending time using the telephone and fax machines to search for products and arrange for purchases, arranging for shipping, and receiving the goods. Across the economy, this adds up to trillions of dollars annually being spent for procurement processes that could potentially be automated. If even just a portion of inter-firm trade were automated, and parts of the entire procurement process assisted by the Internet, literally trillions of dollars might be released for more productive uses, consumer prices potentially would fall, productivity would increase, and the economic wealth of the nation would expand. This is the promise of B2B e-commerce. The challenge of B2B e-commerce is changing existing patterns and systems of procurement, and designing and implementing new Internet-based B2B solutions.

ELECTRONIC DATA INTERCHANGE (EDI)

Business-to-business e-commerce refers to the commercial transactions that occur among business firms. Increasingly, these transactions are flowing through a variety of different Internet-enabled mechanisms. About 80 percent of online B2B e-commerce is still based on proprietary systems for **electronic data interchange (EDI)**. Electronic data interchange enables the computer-to-computer exchange between two organizations of standard transactions such as invoices, bills of lading, shipment schedules, or purchase orders. Transactions are automatically transmitted from one information system to another through a network, eliminating the printing and handling of paper at one end and the inputting of data at the other. Each major industry in the United States and much of the rest of the world has EDI standards that define the structure and information fields of electronic documents for that industry.

EDI originally automated the exchange of documents such as purchase orders, invoices, and shipping notices. Although many companies still use EDI for document automation, firms engaged in just-in-time inventory replenishment and continuous production use EDI as a system for continuous replenishment. Suppliers have online access to selected parts of the purchasing firm's production and delivery schedules and automatically ship materials and goods to meet prespecified targets without intervention by firm purchasing agents (see Figure 10.6).

FIGURE 10.6 ELECTRONIC DATA INTERCHANGE (EDI)

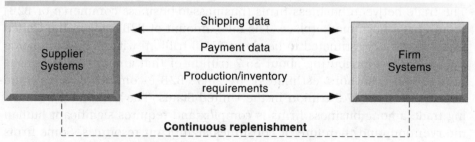

Companies use EDI to automate transactions for B2B e-commerce and continuous inventory replenishment. Suppliers can automatically send data about shipments to purchasing firms. The purchasing firms can use EDI to provide production and inventory requirements and payment data to suppliers.

Although many organizations still use private networks for EDI, they are increasingly Web-enabled because Internet technology provides a much more flexible and low-cost platform for linking to other firms. Businesses are able to extend digital technology to a wider range of activities and broaden their circle of trading partners.

Take procurement, for example. Procurement involves not only purchasing goods and materials but also sourcing, negotiating with suppliers, paying for goods, and making delivery arrangements. Businesses can now use the Internet to locate the lowest-cost supplier, search online catalogs of supplier products, negotiate with suppliers, place orders, make payments, and arrange transportation. They are not limited to partners linked by traditional EDI networks.

NEW WAYS OF B2B BUYING AND SELLING

The Internet and Web technology enable businesses to create new electronic storefronts for selling to other businesses with multimedia graphic displays and interactive features similar to those for B2C commerce. Alternatively, businesses can use Internet technology to create extranets or electronic marketplaces for linking to other businesses for purchase and sale transactions.

Private industrial networks typically consist of a large firm using a secure Web site to link to its suppliers and other key business partners (see Figure 10.7). The network is owned by the buyer, and it permits the firm and designated suppliers, distributors, and other business partners to share

FIGURE 10.7 A PRIVATE INDUSTRIAL NETWORK

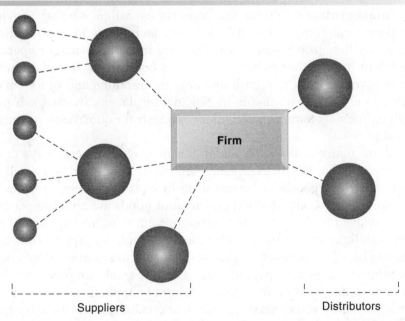

A private industrial network, also known as a private exchange, links a firm to its suppliers, distributors, and other key business partners for efficient supply chain management and other collaborative commerce activities.

FIGURE 10.8 A NET MARKETPLACE

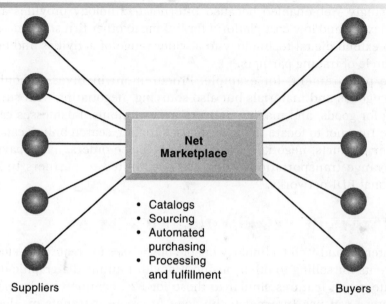

Suppliers

Buyers

Net marketplaces are online marketplaces where multiple buyers can purchase from multiple sellers.

product design and development, marketing, production scheduling, inventory management, and unstructured communication, including graphics and e-mail. Another term for a private industrial network is a **private exchange**.

An example is VW Group Supply, which links the Volkswagen Group and its suppliers. VW Group Supply handles 90 percent of all global purchasing for Volkswagen, including all automotive and parts components.

Net marketplaces, which are sometimes called e-hubs, provide a single, digital marketplace based on Internet technology for many different buyers and sellers (see Figure 10.8). They are industry-owned or operate as independent intermediaries between buyers and sellers. Net marketplaces generate revenue from purchase and sale transactions and other services provided to clients. Participants in Net marketplaces can establish prices through online negotiations, auctions, or requests for quotations, or they can use fixed prices.

There are many different types of Net marketplaces and ways of classifying them. Some Net marketplaces sell direct goods and some sell indirect goods. **Direct goods** are goods used in a production process, such as sheet steel for auto body production. **Indirect goods** are all other goods not directly involved in the production process, such as office supplies or products for maintenance and repair. Some Net marketplaces support contractual purchasing based on long-term relationships with designated suppliers, and others support short-term spot purchasing, where goods are purchased based on immediate needs, often from many different suppliers.

Some Net marketplaces serve vertical markets for specific industries, such as automobiles, telecommunications, or machine tools, whereas others serve horizontal markets for goods and services that can be found in many different industries, such as office equipment or transportation.

Exostar is an example of an industry-owned Net marketplace, focusing on long-term contract purchasing relationships and on providing common networks and computing platforms for reducing supply chain inefficiencies. This aerospace and defense industry-sponsored Net marketplace was founded jointly by BAE Systems, Boeing, Lockheed Martin, Raytheon, and Rolls-Royce PLC to connect these companies to their suppliers and facilitate collaboration. More than 70,000 trading partners in the commercial, military, and government sectors use Exostar's sourcing, e-procurement, and collaboration tools for both direct and indirect goods.

Exchanges are independently owned third-party Net marketplaces that connect thousands of suppliers and buyers for spot purchasing. Many exchanges provide vertical markets for a single industry, such as food, electronics, or industrial equipment, and they primarily deal with direct inputs. For example, Go2Paper enables a spot market for paper, board, and craft among buyers and sellers in the paper industries from over 75 countries.

Exchanges proliferated during the early years of e-commerce but many have failed. Suppliers were reluctant to participate because the exchanges encouraged competitive bidding that drove prices down and did not offer any long-term relationships with buyers or services to make lowering prices worthwhile. Many essential direct purchases are not conducted on a spot basis because they require contracts and consideration of issues such as delivery timing, customization, and quality of products.

10.5 WHAT IS THE ROLE OF M-COMMERCE IN BUSINESS AND WHAT ARE THE MOST IMPORTANT M-COMMERCE APPLICATIONS?

Walk down the street in any major metropolitan area and count how many people are pecking away at their iPhones, Samsungs or BlackBerrys. Ride the trains, fly the planes, and you'll see your fellow travelers reading an online newspaper, watching a video on their phone, or reading a novel on their Kindle. In five years, the majority of Internet users in the United States will rely on mobile devices as their primary device for accessing the Internet. As the mobile audience expands in leaps and bounds, mobile advertising and m-commerce have taken off.

In 2014, m-commerce constitute about 19 percent of all e-commerce, with about $57 billion in annual revenues generated by retail goods and services, apps, advertising, music, videos, ring tones, applications, movies, television, and location-based services like local restaurant locators and traffic updates. However, m-commerce is the fastest growing form of e-commerce, with some areas expanding at a rate of 50 percent or more per year, and is estimated to grow to $132 billion in 2018 (see Figure 10.9) (eMarketer, 2014d). It is becoming especially popular in the online travel industry, as discussed in the Interactive Session on Technology.

The main areas of growth in mobile e-commerce are retail sales at the top Mobile 400 companies, including Amazon ($4 billion) and Apple (about $1.1 billion); and sales of digital content music, TV shows and movies (about

INTERACTIVE SESSION: TECHNOLOGY

SOCIAL MEDIA ANALYTICS IN INDIAN POLITICS

India, the world's largest democracy, holds Lok Sabha (or parliamentary) elections every five years. With over 500 constituencies going to vote, it is fair to say that this is the most grandiose event in which the entire country participates. What made the General Elections of 2014 more special was the fact that out of the 800 million eligible voters, over a 100 million were first-time voters and 23 million were between 18 and 19 years of age. India, which has the second-largest population in the world, has the third-largest Internet-user base of 238 million people. Contrary to the popular belief that Internet usage is restricted to the Indian metros, the use of social media is rapidly spreading beyond the top eight cities. One-third of the users now reside in towns having a population of under five lakh people, while 25% of them live in cities with a population of less than two lakh people. This has had widespread consequences for the political campaign strategies during the General Elections of 2014.

Narendra Modi, the prime ministerial candidate for the National Democratic Alliance (NDA) led by the Bharatiya Janata Party (BJP), was one of the first political leaders to use Twitter in order to reach the masses. Modi joined Twitter in January 2009, and all the other BJP leaders were also encouraged to interact with voters through this social media platform. However, there was a need to professionally manage all the social media content, and to do this, the party appointed Arvind Gupta as its national technology head.

Prior to the elections, a centralized IT cell was formed in New Delhi comprising a team of 40 professionals from premier institutes of technology and management education, IITs and IIMs, respectively. They worked tirelessly to manage BJP's social media content. In addition, volunteers were brought in to click photos at Modi's rallies and post them on social networks. For better coordination between the volunteers and the IT cell at New Delhi, a WhatsApp group of 150 people was created. The party explored every online opportunity to engage with voters, be it Google Plus, Hangouts, Twitter, or Facebook. Taglines like "*Abki*

bar Modi sarkar" became viral on Facebook, Twitter, and Instagram. Facebook pages such as "I want Narendra Modi as next PM of India" and "I support Narendra Modi" were created to attract voters and gauge their mood. Trending hashtags like #NaMo and #SelfieWithModi became the main topics of discussion. The IT cell regularly posted images, videos, and details about Modi's upcoming rallies. They also ran analytics on the huge data collected from social networking sites so as to increase the impact of Modi's speeches at the rallies.

Gupta laid emphasis on the need for analytics in managing such a huge campaign because he felt that this tool could help shape the campaign. For example, in October 2013, speaking at a youth function in New Delhi, Modi commented, "I am known to be a Hindutva leader. My image does not permit to say so, but I dare to say. My real thought is: *pehle shauchalaya, phir devalaya* (toilet first, temple later)." Analytics results showed that 45% of the social media users saw this statement in a favorable light. This gave Modi's team a clue that this could become one of the leading issues of the election. To spread this message further, the core IT team started engaging more users on social networking sites and found that now 68% of the people agreed with Modi's statement. After the elections, Modi started the Swachh Bharat Abhiyan on Gandhi Jayanti in New Delhi.

The Aam Aadmi Party (AAP), established in 2012 and headed by Arvind Kejriwal, also used social networking sites extensively to campaign for the elections. The main aim of the party was to share its honest opinion about important issues with the masses, spread awareness about party movements, display a common voice that would be coherent with the party's offline objectives, and connect with the youth. Consequently, Twitter hashtags like #VoteForAAP were strategically used by the party to gain political ground. In response to the rising digital popularity of the competitor, Modi, AAP created hashtags like #KejriwalAtKanpur to counter the leading one #NaMoInLucknow. Other hashtags such as #Internship4AAP and #Donate4CleanPoltics also ended up trending on Twitter. Rahul Jain, the director of digital marketing and sales at Social Rajneeti, an online reputation management and political promotions firm, said, "Aam Aadmi Party has been instrumental in shaping the revolutionary Indian politics since 2014 and has taken a prime position among the leading parties in the General Election, 2014. On social media, the party gets every aspect right from communication to uploading effective, thought-provoking videos and closely connecting with their audience through Google Hangouts." With the growing effectiveness of online campaigns, it comes as no surprise that political parties like the Congress, which didn't deploy as much time and effort on social media to engage with the tech-savvy, eligible young voters, lost the General Elections in 2014.

Sources: Rajan, Nandagopal, "SMW: Social media has changed political discourse like never before", *Financial Express* (2014). Retrieved from http://computer.financialexpress.com/events/smw-social-media-has-changed-political-discourse-like-never-before/3703/; http://www.cioandleader.com/news/38911/google-launches-candidates-tool-lok-sabha-elections-2014; "Social Media & Lok Sabha Elections: A study finds that Facebook users may be the new votebank Indian politicians have to now worry about", IRIS Knowledge Foundation and Internet and Mobile Association of India. Retrieved from http://www.esocialsciences.org/General/A2013412184534_19.pdf; Daxina Pathak, "A Study on

Use of Social Networking sites during Lok Sabha Elections-2014 by the Bhartiya Janta Party", *Altius Shodh Journal of Management & Commerce* (http://www.altius.ac.in/pdf/53.pdf); Surjit Kaur and Manpreet Kaur, "Impact of Social Media on Politics", *GIAN JYOTI E-JOURNAL*, Volume 3, Issue 4, Oct-Dec 2013 (http://www.gjimt.ac.in/wp-content/uploads/2013/12/3_Surjit-Kaur_Manpreet-Kaur_Impact_of_social_Media_on_Politics.pdf); "Social Media Played a Key Role in Lok Sabha Polls: Rajnath Singh", *NDTV* (2014). Retrieved from http://www.ndtv.com/article/india/social-media-played-a-key-role-in-lok-sabha-polls-rajnath-singh-557174; "Social Media: The Game Changer of Lok Sabha Elections 2014", *Centrac*. Retrieved from http://centerac.com/social-media-the-game-changer-of-lok-sabha-elections-2014/; "The role of social media in 2014 Lok Sabha elections", IBNLive (2014). Retrieved from http://ibnlive.in.com/news/the-role-of-social-media-in-2014-lok-sabha-elections/460803-3.html; "Build toilets first and temples later, Narendra Modi says", The Times of India (2013). Retrieved from http://timesofindia.indiatimes.com/india/Build-toilets-first-and-temples-later-Narendra-Modi-says/articleshow/23422631.cms; Kumar, Vikram, "Inside the BJP's war room where a team of 40 experts keeps an eye on the latest voting trends", *Daily Mail* (2014). Retrieved from http://www.dailymail.co.uk/indiahome/indianews/article-2608582/Inside-BJPs-war-room-team-40-experts-keeps-eye-latest-voting-trends.html; Chopra, Raahil, "'Big data is like teenage sex': BJP's Arvind Gupta", *CampaignIndia* (2014). Retrieved from http://www.campaignindia.in/Article/390271,8216big-data-is-like-teenage-sex8217-bjp8217s-arvind-gupta.aspx; "Social Media Strategy Review: Aam Aadmi Party", *Social Samosa* (2014). Retrieved from http://www.socialsamosa.com/2014/03/social-media-strategy-review-aam-aadmi-party/.

CASE STUDY QUESTIONS

1. What are the factors that led to the widespread adoption of social media in India?

2. How did BJP utilize social media and analytics for its political campaign in 2014?

3. Which other political party used social media and how?

$4 billion) (Internet Retailer, 2013). These estimates do not include mobile advertising or location-based services.

M-commerce applications have taken off for services that are time-critical, that appeal to people on the move, or that accomplish a task more efficiently than other methods. The Interactive Session on Technology describes how initiatives on the social media platforms are helping political parties establish an interactive relationship with the public.

LOCATION-BASED SERVICES AND APPLICATIONS

Location-based services include geosocial services, geoadvertising, and geoinformation services. Seventy-four percent of smartphone owners use location-based services. What ties these activities together and is the foundation for mobile commerce is the global positioning system (GPS) enabled

FIGURE 10.9 CONSOLIDATED MOBILE COMMERCE REVENUES

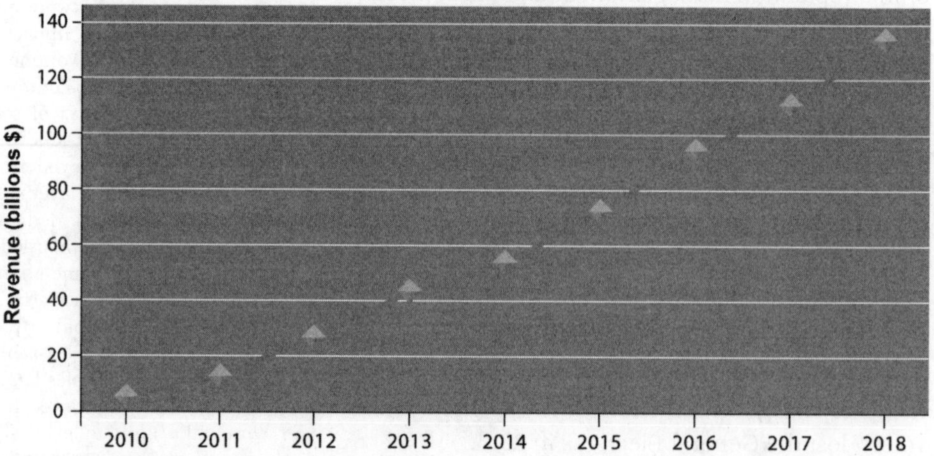

Mobile e-commerce is the fastest growing type of B2C e-commerce and represents about 19 percent of all e-commerce in 2014.

map services available on smartphones. A **geosocial service** can tell you where your friends are meeting. **Geoadvertising services** can tell you where to find the nearest Italian restaurant, and **geoinformation services** can tell you the price of a house you are looking at, or about special exhibits at a museum you are passing.

Wikitude.me is an example of a geoinformation service. Wikitude.me provides a special kind of browser for smartphones equipped with a built-in GPS and compass that can identify your precise location and where the phone is pointed. Using information from over 800,000 points of interest available on Wikipedia, plus thousands of other local sites, the browser overlays information about points of interest you are viewing, and displays that information on your smartphone screen, superimposed on a map or photograph that you just snapped. For example, users can point their smartphone cameras towards mountains from a tour bus and see the names and heights of the mountains displayed on the screen. Wikitude.me also allows users to geo-tag the world around them, and then submit the tags to Wikitude in order to share content with other users.

Foursquare, Loopt, and new offerings by Facebook and Google are examples of geosocial services. Geosocial services help you find friends, or be found by your friends, by "checking in" to the service, announcing your presence in a restaurant or other place. Your friends are instantly notified. About 20 percent of smartphone owners use geosocial services. The popularity of specialized sites like Foursquare has waned as Facebook and Google + have moved into geosocial services and turned them into extensions of their larger social networks.

Loopt claimed more than 5 million users in 2014. The service doesn't sell information to advertisers, but does post ads based on user location. Loopt's target is to deal with advertisers at the walking level (within 200 to 250 meters). Foursquare provides a similar location-based social networking service to 22 million registered users, who may connect with friends and update their location. Points are awarded for checking in at designated venues. Users choose to have their check-ins posted on their accounts on Twitter, Facebook, or both. Users also earn badges by checking in at locations with certain tags, for check-in frequency, or for the time of check-in. More than 500,000 local merchants worldwide use the merchant platform for marketing.

Connecting people to local merchants in the form of geoadvertising is the economic foundation for mobile commerce. Mobile advertising will reach $17.7 billion in 2014, up 83 percent from 2013. Geoadvertising sends ads to users based on their GPS locations. Smartphones report their locations back to Google and Apple. Merchants buy access to these consumers when they come within range of a merchant. For instance, Kiehl Stores, a cosmetics retailer, sent special offers and announcements to customers who came within 100 yards of their store.

OTHER MOBILE COMMERCE SERVICES

Banks and credit card companies are rolling out services that let customers manage their accounts from their mobile devices. JPMorgan Chase and Bank of America customers can use their cell phones to check account balances, transfer funds, and pay bills. Apple Pay for the iPhone 6 and Apple Watch, along with other Android and Windows smartphone models, allows users to charge items to their credit card accounts with a swipe of their phone. (See our Learning Track on mobile payment systems.)

Although the mobile advertising market is currently small, it is rapidly growing (up 75 percent from last year and expected to grow to over $47 billion by 2017), as more and more companies seek ways to exploit new databases of location-specific information. The largest providers of mobile display advertising are Apple's iAd platform and Google's AdMob platform (both with a 21 percent market share) followed by Millenial Media. Facebook is a distant fourth but moving rapidly to catch up. Alcatel-Lucent offers a new service to be managed by Placecast that will identify cell phone users within a specified distance of an advertiser's nearest outlet and notify them about the outlet's address and phone number, perhaps including a link to a coupon or other promotion. Placecast's clients include Hyatt, FedEx, and Avis Rent-A-Car.

Yahoo displays ads on its mobile home page for companies such as Pepsi, Procter & Gamble, Hilton, Nissan, and Intel. Google is displaying ads linked to cell phone searches by users of the mobile version of its search engine, while Microsoft offers banner and text advertising on its MSN Mobile portal in the United States. Ads are embedded in games, videos, and other mobile applications.

Shopkick is a mobile application that enables retailers such as Best Buy, Sports Authority, and Macy's to offer coupons to people when they walk into their stores. The Shopkick app automatically recognizes when the user has entered a partner retail store and offers a new virtual currency called "kick-bucks," which can be redeemed for Facebook credits, iTunes Gift Cards, travel vouchers, DVDs, or immediate cash-back rewards at any of the partner stores.

Fifty-five percent of online retailers now have m-commerce Web sites—simplified versions of their Web sites that make it possible for shoppers to use cell phones to place orders. Clothing retailers Lilly Pulitzer and Armani Exchange, Home Depot, Amazon, Walmart, and 1–800-Flowers are among those companies with apps for m-commerce sales.

10.6   WHAT ISSUES MUST BE ADDRESSED WHEN BUILDING AN E-COMMERCE PRESENCE?

Building a successful e-commerce presence requires a keen understanding of business, technology, and social issues, as well as a systematic approach. Today, an e-commerce presence is not just a corporate Web site, but may also include a social network site on Facebook, a Twitter feed, and smartphone apps where customers can access your services. Developing and coordinating all these different customer venues can be difficult. A complete treatment of the topic is beyond the scope of this text, and students should consult books devoted to just this topic (Laudon and Traver, 2015). The two most important management challenges in building a successful e-commerce presence are (1) developing a clear understanding of your business objectives and (2) knowing how to choose the right technology to achieve those objectives.

DEVELOP AN E-COMMERCE PRESENCE MAP

E-commerce has moved from being a PC-centric activity on the Web to a mobile and tablet-based activity. While 80 percent or more of e-commerce today is conducted using PCs, increasingly smartphones and tablets will be used for purchasing. Currently, smartphones and tablets are used by a majority of Internet users in the United States to shop for goods and services, look up prices, enjoy entertainment, and access social sites, less so to make purchases. Your potential customers use these various devices at different times during the day, and involve themselves in different conversations depending what they are doing—touching base with friends, tweeting, or reading a blog. Each of these are "touch points" where you can meet the customer, and you have to think about how you develop a presence in these different virtual places. Figure 10.10 provides a roadmap to the platforms and related activities you will need to think about when developing your e-commerce presence.

Figure 10.10 illustrates four different kinds of e-commerce presence: Web sites, e-mail, social media, and offline media. For each of these types there are different platforms that you will need to address. For instance, in the case of Web site presence, there are three different platforms: traditional desktop, tablets, and smartphones, each with different capabilities. And for each type of e-commerce presence there are related activities you will need to consider. For instance, in the case of Web sites, you will want to engage in search engine marketing, display ads, affiliate programs, and sponsorships. Offline media, the fourth type of e-commerce presence, is included here because many firms use multiplatform or integrated marketing where print ads refer customers to Web sites.

DEVELOP A TIMELINE: MILESTONES

Where would you like to be a year from now? It's a good idea for you to have a rough idea of the time frame for developing your e-commerce presence when you begin. You should break your project down into a small number of phases

FIGURE 10.10 E-COMMERCE PRESENCE MAP

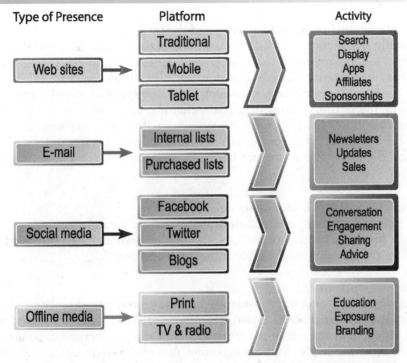

An e-commerce presence requires firms to consider the four different types of presence, with specific platforms and activities associated with each.

that could be completed within a specified time. Table 10.8 illustrates a one-year timeline for the development of an e-commerce presence for a start-up company devoted to teenage fashions. You can also find more detail about developing an e-commerce Web site in the Learning Tracks for this chapter.

TABLE 10.8 E-COMMERCE PRESENCE TIMELINE

PHASE	ACTIVITY	MILESTONE
Phase 1: Planning	Envision Web presence; determine personnel	Web mission statement
Phase 2: Web site development	Acquire content; develop a site design; arrange for hosting the site	Web site plan
Phase 3: Web Implementation	Develop keywords and metatags; focus on search engine optimization; identify potential sponsors	A functional Web site
Phase 4: Social media plan	Identify appropriate social platforms and content for your products and services	A social media plan
Phase 5: Social media implementation	Develop Facebook, Twitter, and Pinterest presence	Functioning social media presence
Phase 6: Mobile plan	Develop a mobile plan; consider options for porting your Web site to smartphones	A mobile media plan

Review Summary

1. **What are the unique features of e-commerce, digital markets, and digital goods?**

   E-commerce involves digitally enabled commercial transactions between and among organizations and individuals. Unique features of e-commerce technology include ubiquity, global reach, universal technology standards, richness, interactivity, information density, capabilities for personalization and customization, and social technology. E-commerce is becoming increasingly social, mobile, and local.

   Digital markets are said to be more "transparent" than traditional markets, with reduced information asymmetry, search costs, transaction costs, and menu costs, along with the ability to change prices dynamically based on market conditions. Digital goods, such as music, video, software, and books, can be delivered over a digital network. Once a digital product has been produced, the cost of delivering that product digitally is extremely low.

2. **What are the principal e-commerce business and revenue models?**

   E-commerce business models are e-tailers, transaction brokers, market creators, content providers, community providers, service providers, and portals. The principal e-commerce revenue models are advertising, sales, subscription, free/freemium, transaction fee, and affiliate.

3. **How has e-commerce transformed marketing?**

   The Internet provides marketers with new ways of identifying and communicating with millions of potential customers at costs far lower than traditional media. Crowdsourcing utilizing the "wisdom of crowds" helps companies learn from customers in order to improve product offerings and increase customer value. Behavioral targeting techniques increase the effectiveness of banner, rich media, and video ads. Social commerce uses social networks and social network sites to improve targeting of products and services.

4. **How has e-commerce affected business-to-business transactions?**

   B2B e-commerce generates efficiencies by enabling companies to locate suppliers, solicit bids, place orders, and track shipments in transit electronically. Net marketplaces provide a single, digital marketplace for many buyers and sellers. Private industrial networks link a firm with its suppliers and other strategic business partners to develop highly efficient and responsive supply chains.

5. **What is the role of m-commerce in business, and what are the most important m-commerce applications?**

   M-commerce is especially well suited for location-based applications, such as finding local hotels and restaurants, monitoring local traffic and weather, and providing personalized location-based marketing. Mobile phones and handhelds are being used for mobile bill payment, banking, securities trading, transportation schedule updates, and downloads of digital content, such as music, games, and video clips. M-commerce requires wireless portals and special digital payment systems that can handle micropayments. The GPS capabilities of smartphones make possible geoadvertising, geosocial, and geoinformation services.

6. **What issues must be addressed when building an e-commerce presence?**

   Building a successful e-commerce presence requires a clear understanding of the business objectives to be achieved and selection of the right platforms, activities, and timeline to achieve those objectives. An e-commerce presence includes not only a corporate Web site but also a presence on Facebook, Twitter, and other social networking sites and smartphone apps.

Key Terms

Advertising revenue model, 423
Affiliate revenue model, 425
Behavioral targeting, 428
Business-to-business (B2B), 419
Business-to-consumer (B2C), 419
Community providers, 423
Consumer-to-consumer (C2C), 419
Cost transparency, 414
Crowdsourcing, 435
Customization, 414
Digital goods, 416
Direct goods, 438
Disintermediation, 416
Dynamic pricing, 416
Electronic data interchange (EDI), 436
E-tailer, 421
Exchanges, 439
Free/freemium revenue model, 424
Geoadvertising services, 442
Geoinformation services, 442
Geosocial services, 442
Indirect goods, 438
Information asymmetry, 415
Information density, 414
Intellectual property, 421
Location-based services, 442
Long tail marketing, 428

Market creator, 422
Market entry costs, 413
Marketspace, 412
Menu costs, 416
Micropayment systems, 424
Mobile commerce
   (m-commerce), 420
Net marketplaces, 438
Personalization, 414
Podcasting, 422
Prediction market, 435
Price discrimination, 414
Price transparency, 414
Private exchange, 438
Private industrial networks, 437
Revenue model, 423
Richness, 413
Sharing economy, 422
Sales revenue model, 424
Search costs, 413
Social graph, 432
Social shopping, 434
Streaming, 422
Subscription revenue model, 424
Transaction costs, 412
Transaction fee revenue model, 425
Wisdom of crowds, 434

Review Questions

10-1 What are the unique features of e-commerce, digital markets, and digital goods?
- Name and describe four business trends and three technology trends shaping e-commerce today.
- List and describe the eight unique features of e-commerce.
- Define a digital market and digital goods and describe their distinguishing features.

10-2 What are the principal e-commerce business and revenue models?
- Name and describe the principal e-commerce business models.
- Name and describe the e-commerce revenue models.

10-3 How has e-commerce transformed marketing?
- Explain how social networking and the "wisdom of crowds" help companies improve their marketing.

- Define behavioral targeting and explain how it works at individual Web sites and on advertising networks.
- Define the social graph and explain how it is used in e-commerce marketing.

10-4 How has e-commerce affected business-to-business transactions?
- Explain how Internet technology supports business-to-business electronic commerce.
- Define and describe Net marketplaces and explain how they differ from private industrial networks (private exchanges).

10-5 What is the role of m-commerce in business, and what are the most important m-commerce applications?
- List and describe important types of m-commerce services and applications.

10-6 What issues must be addressed when building an e-commerce presence?
- List and describe the four types of e-commerce presence.

Discussion Questions

10-7 How does the Internet change consumer and supplier relationships?

10-8 The Internet may not make corporations obsolete, but the corporations will have to change their business models. Do you agree? Why or why not?

10-9 How have social technologies changed e-commerce?

Hands-On MIS Projects

The projects in this section give you hands-on experience developing e-commerce strategies for businesses, using spreadsheet software to research the profitability of an e-commerce company, and using Web tools to research and evaluate e-commerce hosting services.

Management Decision Problems

10-10 Columbiana is a small, independent island in the Caribbean that has many historical buildings, forts, and other sites, along with rain forests and striking mountains. A few first-class hotels and several dozen less expensive accommodations can be found along its beautiful white sand beaches. The major airlines have regular flights to Columbiana, as do several small airlines. Columbiana's government wants to increase tourism and develop new markets for the country's tropical agricultural products. How can a Web presence help? What Internet business model would be appropriate? What functions should the Web site perform?

10-11 Explore the Web sites of the following companies: Blue Nile, Swatch, Lowe's, and Priceline. Determine which of these Web sites would benefit most from adding a company-sponsored blog to the Web site.

List the business benefits of the blog. Specify the intended audience for the blog. Decide who in the company should author the blog, and select some topics for the blog.

Achieving Operational Excellence: Evaluating E-Commerce Hosting Services

Software skills: Web browser software
Business skills: Evaluating e-commerce hosting services

10-12 This project will help develop your Internet skills in commercial services for hosting an e-commerce site for a small start-up company.

You would like to set up a Web site to sell towels, linens, pottery, and tableware from Portugal and are examining services for hosting small business Internet storefronts. Your Web site should be able to take secure credit card payments and to calculate shipping costs and taxes. Initially, you would like to display photos and descriptions of 40 different products. Visit Yahoo! Small Business, GoDaddy, and iPage and compare the range of e-commerce hosting services they offer to small businesses, their capabilities, and costs. Also examine the tools they provide for creating an e-commerce site. Compare these services and decide which you would use if you were actually establishing a Web store. Write a brief report indicating your choice and explaining the strengths and weaknesses of each.

Mobile Commerce with Airtel Money
CASE STUDY

Mobiles phones are becoming indispensable in our lives. Service providers are constantly trying to innovate to provide value-added services to customers. India, an emerging leader in the smartphone market, is witnessing competition among cellular service providers to woo customers.

Bharti Airtel is one of the top telecom service providers in India. In 2010, it felt that the urban Indian cellular service market was fast approaching a saturation point, and it decided to turn its attention to the rural market which comprises 70% of India's population. While brainstorming about the kind of value-added services that could be provided to rural subscribers, Airtel realized that these areas had limited banking facilities, with only 5% of the total ATM coverage.

Airtel launched the pioneering mobile commerce service, Airtel Money, which uses the mobile money transfer (MMT) technology to allow users to send money to one another through their phones *via* a highly secured network. Airtel felt that several groups of customers would find value in this facility. First, the large rural workforce that migrates to the cities for jobs would be able to use Airtel Money to remit their wages back home. Even the young urban working population could use their cell phones to pay bills. Sanjay Kapoor, the CEO of Bharti Airtel in India and South Asia, said, "While an estimated 24 crore people across India hold bank accounts, more than 90% of the country's population uses cash to pay for its daily needs. Additionally, a majority of customers continue to rely on traditional or time-consuming methods like money orders and cheque remittances when it comes to transferring funds. On the other hand, the penetration of mobile telephony currently enriches the lives of over 90 crore people in our country and can facilitate a paradigm shift in the way India transacts. We see the national rollout of Airtel Money playing a pivotal role in accelerating mobile-based commerce in India and look forward to further extending the availability of this

service in deeper pockets of the country in weeks to come."

In 2011, Airtel Money was launched as a pilot project through which Airtel M Commerce Services Limited (AMSL) started collecting data regarding the transfer of money across India. The success of the pilot service and the analysis of the corresponding data revealed that Airtel Money held a promising future. The only major hurdle was getting the required clearances from the Reserve Bank of India (RBI).

The implementation of such a project demanded changes in the organizational structure at Airtel. Airtel was operating on systems, which though completely stable, were not geared towards supporting monetary transactions or mCommerce. The company felt that making a change to stable systems made no sense and would impact existing business. A separate niche system had to be developed from scratch. In June 2010, AMSL got a certificate of authorization from the RBI to operate a payment system and issue a stored-value wallet to its subscribers. Airtel also went on to create a parallel sales and marketing hierarchy for the new company.

The low data coverage in rural areas proved yet another challenge for AMSL. It needed an application which could enable GSM cell phones to communicate with service providers without Internet data connectivity. A technology like J2ME, which required GPRS download and large memory, was not a preferred option for the Indian rural market. Hence, AMSL implemented the unstructured service supplementary data (USSD), which, along with SMS, supported the Airtel Money application. USSD is a protocol used for GSM cell phones to communicate with the service provider's computers. USSD applies 182 alphanumeric characters and creates a real-time connection, which allows a two-way exchange of data.

AMSL also needed a framework which could necessitate the transfer of payment from one mobile phone to another in a cost-efficient and convenient manner. AMSL joined hands with Infosys to provide this framework in the form of a private cloud. To start the Airtel Money application on a mobile phone, the customer first needs to register for it. The customer is given four-digit personal identification mPin, which must be changed within 48 hours to another secure four-digit mPin of the user's choice. This mPin will authenticate all future financial transactions. Once registered, customer can load money on their mobile devices and can create three types of wallets: the Express Wallet, the Power Wallet, and the Super Wallet. From these Wallets, the customers can pay off mobile, land-line or DTH bills, purchase movie tickets, and so on. The star feature of Airtel Money is its ability to transfer money from one Wallet to another. The types of transfer facilities depend on the kind of Wallet the user creates. Money can be sent either to the receiver's bank account or to their Airtel Money Wallet. For the latter, all the sender needs to do is enter the receiver's mobile phone number, amount, and the mPin.

There was special provision in the Airtel Money app to cater to the needs of unbanked rural populations. Senders would need to use the Super Wallet to send money. The receiver would get an SMS on their mobile phone with a unique code. This code could be presented to any Airtel Money Axis Bank retailer to withdraw money. The customer would also get a 4% interest on the balance in their Super Wallet. Airtel Money is now available in more than 300 locations across the country.

Sources: Saxena, Anupam, "Airtel Signs Up As Banking Correspondent For Axis Bank; Supports Cash Withdrawals", *Nedianama* (2012). Retrieved from http://www.medianama.com/2012/05/223-airtel-signs-up-as-banking-correspondent-for-axis-bank-no-open-wallet/; "'Airtel money' empowers customers with mobile currency". Retrieved from http://www.infosys.com/newsroom/features/Pages/telecom-mobile-wallet-service.aspx; "A Sneak Peek into airtel money: Changing the Way You Pay", *Telecomtalk* (2013). Retrieved from http://telecomtalk.info/a-sneak-peek-into-airtel-money-changing-the-way-you-pay/106083/; "Bharti Airtel selects Infosys as its technology partner for 'airtel money'". Retrieved from http://www.airtel.in/about-bharti/media-centre/bharti-airtel-news/mobile/bharti-airtel-selects-infosys-as-its-technology-partner-for-airtel-money;Van, Long, "Use of USSD technology in Mobile Banking", *Mobile-Financial.Com* (2009). Retrieved from http://mobile-financial.com/blogs/use-ussd-technology-mobile-banking; "An Overview of the different mobile banking technology options, and their impact on the mobile banking market", FinMark Trust (2007) http://www.gsma.com/mobilefordevelopment/wp-content/uploads/2012/06/finmark_mbt_aug_07.pdf.

CASE STUDY QUESTIONS

10-13 What was the reason behind the conception of a service like Airtel Money?

10-14 Although voice connectivity in India is high, data connectivity is low. How did Airtel Money overcome this problem?

10-15 Discuss how subscribers use Airtel Money on their phones.

10-16 Discuss the different options available for the transfer of balance through Airtel Money. Which option is most beneficial for rural users?

Chapter 10 References

Arazy, Ofer and Ian R. Gallatly. "Corporate Wikis: The Effects of Owners' Motivation and Behavior on Group Members' Engagement" Journal of Management Information Systems 29, No. 3 (Winter 2013).

Brynjolfsson, Erik, Yu Jeffrey Hu, and Mohammad S. Rahman. "Competing in the Age of Multichannel Retailing." *MIT Sloan Management Review* (May 2013).

Butler, Brian S., Patrick J. Bateman, Peter H. Gray, and E. Ilana Diamant. "An Attraction-Selection-Attrition Theory of Online Community Size and Resilience." *MIS Quarterly* 38, No. 3 (September 2014).

Brynjolfsson, Erik,Yu Hu, and Michael D. Smith. "Consumer Surplus in the Digital Economy: Estimating the Value of Increased Product Variety at Online Booksellers." *Management Science* 49, No. 11 (November 2003).

Blake Chandlee, Blake and Gerald C. (Jerry) Kane. "How Facebook Is Delivering Personalization on a Whole New Scale." *MIT Sloan Management Review* 55, No. 4 (August 5, 2014).

Carol Xiaojuan Ou, Paul A. Pavlou, and Robert M. Davison. "Swift Guanxi in Online Marketplaces: The Role of Computer-Mediated Communication Technologies." *MIS Quarterly* 38, No. 1 (March 2014).

Chen, Jianquing and Jan Stallaert. "An Economic Analysis of Online Advertising Using Behavioral Targeting." *MIS Quarterly* 38, No. 2 (June 2014).

comScore Inc. "ComScore Media Metrix Ranks Top 50 U.S. Web Properties for July 2013." (August 18, 2014a).

comScore Inc. "ComScore 2013 US Digital Future in Focus." [Nick Mulligan]. (April 2, 2014b).

Dewan, Sanjeev and Jui Ramaprasad."Anxious or Angry? Effects of Discrete Emotions on the Perceived Helpfulness of Online Reviews." *MIS Quarterly* 38, No. 1 (March 2014).

eMarketer, "US Retail Ecommerce: 2014 Trends and Forecast." (Yory Wurmser), Report, April 2014a.

eMarketer, "US Ad Spending 2014 Forecast and Comparative Estimates," eMarketer Report, Alison McCarthy, July 2014b

eMarketer, "US Fixed Broadband Households, 2012–2018, chart, Feb 2014 in in "US Internet Users: 2014 CompleteForecast." (Alison McCarthy), March 20, 2014c

eMarketer, Mobile Commerce Deep Dive: The Products, Channels and Tactics Fueling Growth (Cathy Boyle). Report. July 2014d.

eMarketer, "Mobile Phone Internet Users and Penetration Worldwide, 2012-2018," Chart. June 2014d.

Facebook, About, http://newsroom.fb.com/company-info/, 2014

Federal Trade Commission, "Data Brokers: A Call for Transparency and Accountability," Federal Trade Commission, May 2014.

Fang, Yulin, Israr Qureshi, Heshan Sun, Patrick McCole, Elaine Ramsey, and Kai H. Lim. "Trust, Satisfaction, and Online Repurchase Intention: The Moderating Role of Perceived Effectiveness of E-Commerce Institutional Mechanisms." *MIS Quarterly* 38, No. 2 (June 2014).

Gast, Arne and Michele Zanini. "The Social Side of Strategy." *McKinsey Quarterly* (May 2012).

eMarketer, "US Retail E-commerce Forecast: Entering the Age of Omnichannel Retailing." (Jeffrey Grau). eMarketer Report. (March 1, 2012).

Gupta, Sunil. "For Mobile Devices, Think Apps, Not Ads." *Harvard Business Review* (March 2013).

Hinz, Oliver , Jochen Eckert, and Bernd Skiera. "Drivers of the Long Tail Phenomenon: An Empirical Analysis." *Journal of Management Information Systems* 27, No. 4 (Spring 2011).

Hinz, Oliver, Il-Horn Hann, and Martin Spann. "Price Discrimination in E-Commerce? An Examination of Dynamic Pricing in Name-Your-Own Price Markets." *MIS Quarterly* 35, No. 1 (March 2011).

Hoofnagle, Chris Jay, Jennifer M. Urban, & Su Li. Privacy and Modern Advertising: Most US Internet Users Want "Do Not Track" to Stop Collection of Data About their Online Activities. Berkeley Consumer Privacy Survey. BCLT Research Paper, October 8, 2012.

Howe, Heff. *Crowdsourcing: Why the Power of the Crowd Is Driving the Future of Business.* New York: Random House (2008).

Internet Retailer. "Mobile Commerce Top 400 2013." (2013).

Internet World Stats. "Internet Users in the World." (Internetworldstats.com, 2014).

Kumar, V. and Rohan Mirchandan "Increasing the ROI of Social Media Marketing." *MIT Sloan Management Review* 54, No. 1 (Fall 2012).

Laudon, Kenneth C. and Carol Guercio Traver. *E-Commerce: Business, Technology, Society*, 11th edition. Upper Saddle River, NJ: Prentice-Hall (2015).

Lin, Mei , Ke, Xuqing and Whinston, Andrew B. "Vertical Differentiation and a Comparison of Online Advertising Models ." *Journal of Management Information Systems* 29, No. 1 (Summer 2012).

Oestreicher-Singer, Gal and Arun Sundararajan. "Recommendation Networks and the Long Tail of Electronic Commerce." *MIS Quarterly* 36, No. 1 (March 2012).

Pew Internet and American Life Project. "Daily Internet Activities." (January 6, 2014.)

Pew Internet and American Life Project. " Internet Users Don't like Targeted Ads." (March 13, 2012).

Qiu, Liangfei , Huaxia Rui, and Andrew B. Whinston. "Effects of Social Networks on Prediction Markets: Examination in a Controlled Experiment " *Journal of Management Information Systems* 30, No. 4 (Spring 2014).

Rigby, Darrell K. "Digital Physical Mashups." *Harvard Business Review* (September 2014).

Shuk, Ying Ho and David Bodoff. "The Effects of Web Personalization on User Attitude and Behavior: An Integration of the Elaboration Likelihood Model and Consumer Search Theory." *MIS Quarterly* 38, No. 2 (June 2014).

US Bureau of the Census. "E-Stats. 2014" http://www.census.gov/econ/index.html (May 22, 2014).

Wood, Molly. "Facebook Generation Rekindles Expectation of Privacy Online," New York Times, September 7, 2014.

Yin, Dezhi, Samuel D. Bond, and Han Zhang. "Anxious or Angry? Effects of Discrete Emotions on the Perceived Helpfulness of Online Reviews." *MIS Quarterly* 38, No. 2 (June 2014).

Managing Knowledge | **C H A P T E R 11**

LEARNING OBJECTIVES

After reading this chapter, you will be able to answer the following questions:

1. What is the role of knowledge management systems in business?

2. What types of systems are used for enterprise-wide knowledge management and how do they provide value for businesses?

3. What are the major types of knowledge work systems and how do they provide value for firms?

4. What are the business benefits of using intelligent techniques for knowledge management?

CHAPTER CASES

Connecting Unisys Globally
    Through Social Collaboration
    Information Systems
Is 3-D Printing a Game-Changer?

Facial Recognition Systems:
    Another Threat to Privacy?
What's Up with IBM's Watson?

CONNECTING UNISYS GLOBALLY THROUGH SOCIAL COLLABORATION INFORMATION SYSTEMS

Unisys Corporation has global presence in more than 100 countries, including India. The company provides a range of IT, software, and technology services to commercial organizations and government agencies throughout the world. In its 140 years of existence, the firm has had approximately 23,000 employees. As a services firm, the harnessing and sharing of intellectual capital are vital to its operations. A quick response to customer queries is essential when it comes to tapping market opportunities. However, the management at Unisys felt that the lack of platforms to share knowledge among its employees limited the firm's ability to leverage its expertise to respond to the dynamic business environment.

It was discovered that the company had multiple information silos within its system, which prevented enterprise-wide sharing of knowledge. The model of communication was traditional and top-down. There was no way for employees to find and connect with subject-matter experts. Unisys wished to achieve true enterprise collaboration through an information system to sort out all these problems. This vision was shared by the company's CEO, Ed Coleman, who had already leveraged the value of social media for brand

© Shawn Hempel/Shutterstock

promotion and reaching out to customers. The firm then decided to once again adopt social media to empower its employees and increase their efficiency in the workplace.

This model, however, had to be implemented with care. Unisys first started by conducting leadership interviews to understand how the adoption of social business could add value to their enterprise. Through this, areas were identified where social technology could deliver value to customers and provide improved capabilities. An advisory council of stakeholders across the organization was formed that could address potential barriers to implementation. Based on the recommendations of the advisory council, Unisys redesigned its intranet, Inside Unisys, by adding a new feature called NewsGator.

NewsGator is a social engine that enabled employees to create their individual profiles and 'follow' colleagues to build valuable networks. Other features included transparent newsfeeds and blogs, which enabled the employees to communicate and learn through sharing. To facilitate the adoption of social business, Unisys launched strategic communities at different levels of the firm, which were termed as the hub for social collaboration. 'Organic communities' were given the task of developing expertise through interaction with like-minded people. 'Business unit communities' were responsible for the disbursal of the latest news and alerts among employees. 'Role-based communities' and 'industry or vertical communities' were Unisys-sponsored communities of excellence. They primarily dealt with the development and dissemination of essential knowledge in sales, delivery, and market trends. 'Areas of strength communities' were authoritative communities that leveraged knowledge in Unisys' key solutions and offerings. Additionally, employees could crowd-source ideas into communities, which led the firm to innovations. Unisys hard aligned its employees to their business unit communities, so that the firm could push important news and information through these communities. The employees could also subscribe to other communities, which updated them with information in their areas of interest. This was also integrated into a new hire orientation program to increase their engagement and facilitate in quick on-boarding. From time to time, the firm also launched targeted role-based awareness campaigns to educate and train employees on the usage of enterprise collaboration.

The results of adopting this system were enormous. Within the first 18 months of implementation, 91 per cent of the targeted base of 16,000 employees adopted this system. In its global workforce, this percentage stood at 78. All members of the senior leadership of Unisys used this system and promoted social collaboration within their organizations. Thirteen strategic communities and 120 organic communities have been developed since. Social exchanges on newsfeed and blogs are populated with high-value business content. This rapid adoption of social technologies has fuelled the innovative culture at Unisys, increased workplace efficiency, facilitated employee development, and improved market agility and customer service. This has also increased the efficiency of virtual teams, which comprises remote, home-based employees, who can feel connected to their business environment through Unisys' social tools and processes.

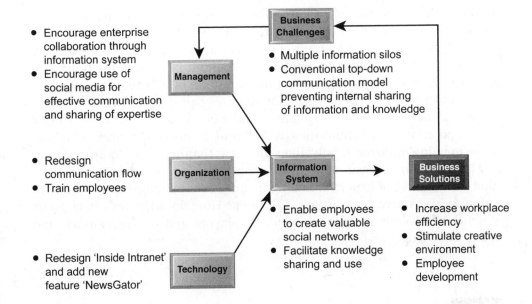

- Encourage enterprise collaboration through information system
- Encourage use of social media for effective communication and sharing of expertise

Management

Business Challenges
- Multiple information silos
- Conventional top-down communication model preventing internal sharing of information and knowledge

- Redesign communication flow
- Train employees

Organization

Information System

Business Solutions

- Enable employees to create valuable social networks
- Facilitate knowledge sharing and use

- Increase workplace efficiency
- Stimulate creative environment
- Employee development

- Redesign 'Inside Intranet' and add new feature 'NewsGator'

Technology

Sources: 'Unisys Case Study: Best Practices in Socially Enabling a Global Workforce' (2013). Retrieved from http://www.apqc.org/sites/default/files/files/UPDATED_APQC_Unisys_SC_Case_Presentation_FINAL(3).pdf; 'Unisys Unified Social Business Overview' (2014). Retrieved from https://www.youtube.com/watch?v = muEz5GMiunk; Kass, Kelly, 'From Silos to Social: How Unisys socially-enabled its global enterprise'. Retrieved from https://www.simply-communicate.com/case-studies/collaboration/silos-social-how-unisys-socially-enabled-its-global-enterprise; *Unisys*. Retried from http://www.unisys.com/; 'Great Intranets: Unisys'. Retrieved from http://www.prescientdigital.com/articles/great-intranets-unisys; Lightman, Stefanie, NewsGator's Free Adoption Framework Gains Momentum', *Sitrion* (2013). Retrieved from http://www.sitrion.com/blog/newsgators-free-adoption-framework-gains-momentum.

The experience of Unisys described in this case shows how business performance can benefit from new communication media to facilitate acquisition and sharing of knowledge. Facilitating access to knowledge, and harnessing and using that knowledge to improve business processes are vital to success and survival of all areas of business.

The chapter-opening diagram calls attention to the important points raised by this case and this chapter. Constant communication and sharing of expertise among its employees are essential tools for any firm, especially if it is offering innovative services and solutions. However, Unisys had multiple information silos within its system, which prevented the enterprise-wide sharing of knowledge. The model of communication was the conventional top-down one. There was no way for employees to find and connect with subject-matter experts to resolve problems. There was an urgent need to achieve true enterprise collaboration through an information system. To achieve enterprise-wide collaboration, Unisys decided to change its internal communication system by using social media to empower employees and increase efficiency in the workplace. Unisys redesigned its Intranet, Inside Unisys, with the aim to provide a platform where the employees can interact with each other. The result was addition of a key feature in the company's intranet, known as NewsGator. Thanks to this new social media platform, employees can create their profiles and 'follow' other colleagues to build a valuable network. Other features of this platform are transparent newsfeeds and blogs which enabled the employees to communicate and learn through sharing. However, realizing the fact that adoption of new technology in the form of social media based interaction requires cultural changes in the organizational mindset, and to facilitate the adoption of social business, Unisys launched strategic communities at different levels of the firm. This was done to help employees easily adopt the new channel of communication.

Here are some questions to think about: Why are constant communication and sharing of expertise among its employees so important for a firm offering innovative services and solutions? How does Unisys's new social engine, NewsGator, make it easier for employees and managers to use and share knowledge?

11.1 WHAT IS THE ROLE OF KNOWLEDGE MANAGEMENT SYSTEMS IN BUSINESS?

Knowledge management and collaboration systems are among the fastest growing areas of corporate and government software investment. The past decade has shown an explosive growth in research on knowledge and knowledge management in the economics, management, and information systems fields.

Knowledge management and collaboration are closely related. Knowledge that cannot be communicated and shared with others is nearly useless. Knowledge becomes useful and actionable when shared throughout the firm. We have already described the major tools for collaboration and social business in Chapter 2. In this chapter, we will focus on knowledge management systems, and be mindful that communicating and sharing knowledge are becoming increasingly important.

We live in an information economy in which the major source of wealth and prosperity is the production and distribution of information and knowledge. An estimated 37 percent of the U.S. labor force consists of knowledge and information workers, the largest single segment of the labor force. About 45 percent of the gross domestic product (GDP) of the United States is generated by the knowledge and information sectors (U.S. Department of Commerce, 2012).

Knowledge management has become an important theme at many large business firms as managers realize that much of their firm's value depends on the firm's ability to create and manage knowledge. Studies have found that a substantial part of a firm's stock market value is related to its intangible assets, of which knowledge is one important component, along with brands, reputations, and unique business processes. Well-executed knowledge-based projects have been known to produce extraordinary returns on investment, although the impacts of knowledge-based investments are difficult to measure (Gu and Lev, 2001).

IMPORTANT DIMENSIONS OF KNOWLEDGE

There is an important distinction between data, information, knowledge, and wisdom. Chapter 1 defines **data** as a flow of events or transactions captured by an organization's systems that, by itself, is useful for transacting but little else. To turn data into useful *information*, a firm must expend resources to organize data into categories of understanding, such as monthly, daily, regional, or store-based reports of total sales. To transform information into **knowledge**, a firm must expend additional resources to discover patterns, rules, and contexts where the knowledge works. Finally, **wisdom** is thought to be the collective and individual experience of applying knowledge to the solution of problems. Wisdom involves where, when, and how to apply knowledge.

Knowledge is both an individual attribute and a collective attribute of the firm. Knowledge is a cognitive, even a physiological, event that takes place inside people's heads. It is also stored in libraries and records, shared in lectures, and stored by firms in the form of business processes and employee know-how. Knowledge residing in the minds of employees that has not been documented is called **tacit knowledge**, whereas knowledge that has been documented is called **explicit knowledge**. Knowledge can reside in e-mail, voice mail, graphics, and unstructured documents as well as structured documents. Knowledge is generally believed to have a location, either in the minds of humans or in specific business processes. Knowledge is "sticky" and not universally applicable or easily moved. Finally, knowledge is thought to be situational and contextual. For example, you must know when to perform a procedure as well as how to perform it. Table 11.1 reviews these dimensions of knowledge.

We can see that knowledge is a different kind of firm asset from, say, buildings and financial assets; that knowledge is a complex phenomenon; and that there are many aspects to the process of managing knowledge. We can also recognize that knowledge-based core competencies of firms—the two or three things that an organization does best—are key organizational assets. Knowing how to do things effectively and efficiently in ways that other organizations cannot duplicate is a primary source of profit and competitive advantage that cannot be purchased easily by competitors in the marketplace.

For instance, having a unique build-to-order production system constitutes a form of knowledge and perhaps a unique asset that other firms cannot copy easily. With knowledge, firms become more efficient and effective in their use of scarce resources. Without knowledge, firms become less efficient and less effective in their use of resources and ultimately fail.

Organizational Learning and Knowledge Management

Like humans, organizations create and gather knowledge using a variety of organizational learning mechanisms. Through collection of data, careful measurement of planned activities, trial and error (experiment), and feedback from customers and the environment in general, organizations gain experience. Organizations that learn adjust their behavior to reflect that learning by creating new business processes and by changing patterns of management decision making. This process of change is called **organizational learning**. Arguably, organizations that can sense and respond to

TABLE 11.1 IMPORTANT DIMENSIONS OF KNOWLEDGE

KNOWLEDGE IS A FIRM ASSET

Knowledge is an intangible asset.

The transformation of data into useful information and knowledge requires organizational resources.

Knowledge is not subject to the law of diminishing returns as are physical assets, but instead experiences network effects as its value increases as more people share it.

KNOWLEDGE HAS DIFFERENT FORMS

Knowledge can be either tacit or explicit (codified).

Knowledge involves know-how, craft, and skill.

Knowledge involves knowing how to follow procedures.

Knowledge involves knowing why, not simply when, things happen (causality).

KNOWLEDGE HAS A LOCATION

Knowledge is a cognitive event involving mental models and maps of individuals.

There is both a social and an individual basis of knowledge.

Knowledge is "sticky" (hard to move), situated (enmeshed in a firm's culture), and contextual (works only in certain situations).

KNOWLEDGE IS SITUATIONAL

Knowledge is conditional; knowing when to apply a procedure is just as important as knowing the procedure (conditional).

Knowledge is related to context; you must know how to use a certain tool and under what circumstances.

their environments rapidly will survive longer than organizations that have poor learning mechanisms.

THE KNOWLEDGE MANAGEMENT VALUE CHAIN

Knowledge management refers to the set of business processes developed in an organization to create, store, transfer, and apply knowledge. Knowledge management increases the ability of the organization to learn from its environment and to incorporate knowledge into its business processes. Figure 11.1 illustrates the five value-adding steps in the knowledge management value chain. Each stage in the value chain adds value to raw data and information as they are transformed into usable knowledge.

In Figure 11.1, information systems activities are separated from related management and organizational activities, with information systems activities on the top of the graphic and organizational and management activities below. One apt slogan of the knowledge management field is, "Effective knowledge management is 80 percent managerial and organizational, and 20 percent technology."

In Chapter 1, we define *organizational and management capital* as the set of business processes, culture, and behavior required to obtain value from investments in information systems. In the case of knowledge management, as with other information systems investments, supportive values,

FIGURE 11.1 THE KNOWLEDGE MANAGEMENT VALUE CHAIN

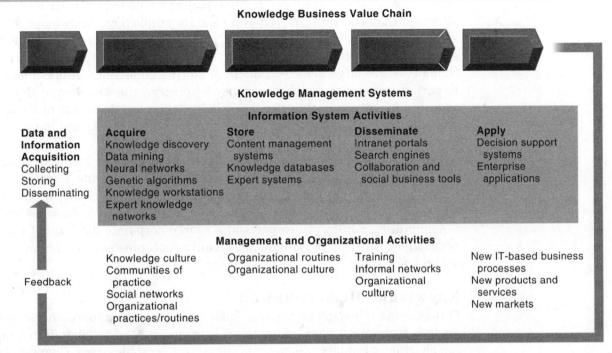

Knowledge management today involves both information systems activities and a host of enabling management and organizational activities.

structures, and behavior patterns must be built to maximize the return on investment in knowledge management projects. In Figure 11.1, the management and organizational activities in the lower half of the diagram represent the investment in organizational capital required to obtain substantial returns on the information technology (IT) investments and systems shown in the top half of the diagram.

Knowledge Acquisition

Organizations acquire knowledge in a number of ways, depending on the type of knowledge they seek. The first knowledge management systems sought to build corporate repositories of documents, reports, presentations, and best practices. These efforts have been extended to include unstructured documents (such as e-mail). In other cases, organizations acquire knowledge by developing online expert networks so that employees can "find the expert" in the company who is personally knowledgeable.

In still other cases, firms must create new knowledge by discovering patterns in corporate data or by using knowledge workstations where engineers can discover new knowledge. These various efforts are described throughout this chapter. A coherent and organized knowledge system also requires systematic data from the firm's transaction processing systems that track sales, payments, inventory, customers, and other vital data, as well as data from external sources such as news feeds, industry reports, legal opinions, scientific research, and government statistics.

Knowledge Storage

Once they are discovered, documents, patterns, and expert rules must be stored so they can be retrieved and used by employees. Knowledge storage generally involves the creation of a database. Document management systems that digitize, index, and tag documents according to a coherent framework are large databases adept at storing collections of documents. Expert systems also help corporations preserve the knowledge that is acquired by incorporating that knowledge into organizational processes and culture. Each of these is discussed later in this chapter and in the following chapter.

Management must support the development of planned knowledge storage systems, encourage the development of corporate-wide schemas for indexing documents, and reward employees for taking the time to update and store documents properly. For instance, it would reward the sales force for submitting names of prospects to a shared corporate database of prospects where all sales personnel can identify each prospect and review the stored knowledge.

Knowledge Dissemination

Portals, e-mail, instant messaging, wikis, social business tools, and search engines technology have added to an existing array of collaboration tools for sharing calendars, documents, data, and graphics (see Chapter 2). Contemporary technology seems to have created a deluge of information and knowledge. How can managers and employees discover, in a sea of information and knowledge, that which is really important for their decisions and their work? Here, training programs, informal networks, and shared management experience communicated through a supportive culture help managers focus their attention on the important knowledge and information.

Knowledge Application

Regardless of what type of knowledge management system is involved, knowledge that is not shared and applied to the practical problems facing firms and managers does not add business value. To provide a return on investment, organizational knowledge must become a systematic part of management decision making and become situated in systems for decision support (described in Chapter 12). Ultimately, new knowledge must be built into a firm's business processes and key application systems, including enterprise applications for managing key internal business processes and relationships with customers and suppliers. Management supports this process by creating—based on new knowledge—new business practices, new products and services, and new markets for the firm.

Building Organizational and Management Capital: Collaboration, Communities of Practice, and Office Environments

In addition to the activities we have just described, managers can help by developing new organizational roles and responsibilities for the acquisition of knowledge, including the creation of chief knowledge officer executive positions, dedicated staff positions (knowledge managers), and communities of practice. **Communities of practice (COPs)** are informal social networks of professionals and employees within and outside the firm who have similar work-related activities and interests. The activities of these communities include self-education and group education, conferences, online newsletters, and day-to-day sharing of experiences and techniques to solve specific work problems. Many organizations, such as IBM, the U.S. Federal Highway Administration, and the World Bank have encouraged the development of thousands of online communities of practice. These communities of practice depend greatly on software environments that enable collaboration and communication.

COPs can make it easier for people to reuse knowledge by pointing community members to useful documents, creating document repositories, and filtering information for newcomers. COPs members act as facilitators, encouraging contributions and discussion. COPs can also reduce the learning curve for new employees by providing contacts with subject matter experts and access to a community's established methods and tools. Finally, COPs can act as a spawning ground for new ideas, techniques, and decision-making behavior.

TYPES OF KNOWLEDGE MANAGEMENT SYSTEMS

There are essentially three major types of knowledge management systems: enterprise-wide knowledge management systems, knowledge work systems, and intelligent techniques. Figure 11.2 shows the knowledge management system applications for each of these major categories.

FIGURE 11.2 MAJOR TYPES OF KNOWLEDGE MANAGEMENT SYSTEMS

Enterprise-Wide Knowledge Management Systems

Knowledge Work Systems

Intelligent Techniques

General-purpose, integrated, firmwide efforts to collect, store, disseminate, and use digital content and knowledge

Enterprise content management systems
Collaboration and social tools
Learning management systems

Specialized workstations and systems that enable scientists, engineers, and other knowledge workers to create and discover new knowledge

Computer-aided design (CAD)
3-D virtualization
Virtual reality
Investment workstations

Tools for discovering patterns and applying knowledge to discrete decisions and knowledge domains

Data mining
Neural networks
Expert systems
Case-based reasoning
Fuzzy logic
Genetic algorithms
Intelligent agents

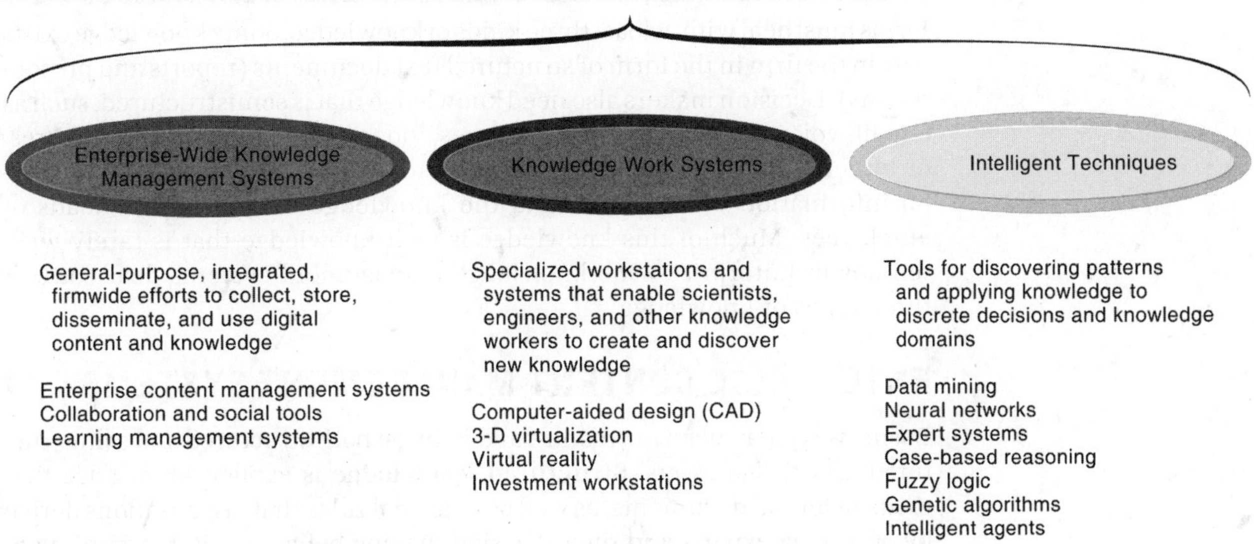

There are three major categories of knowledge management systems, and each can be broken down further into more specialized types of knowledge management systems.

Enterprise-wide knowledge management systems are general-purpose firmwide efforts to collect, store, distribute, and apply digital content and knowledge. These systems include capabilities for searching for information, storing both structured and unstructured data, and locating employee expertise within the firm. They also include supporting technologies such as portals, search engines, collaboration and social business tools, and learning management systems.

The development of powerful networked workstations and software for assisting engineers and scientists in the discovery of new knowledge has led to the creation of knowledge work systems such as computer-aided design (CAD), visualization, simulation, and virtual reality systems. **Knowledge work systems (KWS)** are specialized systems built for engineers, scientists, and other knowledge workers charged with discovering and creating new knowledge for a company. We discuss knowledge work applications in detail in Section 11.3.

Knowledge management also includes a diverse group of **intelligent techniques**, such as data mining, expert systems, neural networks, fuzzy logic, genetic algorithms, and intelligent agents. These techniques have different objectives, from a focus on discovering knowledge (data mining and neural networks), to distilling knowledge in the form of rules for a computer program (expert systems and fuzzy logic), to discovering optimal solutions for problems (genetic algorithms). Section 11.4 provides more detail about these intelligent techniques.

11.2 WHAT TYPES OF SYSTEMS ARE USED FOR ENTERPRISE-WIDE KNOWLEDGE MANAGEMENT AND HOW DO THEY PROVIDE VALUE FOR BUSINESSES?

Firms must deal with at least three kinds of knowledge. Some knowledge exists within the firm in the form of structured text documents (reports and presentations). Decision makers also need knowledge that is semistructured, such as e-mail, voice mail, chat room exchanges, videos, digital pictures, brochures, or bulletin board postings. In still other cases, there is no formal or digital information of any kind, and the knowledge resides in the heads of employees. Much of this knowledge is tacit knowledge that is rarely written down. Enterprise-wide knowledge management systems deal with all three types of knowledge.

ENTERPRISE CONTENT MANAGEMENT SYSTEMS

Businesses today need to organize and manage both structured and semistructured knowledge assets. **Structured knowledge** is explicit knowledge that exists in formal documents, as well as in formal rules that organizations derive by observing experts and their decision-making behaviors. But, according to experts, at least 80 percent of an organization's business content is semistructured or unstructured—information in folders, messages, memos, proposals,

FIGURE 11.3 AN ENTERPRISE CONTENT MANAGEMENT SYSTEM

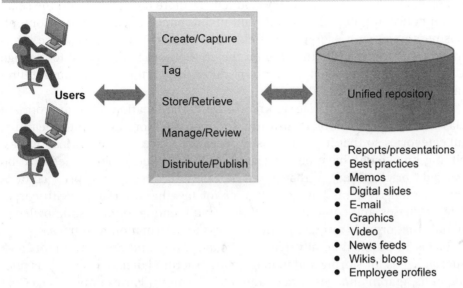

An enterprise content management system has capabilities for classifying, organizing, and managing structured and semistructured knowledge and making it available throughout the enterprise.

e-mails, graphics, electronic slide presentations, and even videos created in different formats and stored in many locations.

Enterprise content management systems help organizations manage both types of information. They have capabilities for knowledge capture, storage, retrieval, distribution, and preservation to help firms improve their business processes and decisions. Such systems include corporate repositories of documents, reports, presentations, and best practices, as well as capabilities for collecting and organizing semistructured knowledge such as e-mail (see Figure 11.3). Major enterprise content management systems also enable users to access external sources of information, such as news feeds and research, and to communicate via e-mail, chat/instant messaging, discussion groups, and videoconferencing. They are starting to incorporate blogs, wikis, and other enterprise social networking tools. Open Text Corporation, EMC (Documentum), IBM, and Oracle Corporation are leading vendors of enterprise content management software.

Calgary is the largest city in Alberta and the third largest municipality in Canada, with a population exceeding 1.1 million. Its 15,000 employees use OpenText Content Suite Platform to manage and share many different kinds of documents to provide essential services to citizens. Content Suite helps the city capture content it can actually track. Once a workspace is established in Content Server, the system automatically classifies documents, including graphic content, according to record type, retention requirements, and who in the organization is responsible for the document. Content created by one workgroup is easily accessible by other workgroups. Content Suite helped the city establish a strong records management program that supports groups with different needs. For example, Calgary's legal department and Freedom of Information Group places top priority on control and governance. Its Security team and City Council are more concerned with the separation between public documents and maintenance of confidential content. Business units with users in the field need an easy way to access the information they need while they are on the go. Content Suite is able to manage Calgary's content to meet each group's most important information requirements (OpenText 2013–2014).

A key problem in managing knowledge is the creation of an appropriate classification scheme, or **taxonomy**, to organize information into meaningful categories so that it can be easily accessed. Once the categories for classifying knowledge have been created, each knowledge object needs to be "tagged," or classified, so that it can be easily retrieved. Enterprise content management systems have capabilities for tagging, interfacing with corporate databases and content repositories, and creating enterprise knowledge portals that provide a single point of access to information resources.

Firms in publishing, advertising, broadcasting, and entertainment have special needs for storing and managing unstructured digital data such as photographs, graphic images, video, and audio content. For example, Coca-Cola must keep track of all the images of the Coca-Cola brand that have been created in the past at all of the company's worldwide offices, to prevent both redundant work and variation from a standard brand image. **Digital asset management systems** help companies classify, store, and distribute these digital objects.

LOCATING AND SHARING EXPERTISE

Some of the knowledge businesses need is not in the form of a digital document but instead resides in the memory of individual experts in the firm. Contemporary enterprise content management systems, along with the systems for collaboration and social business introduced in Chapter 2, have capabilities for locating experts and tapping their knowledge. These include online directories of corporate experts and their profiles, with details about their job experience, projects, publications, and educational degrees, and repositories of expert-generated content. Specialized search tools make it easier for employees to find the appropriate expert in a company.

For knowledge resources outside the firm, social networking and social business tools enable users to bookmark Web pages of interest, tag these bookmarks with keywords, and share the tags and Web page links with other people. These bookmarks are often public on sites such as Delicious and Reddit, but some can be saved privately and shared only with specified people or groups.

LEARNING MANAGEMENT SYSTEMS

Companies need ways to keep track of and manage employee learning and to integrate it more fully into their knowledge management and other corporate systems. A **learning management system (LMS)** provides tools for the management, delivery, tracking, and assessment of various types of employee learning and training.

Contemporary LMS support multiple modes of learning, including CD-ROM, downloadable videos, Web-based classes, live instruction in classes or online, and group learning in online forums and chat sessions. The LMS consolidates mixed-media training, automates the selection and administration of courses, assembles and delivers learning content, and measures learning effectiveness.

CVM Solutions, LLC (CVM) uses Digitec's Knowledge Direct learning management system to provide training about how to manage suppliers for clients such as Procter & Gamble, Colgate-Palmolive, and Delta Airlines. Knowledge Direct provides a portal for accessing course content online, along with hands-free administration features such as student registration and assessment tools, built-in Help and Contact Support, automatic e-mail triggers to remind users of courses or deadlines, automatic e-mail acknowledgement of course completions, and Web-based reporting for courses accessed.

Businesses run their own learning management systems, but they are also turning to publicly-available **massive open online courses (MOOCs)** to educate their employees. A MOOC is an online course made available via the Web to very large numbers of participants. For example, in March 2013 employees from General Electric, Johnson & Johnson, Samsung, and Walmart were among over 90,000 learners from 143 countries enrolled in Foundations for Business Strategy, a MOOC offered through the Coursera online learning platform by the University of Virginia's Darden School of Business (Nurmohamed, Gillani, and Lenox, 2013).

11.3 WHAT ARE THE MAJOR TYPES OF KNOWLEDGE WORK SYSTEMS AND HOW DO THEY PROVIDE VALUE FOR FIRMS?

The enterprise-wide knowledge systems we have just described provide a wide range of capabilities that can be used by many if not all the workers and groups in an organization. Firms also have specialized systems for knowledge workers to help them create new knowledge and to ensure that this knowledge is properly integrated into the business.

KNOWLEDGE WORKERS AND KNOWLEDGE WORK

Knowledge workers, which we introduced in Chapter 1, include researchers, designers, architects, scientists, and engineers who primarily create knowledge and information for the organization. Knowledge workers usually have high levels of education and memberships in professional organizations and are often asked to exercise independent judgment as a routine aspect of their work. For example, knowledge workers create new products or find ways of improving existing ones. Knowledge workers perform three key roles that are critical to the organization and to the managers who work within the organization:

- Keeping the organization current in knowledge as it develops in the external world—in technology, science, social thought, and the arts
- Serving as internal consultants regarding the areas of their knowledge, the changes taking place, and opportunities
- Acting as change agents, evaluating, initiating, and promoting change projects

REQUIREMENTS OF KNOWLEDGE WORK SYSTEMS

Most knowledge workers rely on office systems, such as word processors, voice mail, e-mail, videoconferencing, and scheduling systems, which are designed to increase worker productivity in the office. However, knowledge workers also require highly specialized knowledge work systems with powerful graphics, analytical tools, and communications and document management capabilities.

These systems require sufficient computing power to handle the sophisticated graphics or complex calculations necessary for such knowledge workers as scientific researchers, product designers, and financial analysts. Because knowledge workers are so focused on knowledge in the external world, these systems also must give the worker quick and easy access to external databases. They typically feature user-friendly interfaces that enable users to perform needed tasks without having to spend a great deal of time learning how to use the system. Knowledge workers are highly paid—wasting a knowledge worker's time is simply too expensive. Figure 11.4 summarizes the requirements of knowledge work systems.

FIGURE 11.4 REQUIREMENTS OF KNOWLEDGE WORK SYSTEMS

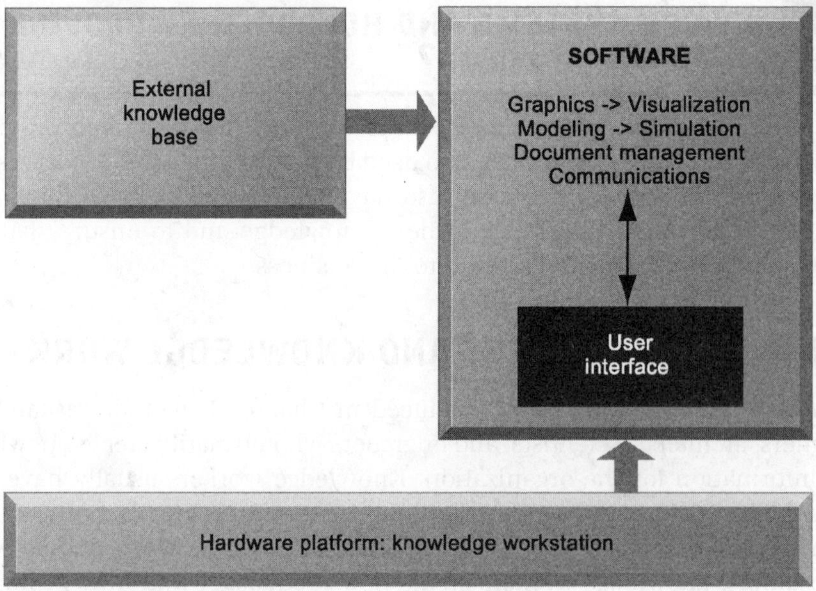

Knowledge work systems require strong links to external knowledge bases in addition to specialized hardware and software.

Knowledge workstations often are designed and optimized for the specific tasks to be performed; so, for example, a design engineer requires a different workstation setup than a financial analyst. Design engineers need graphics with enough power to handle three-dimensional (3-D) CAD systems. However, financial analysts are more interested in access to a myriad number of external databases and large databases for efficiently storing and accessing massive amounts of financial data.

EXAMPLES OF KNOWLEDGE WORK SYSTEMS

Major knowledge work applications include CAD systems, virtual reality systems for simulation and modeling, and financial workstations. **Computer-aided design (CAD)** automates the creation and revision of designs, using computers and sophisticated graphics software. Using a more traditional physical design methodology, each design modification requires a mold to be made and a prototype to be tested physically. That process must be repeated many times, which is a very expensive and time-consuming process. Using a CAD workstation, the designer need only make a physical prototype toward the end of the design process because the design can be easily tested and changed on the computer. The ability of CAD software to provide design specifications for the tooling and manufacturing processes also saves a great deal of time and money while producing a manufacturing process with far fewer problems.

For example, Ford Motor Company used a computer simulation to create an engine cylinder that came up with the most efficient design possible. Engineers altered that design to account for manufacturing constraints and tested the revised design virtually in models that used decades of data on material properties and engine performance. Ford then created the mold to make a real part that could be bolted onto an engine for further testing. The entire process took days instead of months and cost thousands of dollars instead of millions. CAD systems have provided similar benefits to Jaguar Land Rover, as described in the chapter-opening case.

CAD systems are able to supply data for **3-D printing**, also known as additive manufacturing, which uses machines to make solid objects, layer by layer, from specifications in a digital file. 3-D printing is currently being used for producing prototypes and customized manufacturing work (see the Interactive Session on Technology).

Virtual reality systems have visualization, rendering, and simulation capabilities that go far beyond those of conventional CAD systems. They use interactive graphics software to create computer-generated simulations that are so close to reality that users almost believe they are participating in a real-world situation. In many virtual reality systems, the user dons special clothing, headgear, and equipment, depending on the application. The clothing contains sensors that record the user's movements and immediately transmit that information back to the computer. For instance, to walk through a virtual reality simulation of a house, you would need garb that monitors the movement of your feet, hands, and head. You also would need goggles containing video screens and sometimes audio attachments and feeling gloves so that you can be immersed in the computer feedback.

INTERACTIVE SESSION: TECHNOLOGY

IS 3-D PRINTING A GAME-CHANGER?

There's a lot of talk about 3-D printing and it is one of today's hottest new technologies. 3-D printing, or additive manufacturing, is a process for making three dimensional solid objects from a digital file. The creation of a 3-D printed object is achieved using additive processes in which an object is created by laying down successive layers of materials. Each of these layers can be seen as a thinly sliced horizontal cross-section of the eventual object.

A virtual design of the object is made in a CAD (Computer Aided Design) file using a 3-D modeling program. The software slices the model of the object into hundreds or thousands of horizontal layers, each of which is a thinly-sliced horizontal cross-section of the final object. The software creates a digital file that instructs a 3-D printer how to create the object layer by layer, with no sign of the layering visible. The output is a single three-dimensional object.

There are several different ways in which 3-D printers build layers to create the final object. Some methods use melting or softening material to produce the layers (selective laser sintering and fused deposition modeling), while others lay liquid materials that are cured with different technologies (stereolithography).

Today's 3-D printers can handle materials including plastic, titanium, and human cartilage, and produce fully functional components, including batteries, transistors, LEDs, and other complex mechanisms. Costs have dropped dramatically, with basic 3-D printers for hobbyists selling as low as $250, although industrial 3-D printers may run up to $800,000.

Need a part for your washing machine? Right now, you'd order it from your repairman, who would get it from a distributor, who would have it shipped from China, where thousands of these parts were mass-produced at the same time, probably injection-molded from a very expensive mold. In the future, you might be able to 3-D print the part in your home, using a CAD file you

downloaded. If you didn't have a 3-D printer, you could print it out at a local 3-D printing facility similar to Kinko's or transmit the CAD file over the Internet for printing by a cloud-based 3-D printing service such as Shapeways.

3-D printing eliminates the need for expensive customized tooling, using less material per object. With injection molding, companies must create a different physical mold for every different part they want to produce. If the specifications for a part change, they must create a new mold for the part. With 3-D printing there's no mold, just a computer model of the part that can be updated any time.

This was an advantage for Chris Milnes, who manufactures the Square Helper—a plastic clip the size of a quarter that holds a credit card reader in place on an iPhone or iPad. If Mr. Milnes had the clip made in China, it would have cost $6,000 for the tooling to build an injection mold, plus 25 to 30 cents per unit. Instead, he uses a MakerBot Replicator 2 purchased for $2,000, and the plastic for 3-D printing the reader costs 3 cents apiece. Using a 3-D printer also makes it much easier to adjust the part when Apple updates the iPhone. All Milnes has to do is to change a few lines of software. So far, Milnes has sold about 2,000 clips for $7.95 each.

Some say 3-D printing has potential to reshape manufacturing and even usher in a Third Industrial Revolution in which customizable one-off production supplants mass production. For some types of manufacturing work, this could be true, and there will be profound changes in some companies' business models and production locations. Don't expect a seismic shift, however.

It takes much more than pressing a button to create a part using 3-D printing. A 3-D printer is much more complicated to use than a desktop printer, with much more technical know-how required to operate the device and software. The outputs are much more specialized. A printer for metal can't print plastic and a printer for ABS plastic, for example, may not print any other type of plastic. Plastics are relatively straightforward to work with, but metals are more difficult.

Fashioning something using 3-D printing is extremely slow and cumbersome. It can take an entire day or longer for printouts to cool. 3-D printing doesn't scale well if you have to churn out thousands of items in a short time. A startup called Rest Devices was using 3-D printing to design and manufacture the Mimo, an infant's one piece outfit with a built-in sensor that lets parents monitor their newborns' breathing. When Babies "R" Us ordered 7,000 pieces, their MakerBot 3-D printer simply couldn't produce the items fast enough. Rest Devices then turned to traditional injection molding to make key plastic parts. A part comes out of injection molding every 20-30 seconds, whereas the 3-D printer could only produce one in 15-20 minutes.

It looks like 3-D printing is better suited for jobs involving complex designs or limited production runs. 3-D printing is very useful for helping designers test ideas and speed product development, not replacing large-scale manufacturing. For example, Ford Motor Company is using 3-D printing to test parts of new cars. An engine prototype printed from sand-based material cost $3000 to make and is available in 4 days. A traditional prototype used to require months to create and cost half-million dollars. Nike uses 3-D print-

ers to create multi-colored prototypes of shoes. The company used to spend thousands of dollars on a physical prototype and wait weeks for it to be produced. Now, the prototype cost is only in the hundreds of dollars. Changes can be made instantly on the computer and the prototype reprinted on the same day.

Some companies are using 3-D printers for short-run or custom manufacturing, where the printed objects are not prototypes, but the actual end user product. GE Aviation using 3-D printers to manufacture more than 85,000 fuel nozzles for its Leap jet engines. (There are 19 nozzles per engine.) Rather than assembling finely-honed metal parts, GE printed the engine's fuel nozzles layer by layer. Earlier fuel nozzles had 20 different parts, whereas the 3-D printed version is a single piece optimized to spray fuel into engines. The new version is 25 percent lighter than current models, and is capable of lasting five times longer before servicing. Transforming multiple parts into a single part results in a final assembly that is less susceptible to errors.

Sources: Lyndsey Gilpin, "3-D printing: 10 companies using it in ground-breaking ways, TechRepublic, March 26, 2014; Peter S. Green, "3-D Printing's Promise-and Limits," *Wall Street Journal*, June 1, 2014; Daniel Cohen, Matthew Sargeant, and Ken Somers, "3-D Printing Takes Shape," McKinsey Quarterly, January 2014; Alexander Eule," Beware 3-D Printing!" Barrons, March 8, 2014; Tim Laseter and Jeremy Hutchison-Krupat, "A Skeptic's Guide to 3-D Printing," Strategy + Business, Winter 2013.

CASE STUDY QUESTIONS

1. Describe the technologies used in 3-D printing. How does 3-D printing differ from CAD?

2. What are the advantages and disadvantages of using 3-D printing?

3. What kinds of businesses are most likely to benefit from 3-D printing? Why? Give 2 examples.

4. How could 3-D printing impact companies' supply chains and business models?

At NYU Langone Medical Center in New York City, students wearing 3-D glasses are able to "dissect" a virtual cadaver projected on a screen. With the help of a computer, they can move through the virtual body, scrutinizing layers of muscles or watching a close-up of a pumping heart along with bright red arteries and deep blue veins. The virtual human body was created by BioDigital Systems, a New York City medical visualization firm. The virtual cadaver being used at Langone is a beta version that BioDigital plans to develop into a searchable, customizable map of the human body for medical educators and physicians. NYU medical school has no current plans to phase out dissection, but the 3-D virtual cadaver is a valuable complementary teaching tool (Singer, 2012).

Ford Motor Company has been using virtual reality to help design its vehicles. In one example of Ford's Immersive Virtual Environment, a designer was presented with a car seat, steering wheel, and blank dashboard. Wearing virtual reality glasses and gloves with sensors, the designer was able to "sit" in the seat surrounded by the vehicle's 3-D design to experience how a proposed interior would look and feel. The designer would be able to identify blind spots or see if knobs were in an awkward place. Ford's designers could also use this technology to see the impact of a design on manufacturing. For example, is a bolt that assembly line workers need to tighten too hard to reach?

Augmented reality (AR) is a related technology for enhancing visualization. AR provides a live direct or indirect view of a physical real-world environment whose elements are augmented by virtual computer-generated imagery. The user is grounded in the real physical world, and the virtual images are merged with the real view to create the augmented display. The digital technology provides additional information to enhance the perception of reality, making the surrounding real world of the user more interactive and meaningful. The yellow first-down markers shown on televised football games are examples of augmented reality as are medical procedures like image-guided surgery, where data acquired from computerized tomography (CT) and magnetic resonance imaging (MRI) scans or from ultrasound imaging are superimposed on the patient in the operating room. Other industries where AR has caught on include military training, engineering design, robotics, and consumer design.

Virtual reality applications developed for the Web use a standard called **Virtual Reality Modeling Language (VRML)**. VRML is a set of specifications for interactive, 3-D modeling on the World Wide Web that can organize multiple media types, including animation, images, and audio to put users in a simulated real-world environment. VRML is platform independent, operates over a desktop computer, and requires little bandwidth.

DuPont, the Wilmington, Delaware, chemical company, created a VRML application called HyperPlant, which enables users to access 3-D data over the Internet using Web browser software. Engineers can go through 3-D models as if they were physically walking through a plant, viewing objects at eye level. This level of detail reduces the number of mistakes they make during construction of oil rigs, oil plants, and other structures.

The financial industry is using specialized **investment workstations** such as Bloomberg Terminals to leverage the knowledge and time of its

TABLE 11.2 EXAMPLES OF KNOWLEDGE WORK SYSTEMS

KNOWLEDGE WORK SYSTEM	FUNCTION IN ORGANIZATION
CAD/CAM (computer-aided manufacturing)	Provides engineers, designers, and factory managers with precise control over industrial design and manufacturing
Virtual reality systems	Provide drug designers, architects, engineers, and medical workers with precise, photorealistic simulations of objects
Investment workstations	High-end PCs and workstations used in the financial sector to analyze trading situations instantaneously and facilitate portfolio management

brokers, traders, and portfolio managers. Firms such as Merrill Lynch and UBS Financial Services have installed investment workstations that integrate a wide range of data from both internal and external sources, including contact management data, real-time and historical market data, and research reports. Previously, financial professionals had to spend considerable time accessing data from separate systems and piecing together the information they needed. By providing one-stop information faster and with fewer errors, the workstations streamline the entire investment process from stock selection to updating client records. Table 11.2 summarizes the major types of knowledge work systems.

11.4 WHAT ARE THE BUSINESS BENEFITS OF USING INTELLIGENT TECHNIQUES FOR KNOWLEDGE MANAGEMENT?

Artificial intelligence and database technology provide a number of intelligent techniques that organizations can use to capture individual and collective knowledge and to extend their knowledge base. Expert systems, case-based reasoning, and fuzzy logic are used for capturing tacit knowledge. Neural networks and data mining are used for **knowledge discovery**. They can discover underlying patterns, categories, and behaviors in large data sets that could not be discovered by managers alone or simply through experience. Genetic algorithms are used for generating solutions to problems that are too large and complex for human beings to analyze on their own. Intelligent agents can automate routine tasks to help firms search for and filter information for use in electronic commerce, supply chain management, and other activities.

Data mining, which we introduced in Chapter 6, helps organizations capture undiscovered knowledge residing in large databases, providing managers with new insight for improving business performance. It has become an important tool for management decision making, and we provide a detailed discussion of data mining for management decision support in Chapter 12.

The other intelligent techniques discussed in this section are based on **artificial intelligence (AI)** technology, which consists of computer-based systems (both hardware and software) that attempt to emulate human behavior. Such systems would be able to learn languages, accomplish physical tasks, use a perceptual apparatus, and emulate human expertise and decision making. Although AI applications do not exhibit the breadth, complexity, originality, and generality of human intelligence, they play an important role in contemporary knowledge management.

CAPTURING KNOWLEDGE: EXPERT SYSTEMS

Expert systems are an intelligent technique for capturing tacit knowledge in a very specific and limited domain of human expertise. These systems capture the knowledge of skilled employees in the form of a set of rules in a software system that can be used by others in the organization. The set of rules in the expert system adds to the memory, or stored learning, of the firm.

Expert systems lack the breadth of knowledge and the understanding of fundamental principles of a human expert. They typically perform very limited tasks that can be performed by professionals in a few minutes or hours, such as diagnosing a malfunctioning machine or determining whether to grant credit for a loan. Problems that cannot be solved by human experts in the same short period of time are far too difficult for an expert system. However, by capturing human expertise in limited areas, expert systems can provide benefits, helping organizations make high-quality decisions with fewer people. Today, expert systems are widely used in business in discrete, highly structured decision-making situations.

How Expert Systems Work

Human knowledge must be modeled or represented in a way that a computer can process. Expert systems model human knowledge as a set of rules that collectively are called the **knowledge base**. The rules are obtained by carefully interviewing one or several "experts" who have a thorough command of the knowledge base for the system or by documenting business rules found in manuals, books, or reports. Expert systems have from 200 to many thousands of these rules, depending on the complexity of the problem. These rules are much more interconnected and nested than in a traditional software program (see Figure 11.5).

The strategy used to search through the knowledge base is called the **inference engine**. Two strategies are commonly used: forward chaining and backward chaining (see Figure 11.6).

In **forward chaining,** the inference engine begins with the information entered by the user and searches the rule base to arrive at a conclusion. The strategy is to fire, or carry out, the action of the rule when a condition is true. In Figure 11.6, beginning on the left, if the user enters a client's name with income greater than $100,000, the engine will fire all rules in sequence from left to right. If the user then enters information indicating that the same client owns real estate, another pass of the rule base will occur and more rules will fire. Processing continues until no more rules can be fired.

FIGURE 11.5 RULES IN AN EXPERT SYSTEM

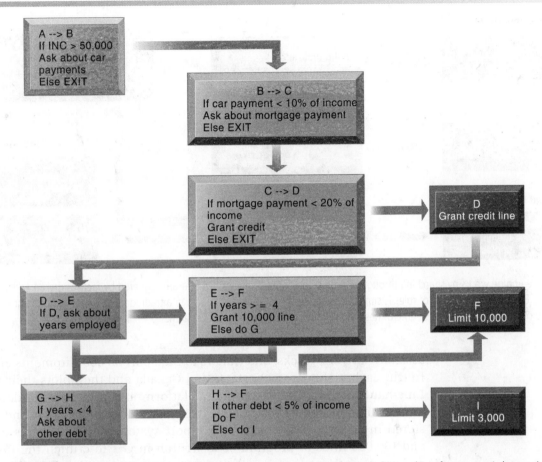

An expert system contains a number of rules to be followed. The rules are interconnected; the number of outcomes is known in advance and is limited; there are multiple paths to the same outcome; and the system can consider multiple rules at a single time. The rules illustrated are for simple credit-granting expert systems.

In **backward chaining,** the strategy for searching the rule base starts with a hypothesis and proceeds by asking the user questions about selected facts until the hypothesis is either confirmed or disproved. In our example, in Figure 11.6, ask the question, "Should we add this person to the prospect database?" Begin on the right of the diagram and work toward the left. You can see that the person should be added to the database if a sales representative is sent, term insurance is granted, or a financial adviser visits the client.

Examples of Successful Expert Systems

Expert systems provide businesses with an array of benefits including improved decisions, reduced errors, reduced costs, reduced training time, and higher levels of quality and service. Con-Way Transportation built an expert system called Line-haul to automate and optimize planning of overnight shipment routes for its nationwide freight-trucking business. The expert system captures the business rules that dispatchers follow when

FIGURE 11.6 INFERENCE ENGINES IN EXPERT SYSTEMS

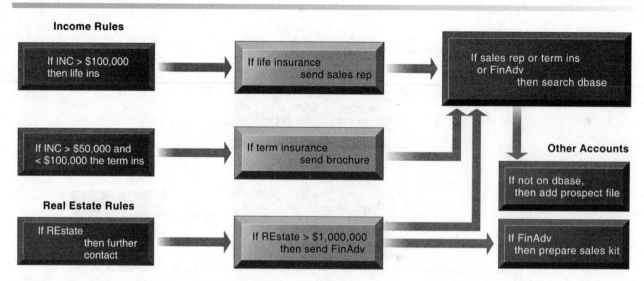

An inference engine works by searching through the rules and "firing" those rules that are triggered by facts gathered and entered by the user. Basically, a collection of rules is similar to a series of nested IF statements in a traditional software program; however, the magnitude of the statements and degree of nesting are much greater in an expert system.

assigning drivers, trucks, and trailers to transport 50,000 shipments of heavy freight each night across 25 states and Canada and then plots their routes. Line-haul runs on a Sun computer platform and uses data on daily customer shipment requests, available drivers, trucks, trailer space, and weight stored in an Oracle database. The expert system uses thousands of rules and 100,000 lines of program code written in C++ to crunch the numbers and create optimum routing plans for 95 percent of daily freight shipments. Con-Way dispatchers tweak the routing plan provided by the expert system and relay final routing specifications to field personnel responsible for packing the trailers for their nighttime runs. Con-Way recouped its $3 million investment in the system within two years by reducing the number of drivers, packing more freight per trailer, and reducing damage from rehandling. The system also reduces dispatchers' arduous nightly tasks.

Although expert systems lack the robust and general intelligence of human beings, they can provide benefits to organizations if their limitations are well understood. Only certain classes of problems can be solved using expert systems. Virtually all successful expert systems deal with problems of classification in limited domains of knowledge where there are relatively few alternative outcomes and these possible outcomes are all known in advance. Expert systems are much less useful for dealing with unstructured problems typically encountered by managers.

Many expert systems require large, lengthy, and expensive development efforts. Hiring or training more experts may be less expensive than building an expert system. Typically, the environment in which an expert system operates is continually changing so that the expert system must also continually change. Some expert systems, especially large ones, are so complex that in a few years the maintenance costs equal the development costs.

ORGANIZATIONAL INTELLIGENCE: CASE-BASED REASONING

Expert systems primarily capture the tacit knowledge of individual experts, but organizations also have collective knowledge and expertise that they have built up over the years. This organizational knowledge can be captured and stored using case-based reasoning. In **case-based reasoning (CBR)**, descriptions of past experiences of human specialists, represented as cases, are documented and stored in a database for later retrieval when the user encounters a new case with similar parameters. The system searches for stored cases with problem characteristics similar to the new one, finds the closest fit, and applies the solutions of the old case to the new case. Successful solutions are tagged to the new case and both are stored together with the other cases in the knowledge base. Unsuccessful solutions also are appended to the case database along with explanations as to why the solutions did not work (see Figure 11.7).

Expert systems work by applying a set of IF-THEN-ELSE rules extracted from human experts. Case-based reasoning, in contrast, represents knowledge as a series of cases, and this knowledge base is continuously expanded and refined by users. You'll find case-based reasoning in diagnostic systems in medicine or customer support where users can retrieve past cases whose characteristics are similar to the new case. The system suggests a solution or diagnosis based on the best-matching retrieved case.

FUZZY LOGIC SYSTEMS

Most people do not think in terms of traditional IF-THEN rules or precise numbers. Humans tend to categorize things imprecisely using rules for making decisions that may have many shades of meaning. For example, a man or a woman can be *strong* or *intelligent*. A company can be *large, medium,* or *small* in size. Temperature can be *hot, cold, cool,* or *warm*. These categories represent a range of values.

Fuzzy logic is a rule-based technology that can represent such imprecision by creating rules that use approximate or subjective values. It can describe a particular phenomenon or process linguistically and then represent that description in a small number of flexible rules. Organizations can use fuzzy logic to create software systems that capture tacit knowledge where there is linguistic ambiguity.

Let's look at the way fuzzy logic would represent various temperatures in a computer application to control room temperature automatically. The terms (known as *membership functions*) are imprecisely defined so that, for example, in Figure 11.8, cool is between 45 degrees and 70 degrees, although the temperature is most clearly cool between about 60 degrees and 67 degrees. Note that *cool* is overlapped by *cold* or *norm*. To control the room environment using this logic, the programmer would develop similarly imprecise definitions for humidity and other factors, such as outdoor wind and temperature. The rules might include one that says: "If the temperature is *cool* or *cold* and the humidity is low while the outdoor wind is

FIGURE 11.7 HOW CASE-BASED REASONING WORKS

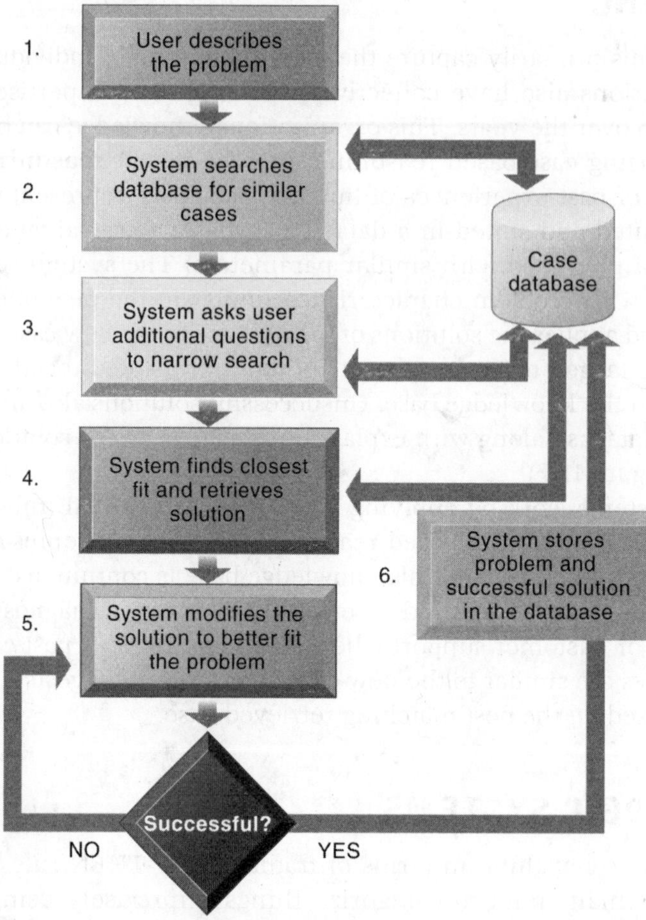

Case-based reasoning represents knowledge as a database of past cases and their solutions. The system uses a six-step process to generate solutions to new problems encountered by the user.

high and the outdoor temperature is low, raise the heat and humidity in the room." The computer would combine the membership function readings in a weighted manner and, using all the rules, raise and lower the temperature and humidity.

Fuzzy logic provides solutions to problems requiring expertise that is difficult to represent in the form of crisp IF-THEN rules. In Japan, Sendai's subway system uses fuzzy logic controls to accelerate so smoothly that standing passengers need not hold on. Mitsubishi Heavy Industries in Tokyo has been able to reduce the power consumption of its air conditioners by 20 percent by implementing control programs in fuzzy logic. The autofocus device in cameras is only possible because of fuzzy logic. In these instances, fuzzy logic allows incremental changes in inputs to produce smooth changes in outputs instead of discontinuous ones, making it useful for consumer electronics and engineering applications.

FIGURE 11.8 FUZZY LOGIC FOR TEMPERATURE CONTROL

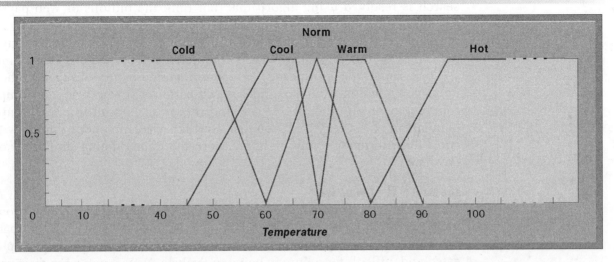

The membership functions for the input called temperature are in the logic of the thermostat to control the room temperature. Membership functions help translate linguistic expressions such as *warm* into numbers that the computer can manipulate.

Management also has found fuzzy logic useful for decision making and organizational control. A Wall Street firm created a system that selects companies for potential acquisition, using the language stock traders understand. A fuzzy logic system has been developed to detect possible fraud in medical claims submitted by health care providers anywhere in the United States.

MACHINE LEARNING

Machine learning is the study of how computer programs can improve their performance without explicit programming. Why does this constitute learning? A machine that learns is a machine that, like a human being, can recognize patterns in data, and change its behavior based on its recognition of patterns, experience, or prior learnings (a database). For instance, a car-driving robot should be able to recognize the presence of other cars and objects (people), and change its behavior accordingly (stop, go, slow down, speed up, or turn). The idea of a self-taught, self-correcting, computer program is not new, and has been a part of the artificial intelligence field at least since the 1970s. Up until the 1990s, however, machine learning was not very capable of producing useful devices or solving interesting, business problems.

Machine learning has expanded greatly in the last ten years because of the growth in computing power available to scientists and firms and its falling cost, along with advances in the design of algorithms, databases, and robots (see the chapter-ending case on IBM's Watson). The Internet and the big data (see Chapter 6) made available on the Internet have proved to be very useful testing and proving grounds for machine learning.

We use machine learning every day but don't recognize it. Every Google search is resolved using algorithms that rank the billions of Web pages based on your query, and change the results based on any changes you make in your search, all in a few milliseconds. Search results also vary according to your prior searches and the items you clicked on. Every time you buy something on Amazon, its recommender engine will suggest other items you might be interested in based on patterns in your prior consumption, behavior on other Web sites, and the purchases of others who are "similar" to you. Every time you visit Netflix, a recommender system will come up with movies you might be interested in based on a similar set of factors.

Neural Networks

Neural networks are used for solving complex, poorly understood problems for which large amounts of data have been collected. They find patterns and relationships in massive amounts of data that would be too complicated and difficult for a human being to analyze. Neural networks discover this knowledge by using hardware and software that parallel the processing patterns of the biological or human brain. Neural networks "learn" patterns from large quantities of data by sifting through data, searching for relationships, building models, and correcting over and over again the model's own mistakes.

A neural network has a large number of sensing and processing nodes that continuously interact with each other. Figure 11.9 represents one type of neural network comprising an input layer, an output layer, and a hidden processing layer. Humans "train" the network by feeding it a set of training data for which the inputs produce a known set of outputs or conclusions. This helps the computer learn the correct solution by example. As the

FIGURE 11.9 HOW A NEURAL NETWORK WORKS

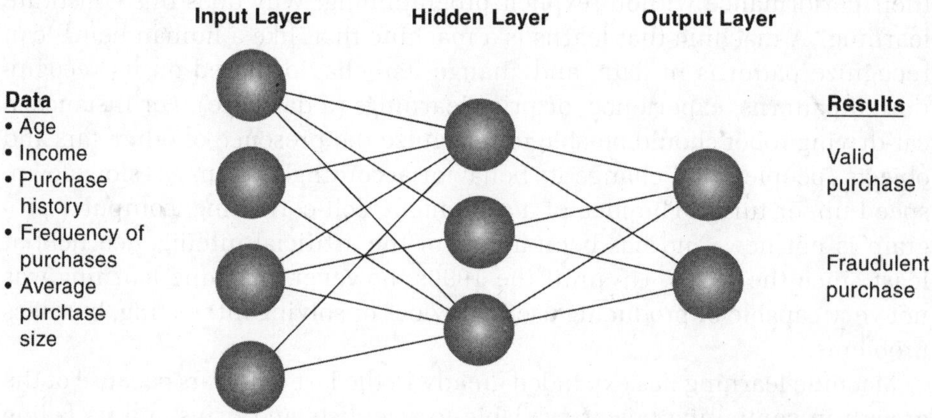

A neural network uses rules it "learns" from patterns in data to construct a hidden layer of logic. The hidden layer then processes inputs, classifying them based on the experience of the model. In this example, the neural network has been trained to distinguish between valid and fraudulent credit card purchases.

computer is fed more data, each case is compared with the known outcome. If it differs, a correction is calculated and applied to the nodes in the hidden processing layer. These steps are repeated until a condition, such as corrections being less than a certain amount, is reached. The neural network in Figure 11.9 has learned how to identify a fraudulent credit card purchase. Also, self-organizing neural networks can be trained by exposing them to large amounts of data and allowing them to discover the patterns and relationships in the data.

A Google research team headed by Stanford University computer scientist Andrew Y. Ng and Google fellow Jeff Dean recently created a neural network with more than one billion connections that could identify cats. The network used an array of 16,000 processors and was fed random thumbnails of images, each extracted from a collection of 10 million YouTube videos. The neural network taught itself to recognize cats, without human help in identifying specific features during the learning process. Google believes this neural network has promising applications in image search, speech recognition, and machine language translation (Markoff, 2013). IBM has developed an energy-efficient processor chip that relies on a dense web of transistors similar to the brain's neural network. It is still in experimental mode, with great promise for pattern recognition (Markoff, 2014). The Interactive Session on Organizations describes neural network applications for facial recognition and their potential impact on individual privacy.

Whereas expert systems seek to emulate or model a human expert's way of solving problems, neural network builders claim that they do not program solutions and do not aim to solve specific problems. Instead, neural network designers seek to put intelligence into the hardware in the form of a generalized capability to learn. In contrast, the expert system is highly specific to a given problem and cannot be retrained easily.

Neural network applications in medicine, science, and business address problems in pattern classification, prediction, financial analysis, and control and optimization. In medicine, neural network applications are used for screening patients for coronary artery disease, for diagnosing patients with epilepsy and Alzheimer's disease, and for performing pattern recognition of pathology images. The financial industry uses neural networks to discern patterns in vast pools of data that might help predict the performance of equities, corporate bond ratings, or corporate bankruptcies. Visa International uses a neural network to help detect credit card fraud by monitoring all Visa transactions for sudden changes in the buying patterns of cardholders.

There are many puzzling aspects of neural networks. Unlike expert systems, which typically provide explanations for their solutions, neural networks cannot always explain why they arrived at a particular solution. Moreover, they cannot always guarantee a completely certain solution, arrive at the same solution again with the same input data, or always guarantee the best solution. They are very sensitive and may not perform well if their training covers too little or too much data. In most current applications, neural networks are best used as aids to human decision makers instead of substitutes for them.

INTERACTIVE SESSION: ORGANIZATIONS

FACIAL RECOGNITION SYSTEMS: ANOTHER THREAT TO PRIVACY?

Are you on Facebook? Do you worry about how much Facebook knows about you? Well, as much as it knows now, it's about to know much more. Facebook has been investing heavily in artificial intelligence technology to uniquely identify your face and to track your behavior more precisely.

Facebook's facial recognition tool, called DeepFace is nearly as accurate as the human brain in recognizing a face. DeepFace can compare two photos and state with 97.25% accuracy whether the photos show the same face. Humans are able to perform the same task with 97.53% accuracy.

DeepFace was developed by Facebook's AI research group in Menlo Park, California and is based on an advanced deep-learning neural network. Deep learning looks at a large body of data, including human faces, and tries to develop a high-level abstraction of a human face by looking for recurring patterns (cheeks, eyebrows, etc). The DeepFace neural network consists of nine layers of "neurons." Its learning process has created 120 million connections (synapses) between those neurons using four million photos of faces.

Once the learning process is complete, every image fed into the system passes through the synapses in a different way, producing a unique fingerprint among the layers of neurons. For example, a neuron might ask if a particular face has a heavy brow. If so, one synapse would be followed, if not, another path would be taken.

DeepFace soon will be ready for commercial use, most likely to help Facebook improve the accuracy of its existing facial recognition capabilities to ensure that every photo of you on Facebook is connected to your account. (Facebook has one of the largest facial databases in the world for its photo tagging service.) DeepFace might also be used for real-world facial tracking, for example monitoring someone's shopping habits as that person moves from physical store to store. Facebook could profit handsomely from the detailed behavioral tracking data collected via DeepFace.

Facebook is one of many organizations using facial recognition systems, and neural networks are one of several techniques for this purpose. The Oregon Department of Motor Vehicles (DMV) uses facial recognition software to ensure that driver's licenses, instruction permits, and ID cards are not issued under false names. In Pinellas County, Florida, police can capture a 3-D video and upload it to an image gallery for comparison to identify people with prior criminal records or outstanding warrants.

Whatever the technology foundation, facial recognition systems are raising alarm among privacy advocates, who are worried about the far-reaching use of people's facial photos without their knowledge or consent. Although police departments and DMVs have strict limits on the use of their facial recognition software, casinos are beginning to faceprint their visitors to identify high rollers to pamper, and some Japanese grocery stores now use face-matching to identify shoplifters.

Dr. Joseph J. Atick, one of the pioneers of facial recognition technology, is at the forefront of these concerns. Atick is in favor of facial recognition for specific purposes such as law and immigration enforcement, motor vehicle department authentication, and airport entry, but he warns about its use for mass surveillance. Atick has been encouraging companies to adopt policies that safeguard the retention and reuse of facial data, stipulating that it cannot be matched, shared, or sold without permission. Another concern is the lack of a legal framework for complying with requests for facial matching from government agencies.

The impending release of a Google Glass app (glassware) called NameTag underscores Atick's concerns about unregulated facial recognition software. The name, occupation, and public Facebook profile of any passerby on the street can be obtained by momentarily focusing on his or her face. Google announced that it would not authorize any facial recognition apps, but an alternative operating system that bypasses Glass's swiping and voice commands allows a picture to be snapped with a wink. A facial recognition app records the names of people to whom you have been introduced, and a beta version of NameTag has been released.

Facial analysis has progressed beyond scrutinizing static features. Frame-by-frame analysis can isolate involuntary millisecond-long expressions, revealing private sentiments. While these insights can drive productive endeavors, they are fraught with privacy implications. For example, do you want the person conducting your job interview to be able to review a videotape, identify fleeting moments of confusion or indecision, and decide against hiring you?

Psychologist Paul Eckman studied these fleeting microexpressions that surface when people are attempting to suppress an emotion and devised the Facial Action Coding System (FACS). Forty-three facial muscles control seven primary expressions—happiness, sadness, fear, anger, disgust, contempt, and surprise. Combinations of other basic muscle movements signal more advanced emotions such as frustration and confusion. People, and now computer programs, can be trained to recognize the universal spontaneous micromovements that divulge peoples' true feelings—narrowed eyelids, raised eyebrows, wrinkled forehead, scrunched nose, flared nostrils, or tensed lips.

Large datasets of FACS-catalogued video will soon be incorporated into computer games. Measuring player reactions to game activity can, for example, prompt developers to add features or increase game speed at junctures where players exhibit boredom.

Emotient, another expression analysis start-up located in San Diego, California, received a $6 million infusion of funds in early 2014 to support glassware for retail salespeople. Customer responses to everyday exchanges will be measured and evaluated to develop training programs aimed at optimizing customer service, product offerings, and merchandising techniques.

Emotient is confident that the ability to objectively and accurately gauge customer emotions will give retail teams more tools to increase sales, but customer response to being recorded by cameras embedded in smartglasses is uncertain. The increasingly common tradeoff between an improved customer selling experience and privacy will have to be astutely navigated, with the additional burden of gaining customer acceptance for being recorded.

Although facial expression analysis will likely never be an exact science, academics, business people, and, certainly, government agencies are intrigued by its possible applications. Online learning could be improved using Webcams that perceive confusion in a student's expression, and trigger additional tutoring sessions. Instantaneous feedback from smartglasses could help people with autism to navigate a world that is often baffling to them due to their inability to interpret social cues. And when voice and gesture analysis and gaze tracking can be combined with facial expression analysis, the possibilities will explode, along with the privacy implications.

Sources: Sebastian Anthony, "Facebook's facial recognition software is now as accurate as the human brain, but what now?" ExtremeTech, March 19, 2014; Natasha Singer, "Never Forgetting a Face," New York Times, May 17, 2014; Ingrid Lunden, "Emotient Raises $6M For Facial Expression Recognition Tech, Debuts Google Glass Sentiment Analysis App," techcrunch.com, March 6, 2014; Anne Eisenberg, "When Algorithms Grow Accustomed to Your Face," New York Times, November 30, 2013; and Doug Smith, "Privacy Concerns over Facial Recognition Software," myfoxtampabay.com, November 12, 2013.

CASE STUDY QUESTIONS

1. What are some of the benefits of using facial recognition technology? Describe some current and future applications of this technology.

2. How does facial recognition technology threaten the protection of individual privacy? Give several examples.

3. Would you like DeepFace to track your activities on Facebook and in the physical world? Why or why not?

FIGURE 11.10 THE COMPONENTS OF A GENETIC ALGORITHM

		Length	Width	Weight	Fitness
	1	Long	Wide	Light	55
	2	Short	Narrow	Heavy	49
	3	Long	Narrow	Heavy	36
	4	Short	Medium	Light	61
	5	Long	Medium	Very light	74
A population of chromosomes			**Decoding of chromosomes**		**Evaluation of chromosomes**

This example illustrates an initial population of "chromosomes," each representing a different solution. The genetic algorithm uses an iterative process to refine the initial solutions so that the better ones, those with the higher fitness, are more likely to emerge as the best solution.

Genetic Algorithms

Genetic algorithms are useful for finding the optimal solution for a specific problem by examining a very large number of possible solutions for that problem. They are based on techniques inspired by evolutionary biology, such as inheritance, mutation, selection, and crossover (recombination).

A genetic algorithm works by representing information as a string of 0s and 1s. The genetic algorithm searches a population of randomly generated strings of binary digits to identify the right string representing the best possible solution for the problem. As solutions alter and combine, the worst ones are discarded and the better ones survive to go on to produce even better solutions.

In Figure 11.10, each string corresponds to one of the variables in the problem. One applies a test for fitness, ranking the strings in the population according to their level of desirability as possible solutions. After the initial population is evaluated for fitness, the algorithm then produces the next generation of strings, consisting of strings that survived the fitness test plus off-spring strings produced from mating pairs of strings, and tests their fitness. The process continues until a solution is reached.

Genetic algorithms are used to solve problems that are very dynamic and complex, involving hundreds or thousands of variables or formulas. The problem must be one where the range of possible solutions can be represented genetically and criteria can be established for evaluating fitness. Genetic algorithms expedite the solution because they are able to evaluate many solution alternatives quickly to find the best one. For example, General Electric engineers used genetic algorithms to help optimize the design for jet turbine aircraft engines, where each design change required changes in up to 100 variables. The supply chain management software from i2 Technologies uses genetic algorithms to optimize production-scheduling models incorporating hundreds of thousands of details about customer orders, material and resource availability, manufacturing and distribution capability, and delivery dates.

INTELLIGENT AGENTS

Intelligent agent technology helps businesses navigate through large amounts of data to locate and act on information that is considered important. **Intelligent agents** are software programs that work without direct human intervention to carry out specific tasks for an individual user, business process, or software application. The agent uses a built-in or learned knowledge base to accomplish tasks or make decisions on the user's behalf, such as deleting junk e-mail, scheduling appointments, or traveling over interconnected networks to find the cheapest airfare to California.

There are many intelligent agent applications today in operating systems, application software, e-mail systems, mobile computing software, and network tools. For example, the wizards found in Microsoft Office software tools have built-in capabilities to show users how to accomplish various tasks, such as formatting documents or creating graphs, and to anticipate when users need assistance. Chapter 10 describes how intelligent agent shopping bots can help consumers find products they want and assist them in comparing prices and other features.

Although some intelligent agents are programmed to follow a simple set of rules, others are capable of learning from experience and adjusting their behavior. Siri, an application on Apple's iOS operating system for the iPhone and iPad, is an example. Siri is an intelligent personal assistant that uses voice recognition technology to answer questions, make recommendations, and perform actions. The software adapts to the user's individual preferences over time and personalizes results, performing tasks such as finding nearby restaurants, purchasing movie tickets, getting directions, scheduling appointments, and sending messages. Siri understands natural speech, and it asks the user questions if it needs more information to complete a task. Siri does not process speech input locally on the users's device. Instead, it sends commands through a remote server, so users have to be connected to Wi-Fi or a 3G signal.

Many complex phenomena can be modeled as systems of autonomous agents that follow relatively simple rules for interaction. **Agent-based modeling** applications have been developed to model the behavior of consumers, stock markets, and supply chains and to predict the spread of epidemics.

Procter & Gamble (P&G) used agent-based modeling to improve coordination among different members of its supply chain in response to changing business conditions (see Figure 11.11). It modeled a complex supply chain as a group of semiautonomous "agents" representing individual supply chain components, such as trucks, production facilities, distributors, and retail stores. The behavior of each agent is programmed to follow rules that mimic

FIGURE 11.11 **INTELLIGENT AGENTS IN P&G'S SUPPLY CHAIN NETWORK**

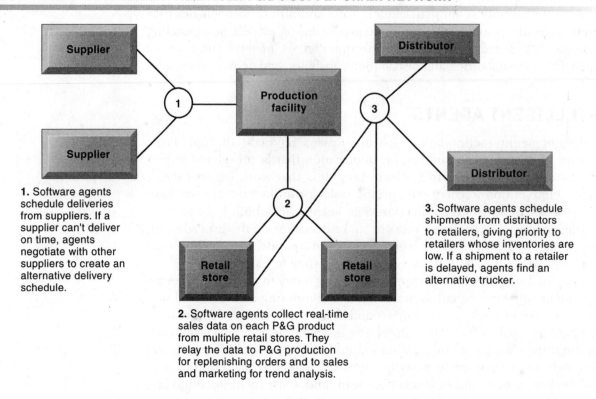

1. Software agents schedule deliveries from suppliers. If a supplier can't deliver on time, agents negotiate with other suppliers to create an alternative delivery schedule.

2. Software agents collect real-time sales data on each P&G product from multiple retail stores. They relay the data to P&G production for replenishing orders and to sales and marketing for trend analysis.

3. Software agents schedule shipments from distributors to retailers, giving priority to retailers whose inventories are low. If a shipment to a retailer is delayed, agents find an alternative trucker.

Intelligent agents are helping P&G shorten the replenishment cycles for products such as a box of Tide.

actual behavior, such as "order an item when it is out of stock." Simulations using the agents enable the company to perform what-if analyses on inventory levels, in-store stockouts, and transportation costs.

Using intelligent agent models, P&G discovered that trucks should often be dispatched before being fully loaded. Although transportation costs would be higher using partially loaded trucks, the simulation showed that retail store stockouts would occur less often, thus reducing the amount of lost sales, which would more than make up for the higher distribution costs. Agent-based modeling has saved P&G $300 million annually on an investment of less than 1 percent of that amount.

HYBRID AI SYSTEMS

Genetic algorithms, fuzzy logic, neural networks, and expert systems can be integrated into a single application to take advantage of the best features of these technologies. Such systems are called **hybrid AI systems**. Hybrid applications in business are growing. In Japan, Hitachi, Mitsubishi, Ricoh, Sanyo, and others are starting to incorporate hybrid AI in products such as home appliances, factory machinery, and office equipment. Matsushita has developed a "neurofuzzy" washing machine that combines fuzzy logic with neural networks. Nikko Securities has been working on a neurofuzzy system to forecast convertible-bond ratings.

Review Summary

1. **What is the role of knowledge management systems in business?**

   Knowledge management is a set of processes to create, store, transfer, and apply knowledge in the organization. Much of a firm's value depends on its ability to create and manage knowledge. Knowledge management promotes organizational learning by increasing the ability of the organization to learn from its environment and to incorporate knowledge into its business processes. There are three major types of knowledge management systems: enterprise-wide knowledge management systems, knowledge work systems, and intelligent techniques.

2. **What types of systems are used for enterprise-wide knowledge management and how do they provide value for businesses?**

   Enterprise-wide knowledge management systems are firmwide efforts to collect, store, distribute, and apply digital content and knowledge. Enterprise content management systems provide databases and tools for organizing and storing structured documents and tools for organizing and storing semistructured knowledge, such as e-mail or rich media. Knowledge network systems provide directories and tools for locating firm employees with special expertise who are important sources of tacit knowledge. Often these systems include group collaboration tools (including wikis and social bookmarking), portals to simplify information access, search tools, and tools for classifying information based on a taxonomy that is appropriate for the organization. Enterprise-wide knowledge management systems can provide considerable value if they are well designed and enable employees to locate, share, and use knowledge more efficiently.

3. **What are the major types of knowledge work systems and how do they provide value for firms?**

   Knowledge work systems (KWS) support the creation of new knowledge and its integration into the organization. KWS require easy access to an external knowledge base; powerful computer hardware that can support software with intensive graphics, analysis, document management, and communications capabilities; and a user-friendly interface. Computer-aided design (CAD) systems, augmented reality applications, and virtual reality systems, which create interactive simulations that behave like the real world, require graphics and powerful modeling capabilities. KWS for financial professionals provide access to external databases and the ability to analyze massive amounts of financial data very quickly.

4. **What are the business benefits of using intelligent techniques for knowledge management?**

   Artificial intelligence lacks the flexibility, breadth, and generality of human intelligence, but it can be used to capture, codify, and extend organizational knowledge. Expert systems capture tacit knowledge from a limited domain of human expertise and express that knowledge in the form of rules. Expert systems are most useful for problems of classification or diagnosis. Case-based reasoning represents organizational knowledge as a database of cases that can be continually expanded and refined.

   Fuzzy logic is a software technology for expressing knowledge in the form of rules that use approximate or subjective values. Fuzzy logic has been used for controlling physical devices and is starting to be used for limited decision-making applications.

   Machine learning refers to the ability of computer programs to automatically learn and improve with experience. Neural networks consist of hardware and software that attempt to mimic the thought processes of the human brain. Neural networks are notable for their ability to learn without programming and to recognize patterns that cannot be easily described by humans. They are being used in science, medicine, and business to discriminate patterns in massive amounts of data.

   Genetic algorithms develop solutions to particular problems using genetically based processes such as fitness, crossover, and mutation. Genetic algorithms are beginning to be applied to problems involving optimization, product design, and monitoring industrial systems where many alternatives or variables must be evaluated to generate an optimal solution.

Intelligent agents are software programs with built-in or learned knowledge bases that carry out specific tasks for an individual user, business process, or software application. Intelligent agents can be programmed to navigate through large amounts of data to locate useful information and in some cases act on that information on behalf of the user.

Key Terms

3-D printing, 467

Agent-based modeling, 483

Artificial intelligence (AI), 471

Augmented reality (AR), 470

Backward chaining, 473

Case-based reasoning (CBR), 475

Communities of practice (COPs), 461

Computer-aided design (CAD), 467

Data, 457

Digital asset management systems, 464

Enterprise content management systems, 463

Enterprise-wide knowledge management systems, 462

Expert systems, 472

Explicit knowledge, 457

Forward chaining, 472

Fuzzy logic, 475

Genetic algorithms, 479

Hybrid AI systems, 484

Inference engine, 472

Intelligent agents, 483

Intelligent techniques, 462

Investment workstations, 470

Knowledge, 457

Knowledge base, 472

Knowledge discovery, 471

Knowledge management, 458

Knowledge work systems (KWS), 462

Learning management system (LMS), 464

Machine learning, 477

Massive open online course (MOOC), 465

Neural networks, 478

Organizational learning, 457

Structured knowledge, 462

Tacit knowledge, 457

Taxonomy, 464

Virtual Reality Modeling Language (VRML), 470

Virtual reality systems, 467

Wisdom, 457

Review Questions

11-1 What is the role of knowledge management systems in business?

- Define knowledge management and explain its value to businesses.
- Describe the important dimensions of knowledge.
- Distinguish between data, knowledge, and wisdom and between tacit knowledge and explicit knowledge.
- Describe the stages in the knowledge management value chain.

11-2 What types of systems are used for enterprise-wide knowledge management and how do they provide value for businesses?

- Define and describe the various types of enterprise-wide knowledge management systems and explain how they provide value for businesses.
- Describe the role of the following in facilitating knowledge management: taxonomies, MOOCs, and learning management systems.

11-3 What are the major types of knowledge work systems and how do they provide value for firms?

- Define knowledge work systems and describe the generic requirements of knowledge work systems.
- Describe how the following systems support knowledge work: CAD, virtual reality, augmented reality, and investment workstations.

11-4 What are the business benefits of using intelligent techniques for knowledge management?

- Define an expert system, describe how it works, and explain its value to business.
- Define case-based reasoning and explain how it differs from an expert system.
- Define machine learning and give some examples.

- Define a neural network, and describe how it works and how it benefits businesses.

- Define and describe fuzzy logic, genetic algorithms, and intelligent agents. Explain how each works and the kinds of problems for which each is suited.

Discussion Questions

11-5 Knowledge management is a business process, not a technology. Discuss.

11-6 Describe various ways that knowledge management systems could help firms with sales and marketing or with manufacturing and production.

11-7 Your company wants to do more with knowledge management. Describe the steps it should take to develop a knowledge management program and select knowledge management applications.

Hands-On MIS Projects

The projects in this section give you hands-on experience designing a knowledge portal, identifying opportunities for knowledge management, creating a simple expert system, and using intelligent agents to research products for sale on the Web.

Management Decision Problems

11-8   U.S. Pharma Corporation is headquartered in New Jersey but has research sites in Germany, France, the United Kingdom, Switzerland, and Australia. Research and development of new pharmaceuticals is key to ongoing profits, and U.S. Pharma researches and tests thousands of possible drugs. The company's researchers need to share information with others within and outside the company, including the U.S. Food and Drug Administration, the World Health Organization, and the International Federation of Pharmaceutical Manufacturers & Associations. Also critical is access to health information sites, such as the U.S. National Library of Medicine, and to industry conferences and professional journals. Design a knowledge portal for U.S. Pharma's researchers. Include in your design specifications relevant internal systems and databases, external sources of information, and internal and external communication and collaboration tools. Design a home page for your portal.

11-9   Canadian Tire is one of Canada's largest companies, with 57,000 employees and 1,200 stores and gas bars (gas stations) across Canada selling sports, leisure, home products, apparel, and financial services as well as automotive and petroleum products. The retail outlets are independently owned and operated. Canadian Tire has been using daily mailings and thick product catalogs to inform its dealers about new products, merchandise setups, best practices, product ordering, and problem resolution and it is looking for a better way to provide employees with human resources and administrative documents. Describe the problems created by this way of doing business and how knowledge management systems might help.

Improving Decision Making: Building a Simple Expert System for Retirement Planning

Software skills: Spreadsheet formulas and IF function or expert system tool
Business skills: Benefits eligibility determination

11-10   Expert systems typically use a large number of rules. This project has been simplified to reduce the number of rules, but it will give you experience working with a series of rules to develop an application.

When employees at your company retire, they are given cash bonuses. These cash bonuses are based on the length of employment and the retiree's age. To receive a bonus, an employee must be at least 50 years of age and have worked for the company for more than five years. The following table summarizes the criteria for determining bonuses.

LENGTH OF EMPLOYMENT	BONUS
<5 years	No bonus
5–10 years	20 percent of current annual salary
11–15 years	30 percent of current annual salary
16–20 years	40 percent of current annual salary
20–25 years	50 percent of current annual salary
26 or more years	100 percent of current annual salary

Using the information provided, build a simple expert system. Find a demonstration copy of an expert system software tool on the Web that you can download. Alternatively, use your spreadsheet software to build the expert system. (If you are using spreadsheet software, we suggest using the IF function so you can see how rules are created.)

Improving Decision Making: Using Intelligent Agents for Comparison Shopping

Software skills: Web browser and shopping bot software
Business skills: Product evaluation and selection

11-11 This project will give you experience using shopping bots to search online for products, find product information, and find the best prices and vendors. Select a digital camera you might want to purchase, such as the Canon PowerShot S110 or the Olympus Tough TG-3. Visit MySimon (www.mysimon.com), BizRate.com (www.bizrate.com), and Google Shopping to do price comparisons for you. Evaluate these shopping sites in terms of their ease of use, number of offerings, speed in obtaining information, thoroughness of information offered about the product and seller, and price selection. Which site or sites would you use and why? Which camera would you select and why? How helpful were these sites for making your decision?

What's Up with IBM's Watson?
CASE STUDY

In February, 2011 an IBM computer named Watson made history by handily defeating the two most decorated champions of the game show Jeopardy, Ken Jennings and Brad Rutter. Watson was named after IBM's founder, Thomas J. Watson, and its achievement marked a milestone in the ability of computers to process and interpret human language.

IBM had been working on Watson for years. The project's goal was to develop a more effective set of techniques that computers can use to process *natural language* – language that human beings instinctively use, not language specially formatted to be understood by computers. Watson had to be able to register the intent of a question, search through millions of lines of text and data, pick up nuances of meaning and context, and rank potential responses for a user to select, all in less than three seconds.

The hardware for Watson used in Jeopardy consisted of 10 racks of IBM POWER 750 servers running Linux, with 15 terabytes of RAM and 2,880 processor cores (equivalent to 6,000 top-end home computers), and operated at 80 teraflops. Watson needed this amount of power to quickly scan its enormous database of information, including information from the Internet. To prepare for Jeopardy, the IBM researchers downloaded over 10 million documents, including encyclopedias and Wikipedia, the Internet Movie Database (IMDB), and the entire archive of *The New York Times*. All of the data sat in Watson's primary memory, as opposed to a much slower hard drive, so that Watson could find the data it needed within three seconds.

Watson is able to learn from its mistakes as well as its successes. To solve a typical problem, Watson tries many of the thousands of algorithms that the team has programmed it to use. The algorithms evaluate the language used in each clue, gather information about the important people and places mentioned in the clue, and generate hundreds of solutions. Human beings don't need to take such a formal approach to generate the solutions that fit a question best, but Watson compensates for this with superior computing power and speed. If a certain algorithm works to solve a problem, Watson remembers what type of question it was and the algorithm it used to get the right answer. In this way, Watson improves at answering questions over time. Watson also learns another way — the team gave Watson thousands of old Jeopardy questions to process. Watson analyzed both questions and answers to determine patterns or similarities between clues, and using these patterns, it assigns varying degrees of confidence to the answers it gives.

Although Watson was only able to correctly answer a small fraction of the questions it was initially given, machine learning allowed the system to continue to improve until it reached Jeopardy champion level. IBM term cognitive computing to refer to Watson's ability to interpret speech and text, rapidly mine large volumes of data, answer questions, draw conclusions, and learn from its mistakes.

The Watson version used in Jeopardy took 20 IBM engineers three years to build at an $18 million labor cost, and an estimated $1 million in equipment. IBM saw the investment as a stepping stone to broader commercial uses of its AI technology, including applications for health care, financial services, or any industry where sifting through large amounts of data (including unstructured data) to answer questions is important. Watson is expected to become more useful and powerful by learning from new sets of experts in new fields of knowledge. In January 2014 the company created a new division, the Watson Business Group, which will have 2500 employees working largely in New York City's Silicon Alley. IBM has invested more than $1 billion in this Group, and has allocated one-third of its overall research efforts to Watson.

In September 2011, WellPoint Inc., the largest U.S. health care provider, with 34.2 million members, enlisted Watson for utilization management. The WellPoint Interactive Care Reviewer application is designed to determine if physicians' requested treatment meets the guidelines of the company and a patient's insurance policy. The Watson WellPoint application combines data from three sources: a patient's chart and electronic records maintained by a physician or hospital, the insurance company's history of medicines and treatments, and Watson's huge library of textbooks and medical journals. According to WellPoint vice president Elizabeth Bingham, Watson initially took too long to "learn" WellPoint's policies. IBM was able to improve the system by revising the Watson training routine for WellPoint, and the Interactive Care Reviewer is being adopted by 1600 health care providers.

Cancer treatment appears to be an especially promising application for Watson. Current guidelines aren't precise enough to determine treatments that are most appropriate for a specific patient. For example, the recommended treatment may be chemotherapy, but how do you pick among ten or more possible chemotherapy options? How do you choose the dosage? What treatment frequency would work best? Oncologists also can't keep pace with the torrent of cancer research findings and therapies, genomic techniques, and patient record data. It is just too much for even a highly-trained scientist to manage.

In 2012 Memorial Sloan-Kettering Cancer Center began work on a Watson application to recommend cancer treatments, using data from Sloan-Kettering's clinical database of over one million patients along with treatment guidelines and published research to help Sloan-Kettering researchers to recommend personalized treatment options for lung cancer patients. The Watson application needs to pass a series of tests in order to be used on cancer patients, and actually being able to use Watson is more complex than originally envisioned. For instance, Sloan-Kettering oncologist Dr. Mark Kris displayed a screen from Watson that listed three potential treatments, but Watson was less than 32 percent confident that any of them were correct.

Ari Caroline, director of Sloan Kettering's quantitative analysis and strategic initiatives group has tutored Watson and has said that system was still in pilot mode. But progress is genuine, and Caroline believes Watson will soon be able to guide oncologists in selecting treatment options and tackling new research. A final version of the system has not yet been released.

Researchers at the University of Texas MD Anderson Cancer Center worked with IBM for a year to build a version of Watson called Oncology Expert Advisor (OEA) to recommend cancer treatments by mining medical literature, with an initial focus on acute leukemia. Watson learned from a variety of data about which cancer treatments worked best and which should be avoided for specific patients. OEA "reads" the medical records of patients to generate case summaries. It then weighs the patient profile against its knowledge base to suggest treatment options relevant to that particular patient, based on literature, guidelines and expert recommendations. When asked by a doctor about a patient, Watson's algorithms search for possible treatments and rank them according to levels of confidence up to 100%, with each option linked to supporting evidence.

The project initially stumbled because IBM engineers and Anderson doctors couldn't understand each other. IBM developers worked elsewhere and only visited Anderson every few weeks to talk to doctors. When IBM developers and doctors started meeting several times a week, the application became much better and the leukemia advisor is nearly ready for use. However, it might take two more years before Watson could handle other types of cancer. And although Watson might help oncology specialists at M.D. Anderson identify leukemia treatment options, it can't substitute for the expertise of an experienced doctor, according to Lynda Chin, chairperson of the M.D. Anderson genomic department. The cancer experts have seen patients a thousand times, and sometimes their decisions are based on intuition that's difficult to explain. The Anderson project was valued at nearly $15 million, and IBM management is hoping it could grow to $100 million. The Anderson project plans to expand to other cancer types once the prototype becomes more developed.

In November 2013 IBM announced it would make Watson technology available via the Internet as a cloud service that could be used by many different industries. IBM will open parts of the system to outside developers to create businesses and mobile applications based on cognitive computing. A Watson Developer Cloud provides tools and methodologies for developers to work with a Watson system, a content store supplying both free and fee-based data for new applications, and about five hundred subject matter experts from IBM and third parties. Welltok used these tools to create a mobile Watson app called CareWell Concierge for Intelligent Health Itineraries for consumers. Users will be able to participate with Watson in conversations about their health. Fluid Retail is developing a personalized shopping assistant. MD Buyline is developing a Watson app to advise hospital managers about procurement of medical equipment and supplies.

IBM will deliver three new cloud-based products based on Watson's cognitive intelligence and capabilities. IBM Watson Discovery Advisor is aimed at the pharmaceutical, publishing, and education industries, and will wade through search results to deliver data faster and help researchers formulate conclusions. IBM Watson Analytics is a cloud-based service that provides insights, including visual representations, based on raw big data enterprises send to Watson. IBM Watson Explorer is a cloud service that will provide a unified view of a user's information, facilitating the revelation and sharing of data-driven insights

IBM has also made Watson easier and less expensive to use. The latest version of Watson is 24 times faster than the version used in the 2011 Jeopardy contest, using only 10 percent of the hardware used in the Jeopardy version.

Nevertheless, Watson thus far has not produced much revenue for IBM—only about $100 million from commercialization efforts between 2011 and 2014. IBM CEO Virginia Rometty is hoping Watson will be able to produce $10 billion in annual revenue within a decade, and that Watson will bring in $1 billion in revenue per year by 2018.

In order to effectively commercialize the technology, IBM will need to expand Watson's knowledge domains, and this is its greatest challenge. Turning Watson into a useful business tool requires an enormous amount of work. Watson has to learn the terminology and master the domains of expertise in many different areas, including health care and scientific research, understand the context of how that language is used, and how to correlate questions with the correct answers. Watson doesn't work yet with data from audio, video, and animations and with languages other than English. It can't come up yet with its own ideas.

IBM will have to be careful not to oversell what Watson can do, so that Watson does not end up like other artificial intelligence systems where expectations were way overblown. Making machines that beat humans at chess or a TV game show is much easier than solving problems in the real world. According to Curt Monash, president of Monash Research, Watson hasn't yet overcome the hurdle that derailed AI in the 1980s, which was that AI was only able to capture small pieces of a limited knowledge domain for a single-purpose use. Watson is having more trouble solving real-life problems than Jeopardy questions. Watson's basic learning process requiring IBM engineers to master the technicalities of a customer's business and translate those requirements into usable software has been very arduous. It remains to be seen whether the complexity of establishing a body of knowledge and training an intelligent system is repeatable and scalable for other types of work and whether it creates an opportunities for differentiation and competitive advantage. Watson is very much a work in progress.

Sources: Mohana Ravindranath, "How IBM Is Trying to Commercialize Watson," *Washington Post*, May 11, 2014; Spencer E. Ante, "IBM Struggles to Turn Watson Computer Into Big Business, Wall Street Journal, January 7, 2014; Lynda Chin, "IBM Watson: Providing a Second Opinion for Oncologists," www.ibm.com, accessed July 9, 2014; George Lawton, "IBM's Watson Supercomputer Gives Developers Access to Cognitive Cloud," SearchCloudApplications.com, March 28, 2014; Jack Vaughan, "For IBM Watson, No easy Answers on Commercial Cognitive Computing," Searchdatamanagement.com, January 10, 2014; Michael Goldberg, "Five Things to Know about IBM Watson, Where

It Is and Where It's Going," DataInformed, January 14, 2014; Larry Dignan, "IBM Forms Watson Business Group: Will Commercialization Follow?," ZDNet, January 9, 2014; Quentin Hardy, "IBM Bets Watson Can Earn Its Keep," *New York Times*, January 8, 2014 and "IBM to Announce More Powerful Watson via the Internet," *New York Times*, November 13, 2013; Ian B Murphy, "Predictive Analytics in Development: IBM Watson at Memorial Sloan-Kettering, RPI Research Lab," DataInformed, February 20, 2013; Anna Wilde Mathews, John Markoff, "Computer Wins on 'Jeopardy!': Trivial, It's Not," *The New York Times*, February 16, 2011; Stanley Fish, "What Did Watson the Computer Do?" *The New York Times*, February 21, 2011; and Stephen Baker, "The Programmer's Dilemma: Building a Jeopardy! Champion," *McKinsey Quarterly*, February 2011.

CASE STUDY QUESTIONS

11-12 How powerful is Watson? Describe its technology. Why does it require so much powerful hardware?

11-13 How "intelligent" is Watson? What can it do? What can't it do?

11-14 What kinds of problems is Watson able to solve? How useful a tool is it for knowledge management and decision making?

11-15 Do you think Watson will be as useful in other industries and disciplines as IBM hopes? Will it be beneficial to everyone? Explain your answer.

Chapter 11 References

Alavi, Maryam and Dorothy Leidner. "Knowledge Management and Knowledge Management Systems: Conceptual Foundations and Research Issues," *MIS Quarterly 25*, No. 1(March 2001).

Althuizen, Niek and Berend Wierenga ."Supporting Creative Problem Solving with a Case-Based Reasoning System." Journal of Management Information Systems 31. No. 1 (Summer 2014).

Boutin, Paul. "A New Reality." Technology Review (May/June 2011).

Burtka, Michael. "Generic Algorithms." *The Stern Information Systems Review* 1, No. 1 (Spring 1993).

Clark, Don. "IBM Unveils Chip Simulating Brain Functions." Wall Street Journal (August 7, 2014).

Davenport, Thomas H., and Lawrence Prusak. *Working Knowledge: How Organizations Manage What They Know*. Boston, MA: Harvard Business School Press (1997).

Davenport, Thomas H., Laurence Prusak, and Bruce Strong. "Putting Ideas to Work." The Wall Street Journal (March 10, 2008).

Davenport, Thomas H., Robert J. Thomas and Susan Cantrell. "The Mysterious Art and Science of Knowledge-Worker Performance." *MIT Sloan Management Review* 44, No. 1 (Fall 2002).

Dhar, Vasant, and Roger Stein. Intelligent Decision Support Methods: The Science of Knowledge Work. Upper Saddle River, NJ: Prentice Hall (1997).

El Najdawi, M. K., and Anthony C. Stylianou. "Expert Support Systems: Integrating AI Technologies." *Communications of the ACM* 36, No. 12 (December 1993).

Grover, Varun and Thomas H. Davenport. "General Perspectives on Knowledge Management: Fostering a Research Agenda." Journal of Management Information Systems 18, No. 1 (Summer 2001).

Gu, Feng and Baruch Lev. "Intangible Assets. Measurements, Drivers, Usefulness." http://pages.stern.nyu.edu/~blev/.

Hagerty, James R. and Kate Linebaugh. "Next 3-D Frontier: Printed Plane Parts." The Wall Street Journal (July 14, 2012).

Holland, John H. "Genetic Algorithms." *Scientific American* (July 1992).

Housel Tom and Arthur A. Bell. *Measuring and Managing Knowledge*. New York: McGraw-Hill (2001).

Jones, Quentin, Gilad Ravid, and Sheizaf Rafaeli. "Information Overload and the Message Dynamics of Online Interaction Spaces: A Theoretical Model and Empirical Exploration." *Information Systems Research* 15, No. 2 (June 2004).

Leonard-Barton, Dorothy and Walter Swap. "Deep Smarts." Harvard Business Review (September 1, 2004).

Leonard-Barton, Dorothy, and John J. Sviokla. "Putting Expert Systems to Work." *Harvard Business Review* (March–April 1988).

Lev, Baruch. "Sharpening the Intangibles Edge." *Harvard Business Review* (June 1, 2004).

Malone, Thomas W., Robert Laubacher, and Chrysanthos Dellarocas. "The Collective Intelligence Genome." *MIT Sloan Management Review* 51, No. 3 (Spring 2010).

Markoff, John. "Brainlike Computers, Learning from Experience." New York Times (December 28, 2013).

Markoff, John. "How Many Computers to Identify a Cat? 16,000." New York Times (June 26, 2012).

Markoff, John. "The Rapid Advance of Artificial Intelligence." New York Times (October 14, 2013).

Markus, M. Lynne, Ann Majchrzak, and Less Gasser."A Design Theory for Systems that Support Emergent Knowledge Processes." *MIS Quarterly* 26, No. 3 (September 2002).

McCarthy, John. "Generality in Artificial Intelligence." *Communications of the ACM* (December 1987).

Mehra, Amit, Nishtha Langer, Ravi Bapna, and Ram Gopal. "Estimating Returns to Training in the Knowledge Economy: A Firm-Level Analysis of Small and Medium Enterprises." *MIS Quarterly* 38, No. 3 (September 2014).

Murphy, Chris "4 Ways Ford Is Exploring Next-Gen Car Tech." Information Week (July 27, 2012).

Nurmohamed, Zafred, Nabeel Gillani, and Michael Lenox. "New Use for MOOCs: Real-World Problem-Solving." *Harvard Business Review* (July 2013).

OpenText Corporation. "The City of Calgary Streamlines Content Access and Compliance." (2013–2014).

Orlikowski, Wanda J. "Knowing in Practice: Enacting a Collective Capability in Distributed Organizing." *Organization Science* 13, No. 3 (May-June 2002).

Ramsey, Mike. "Design Revolution Sweeps the Auto Industry." *Wall Street Journal* (October 20, 2013).

Rosman, Katherine. "Augmented Reality Finally Starts to Gain Traction. Wall Street Journal (March 3, 2014).

Sadeh, Norman, David W. Hildum, and Dag Kjenstad." Agent-Based E-Supply Chain Decision Support." *Journal of*

Organizational Computing and Electronic Commerce 13, No. 3 & 4 (2003)

Singer, Natasha. "The Virtual Anatomy, Ready for Dissection." *The New York Times* (January 7, 2012).

U.S. Department of Commerce, Bureau of the Census. Statistical Abstract of the United States, 2012 Table 616. Washington, D.C. (2012).

Weill, Peter, Thomas Malone, and Thomas G. Apel. "The Business Models Investors Prefer." *MIT Sloan Management Review* 52, No. 4 (Summer 2011).

Zadeh, Lotfi A. "Fuzzy Logic, Neural Networks, and Soft Computing." *Communications of the ACM* 37, No. 3 (March 1994).

Zadeh, Lotfi A. "The Calculus of Fuzzy If/Then Rules." *AI Expert* (March 1992).

Zeying Wan, Deborah Compeau and Nicole Haggerty. "The Effects of Self- Regulated Learning Processes on E-Learning Outcomes in Organizational Settings." Journal of Management Information Systems 29, No. 1 (Summer 2012).

CHAPTER 12

LEARNING OBJECTIVES

After reading this chapter, you will be able to answer the following questions:

1. What are the different types of decisions and how does the decision-making process work? How do information systems support the activities of managers and management decision making?

2. How do business intelligence and business analytics support decision making?

3. How do different decision-making constituencies in an organization use business intelligence? What is the role of information systems in helping people working in a group make decisions more efficiently?

CHAPTER CASES

Germany Wins the World Cup with Big Data at Its Side

The Analytics behind Matrimony.com

America's Cup: The Tension between Technology and Human Decision Makers

How Much Does Data-Driven Planting Help Farmers?

GERMANY WINS THE WORLD CUP WITH BIG DATA AT ITS SIDE

In a stunning display of talent, resilience, and teamwork, Germany won the 2014 World Cup, defeating Argentina 1–0. Argentina had Lionel Messi, the 2014 World Cup's best player. Brazil, whom the Germans defeated 7–1 in the semi-finals, was considered the overwhelming favorite. Exactly how did Germany pull this off?

The German team sparkled with individual talent in every position, and was praised for playing brilliantly as a team. But the winners had another behind-the-scenes advantage: Big data was at their side. The German team was able to use information technology to analyze massive amounts of data about teams' performance and then use what it had learned to improve how it played. Each of the 32 competing 2014 World Cup teams had a dedicated video and performance analyst, but Germany appears to have been the only one that employed a special database and software to measure and analyze individual and team performance and strategies.

In 2012, the German Football Association partnered with German software giant SAP AG to create a custom match analysis tool called Match Insights that collects and analyzes massive amounts of player performance data. Match Insights analyzes video data from on-field

© Ralf Falbe/Alamy

495

cameras that capture thousands of data points per second, including player speed and position. These data are organized and stored in an SAP database. Match Insights uses SAP HANA in-memory computing and analytic software to analyze vast quantities of data in real time (see Chapter 6). Match Insights allows coaches to target performance metrics for specific players and give them feedback via their mobile devices.

About 50 students at Deutsche Sporthochschule Köln (a sports university in Cologne) started compiling data about the teams and players that would be competing for the next World Cup, including every play they had run, and input the data into the Match Insights database. These data included video from eight on-field cameras that surround the area where the match is played, which the database views as a grid. The system assigns each German and opposing soccer player a unique identifier, so that their movements can be tracked digitally. Match Insights analyzes these data to measure key performance indicators, such as possession time (the percentage of time a team has the ball in a match), the number of touches controlling the ball, and movement speeds.

Improving speed was a major objective for the German team in 2014. Match Insights enabled the team to analyze statistics about average possession time and reduce it from 3.4 seconds to about 1.1 seconds. Better possession time enabled the German team to improve on their aggressive, fast-paced style of playing that brought them to World Cup victory.

Match Insights can show the team virtual "defensive shadows" that indicate how much area a player can protect with his own body. This information helps the team visualize and exploit weak links in an opponent's setup.

The German team also used Match Insights to evaluate the performance of its competitors. For example, the Germans were able to see before playing against the French that this team was very concentrated in the middle but left spaces on the flanks because their full-backs did not push up properly. The German team also reviewed extensive data about how Brazil's players reacted in pressure situations, their preferred routes, and how they responded when fouled.

Match Insights was able to make its vast trove of performance data available to team members' mobile phones or tablets. With help from SAP, the team developed a mobile app that sends short clips of analysis to individual players or groups of players. Right after a game, every player receives several visual examples of him doing things well and poorly and may also receive visual data about the opposition. Players can also view their performance data in the players' lounge.

Some commentators have described Match Insights as Germany's 12th man. SAP plans to offering Match Insights to other clubs and soccer federations.

Sources: Jack Rosenberger, "Germany's Secret World Cup Weapon: Big Data," *CIO Insight*, July 18, 2014; Steven Norton, "Germany's 12th Man at the World Cup: Big Data," *Wall Street Journal*, July 10, 2014; and SAP News, "SAP and the German Football Association Turn Big Data into Smart Decisions to Improve Player Performance at the World Cup in Brazil," June 11, 2014.

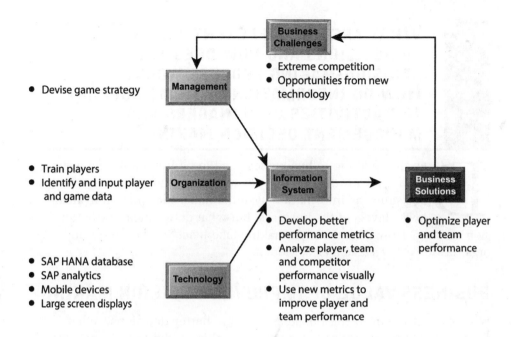

- Devise game strategy

Management

Business Challenges
- Extreme competition
- Opportunities from new technology

- Train players
- Identify and input player and game data

Organization

Information System

Business Solutions
- Optimize player and team performance

- SAP HANA database
- SAP analytics
- Mobile devices
- Large screen displays

Technology

- Develop better performance metrics
- Analyze player, team and competitor performance visually
- Use new metrics to improve player and team performance

Soccer is one of a growing number of sports being transformed by big data. Others include baseball (think Moneyball), basketball, and tennis. Data analytics are just starting to be used in soccer, and the German team appears to have been in the forefront for the 2014 World Cup soccer competition. The chapter-opening case shows how advanced analytics helped this team come out on top by providing very detailed information about individual player and team performance that could help the team make better decisions about how to improve its game. The opening case has important lessons for other organizations and businesses as well: You can be more efficient and competitive if, like the German World Cup team, you know how to use data to drive your decisions.

The chapter-opening diagram calls attention to important points raised by this case and this chapter. World Cup Soccer is one of the globe's most competitive and highly-charged sports, and the German team was not favored to win the 2014 competition. However, it appears to be the first World Cup team to take advantage of new opportunities from information technology, including tools for capturing, storing, and analyzing big data regarding player and team performance. Other teams were hamstrung by earlier models of decision making that didn't take advantage of available technology. The German World Cup team collected vast quantities of detailed statistical and visual data and was able to devise a better set of metrics for analyzing player and team performance. Match Insights helped World Cup managers, coaches, and players make more precise, fine-grained decisions on how to best play the game.

Here are some questions to think about: How did using Match Insights change the way the German World Cup team made decisions? Give examples of two decisions that were improved by using Match Insights. What can businesses learn from the German 2014 World Cup victory?

12.1 WHAT ARE THE DIFFERENT TYPES OF DECISIONS AND HOW DOES THE DECISION-MAKING PROCESS WORK? HOW DO INFORMATION SYSTEMS SUPPORT THE ACTIVITIES OF MANAGERS AND MANAGEMENT DECISION MAKING?

D ecision making in businesses used to be limited to management. Today, lower-level employees are responsible for some of these decisions, as information systems make information available to lower levels of the business. But what do we mean by better decision making? How does decision making take place in businesses and other organizations? Let's take a closer look.

BUSINESS VALUE OF IMPROVED DECISION MAKING

What does it mean to the business to make better decisions? What is the monetary value of improved decision making? Table 12.1 attempts to measure the monetary value of improved decision making for a small U.S. manufacturing firm with $280 million in annual revenue and 140 employees. The firm has identified a number of key decisions where new system investments might improve the quality of decision making. The table provides selected estimates of annual value (in the form of cost savings or increased revenue) from improved decision making in selected areas of the business.

We can see from Table 12.1 that decisions are made at all levels of the firm and that some of these decisions are common, routine, and numerous. Although the value of improving any single decision may be small, improving hundreds of thousands of "small" decisions adds up to a large annual value for the business.

TABLE 12.1 BUSINESS VALUE OF ENHANCED DECISION MAKING

EXAMPLE DECISION	DECISION MAKER	NUMBER OF ANNUAL DECISIONS	ESTIMATED VALUE TO FIRM OF A SINGLE IMPROVED DECISION	ANNUAL VALUE
Allocate support to most valuable customers	Accounts manager	12	$100,000	$1,200,000
Predict call center daily demand	Call center management	4	$150,000	$600,000
Decide parts inventory levels daily	Inventory manager	365	$5,000	$1,825,000
Identify competitive bids from major suppliers	Senior management	1	$2,000,000	$2,000,000
Schedule production to fill orders	Manufacturing manager	150	$10,000	$1,500,000
Allocate labor to complete a job	Production floor manager	100	$4,000	$400,000

TYPES OF DECISIONS

Chapters 1 and 2 showed that there are different levels in an organization. Each of these levels has different information requirements for decision support and responsibility for different types of decisions (see Figure 12.1). Decisions are classified as structured, semistructured, and unstructured.

Unstructured decisions are those in which the decision maker must provide judgment, evaluation, and insight to solve the problem. Each of these decisions is novel, important, and nonroutine, and there is no well-understood or agreed-on procedure for making them.

Structured decisions, by contrast, are repetitive and routine, and they involve a definite procedure for handling them so that they do not have to be treated each time as if they were new. Many decisions have elements of both types of decisions and are **semistructured**, where only part of the problem has a clear-cut answer provided by an accepted procedure. In general, structured decisions are more prevalent at lower organizational levels, whereas unstructured problems are more common at higher levels of the firm.

Senior executives face many unstructured decision situations, such as establishing the firm's 5- or 10-year goals or deciding new markets to enter. Answering the question "Should we enter a new market?" would require access to news, government reports, and industry views as well as high-level summaries of firm performance. However, the answer would also require

FIGURE 12.1 INFORMATION REQUIREMENTS OF KEY DECISION-MAKING GROUPS IN A FIRM

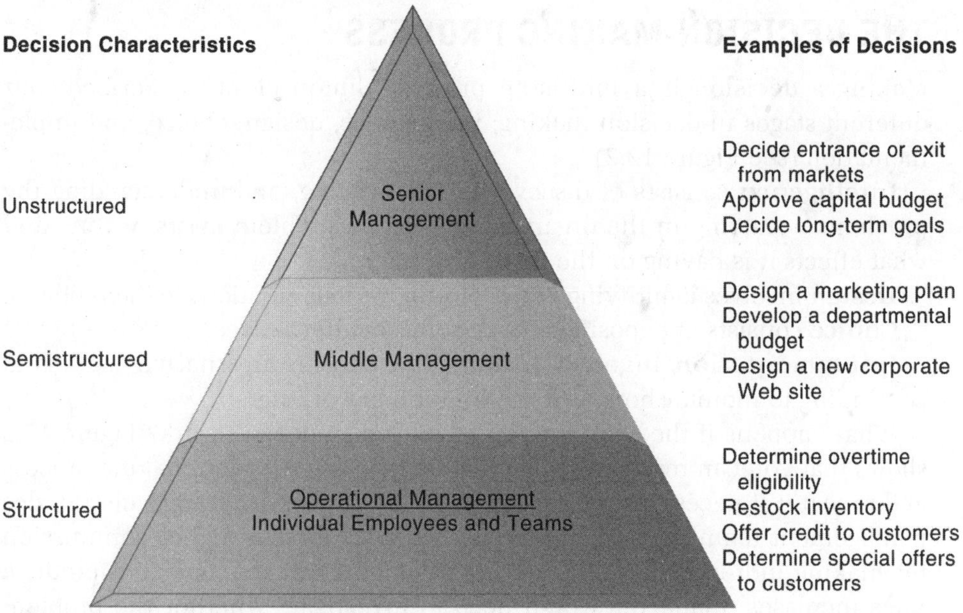

Decision Characteristics		Examples of Decisions
Unstructured	Senior Management	Decide entrance or exit from markets Approve capital budget Decide long-term goals
Semistructured	Middle Management	Design a marketing plan Develop a departmental budget Design a new corporate Web site
Structured	Operational Management Individual Employees and Teams	Determine overtime eligibility Restock inventory Offer credit to customers Determine special offers to customers

Senior managers, middle managers, operational managers, and employees have different types of decisions and information requirements.

senior managers to use their own best judgment and poll other managers for their opinions.

Middle management faces more structured decision scenarios but their decisions may include unstructured components. A typical middle-level management decision might be "Why is the reported order fulfillment report showing a decline over the past six months at a distribution center in Minneapolis?" This middle manager will obtain a report from the firm's enterprise system or distribution management system on order activity and operational efficiency at the Minneapolis distribution center. This is the structured part of the decision. But before arriving at an answer, this middle manager will have to interview employees and gather more unstructured information from external sources about local economic conditions or sales trends.

Operational management and rank-and-file employees tend to make more structured decisions. For example, a supervisor on an assembly line has to decide whether an hourly paid worker is entitled to overtime pay. If the employee worked more than eight hours on a particular day, the supervisor would routinely grant overtime pay for any time beyond eight hours that was clocked on that day.

A sales account representative often has to make decisions about extending credit to customers by consulting the firm's customer database that contains credit information. If the customer met the firm's prespecified criteria for granting credit, the account representative would grant that customer credit to make a purchase. In both instances, the decisions are highly structured and are routinely made thousands of times each day in most large firms. The answer has been preprogrammed into the firm's payroll and accounts receivable systems.

THE DECISION-MAKING PROCESS

Making a decision is a multistep process. Simon (1960) described four different stages in decision making: intelligence, design, choice, and implementation (see Figure 12.2).

Intelligence consists of discovering, identifying, and understanding the problems occurring in the organization—why a problem exists, where, and what effects it is having on the firm.

Design involves identifying and exploring various solutions to the problem.

Choice consists of choosing among solution alternatives.

Implementation involves making the chosen alternative work and continuing to monitor how well the solution is working.

What happens if the solution you have chosen doesn't work? Figure 12.2 shows that you can return to an earlier stage in the decision-making process and repeat it if necessary. For instance, in the face of declining sales, a sales management team may decide to pay the sales force a higher commission for making more sales to spur on the sales effort. If this does not produce sales increases, managers would need to investigate whether the problem stems from poor product design, inadequate customer support, or a host of other causes that call for a different solution.

FIGURE 12.2 STAGES IN DECISION MAKING

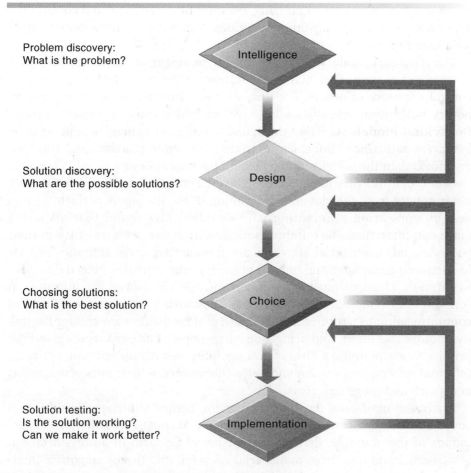

Problem discovery:
What is the problem?

Intelligence

Solution discovery:
What are the possible solutions?

Design

Choosing solutions:
What is the best solution?

Choice

Solution testing:
Is the solution working?
Can we make it work better?

Implementation

The decision-making process is broken down into four stages.

MANAGERS AND DECISION MAKING IN THE REAL WORLD

The premise of this book and this chapter is that systems to support decision making produce better decision making by managers and employees, above average returns on investment for the firm, and ultimately higher profitability. However, information systems cannot improve all the different kinds of decisions taking place in an organization. Let's examine the role of managers and decision making in organizations to see why this is so.

Managerial Roles

Managers play key roles in organizations. Their responsibilities range from making decisions, to writing reports, to attending meetings, to arranging birthday parties. We are able to better understand managerial functions and roles by examining classical and contemporary models of managerial behavior.

The **classical model of management**, which describes what managers do, was largely unquestioned for the more than 70 years since the 1920s.

Henri Fayol and other early writers first described the five classical functions of managers as planning, organizing, coordinating, deciding, and controlling. This description of management activities dominated management thought for a long time, and it is still popular today.

The classical model describes formal managerial functions but does not address exactly what managers do when they plan, decide things, and control the work of others. For this, we must turn to the work of contemporary behavioral scientists who have studied managers in daily action. **Behavioral models** state that the actual behavior of managers appears to be less systematic, more informal, less reflective, more reactive, and less well organized than the classical model would have us believe.

Observers find that managerial behavior actually has five attributes that differ greatly from the classical description. First, managers perform a great deal of work at an unrelenting pace—studies have found that managers engage in more than 600 different activities each day, with no break in their pace. Second, managerial activities are fragmented; most activities last for less than nine minutes, and only 10 percent of the activities exceed one hour in duration. Third, managers prefer current, specific, and ad hoc information (printed information often will be too old). Fourth, they prefer oral forms of communication to written forms because oral media provide greater flexibility, require less effort, and bring a faster response. Fifth, managers give high priority to maintaining a diverse and complex web of contacts that act as an informal information system and helps them execute their personal agendas and short- and long-term goals.

Analyzing managers' day-to-day behavior, Henry Mintzberg found that it could be classified into 10 managerial roles. **Managerial roles** are expectations of the activities that managers should perform in an organization. Mintzberg found that these managerial roles fell into three categories: interpersonal, informational, and decisional.

Interpersonal Roles. Managers act as figureheads for the organization when they represent their companies to the outside world and perform symbolic duties, such as giving out employee awards, in their **interpersonal role**. Managers act as leaders, attempting to motivate, counsel, and support subordinates. Managers also act as liaisons between various organizational levels; within each of these levels, they serve as liaisons among the members of the management team. Managers provide time and favors, which they expect to be returned.

Informational Roles. In their **informational role,** managers act as the nerve centers of their organizations, receiving the most concrete, up-to-date information and redistributing it to those who need to be aware of it. Managers are therefore information disseminators and spokespersons for their organizations.

Decisional Roles. Managers make decisions. In their **decisional role**, they act as entrepreneurs by initiating new kinds of activities; they handle disturbances arising in the organization; they allocate resources to staff members who need them; and they negotiate conflicts and mediate between conflicting groups.

TABLE 12.2 MANAGERIAL ROLES AND SUPPORTING INFORMATION SYSTEMS

ROLE	BEHAVIOR	SUPPORT SYSTEMS
Interpersonal Roles		
Figurehead		Telepresence systems
Leader	Interpersonal	Telepresence, social networks, Twitter
Liaison		Smartphones, social networks
Informational Roles		
Nerve center		Management information systems, executive support system
Disseminator	Information	E-mail, social networks
Spokesperson	processing	Webinars, telepresence
Decisional Roles		
Entrepreneur	Decision	None exist
Disturbance handler	making	None exist
Resource allocator		Business intelligence, decision-support system
Negotiator		None exist

Sources: Kenneth C. Laudon and Jane P. Laudon; and Mintzberg, 1971.

Table 12.2, based on Mintzberg's role classifications, is one look at where systems can and cannot help managers. The table shows that information systems are now capable of supporting most, but not all, areas of managerial life.

Real-World Decision Making

We now see that information systems are not helpful for all managerial roles. And in those managerial roles where information systems might improve decisions, investments in information technology do not always produce positive results. There are three main reasons: information quality, management filters, and organizational culture (see Chapter 3).

Information Quality. High-quality decisions require high-quality information. Table 12.3 describes information quality dimensions that affect the quality of decisions.

If the output of information systems does not meet these quality criteria, decision making will suffer. Chapter 6 has shown that corporate databases and files have varying levels of inaccuracy and incompleteness, which in turn will degrade the quality of decision making.

Management Filters. Even with timely, accurate information, some managers make bad decisions. Managers (like all human beings) absorb information through a series of filters to make sense of the world around them. Managers have selective attention, focus on certain kinds of problems and solutions, and have a variety of biases that reject information that does not conform to their prior conceptions.

TABLE 12.3 INFORMATION QUALITY DIMENSIONS

QUALITY DIMENSION	DESCRIPTION
Accuracy	Do the data represent reality?
Integrity	Are the structure of data and relationships among the entities and attributes consistent?
Consistency	Are data elements consistently defined?
Completeness	Are all the necessary data present?
Validity	Do data values fall within defined ranges?
Timeliness	Are data available when needed?
Accessibility	Are the data accessible, comprehensible, and usable?

For instance, Wall Street firms such as Bear Stearns and Lehman Brothers imploded in 2008 because they underestimated the risk of their investments in complex mortgage securities, many of which were based on subprime loans that were more likely to default. The computer models they and other financial institutions used to manage risk were based on overly optimistic assumptions and overly simplistic data about what might go wrong. Management wanted to make sure that their firms' capital was not all tied up as a cushion against defaults from risky investments, preventing them from investing it to generate profits. So the designers of these risk management systems were encouraged to measure risks in a way that minimzed their importance. Some trading desks also oversimplified the information maintained about the mortgage securities to make them appear as simple bonds with higher ratings than were warranted by their underlying components.

Organizational Inertia and Politics. Organizations are bureaucracies with limited capabilities and competencies for acting decisively. When environments change and businesses need to adopt new business models to survive, strong forces within organizations resist making decisions calling for major change. Decisions taken by a firm often represent a balancing of the firm's various interest groups rather than the best solution to the problem.

Studies of business restructuring find that firms tend to ignore poor performance until threatened by outside takeovers, and they systematically blame poor performance on external forces beyond their control—such as economic conditions (the economy), foreign competition, and rising prices—rather than blaming senior or middle management for poor business judgment.

HIGH-VELOCITY AUTOMATED DECISION MAKING

Today, many decisions made by organizations are not made by managers, or any humans. For instance, when you enter a query into Google's search engine, Google has to decide which URLs to display in about half a second on average (500 milliseconds). The New York Stock Exchange spent over

$450 million in 2010–2011 to build a trading platform that executes incoming orders in less than 50 milliseconds. High frequency traders at electronic stock exchanges execute their trades in under 30 milliseconds.

The class of decisions that are highly structured and automated is growing rapidly. What makes this kind of automated high-speed decision making possible are computer algorithms that precisely define the steps to be followed to produce a decision, very large databases, very high-speed processors, and software optimized to the task. In these situations, humans (including managers) are eliminated from the decision chain because they are too slow.

This also means organizations in these areas are making decisions faster than what managers can monitor or control. Inability to control automated decisions was a major factor in the "Flash Crash" experienced by U.S. stock markets on May 6, 2010, when the Dow Jones Industrial Average fell over 600 points in a matter of minutes before rebounding later that day. The stock market was overwhelmed by a huge wave of sell orders triggered primarily by high-speed computerized trading programs within a few seconds, causing shares of some companies like Procter & Gamble to sell for pennies. The past few years have seen a series of similar breakdowns in computerized trading systems, including one on August 1, 2012 when a software error caused Knight Capital to enter millions of faulty trades in less than an hour. The trading glitch created wild surges and plunges in nearly 150 stocks and left Knight with $440 million in losses.

How does the Simon framework of intelligence-design-choice-implementation work in high-velocity decision environments? Essentially, the intelligence, design, choice, and implementation parts of the decision-making process are captured by the software's algorithms. The humans who wrote the software have already identified the problem, designed a method for finding a solution, defined a range of acceptable solutions, and implemented the solution. Obviously, with humans out of the loop, great care needs to be taken to ensure the proper operation of these systems lest they do significant harm to organizations and humans.

12.2 HOW DO BUSINESS INTELLIGENCE AND BUSINESS ANALYTICS SUPPORT DECISION MAKING?

Chapter 2 introduced you to the different types of systems used for supporting management decision making. At the foundation of all of these decision support systems are a business intelligence and business analytics infrastructure that supplies the data and the analytic tools for supporting decision making. In this section, we want to answer the following questions:

- What are business intelligence (BI) and business analytics (BA)
- Who makes business intelligence and business analytics hardware and software?
- Who are the users of business intelligence?
- What kinds of analytical tools come with a BI/BA suite?

- How do managers use these tools?
- What are some examples of firms who have used these tools?
- What management strategies are used for developing BI/BA capabilities?

WHAT IS BUSINESS INTELLIGENCE?

"Business intelligence (BI)" is a term used by hardware and software vendors and information technology consultants to describe the infrastructure for warehousing, integrating, reporting, and analyzing data that come from the business environment, including big data. The foundation infrastructure collects, stores, cleans, and makes relevant information available to managers. Think databases, data warehouses, data marts, Hadoop, and analytic platforms, which we described in Chapter 6. "Business analytics (BA)" is also a vendor-defined term that focuses more on tools and techniques for analyzing and understanding data. Think online analytical processing (OLAP), statistics, models, and data mining, which we also introduced in Chapter 6.

Business intelligence and analytics are essentially about integrating all the information streams produced by a firm into a single, coherent enterprise-wide set of data, and then, using modeling, statistical analysis tools (like normal distributions, correlation and regression analysis, Chi square analysis, forecasting, and cluster analysis), and data mining tools to make sense out of all these data so managers can make better decisions and plans. The German World Cup soccer team described in the chapter-opening case is using business intelligence and analytics to make some very fine-grained decisions about how to improve team and player performance.

Business Intelligence Vendors

It is important to remember that business intelligence and analytics are products defined by technology vendors and consulting firms. They consist of hardware and software suites sold primarily by large system vendors to very large Fortune 500 firms. The largest five providers of these products are Oracle, SAP, IBM, Microsoft, and SAS. Microsoft's products are aimed at small to medium-sized firms, and they are based on desktop tools familiar to employees (such as Excel spreadsheet software), Microsoft SharePoint collaboration tools, and Microsoft SQL Server database software. According to Gartner Inc., the global business intelligence and analytics market was $14.4 billion in 2013 (Gartner, 2014). This makes business intelligence and business analytics one of the fastest growing and largest segments in the U.S. software market.

THE BUSINESS INTELLIGENCE ENVIRONMENT

Figure 12.3 gives an overview of a business intelligence environment, highlighting the kinds of hardware, software, and management capabilities that the major vendors offer and that firms develop over time. There are six elements in this business intelligence environment:

FIGURE 12.3 BUSINESS INTELLIGENCE AND ANALYTICS FOR DECISION
SUPPORT

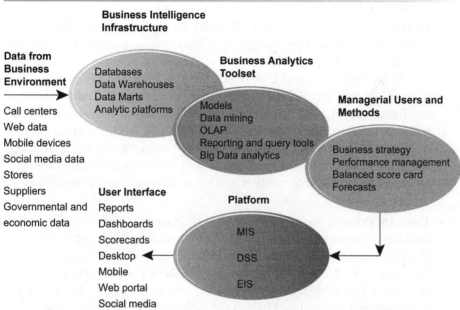

Business intelligence and analytics requires a strong database foundation, a set of analytic tools,
and an involved management team that can ask intelligent questions and analyze data.

- **Data from the business environment:** Businesses must deal with
  both structured and unstructured data from many different sources,
  including big data. The data need to be integrated and organized so
  that they can be analyzed and used by human decision makers.

- **Business intelligence infrastructure:** The underlying foundation
  of business intelligence is a powerful database system that captures all
  the relevant data to operate the business. The data may be stored in
  transactional databases or combined and integrated into an enterprise-
  data warehouse or series of interrelated data marts.

- **Business analytics toolset:** A set of software tools are used to
  analyze data and produce reports, respond to questions posed by managers, and track the progress of the business using key indicators of
  performance.

- **Managerial users and methods:** Business intelligence hardware
  and software are only as intelligent as the human beings who use
  them. Managers impose order on the analysis of data using a variety
  of managerial methods that define strategic business goals and specify
  how progress will be measured. These include business performance
  management and balanced scorecard approaches focusing on key
  performance indicators and industry strategic analyses focusing on
  changes in the general business environment, with special attention
  to competitors. Without strong senior management oversight, business
  analytics can produce a great deal of information, reports, and online

screens that focus on the wrong matters and divert attention from the real issues. You need to remember that, so far, only humans can ask intelligent questions.

- **Delivery platform—MIS, DSS, ESS:** The results from business intelligence and analytics are delivered to managers and employees in a variety of ways, depending on what they need to know to perform their jobs. MIS, DSS, and ESS, which we introduced in Chapter 2, deliver information and knowledge to different people and levels in the firm—operational employees, middle managers, and senior executives. In the past, these systems could not share data and operated as independent systems. Today, one suite of hardware and software tools in the form of a business intelligence and analytics package is able to integrate all this information and bring it to managers' desktop or mobile platforms.

- **User interface:** Business people are no longer tied to their desks and desktops. They often learn quicker from a visual representation of data than from a dry report with columns and rows of information. Today's business analytics software suites feature **data visualization** tools, such as rich graphs, charts, dashboards, and maps. They also are able to deliver reports on BlackBerrys, iPhones, iPads, and other mobile handhelds as well as on the firm's Web portal. BA software is adding capabilities to post information on Twitter, Facebook, or internal social media to support decision making in an online group setting rather than in a face-to-face meeting.

BUSINESS INTELLIGENCE AND ANALYTICS CAPABILITIES

Business intelligence and analytics promise to deliver correct, nearly real-time information to decision makers, and the analytic tools help them quickly understand the information and take action. There are six analytic functionalities that BI systems deliver to achieve these ends:

- **Production reports:** These are predefined reports based on industry-specific requirements (see Table 12.4).

- **Parameterized reports:** Users enter several parameters as in a pivot table to filter data and isolate impacts of parameters. For instance, you might want to enter region and time of day to understand how sales of a product vary by region and time. If you were Starbucks, you might find that customers in the East buy most of their coffee in the morning, whereas in the Northwest customers buy coffee throughout the day. This finding might lead to different marketing and ad campaigns in each region. (See the discussion of pivot tables in Section 12.3.)

- **Dashboards/scorecards:** These are visual tools for presenting performance data defined by users.

- **Ad hoc query/search/report creation:** These allow users to create their own reports based on queries and searches.

TABLE 12.4 EXAMPLES OF BUSINESS INTELLIGENCE PREDEFINED PRODUCTION REPORTS

BUSINESS FUNCTIONAL AREA	PRODUCTION REPORTS
Sales	Forecast sales; sales team performance; cross-selling; sales cycle times
Service/Call Center	Customer satisfaction; service cost; resolution rates; churn rates
Marketing	Campaign effectiveness; loyalty and attrition; market basket analysis
Procurement and Support	Direct and indirect spending; off-contract purchases; supplier performance
Supply Chain	Backlog; fulfillment status; order cycle time; bill of materials analysis
Financials	General ledger; accounts receivable and payable; cash flow; profitability
Human Resources	Employee productivity; compensation; workforce demographics; retention

- **Drill down:** This is the ability to move from a high-level summary to a more detailed view.
- **Forecasts, scenarios, models:** These include the ability to perform linear forecasting, what-if scenario analysis, and analyze data using standard statistical tools.

Who Uses Business Intelligence and Business Analytics?

In previous chapters, we have described the different information constituencies in business firms—from senior managers to middle managers, analysts, and operational employees. This also holds true for BI and BA systems (see Figure 12.4). Over 80 percent of the audience for BI consists of casual users who rely largely on production reports. Senior executives tend to use BI to monitor firm activities using visual interfaces like dashboards and scorecards. Middle managers and analysts are much more likely to be immersed in the data and software, entering queries and slicing and dicing the data along different dimensions. Operational employees will, along with customers and suppliers, be looking mostly at prepackaged reports.

Predictive Analytics

An important capability of business intelligence analytics is the ability to model future events and behaviors, such as the probability that a customer will respond to an offer to purchase a product. **Predictive analytics** use statistical analysis, data mining techniques, historical data, and assumptions about future conditions to predict future trends and behavior patterns. Variables that can be measured to predict future behavior are identified. For example, an insurance company might use variables such as age, gender, and driving record as predictors of driving safety when issuing auto insurance policies. A collection of such predictors is combined into

FIGURE 12.4 BUSINESS INTELLIGENCE USERS

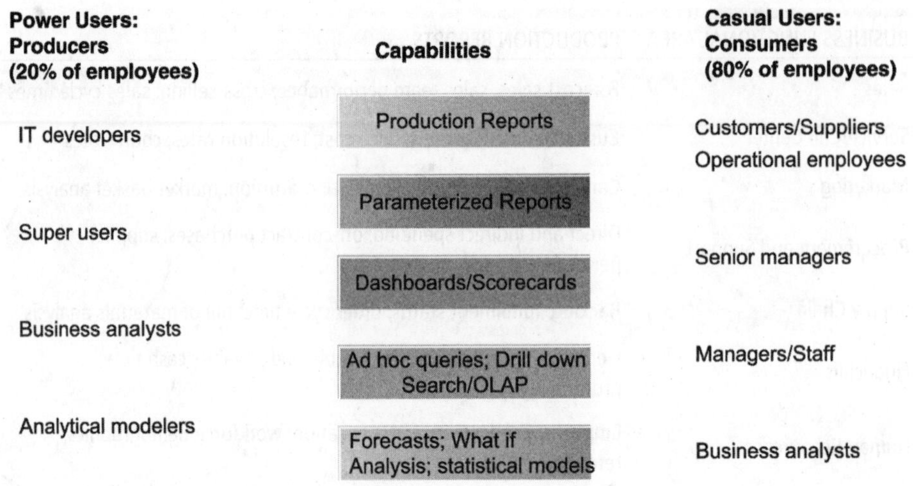

Power Users: Producers (20% of employees)	Capabilities	Casual Users: Consumers (80% of employees)
IT developers	Production Reports	Customers/Suppliers Operational employees
Super users	Parameterized Reports	Senior managers
Business analysts	Dashboards/Scorecards	Managers/Staff
Analytical modelers	Ad hoc queries; Drill down Search/OLAP	Business analysts
	Forecasts; What if Analysis; statistical models	

Casual users are consumers of BI output, while intense power users are the producers of reports, new analyses, models, and forecasts.

a predictive model for forecasting future probabilities with an acceptable level of reliability.

FedEx has been using predictive analytics to develop models that predict how customers will respond to price changes and new services, which customers are most at risk of switching to competitors, and how much revenue will be generated by new storefront or drop-box locations. The accuracy rate of FedEx's predictive analytics system ranges from 65 to 90 percent.

Predictive analytics are being incorporated into numerous business intelligence applications for sales, marketing, finance, fraud detection, and health care. One of the most well-known applications is credit scoring, which is used throughout the financial services industry. When you apply for a new credit card, scoring models process your credit history, loan application, and purchase data to determine your likelihood of making future credit payments on time. Telecommunications companies use predictive analytics to identify which customers are most profitable, which are most likely to leave, and which new services and plans will be most likely to retain customers. Health care insurers have been analyzing data for years to identify which patients are most likely to generate high costs.

Many companies employ predictive analytics to predict response to direct marketing campaigns. By identifying customers less likely to respond, companies are able to lower their marketing and sales costs by bypassing this group and focusing their resources on customers who have been identified as more promising. For instance, the U.S. division of The Body Shop PLC used predictive analytics and its database of catalog, Web, and retail store customers to identify customers who were more likely to make catalog purchases. That information helped the company build a more precise and targeted mailing list for its catalogs, improving the response rate for catalog mailings and catalog revenues.

Big Data Analytics

Predictive analytics are starting to use big data from both private and public sectors, including data from social media, customer transactions, and output from sensors and machines. In e-commerce, many online retailers have capabilities for making personalized online product recommendations to their Web site visitors to help stimulate purchases and guide their decisions about what merchandise to stock. However, most of these product recommendations have been based on the behaviors of similar groups of customers, such as those with incomes under $50,000 or whose ages are between 18–25 years. Now some retailers are starting to analyze the tremendous quantities of online and in-store customer data they collect along with social media data to make these recommendations more individualized. These efforts are translating into higher customer spending and customer retention rates. Table 12.5 provides examples of companies using big data analytics.

In the public sector, big-data analytics has been driving the movement toward "smart cities," which make intensive use of digital technology to make better decisions about running cities and serving their residents. Public recordkeeping has produced warehouses full of property transfers, tax records, corporate filings, environmental compliance audits, restaurant inspections, building maintenance reports, mass transit appraisals, crime data, health department stats, public education records, utility reviews, and more. Municipalities are adding more data captured through sensors, location data from mobile phones, and targeted smartphone apps. Predictive modeling programs now inform public policy decisions on utility management,

TABLE 12.5 WHAT BIG DATA ANALYTICS CAN DO

Bank of America	Able to analyze all of its 50 million customers at once to understand each customer across all channels and interactions, and present consistent, finely-customized offers. Can determine which of its customers has a credit card, or a mortgage loan that could benefit from refinancing at a competitor. When the customer visits BofA online, calls a call center, or visits a branch, that information is available for the online app or sales associate to present BofA's competing offer.
Vestas Wind Systems	Improves wind turbine placement for optimal energy output using IBM BigInsights software and an IBM "Firestorm" supercomputer to analyze 2.8 petabytes of structured and unstructured data such as weather reports, tidal phases, geospatial and sensor data, satellite images, deforestation maps, and weather modeling research. The analysis, which used to take weeks, can now be completed in less than one hour.
Hunch.com	Analyzes massive database with data from customer purchases, social networks and signals from around the Web to produce a "taste graph" that maps users with their predicted affinity to products, services, and Web sites. The taste graph includes predictions about 500 million people, 200 million objects (videos, gadgets, books), and 30 billion connections between people and objects. Helps eBay develop more finely customized recommendations on items to offer.
Actian	Provides Fidelity National Information Services and other financial companies with platform to run fraud analytics against 440,000 ATMs, supporting 95 million cards and over 2 million point-of-sale locations.

INTERACTIVE SESSION: TECHNOLOGY

THE ANALYTICS BEHIND MATRIMONY.COM

The booming Indian economy has opened up job avenues for young Indian women and men. The technology-savvy youth today prefers using trusted Internet sites to find themselves suitable matches. The popularity of sites like Matrimomy.com, Shaadi.com, Tambulya.com, and AssistedMatrimony.com has increased in recent past. According to the Associated Chambers of Commerce of India (ASSOCHAM), the e-Matrimony space will grow to a ₹1,500-crore industry by 2017.

Matrimony.com, a Chennai-based company, is one of the leading Indian online matrimony sites. It sees an influx of over 8,000 new subscribers daily. Matrimony.com also has a strong presence across South Asia, and in the U.K., U.S., Dubai, Sri Lanka, and Malaysia. Even though it employs a fairly large sales team, both on the ground and over the telephone, its Web site remains the major source of its revenue. Once logged in, the online user needs to fill out their profile and get registered as a member. The rate of getting a positive response on the site is considered to be directly related to the quality of information the user supplies in their profile.

However, over time, Matrimony.com noticed that a majority of the male members were not filling the non-mandatory fields in their profile. For example, the 'About Me' section, which was not a mandatory field, went unanswered by most because filling it up was a time-consuming exercise. As a result, those profiles were not getting the kind of views and responses that the members hoped for. Members also complained that the profile information form had a large number of fields, which they felt, could be reduced. Moreover, since Matrimony.com collected information about new members through various channels (the Web site, telesales, and field sales), it was difficult to maintain a comprehensive database for all this information.

In an effort to address the problem of low profile responses, Matrimony.com wanted to find out if there was a correlation between the information in the mandatory and non-mandatory fields in getting positive responses. The company undertook the task of advising its members on the most effective way to fill out their profiles so as to attract maximum responses. Matrimony.com took this a step further by analyzing the data and comparing it to the richness of profile information and response rates to offer customized services to its members. What the company needed was an enterprise-wise marketing suite that would have the right analytics tools to maximize customer satisfaction. Matrimony.com decided to go with IBM's solution for the implementation of advanced analytics on their Web site. These included the IBM ExperienceOne and the SPSS predictive tools for data analysis.

IBM ExperienceOne combines the applications of IBM Enterprise Marketing Management, WebSphere Commerce, and IBM Customer Experience to understand the needs of its users for active customer engagement. However, all the current data of the site was located in an open-source database called MySQL, which was not compatible with the IBM suite of applications. Migrating all this data to a suitable database wasn't an option either, as doing so would disrupt the firm's marketing plans, increase costs, and take time. So, with the involvement of a company called Xerago, Matrimony.com was able to customize and re-configure the database drivers to build a perfect handshake between the MySQL database and the IBM suite.

Next, the SPSS predictive analytical tools of IBM were deployed to generate descriptive statistics-based reports and create predictive marketing models. A tool called Cognos was used for score-carding, monitoring, and reporting. The enterprise marketing management suite included IBM Campaign, which was used to build cross-channel campaigns for Matrimony.com. IBM eMessage was put in place to send and track email to all inbound and outbound channels, while IBM Interact offered personalized marketing to customers. This empowered Matrimony.com to run analytics on customer data like never before and find answers to its marketing problems. The results were indeed revelatory.

The analysis of data showed that men who smoked regularly made an attempt to state that they were "social smokers" in order to hide their habit. Even more surprisingly, it was revealed that women responded better to profiles that stated that the candidate was a regular smoker, rather than those that stated that the user was a social smoker. Consequently, Matrimony.com was able to advise its male members to be honest in revealing their smoking habits. Jayaram K. Iyer, the chief strategy and analytics officer at Matrimony.com, says, "We analyzed volumes of text data and figured that women are most interested when men write about their hobbies—and least when they write about their expectations. This is extremely crucial intelligence about what should be included in profile descriptions." Moreover, the fields that bore no correlation to getting a positive response from members were removed from the profile information form. With the implementation of these small but crucial changes powered by the information generated through data analysis, sales of the company grew by 8%, while alliance interests showed a 5% rise in merely two weeks.

Sources: Jha, Sneha, "Matrimony.com Uses Analytics to Figure Out What Women Want", *Cio.In* (2014). Retrieved from http://www.cio.in/case-study/matrimonycom-uses-analytics-figure-out-what-women-want; "Matrimony.com finds a Match with IBM Big Data and Analytics", IBM (2014). Retrieved from http://www-03.ibm.com/press/in/en/pressrelease/44120.wss; http://www.informationweek.in/informationweek/news-analysis/296152/analytics-match; "Bharat Matrimony makes the most of IBM EMM". Retrieved from http://www.xerago.com/bharat-matrimony-for-my-sql.html; "Matrimony.com & IBM collaboration" (2014). Retrieved from https://www.youtube.com/watch?v = VrHyN1NPt-I.

CASE STUDY QUESTIONS

1. What were the challenges faced by Matrimony.com?

2. In your opinion, how can data analysis rescue a firm from such challenges?

3. Discuss the features of IBM ExperienceOne and the marketing management suite as understood from the text.

transportation operation, healthcare delivery, and public safety. What's more, the ability to evaluate how changes in one service impact the operation and delivery of other services enables holistic problem-solving that could only be dreamed of a generation ago.

Operational Intelligence and Analytics

Some of the decisions described in the Interactive Session on smart cities deal with how to run the business of these cities on a day-to-day basis. These are largely operational decisions, and this type of business activity monitoring is called **operational intelligence**. Another example of operational intelligence is the use of data generated by sensors on trucks, trailers, and intermodal containers owned by Schneider National, one of North America's largest truckload, logistics and intermodal services providers. The sensors monitor location, driving behaviors, fuel levels and whether a trailer or container is loaded or empty. Data from fuel tank sensors help Schneider identify the optimal location at which a driver should stop for fuel based on how much is left in the tank, the truck's destination, and fuel prices en route. General Electric Company (GE) is using myriad sensors to collect data about heat, vibrations, and pressure inside a massive steam-driven

GE generator capable of powering 750,000 homes. These sensor data are analyzed along with data on fuel costs, local weather, demand for power, and alternative supplies of electricity to determine the optimal generator performance for the conditions of the moment (Davenport, 2014).

The Internet of Things is creating huge streams of data from Web activities, smartphones, sensors, gauges, and monitoring devices that can be used for operational intelligence about activities inside and outside the organization. Software for operational intelligence and analytics enables organizations to analyze these streams of big data as they are generated in real time. Companies can set trigger alerts on events or have them fed into live dashboards to help managers with their decisions. For example, Schneider's sensors capture hard braking in a moving truck and relay the data to corporate headquarters, where the data are tracked in dashboards monitoring safety metrics. The event initiates a conversation between the driver and that person's supervisor.

Another example of operational intelligence is the use of real-time data in the 34th America's Cup race, as described in the Interactive Session on Management. As you read this case, try to determine the extent to which information technology was able to replace human decision-makers.

Location Analytics and Geographic Information Systems

The Interactive Session on smart cities also describes data and decisions based on location data. BI analytics include **location analytics**, the ability to gain business insight from the location (geographic) component of data, including location data from mobile phones, output from sensors or scanning devices, and data from maps. For example, location analytics might help a marketer determine which people to target with mobile ads about nearby restaurants and stores, or quantify the impact of mobile ads on in-store visits. Location analytics would help a utility company view and measure outages and their associated costs as related to customer location to help prioritize marketing, system upgrades and customer service efforts. UPS's package tracking and delivery-routing systems described in Chapter 1 use location analytics, as does an application used by Starbucks to determine where to open new stores. The Starbucks application identifies geographic locations that will produce a high sales-to-investment ratio and per-store sales volume.

The Starbucks application and some of the New York City systems described earlier are examples of **geographic information systems (GIS)**. GIS provide tools to help decision makers visualize problems that benefit from mapping. GIS software ties location data about the distribution of people or other resources to points, lines, and areas on a map. Some GIS have modeling capabilities for changing the data and automatically revising business scenarios.

GIS might be used to help state and local governments calculate response times to natural disasters and other emergencies or to help banks identify the best location for new branches or ATM terminals. For example, Columbia, South Carolina-based First Citizens Bank uses MapInfo GIS software to determine which markets to focus on for retaining customers and which to focus on for acquiring new customers. The GIS software also lets

INTERACTIVE SESSION: MANAGEMENT

AMERICA'S CUP: THE TENSION BETWEEN TECHNOLOGY AND HUMAN DECISION MAKERS

On September 25, 2013, Oracle Team USA pulled off one of the greatest comebacks in organized sports by winning the last race of the 34th America's Cup Race on breezy San Francisco Bay. Oracle was down 8–1 to its archrival New Zealand in the previous week after losing seven races in a row. Looked like a rout. But then a miracle: Oracle won seven races in a row. And in a winner-take-all finale, Oracle beat Team New Zealand by 44 seconds over the 12-mile race course before thousands of spectators lined up along San Francisco Bay. Both Team USA and Team New Zealand were the highest of high-tech boats ever to leave a designer's computer screen.

In earlier days, America's Cup races were typically among single-hulled sailboats in the 70-foot range that looked like sailboats in the local yacht club, just more so: a single, long, narrow hull, and a really tall mast to hold the sails up. They might get up to 10 miles an hour on the race course.

In 2010, software billionaire Larry Ellison, founder of Oracle, changed all that by spending over $300 million on a new kind of Cup racer: a three-hulled catamaran made of carbon fiber with what looked like an aircraft wing instead of a mast with sails. In two races, the boat, BMW Oracle USA, beat its Swiss contender, Alinghi. Having won the 33rd America's Cup, Ellison could set the boat design and rules for the 34th race in 2013.

The 2013 design was a spectacular jump from traditional sailboats to 21st Century sailing machines. The 2013 boats were 72-foot, twin-hull catamarans dubbed AC72s, capable of over 50 miles per hour—among the fastest sail boats ever built. The AC72 used small hydrofoils underneath the hulls that provided over 12,000 pounds of lift, bringing the boats out of the water completely, and flying like an airplane. In the end, it was unclear to seasoned sailors worldwide whether the AC72 was really a sailboat at all, but rather more aptly called a "sailing machine."

The 34th America's Cup campaign cost Ellison $100 million, including the cost of a single boat pegged at about $8 million. Oracle had two identical boats built. The new boats were also capable of going completely out of control, usually by digging their bows into the water, and then flipping.

Controlling this wickedly sleek sailing machine requires a lightning-fast collection of massive amounts of data, powerful data management, rapid real-time data analysis, quick decision making, and immediate measurement of the results. In short, all the information technologies needed by a modern business firm. When you can perform all these tasks thousands of times in an hour, you can incrementally improve your performance and have an overwhelming advantage over less IT-savvy opponents on race day. For Team USA, this meant using 250 sensors on the wing, hull, and rudder to gather real-time data on pressure, angles, loads, and strains to monitor the effectiveness of each adjustment. The sensors track 4,000 variables, 10 times a second, producing 90 million data points an hour. The sensors are wired to an onboard server that processes the information, and sends it out on a wireless network to crew member wrist displays. Managing all these data is Oracle Database 11g data management software. The data are also wirelessly transferred to a tender ship running Oracle 11g for near real-time analysis using a family of formulas (called velocity prediction formulas) geared to understanding what makes the boat go fast. Oracle's Application Express presentation graphics summarize the millions of data points and present the boat managers with charts that make sense of the information. The data are also sent to Oracle's Austin data center for more in-depth analysis. Using powerful data analysis tools, USA managers were able to find relationships they had never thought about before. Over several months of practice, from day one to the day before the race, the crew of Team

USA could chart a steady improvement in performance. For the first time in history, it seemed possible to leave sailing to the computer hardware and software.

Each Team USA crew member wore a small mobile handheld computer on his wrist to display data on the key performance variables customized for that person's responsibilities, such as the load balance on a specific rope or the current aerodynamic performance of the wing sail. The captain and tactician had data displayed on their sunglasses. In this way, each crew member gets the data he needs instantly to perform his job. The crew was trained to sail like pilots looking at instruments, rather than sailors looking at the boat and sea for clues. Professional and amateur sailors across the world wondered if the technology had transformed sailing into something else, something akin to flying drones from a desk.

So, why did Team USA lose seven races in a row, and how was Oracle able to pull out a victory? After the seventh loss, skipper James Spithill called for a one-day "time-out" allowed by the rules. Team USA was losing the upwind legs of all the races where Team New Zealand had the edge. The sailors and engineers disagreed about the solution. The engineers called for boat modifications, while the sailors called for more attention to be paid to sailing and less attention to monitoring their wrist computers.

In training for the races, the sailors were told to listen to the engineers who had the best technology to predict boat speeds. The engineers' software program told them to sail Team USA as close as possible to wind on the upwind legs (about 45 degrees to the wind), but the sailors' observations of the actual races suggested New Zealand was winning because it sailed five degrees off the wind at about 50 degrees, sailing a longer but faster upwind course. The difference was seconds per mile, which, all other things being equal, adds up to victory in a 12-mile race. The sailors claimed the engineers' software was just wrong.

In the end, Team USA pursued both solutions: multiple small changes were made in the boat hull and underwater foils, and on the race course. Spithill and his team stopped looking so much at their wrist computer screens, and started to act like sailors on a race course rather than drone pilots in an office. Team USA won every upwind leg of the last eight races. The engineers admitted their software models were not providing accurate advice.

Sources: Stu Wood, "Against the Wind, One of the Greatest Comebacks in Sports History," *Wall Street Journal*, Feb. 28, 2014 and "America's Cup: Resolving the Tension Between Man and Technology," *Wall Street Journal*, March 3, 2014; Christopher Carey, "Oracle Completes Voyage to History, Winning America's Cup," *New York Times*, September 25, 2013; Christopher Carey, "After Comeback for the Ages, a Last Dash for America's Cup," *New York Times*, September 25, 2013; and Joe Schneider, "Team New Zealand Gets Last Shot at America's Cup as Costs Surge," Bloomberg News, Feb 7, 2013.

CASE STUDY QUESTIONS

1. How did information technology change the way America's Cup boats were managed and sailed?

2. How did information technology impact decision making at Team USA?

3. How much was technology responsible for Team USA's America's Cup victory? Explain your answer.

4. Compare the role of big data in Team USA's America's Cup victory with its role in the German team's 2014 World Cup victory described in the chapter-opening case.

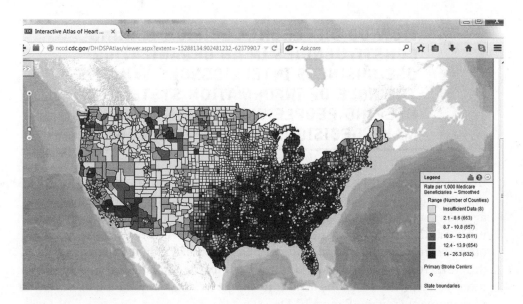

The U.S. Centers for Disease Control and Prevention created a GIS for identifying the stroke hospitalization rate per 1000 Medicare beneficiaries (age 65 and older) in various parts of the United States. The small yellow triangles designate primary stroke care centers.

the bank drill down into details at the individual branch level and individualize goals for each branch. Each branch is able to see whether the greatest revenue opportunities are from mining its database of existing customers or from finding new customers.

MANAGEMENT STRATEGIES FOR DEVELOPING BI AND BA CAPABILITIES

There are two different strategies for adopting BI and BA capabilities for the organization: one-stop integrated solutions versus multiple best-of-breed vendor solutions. The hardware firms (IBM, HP, and now Oracle, which owns Sun Microsystems) want to sell your firm integrated hardware/software solutions that tend to run only on their hardware (the totally integrated solution). It's called "one-stop shopping." The software firms (SAP, SAS, and Microsoft) encourage firms to adopt the "best-of-breed" software that runs on any machine they want. In this strategy, you adopt the best database and data warehouse solution, and select the business intelligence and analytics package from whatever vendor you believe is best.

The first solution carries the risk that a single vendor provides your firm's total hardware and software solution, making your firm dependent on its pricing power. However, it offers the advantage of dealing with a single vendor who can deliver on a global scale. The second solution offers greater flexibility and independence, but with the risk of potential difficulties integrating the software to the hardware platform, as well as to other software. Vendors always claim their software is "compatible" with other software, but the reality is that it can be very difficult to integrate software from different vendors.

Regardless of which strategy your firm adopts, all BI and BA systems lock the firm into a set of vendors and switching is very costly. Once you train thousands of employees across the world on using a particular set of tools, it is extremely difficult to switch. When you adopt these systems, you are in essence taking in a new partner.

12.3 HOW DO DIFFERENT DECISION-MAKING CONSTITUENCIES IN AN ORGANIZATION USE BUSINESS INTELLIGENCE? WHAT IS THE ROLE OF INFORMATION SYSTEMS IN HELPING PEOPLE WORKING IN A GROUP MAKE DECISIONS MORE EFFICIENTLY?

There are many different constituencies that make up a modern business firm. Earlier in this text and in this chapter we identified three levels of management: lower supervisory (operational) management, middle management, and senior management (vice president and above, including executive or "C level" management, e.g. chief executive officer, chief financial officers, and chief operational officer.) Each of these management groups has different responsibilities and different needs for information and business intelligence, with decisions becoming less structured among higher levels of management (review Figure 12.1).

DECISION SUPPORT FOR OPERATIONAL AND MIDDLE MANAGEMENT

Operational and middle management are generally charged with monitoring the performance of key aspects of the business, ranging from the down-time of machines on a factory floor, to the daily or even hourly sales at franchise food stores, to the daily traffic at a company's Web site. Most of the decisions they make are fairly structured. Management information systems (MIS) are typically used by middle managers to support this type of decision making, and their primary output is a set of routine production reports based on data extracted and summarized from the firm's underlying transaction processing systems (TPS). Increasingly, middle managers receive these reports online on the company portal, and are able to interactively query the data to find out why events are happening. To save even more analysis time, managers turn to exception reports, which highlight only exceptional conditions, such as when the sales quotas for a specific territory fall below an anticipated level or employees have exceeded their spending limits in a dental care plan. Table 12.6 provides some examples of MIS applications.

Support for Semistructured Decisions

Some managers are "super users" and keen business analysts who want to create their own reports, and use more sophisticated analytics and models to find patterns in data, to model alternative business scenarios, or to test specific hypotheses. Decision-support systems (DSS) are the BI delivery platform for this category of users, with the ability to support semistructured decision making.

DSS rely more heavily on modeling than MIS, using mathematical or analytical models to perform what-if or other kinds of analysis. "What-if" analysis, working forward from known or assumed conditions, allows the user to vary certain values to test results to predict outcomes if changes occur

TABLE 12.6 EXAMPLES OF MIS APPLICATIONS

COMPANY	MIS APPLICATION
California Pizza Kitchen	Inventory Express application "remembers" each restaurant's ordering patterns and compares the amount of ingredients used per menu item to predefined portion measurements established by management. The system identifies restaurants with out-of-line portions and notifies their managers so that corrective actions will be taken.
PharMark	Extranet MIS identifies patients with drug-use patterns that place them at risk for adverse outcomes.
Black & Veatch	Intranet MIS tracks construction costs for various projects across the United States.
Taco Bell	Total Automation of Company Operations (TACO) system provides information on food, labor, and period-to-date costs for each restaurant.

in those values. What happens if we raise product prices by 5 percent or increase the advertising budget by $1 million? **Sensitivity analysis** models ask what-if questions repeatedly to predict a range of outcomes when one or more variables are changed multiple times (see Figure 12.5). Backward sensitivity analysis helps decision makers with goal seeking: If I want to sell 1 million product units next year, how much must I reduce the price of the product?

Chapter 6 described multidimensional data analysis and OLAP as one of the key business intelligence technologies. Spreadsheets have a similar feature for multidimensional analysis called a **pivot table**, which manager "super users" and analysts employ to identify and understand patterns in business information that may be useful for semistructured decision making.

Figure 12.6 illustrates a Microsoft Excel pivot table that examines a large list of order transactions for a company selling online management training videos and books. It shows the relationship between two dimensions: the

FIGURE 12.5 SENSITIVITY ANALYSIS

		Variable Cost per Unit				
Total fixed costs	19000					
Variable cost per unit	3					
Average sales price	17					
Contribution margin	14					
Break-even point	1357					
Sales	1357	2	3	4	5	6
Price	14	1583	1727	1900	2111	2375
	15	1462	1583	1727	1900	2111
	16	1357	1462	1583	1727	1900
	17	1267	1357	1462	1583	1727
	18	1188	1267	1357	1462	1583

This table displays the results of a sensitivity analysis of the effect of changing the sales price of a necktie and the cost per unit on the product's break-even point. It answers the question, "What happens to the break-even point if the sales price and the cost to make each unit increase or decrease?"

FIGURE 12.6 A PIVOT TABLE THAT EXAMINES CUSTOMER REGIONAL DISTRIBUTION AND ADVERTISING SOURCE

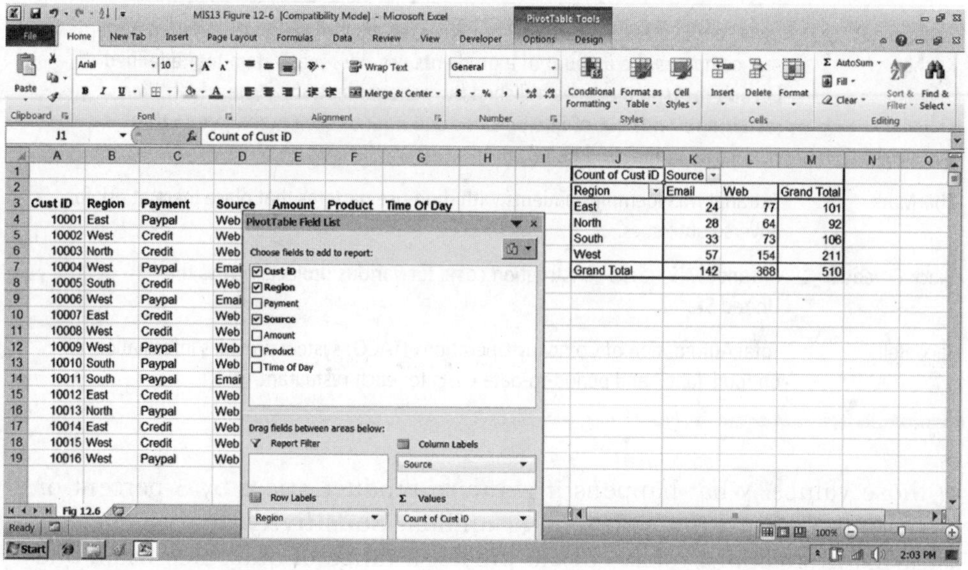

In this pivot table, we are able to examine where an online training company's customers come from in terms of region and advertising source.

sales region and the source of contact (Web banner ad or e-mail) for each customer order. It answers the question: does the source of the customer make a difference in addition to region? The pivot table in this figure shows that most customers come from the West and that banner advertising produces most of the customers in all the regions.

One of the Hands-On MIS projects for this chapter asks you to use a pivot table to find answers to a number of other questions using the same list of transactions for the online training company as we used in this discussion. The complete Excel file for these transactions is available in MyMISLab. We have also added a Learning Track on creating pivot tables using Excel.

In the past, much of this modeling was done with spreadsheets and small stand-alone databases. Today these capabilities are incorporated into large enterprise BI systems where they are able to analyze data from large corporate databases. BI analytics include tools for intensive modeling, some of which we described earlier. Such capabilities help Progressive Insurance identify the best customers for its products. Using widely available insurance industry data, Progressive defines small groups of customers, or "cells," such as motorcycle riders aged 30 or above with college educations, credit scores over a certain level, and no accidents. For each "cell," Progressive performs a regression analysis to identify factors most closely correlated with the insurance losses that are typical for this group. It then sets prices for each cell, and uses simulation software to test whether this pricing arrangement will enable the company to make a profit. These analytic techniques, make it possible for Progressive to profitably insure customers in traditionally high-risk categories that other insurers would have rejected.

DECISION SUPPORT FOR SENIOR MANAGEMENT: BALANCED SCORECARD AND ENTERPRISE PERFORMANCE MANAGEMENT METHODS

The purpose of executive support systems (ESS), introduced in Chapter 2, is to help C-level executive managers focus on the really important performance information that affect the overall profitability and success of the firm. There are two parts to developing ESS. First, you will need a methodology for understanding exactly what is "the really important performance information" for a specific firm that executives need, and second, you will need to develop systems capable of delivering this information to the right people in a timely fashion.

Currently, the leading methodology for understanding the really important information needed by a firm's executives is called the **balanced scorecard method** (Kaplan and Norton, 2004; Kaplan and Norton, 1992). The balanced score card is a framework for operationalizing a firm's strategic plan by focusing on measurable outcomes on four dimensions of firm performance: financial, business process, customer, and learning and growth (Figure 12.7).

Performance on each dimension is measured using **key performance indicators (KPIs)**, which are the measures proposed by senior management for understanding how well the firm is performing along any given dimension. For instance, one key indicator of how well an online retail firm is meeting its customer performance objectives is the average length of time required to deliver a package to a consumer. If your firm is a bank, one KPI

FIGURE 12.7 THE BALANCED SCORECARD FRAMEWORK

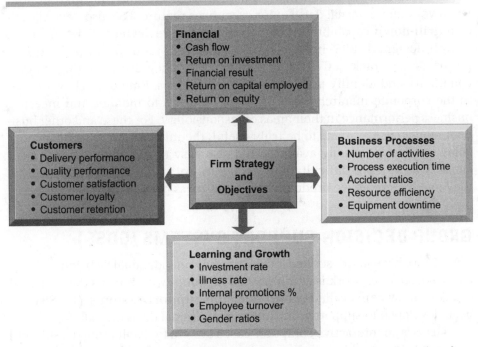

In the balanced scorecard framework, the firm's strategic objectives are operationalized along four dimensions: financial, business process, customer, and learning and growth. Each dimension is measured using several KPIs.

of business process performance is the length of time required to perform a basic function like creating a new customer account.

The balanced scorecard framework is thought to be "balanced" because it causes managers to focus on more than just financial performance. In this view, financial performance is past history—the result of past actions—and managers should focus on the things they are able to influence today, such as business process efficiency, customer satisfaction, and employee training. Once a scorecard is developed by consultants and senior executives, the next step is automating a flow of information to executives and other managers for each of the key performance indicators. There are literally hundreds of consulting and software firms that offer these capabilities, which are described below. Once these systems are implemented, they are often referred to as ESS.

Another closely related popular management methodology is **business performance management (BPM)**. Originally defined by an industry group in 2004 (led by the same companies that sell enterprise and database systems like Oracle, SAP, and IBM), BPM attempts to systematically translate a firm's strategies (e.g., differentiation, low-cost producer, market share growth, and scope of operation) into operational targets. Once the strategies and targets are identified, a set of KPIs are developed that measure progress towards the targets. The firm's performance is then measured with information drawn from the firm's enterprise database systems. BPM uses the same ideas as balanced scorecard but with a stronger strategy flavor.

Corporate data for contemporary ESS are supplied by the firm's existing enterprise applications (enterprise resource planning, supply chain management, and customer relationship management). ESS also provide access to news services, financial market databases, economic information, and whatever other external data senior executives require. ESS also have significant **drill-down** capabilities if managers need more detailed views of data.

Well-designed ESS help senior executives monitor organizational performance, track activities of competitors, recognize changing market conditions, and identify problems and opportunities. Employees lower down in the corporate hierarchy also use these systems to monitor and measure business performance in their areas of responsibility. For these and other business intelligence systems to be truly useful, the information must be "actionable"—it must be readily available and also easy to use when making decisions. If users have difficulty identifying critical metrics within the reports they receive, employee productivity and business performance will suffer.

GROUP DECISION-SUPPORT SYSTEMS (GDSS)

The DSS we have just described focus primarily on individual decision making. However, so much work is accomplished in groups within firms that a special category of systems called **group decision-support systems (GDSS)** has been developed to support group and organizational decision making.

A GDSS is an interactive computer-based system for facilitating the solution of unstructured problems by a set of decision makers working together as a group in the same location or in different locations. Collaboration systems and Web-based tools for videoconferencing and electronic meetings described earlier in this text support some group decision processes, but their focus is primarily on communication. GDSS, however, provide tools and technologies geared explicitly toward group decision making.

GDSS-guided meetings take place in conference rooms with special hardware and software tools to facilitate group decision making. The hardware includes computer and networking equipment, overhead projectors, and display screens. Special electronic meeting software collects, documents, ranks, edits, and stores the ideas offered in a decision-making meeting. The more elaborate GDSS use a professional facilitator and support staff. The facilitator selects the software tools and helps organize and run the meeting.

A sophisticated GDSS provides each attendee with a dedicated desktop computer under that person's individual control. No one will be able to see what individuals do on their computers until those participants are ready to share information. Their input is transmitted over a network to a central server that stores information generated by the meeting and makes it available to all on the meeting network. Data can also be projected on a large screen in the meeting room.

GDSS make it possible to increase meeting size while at the same time increasing productivity because individuals contribute simultaneously rather than one at a time. A GDSS promotes a collaborative atmosphere by guaranteeing contributors' anonymity so that attendees focus on evaluating the ideas themselves without fear of personally being criticized or of having their ideas rejected based on the contributor. GDSS software tools follow structured methods for organizing and evaluating ideas and for preserving the results of meetings, enabling nonattendees to locate needed information after the meeting. GDSS effectiveness depends on the nature of the problem and the group and on how well a meeting is planned and conducted.

Review Summary

1. *What are the different types of decisions and how does the decision-making process work? How do information systems support the activities of managers and management decision making?*

   The different levels in an organization (strategic, management, operational) have different decision-making requirements. Decisions can be structured, semistructured, or unstructured, with structured decisions clustering at the operational level of the organization and unstructured decisions at the strategic level. Decision making can be performed by individuals or groups and includes employees as well as operational, middle, and senior managers. There are four stages in decision making: intelligence, design, choice, and implementation. Systems to support decision making do not always produce better manager and employee decisions that improve firm performance because of problems with information quality, management filters, and organizational culture.

   Early classical models of managerial activities stress the functions of planning, organizing, coordinating, deciding, and controlling. Contemporary research looking at the actual behavior of managers has found that managers' real activities are highly fragmented, variegated, and brief in duration and that managers shy away from making grand, sweeping policy decisions.

   Information technology provides new tools for managers to carry out both their traditional and newer roles, enabling them to monitor, plan, and forecast with more precision and speed than ever before and to respond more rapidly to the changing business environment. Information systems have been most helpful to managers by providing support for their roles in disseminating information, providing liaisons between organizational levels, and allocating resources. However, information systems are less successful at supporting unstructured decisions. Where information systems are useful, information quality, management filters, and organizational culture can degrade decision making.

2. *How do business intelligence and business analytics support decision making?*

Business intelligence and analytics promise to deliver correct, nearly real-time information to decision makers, and the analytic tools help them quickly understand the information and take action. A business intelligence environment consists of data from the business environment, the BI infrastructure, a BA toolset, managerial users and methods, a BI delivery platform (MIS, DSS, or ESS), and the user interface. There are six analytic functionalities that BI systems deliver to achieve these ends: predefined production reports, parameterized reports, dashboards and scorecards, ad hoc queries and searches, the ability to drill down to detailed views of data, and the ability to model scenarios and create forecasts.

3. *How do different decision-making constituencies in an organization use business intelligence? What is the role of information systems in helping people working in a group make decisions more efficiently?*

Operational and middle management are generally charged with monitoring the performance of their firm. Most of the decisions they make are fairly structured. Management information systems (MIS) producing routine production reports are typically used to support this type of decision making. For making unstructured decisions, middle managers and analysts will use decision-support systems (DSS) with powerful analytics and modeling tools, including spreadsheets and pivot tables. Senior executives making unstructured decisions use dashboards and visual interfaces displaying key performance information affecting the overall profitability, success, and strategy of the firm. The balanced scorecard and business performance management are two methodologies used in designing executive support systems (ESS).

Group decision-support systems (GDSS) help people working together in a group arrive at decisions more efficiently. GDSS feature special conference room facilities where participants contribute their ideas using networked computers and software tools for organizing ideas, gathering information, making and setting priorities, and documenting meeting sessions.

Key Terms

Balanced scorecard method, 521
Behavioral models, 502
Business performance management
 (BPM), 522
Choice, 500
Classical model of management, 501
Data visualization, 508
Decisional role, 502
Design, 500
Drill down, 522
Geographic information systems (GIS), 514
Group decision-support systems (GDSS), 522
Implementation, 500

Informational role, 502
Intelligence, 500
Interpersonal role, 502
Key performance indicators (KPIs), 521
Managerial roles, 502
Location analytics, 513
Operational intelligence, 512
Pivot table, 519
Predictive analytics, 509
Semistructured decisions, 499
Sensitivity analysis, 519
Structured decisions, 499
Unstructured decisions, 499

Review Questions

12-1 What are the different types of decisions and how does the decision-making process work? How do information systems support the activities of managers and management decision making?

- List and describe the different levels of decision making and decision-making

constituencies in organizations. Explain how their decision-making requirements differ.

- Distinguish between an unstructured, semistructured, and structured decision.

- List and describe the stages in decision making.

- Compare the descriptions of managerial behavior in the classical and behavioral models.
- Identify the specific managerial roles that can be supported by information systems.

12-2 How do business intelligence and business analytics support decision making?

- Define and describe business intelligence and business analytics.
- List and describe the elements of a business intelligence environment.
- List and describe the analytic functionalities provided by BI systems.
- Compare two different management strategies for developing BI and BA capabilities.

12-3 How do different decision-making constituencies in an organization use business intelligence? What is the role of information systems in helping people working in a group make decisions more efficiently?

- List each of the major decision-making constituencies in an organization and describe the types of decisions each makes.
- Describe how MIS, DSS, or ESS provide decision support for each of these groups.
- Define and describe the balanced scorecard method and business performance management.
- Define a group decision-support system (GDSS) and explain how it differs from a DSS.
- Explain how a GDSS works and how it provides value for a business.

Discussion Questions

12-4 As a manager or user of information systems, what would you need to know to participate in the design and use of a DSS or an ESS? Why?

12-5 If businesses used DSS, GDSS, and ESS more widely, would managers and employees make better decisions? Why or why not?

12-6 How much can business intelligence and business analytics help companies refine their business strategy? Explain your answer.

Hands-On MIS Projects

The projects in this section give you hands-on experience identifying opportunities for DSS, using a spreadsheet pivot table to analyze sales data, and online retirement planning tools for financial planning.

Management Decision Problems

12-7 Dealerships for Subaru and other automobile manufacturers keep records of the mileage of cars they sell and service. Mileage data are used to remind customers of when they need to schedule service appointments, but they are used for other purposes as well. What kinds of decisions does this piece of data support at the local level and at the corporate level? What would happen if this piece of data were erroneous, for example, showing mileage of 130,000 instead of 30,000? How would it affect decision making? Assess its business impact.

12-8 Applebee's is the largest casual dining chain in the world, with over 1,800 locations throughout the U.S. and also in 20 other countries. The menu features beef, chicken, and pork items, as well as burgers, pasta, and seafood. Applebee's CEO wants to make the restaurant more profitable by developing menus that are tastier and contain more items that customers want and are willing to pay for despite rising costs for gasoline and agricultural products. How might business intelligence help management implement this strategy? What pieces of data would Applebee's need to collect? What kinds of reports would be useful to help management make decisions on how to improve menus and profitability?

Improving Decision Making: Using a Web-Based DSS for Retirement Planning

Software skills: Internet-based software
Business skills: Financial planning

12-9 This project will help develop your skills in using Web-based DSS for financial planning.

The Web sites for CNN Money and Kiplinger feature Web-based DSS for financial planning and decision making. Select either site to plan for retirement. Use your chosen site to determine how much you need to save to have enough income for your retirement. Assume that you are 50 years old, single and plan to retire in 16 years. You have $100,000 in savings. Your current annual income is $85,000. Your goal is to be able to generate an annual retirement income of $60,000, including Social Security benefit payments.

Use the Web site you have selected to determine how much money you need to save to help you achieve your retirement goal. If you need to calculate your estimated Social Security benefit, use the Quick Calculator at the Social Security Administration Web site

Critique the site—its ease of use, its clarity, the value of any conclusions reached, and the extent to which the site helps investors understand their financial needs and the financial markets.

How Much Does Data-Driven Planting Help Farmers?
CASE STUDY

Like many other businesses, farming is being reshaped by information technology. Many tractors and combines today are guided by Global Positioning System (GPS) satellite-based navigation systems. The GPS computer receives signals from earth-orbiting satellites to track each piece of equipment's location and where it has gone. The system issues instructions for hoses to deliver precise amounts of fertilizer right into the grooves cut by the tiller. The system helps steer the equipment, so farmers are able to monitor progress on iPads and other tablet computers in their tractor cabs. Placing seed and fertilizer together with this level of precision means farmers need to use fewer loads of fertilizer, potentially saving an individual farmer tens of thousands of dollars.

Now big agricultural companies like Monsanto and Dupont want to do more. Since adjustments in planting depth or the distance between crop rows can make a big difference in crop yields, these companies want their computers to analyze the data generated during this computerized planting work to show farmers how to further increase their crop output. This practice is also known as predictive planting. Proponents say prescriptive planting will spark an agricultural revolution rivalling the introduction of mechanized tractors in the first half of the 20th century and the rise of genetically modified seeds in the 1990s.

Here's how prescriptive planting works: The farmer provides data on field boundaries, historic crop yields, and soil conditions to an agricultural data analysis company, which analyzes the data along with other data it has collected about seed performance and soil types in different areas. The company then sends a computer file with recommendations back to the farmer, who uploads the data into computerized planting equipment. The farmer's planting equipment follows the recommendations as it plants fields. For example, the recommendations might tell an Iowa corn farmer to lower the number of seeds planted per acre or to plant more seeds per acre in specified portions of

the field capable of growing more corn. The farmer might also receive advice on the exact type of seed to plant in different areas. The data analysis company monitors weather and other factors to advise farmers how to manage crops as they grow.

A new software application developed by Monsanto called FieldScripts takes into account variables such as the amount of sunlight and shade, and variations in soil nitrogen and phosphorous content down to an area as small as a 10-meter by 10-meter grid. Monsanto then analyzes the data in conjunction with the genetic properties of their seeds, combines all this information with climate predictions, and delivers precise planting instructions or "scripts" to iPads connected to planting equipment in the field. Tools such as FieldScripts would allow farmers to pinpoint areas that need more or less fertilizer, saving them the cost of spreading fertilizer everywhere, while boosting their yields in areas that have performed more poorly and reducing the amount of excess fertilizer that enters the water table. So, predictive planting could also be good for the environment.

Prescriptive planting could help improve the average corn harvest to more than 200 bushels an acre from the current 160 bushels, some experts say. Such a gain would generate an extra $182 an acre in revenue for farmers, based on recent prices. (Iowa corn farmers received about $759 an acre in 2013.) On a larger scale, according to Monsanto, the world's largest seed company, data-driven planting advice to farmers could increase worldwide crop production by about $20 billion a year. So far, output from predictive planting systems has not achieved those spectacular levels. Farmers who use prescriptive planting report their yields rising by 5 to 10 bushels per acre.

The costs of investing in the new technology and vendor service fees can amount to more than what many small farmers can earn in extra yield from their farms. According to Sara Olson of Lux Research Inc., the problem with precision agriculture is the diminishing returns that come along with costly technologies on smaller farms. That means that only the really big farms are likely to benefit.

Monsanto estimates that FieldScripts will improve yields by 5 to 10 bushels per acre. With corn at around $4 per bushel, that's an increase of $20–$40 per acre. A small farm, of about 500 acres, could get anywhere from $10,000 to $20,000 in extra revenue. Monsanto charges around $10 per acre for the service, so the farm will wind up paying around $5,000—in addition to paying tens of thousands of dollars to either retrofit its existing planting equipment or buy more modern tractors that include the electronics gear that syncs the "scripts" provided by the Monsanto online service with the planter's onboard navigation systems. Monsanto also charges an extra $15 per acre for its local climate prediction service. A small farm will most likely lose money or break even for the first two years of using a service like FieldScripts, according to Olson.

For large farm of about 5,000 acres, FieldScripts could increase revenues increase by between $100,000 and $200,000. With Monsanto's service costing around $50,000, that farm's total profits will run between $50,000 to $150,000, more than sufficient to offset the cost of updating farm machinery. Whether a farm is big or small the impact of FieldScripts would be minimal in good years because yields would be high regardless. Steve Pitstick, who owns a 2,600-acre corn and soybean farm near DeKalb, Ill., said that the technology is likely to have a bigger impact in years when conditions aren't so good. Since Midwest farming conditionswere good in 2013, Pitstick found that yields from fields that he managed using FieldScripts were only between 1 percent and 2 percent higher than fields where he didn't use the service.

A spokesperson for Monsanto stated that the outcome of predictive planting is less about the size of the farm and more about the farmer's technology know-how. A wide range of farmers are currently using various types of precision agriculture technology. Both small-and large-scale farmers dealing with various crops and production methods are increasingly looking for new technologies and tools that can improve their yields while managing their overall risk. According to Michael Cox, co-director of investment research at securities firm Piper Jaffray Cos., revenue from FieldScripts

and other technology-driven products and services could account for 20 percent of Monsanto's projected growth in per-share earnings by 2018.

Although some farmers have embraced predictive planting, others are critical. Many farmers are worried about the intrusion of big data into their once-insular businesses and are especially suspicious of what Monsanto and DuPont might do with the collected data. Others worry about seed prices rising too much, since the companies that developed predictive planting technology are the same ones that sell seeds. Farmers also fear that rivals could use the data to their own advantage. For instance, if nearby farmers saw crop-yield information, they might rush to rent farmland, pushing land and other costs higher. Other farmers worry that Wall Street traders could use the data to make bets on futures contracts. If such bets push futures-contract prices lower early in the growing season, it might squeeze the profits farmers could lock in for their crops by selling futures.

There are not yet any publicly known examples where a farmer's prescriptive-planting information has been misused. Monsanto and DuPont officials say the companies have no plans to sell data gathered from farmers. Deere& Co., which working with DuPont and Dow Chemical Co. to formulate specialized seed-planting recommendations based on data from its tractors, combines and other machinery, says it obtains consent from customers before sharing any of their data.

Kip Tom has been testing Monsanto's system on his 20,000-acre farm near Leesburg, Indiana, for about three years. He claims he would not plant a single acre without it. But he keeps close tabs on how data flow from and to his farm machinery. In 2013, Mr. Tom unplugged a cable inside one of his combine to prevent it from capturing details of his planting algorithm as he harvested corn. The combine's manufacturer didn't develop that information, so Tom didn't believe it should have access to it.

Some farmers have discussed aggregating planting data on their own so they could decide what information to sell and at what price. Other farmers are working with smaller technology companies that are trying to keep agricultural giants from dominating the prescriptive-planting business. Steve Cubbage, owner of Prime Meridian

LLC in Nevada, Missouri, one of these small companies, says his company's independence from the seed, machinery and chemical industry adds credibility. About one hundred farmers use Prime Meridian's precision-seeding service, and Cubbage expects the number to increase dramatically. The company is developing a system to store farm-by-farm information on an online Web-based service that could give access to seed dealers, financial advisers and other outsiders approved by farmers.

The American Farm Bureau Federation, a trade group for farmers, has warned members that seed companies touting higher crop yields from prescriptive planting have a vested interest in persuading farmers to plant more. The Federation also says the services might steer farmers to buy certain seeds, sprays and equipment for their land. The Farm Bureau has held internal talks about whether the trade group should set up its own computer servers as a data storehouse, but no decision has been reached.

Brian Dunn, who grows wheat, corn and sorghum on 2,500 acres near St. John, Kansas, believes that big companies can help in the short-term, but is skeptical about the long-term. He uses Prime Meridian's service.

In a move to ease farmers' worries, Monsanto said last month that it supports industrywide standards for managing information collected from fields. The company aims to build a free online data storehouse where farmers could upload information ranging from crop yields to planting dates. Monsanto says it wouldn't access the data without permission from farmers.

One reason that suspicions run deep among some farmers: a surge in seed prices as the biggest companies increased their market share during the past fifteen years, largely through takeovers. Monsanto and DuPont now sell about 70 percent of all corn seed in the U.S. In 2013, farmers paid about $118 an acre for corn seed, up 166 percent from the inflation-adjusted cost of $45 an acre in 2005, according to Purdue University estimates. The seed companies say the higher prices reflect the benefits of using their genetically modified seeds, including bigger crops and resistance to insects and weed-killing sprays that have helped reduce the usage of harmful pesticides.

Sources: Jacob Bunge, "On the Farm Data Harvesting Sows Seeds of Mistrust," *Wall Street Journal*, February 25, 2014; Michael Hickins, "For Small Farmers, Big Data Adds Modern Problems to Ancient Ones," *Wall Street Journal*, February 25, 2014; www.monsanto.com, accessed March 4, 2014; Drake Bennett, "Inside Monsanto, America's Third-Hated Company," Business Week, July 3, 2014; and Christopher Eutaw, "The Biggest Revolution Since Louis XVI Was Beheaded," Capital Hill Daily, February 27, 2014.

CASE STUDY QUESTIONS

12-10 List and describe the technologies used in this case study.

12-11 How do the systems described in this case provide operational intelligence?

12-12 How does predictive planting support decision making? Identify three different decisions that can be supported.

12-13 How helpful is predictive planting to individual farmers and the agricultural industry? Explain your answer.

Chapter 12 References

Bhandari, Rishi, Marc Singer, and Hiek van der Scheer. "Using Marketing Analytics to Drive Superior Growth." McKinsey & Co. (June 2014).

Clark, Thomas D., Jr., Mary C. Jones, and Curtis P. Armstrong. "The Dynamic Structure of Management Support Systems: Theory Development, Research Focus, and Direction." MIS Quarterly 31, No. 3 (September 2007).

Davenport, Thomas H. "Analytics 3.0." Harvard Business Review (December 2013).

Davenport, Thomas H. Big Data at Work: Dispelling the Myths, Uncovering the Opportunities. Harvard Business Review Press (2014).

Davenport, Thomas H. and Jill Dyche. "Big Data in Big Companies." International Institute of Analytics (May 2013).

Davenport, Thomas H. and Jinho Kim. Keeping Up with the Quants: Your Guide to Understanding and Using Analytics. Harvard Business Press Books (2013).

Davenport, Thomas H., Jeanne G. Harris, and Robert Morison. Analytics at Work: Smarter Decisions, Better Results. Boston: Harvard Business Press (2010).

De la Merced, Michael J. and Ben Protess. "A Fast-Paced Stock Exchange Trips Over Itself." The New York Times (March 23, 2012)

Dennis, Alan R., Jay E. Aronson, William G. Henriger, and Edward D. Walker III. "Structuring Time and Task in Electronic Brainstorming." MIS Quarterly 23, No. 1 (March 1999).

Devlin, Barry. "Operational Analytics from A to Z." 9 sight Consulting (May 2013).

Fogarty, David and Peter C. Bell. "Should You Outsource Analytics?" MIT Sloan Management Review (Winter 2014).

Gallupe, R. Brent, Geraldine DeSanctis, and Gary W. Dickson. "Computer-Based Support for Group Problem-Finding: An Experimental Investigation." MIS Quarterly 12, No. 2 (June 1988).

Gartner. "Gartner Says Worldwide Business Intelligence and Analytics Software Market Grew 8 Percent in 2013." (April 29, 2014).

Grau, Jeffrey. "How Retailers Are Leveraging 'Big Data' to Personalize Ecommerce." eMarketer (2012).

Harris, Jeanne G. and Vijay Mehrotra. "Getting Value from Your Data Scientists." MIT Sloan Management Review (Fall 2014).

Hurst, Cameron with Michael S. Hopkins and Leslie Brokaw. "Matchmaking With Math: How Analytics Beats Intuition to Win Customers." MIT Sloan Management Review 52, No. 2 (Winter 2011).

Jensen, Matthew, Paul Benjamin Lowry, Judee K. Burgoon, and Jay Nunamaker. "Technology Dominance in Complex Decision making." Journal of Management Information Systems 27, No. 1 (Summer 2010).

Kaplan, Robert S. and David P. Norton. "The Balanced Scorecard: Measures that Drive Performance", Harvard Business Review (Jan – Feb 1992).

Kaplan, Robert S. and David P. Norton. Strategy Maps: Converting Intangible Assets into Tangible Outcomes. Boston: Harvard Business School Press (2004).

Kiron, David, Pamela Kirk Prentice, and Renee Boucher Ferguson. "Raising the Bar with Analytics." MIT Sloan Management Review (Winter 2014).

Kiron, David, Pamela Kirk, and Renee Boucher Ferguson. "Innovating with Analytics." MIT Sloan Management Review 54, No. 1 (Fall 2012).

Lauricella, Tom and Scott Patterson. "With Knight Wounded, Traders Ask If Speed Kills." Wall Street Journal (August 2, 2012).

LaValle, Steve, Eric Lesser, Rebecca Shockley, Michael S. Hopkins and Nina Kruschwitz. "Big Data, Analytics, and the Path from Insights to Value." MIT Sloan Management Review 52, No. 2 (Winter 2011).

Leidner, Dorothy E., and Joyce Elam. "The Impact of Executive Information Systems on Organizational Design, Intelligence, and Decision Making." Organization Science 6, No. 6 (November–December 1995).

Marchand, Donald A. and Joe Peppard. "Why IT Fumbles Analytics." Harvard Business Review (January-February 2013).

Mintzberg, Henry. "Nichols, Wes. "Advertising Analytics 2.0." Harvard Business Review (March 2013).

Nystrom, Paul C., and William H. Starbuck. "To Avoid Organizational Crises, Unlearn." Organizational Dynamics, Spring 1984.

Rockart, John F., and David W. DeLong. Executive Support Systems: The Emergence of Top Management Computer Use. Homewood, IL: Dow-Jones Irwin (1988).

Simon, H. A. The New Science of Management Decision. New York: Harper & Row (1960).

Starbuck, William H. and Bo Hedberg. "How Organizations Learn from Success and Failure," The Handbook of Organizational Learning and Knowledge. 1985.

Tversky, A. and D. Kahneman. "The Framing of Decisions and the Psychology of Choice." Science 211 (January 1981).

PART FOUR

Building and Managing Systems

Part Four focuses on building and managing systems in organizations. This part answers questions such as: What activities are required to build a new information system? What alternative approaches are available for building system solutions? How should information systems projects be managed to ensure that new systems provide genuine business benefits and work successfully in the organization? What issues must be addressed when building and managing global systems?

Building Information Systems

13

LEARNING OBJECTIVES

After reading this chapter, you will be able to answer the following questions:

1. How does building new systems produce organizational change?
2. What are the core activities in the systems development process?
3. What are the principal methodologies for modeling and designing systems?
4. What are alternative methods for building information systems?
5. What are new approaches for system building in the digital firm era?

CHAPTER CASES

New Systems Help Work Flow More
  Smoothly at Moen
Centralization of Operations
  at Tata Power

The Challenge of Mobile Application
  Development
SourceGas Goes for Better Workforce
  Scheduling Systems

NEW SYSTEMS HELP WORK FLOW MORE SMOOTHLY AT MOEN

Does your kitchen sink have a single-handle faucet or two faucets? If it's one with a single handle, it was invented in 1939 by Al Moen, founder of Moen, Incorporated, the number one faucet brand in North America. Based in North Olmsted, Ohio, Moen manufactures and sells a wide range of kitchen and bath products, including sinks, showerheads, and numerous accessories. New products are constantly being launched, and each requires numerous capital expense requests throughout the product development process.

Moen has three manufacturing facilities in the U.S. and one in China, as well as two distribution facilities in the U.S., one in China, and one in Canada and Mexico. The company had implemented a single instance of the SAP enterprise resource planning (ERP) system for nearly every line of its business worldwide, including supply chain, sales, service, and manufacturing. As a result, many of Moen's automated business processes were streamlined and efficient. Until recently, the process for initiating a capital expense request was one of the exceptions.

Moen's process to initiate a capital expense request (CER) was heavily manual. First, a user submitted a paper form that was routed man-

© Dusit/Shutterstock

ually through the corporate office from inbox to inbox to obtain the proper supporting documentation and approvals. The exact route differed, depending on factors such as type and amount of funds requested, department of origin, and level of approval needed. This process was very inefficient and uncertain. Among Moen's 300 employees involved in the capital expense request process, only a few outside of the finance department understood where and how the request was being routed. Finance would know if required approvals were insufficient, but getting to that department involved a great deal of guesswork from people who weren't sure of exactly where a form needed to go. Manually-routed documents could be easily lost or misplaced, leaving the other people along the approval chain completely unaware of the request. Making matters worse, CERs originating in Moen's Chinese manufacturing facility had to be mailed to the corporate office, increasing chances of getting lost. The recipient of these overseas requests couldn't just walk down the hallway to ask the sender a question.

Moen needed a solution that automated business form development and routing and that could easily integrate with its global SAP ERP system and support yearly upgrades to the SAP software. There were other requirements: The system had to be easy to use, with business users capable of automating select processes with a minimum of IT support. The solution also had to easily integrate with Microsoft SharePoint, which was supporting other internal Moen processes. And management did not want to limit the solution to CERs; it wanted the selected tool to automate other processes as well.

With assistance from Clear Process Solutions as consultants, Moen selected Winshuttle workflow software in November 2013. Winshuttle enables users to build and adapt Excel and SharePoint-based interactive forms and workflows for SAP without costly custom development and without compromising on security or control. The software integrates easily with both SharePoint and SAP, and can be tailored to Moen's processes. It is able to provide complete visibility into exactly where a request is located within the routing process.

It took five months to implement Winshuttle. During that time, users were given training classes on how to build a workflow using the software. Gina Carlson, Moen's Director of Asia Pacific Customer Relationship and Financial Systems, also instituted a formal communication plan with additional training documents, Webinars, and IT town halls.

Before automation, the CER process took anywhere from four to ten business days, depending on the number of approvals required. After Winshuttle was implemented, even complex and high-profile CERs can be processed in one to two business days. Moen is able to see the status of a particular CER at any point in the processing cycle. Carlson and her colleagues are able to know at any time where a specific funding request is in the pipeline, who has seen it, and who needs to approve it.

Within the first month after the system went live, almost 70 Moen employees used the new automated CER process. With management anticipating savings from automating CER of two hours per person, the project is expected to pay for itself within three months. The days of tracking down paper-based forms at Moen are coming to an end.

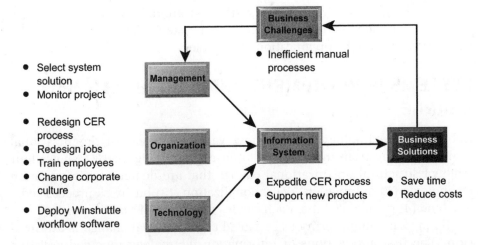

- Select system solution
- Monitor project

- Redesign CER process
- Redesign jobs
- Train employees
- Change corporate culture

- Deploy Winshuttle workflow software

Business Challenges

- Inefficient manual processes

Management

Organization

Information System

Technology

- Expedite CER process
- Support new products

Business Solutions

- Save time
- Reduce costs

Sources: Ken Murphy, "Capital Request Processes Now Flow as Smoothly as Water from a New Faucet," SAP Insider Profiles, July-September 2014; www.moen.com, accessed September 8, 2014; and www.winshuttle.com, accessed September 8, 2014.

The experience of Moen illustrates some of the steps required to design and build new information systems. Building a new system for processing capital expense requests entailed analyzing the organization's problems with existing systems, assessing information requirements, selecting appropriate technology, and redesigning business processes and jobs. Management had to oversee the systems-building effort and evaluate benefits and costs. The new information system represented a process of planned organizational change.

The chapter-opening case calls attention to important points raised by this case and this chapter. Moen's process for handling capital expense requests was hampered by outdated and inefficient manual processes, which raised costs, slowed down work, and limited the company's ability to develop new products.

Management decided to redesign and automate this process using new workflow software that enables users to create interactive forms and workflows for SAP without costly custom development. The solution encompassed not just the application of new technology, but changes to corporate culture, business processes, and job functions. Moen's pace of work and approvals for new capital expenditures have become much faster.

Here are some questions to think about: Why was Winshuttle software a good choice for Moen? How much did the new system change the way Moen ran its business?

13.1 HOW DOES BUILDING NEW SYSTEMS PRODUCE ORGANIZATIONAL CHANGE?

Building a new information system is one kind of planned organizational change. The introduction of a new information system involves much more than new hardware and software. It also includes changes in jobs, skills, management, and organization.

When we design a new information system, we are redesigning the organization. System builders must understand how a system will affect specific business processes and the organization as a whole.

SYSTEMS DEVELOPMENT AND ORGANIZATIONAL CHANGE

Information technology can promote various degrees of organizational change, ranging from incremental to far-reaching. Figure 13.1 shows four kinds of structural organizational change that are enabled by information technology: (1) automation, (2) rationalization, (3) business process redesign, and (4) paradigm shifts. Each carries different risks and rewards.

The most common form of IT-enabled organizational change is **automation**. The first applications of information technology involved assisting employees with performing their tasks more efficiently and effectively. Calculating paychecks and payroll registers, giving bank tellers instant access to customer deposit records, and developing a nationwide reservation network for airline ticket agents are all examples of early automation.

A deeper form of organizational change—one that follows quickly from early automation—is **rationalization of procedures**. Automation

FIGURE 13.1 ORGANIZATIONAL CHANGE CARRIES RISKS AND REWARDS

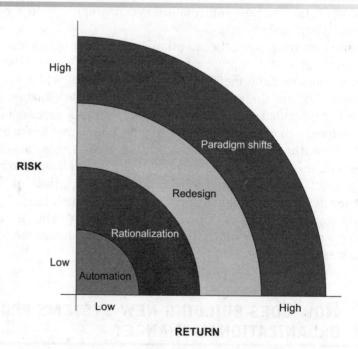

The most common forms of organizational change are automation and rationalization. These relatively slow-moving and slow-changing strategies present modest returns but little risk. Faster and more comprehensive change—such as redesign and paradigm shifts—carries high rewards but offers substantial chances of failure.

frequently reveals new bottlenecks in production and makes the existing arrangement of procedures and structures painfully cumbersome. Rationalization of procedures is the streamlining of standard operating procedures. For example, Moen's new system for capital expense requests is effective not only because it uses computer technology but also because the company simplified its business processes for this function. Fewer manual steps are required.

Rationalization of procedures is often found in programs for making a series of continuous quality improvements in products, services, and operations, such as total quality management (TQM) and six sigma. **Total quality management (TQM)** makes achieving quality an end in itself and the responsibility of all people and functions within an organization. TQM derives from concepts developed by American quality experts such as W. Edwards Deming and Joseph Juran, but it was popularized by the Japanese. **Six sigma** is a specific measure of quality, representing 3.4 defects per million opportunities. Most companies cannot achieve this level of quality, but use six sigma as a goal for driving ongoing quality improvement programs.

A more powerful type of organizational change is **business process redesign**, in which business processes are analyzed, simplified, and redesigned. Business process redesign reorganizes workflows, combining steps to cut waste and eliminate repetitive, paper-intensive tasks. (Sometimes the new design eliminates jobs as well.) It is much more ambitious than rationalization of procedures, requiring a new vision of how the process is to be organized.

A widely cited example of business process redesign is Ford Motor Company's invoiceless processing, which reduced headcount in Ford's North American Accounts Payable organization of 500 people by 75 percent. Accounts payable clerks used to spend most of their time resolving discrepancies between purchase orders, receiving documents, and invoices. Ford redesigned its accounts payable process so that the purchasing department enters a purchase order into an online database that can be checked by the receiving department when the ordered items arrive. If the received goods match the purchase order, the system automatically generates a check for accounts payable to send to the vendor. There is no need for vendors to send invoices.

Rationalizing procedures and redesigning business processes are limited to specific parts of a business. New information systems can ultimately affect the design of the entire organization by transforming how the organization carries out its business or even the nature of the business. For instance, the long-haul trucking and transportation firm Schneider National used new information systems to change its business model. Schneider created a new business managing logistics for other companies. This more radical form of business change is called a **paradigm shift**. A paradigm shift involves rethinking the nature of the business and the nature of the organization.

Paradigm shifts and business process redesign often fail because extensive organizational change is so difficult to orchestrate (see Chapter 14). Why, then, do so many corporations contemplate such radical change? Because the rewards are equally high (see Figure 13.1). In many instances, firms seeking paradigm shifts and pursuing reengineering strategies achieve stunning, order-of-magnitude increases in their returns on investment (or productivity). Some of these success stories, and some failure stories, are included throughout this book.

BUSINESS PROCESS REDESIGN

Like Moen, described in the chapter-opening case, many businesses today are trying to use information technology to improve their business processes. Some of these systems entail incremental process change, but others require more far-reaching redesign of business processes. To deal with these changes, organizations are turning to business process management. **Business process management (BPM)** provides a variety of tools and methodologies to analyze existing processes, design new processes, and optimize those processes. BPM is never concluded because process improvement requires continual change. Companies practicing business process management go through the following steps:

1. **Identify processes for change:** One of the most important strategic decisions that a firm can make is not deciding how to use computers to improve business processes, but understanding what business processes need improvement. When systems are used to strengthen the wrong business model or business processes, the business can become more efficient at doing what it should not do. As a result, the firm becomes vulnerable to competitors who may have discovered the right business model. Considerable time and cost may also be spent improving business processes that have little impact on overall firm performance and revenue. Managers need to determine what business processes are the most important and how improving these processes will help business performance.

2. **Analyze existing processes:** Existing business processes should be modeled and documented, noting inputs, outputs, resources, and the sequence of activities. The process design team identifies redundant steps, paper-intensive tasks, bottlenecks, and other inefficiencies.

Figure 13.2 illustrates the "as-is" process for purchasing a book from a physical bookstore. Consider what happens when a customer visits a physical bookstore and searches its shelves for a book. If he or she finds the book, that person takes it to the checkout counter and pays for it via credit card, cash, or check. If the customer is unable to locate the book, he or she must ask a bookstore clerk to search the shelves or check the bookstore's inventory records to see if it is in stock. If the clerk finds the book, the customer purchases it and leaves. If the book is not available locally, the clerk inquires about ordering it for the customer, from the bookstore's warehouse or from the book's distributor or publisher. Once the ordered book arrives at the bookstore, a bookstore employee telephones the customer with this information. The customer would have to go to the bookstore again to pick up the book and pay for it. If the bookstore is unable to order the book for the customer, the customer would have to try another bookstore. You can see

FIGURE 13.2 AS-IS BUSINESS PROCESS FOR PURCHASING A BOOK FROM A PHYSICAL BOOKSTORE

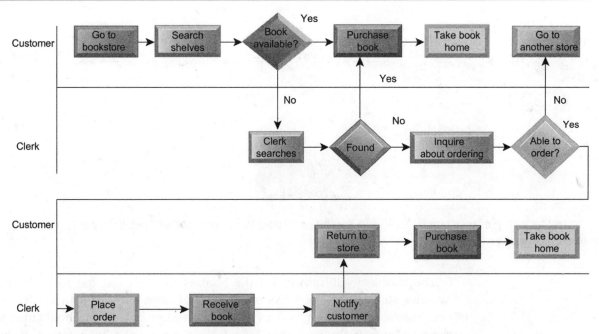

Purchasing a book from a physical bookstore requires many steps to be performed by both the seller and the customer.

that this process has many steps and might require the customer to make multiple trips to the bookstore.

3. **Design the new process:** Once the existing process is mapped and measured in terms of time and cost, the process design team will try to improve the process by designing a new one. A new streamlined "to-be" process will be documented and modeled for comparison with the old process.

Figure 13.3 illustrates how the book-purchasing process can be redesigned by taking advantage of the Internet. The customer accesses an online bookstore over the Internet from his or her computer. He or she searches the bookstore's online catalog for the book he or she wants. If the book is available, the customer orders the book online, supplying credit card and shipping address information, and the book is delivered to the customer's home. If the online bookstore does not carry the book, the customer selects another online bookstore and searches for the book again. This process has far fewer steps than that for purchasing the book in a physical bookstore, requires much less effort on the part of the customer, and requires less sales staff for customer service. The new process is therefore much more efficient and time-saving.

The new process design needs to be justified by showing how much it reduces time and cost or enhances customer service and value. Management first measures the time and cost of the existing process as a baseline. In our example, the time required for purchasing a book from a physical bookstore might range from 15 minutes (if the customer immediately finds what he

FIGURE 13.3 REDESIGNED PROCESS FOR PURCHASING A BOOK ONLINE

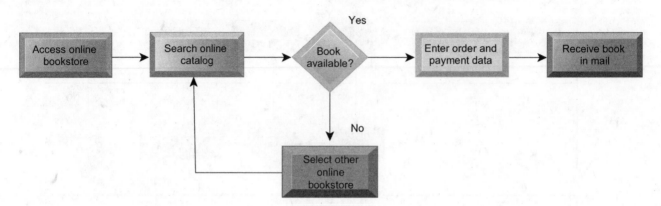

Using Internet technology makes it possible to redesign the process for purchasing a book so that it requires fewer steps and consumes fewer resources.

or she wants) to 30 minutes if the book is in stock but has to be located by sales staff. If the book has to be ordered from another source, the process might take one or two weeks and another trip to the bookstore for the customer. If the customer lives far away from the bookstore, the time to travel to the bookstore would have to be factored in. The bookstore will have to pay the costs for maintaining a physical store and keeping the book in stock, for sales staff on site, and for shipment costs if the book has to be obtained from another location.

The new process for purchasing a book online might only take several minutes, although the customer might have to wait several days or a week to receive the book in the mail and will have to pay a shipping charge. But the customer saves time and money by not having to travel to the bookstore or make additional visits to pick up the book. Booksellers' costs are lower because they do not have to pay for a physical store location or for local inventory.

4. **Implement the new process:** Once the new process has been thoroughly modeled and analyzed, it must be translated into a new set of procedures and work rules. New information systems or enhancements to existing systems may have to be implemented to support the redesigned process. The new process and supporting systems are rolled out into the business organization. As the business starts using this process, problems are uncovered and addressed. Employees working with the process may recommend improvements.

5. **Continuous measurement:** Once a process has been implemented and optimized, it needs to be continually measured. Why? Processes may deteriorate over time as employees fall back on old methods, or they may lose their effectiveness if the business experiences other changes.

Although many business process improvements are incremental and ongoing, there are occasions when more radical change must take place. Our example of a physical bookstore redesigning the book-purchasing process so that it can be carried out online is an example of this type of radical, far-reaching change. When properly implemented, business process redesign produces dramatic gains in productivity and efficiency, and may even change the way the business is run. In some instances, it drives a "paradigm shift" that transforms the nature of the business itself.

This actually happened in book retailing when Amazon challenged traditional physical bookstores with its online retail model. By radically rethinking the way a book can be purchased and sold, Amazon and other online bookstores have achieved remarkable efficiencies, cost reductions, and a whole new way of doing business.

BPM poses challenges. Executives report that the largest single barrier to successful business process change is organizational culture. Employees do not like unfamiliar routines and often try to resist change. This is especially true of projects where organizational changes are very ambitious and far-reaching. Managing change is neither simple nor intuitive, and companies committed to extensive process improvement need a good change management strategy (see Chapter 14).

Tools for Business Process Management

Over 100 software firms provide tools for various aspects of BPM, including IBM, Oracle, and TIBCO. These tools help businesses identify and document processes requiring improvement, create models of improved processes, capture and enforce business rules for performing processes, and integrate existing systems to support new or redesigned processes. BPM software tools also provide analytics for verifying that process performance has been improved and for measuring the impact of process changes on key business performance indicators.

Some BPM tools document and monitor business processes to help firms identify inefficiencies, using software to connect with each of the systems a company uses for a particular process to identify trouble spots. Another category of tools automate some parts of a business process and enforce business rules so that employees perform that process more consistently and efficiently.

For example, American National Insurance Company (ANCO), which offers life insurance, medical insurance, property casualty insurance, and investment services, used Pega BPM workflow software to streamline customer service processes across four business groups. The software built rules to guide customer service representatives through a single view of a customer's information that was maintained in multiple systems. By eliminating the need to juggle multiple applications simultaneously to handle customer and agent requests, the improved process increased customer service representative workload capacity by 192 percent.

A third category of tools helps businesses integrate their existing systems to support process improvements. They automatically manage processes across the business, extract data from various sources and databases, and generate transactions in multiple related systems (see the Interactive Session on Organizations).

INTERACTIVE SESSION: ORGANIZATIONS

CENTRALIZATION OF OPERATIONS AT TATA POWER

Prior to 2002, Delhi was plagued with frequent power cuts and blackouts. There were regular power thefts, and each year, the government had to provide a subsidy of approximately ₹1,500 to the Delhi Vidyut Board (DVB). Subsidies, however, are not a long-term solution to cut losses. The electric supply situation in Delhi needed to improve. For this to happen, the power sector needed to become self-sufficient. To reform the DVB, the board was unbundled in 2002 into three distribution companies, one generation unit, and one transmission company. The Tata Power Delhi Distribution Limited (TPDDL), a joint venture between Tata Power and the government of the National Capital Territory of Delhi, was formed as a result of this unbundling. Even though it inherited losses from the DVB, the TPDDL now has an annual turnover of ₹5,979 crore. It has a registered consumer base of 14 lakh and operates over an area of 510 square kilometers in north and north-west Delhi. This turnaround has largely been accredited to the several IT initiatives undertaken by TPDDL after its formation.

At the time of its formation, the TPDDL was burdened with losses of approximately ₹10 crore a day. It received around 10,000 complaints each day regarding the lack of power supply. It had a backlog of 100,000 consumer complaints and 20,000 new connections. It employed a large workforce of over 5,000 employees, who were not skilled enough to deal with the situation. Consumer records were erroneous and ill-maintained, and there was no system of management for functions such as human resources, finance, and governance. There was no proper consumer service interface either.

Within a span of 10 years, TPDDL overhauled the entire system and reduced the aggregate commercial and technical (AT&C) losses to less than 10%. Consumers now interact with the firm through a one-stop state-of-the-art integrated call center. The reliability of the power supply increased significantly because of these initiatives, and so did the profits. The company's operational performance is shown in Figure 13.4.

This change in the company's fortunes can be attributed to the adoption of innovative technology and the deployment of a skilled workforce. TPDDL knew that it needed to re-engineer its business processes in order to bring in sustainability. The first step was to address the AT&C losses and find solutions to overcome them. TPDDL soon discovered that these losses occurred due to thefts, unauthorized use of meters, tampering of meters by direct hooking, deficiencies in the metering process, slow or defective meters, or deficiencies in the billing process. Bills often did not get delivered correctly and went unpaid by customers. The company decided to replace the electromechanical meters with electronic meters to enable automatic meter reading (AMR). This was done for all high-revenue customers who contributed at least 60% of the total revenue. A software was developed in-house for analyzing the data downloaded through AMR. Besides, a high-voltage distribution system (HVDS) was installed in more than 250 areas. This system prevented electrical losses owing to the fact that it is deployed nearer to load centers and covers a reduced number of customers. This way, faults can be localized. Since this system transmits power at a high voltage, it also eliminates the need for long low-tension lines.

Accounting of energy at TPDDL has also been re-engineered to flow smoothly from the transmission level at the grids to the distribution level at the consumer premises. TPDDL automated the grids within its distribution area to form "smart grids". It implemented the supervisory control and data acquisition system (SCADA), which connected all the automated grids together. These grids are remotely monitored from a SCADA master-control center at Pitampura in north-west Delhi. This enabled centralized control and monitoring of the entire electrical network. TPDDL also used geographic information systems (GIS) to map all its assets including transformers, buildings, poles, cables, and so on. For better connectivity and communication between the power grids and the commercial offices, a strong optical fiber cable

FIGURE 13.4 SNAPSHOT OF TPDDL'S OPERATIONAL PERFORMANCE

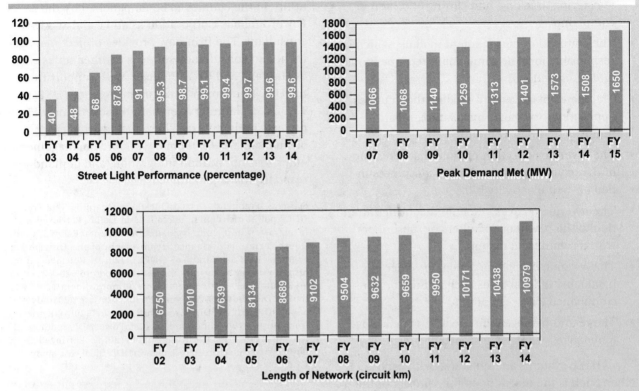

Source: Tata Power Delhi Distribution System, "TPDDL Excellence Journey," (2014); Retrieved from http://www.slideshare.net/TataPowerDDL/tpddl-excellence-journey

was deployed. A distribution management system (DMS) was also installed to centrally monitor all distribution networks. Prior to the use of this system, networks were managed manually. This meant that it was not possible to obtain any real-time network data. But with the presence of a DMS, network decisions can be taken by the control-center executives based on real-time network information. Centralization of operations and mapping through GIS has enabled quicker identification of fault locations and timely redressal of issues.

An outage management system (OMS) has also been deployed. An OMS is an automation solution which aids in the prompt restoration of outages affecting the customers. The system provides geo-referenced network details to the field crew that is responsible for restoring power in the impacted area. The historical data collected by this system also helps the management predict power outages. The CRM is updated on any planned outage and consumers are intimated accordingly.

Further, TPDDL launched an SMS-based fault management system that uses the GSM technology to log the "no supply" complaints. This has led to a speedy redressal of issues. The system also has provision for collecting customer feedback on the service provided. Apart from this system, Sampark Kendras with a seating capacity of 65 were also set up. Now, in each of the 12 districts where TPDDL distributes power, there is an online customer-care center with an individual customer-care executive for each district. Besides, TPDDL now uploads the billing details of all subscribers on its official Web site, where consumers can view, print, and make online payments. TPDDL has also set up ATM-like kiosks in Delhi, where both cash and cheque payment towards electricity bills are accepted. These machines operate round the year, from 8 a.m. to 8 p.m.

An in-house CRM application, called Sambandh, serves a lot of different functions through its various modules. These are:

- The customer-care module, which is used for registering, tracking, and closing of customer complaints.

- The connection management module, which is responsible for new connection, reconnections, or disconnections.

- The meter management module that handles applications for meter installation, repair, removal, and replacement.

- The revenue collection module that takes care of the payments received from consumers in lieu of their electricity bills.

- The revenue recovery module that brings attention to the payment defaulters or subscribers with disconnected meters.

- The revenue disciplinary module, which is invaluable in legal cases such as theft or non-compliance with regulations.

- The record management module, which is used to manage records of customer requests.

All these systems are integrated with each other. Such is the magnitude of the impact of the reforms brought in by TPDDL that it is the only utility in the country to be empanelled by the Power Finance Corporation as an IT and SCADA consultant. The firm now provides project management and consultancy services to other states such as Haryana and Uttar Pradesh. With support from the U.S. Trade and Development Agency (USTDA), TPDDL is planning to embark on several new IT projects in the future. These include the use of business analytics, mobile workforce management, enterprise application integration, and demand response management.

Sources: "Frequently Asked Questions regarding Tata Power-DDL's power distribution operations in Delhi". Retrieved from http://www.ndpl.com/UploadedDocuments/FAQ%27s.pdf; Ghosh, Arup, "Performance Improvement of the Distribution Segment (A Case Study of NDPL)" (2010). Retrieved from http://www.iitk.ac.in/ime/anoops/for10/pdf/16%20-%20Y%20S%20Butola%20-%20Performance%20Improvement%20of%20the%20Distribution%20Segment%20A%20Case%20Study%20of%20NDPL.pdf; "TPDDL Excellence Journey" (2014). Retrieved from http://www.slideshare.net/TataPowerDDL/tpddl-excellence-journey; "TPDDL Case Study" (2014). Retrieved from http://www.slideshare.net/TataPowerDDL/tpddl-case-study.

CASE STUDY QUESTIONS

1. What was the need for the formation of TPDDL? Discuss the challenges faced by the company.

2. What was the role of business process re-engineering to overcome the AT&C losses that were handed down to TPDDL?

3. Discuss the role of IT in the centralization of operations at TPDDL and list advantages of doing so.

4. How did TPDDL use information technology to deliver better services to customers?

13.2 WHAT ARE THE CORE ACTIVITIES IN THE SYSTEMS DEVELOPMENT PROCESS?

New information systems are an outgrowth of a process of organizational problem solving. A new information system is built as a solution to some type of problem or set of problems the organization perceives it is facing. The problem may be one in which managers and employees realize that the organization is not performing as well as expected, or that the organization should take advantage of new opportunities to perform more successfully.

The activities that go into producing an information system solution to an organizational problem or opportunity are called **systems development**.

FIGURE 13.5 THE SYSTEMS DEVELOPMENT PROCESS

Building a system can be broken down into six core activities.

Systems development is a structured kind of problem solved with distinct activities. These activities consist of systems analysis, systems design, programming, testing, conversion, and production and maintenance.

Figure 13.5 illustrates the systems development process. The systems development activities depicted usually take place in sequential order. But some of the activities may need to be repeated or some may take place simultaneously, depending on the approach to system building that is being employed (see Section 13.4).

SYSTEMS ANALYSIS

Systems analysis is the analysis of a problem that a firm tries to solve with an information system. It consists of defining the problem, identifying its causes, specifying the solution, and identifying the information requirements that must be met by a system solution.

The systems analyst creates a road map of the existing organization and systems, identifying the primary owners and users of data along with existing hardware and software. The systems analyst then details the problems of existing systems. By examining documents, work papers, and procedures, observing system operations, and interviewing key users of the systems, the analyst can identify the problem areas and objectives a solution would achieve. Often, the solution requires building a new information system or improving an existing one.

The systems analysis also includes a **feasibility study** to determine whether that solution is feasible, or achievable, from a financial, technical, and organizational standpoint. The feasibility study determines whether the proposed system is expected to be a good investment, whether the technology needed for the system is available and can be handled by the firm's information systems specialists, and whether the organization can handle the changes introduced by the system.

Normally, the systems analysis process identifies several alternative solutions that the organization can pursue and assess the feasibility of each. A written systems proposal report describes the costs and benefits, and the advantages and disadvantages, of each alternative. It is up to management to determine which mix of costs, benefits, technical features, and organizational impacts represents the most desirable alternative.

Establishing Information Requirements

Perhaps the most challenging task of the systems analyst is to define the specific information requirements that must be met by the chosen system solution. At the most basic level, the **information requirements** of a new system involve identifying who needs what information, where, when, and how. Requirements analysis carefully defines the objectives of the new or modified system and develops a detailed description of the functions that the new system must perform. Faulty requirements analysis is a leading cause of systems failure and high systems development costs (see Chapter 14). A system designed around the wrong set of requirements will either have to be discarded because of poor performance or will need to undergo major modifications. Section 13.3 describes alternative approaches to eliciting requirements that help minimize this problem.

Some problems do not require an information system solution but instead need an adjustment in management, additional training, or refinement of existing organizational procedures. If the problem is information related, systems analysis still may be required to diagnose the problem and arrive at the proper solution.

SYSTEMS DESIGN

Systems analysis describes what a system should do to meet information requirements, and **systems design** shows how the system will fulfill this objective. The design of an information system is the overall plan or model for that system. Like the blueprint of a building or house, it consists of all the specifications that give the system its form and structure.

The systems designer details the system specifications that will deliver the functions identified during systems analysis. These specifications should address all of the managerial, organizational, and technological components of the system solution. Table 13.1 lists the types of specifications that would be produced during systems design.

Like houses or buildings, information systems may have many possible designs. Each design represents a unique blend of all technical and organizational components. What makes one design superior to others is the ease and efficiency with which it fulfills user requirements within a specific set of technical, organizational, financial, and time constraints.

The Role of End Users

User information requirements drive the entire system-building effort. Users must have sufficient control over the design process to ensure that the system reflects their business priorities and information needs,

TABLE 13.1 DESIGN SPECIFICATIONS

OUTPUT	PROCESSING	DOCUMENTATION
Medium	Computations	Operations documentation
Content	Program modules	Systems documentation
Timing	Required reports	User documentation
INPUT	Timing of outputs	CONVERSION
Origins	MANUAL PROCEDURES	Transfer files
Flow	What activities	Initiate new procedures
Data entry	Who performs them	Select testing method
USER INTERFACE	When	Cut over to new system
Simplicity	How	TRAINING
Efficiency	Where	Select training techniques
Logic	CONTROLS	Develop training modules
Feedback	Input controls (characters, limit,	Identify training facilities
Errors	reasonableness)	ORGANIZATIONAL CHANGES
DATABASE DESIGN	Processing controls (consistency, record counts)	Task redesign
Logical data model	Output controls (totals, samples of output)	Job design
Volume and speed requirements	Procedural controls (passwords, special forms)	Process design
File organization and design	SECURITY	Organization structure design
Record specifications	Access controls	Reporting relationships
	Catastrophe plans	
	Audit trails	

not the biases of the technical staff. Working on design increases users' understanding and acceptance of the system. As we describe in Chapter 14, insufficient user involvement in the design effort is a major cause of system failure. However, some systems require more user participation in design than others, and Section 13.3 shows how alternative systems development methods address the user participation issue.

COMPLETING THE SYSTEMS DEVELOPMENT PROCESS

The remaining steps in the systems development process translate the solution specifications established during systems analysis and design into a fully operational information system. These concluding steps consist of programming, testing, conversion, production, and maintenance.

Programming

During the **programming** stage, system specifications that were prepared during the design stage are translated into software program code. Today, many organizations no longer do their own programming for new systems. Instead, they purchase the software that meets the requirements for a new system from external sources such as software packages from a commercial software vendor, software services from an application service provider, or outsourcing firms that develop custom application software for their clients (see Section 13.3).

Testing

Exhaustive and thorough **testing** must be conducted to ascertain whether the system produces the right results. Testing answers the question, "Will the system produce the desired results under known conditions?" As Chapter 5 noted, some companies are starting to use cloud computing services for this work.

The amount of time needed to answer this question has been traditionally underrated in systems project planning (see Chapter 14). Testing is time-consuming: Test data must be carefully prepared, results reviewed, and corrections made in the system. In some instances, parts of the system may have to be redesigned. The risks resulting from glossing over this step are enormous.

Testing an information system can be broken down into three types of activities: unit testing, system testing, and acceptance testing. **Unit testing**, or program testing, consists of testing each program separately in the system. It is widely believed that the purpose of such testing is to guarantee that programs are error-free, but this goal is realistically impossible. Testing should be viewed instead as a means of locating errors in programs, focusing on finding all the ways to make a program fail. Once they are pinpointed, problems can be corrected.

System testing tests the functioning of the information system as a whole. It tries to determine whether discrete modules will function together as planned and whether discrepancies exist between the way the system actually works and the way it was conceived. Among the areas examined are performance time, capacity for file storage and handling peak loads, recovery and restart capabilities, and manual procedures.

Acceptance testing provides the final certification that the system is ready to be used in a production setting. Systems tests are evaluated by users and reviewed by management. When all parties are satisfied that the new system meets their standards, the system is formally accepted for installation.

The systems development team works with users to devise a systematic test plan. The **test plan** includes all of the preparations for the series of tests we have just described.

Figure 13.6 shows an example of a test plan. The general condition being tested is a record change. The documentation consists of a series of test plan screens maintained on a database (perhaps a PC database) that is ideally suited to this kind of application.

Conversion is the process of changing from the old system to the new system. Four main conversion strategies can be employed: the parallel strategy, the direct cutover strategy, the pilot study strategy, and the phased approach strategy.

In a **parallel strategy,** both the old system and its potential replacement are run together for a time until everyone is assured that the new one functions correctly. This is the safest conversion approach because, in the event of errors or processing disruptions, the old system can still be used as a backup. However, this approach is very expensive, and additional staff or resources may be required to run the extra system.

FIGURE 13.6 A SAMPLE TEST PLAN TO TEST A RECORD CHANGE

Procedure	Address and Maintenance "Record Change Series"		Test Series 2		
Prepared By:		Date:	Version:		
Test Ref.	Condition Tested	Special Requirements	Expected Results	Output On	Next Screen
2.0	Change records				
2.1	Change existing record	Key field	Not allowed		
2.2	Change nonexistent record	Other fields	"Invalid key" message		
2.3	Change deleted record	Deleted record must be available	"Deleted" message		
2.4	Make second record	Change 2.1 above	OK if valid	Transaction file	V45
2.5	Insert record		OK if valid	Transaction file	V45
2.6	Abort during change	Abort 2.5	No change	Transaction file	V45

When developing a test plan, it is imperative to include the various conditions to be tested, the requirements for each condition tested, and the expected results. Test plans require input from both end users and information systems specialists.

The **direct cutover strategy** replaces the old system entirely with the new system on an appointed day. It is a very risky approach that can potentially be more costly than running two systems in parallel if serious problems with the new system are found. There is no other system to fall back on. Dislocations, disruptions, and the cost of corrections may be enormous.

The **pilot study strategy** introduces the new system to only a limited area of the organization, such as a single department or operating unit. When this pilot version is complete and working smoothly, it is installed throughout the rest of the organization, either simultaneously or in stages.

The **phased approach strategy** introduces the new system in stages, either by functions or by organizational units. If, for example, the system is introduced by function, a new payroll system might begin with hourly workers who are paid weekly, followed six months later by adding salaried employees (who are paid monthly) to the system. If the system is introduced by organizational unit, corporate headquarters might be converted first, followed by outlying operating units four months later.

Moving from an old system to a new one requires that end users be trained to use the new system. Detailed **documentation** showing how the system works from both a technical and end-user standpoint is finalized during conversion time for use in training and everyday operations. Lack of proper training and documentation contributes to system failure, so this portion of the systems development process is very important.

Production and Maintenance

After the new system is installed and conversion is complete, the system is said to be in **production**. During this stage, the system will be reviewed by both users and technical specialists to determine how well it has met its

TABLE 13.2 SYSTEMS DEVELOPMENT

CORE ACTIVITY	DESCRIPTION
Systems analysis	Identify problem(s) Specify solutions Establish information requirements
Systems design	Create design specifications
Programming	Translate design specifications into program code
Testing	Perform unit testing Perform systems testing Perform acceptance testing
Conversion	Plan conversion Prepare documentation Train users and technical staff
Production and maintenance	Operate the system Evaluate the system Modify the system

original objectives and to decide whether any revisions or modifications are in order. In some instances, a formal **post-implementation audit** document is prepared. After the system has been fine-tuned, it must be maintained while it is in production to correct errors, meet requirements, or improve processing efficiency. Changes in hardware, software, documentation, or procedures to a production system to correct errors, meet new requirements, or improve processing efficiency are termed **maintenance**.

Approximately 20 percent of the time devoted to maintenance is used for debugging or correcting emergency production problems. Another 20 percent is concerned with changes in data, files, reports, hardware, or system software. But 60 percent of all maintenance work consists of making user enhancements, improving documentation, and recoding system components for greater processing efficiency. The amount of work in the third category of maintenance problems could be reduced significantly through better systems analysis and design practices. Table 13.2 summarizes the systems development activities.

 WHAT ARE THE PRINCIPAL METHODOLOGIES FOR MODELING AND DESIGNING SYSTEMS?

There are alternative methodologies for modeling and designing systems. Structured methodologies and object-oriented development are the most prominent.

STRUCTURED METHODOLOGIES

Structured methodologies have been used to document, analyze, and design information systems since the 1970s. **Structured** refers to the fact that the

Chapter 13 Building Information Systems **551**

techniques are step by step, with each step building on the previous one. Structured methodologies are top-down, progressing from the highest, most abstract level to the lowest level of detail—from the general to the specific.

Structured development methods are process-oriented, focusing primarily on modeling the processes, or actions that capture, store, manipulate, and distribute data as the data flow through a system. These methods separate data from processes. A separate programming procedure must be written every time someone wants to take an action on a particular piece of data. The procedures act on data that the program passes to them.

The primary tool for representing a system's component processes and the flow of data between them is the **data flow diagram (DFD)**. The data flow diagram offers a logical graphic model of information flow, partitioning a system into modules that show manageable levels of detail. It rigorously specifies the processes or transformations that occur within each module and the interfaces that exist between them.

Figure 13.7 shows a simple data flow diagram for a mail-in university course registration system. The rounded boxes represent processes, which portray the transformation of data. The square box represents an external entity, which is an originator or receiver of information located outside the boundaries of the system being modeled. The open rectangles represent data stores, which are either manual or automated inventories of data. The arrows represent data flows, which show the movement between processes, external entities, and data stores. They contain packets of data with the name or content of each data flow listed beside the arrow.

FIGURE 13.7 DATA FLOW DIAGRAM FOR MAIL-IN UNIVERSITY REGISTRATION SYSTEM

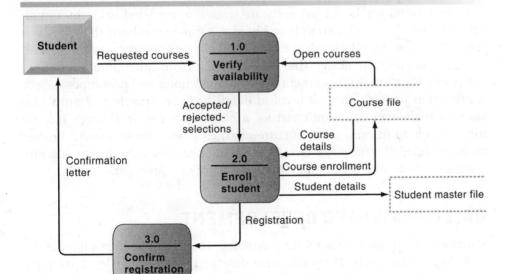

The system has three processes: Verify availability (1.0), Enroll student (2.0), and Confirm registration (3.0). The name and content of each of the data flows appear adjacent to each arrow. There is one external entity in this system: the student. There are two data stores: the student master file and the course file.

This data flow diagram shows that students submit registration forms with their name, identification number, and the numbers of the courses they wish to take. In process 1.0, the system verifies that each course selected is still open by referencing the university's course file. The file distinguishes courses that are open from those that have been canceled or filled. Process 1.0 then determines which of the student's selections can be accepted or rejected. Process 2.0 enrolls the student in the courses for which he or she has been accepted. It updates the university's course file with the student's name and identification number and recalculates the class size. If maximum enrollment has been reached, the course number is flagged as closed. Process 2.0 also updates the university's student master file with information about new students or changes in address. Process 3.0 then sends each student applicant a confirmation of registration letter listing the courses for which he or she is registered and noting the course selections that could not be fulfilled.

The diagrams can be used to depict higher-level processes as well as lower-level details. Through leveled data flow diagrams, a complex process can be broken down into successive levels of detail. An entire system can be divided into subsystems with a high-level data flow diagram. Each subsystem, in turn, can be divided into additional subsystems with second-level data flow diagrams, and the lower-level subsystems can be broken down again until the lowest level of detail has been reached.

Another tool for structured analysis is a data dictionary, which contains information about individual pieces of data and data groupings within a system (see Chapter 6). The data dictionary defines the contents of data flows and data stores so that systems builders understand exactly what pieces of data they contain. **Process specifications** describe the transformation occurring within the lowest level of the data flow diagrams. They express the logic for each process.

In structured methodology, software design is modeled using hierarchical structure charts. The **structure chart** is a top-down chart, showing each level of design, its relationship to other levels, and its place in the overall design structure. The design first considers the main function of a program or system, then breaks this function into subfunctions, and decomposes each subfunction until the lowest level of detail has been reached. Figure 13.8 shows a high-level structure chart for a payroll system. If a design has too many levels to fit onto one structure chart, it can be broken down further on more detailed structure charts. A structure chart may document one program, one system (a set of programs), or part of one program.

OBJECT-ORIENTED DEVELOPMENT

Structured methods are useful for modeling processes, but do not handle the modeling of data well. They also treat data and processes as logically separate entities, whereas in the real world such separation seems unnatural. Different modeling conventions are used for analysis (the data flow diagram) and for design (the structure chart).

Object-oriented development addresses these issues. Object-oriented development uses the **object** as the basic unit of systems analysis and

FIGURE 13.8 HIGH-LEVEL STRUCTURE CHART FOR A PAYROLL SYSTEM

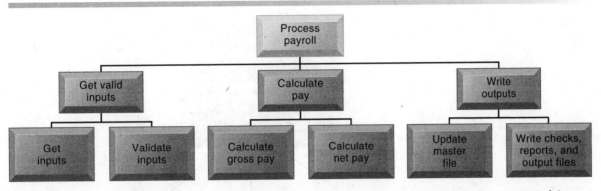

This structure chart shows the highest or most abstract level of design for a payroll system, providing an overview of the entire system.

design. An object combines data and the specific processes that operate on those data. Data encapsulated in an object can be accessed and modified only by the operations, or methods, associated with that object. Instead of passing data to procedures, programs send a message for an object to perform an operation that is already embedded in it. The system is modeled as a collection of objects and the relationships among them. Because processing logic resides within objects rather than in separate software programs, objects must collaborate with each other to make the system work.

Object-oriented modeling is based on the concepts of *class* and *inheritance*. Objects belonging to a certain class, or general categories of similar objects, have the features of that class. Classes of objects in turn can inherit all the structure and behaviors of a more general class and then add variables and behaviors unique to each object. New classes of objects are created by choosing an existing class and specifying how the new class differs from the existing class, instead of starting from scratch each time.

We can see how class and inheritance work in Figure 13.9, which illustrates the relationships among classes concerning employees and how they are paid. Employee is the common ancestor, or superclass, for the other three classes. Salaried, Hourly, and Temporary are subclasses of Employee. The class name is in the top compartment, the attributes for each class are in the middle portion of each box, and the list of operations is in the bottom portion of each box. The features that are shared by all employees (ID, name, address, date hired, position, and pay) are stored in the Employee superclass, whereas each subclass stores features that are specific to that particular type of employee. Specific to hourly employees, for example, are their hourly rates and overtime rates. A solid line from the subclass to the superclass is a generalization path showing that the subclasses Salaried, Hourly, and Temporary have common features that can be generalized into the superclass Employee.

Object-oriented development is more iterative and incremental than traditional structured development. During analysis, systems builders document the functional requirements of the system, specifying its most important properties and what the proposed system must do. Interactions between the system and its users are analyzed to identify objects, which include

FIGURE 13.9 CLASS AND INHERITANCE

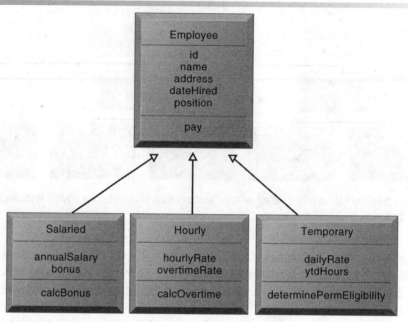

This figure illustrates how classes inherit the common features of their superclass.

both data and processes. The object-oriented design phase describes how the objects will behave and how they will interact with one another. Similar objects are grouped together to form a class, and classes are grouped into hierarchies in which a subclass inherits the attributes and methods from its superclass.

The information system is implemented by translating the design into program code, reusing classes that are already available in a library of reusable software objects, and adding new ones created during the object-oriented design phase. Implementation may also involve the creation of an object-oriented database. The resulting system must be thoroughly tested and evaluated.

Because objects are reusable, object-oriented development could potentially reduce the time and cost of writing software because organizations can reuse software objects that have already been created as building blocks for other applications. New systems can be created by using some existing objects, changing others, and adding a few new objects. Object-oriented frameworks have been developed to provide reusable, semicomplete applications that the organization can further customize into finished applications.

COMPUTER-AIDED SOFTWARE ENGINEERING

Computer-aided software engineering (CASE)—sometimes called *computer-aided systems engineering*—provides software tools to automate the methodologies we have just described to reduce the amount of repetitive work the developer needs to do. CASE tools also facilitate the creation of clear documentation and the coordination of team development efforts.

Team members can share their work easily by accessing each other's files to review or modify what has been done. Modest productivity benefits can also be achieved if the tools are used properly.

CASE tools provide automated graphics facilities for producing charts and diagrams, screen and report generators, data dictionaries, extensive reporting facilities, analysis and checking tools, code generators, and documentation generators. In general, CASE tools try to increase productivity and quality by:

- Enforcing a standard development methodology and design discipline
- Improving communication between users and technical specialists
- Organizing and correlating design components and providing rapid access to them using a design repository
- Automating tedious and error-prone portions of analysis and design
- Automating code generation and testing and control rollout

CASE tools contain features for validating design diagrams and specifications. CASE tools thus support iterative design by automating revisions and changes and providing prototyping facilities. A CASE information repository stores all the information defined by the analysts during the project. The repository includes data flow diagrams, structure charts, entity-relationship diagrams, data definitions, process specifications, screen and report formats, notes and comments, and test results.

To be used effectively, CASE tools require organizational discipline. Every member of a development project must adhere to a common set of naming conventions and standards as well as to a development methodology. The best CASE tools enforce common methods and standards, which may discourage their use in situations where organizational discipline is lacking.

13.4 WHAT ARE ALTERNATIVE METHODS FOR BUILDING INFORMATION SYSTEMS?

Systems differ in terms of their size and technological complexity and in terms of the organizational problems they are meant to solve. A number of systems-building approaches have been developed to deal with these differences. This section describes these alternative methods: the traditional systems life cycle, prototyping, application software packages, end-user development, and outsourcing.

TRADITIONAL SYSTEMS LIFE CYCLE

The **systems life cycle** is the oldest method for building information systems. The life cycle methodology is a phased approach to building a system, dividing systems development into formal stages, as illustrated in Figure 13.10. Systems development specialists have different opinions on how to partition the systems-building stages, but they roughly correspond to the stages of systems development we have just described.

FIGURE 13.10 THE TRADITIONAL SYSTEMS DEVELOPMENT LIFE CYCLE

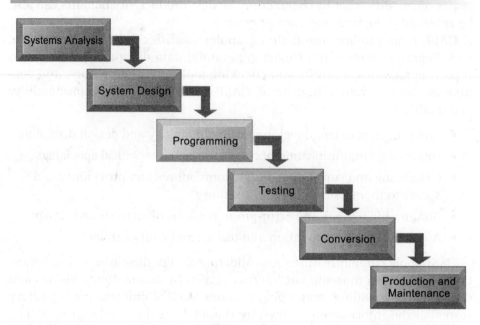

The systems development life cycle partitions systems development into formal stages, with each stage requiring completion before the next stage can begin.

The systems life cycle methodology maintains a formal division of labor between end users and information systems specialists. Technical specialists, such as systems analysts and programmers, are responsible for much of the systems analysis, design, and implementation work; end users are limited to providing information requirements and reviewing the technical staff's work. The life cycle also emphasizes formal specifications and paperwork, so many documents are generated during the course of a systems project.

The systems life cycle is still used for building large complex systems that require a rigorous and formal requirements analysis, predefined specifications, and tight controls over the system-building process. However, the systems life cycle approach can be costly, time-consuming, and inflexible. Although systems builders can go back and forth among stages in the life cycle, the systems life cycle is predominantly a "waterfall" approach in which tasks in one stage are completed before work for the next stage begins. Activities can be repeated, but volumes of new documents must be generated and steps retraced if requirements and specifications need to be revised. This encourages freezing of specifications relatively early in the development process. The life cycle approach is also not suitable for many small desktop systems, which tend to be less structured and more individualized.

PROTOTYPING

Prototyping consists of building an experimental system rapidly and inexpensively for end users to evaluate. By interacting with the prototype, users can get a better idea of their information requirements. The proto-type endorsed by the users can be used as a template to create the final system.

The **prototype** is a working version of an information system or part of the system, but it is meant to be only a preliminary model. Once opera-tional, the prototype will be further refined until it conforms precisely to users' requirements. Once the design has been finalized, the prototype can be converted to a polished production system.

The process of building a preliminary design, trying it out, refining it, and trying again has been called an **iterative** process of systems develop-ment because the steps required to build a system can be repeated over and over again. Prototyping is more explicitly iterative than the conventional life cycle, and it actively promotes system design changes. It has been said that prototyping replaces unplanned rework with planned iteration, with each version more accurately reflecting users' requirements.

Steps in Prototyping

Figure 13.11 shows a four-step model of the prototyping process, which con-sists of the following:

FIGURE 13.11 THE PROTOTYPING PROCESS

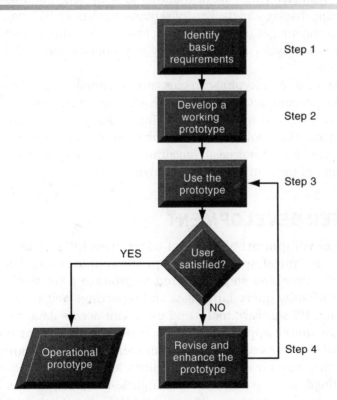

The process of developing a prototype can be broken down into four steps. Because a prototype can be developed quickly and inexpensively, systems builders can go through several iterations, repeating steps 3 and 4, to refine and enhance the prototype before arriving at the final operational one.

Step 1: *Identify the user's basic requirements.* The systems designer (usually an information systems specialist) works with the user only long enough to capture the user's basic information needs.

Step 2: *Develop an initial prototype.* The systems designer creates a working prototype quickly, using tools for rapidly generating software.

Step 3: *Use the prototype.* The user is encouraged to work with the system to determine how well the prototype meets his or her needs and to make suggestions for improving the prototype.

Step 4: *Revise and enhance the prototype.* The system builder notes all changes the user requests and refines the prototype accordingly. After the prototype has been revised, the cycle returns to Step 3. Steps 3 and 4 are repeated until the user is satisfied.

When no more iterations are required, the approved prototype then becomes an operational prototype that furnishes the final specifications for the application. Sometimes the prototype is adopted as the production version of the system.

Advantages and Disadvantages of Prototyping

Prototyping is most useful when there is some uncertainty about requirements or design solutions and often used for designing an information system's **end-user interface** (the part of the system with which end users interact, such as online display and data entry screens, reports, or Web pages). Because prototyping encourages intense end-user involvement throughout the systems development life cycle, it is more likely to produce systems that fulfill user requirements.

However, rapid prototyping can gloss over essential steps in systems development. If the completed prototype works reasonably well, management may not see the need for reprogramming, redesign, or full documentation and testing to build a polished production system. Some of these hastily constructed systems may not easily accommodate large quantities of data or a large number of users in a production environment.

END-USER DEVELOPMENT

End-user development allows end users, with little or no formal assistance from technical specialists, to create simple information systems, reducing the time and steps required to produce a finished application. Using user-friendly query languages and reporting, Web site development, graphics, and PC software tools, end users can access data, create reports, and develop simple applications on their own, with little or no help from professional systems analysts or programmers. A **query language** is a software tool that provides immediate online answers to questions that are not predefined, such as "Who are the highest-performing sales representatives?" Query languages are often tied to data management software (see Chapter 6).

For example, Neways Enterprise, a multinational firm which designs, manufactures, and sells personal care, household and nutritional products that are free of harmful ingredients, used Information Builders WEBFOCUS to create an online self-service reporting system for its thousands of independent distributors and its business analysts. The business analysts use the self-service reports to monitor finances, anticipate trends, and predict results based on current insights. Neways' globally dispersed independent distributors use the system to access real-time production data to support sales efforts and track qualification for monthly bonuses. The system's reporting tools let them decide how deeply they want to drill into the data (Information Builders, 2014).

On the whole, end-user-developed systems can be completed more rapidly than those developed through the conventional systems life cycle. Allowing users to specify their own business needs improves requirements gathering and often leads to a higher level of user involvement and satisfaction with the system. However, end-user software tools still cannot replace conventional tools for some business applications because they cannot easily handle the processing of large numbers of transactions or applications with extensive procedural logic and updating requirements.

End-user computing also poses organizational risks because it occurs outside of traditional mechanisms for information systems management and control. When systems are created rapidly, without a formal development methodology, testing and documentation may be inadequate. Control over data can be lost in systems outside the traditional information systems department. To help organizations maximize the benefits of end-user applications development, management should control the development of end-user applications by requiring cost justification of end-user information system projects and by establishing hardware, software, and quality standards for user-developed applications.

APPLICATION SOFTWARE PACKAGES AND OUTSOURCING

Chapter 5 points out that much of today's software is not developed in-house but is purchased from external sources. Firms can rent the software from a software service provider, they can purchase a software package from a commercial vendor, or they can have a custom application developed by an outside outsourcing firm.

Application Software Packages

During the past several decades, many systems have been built on an application software package foundation. Many applications are common to all business organizations—for example, payroll, accounts receivable, general ledger, or inventory control. For such universal functions with standard processes that do not change a great deal over time, a generalized system will fulfill the requirements of many organizations.

If a software package can fulfill most of an organization's requirements, the company does not have to write its own software. The company can save time and money by using the prewritten, predesigned, pretested software programs from the package. Package vendors supply much of the ongoing maintenance and support for the system, including enhancements to keep the system in line with ongoing technical and business developments. When a package solution is pursued, end users will be responsible for supplying the business information requirements for the system and information systems specialists will provide technical requirements.

If an organization has unique requirements that the package does not address, many packages include capabilities for customization. **Customization** features allow a software package to be modified to meet an organization's unique requirements without destroying the integrity of the packaged software. If a great deal of customization is required, additional programming and customization work may become so expensive and time-consuming that they negate many of the advantages of software packages.

When a system is developed using an application software package, systems analysis will include a package evaluation effort, in which both end users and information systems specialists will participate. The most important evaluation criteria are the functions provided by the package, flexibility, user-friendliness, hardware and software resources, database requirements, installation and maintenance efforts, documentation, vendor quality, and cost. The package evaluation process often is based on a **Request for Proposal (RFP)**, which is a detailed list of questions submitted to packaged-software vendors.

When a software package is selected, the organization no longer has total control over the systems design process. Instead of tailoring the systems design specifications directly to user requirements, the design effort will consist of trying to mold user requirements to conform to the features of the package. If the organization's requirements conflict with the way the package works and the package cannot be customized, the organization will have to adapt to the package and change its procedures.

Outsourcing

If a firm does not want to use its internal resources to build or operate information systems, it can outsource the work to an external organization that specializes in providing these services. Cloud computing and software as a service (SaaS) providers, which we described in Chapter 5, are one form of outsourcing. Subscribing companies use the software and computer hardware provided by the service as the technical platform for their systems. In another form of outsourcing, a company could hire an external vendor to design and create the software for its system, but that company would operate the system on its own computers. The outsourcing vendor might be domestic or in another country.

Domestic outsourcing is driven primarily by the fact that outsourcing firms possess skills, resources, and assets that their clients do not have. Installing a new supply chain management system in a very large company might require hiring an additional 30 to 50 people with specific expertise in supply chain management software, licensed from a vendor. Rather than hire permanent new employees, most of whom would need extensive training in the software package, and then release them after the new system is built, it makes more sense, and is often less expensive, to outsource this work for a 12-month period.

In the case of **offshore outsourcing**, the decision tends to be much more cost-driven. A skilled programmer in India or Russia earns about USD $10,000–$20,000 per year, compared to about $60,000 per year for a comparable programmer in the United States. The Internet and low-cost communications technology have drastically reduced the expense and difficulty of coordinating the work of global teams in faraway locations. In addition to cost savings, many offshore outsourcing firms offer world-class technology assets and skills. Wage inflation outside the United States has recently eroded some of these advantages, and some jobs have moved back to the United States.

Nevertheless, there is a very strong chance that at some point in your career, you'll be working with offshore outsourcers or global teams. Your firm is most likely to benefit from outsourcing if it takes the time to evaluate all the risks and to make sure outsourcing is appropriate for its particular needs. Any company that outsources its applications must thoroughly understand the project, including its requirements, method of implementation, anticipated benefits, cost components, and metrics for measuring performance.

Many firms underestimate costs for identifying and evaluating vendors of information technology services, for transitioning to a new vendor, for improving internal software development methods to match those of outsourcing vendors, and for monitoring vendors to make sure they are fulfilling their contractual obligations. Companies will need to allocate resources for documenting requirements, sending out RFPs, handling travel expenses, negotiating contracts, and project management. Experts claim it takes from three months to a full year to fully transfer work to an offshore partner and make sure the vendor thoroughly understands your business.

Outsourcing offshore incurs additional costs for coping with cultural differences that drain productivity and dealing with human resources issues, such as terminating or relocating domestic employees. All of these hidden costs undercut some of the anticipated benefits from outsourcing. Firms should be especially cautious when using an outsourcer to develop or to operate applications that give it some type of competitive advantage.

General Motors Corporation (GM) had outsourced 90 percent of its IT services, including its data centers and application development. The company recently decided to bring 90 percent of its IT infrastructure in-house, with only 10 percent managed by outsourcers. Lowering costs is important, but GM's primary reason for cutting back outsourcing is to take back control of its information systems, which it believes were preventing the company from responding quickly to competitive opportunities. Bringing information systems in-house will make it easier for GM to cut its sprawling list of IT applications by at least 40 percent, move to a more standardized platform, complete innovative IT projects more quickly, and get a better grip on customer and production data, which had been housed in too many different systems. The automaker is consolidating 23 data centers worldwide

FIGURE 13.12 TOTAL COST OF OFFSHORE OUTSOURCING

TOTAL COST OF OFFSHORE OUTSOURCING				
Cost of outsourcing contract			$10,000,000	
Hidden Costs	Best Case	Additional Cost ($)	Worst Case	Additional Cost ($)
1. Vendor selection	0%	20,000	2%	200,000
2. Transition costs	2%	200,000	3%	300,000
3. Layoffs & retention	3%	300,000	5%	500,000
4. Lost productivity/cultural issues	3%	300,000	27%	2,700,000
5. Improving development processes	1%	100,000	10%	1,000,000
6. Managing the contract	6%	600,000	10%	1,000,000
Total additional costs		1,520,000		5,700,000
	Outstanding Contract ($)	Additional Cost ($)	Total Cost ($)	Additional Cost
Total cost of outsourcing (TCO) best case	10,000,000	1,520,000	11,520,000	15.2%
Total cost of outsourcing (TCO) worst case	10,000,000	5,700,000	15,700,000	57.0%

If a firm spends $10 million on offshore outsourcing contracts, that company will actually spend 15.2 percent in extra costs even under the best-case scenario. In the worst-case scenario, where there is a dramatic drop in productivity along with exceptionally high transition and layoff costs, a firm can expect to pay up to 57 percent in extra costs on top of the $10 million outlay for an offshore contract.

into just two, both in Michigan, and running four software development centers (Murphy, 2012).

Figure 13.12 shows best- and worst-case scenarios for the total cost of an offshore outsourcing project. It shows how much hidden costs affect the total project cost. The best case reflects the lowest estimates for additional costs, and the worst case reflects the highest estimates for these costs. As you can see, hidden costs increase the total cost of an offshore outsourcing project by an extra 15 to 57 percent. Even with these extra costs, many firms will benefit from offshore outsourcing if they manage the work well. Under the worst-case scenario, a firm would still save about 15 percent.

13.5 WHAT ARE NEW APPROACHES FOR SYSTEM BUILDING IN THE DIGITAL FIRM ERA?

In the digital firm environment, organizations need to be able to add, change, and retire their technology capabilities very rapidly to respond to new opportunities, including the need to provide applications for mobile platforms. Companies are starting to use shorter, more informal development processes that provide fast solutions. In addition to using software packages and external service providers, businesses are relying more heavily on fast-cycle techniques such as rapid application development, joint application design, agile development, and reusable standardized software components that can be assembled into a complete set of services for e-commerce and e-business.

RAPID APPLICATION DEVELOPMENT (RAD)

Object-oriented software tools, reusable software, prototyping, and fourth-generation language tools are helping systems builders create working systems much more rapidly than they could using traditional systems-building methods and software tools. The term **rapid application development (RAD)** is used to describe this process of creating workable systems in a very short period of time. RAD can include the use of visual programming and other tools for building graphical user interfaces, iterative prototyping of key system elements, the automation of program code generation, and close teamwork among end users and information systems specialists. Simple systems often can be assembled from prebuilt components. The process does not have to be sequential, and key parts of development can occur simultaneously.

Sometimes a technique called **joint application design (JAD)** is used to accelerate the generation of information requirements and to develop the initial systems design. JAD brings end users and information systems specialists together in an interactive session to discuss the system's design. Properly prepared and facilitated, JAD sessions can significantly speed up the design phase and involve users at an intense level.

Agile development focuses on rapid delivery of working software by breaking a large project into a series of small subprojects that are completed in short periods of time using iteration and continuous feedback. Each mini-project is worked on by a team as if it were a complete project, including planning, requirements analysis, design, coding, testing, and documentation. Improvement or addition of new functionality takes place within the next iteration as developers clarify requirements. This helps to minimize the overall risk, and allows the project to adapt to changes more quickly. Agile methods emphasize face-to-face communication over written documents, encouraging people to collaborate and make decisions quickly and effectively.

COMPONENT-BASED DEVELOPMENT AND WEB SERVICES

We have already described some of the benefits of object-oriented development for building systems that can respond to rapidly changing business environments, including Web applications. To further expedite software creation, groups of objects have been assembled to provide software components for common functions such as a graphical user interface or online ordering capability that can be combined to create large-scale business applications. This approach to software development is called **component-based development**, and it enables a system to be built by assembling and integrating existing software components. Increasingly, these software components are coming from cloud services. Businesses are using component-based development to create their e-commerce applications by combining commercially available components for shopping carts, user authentication, search engines, and catalogs with pieces of software for their own unique business requirements.

Web Services and Service-Oriented Computing

Chapter 5 introduced *Web services* as loosely coupled, reusable software components delivered using Extensible Markup Language (XML) and other open protocols and standards that enable one application to communicate with another with no custom programming required to share data and services. In addition to supporting internal and external integration of systems, Web services can be used as tools for building new information system applications or enhancing existing systems. Because these software services use a universal set of standards, they promise to be less expensive and less difficult to weave together than proprietary components.

Web services can perform certain functions on their own, and they can also engage other Web services to complete more complex transactions, such as checking credit, procurement, or ordering products. By creating software components that can communicate and share data regardless of the operating system, programming language, or client device, Web services can provide significant cost savings in systems building while opening up new opportunities for collaboration with other companies.

MOBILE APPLICATION DEVELOPMENT: DESIGNING FOR A MULTI-SCREEN WORLD

Today, employees and customers expect, and even demand, to be able to use a mobile device of their choice to obtain information or perform a transaction anywhere and at any time. To meet these needs, companies will need to develop mobile Web sites, mobile apps, and native apps as well as traditional information systems. According to digital advertising agency Vertic, mobile app development projects will outnumber native PC projects by a 4-to-1 ratio by 2015 (Greengard, 2013).

Once an organization decides to develop mobile apps, it has to make some important choices, including the technology it will use to implement these apps (whether to write a native app or mobile Web app) and what to do about a mobile Web site. A **mobile Web site** is a version of a regular Web site that is scaled down in content and navigation for easy access and search on a small mobile screen. (Access Amazon's Web site from your computer and then from your smartphone to see the difference from a regular Web site.)

A **mobile Web app** is an Internet-enabled app with specific functionality for mobile devices. Users access mobile Web apps through their mobile device's Web browser. The Web app resides primarily on a server, is accessed via the Internet, and doesn't need to be installed on the device. The same application can be used by most devices that can surf the Web, regardless of their brand.

A **native app** is a standalone application designed to run on a specific platform and device. The native app is installed directly on a mobile device. Native apps can connect to the Internet to download and upload data, and they can also operate on these data even when not connected to the Internet. For example, an e-book reading app such as Kindle software can download a book from the Internet, disconnect from the Internet, and present the book for reading. Native mobile apps provide fast performance and a high degree of reliability. They are also able to take advantage of a mobile device's particular capabilities, such as its camera or touch features. However, native apps are expensive to develop because multiple versions of an app must be programmed for different mobile operating systems and hardware.

Developing applications for mobile platforms is quite different from development for PCs and their much larger screens. The reduced size of mobile devices makes using fingers and multi-touch gestures much easier than typing and using keyboards. Mobile apps need to be optimized for the specific tasks they are to perform; they should not try to carry out too many tasks; and they should be designed for usability. The user experience for mobile interaction is fundamentally different from using a desktop or laptop PC. Saving resources—bandwidth, screen space, memory, processing, data entry, and user gestures—is a top priority.

When a full Web site created for the desktop shrinks to the size of a smartphone screen, it is difficult for the user to navigate through the site. The user must continually zoom in and out and scroll to find relevant material. Therefore, companies need to design Web sites specifically for mobile interfaces and create multiple mobile sites to meet the needs of smartphones, tablets, and desktop browsers. This equates to at least three sites with separate content, maintenance, and costs. Currently, Web sites know what device you are using because your browser will send this information to the server when you log on. Based on this information, the server will deliver the appropriate screen.

One solution to the problem of having multiple Web sites is to use **responsive Web design**. Responsive Web design enables Web sites to automatically change layouts according to the visitor's screen resolution, whether on a desktop, laptop, tablet, or smartphone. Responsive design uses tools such as flexible grid-based layouts, flexible images, and media queries, to optimize the design for different viewing contexts. This eliminates the need for separate design and development work for each new device. HTML5, which we introduced in Chapter 5, is also used for mobile application development because it can support cross-platform mobile applications.

The Interactive Session on Technology describes how some companies have addressed the challenges of mobile development we have just identified.

INTERACTIVE SESSION: TECHNOLOGY

THE CHALLENGE OF MOBILE APPLICATION DEVELOPMENT

Just as everyone today has (or wants) a mobile phone, every business wants mobile apps. Companies of all stripes realize that the target audiences for their applications has shifted from users of personal computers to users of mobile devices. Businesses are frantically struggling to become more mobile, and they want them developed in a very short time frame. That's not so easy.

Developing successful mobile apps poses some unique challenges. The user experience on a mobile device is fundamentally different from that on a PC. There are special features on mobile devices such as location-based services that give firms the potential to interact with customers in meaningful new ways. Firms need to be able to take advantage of those features while delivering an experience that is appropriate to a small screen. There are multiple mobile platforms to work with, including iOS, Android, and Windows 8, and a firm may need a different version of an application to run on each of these. System-builders need to understand how, why, and where customers use mobile devices and how these mobile experiences change business interactions and behavior. You can't just port a Web site or desktop application to a smartphone or tablet. It's a different systems development process.

InterContinental Hotels Group (IHG), which includes InterContinental Hotels, Crowne Plaza Hotels & Resorts, and Holiday Inns clearly needs a mobile app to stay competitive. The Group must compete with other hotel chains and also online services with mobile apps such as Booking.com, Orbitz.com, and Hotels.com, which handle reservations for hundreds of thousands of hotels (see the Chapter 10 Interactive Session on Orbitz). Mobile devices are quickly becoming the preferred method of booking reservations online, and IHG doesn't want to miss the opportunity.

Guests can use IHG's mobile app, IHG Mobile, to book rooms at any of IHG's 4,800 hotels. In addition, the IHG Mobile app includes customer reviews, photos of the hotel and surrounding neighborhood, maps, directions to nearby locales, push notifications, access to special corporate rates, and the ability to manage points for the IHG Rewards program. The app is available for 8 different mobile platforms.

Maintaining this app requires constant teamwork between marketing and mobile application developers. Bill Keen, director of IHG mobile solutions, works with a team of eight product managers and 12 information technology specialists on IHG Mobile. The 12 mobile developers have expertise in mobile application design and building APIs that access IHG's transaction systems and public information services such as weather and maps. An API is an application programming interface that specifies how software components should interact. Both groups are housed in the same building and have face-to-face meetings every morning to test new features and discuss next steps.

The team works on app features and enhancements in two-week sprints. The product managers select the next mobile app feature to work on and the mobile application developers then inform them what can be done in the next two-week sprint. The product managers make the final decision about what to do in that time frame. Both groups use an Agile development process and operate as a single unit sharing responsibilities and accountability.

Supporting the team are an information architect and graphic designer. They analyze what hotel guests need from the app, based on customer feedback, and establish the interactive pattern design, photos, and graphics. The design is then handed to the developers to code into software programs and deploy.

Mobile apps should not be built for the sake of going mobile but for genuinely helping the company become more successful. The mobile app will need to be connected in a meaningful way to the systems that power the business. Alex and Ani learned this when it developed a mobile app for employees in its stores to use to help customers make selections and then complete the purchase transaction.

Alex and Ani, founded in 2004, designs, produces, and sells high-quality, eco-friendly jewelry in the U.S. using artisanal techniques, and is dedicated to helping its customers find inner peace and positive energy. Having customers in Alex and Ani stores wait on long checkout lines ran counter to the company's philosophy and brand image.

Working with Mobiquity, a developer of enterprise mobile solutions, Alex and Ani created a mobile point-of-sales and payment solution where Alex and Ani's Bangle Bartenders can swipe credit cards, scan bar codes, and print, allowing a customer to sign and receive a copy of the credit-card receipt at the time of purchase while they are in the store aisles. They do not have to wait in line for a cashier. The mobile app helps store sales staff to be more attentive to customers while reducing time to pay for purchases. This enhances the in-store customer experience, improves brand perception, and provides better customer service, thereby increasing sales revenues.

The starting point for developing a mobile app is to identify the mobile moments (occasions when someone would pull out a mobile device to get something done) where a mobile app would be especially helpful. Alex and Ani's chief technology officer Joe Lezon and head of retail operations Susan Soards mapped out the mobile moments where employees interact with customers. They then specified the context—the situation, preferences, and attitudes of customers and employees in these mobile moments. Lezon and Soards determined where physically in the store mobile moments occur, how long they last, the stage of the checkout process, what information is available, and customer expectations.

The second step is to design the mobile engagement. Business people, designers, and app developers get together to decide how to engage a customer during mobile moments, and which moments benefit both the customer and the company. A mobile app for moments that benefit both customers and the company is more likely to be successful. Alex and Ani had a small team draw pictures to design the mobile engagement, mapping out exactly how an employee would use an iPod Touch application and a credit card reader/printer linked directly to the company's point-of-sale system to engage customers. The design specifications included screen layouts, the sequence of events, and transactions needed at each step.

The third step is to engineer people, processes, and platforms to deliver the mobile experience. An effective mobile app often requires changing the firm's internal systems, such as those for inventory management, customers, and reservations. Changing those systems typically requires new APIs and tuning the systems to respond more quickly to requests; such changes account for 80 percent of the cost of most mobile projects. Alex and Ani connected their mobile app to the company's point-of-sale systems as well as to systems with detailed product information.

The fourth, final step is to monitor performance and improve outcomes. Alex and Ani analyzed its mobile retail application to determine the length of time for checkouts, whether the app reduces checkout time from minutes to seconds and which customers complete transactions.

Sources: Shane O'Neill, "IHG Builds Hotel App the Agile Way," *Information Week*, May 21, 2014; Ted Schadler and Josh Bernoff, "4 Steps To Build A Better Mobile Business," *Information Week*, July 7, 2014; "Alex and Ani," www.mobiquity.com, accessed July 26, 2014; Art Wittmann "Maximizing Mobility," March 2014; and Leigh Williamson, "A Mobile Application Development Primer," IBM, 2013.

CASE STUDY QUESTIONS

1. What management, organization, and technology issues need to be addressed when building a mobile application?

2. How does user requirement definition for mobile applications differ from traditional systems analysis?

3. Describe Alex and Ani's sales process before and after the mobile application was deployed.

Review Summary

1. **How does building new systems produce organizational change?**

    Building a new information system is a form of planned organizational change. Four kinds of technology-enabled change are (a) automation, (b) rationalization of procedures, (c) business process redesign, and (d) paradigm shift, with far-reaching changes carrying the greatest risks and rewards. Many organizations are using business process management to redesign work flows and business processes in the hope of achieving dramatic productivity breakthroughs. Business process management is also useful for promoting total quality management (TQM), six sigma, and other initiatives for incremental process improvement.

2. **What are the core activities in the systems development process?**

    The core activities in systems development are systems analysis, systems design, programming, testing, conversion, production, and maintenance. Systems analysis is the study and analysis of problems of existing systems and the identification of requirements for their solutions. Systems design provides the specifications for an information system solution, showing how its technical and organizational components fit together.

3. **What are the principal methodologies for modeling and designing systems?**

    The two principal methodologies for modeling and designing information systems are structured methodologies and object-oriented development. Structured methodologies focus on modeling processes and data separately. The data flow diagram is the principal tool for structured analysis, and the structure chart is the principal tool for representing structured software design. Object-oriented development models a system as a collection of objects that combine processes and data. Object-oriented modeling is based on the concepts of class and inheritance.

4. **What are the alternative methods for building information systems?**

    The oldest method for building systems is the systems life cycle, which requires that information systems be developed in formal stages. The stages must proceed sequentially and have defined outputs; each requires formal approval before the next stage can commence. The systems life cycle is useful for large projects that need formal specifications and tight management control over each stage of systems building, but it is very rigid and costly.

    Prototyping consists of building an experimental system rapidly and inexpensively for end users to interact with and evaluate. Prototyping encourages end-user involvement in systems development and iteration of design until specifications are captured accurately. The rapid creation of prototypes can result in systems that have not been completely tested or documented or that are technically inadequate for a production environment.

    Using a software package reduces the amount of design, programming, testing, installation, and maintenance work required to build a system. Application software packages are helpful if a firm does not have the internal information systems staff or financial resources to custom develop a system. To meet an organization's unique requirements, packages may require extensive modifications that can substantially raise development costs.

    End-user development is the development of information systems by end users, either alone or with minimal assistance from information systems specialists. End-user developed systems can be created rapidly and informally using user-friendly software tools. However, end-user development may create information systems that do not necessarily meet quality assurance standards and that are not easily controlled by traditional means.

    Outsourcing consists of using an external vendor to build (or operate) a firm's information systems instead of the organization's internal information systems staff. Outsourcing can save application development costs or enable firms to develop applications without an internal information systems staff. However, firms risk losing control over their information systems and becoming too dependent on external vendors. Outsourcing also entails hidden costs, especially when the work is sent offshore.

5. *What are new approaches for system building in the digital firm era?*

Companies are turning to rapid application design (RAD), joint application design (JAD), agile development, and reusable software components to accelerate the systems development process. RAD uses object-oriented software, visual programming, prototyping, and fourth-generation tools for very rapid creation of systems. Agile development breaks a large project into a series of small subprojects that are completed in short periods of time using iteration and continuous feedback. Component-based development expedites application development by grouping objects into suites of software components that can be combined to create large-scale business applications. Web services provide a common set of standards that enable organizations to link their systems regardless of their technology platform through standard plug-and-play architecture. Mobile application development must pay attention to simplicity, usability, and the need to optimize tasks for tiny screens.

Key Terms

Acceptance testing, 548
Agile development, 563
Automation, 536
Business process management, 538
Business process redesign, 537
Component-based development, 563
Computer-aided software
  engineering (CASE), 554
Conversion, 548
Customization, 560
Data flow diagram (DFD), 551
Direct cutover strategy, 549
Documentation, 549
End-user development, 558
End-user interface, 558
Feasibility study, 545
Information requirements, 546
Iterative, 557
Joint application design (JAD), 563
Maintenance, 550
Mobile Web app, 564
Mobile Web site, 564
Native app, 564
Object, 552
Object-oriented development, 552
Offshore outsourcing, 561
Paradigm shift, 537

Parallel strategy, 548
Phased approach strategy, 549
Pilot study strategy, 549
Post-implementation audit, 550
Process specifications, 552
Production, 549
Programming, 547
Prototype, 557
Prototyping, 556
Query languages, 558
Rapid application development (RAD), 563
Rationalization of procedures, 536
Request for Proposal (RFP), 560
Responsive Web design, 565
Six sigma, 537
Structure chart, 552
Structured, 550
Systems analysis, 545
Systems design, 546
Systems development, 544
Systems life cycle, 555
System testing, 548
Test plan, 548
Testing, 548
Total quality management (TQM), 536
Unit testing, 548

Review Questions

13-1 How does building new systems produce organizational change?

- Describe each of the four kinds of organizational change that can be promoted with information technology.
- Define business process management and describe the steps required to carry it out.

13-2 What are the core activities in the systems development process?

- Distinguish between systems analysis and systems design. Describe the activities for each.
- Define information requirements and explain why they are difficult to determine correctly.
- Explain why the testing stage of systems development is so important. Name and describe the three stages of testing for an information system.

- Describe the role of programming, conversion, production, and maintenance in systems development.

13-3 What are the principal methodologies for modeling and designing systems?

- Compare object-oriented and traditional structured approaches for modeling and designing systems.

13-4 What are alternative methods for building information systems?

- Define the traditional systems life cycle. Describe each of its steps and its advantages and disadvantages for systems building.
- Define information system prototyping. Describe its benefits and limitations. List and describe the steps in the prototyping process.
- Define an application software package. Explain the advantages and disadvantages

of developing information systems based on software packages.

- Define end-user development and describe its advantages and disadvantages. Name some policies and procedures for managing end-user development.
- Describe the advantages and disadvantages of using outsourcing for building information systems.

13-5 What are new approaches for system building in the digital firm era?

- Define rapid application development (RAD) and agile development and explain how they can speed up system-building.
- Explain how component-based development and Web services help firms build and enhance their information systems.
- Explain the features of mobile application development and responsive Web design.

Discussion Questions

13-6 Why is selecting a systems development approach an important business decision? Who should participate in the selection process?

13-7 Some have said that the best way to reduce systems development costs is to use application software packages or user-friendly tools. Do you agree? Why or why not?

13-8 Why is it so important to understand how a business process works when trying to develop a new information system?

Hands-On MIS Projects

The projects in this section give you hands-on experience analyzing business processes, designing and building a customer system for auto sales, and analyzing Web site information requirements.

Management Decision Problems

13-9 For an additional fee, a customer purchasing a Sears Roebuck appliance, such as a washing machine, can purchase a three-year service contract. The contract provides free repair service and parts for the specified appliance using an authorized Sears service provider. When a person with a Sears service contract needs to repair an appliance, such as a washing machine, he or she calls the Sears Repairs & Parts department to schedule an appointment. The department makes the appointment and gives the caller the date and approximate time of the appointment. The repair technician arrives during the designated time framework and diagnoses the problem. If the problem is caused by a faulty part, the technician either replaces the part if he is carrying the part with him or orders the replacement part from Sears. If the part is not in stock at Sears, Sears orders the part and gives the customer an approximate time when the part will arrive. The part is shipped directly to the customer. After the part has arrived, the customer must call Sears to schedule a second appointment for a repair technician to replace the ordered part. This process is very lengthy. It may take two weeks to schedule the first repair visit, another two weeks to order and receive the required part, and another week to schedule a second repair visit after the ordered part has been received.

- Diagram the existing process.

- What is the impact of the existing process on Sears' operational efficiency and customer relationships?

- What changes could be made to make this process more efficient? How could information systems support these changes? Diagram the new, improved process.

13-10 Management at your agricultural chemicals corporation has been dissatisfied with production planning. Production plans are created using best guesses of demand for each product, which are based on how much of each product has been ordered in the past. If a customer places an unexpected order or requests a change to an existing order after it has been placed, there is no way to adjust production plans. The company may have to tell customers it can't fill their orders, or it may run up extra costs maintaining additional inventory to prevent stock-outs.

At the end of each month, orders are totaled and manually keyed into the company's production planning system. Data from the past month's production and inventory systems are manually entered into the firm's order management system. Analysts from the sales department and from the production department analyze the data from their respective systems to determine what the sales targets and production targets should be for the next month. These estimates are usually different. The analysts then get together at a high-level planning meeting to revise the production and sales targets to take into account senior management's goals for market share, revenues, and profits. The outcome of the meeting is a finalized production master schedule.

The entire production planning process takes 17 business days to complete. Nine of these days are required to enter and validate the data. The remaining days are spent developing and reconciling the production and sales targets and finalizing the production master schedule.

- Draw a diagram of the existing production planning process.

- Analyze the problems this process creates for the company.

- How could an enterprise system solve these problems? In what ways could it lower costs? Diagram what the production planning process might look like if the company implemented enterprise software.

Achieving Operational Excellence: Analyzing Web Site Design and Information Requirements

Software skills: Web browser software
Business skills: Information requirements analysis, Web site design

13-11 Visit the Web site of your choice and explore it thoroughly. Prepare a report analyzing the various functions provided by that Web site and its information requirements. Your report should answer these questions: What functions does the Web site perform? What data does it use? What are its inputs, outputs, and processes? What are some of its other design specifications? Does the Web site link to any internal systems or systems of other organizations? What value does this Web site provide the firm?

SourceGas Goes for Better Workforce Scheduling Systems
CASE STUDY

SourceGas is a utility headquartered in Golden, Colorado providing natural gas service to over 413,000 customers in Arkansas, Nebraska, Colorado, and Wyoming. The company has over 1,100 employees and operates nearly 18,000 miles of natural gas transmission and distribution pipeline covering a 332,437-square-mile area—about half the size of Alaska.

The number of work orders (authorizing specific work or repairs to be done) processed per mile traveled is a key performance indicator for utility companies, especially SourceGas. SourceGas's territory includes many large rural areas where re-routing work orders incurs very heavy fuel, maintenance, and other operational costs. The more work orders that can be processed per mile traveled, the lower the cost.

SourceGas's predecessor had installed a mobile information system in 2000 to dispatch approximately 500,000 work orders to approximately 500 field technicians equipped with mobile devices. However, this work order and dispatch system was starting to show its age, and the work order and dispatch processes required too much manual effort. All work was dispatched manually, and there were no systematized scheduling priorities, making it difficult for service technicians to consistently be assigned workloads that were aligned with business objectives.

SourceGas dispatchers were highly experienced and had the requisite knowledge to assign technicians with the appropriate set of skills to perform the work. However, to perform this process successfully, dispatchers had to commit to memory more than 225 different types of work that technicians performed in the field. SourceGas wound up spending a great deal of time and effort clarifying its scheduling policies.

SourceGas's work order process starts with a call from a customer to the SourceGas call center in Fayetteville, Arkansas. Under the company's old system, the company's SAP CRM software created a work order that was sent to the SourceGas dispatch center, where dispatchers assigned the work to technicians who received the assignments using Panasonic Toughbook mobile devices. Although the previous system integrated with SAP CRM software to enable SourceGas to track a work order from start to finish, the work order still had to be initiated manually by the dispatchers.

What's more, the outdated system could no longer be easily modified to keep up with new requirements. SourceGas serves both regulated and non-regulated markets in four states with different business rules, so the system has to be able to accomodate rapid and constant change. Enhancements to the system were just too costly.

SourceGas needed a new system to automate its work order and scheduling processes that could be updated and changed much more easily. Management also wanted a system where SourceGas could make these changes using its own internal resources rather than external consultants, which the company had relied on heavily to make enhancements to its old system. The software for the legacy system had been custom-programmed by third-party vendors, making the system difficult to maintain and enhance.

In the summer of 2011, SourceGas initiated a requirements-gathering workshop with ClickSoftware, the external vendor the company had used in the past to make system enhancements. The objective was to establish system requirements and develop business rules to guide the work order and scheduling processes. SourceGas's biggest priorities were to 1) automate work scheduling; 2) maintain the company's existing timesheet process; and 3) ensure minimal change required for field technicians to use the new system.

For its solution, SourceGas chose SAP Workforce Scheduling & Optimization software package by ClickSoftware, which integrates with its existing SAP systems, including SAP ERP and SAP CRM. SAP Workforce Scheduling & Optimization by ClickSoftware is a real-time optimized scheduling solution for managing scheduling and dispatching, supporting mobile service operations, scheduling service appointments, and monitoring service operations. The software includes capabilities for demand forecasting to determine how much work is set to arrive, when, and where; deploying resources based on knowledge of worker skills, service commitments, location, and customer preferences; responding in real time to on-the-spot issues such as traffic and cancellations; and analyzing service performance by identifying problem areas and methods for improvement. Software users are able to meet anticipated workloads in a specific time frame with better capacity planning and resource allocation. SAP Workforce Scheduling & Optimization software integrates directly with all SAP applications.

An SAP NetWeaver Process Integration adapter automatically handles the messaging between the SAP Workforce Scheduling & Optimization and the SAP CRM system. Work orders are now automatically scheduled and dispatched using the company's business rules configured in the system, with exceptions flagged for dispatchers to handle.

The entire process of implementing the new system-requirements analysis, development, testing, and training, took a little over one year. SourceGas rolled out the system in phases, with its last division going live with the system in December 2012. In implementing the SAP software package, SourceGas faced some special challenges because it had to design the system and configure the software to account for all the special conditions of its unique service area and complex rules for types of work. Some of the questions that had to be addressed were: Are work order priorities the same in an urban area, such as Fayetteville, Arkansas, as they are in rural Wyoming? What constitutes an emergency work order?

The SourceGas system had to be designed to schedule and route all the field technician work according to these various rules and conditions. The design also had to make the system as familiar and easy to use for SourceGas mobile workers as possible, with the new mobile app user experience mirroring field workers' existing user experience as much as possible. This was especially critical for time reporting, which required some simplification while adhering nevertheless to company business rules for proper accounting.

SourceGas was able to enhance the software while maintaining the same user experience. To improve technician efficiency, the software was enhanced to tailor service order completion data sent back to SourceGas's ERP system for each type of service order rather than displaying all data fields on all orders. Another important enhancement was to add audio alerts for dispatchers and technicians' mobile devices to the SAP Workforce Scheduling & Optimization software so that emergency orders receive proper attention. An additional safety feature is the capability for technicians to set a timer to alert dispatch if they haven't returned to their vehicle by a specified time.

SourceGas used an iterative approach and agile development methodology and took user input and user training very seriously. The system project had a committee of super-user technicians as well as an operations team to make sure the system was built to the right specifications. Its technicians had provided important input during the requirements-gathering and design stages of system-building, and they began training on the new application in June 2012. SourceGas trained 20 percent of its workforce to obtain their feedback about the new system (to make sure it met their expectations), and used the experience to create training materials for when the system went totally live. This approach helped ensure users would buy into the new system and that no business process was overlooked.

The testing process had end users on SourceGas's operations team perform all of the approximately 225 types of service orders handled by the company using the new application to make sure the system was able to handle every single business scenario. For example, to test the process of a technician closing out a work order for a meter exchange, the new system must be able to move data from a final reading of the old meter into SourceGas's SAP ERP system, and the system has to perform certain steps before the new meter is recognized and synchronized to a customer account.

What benefits have been produced by the new system? SourceGas's management has received positive feedback about the new system capabilities for automated scheduling, timesheet preparation as well as its improved usability compared to the previous system. Managers can more accurately gauge their workload in their divisions. SourceGas dispatchers can see their workloads more accurately and determine the appropriate resources. The company has already used the new system to complete 400,000 work orders and pay 900,000 timesheet records. However, management would like to see more manpower study reports before it can determine the extent of the new system's operational efficiencies and benefits.

One key benefit that is already apparent, however, is the company's ability to keep a lid on the costs of maintaining and updating the system because it is doing most of that work with in-house staff rather than turning to external vendors, as it had in the past. The SAP Workforce Scheduling and Optimization software package has made it possible for SourceGas to rapidly make changes in-house, which makes it easier for the company to respond to rapid changes in the utility industry.

SourceGas will be further enhancing its SAP Workforce Scheduling and Optimization software to focus more directly on serving customers. Potential changes to the system include allowing customers to place orders online, sending text messages to inform customers when technicians are on the way, and processing payment from customers directly in the field.

Sources: www.sourcegas.com, accessed June 30, 2014; Murphy, Ken "SourceGas Takes the Driver's Seat in Workforce Scheduling," SAP InsiderPROFILES, July 1, 2013; and "SourceGas Implements SAP Workforce Scheduling & Optimization," www.youtube.com, May 14, 2014.

CASE STUDY QUESTIONS

13-12 Analyze SourceGas's problems with its old system. What management, organization, and technology factors were responsible for these problems? What was the business impact of these problems?

13-13 What role did end users play in developing SourceGas's new work order and dispatch system? How did the project team make sure users were involved? What would have happened to the project if they had not done this?

13-14 What types of system-building methods and tools did SourceGas use for building its system?

13-15 Discuss the issue of software package customization at SourceGas.

13-16 What other steps did SourceGas take to make sure the new system was successful?

13-17 What were the benefits of the new system? How did it change the way SourceGas ran its business? How successful was this system solution?

Chapter 13 References

Armstrong, Deborah J. and Bill C. Hardgrove. "Understanding Mindshift Learning: The Transition to Object-Oriented Development." *MIS Quarterly* 31, No. 3 (September 2007).

Aron, Ravi, Eric K.Clemons, and Sashi Reddi. "Just Right Outsourcing: Understanding and Managing Risk." *Journal of Management Information Systems* 22, No. 1 (Summer 2005).

Ashrafi, Noushin and Hessam Ashrafi. *Object-Oriented Systems Analysis and Design*. Upper Saddle River, NY: Prentice-Hall (2009).

Baily, Martin N. and Diana Farrell. "Exploding the Myths of Offshoring." *The McKinsey Quarterly* (July 2004).

Cao, Lan, Kannan Mohan, Balasubramaniam Ramesh and Sumantra Sarkar. "Evolution of Governance: Achieving Ambidexterity in IT Outsourcing." *Journal of Management Information Systems* 30, No. 3 (Winter 2014).

Davidson, Elisabeth J. "Technology Frames and Framing: A Socio-Cognitive Investigation of Requirements Determination." *MIS Quarterly* 26, No. 4 (December 2002).

DeMarco, Tom. *Structured Analysis and System Specification*. New York: Yourdon Press (1978).

Dibbern, Jess, Jessica Winkler, and Armin Heinzl. "Explaining Variations in Client Extra Costs between Software Projects Offshored to India." *MIS Quarterly* 32, No. 2 (June 2008).

Edberg , Dana T., Polina Ivanova and William Kuechler. "Methodology Mashups: An Exploration of Processes Used to Maintain Software ." *Journal of Management Information Systems* 28, No. 4 (Spring 2012).

El Sawy, Omar A. *Redesigning Enterprise Processes for E-Business*. McGraw-Hill (2001).

Feeny, David, Mary Lacity, and Leslie P. Willcocks. "Taking the Measure of Outsourcing Providers." *MIT Sloan Management Review* 46, No. 3 (Spring 2005).

Gefen, David and Erran Carmel. "Is the World Really Flat? A Look at Offshoring in an Online Programming Marketplace." *MIS Quarterly* 32, No. 2 (June 2008).

Greengard, Samuel."Pervasive Mobility Creates New Business Challenges." *Baseline* (June 28, 2013).

Goo, Jahyun, Rajive Kishore, H. R. Rao, and Kichan Nam. "The Role of Service Level Agreements in Relational Management of Information Technology Outsourcing: An Empirical Study." *MIS Quarterly* 33, No. 1 (March 2009).

Hahn, Eugene D., Jonathan P. Doh, and Kraiwinee Bunyaratavej. "The Evolution of Risk in Information Systems Offshoring: The Impact of Home Country Risk, Firm Learning, and Competitive Dynamics." *MIS Quarterly* 33, No. 3 (September 2009).

Hammer, Michael, and James Champy. *Reengineering the Corporation*. New York: HarperCollins (1993).

Hoffer, Jeffrey, Joey George, and Joseph Valacich. *Modern Systems Analysis and Design*, 7th ed. Upper Saddle River, NJ: Prentice Hall (2014).

Information Builders. "WebFOCUS Turns Neways into a Cleaner Data-Driven Company." www.informationbuilders.com, accessed September 3, 2014.

Ivari, Juhani, Rudy Hirscheim, and Heinz K. Klein. "A Dynamic Framework for Classifying Information Systems Development Methodologies and Approaches." *Journal of Management Information Systems* 17, No. 3 (Winter 2000–2001).

Kendall, Kenneth E., and Julie E. Kendall. *Systems Analysis and Design*, 9th ed. Upper Saddle River, NJ: Prentice Hall (2013).

Kindler, Noah B., Vasantha Krishnakanthan, and Ranjit Tinaikar. "Applying Lean to Application Development and Maintenance." *The McKinsey Quarterly* (May 2007).

Kotlarsky, Julia, Harry Scarbrough, and Ilan Oshri. "Coordinating Expertise Across Knowledge Boundaries in Offshore-Outsourcing Projects: The Role of Codification." *MIS Quarterly* 38 No. 2 (June 2014).

Lee, Gwanhoo and Weidong Xia. "Toward Agile: An Integrated Analysis of Quantitative and Qualitative Field Data." *MIS Quarterly* 34, No. 1 (March 2010).

Levina, Natalia, and Jeanne W. Ross. "From the Vendor's Perspective: Exploring the Value Proposition in Information Technology Outsourcing." *MIS Quarterly* 27, No. 3 (September 2003).

Majchrzak, Ann, Cynthia M. Beath, and Ricardo A. Lim. "Managing Client Dialogues during Information Systems Design to Facilitate Client Learning." *MIS Quarterly* 29, No. 4 (December 2005).

Mani, Deepa, Anitesh Barua, and Andrew Whinston. "An Empirical Analysis of the Impact of Information Capabilities Design on Business Process Outsourcing Performance." *MIS Quarterly* 34, No. 1 (March 2010).

Murphy, Chris. "GM's U-Turn." Information Week (July 9, 2012).

Nelson, H. James, Deborah J. Armstrong, and Kay M. Nelson. Patterns of Transition: The Shift from Traditional to Object-Oriented Development." *Journal of Management Information Systems* 25, No. 4 (Spring 2009).

Nidumolu, Sarma R. and Mani Subramani." The Matrix of Control: Combining Process and Structure Approaches to Managing Software Development." *Journal of Management Information Systems* 20, No. 4 (Winter 2004).

Overby, Stephanie. "The Hidden Costs of Offshore Outsourcing," *CIO Magazine* (Sept.1, 2003).

Pollock, Neil and Sampsa Hyysalo. "The Business of Being a User: The Role of the Reference Actor in Shaping Packaged Enterprise System Acquisition and Development." *MIS Quarterly* 38, No. 2 (June 2014).

Sircar, Sumit, Sridhar P. Nerur, and Radhakanta Mahapatra. "Revolution or Evolution?A Comparison of Object-Oriented and Structured Systems Development Methods." *MIS Quarterly* 25, No. 4 (December 2001).

Swanson, E. Burton and Enrique Dans. "System Life Expectancy and the Maintenance Effort: Exploring their Equilibration." *MIS Quarterly* 24, No. 2 (June 2000).

Wittmann, Art. "Maximizing Mobility." *Information Week Tech Digest* (March 2014).

Yourdon, Edward, and L. L. Constantine. *Structured Design*. New York: Yourdon Press (1978).

Managing Projects

LEARNING OBJECTIVES

After reading this chapter, you will be able to answer the following questions:

1. What are the objectives of project management and why is it so essential in developing information systems?

2. What methods can be used for selecting and evaluating information systems projects and aligning them with the firm's business goals?

3. How can firms assess the business value of information systems?

4. What are the principal risk factors in information systems projects, and how can they be managed?

CHAPTER CASES

Harrah's Cherokee Casino Wins with Sound Project Management

New York's CityTime: An IS Project Goes Awry

Reliance Installing the 4G Project in India

A Shaky Start for Healthcare.gov

HARRAH'S CHEROKEE CASINO WINS WITH SOUND PROJECT MANAGEMENT

Harrah's Cherokee Casino Resort in Cherokee, North Carolina is owned by the Eastern Band of Cherokee Indians and is one of the few casinos to have performed well during the 2008 economic downturn and thereafter. As a matter of fact, the casino performed so well that it was able to undertake a US $650 million expansion of its facilities with more game tables and dealers.

The casino's business expansion required an upgrade to the casino's Oracle JD Edwards enterprise resource planning (ERP) system running the company's business operations. The upgrade was designed to maintain existing levels of operational support while providing casino employees with new capabilities to help them in their job.

James Caldwell, Harrah's Cherokee director of information technology and risk control, worked with CSS International consultants to develop a program to complete the upgrade in 100 days. This was an ambitious target for a large software project, but the project came in on time and nearly 15 percent under budget, allowing the company to spend more on streamlining additional human resources processes and automating error-prone, time-consuming tasks. How was Harrah's Cherokee able to pull this off?

© Goodluz/Shutterstock

The answer is: by good project management. Caldwell and his team accurately defined the scope of the project up front, organized project team leaders early on, and worked closely with key users to get a clear understanding of business needs. Caldwell also secured critical management support before moving the project forward.

Managing a world-class casino not only involves keeping game tables active and serving drinks but also managing a hotel, restaurants, nightclub, spas, security, banking operations, housekeeping, and a customer database. An army of employees is required—2,700 at Harrah's Cherokee. Inefficient business processes for hiring and managing these employees was slowing down the business and taking too much time away from the company's core mission of enhancing the customer experience.

Harrah Cherokee's existing ERP system had modules for human resources (HR) and payroll, but they required considerable manual rekeying of data by the casino's HR staff. Data entry tasks were distributed among multiple HR employees. One person would key in data related to new hires and another would be responsible for entering data for job changes. The system's user interface was not user-friendly. HR staff entering data occasionally introduced errors or failed to include critical information, adding to time and operating costs.

For example, if an employee record contains incorrect data, that employee won't get paid on time. Like others companies in service industries, Harrah's Cherokee tends to have higher employee turnover, and that means a steady influx of new employees with data to enter into the system and more opportunities for error.

The solution to this problem was the Pages feature of JD Edwards EnterpriseOne Tools. Pages provides a user-friendly interface for employee self-service applications by giving the information systems department centralized control of users' work screens and letting them customize what employees see. For example, the steps in a specific process can be arranged in a visual process flow instead of just listing menu options on the screen. Page automates previously manual processes, such as a request for personal tie off. Employees are able to log into their self-service portal, submit these requests online, and secure management approval online. Pages also manages employee performance reviews and furnishes online benefits manuals and how-to guides. Since Harrah's Cherokee implemented Pages, help calls to Human Resources have decreased significantly.

Although the benefits of Pages were obvious, the new system represented change, and employees often resist the changes associated with a new information system. Caldwell and his project team proactively engaged with change management. They did not present users with a new system that they had to accept. Instead, they sought active user input on changes to menu design and interface layout. By reaching out to employees and showing they were prepared to support and train them, the project team got them to buy into the new system. Now the company's HR staff can spend more time finding high-quality applications and hiring them more expeditiously instead of spending all day keying in data.

Sources: Tara Swords, "Bonus Payoff," *Profit Magazine*, August 2014; www.cssus.com, accessed September 12, 2014; and www.oracle.com, accessed September 12, 2014.

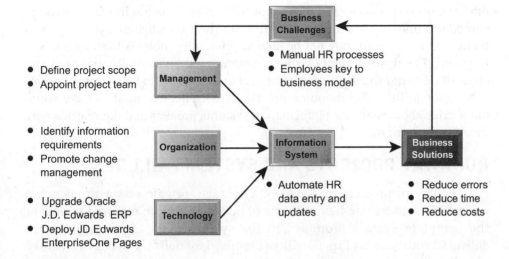

One of the principal challenges posed by information systems is ensuring they deliver genuine business benefits. There is a very high failure rate among information systems projects because organizations have incorrectly assessed their business value or because firms have failed to manage the organizational change surrounding the introduction of new technology.

Harrah Cherokee Casino's management realized this when it undertook its system upgrade. The new system involved changes to important Human Resources (HR) business processes supported by new software. Harrah's Cherokee succeeded with this project because its management clearly understood that strong project management and attention to organizational and "people" issues were essential to success.

The chapter-opening diagram calls attention to important points raised by this case and this chapter. Harrah's Cherokee Casino's expansion plans and future growth called for more streamlined and automated business processes, especially in Human Resources. Outdated manual processes for employee recordkeeping made operations excessively error-prone and inefficient. Management wisely assembled an experienced project team, which took great pains to work carefully with employees to help them deal with the changes in their jobs and routines brought about by the new system.

Here are some questions to think about: Why was it important to have both business users and IT specialists on the project team? What were the risk factors in this project?

14.1   WHAT ARE THE OBJECTIVES OF PROJECT MANAGEMENT AND WHY IS IT SO ESSENTIAL IN DEVELOPING INFORMATION SYSTEMS?

There is a very high failure rate among information systems projects. In nearly every organization, information systems projects take much more time and money to implement than originally anticipated or the completed system does not work properly. When an information system does not meet expectations or costs too much to develop, companies may not realize any benefit from their information system investment, and the system may not be able to solve the problems for which it was intended. The development of a new system must be carefully managed and orchestrated, and the way a project is executed is likely to be the most important factor influencing its outcome. That's why it's essential to have some knowledge about managing information systems projects and the reasons why they succeed or fail.

RUNAWAY PROJECTS AND SYSTEM FAILURE

How badly are projects managed? On average, private sector projects are underestimated by one-half in terms of budget and time required to deliver the complete system promised in the system plan. Many projects are delivered with missing functionality (promised for delivery in later versions). The Standish Group consultancy, which monitors IT project success rates, found that only 32 percent of all technology investments were completed on time, on budget, and with all features and functions originally specified (McCafferty, 2010). A joint study by McKinsey and Oxford University found that large software projects on average run 66 percent over budget and 33 percent over schedule; as many as 17 percent of projects turn out so badly that they can threaten the existence of the company (Chandrasekaran et. al., 2014). Between 30 and 40 percent of all software projects are "runaway" projects that far exceed the original schedule and budget projections and fail to perform as originally specified (see the Interactive Session on Management).

As illustrated in Figure 14.1, a systems development project without proper management will most likely suffer these consequences:

- Costs that vastly exceed budgets
- Unexpected time slippage
- Technical performance that is less than expected
- Failure to obtain anticipated benefits

The systems produced by failed information projects are often not used in the way they were intended, or they are not used at all. Users often have to develop parallel manual systems to make these systems work.

The actual design of the system may fail to capture essential business requirements or improve organizational performance. Information may not be provided quickly enough to be helpful, it may be in a format that is impossible to digest and use, or it may represent the wrong pieces of data.

FIGURE 14.1 CONSEQUENCES OF POOR PROJECT MANAGEMENT

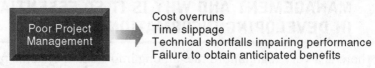

Poor Project Management →
Cost overruns
Time slippage
Technical shortfalls impairing performance
Failure to obtain anticipated benefits

Without proper management, a systems development project takes longer to complete and most often exceeds the allocated budget. The resulting information system most likely is technically inferior and may not be able to demonstrate any benefits to the organization.

INTERACTIVE SESSION: MANAGEMENT

NEW YORK'S CITYTIME: AN IS PROJECT GOES AWRY

New York City's CityTime project started out with good intentions. CityTime was created to automate payroll timekeeping for 80 mayoral and other city agencies and in the process to curb undeserved overtime payments to city workers and improve accountability throughout the government. In an ironic twist, the project instead became permeated with fraud at every level. The original estimated project cost was about US $63 million, but CityTime ended up costing $720 million by the time it became fully operational in 2011.

Project managers from the project's main consulting organization, Science Applications International Corporation (SAIC) were charged and convicted in 2014 of fraud and bribery, as was Mark Mazer, a former consultant to the city's Office of Payroll Administration, who had managed the project for the city. In 2014, along with two others, he received a sentence of twenty years in prison. Manhattan US Attorney Preet Bharara stated that contractors and subcontractors systematically inflated costs, overbilled for consultants' time, and artificially extended the completion date. Again, the biggest reason for the project's unheard-of budget increases was lack of qualified oversight. The few government employees constantly monitoring the project turned a seemingly blind eye on the ballooning costs incurred by SAIC and the lack of progress in the project. Belief that the software developed for the system could be sold to other governments was perhaps another reason why the city let costs run wild.

Mark Page, budget director for New York City Mayor Michael Bloomberg, was reportedly the strongest voice in favor of CityTime. He had hoped to stop the trend of police officers, firefighters, and other aging city workers receiving unnecessary overtime at the end of their careers, presumably to increase their pensions. Page also wanted to limit lawsuits against the city from workers claiming their pay was too low for the hours they had worked. But Page's background was in law, not information systems, making him a poor choice

to oversee CityTime. Other government branches, like the city comptroller, left the project mostly to Page. William C. Thompson, the city comptroller from 2002 to 2009, never audited CityTime despite numerous warnings about the project from staffers. An aide for the mayor did suggest that the comptroller's office had raised concerns about the project to the mayor, but those concerns too were ignored or dismissed by Page.

In 2000, work on the project was transferred to SAIC from the first contractor, a subsidiary of MCI. Instead of the usual competitive bidding process for contracts, the city opted simply to pass it off to SAIC. Shortly after SAIC took control of the contract, work on CityTime was switched from fixed-price to hourly billing. This, in turn, inflated costs from $224 million in 2006 to a total of $628 million by 2009. Thanks to the hourly contracts, the city was on the hook for all of the waste incurred by SAIC. The terms of contracts were also constantly changing: another consulting company hired to provide quality assurance for CityTime had its contract amended 11 times, increasing its value to almost $50 million from its original $3.4 million figure.

SAIC delegated most of the work on CityTime to subcontractors, further complicating the chain of command involved in the project. The most prominent of these, Technodyne, received $450 million in funds from the city. Today, over 150,000 city workers use CityTime to keep track of attendance and leave of absence requests, but the cost per user for the project is estimated to be approximately $4,000. The industry standard for projects of this size at that time was between $200 and $1,000 dollars. New York State had developed a system to perform similar tasks for only $217 million, which makes CityTime's $720 million price tag look even worse by comparison.

In March 2012, the city received some good news—SAIC agreed to repay over $500 million in restitution and penalties back to the city to avoid federal prosecution for various instances of fraud involving the CityTime project. The city recovered most of that money and, according to Mayor Bloomberg, the SAIC repayment meant that taxpayers only had to pay $100 million for CityTime. The scandal nevertheless remained a black mark for Bloomberg and his goals to modernize city information systems.

The New York City Council called a hearing to respond to the budget-crippling cost overruns of both projects. The Bloomberg administration vowed once again to review the way it handles complex, multi-million dollar technology projects. Proposed changes included first looking for commercial software before developing customized software without a real need for it. The city also stated that it would bill contractors as functional benchmarks for projects are achieved instead of hourly, to avoid future partnerships like SAIC, and would ensure that multi-million dollar technology projects are overseen by qualified experts, instead of government administrators from other areas with no project management experience.

According to Mark G. Peters, commissioner of the New York City Investigation Department,

there has been heightened scrutiny of information technology spending in the wake of the CityTime investigation. In March 2014, he directed the agency to design new internal control protocols for technology contracts. Mayor Bill de Blasio has pledged to uphold the highest standards of oversight across government agencies and city services and to prevent costly incidents like the CityTime fraud scandal from happening in the future.

Sources: Reuters, "Three Men Get 20-Year Sentences in New York City Payroll Fraud Case," *New York Times*, April 28, 2014; Robert N. Charette, "Three Guilty Pleas in NYC's CityTime Payroll System Fraud Case, " IEEE Spectrum, June 21, 2013; Jennifer Fermino, "Bloomberg Says New York City 'Lucky' It Had $500 Million CityTime Fraud," New York Daily News, July 26, 2013; www.nyc.gov, accessed August 17, 2013; "CityTime," *New York Times*, March 14, 2012; Michael M. Grynbaum, "Contractor Strikes $500 Million Deal in City Payroll Scandal," *New York Times*, March 14, 2012; Robert Charette, "New York City's $720 Million CityTime Project a Vehicle for Unprecedented Fraud Says US Prosecutor," IEEE Spectrum, June 21, 2011, David W. Chen, Serge F. Kovaleski and John Eligon, Behind Troubled City Payroll Project, Lax Oversight and One Powerful Insider," *New York Times*, March 27, 2011.

CASE STUDY QUESTIONS

1. How important was the CityTime project for New York City? What were its objectives and anticipated business benefits?

2. Evaluate the key risk factors in this project.

3. Classify and describe the problems encountered the CityTime system was being implemented.

What management, organization, and technology factors were responsible for these problems?

4. What was the business impact of CityTime's botched implementation? Explain your answer .

5. Describe the steps that should have been taken to prevent a negative outcomes in this project.

The way in which nontechnical business users must interact with the system may be excessively complicated and discouraging. A system may be designed with a poor user interface. The **user interface** is the part of the system with which end users interact. For example, an online input form or data entry screen may be so poorly arranged that no one wants to submit data or request information. System outputs may be displayed in a format that is too difficult to comprehend.

Web sites may discourage visitors from exploring further if the Web pages are cluttered and poorly arranged, if users cannot easily find the information they are seeking, or if it takes too long to access and display the Web page on the user's computer.

INTERACTIVE SESSION: ORGANIZATIONS

RELIANCE INSTALLING THE 4G PROJECT IN INDIA

Reliance Jio Infocomm Limited (RJIL), a subsidiary of Reliance Industries Limited (RIL), is the first telecom company to obtain a pan-India unified operating license. Reliance plans to commercially launch its 4G broadband services in 2015. The setting up of the network and hardware infrastructure for this project has cost the company ₹40,000 crore in investments. The firm managed to successfully acquire the broadband wireless access (BWA) spectrum through an auction. It also entered into key agreements with several companies such as Tower Vision and Viom Networks for the use of their 8,400 and 42,000 towers, respectively. Contracts have also been signed with companies like Bharti Airtel for fiber utilization and infrastructure sharing, among other things.

There were several challenges that RJIL faced when it decided to embark on this journey. Three types of working processes were to be set up. The first involved negotiations with the infrastructure companies, which would provide the necessary towers, hardware, antennas, microwave, and so on. The second related to discussion with the networking companies, who would be responsible for the provisioning and installation of networking equipment. Finally, a customer-facing operator was needed to take the 4G service to market. Indus Towers, Viom Networks, and BSNL took care of Reliance's infrastructural needs; networking services were provided by Samsung; while Reliance Communications acted as the telecom operator that would provide the 4G service to customers. Indus Towers is the largest provider of telecom towers in the world. It is a joint venture between the Bharti Group, the Aditya Birla Group, and the Vodafone Group. India is divided into 22 circles for telecom operations, and Indus has over one lakh towers in 15 of those circles. These towers can be used by any of the telecom players. This sharing of towers benefits not just the customer (by lowering the price of the service) but also reduces radiation damage on the environment.

Once the infrastructure partner hands over the site to RJIL, Samsung, the networking partner, steps in and surveys the site to determine whether the infrastructure is electronically viable. As part of the survey, the site engineers collect information such as the length of the cable required, height of the antenna, images of the infrastructure site, and so on. They also find a suitable location for installation as per the requirements of the client. All this information is then fed into a material information system, which generates an Excel-based survey report summarizing the findings. This report is then handed over to RJIL to be uploaded it to its geographic information system to get a complete picture of the site. Once Samsung determines the readiness of the site for network installation, RJIL releases payment to the tower infrastructure provider.

An acceptance testing procedure is now conducted on the site. Here, images of the site extracted from the geographic information system (GIS) are uploaded to another software called SiteForge. This makes the real-time sharing of geo-tagged photos possible. Samsung now needs to determine the range of the towers. This is done through the process of linking, where the microwaves installed on each tower are linked to one another. Once this is accomplished (it usually takes 15 days), Samsung performs another survey to test the electromagnetic field, measure the bandwidth of antennas, test antenna radiation, determine the strength of the power transmitted and received, and so on. All this is done to assess the effect of radiation on nearby settlements. This information is again fed into SiteForge, which generates real-time statistics on the health of the network assets at the site. This information system then calculates the impact of the radiation using three techniques: the simple calculation method, the broadband method, and the narrowband method. The simple calculation method is employed first and the results are compared with the effective radiation limit as prescribed by the Department of Telecommunications (DOT). If the radiation limit at this stage exceeds the prescribed limit, the angle of the antenna is modified and the broadband method is applied. If this method also fails to provide results within the prescribed limit, changes are made to the site itself and the narrowband method of calculating radiation is used. Most sites are able to meet the expected radiation limits when tested with these three techniques. If the results still exceed the prescribed values, the site is declared harmful. Based on these findings, the DOT decides whether to give permission for integration or not.

The last step is to conduct a single-cell function test (SCFT) or a drive test. All the sites which receive permission from the DOT need to undergo this test, where the ability of the site to offer the promised Internet speed (which, in RJIL's case, is 50 Mbps) is determined. A stationary test is first conducted by uploading and downloading files. Then the field staff perform a moving test by driving anti-clockwise and clockwise around the site. When the site meets the speed requirements, it is handed over by Samsung to RJIL. The site is then deemed fit for the use of the customer.

Sources: "RJIL signs agreement with Indus Towers to launch 4G services", SmartCity.eletsonline.com. Retrieved from http://smartcity.eletsonline.com/rjil-signs-agreement-with-indus-towers-to-launch-4g-services/; "Reliance Jio Infocomm to launch 4G in 2015: Mukesh Ambani", *The Times of India* (2014). Retrieved from http://timesofindia.indiatimes.com/tech/tech-news/Reliance-Jio-Infocomm-to-launch-4G-in-2015-Mukesh-Ambani/articleshow/36763068.cms; "Core Members". Retrieved from http://www.coai.com/About-Us/Members/Core-Members/Reliance-Jio-Infocomm-Limited; "Looking back, looking forward". Retrieved from http://www.rcom.co.in/Rcom/aboutus/overview/overview_reliancegroup.html.

CASE STUDY QUESTIONS

1. What are the three processes involved in the setting up of any project in the telecom sector?

2. Discuss the role of information systems in conducting the environment-readiness survey on the tower site.

3. How is SiteForge used in the acceptance testing procedure?

4. What do you understand by drive test in the telecom sector?

Additionally, the data in the system may have a high level of inaccuracy or inconsistency. The information in certain fields may be erroneous or ambiguous, or it may not be organized properly for business purposes. Information required for a specific business function may be inaccessible because the data are incomplete.

The Interactive Session on Organizations illustrates that to complete a project, proper coordination between all the executing agencies is very important for implementing the project within the stipulated time frame. As you read this case, try to determine how Reliance Jio Infocomm Limited (RJIL) is able to achieve high level of coordination between three different executing agencies.

PROJECT MANAGEMENT OBJECTIVES

A **project** is a planned series of related activities for achieving a specific business objective. Information systems projects include the development of new information systems, enhancement of existing systems, or upgrade or replacement of the firm's information technology (IT) infrastructure.

Project management refers to the application of knowledge, skills, tools, and techniques to achieve specific targets within specified budget and time constraints. Project management activities include planning the work, assessing risk, estimating resources required to accomplish the work, organizing the work, acquiring human and material resources, assigning tasks, directing activities, controlling project execution, reporting progress, and analyzing the results. As in other areas of business, project management for information systems must deal with five major variables: scope, time, cost, quality, and risk.

Scope defines what work is or is not included in a project. For example, the scope of a project for a new order processing system might be to include new modules for inputting orders and transmitting them to production and accounting but not any changes to related accounts receivable, manufacturing, distribution, or inventory control systems. Project management defines all the work required to complete a project successfully, and should ensure that the scope of a project does not expand beyond what was originally intended.

Time is the amount of time required to complete the project. Project management typically establishes the amount of time required to complete major components of a project. Each of these components is further broken down into activities and tasks. Project management tries to determine the time required to complete each task and establish a schedule for completing the work.

Cost is based on the time to complete a project multiplied by the cost of human resources required to complete the project. Information systems project costs also include the cost of hardware, software, and work space. Project management develops a budget for the project and monitors ongoing project expenses.

Quality is an indicator of how well the end result of a project satisfies the objectives specified by management. The quality of information systems projects usually boils down to improved organizational performance and decision making. Quality also considers the accuracy and timeliness of information produced by the new system and ease of use.

Risk refers to potential problems that would threaten the success of a project. These potential problems might prevent a project from achieving its objectives by increasing time and cost, lowering the quality of project outputs, or preventing the project from being completed altogether. Section 14.4 describes the most important risk factors for information systems.

14.2 WHAT METHODS CAN BE USED FOR SELECTING AND EVALUATING INFORMATION SYSTEMS PROJECTS AND ALIGNING THEM WITH THE FIRM'S BUSINESS GOALS?

Companies typically are presented with many different projects for solving problems and improving performance. There are far more ideas for systems projects than there are resources. Firms will need to select from this group the projects that promise the greatest benefit to the business. Obviously, the firm's overall business strategy should drive project selection. How should managers choose among all the options?

MANAGEMENT STRUCTURE FOR INFORMATION SYSTEMS PROJECTS

Figure 14.2 shows the elements of a management structure for information systems projects in a large corporation. It helps ensure that the most important projects are given priority.

At the apex of this structure is the corporate strategic planning group and the information system steering committee. The corporate strategic planning group is responsible for developing the firm's strategic plan, which may require the development of new systems. Often, this group will have developed objective measures of firm performance (called "key performance indicators," introduced in Chapter 12) and choose to support IT projects which can make a substantial improvement in one or several key performance indicators. These performance indicators are reviewed and discussed by the firm's board of directors.

The information systems steering committee is the senior management group with responsibility for systems development and operation. It is composed of department heads from both end-user and information systems areas. The steering committee reviews and approves plans for systems in all divisions, seeks to coordinate and integrate systems, and occasionally becomes involved in selecting specific information systems projects. This group also has a keen awareness of the key performance indicators decided on by higher level managers and the board of directors.

FIGURE 14.2   MANAGEMENT CONTROL OF SYSTEMS PROJECTS

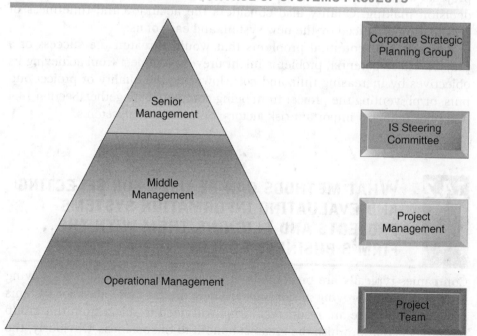

Each level of management in the hierarchy is responsible for specific aspects of systems projects, and this structure helps give priority to the most important systems projects for the organization.

The project team is supervised by a project management group composed of information systems managers and end-user managers responsible for overseeing several specific information systems projects. The project team is directly responsible for the individual systems project. It consists of systems analysts, specialists from the relevant end-user business areas, application programmers, and perhaps database specialists. The mix of skills and the size of the project team depend on the specific nature of the system solution.

LINKING SYSTEMS PROJECTS TO THE BUSINESS PLAN

In order to identify the information systems projects that will deliver the most business value, organizations need to develop an **information systems plan** that supports their overall business plan and in which strategic systems are incorporated into top-level planning. The plan serves as a road map indicating the direction of systems development (the purpose of the plan), the rationale, the current systems/situation, new developments to consider, the management strategy, the implementation plan, and the budget (see Table 14.1).

The plan contains a statement of corporate goals and specifies how information technology will support the attainment of those goals. The report shows how general goals will be achieved by specific systems projects. It identifies specific target dates and milestones that can be used later to evaluate the plan's progress in terms of how many objectives were actually attained in the time frame specified in the plan. The plan indicates the key management decisions concerning hardware acquisition; telecommunications; centralization/decentralization of authority, data, and hardware; and required organizational change. Organizational changes are also usually described, including management and employee training requirements, recruiting efforts, changes in business processes, and changes in authority, structure, or management practice.

In order to plan effectively, firms will need to inventory and document all of their information system applications and IT infrastructure components. For projects in which benefits involve improved decision making, managers should try to identify the decision improvements that would provide the greatest additional value to the firm. They should then develop a set of metrics to quantify the value of more timely and precise information on the outcome of the decision. (See Chapter 12 for more detail on this topic.)

INFORMATION REQUIREMENTS AND KEY PERFORMANCE INDICATORS

To develop an effective information systems plan, the organization must have a clear understanding of both its long- and short-term information requirements. A strategic approach to information requirements, strategic analysis, or critical success factors argues that an organization's information requirements are determined by a small number of **key performance indicators (KPIs)** of managers. KPIs are shaped by the industry, the firm, the manager, and the broader environment. For instance, KPIs for an automobile firm

TABLE 14.1 INFORMATION SYSTEMS PLAN

1. **Purpose of the Plan**
   Overview of plan contents
   Current business organization and future organization
   Key business processes
   Management strategy

2. **Strategic Business Plan Rationale**
   Current situation
   Current business organization
   Changing environments
   Major goals of the business plan
   Firm's strategic plan

3. **Current Systems**
   Major systems supporting business functions and processes
   Current infrastructure capabilities
   > Hardware
   > Software
   > Database
   > Telecommunications and Internet
   Difficulties meeting business requirements
   Anticipated future demands

4. **New Developments**
   New system projects
   > Project descriptions
   > Business rationale
   > Applications' role in strategy
   New infrastructure capabilities required
   > Hardware
   > Software
   > Database
   > Telecommunications and Internet

5. **Management Strategy**
   Acquisition plans
   Milestones and timing
   Organizational realignment
   Internal reorganization
   Management controls
   Major training initiatives
   Personnel strategy

6. **Implementation Plan**
   Anticipated difficulties in implementation
   Progress reports

(continued)

TABLE 14.1 INFORMATION SYSTEMS PLAN (CONTINUED)

7.	Budget Requirements
	Requirements
	Potential savings
	Financing
	Acquisition cycle

might be unit production costs, labor costs, factory productivity, re-work and error rate, customer brand recognition surveys, J.D. Power quality rankings, employee job satisfaction ratings, and health costs. New information systems should focus on providing information that helps the firm meet these goals implied by key performance indicators.

PORTFOLIO ANALYSIS

Once strategic analyses have determined the overall direction of systems development, **portfolio analysis** can be used to evaluate alternative system projects. Portfolio analysis inventories all of the organization's information systems projects and assets, including infrastructure, outsourcing contracts, and licenses. This portfolio of information systems investments can be described as having a certain profile of risk and benefit to the firm (see Figure 14.3) similar to a financial portfolio.

Each information systems project carries its own set of risks and benefits. (Section 14.4 describes the factors that increase the risks of systems projects.) Firms would try to improve the return on their portfolios of IT assets by balancing the risk and return from their systems investments. Although there is no ideal profile for all firms, information-intensive industries (e.g., finance) should have a few high-risk, high-benefit projects to ensure that they stay current with technology. Firms in non-information-intensive industries should focus on high-benefit, low-risk projects.

FIGURE 14.3 A SYSTEM PORTFOLIO

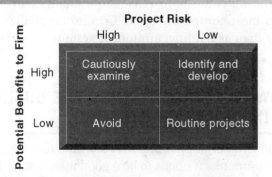

Companies should examine their portfolio of projects in terms of potential benefits and likely risks. Certain kinds of projects should be avoided altogether and others developed rapidly. There is no ideal mix. Companies in different industries have different profiles.

Most desirable, of course, are systems with high benefit and low risk. These promise early returns and low risks. Second, high-benefit, high-risk systems should be examined; low-benefit, high-risk systems should be totally avoided; and low-benefit, low-risk systems should be reexamined for the possibility of rebuilding and replacing them with more desirable systems having higher benefits. By using portfolio analysis, management can determine the optimal mix of investment risk and reward for their firms, balancing riskier high-reward projects with safer lower-reward ones. Firms where portfolio analysis is aligned with business strategy have been found to have a superior return on their IT assets, better alignment of IT investments with business objectives, and better organization-wide coordination of IT investments (Jeffrey and Leliveld, 2004).

SCORING MODELS

A **scoring model** is useful for selecting projects where many criteria must be considered. It assigns weights to various features of a system and then calculates the weighted totals. Using Table 14.2, the firm must decide among two alternative enterprise resource planning (ERP) systems. The first column lists the criteria that decision makers will use to evaluate the systems. These criteria are usually the result of lengthy discussions among the decision-making group. Often the most important outcome of a scoring model is not the score but agreement on the criteria used to judge a system.

Table 14.2 shows that this particular company attaches the most importance to capabilities for sales order processing, inventory management, and warehousing. The second column in Table 14.2 lists the weights that decision makers attached to the decision criteria. Columns 3 and 5 show the percentage of requirements for each function that each alternative ERP system can provide. Each vendor's score can be calculated by multiplying the percentage of requirements met for each function by the weight attached to that function. ERP System B has the highest total score.

As with all "objective" techniques, there are many qualitative judgments involved in using the scoring model. This model requires experts who understand the issues and the technology. It is appropriate to cycle through the scoring model several times, changing the criteria and weights, to see how sensitive the outcome is to reasonable changes in criteria. Scoring models are used most commonly to confirm, to rationalize, and to support decisions, rather than as the final arbiters of system selection.

14.3 HOW CAN FIRMS ASSESS THE BUSINESS VALUE OF INFORMATION SYSTEMS?

Even if a system project supports a firm's strategic goals and meets user information requirements, it needs to be a good investment for the firm. The value of systems from a financial perspective essentially revolves around the issue of return on invested capital. Does a particular information system investment produce sufficient returns to justify its costs?

TABLE 14.2 EXAMPLE OF A SCORING MODEL FOR AN ERP SYSTEM

CRITERIA	WEIGHT	ERP SYSTEM A %	ERP SYSTEM A SCORE	ERP SYSTEM B %	ERP SYSTEM B SCORE
1.0 Order Processing					
1.1 Online order entry	4	67	268	73	292
1.2 Online pricing	4	81	324	87	348
1.3 Inventory check	4	72	288	81	324
1.4 Customer credit check	3	66	198	59	177
1.5 Invoicing	4	73	292	82	328
Total Order Processing			1,370		1,469
2.0 Inventory Management					
2.1 Production forecasting	3	72	216	76	228
2.2 Production planning	4	79	316	81	324
2.3 Inventory control	4	68	272	80	320
2.4 Reports	3	71	213	69	207
Total Inventory Management			1,017		1,079
3.0 Warehousing					
3.1 Receiving	2	71	142	75	150
3.2 Picking/packing	3	77	231	82	246
3.3 Shipping	4	92	368	89	356
Total Warehousing			741		752
Grand Total			3,128		3,300

INFORMATION SYSTEM COSTS AND BENEFITS

Table 14.3 lists some of the more common costs and benefits of systems. **Tangible benefits** can be quantified and assigned a monetary value. **Intangible benefits**, such as more efficient customer service or enhanced decision making, cannot be immediately quantified but may lead to quantifiable gains in the long run. Transaction and clerical systems that displace labor and save space always produce more measurable, tangible benefits than management information systems, decision-support systems, and computer-supported collaborative work systems (see Chapters 2 and 11).

Chapter 5 introduced the concept of total cost of ownership (TCO), which is designed to identify and measure the components of information technology expenditures beyond the initial cost of purchasing and installing hardware and software. However, TCO analysis provides only part of the information needed to evaluate an information technology investment because

TABLE 14.3 COSTS AND BENEFITS OF INFORMATION SYSTEMS

COSTS

Hardware
Telecommunications
Software
Services
Personnel

TANGIBLE BENEFITS (COST SAVINGS)

Increased productivity

Lower operational costs

Reduced workforce

Lower computer expenses

Lower outside vendor costs

Lower clerical and professional costs

Reduced rate of growth in expenses

Reduced facility costs

INTANGIBLE BENEFITS

Improved asset utilization
Improved resource control
Improved organizational planning
Increased organizational flexibility
More timely information
More information
Increased organizational learning
Legal requirements attained
Enhanced employee goodwill
Increased job satisfaction
Improved decision making
Improved operations
Higher client satisfaction
Better corporate image

it does not typically deal with benefits, cost categories such as complexity costs, and "soft" and strategic factors discussed later in this section.

Capital Budgeting for Information Systems

To determine the benefits of a particular project, you'll need to calculate all of its costs and all of its benefits. Obviously, a project where costs exceed benefits should be rejected. But even if the benefits outweigh the costs, additional financial analysis is required to determine whether the project represents a good return on the firm's invested capital. **Capital budgeting** models are one of several techniques used to measure the value of investing in long-term capital investment projects.

Capital budgeting methods rely on measures of cash flows into and out of the firm; capital projects generate those cash flows. The investment cost for information systems projects is an immediate cash outflow caused by expenditures for hardware, software, and labor. In subsequent years, the investment may cause additional cash outflows that will be balanced by cash inflows resulting from the investment. Cash inflows take the form of increased sales of more products (for reasons such as new products, higher quality, or increasing market share) or reduced costs in production and operations. The difference between cash outflows and cash inflows is used for calculating the financial worth of an investment. Once the cash flows have been established, several alternative methods are available for comparing different projects and deciding about the investment.

The principal capital budgeting models for evaluating IT projects are: the payback method, the accounting rate of return on investment (ROI), net present value, and the internal rate of return (IRR). You can find out more about how these capital budgeting models are used to justify information system investments in the Learning Tracks for this chapter.

REAL OPTIONS PRICING MODELS

Some information systems projects are highly uncertain, especially investments in IT infrastructure. Their future revenue streams are unclear and their up-front costs are high. Suppose, for instance, that a firm is considering a $20 million investment to upgrade its IT infrastructure—its hardware, software, data management tools, and networking technology. If this upgraded infrastructure were available, the organization would have the technology capabilities to respond more easily to future problems and opportunities. Although the costs of this investment can be calculated, not all of the benefits of making this investment can be established in advance. But if the firm waits a few years until the revenue potential becomes more obvious, it might be too late to make the infrastructure investment. In such cases, managers might benefit from using real options pricing models to evaluate information technology investments.

Real options pricing models (ROPMs) use the concept of options valuation borrowed from the financial industry. An *option* is essentially the right, but not the obligation, to act at some future date. A typical *call option*, for instance, is a financial option in which a person buys the right (but not the obligation) to purchase an underlying asset (usually a stock) at a fixed price (strike price) on or before a given date.

For instance, let's assume that on September 19, 2014, you could purchase a call option for $31.00 that would give you the right to buy a share of Procter & Gamble (P&G) common stock for $50 per share on a certain date. Options expire over time, and this call option has an expiration date of January 15, 2016. If the price of P&G common stock does not rise above $50 per share by the stock market close on January 15, 2016, you would not exercise the option, and the value of the option would fall to zero on the strike date. If, however, the price of P&G stock rose to, say, $100 per share, you could purchase the stock for the strike price of $50 and retain the profit of $50 per share minus the cost on the option. (Because the option is sold as a 100-share contract, the cost of the contract would be 100 × $31.00 before commissions, or $3100, and you would be purchasing and obtaining a profit from 100 shares of Procter & Gamble.) The stock option enables the owner to benefit from the upside potential of an opportunity while limiting the downside risk.

ROPMs value information systems projects similar to stock options, where an initial expenditure on technology creates the opportunity to obtain the benefits associated with further development and deployment of the technology as long as management has the freedom to cancel, defer, restart, or expand the project. ROPMs give managers the flexibility to stage their IT investment or test the waters with small pilot projects or prototypes to gain more knowledge about the risks of a project before investing in the entire implementation. The disadvantages of this model are primarily in estimating all the key variables affecting option value, including anticipated cash flows from the underlying asset and changes in the cost of implementation. Models for determining option value of information technology platforms are being developed (Fichman, 2004; McGrath and MacMillan, 2000).

LIMITATIONS OF FINANCIAL MODELS

The traditional focus on the financial and technical aspects of an information system tends to overlook the social and organizational dimensions of information systems that may affect the true costs and benefits of the investment. Many companies' information systems investment decisions do not adequately consider costs from organizational disruptions created by a new system, such as the cost to train end users, the impact that users' learning curves for a new system have on productivity, or the time managers need to spend overseeing new system-related changes. Benefits, such as more timely decisions from a new system or enhanced employee learning and expertise, may also be overlooked in a traditional financial analysis (Ryan, Harrison, and Schkade, 2002).

14.4 WHAT ARE THE PRINCIPAL RISK FACTORS IN INFORMATION SYSTEMS PROJECTS, AND HOW CAN THEY BE MANAGED?

We have already introduced the topic of information system risks and risk assessment in Chapter 8. In this chapter, we describe the specific risks to information systems projects and show what can be done to manage them effectively.

DIMENSIONS OF PROJECT RISK

Systems differ dramatically in their size, scope, level of complexity, and organizational and technical components. Some systems development projects are more likely to create the problems we have described earlier or to suffer delays because they carry a much higher level of risk than others. The level of project risk is influenced by project size, project structure, and the level of technical expertise of the information systems staff and project team.

- *Project size.* The larger the project—as indicated by the dollars spent, the size of the implementation staff, the time allocated for implementation, and the number of organizational units affected—the greater the risk. Very large-scale systems projects have a failure rate that is 50 to 75 percent higher than that for other projects because such projects are complex and difficult to control. The organizational complexity of the system—how many units and groups use it and how much it influences business processes—contribute to the complexity of large-scale systems projects just as much as technical characteristics, such as the number of lines of program code, length of project, and budget. In addition, there are few reliable techniques for estimating the time and cost to develop large-scale information systems.

- *Project structure.* Some projects are more highly structured than others. Their requirements are clear and straightforward so outputs and processes can be easily defined. Users know exactly what they want and what the system should do; there is almost no possibility of the users changing their minds. Such projects run a much lower risk than those with relatively undefined, fluid, and constantly changing requirements; with outputs that cannot be fixed easily because they are subject to users' changing ideas; or with users who cannot agree on what they want.

- *Experience with technology.* The project risk rises if the project team and the information system staff lack the required technical expertise. If the team is unfamiliar with the hardware, system software, application software, or database management system proposed for the project, it is highly likely that the project will experience technical problems or take more time to complete because of the need to master new skills.

Although the difficulty of the technology is one risk factor in information systems projects, the other factors are primarily organizational, dealing with the complexity of information requirements, the scope of the project, and how many parts of the organization will be affected by a new information system.

CHANGE MANAGEMENT AND THE CONCEPT OF IMPLEMENTATION

The introduction or alteration of an information system has a powerful behavioral and organizational impact. Changes in the way that information is defined, accessed, and used to manage the organization's resources often lead to new distributions of authority and power. This internal organizational change breeds resistance and opposition and can lead to the demise of an otherwise good system.

A very large percentage of information systems projects stumble because the process of organizational change surrounding system building was not properly addressed. Successful system building requires careful **change management**.

The Concept of Implementation

To manage the organizational change surrounding the introduction of a new information system effectively, you must examine the process of implementation. **Implementation** refers to all organizational activities working toward the adoption, management, and routinization of an innovation, such as a new formation system. In the implementation process, the systems analyst is a **change agent**. The analyst not only develops technical solutions but also redefines the configurations, interactions, job activities, and power relationships of various organizational groups. The analyst is the catalyst for the entire change process and is responsible for ensuring that all parties involved accept the changes created by a new system. The change agent communicates with users, mediates between competing interest groups, and ensures that the organizational adjustment to such changes is complete.

The Role of End Users

System implementation generally benefits from high levels of user involvement and management support. User participation in the design and operation of information systems has several positive results. First, if users are heavily involved in systems design, they have more opportunities to mold the system according to their priorities and business requirements, and more opportunities to control the outcome. Second, they are more likely to react positively to the completed system because they have been active participants in the change process. Incorporating user knowledge and expertise leads to better solutions.

The relationship between users and information systems specialists has traditionally been a problem area for information systems implementation efforts. Users and information systems specialists tend to have different backgrounds, interests, and priorities. This is referred to as the **user-designer communications gap**. These differences lead to divergent organizational loyalties, approaches to problem solving, and vocabularies.

Information systems specialists, for example, often have a highly technical, or machine, orientation to problem solving. They look for elegant and sophisticated technical solutions in which hardware and software efficiency is optimized at the expense of ease of use or organizational effectiveness. Users prefer systems that are oriented toward solving business problems or facilitating organizational tasks. Often the orientations of both groups are so at odds that they appear to speak in different tongues.

These differences are illustrated in Table 14.4, which depicts the typical concerns of end users and technical specialists (information systems designers) regarding the development of a new information system. Communication problems between end users and designers are a major reason why user requirements are not properly incorporated into information systems and why users are driven out of the implementation process.

TABLE 14.4 THE USER DESIGNER COMMUNICATIONS GAP

USER CONCERNS	DESIGNER CONCERNS
Will the system deliver the information we need for our work?	What demands will this system put on our servers?
Can we access the data on our iPhones, BlackBerrys, tablets, and PCs?	What kind of programming demands will this place on our group?
What new procedures do we need to enter data into the system?	Where will the data be stored? What's the most efficient way to store them?
How will the operation of the system change employees' daily routines?	What technologies should we use to secure the data?

Systems development projects run a very high risk of failure when there is a pronounced gap between users and technical specialists and when these groups continue to pursue different goals. Under such conditions, users are often driven away from the project. Because they cannot comprehend what the technicians are saying, users conclude that the entire project is best left in the hands of the information specialists alone.

Management Support and Commitment

If an information systems project has the backing and commitment of management at various levels, it is more likely to be perceived positively by both users and the technical information services staff. Both groups will believe that their participation in the development process will receive higher-level attention and priority. They will be recognized and rewarded for the time and effort they devote to implementation. Management backing also ensures that a systems project receives sufficient funding and resources to be successful. Furthermore, to be enforced effectively, all the changes in work habits and procedures and any organizational realignments associated with a new system depend on management backing. If a manager considers a new system a priority, the system will more likely be treated that way by his or her subordinates.

Change Management Challenges for Business Process Reengineering, Enterprise Applications, and Mergers and Acquisitions

Given the challenges of innovation and implementation, it is not surprising to find a very high failure rate among enterprise application and business process reengineering (BPR) projects, which typically require extensive organizational change and which may require replacing old technologies and legacy systems that are deeply rooted in many interrelated business processes. A number of studies have indicated that 70 percent of all business process reengineering projects fail to deliver promised benefits. Likewise, a high percentage of enterprise applications fail to be fully implemented or to meet the goals of their users even after three years of work.

Many enterprise application and reengineering projects have been undermined by poor implementation and change management practices that failed to address employees' concerns about change. Dealing with fear and anxiety throughout the organization, overcoming resistance by key managers, and changing job functions, career paths, and recruitment practices have posed greater threats to reengineering than the difficulties companies faced visualizing and designing breakthrough changes to business processes. All of the enterprise applications require tighter coordination among different functional groups as well as extensive business process change (see Chapter 9).

Projects related to mergers and acquisitions have a similar failure rate. Mergers and acquisitions are deeply affected by the organizational characteristics of the merging companies as well as by their IT infrastructures. Combining the information systems of two different companies usually requires considerable organizational change and complex systems projects to manage. If the integration is not properly managed, firms can emerge with a tangled hodgepodge of inherited legacy systems built by aggregating the systems of one firm after another. Without a successful systems integration, the benefits anticipated from the merger cannot be realized, or, worse, the merged entity cannot execute its business processes effectively.

CONTROLLING RISK FACTORS

Various project management, requirements gathering, and planning methodologies have been developed for specific categories of implementation problems. Strategies have also been devised for ensuring that users play appropriate roles throughout the implementation period and for managing the organizational change process. Not all aspects of the implementation process can be easily controlled or planned. However, anticipating potential implementation problems and applying appropriate corrective strategies can increase the chances for system success.

The first step in managing project risk involves identifying the nature and level of risk confronting the project (Schmidt et al., 2001). Implementers can then handle each project with the tools and risk management approaches geared to its level of risk (Iversen, Mathiassen, and Nielsen, 2004; Barki, Rivard, and Talbot, 2001; McFarlan, 1981).

Managing Technical Complexity

Projects with challenging and complex technology for users to master benefit from **internal integration tools**. The success of such projects depends on how well their technical complexity can be managed. Project leaders need both heavy technical and administrative experience. They must be able to anticipate problems and develop smooth working relationships among a predominantly technical team. The team should be under the leadership of a manager with a strong technical and project management background, and team members should be highly experienced. Team meetings should take place frequently. Essential technical skills or expertise not available internally should be secured from outside the organization.

Formal Planning and Control Tools

Large projects benefit from appropriate use of **formal planning tools** and **formal control tools** for documenting and monitoring project plans. The two most commonly used methods for documenting project plans are Gantt charts and PERT charts. A **Gantt chart** lists project activities and their corresponding start and completion dates. The Gantt chart visually represents the timing and duration of different tasks in a development project as well as their human resource requirements (see Figure 14.4). It shows each task as a horizontal bar whose length is proportional to the time required to complete it.

Although Gantt charts show when project activities begin and end, they don't depict task dependencies, how one task is affected if another is behind schedule, or how tasks should be ordered. That is where **PERT charts** are useful. PERT stands for Program Evaluation and Review Technique, a methodology developed by the U.S. Navy during the 1950s to manage the Polaris submarine missile program. A PERT chart graphically depicts project tasks and their interrelationships. The PERT chart lists the specific activities that make up a project and the activities that must be completed before a specific activity can start, as illustrated in Figure 14.5.

The PERT chart portrays a project as a network diagram consisting of numbered nodes (either circles or rectangles) representing project tasks. Each node is numbered and shows the task, its duration, the starting date, and the completion date. The direction of the arrows on the lines indicates the sequence of tasks and shows which activities must be completed before the commencement of another activity. In Figure 14.5, the tasks in nodes 2, 3, and 4 are not dependent on each other and can be undertaken simultaneously, but each is dependent on completion of the first task. PERT charts for complex projects can be difficult to interpret, and project managers often use both techniques.

These project management techniques can help managers identify bottlenecks and determine the impact that problems will have on project completion times. They can also help systems developers partition projects into smaller, more manageable segments with defined, measurable business results. Standard control techniques can successfully chart the progress of the project against budgets and target dates, so deviations from the plan can be spotted.

Increasing User Involvement and Overcoming User Resistance

Projects with relatively little structure and many undefined requirements must involve users fully at all stages. Users must be mobilized to support one of many possible design options and to remain committed to a single design. **External integration tools** consist of ways to link the work of the implementation team to users at all organizational levels. For instance, users can become active members of the project team, take on leadership roles, and take charge of installation and training. The implementation team can demonstrate its responsiveness to users, promptly answering questions, incorporating user feedback, and showing their willingness to help.

Participation in implementation activities may not be enough to overcome the problem of user resistance to organizational change. Different users may be affected by the system in different ways. Whereas some users may welcome a new system because it brings changes they perceive as beneficial to

FIGURE 14.4 A GANTT CHART

HRIS COMBINED PLAN–HR	Da	Who
DATA ADMINISTRATION SECURITY		
QMF security review/setup	20	EF TP
Security orientation	2	EF JA
QMF security maintenance	35	TP GL
Data entry sec. profiles	4	EF TP
Data entry sec. views est.	12	EF TP
Data entry security profiles	65	EF TP
DATA DICTIONARY		
Orientation sessions	1	EF
Data dictionary design	32	EFWV
DD prod. coordn-query	20	GL
DD prod. coordn-live	40	EF GL
Data dictionary cleanup	35	EF GL
Data dictionary maint.	35	EF GL
PROCEDURES REVISION DESIGN PREP		
Work flows (old)	10	PK JL
Payroll data flows	31	JL PK
HRIS P/R model	11	PK JL
P/R interface orient. mtg.	6	PK JL
P/R interface coordn. 1	15	PK
P/R interface coordn. 2	8	PK
Benefits interfaces (old)	5	JL
Benefits interfaces (new flow)	8	JL
Benefits communication strategy	3	PK JL
New work flow model	15	PK JL
Posn. data entry flows	14	WV JL

RESOURCE SUMMARY

Name		Code	2014 Oct	Nov	Dec	2015 Jan	Feb	Mar	Apr	May	Jun	Jul	Aug	Sep	Oct	Nov	Dec	2016 Jan	Feb	Mar
Edith Farrell	5.0	EF	2	21	24	24	23	22	22	27	34	34	29	26	28	19	14			
Woody Vinton	5.0	WV	5	17	20	19	12	10	14	10	2							4	3	
Charles Pierce	5.0	CP		5	11	20	13	9	10	7	6	8	4	4	4	4	4			
Ted Leurs	5.0	TL		12	17	17	19	17	14	12	15	16	2	1	1	1	1			
Toni Cox	5.0	TC	1	11	10	11	11	12	19	19	21	21	21	17	17	12	9			
Patricia Knopp	5.0	PC	7	23	30	34	27	25	15	24	25	16	11	13	17	10	3	3	2	
Jane Lawton	5.0	JL	1	9	16	21	19	21	21	20	17	15	14	12	14	8	5			
David Holloway	5.0	DH	4	4	5	5	5	2	7	5	4	16	2							
Diane O'Neill	5.0	DO	6	14	17	16	13	11	9	4										
Joan Albert	5.0	JA	5	6			7	6	2	1				5	5	1				
Marie Marcus	5.0	MM	15	7	2	1	1													
Don Stevens	5.0	DS	4	4	5	4	5	1												
Casual	5.0	CASL		3	4	3			4	7	9	5	3	2						
Kathy Mendez	5.0	KM		1	5	16	20	19	22	19	20	18	20	11	2					
Anna Borden	5.0	AB					9	10	16	15	11	12	19	10	7	1				
Gail Loring	5.0	GL		3	6	5	9	10	17	18	17	10	13	10	10	7	17			
UNASSIGNED	0.0	X												9	236	225	230	14	13	
Co-op	5.0	CO		6	4			2	3	4	4	2	4	16				216	178	
Casual	5.0	CAUL									3	3	3							
TOTAL DAYS			49	147	176	196	194	174	193	195	190	181	140	125	358	288	284	237	196	12

The Gantt chart in this figure shows the task, person-days, and initials of each responsible person, as well as the start and finish dates for each task. The resource summary provides a good manager with the total person-days for each month and for each person working on the project to manage the project successfully. The project described here is a data administration project.

FIGURE 14.5 A PERT CHART

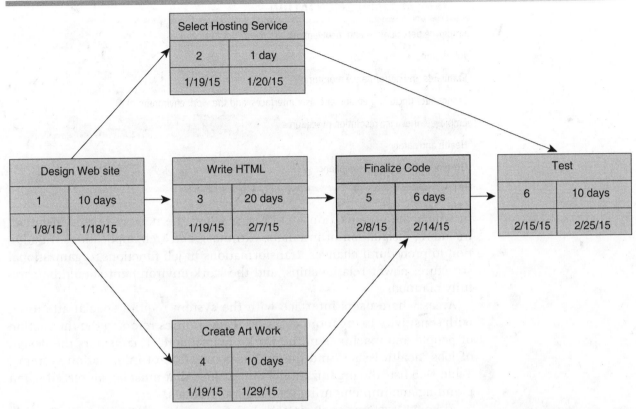

This is a simplified PERT chart for creating a small Web site. It shows the ordering of project tasks and the relationship of a task with preceding and succeeding tasks.

them, others may resist these changes because they believe the shifts are detrimental to their interests.

If the use of a system is voluntary, users may choose to avoid it; if use is mandatory, resistance will take the form of increased error rates, disruptions, turnover, and even sabotage. Therefore, the implementation strategy must not only encourage user participation and involvement, but it must also address the issue of counterimplementation. **Counterimplementation** is a deliberate strategy to thwart the implementation of an information system or an innovation in an organization.

Strategies to overcome user resistance include user participation (to elicit commitment as well as to improve design), user education and training, management edicts and policies, and better incentives for users who cooperate. The new system can be made more user friendly by improving the end-user interface. Users will be more cooperative if organizational problems are solved prior to introducing the new system.

DESIGNING FOR THE ORGANIZATION

Because the purpose of a new system is to improve the organization's performance, information systems projects must explicitly address the ways

TABLE 14.5 ORGANIZATIONAL FACTORS IN SYSTEMS PLANNING AND IMPLEMENTATION

Employee participation and involvement
Job design
Standards and performance monitoring
Ergonomics (including equipment, user interfaces, and the work environment)
Employee grievance resolution procedures
Health and safety
Government regulatory compliance

in which the organization will change when the new system is installed, including installation of intranets, extranets, and Web applications. In addition to procedural changes, transformations in job functions, organizational structure, power relationships, and the work environment should be carefully planned.

Areas where users interface with the system require special attention, with sensitivity to ergonomics issues. **Ergonomics** refers to the interaction of people and machines in the work environment. It considers the design of jobs, health issues, and the end-user interface of information systems. Table 14.5 lists the organizational dimensions that must be addressed when planning and implementing information systems.

Although systems analysis and design activities are supposed to include an organizational impact analysis, this area has traditionally been neglected. An **organizational impact analysis** explains how a proposed system will affect organizational structure, attitudes, decision making, and operations. To integrate information systems successfully with the organization, thorough and fully documented organizational impact assessments must be given more attention in the development effort.

Sociotechnical Design

One way of addressing human and organizational issues is to incorporate **sociotechnical design** practices into information systems projects. Designers set forth separate sets of technical and social design solutions. The social design plans explore different workgroup structures, allocation of tasks, and the design of individual jobs. The proposed technical solutions are compared with the proposed social solutions. The solution that best meets both social and technical objectives is selected for the final design. The resulting sociotechnical design is expected to produce an information system that blends technical efficiency with sensitivity to organizational and human needs, leading to higher job satisfaction and productivity.

PROJECT MANAGEMENT SOFTWARE TOOLS

Commercial software tools that automate many aspects of project management facilitate the project management process. Project management software typically features capabilities for defining and ordering tasks, assigning resources to tasks, establishing starting and ending dates to tasks, tracking progress, and facilitating modifications to tasks and resources. Many automate the creation of Gantt and PERT charts.

Some of these tools are large sophisticated programs for managing very large projects, dispersed work groups, and enterprise functions. These high-end tools can manage very large numbers of tasks and activities and complex relationships.

Microsoft Project has become the most widely used project management software today. It is PC-based, with capabilities for producing PERT and Gantt charts and for supporting critical path analysis, resource allocation, project tracking, and status reporting. Project also tracks the way changes in one aspect of a project affect others. Products such as Easy Projects and Vertabase are useful for firms that want Web-based project management tools.

Going forward, delivery of project management software as a software service (SaaS) will make this technology accessible to more organizations, especially smaller ones. Open source versions of project management software such as Open Workbench and OpenProj will further reduce the total cost of ownership and attract new users. Thanks to the popularity of social media such as Facebook and Twitter, project management software is also likely to become more flexible, collaborative, and user-friendly.

While project management software helps organizations track individual projects, the resources allocated to them, and their costs, **project portfolio management software** helps organizations manage portfolios of projects and dependencies among them. Project portfolio management software helps managers compare proposals and projects against budgets and resource capacity levels to determine the optimal mix and sequencing of projects that best achieves the organization's strategic goals.

Review Summary

1. *What are the objectives of project management and why is it so essential in developing information systems?*
   Good project management is essential for ensuring that systems are delivered on time, on budget, and provide genuine business benefits. Project management activities include planning the work, assessing the risk, estimating and acquiring resources required to accomplish the work, organizing the work, directing execution, and analyzing the results. Project management must deal with five major variables: scope, time, cost, quality, and risk.

2. *What methods can be used for selecting and evaluating information systems projects and aligning them with the firm's business goals?*
   Organizations need an information systems plan that describes how information technology supports the attainment of their business goals and documents all their system applications and IT infrastructure components. Large corporations will have a management structure to ensure the most important systems projects receive priority. Key performance indicators, portfolio analysis, and scoring models can be used to identify and evaluate alternative information systems projects.

3. *How can firms assess the business value of information systems projects?*
   To determine whether an information systems project is a good investment, one must calculate its costs and benefits. Tangible benefits are quantifiable, and intangible benefits that cannot be immediately

quantified may provide quantifiable benefits, in the future. Benefits that exceed costs should be analyzed using capital budgeting methods to make sure a project represents a good return on the firm's invested capital. Real options pricing models, which apply the same techniques for valuing financial options to systems investments, can be useful when considering highly uncertain IT investments.

4. *What are the principal risk factors in information systems projects, and how can they be managed?*

The level of risk in a systems development project is determined by (1) project size, (2) project structure, and (3) experience with technology. IS projects are more likely to fail when there is insufficient or improper user participation in the systems development process, lack of management support, and poor management of the implementation process. There is a very high failure rate among projects involving business process reengineering, enterprise applications, and mergers and acquisitions because they require extensive organizational change.

Implementation refers to the entire process of organizational change surrounding the introduction of a new information system. User support and involvement and management support and control of the implementation process are essential, as are mechanisms for dealing with the level of risk in each new systems project. Project risk factors can be brought under some control by a contingency approach to project management. The risk level of each project determines the appropriate mix of external integration tools, internal integration tools, formal planning tools, and formal control tools to be applied.

Key Terms

Capital budgeting, 592
Change agent, 596
Change management, 596
Counterimplementation, 601
Ergonomics, 602
External integration tools, 599
Formal control tools, 598
Formal planning tools, 598
Gantt chart, 599
Implementation, 596
Information systems plan, 587
Intangible benefits, 591
Internal integration tools, 598
Key performance indicators (KPIs), 587

Organizational impact analysis, 602
PERT chart, 599
Portfolio analysis, 589
Project, 584
Project management, 584
Project portfolio management, 603
Real options pricing models (ROPMs), 593
Scope, 585
Scoring model, 590
Sociotechnical design, 602
Tangible benefits, 591
User-designer communications gap, 596
User interface, 582

Review Questions

14-1 What are the objectives of project management and why is it so essential in developing information systems?

- Describe information system problems resulting from poor project management.

- Define project management. List and describe the project management activities and variables addressed by project management.

14-2 What methods can be used for selecting and evaluating information systems projects and aligning them with the firm's business goals?

- Name and describe the groups responsible for the management of information systems projects.

- Describe the purpose of an information systems plan and list the major categories in the plan.

- Explain how key performance indicators, portfolio analysis, and scoring models can be used to select information systems projects.

14-3 How can firms assess the business value of information systems projects?

- List and describe the major costs and benefits of information systems.

- Distinguish between tangible and intangible benefits.

- Explain how real options pricing models can help manages evaluate information technology investments.

14-4 What are the principal risk factors in information systems projects, and how can they be managed?

- Identify and describe each of the principal risk factors in information systems projects.
- Explain why builders of new information systems need to address implementation and change management.
- Explain why eliciting support of management and end users is so essential for successful implementation of information systems projects.

- Explain why there is such a high failure rate for implementations involving enterprise applications, business process reengineering, and mergers and acquisitions.
- Identify and describe the strategies for controlling project risk.
- Identify the organizational considerations that should be addressed by project planning and implementation.
- Explain how project management software tools contribute to successful project management.

Discussion Questions

14-5 How much does project management impact the success of a new information system?

14-6 It has been said that most systems fail because systems builders ignore organizational behavior problems. Why might this be so?

14-7 What is the role of end users in information systems project management?

Hands-On MIS Projects

The projects in this section give you hands-on experience evaluating information systems projects, using spreadsheet software to perform capital budgeting analyses for new information systems investments, and using Web tools to analyze the financing for a new home.

Management Decision Problems

14-8 The U.S. Census launched an IT project to arm its census takers in the field with high-tech handheld devices that would save taxpayer money by directly beaming population data to headquarters from census takers in the field. Census officials signed a $600 million contract with Harris Corporation in 2006 to build 500,000 devices, but still weren't sure which features they wanted included in the units. Census officials did not specify the testing process to measure the performance of the handheld devices. As the project progressed, 400 change requests to project requirements were added. Two years and hundreds of millions of taxpayer dollars later, the handhelds were far too slow and unreliable to be used for the 2010 U.S. census. What could Census Bureau management and the Harris Corporation have done to prevent this outcome?

14-9 Caterpillar is the world's leading maker of earth-moving machinery and supplier of agricultural equipment. Caterpillar wants to end its support for its Dealer Business System (DBS), which it licenses to its dealers to help them run their businesses. The software in this system is becoming outdated, and senior management wants to transfer support for the hosted version of the software to Accenture Consultants so it can concentrate on its core business. Caterpillar never required its dealers to use DBS, but the system had become a de facto standard for doing business with the company. The majority of the 50 Cat dealers in North America use some version of DBS, as do about half of the 200 or so Cat dealers in the rest of the world. Before Caterpillar turns the product over to Accenture, what factors and issues should it consider? What questions should it ask? What questions should its dealers ask?

Improving Decision Making: Using Web Tools for Buying and Financing a Home

Software skills: Internet-based software
Business skills: Financial planning

14-10 This project will develop your skills using Web-based software for searching for a home and calculating mortgage financing for that home.

You would like to purchase a home in Fort Collins, Colorado. Ideally, it should be a single-family house with at least three bedrooms and one bathroom that costs between $150,000 and $225,000 and finance it with a 30-year fixed rate mortgage. You can afford a down payment that is 20 percent of the value of the house. Before you purchase a house, you would like to find out what homes are available in your price range, find a mortgage, and determine the amount of your monthly payment. Use the Yahoo! Homes site to help you with the following tasks:

- Locate homes in Fort Collins, Colorado, that meet your specifications.
- Find a mortgage for 80 percent of the list price of the home. Compare rates from at least three sites
  (use search engines to find sites other than Yahoo).
- After selecting a mortgage, calculate your closing costs and the monthly payment.

When you are finished, evaluate the whole process. For example, assess the ease of use of the site and your ability to find information about houses and mortgages, the accuracy of the information you found, and the breadth of choice of homes and mortgages.

A Shaky Start for Healthcare.Gov
CASE STUDY

The administration of President Barack Obama has made Patient Protection and Affordable Care Act, often called "Obamacare", its chief domestic accomplishment and the centerpiece of Obama's legacy. Essential to Obama's health care reform plan is Healthcare.gov, a health insurance exchange Web site that facilitates the sale of private health insurance plans to U.S. residents, assists people eligible to sign up for Medicaid, and has a separate marketplace for small businesses.

The site allows users to compare prices on health insurance plans in their states, to enroll in a plan they choose, and to find out if they qualify for government health care subsidies. Users must sign up and create their own specific account first, providing some personal information, in order to receive detailed information about available health care plans in their area.

Healthcare.gov was launched on October 1, 2013, as promised, but visitors quickly encountered numerous technical problems. Software that assigned digital identities to enrollees and ensured that they saw only their own personal data was overwhelmed. Customers encountered cryptic error messages and could not log in to create accounts. There was insufficient computing capacity in the Herndon, Virginia, data center housing the system for the site. Many users received quotes that were incorrect because the feature used prices based on just two age groups.

It was estimated that only 1 percent of interested consumers were able to enroll through the site for the first week of operations, and many applications sent to insurers contained erroneous information. Thousands of enrollees for HealthCare.gov—at least one in five at the height of the problems—received inaccurate assignments to Medicaid or to private health plans. Some people were wrongly denied coverage.

Insurers received enrollment files from the federal exchange that were incomplete or inaccurate—as many as one in ten. The information includes who is enrolling and what subsidies they may receive. Some insurers reported being deluged with phone calls from people who believe they have signed up for a particular health plan, only to find that the company has no record of the enrollment. Enrollment problems with insurers persisted into November.

U.S. chief technology officer Todd Park stated on October 6 that Healthcare.gov's glitches were caused by an unexpectedly high volume of users. About 50,000–60,000 had been expected, but the site had to handle 250,000 simultaneous users. Over 8.1 million people visited Healthcare.gov between October 1 and October, 2013.

White House officials later admitted that Healthcare.gov's problems were not just caused by high traffic volume but also by software and system design issues. Stress tests performed by contractors a day before the launch date revealed the site slowed substantially with only 1,100 simultaneous users, far fewer than the 50,000–60,000 that were anticipated. Technical experts found out that the site was riddled with hardware and software defects, amounting to more than 600 items that needed to be fixed.

A major contributor to these problems was the part of the system's design that requires users to create individual accounts before shopping for health insurance. This means that before users can shop for coverage, they must input personal data that are exchanged among separate computer systems built or run by multiple vendors, including CGI Group, developer of healthcare.gov, Quality Software Services, and credit-checker Experian PLC. If any part of this web of systems fails to work properly, users will be blocked from entering the exchange marketplace. A bottleneck had been created where these systems interacted with a software component called Oracle Identity Manager

supplied by Oracle Corporation that was embedded in the government's identity-checking system. Quality Software Services had subcontracted with Oracle for this part of the system. This problem might have been averted if the system allowed users to browse plans without first going through the complex registration process.

Problems persisted into the third week of operations, including pull-down menus that only worked intermittently and excruciatingly long wait times. For some weeks in October, the site was down 60 percent of the time.

What happened to Healthcare.gov is another example of IT project management gone awry, which often happens with large technology projects, especially those for the U.S. federal government. There was no single leader overseeing the Healthcare.gov implementation. The U.S. Centers for Medicare and Medicaid Services (CMS) coordinated the development effort. However, CMS had a siloed management structure, and no single unit was designated to take charge of the entire project.

CMS parceled out the work for building and implementing the Healthcare.gov system to a number of different outside contractors. The front end of the Web site (including the user interface) was developed by the startup Development Seed. The back end (where all the heavy-duty processing of enrollment data and transactions with insurers takes place) was contracted to CGI Federal, a subsidiary of the Canadian multinational CGI Group, which received $231 million for the project. CGI then subcontracted much of its work to other companies. This is common in large government projects. Functions relating to digital identity authentication were contracted to Experian, the global information services company noted for its credit-checking expertise.

CMS set deadlines for the contractors, who were expected to attend meetings to hammer out the details of the specifications for the Web site. But the computer specialists skipped some of those sessions. Relations between CMS and its primary contractor CGI Federal had deteriorated in the months prior to the Healthcare.gov launch. Contractors for different parts of the system barely communicated with each other.

Some IT experts also criticized CMS's decision to use database software from a company called MarkLogic, which handles data management differently from more mainstream database management systems from companies such as IBM and Oracle. Work proceeded more slowly because so few people were familiar with MarkLogic, and MarkLogic continued to perform below expectations after the Healthcare.gov Web site was launched.

The Web site had not been thoroughly tested before it went live, so a number of software and hardware defects had not been detected. Testing of the system by insurers had been scheduled for July but didn't begin until the third week in September.CMS was responsible for testing the system during the final weeks, not its software developers. Usually software developers handle the portion of the testing for identifying remaining problems before users see the final product.

Fixing the account creation software exposed other problems. As few as 500 users could cripple the system.

Technology experts also faulted Healthcare.gov's developers for trying to go live with all parts of a large and very complex system all at once. It would have been better to roll out system functions gradually. CGI believed that a full-function Healthcare.gov with all the anticipated bells and whistles was an unrealistic target. Given the time required to complete and test the software, it was impossible to launch a full-function exchange by Oct. 1. But government officials insisted that Oct. 1 was not negotiable and had become impatient with CGI's pattern of excuses for missed deadlines. The Obama administration kept on modifying regulations and policies until the summer of 2013, which meant that contractors had to deal with changing requirements.

The Healthcare.gov enrollment system is very complex. It connects to other federal computer networks, including SSA, IRS, VA, Office of Personnel Management, and the Peace Corps. It has to verify a considerable amount of personal information, including income and immigration status.

Vital components were never secured. There was insufficient access to a data center to prevent the Web site from crashing. No backup system for a Web site crash was created. The interaction between the data center where the information is stored and the system was so poorly configured that it had to be redesigned.

CMS had several warnings between March and July that the project was going off-track, but didn't seek deep White House involvement or change the leadership structure, according to officials, congressional aides and e-mails from the period. An administration report noted that inadequate management oversight and coordination among technical teams prevented real-time decision making and efficient responses to address the issues with the site. The House Energy and Commerce Committee, which had been investigating Healthcare.gov, found no evidence of extensive communication between CMS and the White House even in July, when CMS technology official Henry Chao expressed serious concern about the project.

In March, a White House Web site that tracks the status of major government technology projects labeled the project high risk. Officials attributed the downgrade to a lag in submitting information, and the project's status was upgraded the following month. The consulting firm McKinsey & Co. detailed the project's potential risks in a presentation between March 28 and April 8 to the top CMS official, Marilyn Tavenner, to Health and Human Services Secretary Kathleen Sebelius, and to White House Chief Technology Officer Todd Park.

The McKinsey report anticipated many of the site's pitfalls and urged the administration to name a single project leader to streamline decision-making. It also emphasized the importance of White House support for CMS to meet the Oct. 1 launch date. But according to documents from the period and officials, the White House's minimal involvement in the project's details didn't change after the McKinsey report.

By July, CMS officials were growing alarmed about the project's status, including a shortage of staff to address the ever-mounting list of problems. They brought more personnel on board while bickering with contractors over the distribution of resources. But the depth of the website's difficulties still didn't become apparent until weeks after the Oct. 1 launch.

The White House assembled experts from government and industry who worked frantically to fix the system. The Obama administration appointed contractor Quality Software Services Inc. (QSSI) to coordinate the work involved in fixing the Web site. QSSI had worked earlier on the Web site's back-end. Former deputy director of the Office of Management and Budget Jeffrey Zients was appointed to act as the adviser to CMS. In January 2014, Accenture replaced CGI Group as the Web site's lead contractor.

Work on fixing the Web site continued through October and November 2013, and the Web site appeared to be working more smoothly. For the vast majority of users, Healthcare.gov was working more than 90 percent of the time. Response time (the time required for a Web page to load) was reduced from 8 seconds to less than one. The incidence of error messages preventing people from using the site went from 6 percent down to .75 percent. But on November 13, the Obama administration revealed that less than 27,000 people had signed up for private health insurance using Healthcare.gov. Only 137,000 people had done so by November 30. These enrollment numbers were well below what the government had forecast. Healthcare.gov also forced the Obama administration to delay by one year an online exchange for small business.

A spokeswoman for the Centers for Medicare and Medicaid Services said on Nov. 19 that the government had fixed "two-thirds of the high-priority bugs" that were responsible for inaccuracies in enrollment data. Mr. Chao said the government was still working on "back office systems," including those needed to pay insurance companies.

Reuters reported in mid-October 2013, that the total cost of building Healthcare.gov using contractors had tripled from an initial estimate of $93.7 million to about $292 million. Overall cost for building the Web site reached $500 million by October 2013.

By early 2014, Healthcare.gov was working much better, but was not problem-free. The Healthcare.gov site went down shortly after midnight March 30, 2014 and remained unusable until about 7:45 a.m. the following morning. It then experienced another problem around noon that same day that prevented new users from creating accounts, while some people who already had accounts were unable to log in. Some of the hundreds of thousands of Americans trying to sign up for health care at the last minute of the enrollment period were unable to do so. Obama administration officials nevertheless remained confident that they would reach their initial target of seven million health insurance signups by the March 31, 2014 deadline.

On July 30, 2014 the U.S. Government Accountability Office (GAO) released a non-partisan study finding that the Healthcare.gov Web site was developed without effective planning or oversight practices. Kathleen Sibelius resigned as Secretary for Health and Human Services on April 10, 2014 and was replaced by Sylvia Mathews Burwell on June 9 of that year.

Sources: Robert Pear, "Health Website Failures Impede Signup Surge as Deadline Nears," *New York Times*, March 31, 2014; Spencer E. Ante and Louis Radnofsky,"New Technical Woes Hobble Health-Insurance Sign-Ups at Zero Hour," *Wall Street Journal*, March 31, 2014; "How HealthCare.gov Was Supposed to Work and How It Didn't," *New York Times*, December 2, 2013; Sheryl Gay Stolberg and Michael D. Shear, "Inside the Race to Rescue a Health Care Site, and Obama," *New York Times*, November 30, 2013; Gautham Nagesh, "Health Website Problems Weren't Flagged in Time," *Wall Street Journal*, December 2, 2013; Christopher Weaver and Louise Radnofsky, "Healthcare.gov's Flaws Found, Fixes Eyed," *Wall Street Journal*, October 10, 2013 and "Federal Health Site Stymied by Lack of Direction," Wall Street Journal, October 28, 2013; Christopher Weaver, "Errors Continue to Plague Government Health Site," *Wall Street Journal*, December 13, 2013; Jack Gillum and Julie Pace, "Builders of Obama's Health Website Saw Red Flags," Associated Press, October 22, 2013; "Fast Recovery for Health Care Web Site," *New York Times*, December 2, 2013;and Eric Lipton, Jan Austen, and Sharon LaFraniere, "Tension and Flaws Before Health Website Crash," *New York Times*, November 22, 2013.

CASE STUDY QUESTIONS

14-11 Why was the Healthcare.gov project so important?

14-12 Evaluate the key risk factors in this project.

14-13 Classify and describe the problems encountered by this project. What management, organization, and technology factors were responsible for these problems?

14-14 What was the economic, political, and social impact of Healthcare.gov's botched implementation?

14-15 Describe the steps that should have been taken to prevent a negative outcome in this project.

Chapter 14 References

Appan, Radha and Glenn J. Browne. "The Impact of Analyst-Induced Misinformation on the Requirements Elicitation Process." *MIS Quarterly* 36, No 1 (March 2012).

Banker, Rajiv. "Value Implications of Relative Investments in Information Technology." Department of Information Systems and Center for Digital Economy Research, University of Texas at Dallas, January 23, 2001.

Barki, Henri, Suzanne Rivard, and Jean Talbot. "An Integrative Contingency Model of Software Project Risk Management." *Journal of Management Information Systems* 17, No. 4 (Spring 2001).

Benaroch, Michel and Robert J. Kauffman. "Justifying Electronic Banking Network Expansion Using Real Options Analysis." *MIS Quarterly* 24, No. 2 (June 2000).

Benaroch, Michel. "Managing Information Technology Investment Risk: A Real Options Perspective." *Journal of Management Information Systems* 19, No. 2 (Fall 2002).

Bloch, Michael, Sen Blumberg, and Jurgen Laartz. "Delivering Large-Scale IT Projects on Time, on Budget, and on Value." McKinsey Quarterly (October 2012).

Brynjolfsson, Erik, and Lorin M. Hitt. "Information Technology and Organizational Design: Evidence from Micro Data." (January 1998).

Ditmore, Jim. "Why Do Big IT Projects Fail So Often?" *Information Week* (October 29, 2013).

Dubravka Cecez-Kecmanovic, Karlheinz Kautz, and Rebecca Abrahall, "Reframing Success and Failure of Information Systems: A Performative Perspective," *MIS Quarterly* 38, No. 2 (June 2014).

Chandrasekaran, Sriram, Sauri Gudlavalleti, and Sanjay Kaniyar. "Achieving Success in Large Complex Software Projects." McKinsey Quarterly (July 2014).

Clement, Andrew, and Peter Van den Besselaar. "A Retrospective Look at PD Projects." *Communications of the ACM* 36, No. 4 (June 1993).

De Meyer, Arnoud, Christoph H. Loch and Michael T. Pich." Managing Project Uncertainty: From Variation to Chaos." *Sloan Management Review* 43, No. 2 (Winter 2002).

Delone, William H. and Ephraim R. McLean. "The Delone and McLean Model of Information Systems Success: A Ten-Year Update. *Journal of Management Information Systems* 19, No. 4 (Spring 2003).

Fichman, Robert G. "Real Options and IT Platforms Adoption: Implications for Theory and Practice." Information Systems Research 15, No. 2 (June 2004).

Flyvbjerg, Bent and Alexander Budzier. "Why Your IT Project May Be Riskier Than You Think." *Harvard Business Review* (September 2011).

Goff, Stacy A. "The Future of IT Project Management Software." CIO (January 6, 2010).

Hitt, Lorin, D.J. Wu, and Xiaoge Zhou. "Investment in Enterprise Resource Planning: Business Impact and Productivity Measures." *Journal of Management Information Systems* 19, No. 1 (Summer 2002).

Housel, Thomas J., Omar El Sawy, Jianfang Zhong, and Waymond Rodgers. "Measuring the Return on e-Business Initiatives at the Process Level: The Knowledge Value-Added Approach." ICIS (2001).

Iversen, Jakob H., Lars Mathiassen, and Peter Axel Nielsen. "Managing Risk in Software Process Improvement: An Action Research Approach." *MIS Quarterly* 28, No. 3 (September 2004).

Jeffrey, Mark, and Ingmar Leliveld. "Best Practices in IT Portfolio Management." *MIT Sloan Management Review* 45, No. 3 (Spring 2004).

Jiang, James J., Gary Klein, Debbie Tesch, and Hong-Gee Chen. "Closing the User and Provider Service Quality Gap," *Communications of the ACM* 46, No. 2 (February 2003).

Jiang, James J. , Jamie Y.T.Chang , Houn-Gee Chen, Eric T. G. Wang, and Gary Klein, "Achieving IT Program Goals with Integrative Conflict Management." *Journal of Management Information Systems* 31, No. 1 (Summer 2014).

Jun He and William R. King. "The Role of User Participation In Information Systems Development: Implications from a Meta-Analysis." *Journal of Management Information Systems* 25, No. 1 (Summer 2008).

Keen, Peter W. "Information Systems and Organizational Change." *Communications of the ACM* 24 (January 1981).

Keil,Mark, H. Jeff Smith, Charalambos L. Iacovou and Ronald L. Thompson. "The Pitfalls of Project Status Reporting." *MIT Sloan Management Review* 55, No. 3 (Spring 2014).

Keil, Mark, Joan Mann, and Arun Rai. "Why Software Projects Escalate: An Empirical Analysis and Test of Four Theoretical Models." *MIS Quarterly* 24, No. 4 (December 2000).

Kim, Hee Woo and Atreyi Kankanhalli. "Investigating User Resistance to Information Systems Implementation: A Status Quo Bias Perspective." *MIS Quarterly* 33, No. 3 (September 2009).

Kolb, D. A., and A. L. Frohman. "An Organization Development Approach to Consulting." *Sloan Management Review* 12 (Fall 1970).

Lapointe, Liette, and Suzanne Rivard."A Multilevel Model of Resistance to Information Technology Implementation." *MIS Quarterly* 29, No. 3 (September 2005).

Laudon, Kenneth C. "CIOs Beware: Very Large Scale Systems." Center for Research on Information Systems, New York University Stern School of Business, working paper (1989).

Lee, Jong Seok , Keil, Mark and Kasi, Vijay . "The Effect of an Initial Budget and Schedule Goal on Software Project Escalation." *Journal of Management Information Systems* 29, No. 1 (Summer 2012).

Liang, Huigang, Nilesh Sharaf, Qing Hu, and Yajiong Xue. "Assimilation of Enterprise Systems: The Effect of Institutional Pressures and the Mediating Role of Top Management." *MIS Quarterly* 31, no 1 (March 2007).

Mastrogiacomo, Stefano , Missonier, Stephanie and Bonazzi, Riccardo. "Talk Before It's Too Late: Reconsidering the Role of Conversation in Information Systems Project Management." *Journal of Management Information Systems* 31, No. 1 (Summer 2014).

McCafferty, Dennis. "What Dooms IT Projects." *Baseline* (June 10, 2010).

McFarlan, F. Warren. "Portfolio Approach to Information Systems." *Harvard Business Review* (September–October 1981).

McGrath, Rita Gunther and Ian C.McMillan. "Assessing Technology Projects Using Real Options Reasoning." *Industrial Research Institute* (2000).

Mumford, Enid, and Mary Weir. *Computer Systems in Work Design*: The ETHICS Method. New York: John Wiley (1979).

Pfefferman, Mark. "App Development Strategy Cuts Costs, Ensures Compliance," Baseline (September/October 2011).

Polites, Greta L. and Elena Karahanna. "Shackled to the Status Quo: The Inhibiting Effects of Incumbent System Habit, Switching Costs, and Inertia on New System Acceptance." *MIS Quarterly* 36, No. 1 (March 2012).

Rai, Arun, Sandra S. Lang, and Robert B. Welker. "Assessing the Validity of IS Success Models: An Empirical Test and Theoretical Analysis." *Information Systems Research* 13, No. 1 (March 2002).

Rivard, Suzanne and Liette Lapointe. "Information Technology Implementers' Responses to User Resistance: Nature and Effects." *MIS Quarterly* 36, No. 3 (September 2012).

Robey, Daniel, Jeanne W. Ross, and Marie-Claude Boudreau. "Learning to Implement Enterprise Systems: An Exploratory Study of the Dialectics of Change." *Journal of Management Information Systems* 19, No. 1 (Summer 2002).

Ross, Jeanne W. and Cynthia M. Beath." Beyond the Business Case: New Approaches to IT Investment." *Sloan Management Review* 43, No. 2 (Winter 2002).

Ryan, Sherry D., David A. Harrison, and Lawrence L Schkade." Information Technology Investment Decisions: When Do Cost and Benefits in the Social Subsystem Matter?" *Journal of Management Information Systems* 19, No. 2 (Fall 2002).

Sauer, Chris, Andrew Gemino, and Blaize Horner Reich. "The Impact of Size and Volatility on IT Project Performance. "*Communications of the ACM* 50, No. 11 (November 2007).

Schmidt, Roy, Kalle Lyytinen, Mark Keil, and Paul Cule. "Identifying Software Project Risks: An International Delphi Study." *Journal of Management Information Systems* 17, No. 4 (Spring 2001).

Schwalbe, Kathy. *Information Technology Project Management*, 7/e. Cengage (2014).

Sharma, Rajeev and Philip Yetton. "The Contingent Effects of Training, Technical Complexity, and Task Interdependence on Successful Information Systems Implementation." *MIS Quarterly* 31, No. 2 (June 2007).

Smith, H. Jeff, Mark Keil, and Gordon Depledge. "Keeping Mum as the Project Goes Under." *Journal of Management Information Systems* 18, No. 2 (Fall 2001).

Swanson, E. Burton. *Information System Implementation*. Homewood, IL: Richard D. Irwin (1988).

Tiwana, Amrit, and Mark Keil. "Control in Internal and Outsourced Software Projects." *Journal of Management Information Systems* 26, No. 3 (Winter 2010).

Tornatsky, Louis G., J. D. Eveland, M. G. Boylan, W. A. Hetzner, E. C. Johnson, D. Roitman, and J. Schneider. *The Process of Technological Innovation: Reviewing the Literature*. Washington, DC: National Science Foundation (1983).

Vaidyanathan, Ganesh. *Project Management: Process, Technology and Practice*. Upper Saddle River, NJ: Prentice Hall (2013).

Wang, Eric T.G., Gary Klein, and James J. Jiang. "ERP Misfit: Country of Origin and Organizational Factors." *Journal of Management Information Systems* 23, No. 1 (Summer 2006).

Westerman, George. IT is from Venus, Non-IT Is from Mars," *The Wall Street Journal* (April 2, 2012).

Xue, Yajion, Huigang Liang, and William R. Boulton. "Information Technology Governance in Information Technology Investment Decision Processes: The Impact of Investment Characteristics, External Environment, and Internal Context." *MIS Quarterly* 32, No. 1 (March 2008).

Yin, Robert K. "Life Histories of Innovations: How New Practices Become Routinized." *Public Administration Review* (January–February 1981).

Zhu, Kevin and Kenneth L. Kraemer. "E-Commerce Metrics for Net-Enhanced Organizations: Assessing the Value of e-Commerce to Firm Performance in the Manufacturing Sector." *Information Systems Research* 13, No. 3 (September 2002).

Managing Global Systems

LEARNING OBJECTIVES

After reading this chapter, you will be able to answer the following questions:

1. What major factors are driving the internationalization of business?
2. What are the alternative strategies for developing global businesses?
3. What are the challenges posed by global information systems and management solutions for these challenges?
4. What are the issues and technical alternatives to be considered when developing international information systems?

CHAPTER CASES

New Systems Help Fiat Become
    a Global Powerhouse
E-Commerce Russian-Style

One Organization, One Data,
    One Information: ONGC's
    Global System
Unilever's Push Toward Unified
    Global Systems

NEW SYSTEMS HELP FIAT BECOME A GLOBAL POWERHOUSE

Turin, Italy-based Fiat Group Automobiles S.p.A was one of the founders of the European car industry, and is one of the world's leading auto makers. As a result of its partnership with Chrysler, it has the brands and manufacturing capabilities to compete as a global automaker. Worldwide, Fiat manages 215,000 employees, 158 plants, and 77 R&D centers, with 2013 revenues approaching € 90 billion.

Fiat now sells Jeep in Europe and the Fiat 500 in the U.S.A. Management sees even stronger global growth and is working to develop Jeep products for international markets while maintaining a strong global presence in markets for light commercial vehicles and Fiat passenger cars.

As the company expanded globally and added operations and brands, management needed more capabilities for managing the company from a worldwide perspective. These included the ability to easily cross-analyze data among countries, channels, and products and to drill down into variables such as model, power train, and vehicle equipment. Fiat's managers needed to be able to conduct planning and analysis within each region, brand, and legal entity, and senior management wanted to be able to monitor the business with up-to-the-minute information.

© twobee/Shuttertsock

Until recently, this was extremely difficult or nearly impossible. Management had to reconcile information from more than one outdated legacy system and run multiple queries to determine the impact of exchanging products between Fiat's various companies. There was a lack of data consistency between regions and brands.

The solution was to develop new information systems that could provide enterprise-wide data for management reporting and analysis. Working with Techedge SPA consultants, Fiat's information and communications technology team implemented a new group reporting platform based on Oracle Hyperion enterprise performance management and business intelligence software. Fiat now uses Oracle Hyperion Financial Management software to draw data from a third-party ERP system and Microsoft Excel spreadsheets to provide users with pre-aggregated data across countries, legal entities and business functions.

For example, Fiat's finance managers use the system to track profit margins by brand, generate balance sheets, and monitor cash flow across the entire Fiat Group organization. Regional reports break down the data by brand and geographical location to provide management with more precise information about pricing, profit and loss, and dealer incentives. Controllers use the reports to analyze sales activity among dealers as well as fleet, rental car, and government sales channels. The new system delivers information on operational performance, especially all the variables related to new and used cars, plant productions, and after-sales service. The enterprise-wide system allows Fiat managers to analyze the profitability of every type of car sold in each country.

Fiat further enhanced the system to allow managers to perform "what if" analyses by linking Oracle Business Intelligence Enterprise Edition to the Oracle Hyperion Financial Management and Planning applications. This information is displayed through dashboards and parameterized reports, and it provides a more detailed view of profitability. About 50 senior finance professionals now use this system, from regional controllers to the highest officers in the company. Before this system was implemented, it took Fiat several hours running queries just to extract the data.

Today more than 1,500 people in more than 70 business units across Fiat worldwide use the Oracle Hyperion systems for management reporting. Employees can drill down into financial results to analyze profit margins or cash flow at a more minute level, viewing the data in dashboards or exporting the data to Excel spreadsheets for further analysis. Senior management has immediate access to data for strategic planning, forecasting, and budgeting, while marketing and sales department analysts are able to track the effectiveness of promotions and campaigns. With a single common environment for determining pricing, profit and loss, and incentives, Fiat Group is able to engage in planning activities such as product simulation and sales price optimization based on factors such as time, product, and market. Data can be sorted by model and region to obtain consistent answers from anywhere in the world.

Sources: Fiat Group Automobiles Aligns Operational Decisions with Strategy by Using End-to-End Enterprise Performance Management System," www.oracle.com, accessed Sept. 15, 2014; "Techedge and Oracle prove invaluable to Fiat," www.oracle.com, accessed September 15, 2014; David Baum, "Dashboard View," Profit Magazine, May 2013.

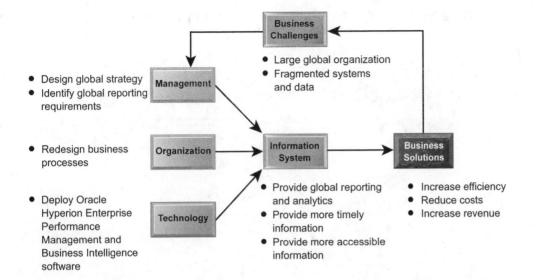

- Design global strategy
- Identify global reporting requirements

Management

Business Challenges
- Large global organization
- Fragmented systems and data

- Redesign business processes

Organization

Information System

Business Solutions

- Deploy Oracle Hyperion Enterprise Performance Management and Business Intelligence software

Technology

- Provide global reporting and analytics
- Provide more timely information
- Provide more accessible information

- Increase efficiency
- Reduce costs
- Increase revenue

Fiat Group's efforts to create global reporting systems identify some of the issues that truly global organizations need to consider if they want to operate worldwide. Like many large, multinational firms, Fiat Group has numerous operating units in many different countries. These units had their own systems, business processes, and reporting standards. As a result, Fiat Group was unable to effectively coordinate global operations or manage its brands across multiple countries and regions. Management was unable to see how Fiat was performing enterprise-wide.

The chapter-opening diagram calls attention to important points raised by this case and this chapter. To solve its global management and business challenges, Fiat Group adopted Oracle Hyperion enterprise performance management and business intelligence software to help integrate information from disparate systems supporting various brands, business regions, and operating units around the globe. Fiat Group's new reporting and business intelligence tools provide managers and employees with enterprise-wide information on firm operations and financial performance so that the company can be more easily managed and coordinated from a global perspective. This will help the company operate more efficiently around the world and also pursue its global growth strategy for its brands.

Here are some questions to think about: How did information technology improve decision making at Fiat Group Automobiles? How would Fiat's new management reporting systems impact operations?

15.1 WHAT MAJOR FACTORS ARE DRIVING THE INTERNATIONALIZATION OF BUSINESS?

In earlier chapters, we describe the emergence of a global economic system and global world order driven by advanced networks and information systems. The new world order is sweeping away many national corporations, national industries, and national economies

FIGURE 15.1 APPLE IPHONE'S GLOBAL SUPPLY CHAIN

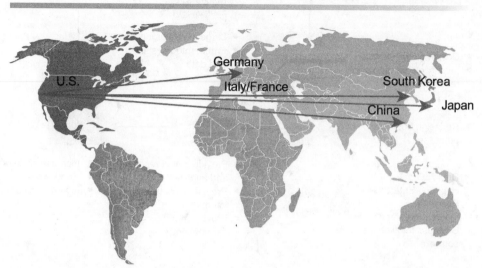

Apple designs the iPhone in the United States, and relies on suppliers in the United States, Germany, Italy, France, and South Korea for other parts. Final assembly occurs in China.

controlled by domestic politicians. Many localized firms will be replaced by fast-moving networked corporations that transcend national boundaries. The growth of international trade has radically altered domestic economies around the globe.

Consider the path to market for an iPhone, which is illustrated in Figure 15.1. The iPhone was designed by Apple engineers in the United States, sourced with more than 100 high-tech components from around the world, and assembled in China. Among the iPhone 5's major suppliers, Samsung Electronics in South Korea has supplied the applications processor. The iPhone 5's accelerator and gyroscope are made in Italy and France by STMicroelectronics, and its electronic compass is made by AKM Semiconductor in Japan. Germany's Dialog Semiconductor designed chips for power management. Texas Instruments (TI) and Broadcom in the United States supply the touch screen controller, Japan's Japan Display and Sharp Electronics and South Korea's LG Display make the high-definition display screen. Foxconn, a Chinese division of Taiwan's Hon Hai Group, is in charge of manufacturing and assembly.

DEVELOPING AN INTERNATIONAL INFORMATION SYSTEMS ARCHITECTURE

This chapter describes how to go about building an international information systems architecture suitable for your international strategy. An **international information systems architecture** consists of the basic information systems required by organizations to coordinate worldwide trade and other activities. Figure 15.2 illustrates the reasoning we follow throughout the chapter and depicts the major dimensions of an international information systems architecture.

FIGURE 15.2 INTERNATIONAL INFORMATION SYSTEMS ARCHITECTURE

The major dimensions for developing an international information systems architecture are the global environment, the corporate global strategies, the structure of the organization, the management and business processes, and the technology platform.

The basic strategy to follow when building an international system is to understand the global environment in which your firm is operating. This means understanding the overall market forces, or business drivers, that are pushing your industry toward global competition. A **business driver** is a force in the environment to which businesses must respond and that influences the direction of the business. Likewise, examine carefully the inhibitors or negative factors that create *management challenges*—factors that could scuttle the development of a global business. Once you have examined the global environment, you will need to consider a corporate strategy for competing in that environment. How will your firm respond? You could ignore the global market and focus on domestic competition only, sell to the globe from a domestic base, or organize production and distribution around the globe. There are many in-between choices.

After you have developed a strategy, it is time to consider how to structure your organization so it can pursue the strategy. How will you accomplish a division of labor across a global environment? Where will production, administration, accounting, marketing, and human resource functions be located? Who will handle the systems function?

Next, you must consider the management issues in implementing your strategy and making the organization design come alive. Key here will be the design of business processes. How can you discover and manage user requirements? How can you induce change in local units to conform to international requirements? How can you reengineer on a global scale, and how can you coordinate systems development?

TABLE 15.1 THE GLOBAL ENVIRONMENT: BUSINESS DRIVERS AND CHALLENGES

GENERAL CULTURAL FACTORS	SPECIFIC BUSINESS FACTORS
Global communication and transportation technologies	Global markets
Development of global culture	Global production and operations
Emergence of global social norms	Global coordination
Political stability	Global workforce
Global knowledge base	Global economies of scale

The last issue to consider is the technology platform. Although changing technology is a key driving factor leading toward global markets, you need to have a corporate strategy and structure before you can rationally choose the right technology.

After you have completed this process of reasoning, you will be well on your way toward an appropriate international information systems portfolio capable of achieving your corporate goals. Let's begin by looking at the overall global environment.

THE GLOBAL ENVIRONMENT: BUSINESS DRIVERS AND CHALLENGES

Table 15.1 lists the business drivers in the global environment that are leading all industries toward global markets and competition.

The global business drivers can be divided into two groups: general cultural factors and specific business factors. Easily recognized general cultural factors have driven internationalization since World War II. Information, communication, and transportation technologies have created a *global village* in which communication (by telephone, television, radio, or computer network) around the globe is no more difficult and not much more expensive than communication down the block. The cost of moving goods and services to and from geographically dispersed locations has fallen dramatically.

The development of global communications has created a global village in a second sense: A **global culture** created by television, the Internet, and other globally shared media such as movies now permits different cultures and peoples to develop common expectations about right and wrong, desirable and undesirable, heroic and cowardly. The collapse of the Eastern bloc has accelerated the growth of a world culture enormously, increased support for capitalism and business, and reduced the level of cultural conflict in Europe considerably.

A last factor to consider is the growth of a global knowledge base. At the end of World War II, knowledge, education, science, and industrial skills were highly concentrated in North America, western Europe, and Japan, with the rest of the world euphemistically called the *Third World*. This is no longer true. Latin America, China, India, southern Asia, and eastern Europe have developed powerful educational, industrial, and scientific centers, resulting in a much more democratically and widely dispersed knowledge base.

These general cultural factors leading toward internationalization result in specific business globalization factors that affect most industries. The growth of powerful communications technologies and the emergence of world cultures lay the groundwork for *global markets*—global consumers interested in consuming similar products that are culturally approved. Coca-Cola, American sneakers (made in Korea but designed in Los Angeles), and Cable News Network (CNN) programming can now be sold in Latin America, Africa, and Asia.

Responding to this demand, global production and operations have emerged with precise online coordination between far-flung production facilities and central headquarters thousands of miles away. At SeaLand Transportation, a major global shipping company based in Newark, New Jersey, shipping managers in Newark can watch the loading of ships in Rotterdam online, check trim and ballast, and trace packages to specific ship locations as the activity proceeds. This is all possible through an international satellite link.

The new global markets and pressure toward global production and operation have called forth whole new capabilities for global coordination. Production, accounting, marketing and sales, human resources, and systems development (all the major business functions) can be coordinated on a global scale.

Frito Lay, for instance, can develop a marketing sales force automation system in the United States and, once provided, may try the same techniques and technologies in Spain. Micromarketing—marketing to very small geographic and social units—no longer means marketing to neighborhoods in the United States, but to neighborhoods throughout the world! Internet-based marketing means marketing to individuals and social networks through out the world. These new levels of global coordination permit for the first time in history the location of business activity according to comparative advantage. Design should be located where it is best accomplished, as should marketing, production, and finance.

Finally, global markets, production, and administration create the conditions for powerful, sustained global economies of scale. Production driven by worldwide global demand can be concentrated where it can best be accomplished, fixed resources can be allocated over larger production runs, and production runs in larger plants can be scheduled more efficiently and precisely estimated. Lower-cost factors of production can be exploited wherever they emerge. The result is a powerful strategic advantage to firms that can organize globally. These general and specific business drivers have greatly enlarged world trade and commerce.

Not all industries are similarly affected by these trends. Clearly, manufacturing has been much more affected than services that still tend to be domestic and highly inefficient. However, the localism of services is breaking down in telecommunications, entertainment, transportation, finance, law, and general business. Clearly, those firms within an industry that can understand the internationalization of the industry and respond appropriately will reap enormous gains in productivity and stability.

TABLE 15.2 CHALLENGES AND OBSTACLES TO GLOBAL BUSINESS SYSTEMS

GLOBAL	SPECIFIC
Cultural particularism: Regionalism, nationalism, language differences	Standards: Different Electronic Data Interchange (EDI), e-mail, telecommunications standards
Social expectations: Brand-name expectations, work hours	Reliability: Phone networks not uniformly reliable
Political laws: Transborder data and privacy laws, commercial regulations	Speed: Different data transfer speeds, many slower than United States
	Personnel: Shortages of skilled consultants

Business Challenges

Although the possibilities of globalization for business success are significant, fundamental forces are operating to inhibit a global economy and to disrupt international business. Table 15.2 lists the most common and powerful challenges to the development of global systems.

At a cultural level, **particularism**, making judgments and taking action on the basis of narrow or personal characteristics, in all its forms (religious, nationalistic, ethnic, regionalism, geopolitical position) rejects the very concept of a shared global culture and rejects the penetration of domestic markets by foreign goods and services. Differences among cultures produce differences in social expectations, politics, and ultimately legal rules. In certain countries, such as the United States, consumers expect domestic name-brand products to be built domestically and are disappointed to learn that much of what they thought of as domestically produced is in fact foreign made.

Different cultures produce different political regimes. Among the many different countries of the world are different laws governing the movement of information, information privacy of their citizens, origins of software and hardware in systems, and radio and satellite telecommunications. Even the hours of business and the terms of business trade vary greatly across political cultures. These different legal regimes complicate global business and must be considered when building global systems.

For instance, European countries have very strict laws concerning transborder data flow and privacy. **Transborder data flow** is defined as the movement of information across international boundaries in any form. Some European countries prohibit the processing of financial information outside their boundaries or the movement of personal information to foreign countries. The European Union Data Protection Directive, which went into effect in October 1998, restricts the flow of any information to countries (such as the United States) that do not meet strict European information laws on personal information. Financial services, travel, and health care companies are often directly affected. In response, most multinational firms develop information systems within each European country to avoid the cost and uncertainty of moving information across national boundaries.

Cultural and political differences profoundly affect organizations' business processes and applications of information technology. A host of specific barriers arise from the general cultural differences, everything from different reliability of phone networks to the shortage of skilled consultants.

National laws and traditions have created disparate accounting practices in various countries, which impact the ways profits and losses are analyzed. German companies generally do not recognize the profit from a venture until the project is completely finished and they have been paid. Conversely, British firms begin posting profits before a project is completed, when they are reasonably certain they will get the money.

These accounting practices are tightly intertwined with each country's legal system, business philosophy, and tax code. British, U.S., and Dutch firms share a predominantly Anglo-Saxon outlook that separates tax calculations from reports to shareholders to focus on showing shareholders how fast profits are growing. Continental European accounting practices are less oriented toward impressing investors, focusing rather on demonstrating compliance with strict rules and minimizing tax liabilities. These diverging accounting practices make it difficult for large international companies with units in different countries to evaluate their performance.

Language remains a significant barrier. Although English has become a kind of standard business language, this is truer at higher levels of companies and not throughout the middle and lower ranks. Software may have to be built with local language interfaces before a new information system can be successfully implemented.

Currency fluctuations can play havoc with planning models and projections. A product that appears profitable in Mexico or Japan may actually produce a loss because of changes in foreign exchange rates.

These inhibiting factors must be taken into account when you are designing and building international systems for your business. For example, companies trying to implement "lean production" systems spanning national boundaries typically underestimate the time, expense, and logistical difficulties of making goods and information flow freely across different countries.

STATE OF THE ART

One might think, given the opportunities for achieving competitive advantages as outlined previously and the interest in future applications, that most international companies have rationally developed marvelous international systems architectures. Nothing could be further from the truth. Most companies have inherited patchwork international systems from the distant past, often based on concepts of information processing developed in the 1960s—batch-oriented reporting from independent foreign divisions to corporate headquarters, manual entry of data from one legacy system to another, with little online control and communication. Corporations in this situation increasingly face powerful competitive challenges in the marketplace from firms that have rationally designed truly international systems. Still other companies have recently built technology platforms for international systems but have nowhere to go because they lack global strategy.

As it turns out, there are significant difficulties in building appropriate international architectures. The difficulties involve planning a system appropriate to the firm's global strategy, structuring the organization of systems and business units, solving implementation issues, and choosing the right technical platform. Let's examine these problems in greater detail.

15.2 WHAT ARE THE ALTERNATIVE STRATEGIES FOR DEVELOPING GLOBAL BUSINESSES?

Three organizational issues face corporations seeking a global position: choosing a strategy, organizing the business, and organizing the systems management area. The first two are closely connected, so we discuss them together.

GLOBAL STRATEGIES AND BUSINESS ORGANIZATION

Four main global strategies form the basis for global firms' organizational structure. These are domestic exporter, multinational, franchiser, and transnational. Each of these strategies is pursued with a specific business organizational structure (see Table 15.3). For simplicity's sake, we describe three kinds of organizational structure or governance: centralized (in the home country), decentralized (to local foreign units), and coordinated (all units participate as equals). Other types of governance patterns can be observed in specific companies (e.g., authoritarian dominance by one unit, a confederacy of equals, a federal structure balancing power among strategic units, and so forth).

The **domestic exporter** strategy is characterized by heavy centralization of corporate activities in the home country of origin. Nearly all international companies begin this way, and some move on to other forms. Production, finance/accounting, sales/marketing, human resources, and strategic management are set up to optimize resources in the home country. International sales are sometimes dispersed using agency agreements or subsidiaries, but even here, foreign marketing relies on the domestic home

TABLE 15.3 GLOBAL BUSINESS STRATEGY AND STRUCTURE

BUSINESS FUNCTION	DOMESTIC EXPORTER	MULTINATIONAL	FRANCHISER	TRANSNATIONAL
Production	Centralized	Dispersed	Coordinated	Coordinated
Finance/Accounting	Centralized	Centralized	Centralized	Coordinated
Sales/Marketing	Mixed	Dispersed	Coordinated	Coordinated
Human Resources	Centralized	Centralized	Coordinated	Coordinated
Strategic Management	Centralized	Centralized	Centralized	Coordinated

base for marketing themes and strategies. Caterpillar Corporation and other heavy capital-equipment manufacturers fall into this category of firm.

The **multinational** strategy concentrates financial management and control out of a central home base while decentralizing production, sales, and marketing operations to units in other countries. The products and services on sale in different countries are adapted to suit local market conditions. The organization becomes a far-flung confederation of production and marketing facilities in different countries. Many financial service firms, along with a host of manufacturers, such as General Motors, Chrysler, and Intel, fit this pattern.

Franchisers are an interesting mix of old and new. On the one hand, the product is created, designed, financed, and initially produced in the home country, but for product-specific reasons must rely heavily on foreign personnel for further production, marketing, and human resources. Food franchisers such as McDonald's, Mrs. Fields Cookies, and KFC fit this pattern. McDonald's created a new form of fast-food chain in the United States and continues to rely largely on the United States for inspiration of new products, strategic management, and financing. Nevertheless, because the product must be produced locally—it is perishable—extensive coordination and dispersal of production, local marketing, and local recruitment of personnel are required.

Generally, foreign franchisees are clones of the mother country units, but fully coordinated worldwide production that could optimize factors of production is not possible. For instance, potatoes and beef can generally not be bought where they are cheapest on world markets but must be produced reasonably close to the area of consumption.

Transnational firms are the stateless, truly globally managed firms that may represent a larger part of international business in the future. Transnational firms have no single national headquarters but instead have many regional headquarters and perhaps a world headquarters. In a **transnational** strategy, nearly all the value-adding activities are managed from a global perspective without reference to national borders, optimizing sources of supply and demand wherever they appear, and taking advantage of any local competitive advantages. Transnational firms take the globe, not the home country, as their management frame of reference. The governance of these firms has been likened to a federal structure in which there is a strong central management core of decision making, but considerable dispersal of power and financial muscle throughout the global divisions. Few companies have actually attained transnational status.

Information technology and improvements in global telecommunications are giving international firms more flexibility to shape their global strategies. Protectionism and a need to serve local markets better encourage companies to disperse production facilities and at least become multinational. At the same time, the drive to achieve economies of scale and take advantage of short-term local advantage moves transnationals toward a global management perspective and a concentration of power and authority. Hence, there are forces of decentralization and dispersal, as well as forces of centralization and global coordination.

GLOBAL SYSTEMS TO FIT THE STRATEGY

Information technology and improvements in global telecommunications are giving international firms more flexibility to shape their global strategies. The configuration, management, and development of systems tend to follow the global strategy chosen. Figure 15.3 depicts the typical arrangements. By *systems* we mean the full range of activities involved in building and operating information systems: conception and alignment with the strategic business plan, systems development, and ongoing operation and maintenance. For the sake of simplicity, we consider four types of systems configuration. *Centralized systems* are those in which systems development and operation occur totally at the domestic home base. *Duplicated systems* are those in which development occurs at the home base but operations are handed over to autonomous units in foreign locations. *Decentralized systems* are those in which each foreign unit designs its own unique solutions and systems. *Networked systems* are those in which systems development and operations occur in an integrated and coordinated fashion across all units.

As can be seen in Figure 15.3, domestic exporters tend to have highly centralized systems in which a single domestic systems development staff develops worldwide applications. Multinationals offer a direct and striking contrast: Here, foreign units devise their own systems solutions based on local needs with few if any applications in common with headquarters (the exceptions being financial reporting and some telecommunications applications). Franchisers have the simplest systems structure: Like the products they sell, franchisers develop a single system usually at the home base and then replicate it around the world. Each unit, no matter where it is located, has identical applications. Last, the most ambitious form of systems development is found in transnational firms: Networked systems are those in which there is a solid, singular global environment for developing and operating systems. This usually presupposes a powerful telecommunications backbone, a culture of shared applications development, and a shared management culture that crosses cultural barriers. The networked systems structure

FIGURE 15.3 GLOBAL STRATEGY AND SYSTEMS CONFIGURATIONS

SYSTEM CONFIGURATION	Strategy			
	Domestic Exporter	Multinational	Franchiser	Transnational
Centralized	X			
Duplicated			X	
Decentralized	x	X	x	
Networked		x		X

The large Xs show the dominant patterns, and the small Xs show the emerging patterns. For instance, domestic exporters rely predominantly on centralized systems, but there is continual pressure and some development of decentralized systems in local marketing regions.

is the most visible in financial services where the homogeneity of the product—money and money instruments—seems to overcome cultural barriers.

REORGANIZING THE BUSINESS

How should a firm organize itself for doing business on an international scale? To develop a global company and information systems support structure, a firm needs to follow these principles:

1. Organize value-adding activities along lines of comparative advantage. For instance, marketing/sales functions should be located where they can best be performed, for least cost and maximum impact; likewise with production, finance, human resources, and information systems.

2. Develop and operate systems units at each level of corporate activity—regional, national, and international. To serve local needs, there should be *host country systems units* of some magnitude. *Regional systems units* should handle telecommunications and systems development across national boundaries that take place within major geographic regions (European, Asian, American). *Transnational systems units* should be established to create the linkages across major regional areas and coordinate the development and operation of international telecommunications and systems development (Roche, 1992).

3. Establish at world headquarters a single office responsible for development of international systems—a global chief information officer (CIO) position.

Many successful companies have devised organizational systems structures along these principles. The success of these companies relies not only on the proper organization of activities, but also on a key ingredient—a management team that can understand the risks and benefits of international systems and that can devise strategies for overcoming the risks. We turn to these management topics next.

 ## 15.3 WHAT ARE THE CHALLENGES POSED BY GLOBAL INFORMATION SYSTEMS AND MANAGEMENT SOLUTIONS FOR THESE CHALLENGES?

Table 15.4 lists the principal management problems posed by developing international systems. It is interesting to note that these problems are the chief difficulties managers experience in developing ordinary domestic systems as well. But these are enormously complicated in the international environment.

A TYPICAL SCENARIO: DISORGANIZATION ON A GLOBAL SCALE

Let's look at a common scenario. A traditional multinational consumer-goods company based in the United States and operating in Europe would

TABLE 15.4 MANAGEMENT CHALLENGES IN DEVELOPING GLOBAL SYSTEMS

Agreeing on common user requirements
Introducing changes in business processes
Coordinating applications development
Coordinating software releases
Encouraging local users to support global systems

like to expand into Asian markets and knows that it must develop a transnational strategy and a supportive information systems structure. Like most multinationals, it has dispersed production and marketing to regional and national centers while maintaining a world headquarters and strategic management in the United States. Historically, it has allowed each of the subsidiary foreign divisions to develop its own systems. The only centrally coordinated system is financial controls and reporting. The central systems group in the United States focuses only on domestic functions and production.

The result is a hodgepodge of hardware, software, and telecommunications. The e-mail systems between Europe and the United States are incompatible. Each production facility uses a different manufacturing resources planning system (or a different version of the same ERP system), and different marketing, sales, and human resource systems. Hardware and database platforms are wildly different. Communications between different sites are poor, given the high cost of European intercountry communications. The central systems group at headquarters in the United States recently was decimated and dispersed to the U.S. local sites in the hope of serving local needs better and reducing costs.

What do you recommend to the senior management leaders of this company, who now want to pursue a transnational strategy and develop an information systems architecture to support a highly coordinated global systems environment? Consider the problems you face by reexamining Table 15.4. The foreign divisions will resist efforts to agree on common user requirements; they have never thought about much other than their own units' needs. The systems groups in American local sites, which have been enlarged recently and told to focus on local needs, will not easily accept guidance from anyone recommending a transnational strategy. It will be difficult to convince local managers anywhere in the world that they should change their business procedures to align with other units in the world, especially if this might interfere with their local performance. After all, local managers are rewarded in this company for meeting local objectives of their division or plant. Finally, it will be difficult to coordinate development of projects around the world in the absence of a powerful telecommunications network and, therefore, difficult to encourage local users to take on ownership in the systems developed.

FIGURE 15.4 LOCAL, REGIONAL, AND GLOBAL SYSTEMS

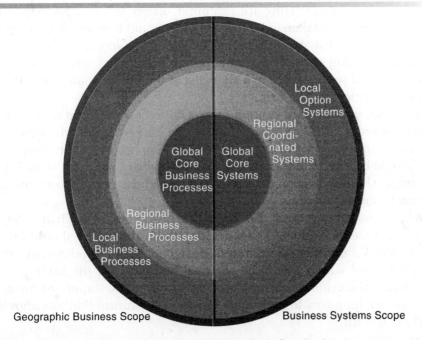

Geographic Business Scope   Business Systems Scope

Agency and other coordination costs increase as the firm moves from local option systems toward regional and global systems. However, transaction costs of participating in global markets probably decrease as firms develop global systems. A sensible strategy is to reduce agency costs by developing only a few core global systems that are vital for global operations, leaving other systems in the hands of regional and local units.

Source: From *Managing Information Technology in Multinational Corporations* by Edward M. Roche, © 1993. Adapted by permission of Prentice Hall, Inc., Upper Saddle River, N.J.

GLOBAL SYSTEMS STRATEGY

Figure 15.4 lays out the main dimensions of a solution. First, consider that not all systems should be coordinated on a transnational basis; only some core systems are truly worth sharing from a cost and feasibility point of view. **Core systems** support functions that are absolutely critical to the organization. Other systems should be partially coordinated because they share key elements, but they do not have to be totally common across national boundaries. For such systems, a good deal of local variation is possible and desirable. A final group of systems is peripheral, truly provincial, and needed to suit local requirements only.

Define the Core Business Processes

How do you identify core systems? The first step is to define a short list of critical core business processes. Business processes are defined and described in Chapter 2, which you should review. Briefly, business processes are sets of logically related tasks to produce specific business results, such as shipping out correct orders to customers or delivering innovative products to the market. Each business process typically involves many functional areas, communicating and coordinating work, information, and knowledge.

The way to identify these core business processes is to conduct a business process analysis. How are customer orders taken, what happens to them once they are taken, who fills the orders, and how are they shipped to the customers? What about suppliers? Do they have access to manufacturing resource planning systems so that supply is automatic? You should be able to identify and set priorities in a short list of ten business processes that are absolutely critical for the firm.

Next, can you identify centers of excellence for these processes? Is the customer order fulfillment superior in the United States, manufacturing process control superior in Germany, and human resources superior in Asia? You should be able to identify some areas of the company, for some lines of business, where a division or unit stands out in the performance of one or several business functions.

When you understand the business processes of a firm, you can rank-order them. You then can decide which processes should be core applications, centrally coordinated, designed, and implemented around the globe, and which should be regional and local. At the same time, by identifying the critical business processes, the really important ones, you have gone a long way to defining a vision of the future that you should be working toward.

Identify the Core Systems to Coordinate Centrally

By identifying the critical core business processes, you begin to see opportunities for transnational systems. The second strategic step is to conquer the core systems and define these systems as truly transnational. The financial and political costs of defining and implementing transnational systems are extremely high. Therefore, keep the list to an absolute minimum, letting experience be the guide and erring on the side of minimalism. By dividing off a small group of systems as absolutely critical, you divide opposition to a transnational strategy. At the same time, you can appease those who oppose the central worldwide coordination implied by transnational systems by permitting peripheral systems development to progress unabated, with the exception of some technical platform requirements.

Choose an Approach: Incremental, Grand Design, Evolutionary

A third step is to choose an approach. Avoid piecemeal approaches. These surely will fail for lack of visibility, opposition from all who stand to lose from transnational development, and lack of power to convince senior management that the transnational systems are worth it. Likewise, avoid grand design approaches that try to do everything at once. These also tend to fail, because of an inability to focus resources. Nothing gets done properly, and opposition to organizational change is needlessly strengthened because the effort requires huge resources. An alternative approach is to evolve transnational applications incrementally from existing applications with a precise and clear vision of the transnational capabilities the organization should have in five years. This is sometimes referred to as the "salami strategy," or one slice at a time.

Make the Benefits Clear

What is in it for the company? One of the worst situations to avoid is to build global systems for the sake of building global systems. From the beginning, it is crucial that senior management at headquarters and foreign division managers clearly understand the benefits that will come to the company as well as to individual units. Although each system offers unique benefits to a particular budget, the overall contribution of global systems lies in four areas.

Global systems—truly integrated, distributed, and transnational systems—contribute to superior management and coordination. A simple price tag cannot be put on the value of this contribution, and the benefit will not show up in any capital budgeting model. It is the ability to switch suppliers on a moment's notice from one region to another in a crisis, the ability to move production in response to natural disasters, and the ability to use excess capacity in one region to meet raging demand in another.

A second major contribution is vast improvement in production, operation, and supply and distribution. Imagine a global value chain, with global suppliers and a global distribution network. For the first time, senior managers can locate value-adding activities in regions where they are most economically performed.

Third, global systems mean global customers and global marketing. Fixed costs around the world can be amortized over a much larger customer base. This will unleash new economies of scale at production facilities.

Last, global systems mean the ability to optimize the use of corporate funds over a much larger capital base. This means, for instance, that capital in a surplus region can be moved efficiently to expand production of capital-starved regions; that cash can be managed more effectively within the company and put to use more effectively.

These strategies will not by themselves create global systems. You will have to implement what you strategize.

THE MANAGEMENT SOLUTION: IMPLEMENTATION

We now can reconsider how to handle the most vexing problems facing managers developing the global information systems architectures that were described in Table 15.4.

Agreeing on Common User Requirements

Establishing a short list of the core business processes and core support systems will begin a process of rational comparison across the many divisions of the company, develop a common language for discussing the business, and naturally lead to an understanding of common elements (as well as the unique qualities that must remain local).

Introducing Changes in Business Processes

Your success as a change agent will depend on your legitimacy, your authority, and your ability to involve users in the change design process. **Legitimacy** is defined as the extent to which your authority is accepted on grounds of competence, vision, or other qualities. The selection of a viable change strategy, which we have defined as evolutionary but with a vision, should assist you in convincing others that change is feasible and desirable. Involving people in change, assuring them that change is in the best interests of the company and their local units, is a key tactic.

Coordinating Applications Development

Choice of change strategy is critical for this problem. At the global level there is far too much complexity to attempt a grand design strategy of change. It is far easier to coordinate change by making small incremental steps toward a larger vision. Imagine a five-year plan of action rather than a two-year plan of action, and reduce the set of transnational systems to a bare minimum to reduce coordination costs.

Coordinating Software Releases

Firms can institute procedures to ensure that all operating units convert to new software updates at the same time so that everyone's software is compatible.

Encouraging Local Users to Support Global Systems

The key to this problem is to involve users in the creation of the design without giving up control over the development of the project to parochial interests. The overall tactic for dealing with resistant local units in a transnational company is cooptation. **Cooptation** is defined as bringing the opposition into the process of designing and implementing the solution without giving up control over the direction and nature of the change. As much as possible, raw power should be avoided. Minimally, however, local units must agree on a short list of transnational systems, and raw power may be required to solidify the idea that transnational systems of some sort are truly required.

How should cooptation proceed? Several alternatives are possible. One alternative is to permit each country unit the opportunity to develop one transnational application first in its home territory, and then throughout the world. In this manner, each major country systems group is given a piece of the action in developing a transnational system, and local units feel a sense of ownership in the transnational effort. On the downside, this assumes the ability to develop high-quality systems is widely distributed, and that, a German team, for example, can successfully implement systems in France and Italy. This will not always be the case.

A second tactic is to develop new transnational centers of excellence, or a single center of excellence. There may be several centers around the globe that focus on specific business processes. These centers draw heavily from local national units, are based on multinational teams, and must report to worldwide management. Centers of excellence perform the initial identification and specification of business processes, define the information requirements, perform the business and systems analysis, and accomplish all design and testing. Implementation, however, and pilot testing are rolled out to other parts of the globe. Recruiting a wide range of local groups to transnational centers of excellence helps send the message that all significant groups are involved in the design and will have an influence.

Even with the proper organizational structure and appropriate management choices, it is still possible to stumble over technology issues. Choices of technology platforms, networks, hardware, and software are the final element in building transnational information systems architectures.

15.4 WHAT ARE THE ISSUES AND TECHNICAL ALTERNATIVES TO BE CONSIDERED WHEN DEVELOPING INTERNATIONAL INFORMATION SYSTEMS?

Once firms have defined a global business model and systems strategy, they must select hardware, software, and networking standards along with key system applications to support global business processes. Hardware, software, and networking pose special technical challenges in an international setting.

One major challenge is finding some way to standardize a global computing platform when there is so much variation from operating unit to operating unit and from country to country. Another major challenge is finding specific software applications that are user friendly and that truly enhance the productivity of international work teams. The universal acceptance of the Internet around the globe has greatly reduced networking problems. But the mere presence of the Internet does not guarantee that information will flow seamlessly throughout the global organization because not all business units use the same applications, and the quality of Internet service can be highly variable (just as with the telephone service). For instance, German business units may use an open source collaboration tool to share documents and communicate, which is incompatible with American headquarters teams, which use Microsoft solutions. Overcoming these challenges requires systems integration and connectivity on a global basis.

COMPUTING PLATFORMS AND SYSTEMS INTEGRATION

The development of a transnational information systems architecture based on the concept of core systems raises questions about how the new core systems will fit in with the existing suite of applications developed around the globe by different divisions, different people, and for different kinds of computing hardware. The goal is to develop global, distributed, and integrated systems to support digital business processes spanning national boundaries. Briefly, these are the same problems faced by any large domestic systems development effort. However, the problems are magnified in an international environment. Just imagine the challenge of integrating systems based on the Windows, Linux, Unix, or proprietary operating systems running on IBM, Sun, HP, and other hardware in many different operating units in many different countries!

Moreover, having all sites use the same hardware and operating system does not guarantee integration. Some central authority in the firm must establish data standards, as well as other technical standards with which sites are to comply. For instance, technical accounting terms such as the beginning and end of the fiscal year must be standardized (review the earlier discussion of the cultural challenges to building global businesses), as well as the acceptable interfaces between systems, communication speeds and architectures, and network software.

CONNECTIVITY

Truly integrated global systems must have connectivity—the ability to link together the systems and people of a global firm into a single integrated network just like the phone system but capable of voice, data, and image transmissions. The Internet has provided an enormously powerful foundation for providing connectivity among the dispersed units of global firms. However, many issues remain. The public Internet does not guarantee any level of service (even in the United States). Few global corporations trust the security of the Internet and generally use private networks to communicate sensitive data, and Internet virtual private networks (VPNs) for communications that require less security. Not all countries support even basic Internet service that requires obtaining reliable circuits, coordinating among different carriers and the regional telecommunications authority, and obtaining standard agreements for the level of telecommunications service provided. Table 15.5 lists the major challenges posed by international networks.

While private networks have guaranteed service levels and better security than the Internet, the Internet is the primary foundation for global corporate networks when lower security and service levels are acceptable. Companies can create global intranets for internal communication or extranets to exchange information more rapidly with business partners in their supply chains. They can use the public Internet to create global networks using VPNs from Internet service providers, which provide many features of a private network using the public Internet (see Chapter 7). However, VPNs may not provide the same level of quick and predictable response as private networks, especially during times of the day when Internet traffic is very congested, and they may not be able to support large numbers of remote users.

TABLE 15.5 CHALLENGES OF INTERNATIONAL NETWORKS

Quality of service
Security
Costs and tariffs
Network management
Installation delays
Poor quality of international service
Regulatory constraints
Network capacity

FIGURE 15.5 INTERNET POPULATION IN SELECTED COUNTRIES

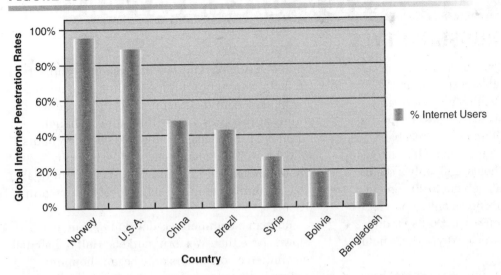

The percentage of the total population using the Internet in developing countries is much smaller than in the United States and Europe, but it is growing rapidly.

Source: Based on data from Internerworldstats.com, 2014, Pew Global Attitudes Project, 2014 and authors.

The high cost of PCs, and low incomes, limit access to Internet service in many developing countries (see Figure 15.5). Where an Internet infrastructure exists in less-developed countries, it often lacks bandwidth capacity, and is unreliable in part due to power grid issues. The purchasing power of most people in developing countries makes access to Internet services very expensive in local currencies. In the case of Russia, uneven Internet service and an undeveloped infrastructure for distributing and paying for goods has hampered the growth of e-commerce (see the Interactive Session on Organizations).

In addition, many countries monitor transmissions (see the Interactive Session on Management). Governments in China, Singapore, Iran, and Saudi Arabia monitor Internet traffic and block access to Web sites considered morally or politically offensive. On the other hand, the rate of growth in the Internet population is far faster in Asia, Africa, and the Middle East than in North America and Europe, where the Internet population is growing slowly if at all. Therefore, in the future, Internet connectivity will be much more widely available and reliable in less-developed regions of the world, and it will play a significant role in integrating these economies with the world economy.

SOFTWARE LOCALIZATION

The development of core systems poses unique challenges for application software: How will the old systems interface with the new? Entirely new interfaces must be built and tested if old systems are kept in local areas (which is common). These interfaces can be costly and messy to build. If new software must be created, another challenge is to build software that can be realistically used by multiple business units from different countries given that business units are accustomed to their unique business processes and definitions of data.

INTERACTIVE SESSION: ORGANIZATIONS

E-COMMERCE RUSSIAN-STYLE

Nearly 63.6 million Russians have Internet access, making Russia the second-largest e-commerce market in all of Europe, behind only Germany. By the end of 2014, Russia will surpass Germany with an estimated 80 million users. Broadband reach is estimated at 40 percent of all households—around 20 million households. Still, only a scant 24 to 26 million—about 38 percent to 40 percent of Internet users—have made an online purchase through 2013 and e-commerce accounts for only 2 percent of Russian retail sales. Why? What's holding e-commerce back?

Russia has expanded its online consumer base faster than any other country, but there are serious barriers to further growth. Russia lacks both logistics infrastructures and online payment systems for e-commerce to flourish. The postal system is both expensive and unreliable, with lost or stolen packages, excessive delivery time, and non-distributed parcel rates of up to 100 percent in remote areas. Cash is the predominant payment method due to an under-developed financial services sector, exorbitant bank charges, and lack of consumer trust in electronic payments. Pre-authorization is often required for card use, merchants lack the infrastructure to store card data, and fraud poses a significant threat to merchants. Combined with the prohibitively expensive investment required to deploy fiber connections across the vast expanses of Russian terrain, the impediments to e-commerce expansion are substantial.

Russian online consumers by and large pay cash-on-delivery (COD) at "pick-up stores" where they collect their purchases. The collection centers accumulate large quantities of cash, which must be deposited every few hours to reduce the risk of theft. A system of payment kiosks has also sprung up on street corners, and in grocery stores, small shops, and convenience stores. These kiosks also serve as bill payment centers and often include multiple terminals from different companies, fashioning a comprehensive payment island. Several online payment systems have been developed including Yandex Money

and WebMoney. These e-wallets, often subject to daily transaction limits, are linked to domestic bank accounts or debit cards or loaded with funds at the kiosks or offline stores. Though Yandex Money has signed up 20,000 merchants and 14 million consumers, and WebMoney 2,200 merchants and 6 million users, 80 percent of all B2C e-commerce in Russia is still conducted in cash.

Russian e-commerce is developing, but at a slower pace than Western markets. Half of habitual e-commerce consumers only began shopping online in the last two years. Card and online payment systems are gaining acceptance for digital goods (software, e-books, and digital music) and travel purchases such as airline tickets and hotel reservations. Shoppers have entered the online sphere for these products as well as for books, and are expanding to electronics, computers, and home appliances, and then jewelry, cosmetics, clothing, and shoes.

Online shopping mall Ozon began in 1998 as an online bookstore but now stocks well over 2 million items. Ozon adopted a multi-pronged strategy to combat Russia's market challenges. In the short-term, it accepted customer preference for COD in order to build trust, expand its customer base, and establish market position. Its delivery service (O'Courier) and 2,100 pick-up centers serve 350 cities throughout Russia and Kazakhstan. This logistics network dwarfs those of its competitors.

Another domestic leader, KupiVIP, has also succeeded largely because it built its own logistics network including multiple warehouses and a fleet of delivery trucks. Centered on its original high-fashion flash sales site, KupiVIP (kupi means buy in Russian) now includes nine white-label sites and ShopTime, a full-priced fashion site. KupiVIP's delivery drivers to double as customer service reps. In addition to collecting COD payments and merchandise for return, they will even wait at the door while customers try on merchandise to decide if they want to keep it.

The unexpected leader of Russian e-commerce, however, is hybrid online-offline retailer Ulmart, which recently became the first Russian e-tailer to surpass $1 billion (USD) in sales. Founded in August 2008 to sell computers online, it quickly expanded into home electronics, household appliances children's goods, auto parts, and tires. Ulmart complements its online selling with 32 Kibermarkets—electronics superstores open 24 hours a day—as well as around 140 pick-up outposts in 150 cities across Russia. Five hubs supply the fulfillment centers, and a fleet of nearly 200 trucks transports merchandise from the warehouses to the outposts and makes home deliveries. Floor space that would traditionally be taken up with row after row of product is instead used for computer terminals and giant state-of-the-art touch screens that serve as virtual display cases. Customers browse and choose products from a virtual catalog, use cash, credit cards, or Yandex Money at a payment zone terminal, and proceed to a comfy waiting zone accoutered with couches and tables for a 15-minute or less wait for their purchases. Ulmart is also at the forefront of Russian m-commerce, building a new Web site for smartphones, even while continuing to support 24-hour call centers.

Ulmart's conspicuous vulnerability is its neglect of the nearly 88 percent of Russia's landmass that lies beyond the reach of its logistics network. To reach these customers, Ulmart must rely on the government-owned Russian Post. Pochta Rossii, still struggles to transport goods between Ulmart's St. Petersburg headquarters and Moscow (400 miles) in less than two weeks, let alone service Novosibirsk, Russia's third most populous city and most populous in Asian Russia, nearly 1,750 miles away.

Russian e-commerce is dominated by a handful of these large companies. Most medium and small domestic retailers have yet to establish an Internet presence. EBay has launched a Russian language site and Amazon is in the process of building one, but their presence is overshadowed by Russian firms, which control 90 percent of the market.

Sources: "Broadband Internet penetration in Russia," themoscownews.com, April 4, 2014;Diane Brady, "Russia's Online Retail Leader Says 'Amazon Has No Chance," Bloomberg Businessweek, February 27, 2014; MaelleGavet, "The CEO of Ozon on Building an e-Commerce Giant in a Cash-Only Economy, " Harvard Business Review (July-August 2014);Ben Hopkins, "The 'good times' could be over for foreign retailers in Russia," rusbase.com, January 29, 2014; James Marson, "At E-Commerce Firms, Russia Rises," by James Marson, Wall Street Journal, Nov. 12, 2013; Juho, "Is E-commerce in Russia Exploding?" magentaadvisory.com, February 4, 2014; "Insight: Online Payment Preferences: Russia," cybersource.com, 2013; Alexi Moskin, "Ulmart and the Benefits of Hybrid Shopping," The St. Petersburg Times, August 14, 2013; "Expansion Ahead for Russian E-commerce," The Moscow News, August 29, 2013;and OlenaSikorska, "E-commerce in Russia: Trends, Problems and Winning Local Players," digital-intheround.com, December 3, 2013.

CASE STUDY QUESTIONS

1. Describe the technical and organizational obstacles to e-commerce growth in Russia.

2. How do these technical and organizational factors hamper companies from doing business in Russia or setting up Russian e-commerce sites?

3. Will non-Russian companies like Amazon.com and eBay flourish in Russia? Explain.

INTERACTIVE SESSION: MANAGEMENT

ONE ORGANIZATION, ONE DATA, ONE INFORMATION: ONGC'S GLOBAL SYSTEM

Oil and Natural Gas Corporation (ONGC) is one of India's most valuable companies, with a market capitalization of ₹2,32,000 crore. ONGC owns and operates more than 11,000 kilometers of gas pipelines in India. Realizing the importance of IT in managing its operations, ONGC embarked on a project called Information Consolidation for Efficiency in the year 2000, with an aim of creating an overarching set-up of "one organization, one data, one information". The target of the project was to achieve global standards in operations and introduce new business processes.

Oil exploration firms collect extensive data, which can be difficult to manage. A lot of the business decisions of such firms depend upon the results of this data. In order to ensure that its managers get an uninhibited view of all the collected information, ONGC chose to leverage state-of-the-art technologies like the supervisory control and data acquisition (SCADA), SAP Enterprise Resource Planning (ERP), and Exposure Prevention Information Network (EPINet) to further its goals. It was believed that these applications would make valuable information available on a real-time basis across the globe and eliminate the problem of data duplicity.

EPINet is a Web-enabled data management system for geophysical as well as exploration and planning data. It provides multiple users, even those who work remotely, simultaneous access to all the assets, logs, drilling data related to exploration and planning, and so on. As a result, the managers at ONGC are now able to take speedy technical and business decisions.

Till the 1990s, all of the firm's exploration and planning data were stored in non-electronic physical forms like tapes and films. Moreover, these were held in different locations around the world with very little centralized access. In order to obtain the older data, manual indexing was done, which often led to the data being inaccurate or difficult to find. The information from oil well surveys was

stored digitally, but since there was no common data store, each team saved it according to its individual preferences. This resulted in multiple versions of unedited data. The legacy system that ONGC used for material management, project monitoring, and maintenance planning often made access to data difficult. Managers weren't sure where to start looking for a piece of information that they needed to make important business decisions. Once the data was located, its collation, consolidation, and analysis proved to be difficult and time consuming. EPINet was judged to be a solution to all these challenges.

EPINet now manages both legacy and current data for the company. The outcome was an integrated exploration and planning database with single, validated exploration and planning database throughout ONGC. EPINet also handles the analysis and interpretation of the data, while the Web-based reporting feature allows all the current data on exploration and planning to flow directly into EPINet for centralized access. Moreover, this software is compliant with industry standards and best practices.

The firm's operations are global in nature and this calls for an IT solution that streamlines its business processes and integrates all the information along business lines. ONGC, with the help of the SAP ERP, went on to standardize more than 100 of its business processes for 13,000 users across all locations in less than 30 months' time. The SAP R/3 ERP was implemented for the finance and HR activities. This led to the automation of several tasks related to payroll and administration. This ERP was then tested at oil-drilling platforms, which required that daily processes be run at specific times.

ONGC undertook another initiative to manage its global operations, this time with the help of the global automation company, ABB Limited. ONGC rolled out the enterprise-wide SCADA system to manage its onshore and offshore assets. This enabled company officials to collect information about the business processes running at various locations. This solution was integrated with the EPINet software and the SAP ERP for a seamless experience.

Sources: "ONGC: Changing the face of the Upstream Oil and Gas Industry in India", https://library.e.abb.com/public/f53d01ec85d7d8e9852571c4007859b2/ONGC%20success%20story.pdf ; Kumar, Sharath, "ONGC's innovative implementation of Wimax based BWA system", *Ciol* (2014). Retrieved from http://www.ciol.com/ongcs-innovative-implementation-wimax-bwa/; "ONGC India chooses ABB Industrial IT for offshore Fire and Gas System Upgrade at the WIN Platform" (2002). Retrieved from http://www.abb.co.in/cawp/seitp202/ c1256c290031524bc1256c02002db8e3.aspx; Mittal, P.K. and Debashis Chatterjee, "EPINET In ONGC India: Transforming E&P Information Into Energy Intelligence", Society of Petroleum Engineers (2006). Retrieved from https://www.onepetro.org/conference-paper/SPE-99336-MS; "Business Process Re-engineering ONGC" (2009). Retrieved from http://www.slideshare.net/swapnilsaurav/business-process-reengineering-ongc.Kumar, C.R. &and M.P. Rao, M.P. (2013). "EPINET—G&G Information Resource Management in ONGC", 10th Biennial International Conference and Exposition, Kochi (2013); "Transforming Asia's largest oil and gas company". Retrieved from http://www.abb.co.in/cawp/seitp202/a22bc1ab5feefe4dc1257546003ad925.aspx.

CASE STUDY QUESTIONS

1. What challenges faced by ONGC led to its adoption of EPINet?

2. Discuss the features of EPINet as a global IT solution.

3. Discuss how SCADA aids ONGC in managing its on-site and offshore assets.

4. How did the SAP ERP streamline the global business processes for the firm?

Aside from integrating the new with the old systems, there are problems of human interface design and functionality of systems. For instance, to be truly useful for enhancing productivity of a global workforce, software interfaces must be easily understood and mastered quickly. Graphical user interfaces are ideal for this but presuppose a common language—often English. When international systems involve knowledge workers only, English may be the assumed international standard. But as international systems penetrate deeper into management and clerical groups, a common language may not be assumed and human interfaces must be built to accommodate different languages and even conventions. The entire process of converting software to operate in a second language is called **software localization**.

What are the most important software applications? Many international systems focus on basic transaction and management reporting systems. Increasingly, firms are turning to supply chain management and enterprise systems to standardize their business processes on a global basis and to create coordinated global supply chains. However, these cross-functional systems are not always compatible with differences in languages, cultural heritages, and business processes in other countries (Martinons, 2004; Liang et al., 2004; Accenture, 2014). Company units in countries that are not technically sophisticated may also encounter problems trying to manage the technical complexities of enterprise applications.

Electronic Data Interchange (EDI) systems and supply chain management systems are widely used by manufacturing and distribution firms to connect to suppliers on a global basis. Collaboration systems, e-mail, and videoconferencing are especially important worldwide collaboration tools for knowledge- and data-based firms, such as advertising firms, research-based firms in medicine and engineering, and graphics and publishing firms. Internet-based tools will be increasingly employed for such purposes.

■ Review Summary ■

1. **What major factors are driving the internationalization of business?**

   The growth of inexpensive international communication and transportation has created a world culture with stable expectations or norms. Political stability and a growing global knowledge base that is widely shared also contribute to the world culture. These general factors create the conditions for global markets, global production, coordination, distribution, and global economies of scale.

2. **What are the alternative strategies for developing global businesses?**

   There are four basic international strategies: domestic exporter, multinational, franchiser, and transnational. In a transnational strategy, all factors of production are coordinated on a global scale. However, the choice of strategy is a function of the type of business and product.

   There is a connection between firm strategy and information systems design. Transnational firms must develop networked system configurations and permit considerable decentralization of development and operations. Franchisers almost always duplicate systems across many countries and use centralized financial controls. Multinationals typically rely on decentralized independence among foreign units with some movement toward development of networks. Domestic exporters typically are centralized in domestic headquarters with some decentralized operations permitted.

3. **What are the challenges posed by global information systems and management solutions for these challenges?**

   Global information systems pose challenges because cultural, political, and language diversity magnifies differences in organizational culture and business processes and encourages proliferation of disparate local information systems that are difficult to integrate. Typically, international systems have evolved without a conscious plan. The remedy is to define a small subset of core business processes and focus on building systems to support these processes. Tactically, managers will have to coopt widely dispersed foreign units to participate in the development and operation of these systems, being careful to maintain overall control.

4. **What are the issues and technical alternatives to be considered when developing international information systems?**

   Implementing a global system requires an implementation strategy that considers both business design and technology platforms. The main hardware and telecommunications issues are systems integration and connectivity. The choices for integration are to go either with a proprietary architecture or with open systems technology. Global networks are extremely difficult to build and operate. Firms can build their own global networks or they can create global networks based on the Internet (intranets or virtual private networks). The main software issues concern building interfaces to existing systems and selecting applications that can work with multiple cultural, language, and organizational frameworks.

Key Terms

Business driver, 617
Cooptation, 630
Core systems, 627
Domestic exporter, 622
Franchisers, 623
Global culture, 618
International information systems architecture, 616

Legitimacy, 629
Multinational, 623
Particularism, 620
Software localization, 637
Transborder data flow, 620
Transnational, 623

Review Questions

15-1 What major factors are driving the internationalization of business?

- List and describe the five major dimensions for developing an international information systems architecture.
- Describe the five general cultural factors leading toward growth in global business and the four specific business factors. Describe the interconnection among these factors.
- List and describe the major challenges to the development of global systems.
- Explain why some firms have not planned for the development of international systems.

15-2 What are the alternative strategies for developing global businesses?

- Describe the four main strategies for global business and organizational structure.
- Describe the four different system configurations that can be used to support different global strategies.

15-3 What are the challenges posed by global information systems and management solutions for these challenges?

- List and describe the major management issues in developing international systems.
- Identify and describe three principles to follow when organizing the firm for global business.
- Identify and describe three steps of a management strategy for developing and implementing global systems.
- Define cooptation and explain how can it be used in building global systems.

15-4 What are the issues and technical alternatives to be considered when developing international information systems?

- Describe the main technical issues facing global systems.
- Identify some technologies that will help firms develop global systems.

Discussion Questions

15-5 If you were a manager in a company that operates in many countries, what criteria would you use to determine whether an application should be developed as a global application or as a local application?

15-6 Describe ways the Internet can be used in international information systems.

Hands-On MIS Projects

The projects in this section give you hands-on experience conducting international market research, analyzing international systems issues for an expanding business, and building a job posting database and Web page for an international company.

Management Decision Problems

15-7 United Parcel Service (UPS) has been expanding its package delivery and logistics services in China, serving both multinational companies and local businesses. UPS drivers in China need to use UPS systems and tools such as its handheld Driver Information and Delivery Acquisition Device for capturing package delivery data. UPS wants to make its WorldShip, CampusShip, and other shipping-management services accessible to Chinese and multinational customers via the Web. What are some of the international systems issues UPS must consider in order to operate successfully in China?

15-8 Your company manufactures and sells tennis rackets and would like to start selling outside the United States. You are in charge of developing a global Web strategy and the first countries you are thinking of targeting are Brazil, China, Germany, Italy, and Japan. Using the statistics in the CIA World Factbook, which of these countries would you target first? What criteria did you use? What other considerations should you address in your Web strategy? What features would you put on your Web site to attract buyers from the countries you target?

Achieving Operational Excellence: Building a Job Database and Web Page for an International Consulting Firm

Software skills: Database and Web page design
Business skills: Human resources internal job postings

15-9 Companies with many overseas locations need a way to inform employees about available job openings in these locations. In this project you'll use database software to design a database for posting internal job openings and a Web page for displaying this information.

KTP Consulting operates in various locations around the world. KTP specializes in designing, developing, and implementing enterprise systems for medium- to large-size companies. KTP offers its employees opportunities to travel, live, and work in various locations throughout the United States, Europe, and Asia. The firm's human resources department has a simple database that enables its staff to track job vacancies. When an employee is interested in relocating, she or he contacts the human resources department for a list of KTP job vacancies. KTP also posts its employment opportunities on the company Web site.

What type of data should be included in the KTP job vacancies database? What information should not be included in this database? Based on your answers to these questions, build a job vacancies database for KTP. Populate the database with at least 20 records. You should also build a simple Web page that incorporates job vacancy data from your newly created database. Submit a copy of the KTP database and Web page to your professor.

Improving Decision Making: Conducting International Marketing and Pricing Research

Software skills: Internet-based software
Business skills: International pricing and marketing

15-10 In this project you'll use the Web to research overseas distributors and customs regulations and use Internet-based software to calculate prices in foreign currencies.

You are in charge of marketing for a U.S. manufacturer of office furniture that has decided to enter the international market. You have been given the name of Sorin SRL, a major Italian office furniture retailer, but your source had no other information. You want to test the market by contacting this firm to offer it a specific desk chair that you have to sell at about $125. Using the Web, locate the information needed to contact this firm and to find out how many European euros you would need to get for the chair in the current market. One source for locating European companies is the Europages Business Directory. In addition, consider using the Universal Currency Converter Web site, which determines the value of one currency expressed in other currencies. Obtain both the information needed to contact the firm and the price of your chair in their local currency. Then locate and obtain customs and legal restrictions on the products you will export from the United States and import into Italy. Finally, locate a company that will represent you as a customs agent and gather information on shipping costs.

Unilever's Push Toward Unified Global Systems
CASE STUDY

Palm oil was the driving force behind the 1929 merger that created what is today the third largest consumer goods company in the world behind Proctor Gamble and Nestlé. What may have seemed an odd marriage between British soap maker, Lever Brothers, and Dutch margarine producer, Margarine Unie, provided new company, Unilever, unprecedented purchasing power for the primary raw material of both products. Today Unilever focuses on 14 brands, each netting more than €1 billion annually including laundry soap Surf (Omo), soap, shower gel, shampoo and conditioner brands Lux, Dove, and Sunsilk, and deodorant and personal care brands Axe (Lynx) and Rexona, also sold as Sure, Degree, Shield, and Rexena. On the edible side, top sellers include ice cream brands Magnum and Heartbrand, margarine brands Becel (Flora/Promise/Fruit d'Or) and Rama, mayonnaise brands Hellmann's and Best Foods, and soup, seasonings, and tea brands Lipton and Knorr. All told, the Anglo-Dutch multinational boasts over 400 brands, sells its products in over 190 countries, and employs more than 175, 000 people worldwide.

Unilever is organized as two separate holding companies: Unilever PLC (public limited company), headquartered in London, United Kingdom, and Unilever N.V., headquartered in Rotterdam, The Netherlands. The two legal divisions operate as nearly as possible to a single economic entity— The Unilever Group—with unity of management, operations, purpose, and mission.

Since 2009, when Dutchman Paul Polman took the reins as CEO, The Unilever Group has made sustainable living the core goal of its business model. Using the inputs common to all major packaged goods manufacturers—brands, people, and operations—Unilever's Compass strategy focuses on using cost leveraging and cost efficiencies, innovation in marketing and marketing investment, and profitable volume growth to yield sustained growth, lowered environmental impact, and positive social impact.

By 2010, a 10 year plan quantified the goals: to double sales from €40 billion to €80 billion, halve its environmental footprint, reach 4 billion of the world's estimated 9 billion 2020 citizens, bring safe drinking water to 500 million people, source 100 percent of its raw materials sustainably, and improve the lives of 500,000 small farmers and distributors by bringing them into its supply chain. Given the reality of climate change and the growing scarcity of water and other natural resources, Polman believes viable business models for the 21st century must include strategies for maximizing social and environmental returns along with profits and investor returns.

In order to grow its business in developing and emerging markets, Unilever needed to unify its core business processes, including supply chain management. Standardized processes were essential to effectively manage volatile prices and changing commodity supplies. However, ambitious company-wide goal setting such as this was not feasible prior to 2007. At that point, almost every business in each of the more than 190 countries in which Unilever operated functioned as an independent division. Approximately 30,000 transactions per minute, including every order received, invoice issued, material produced, and product shipped were processed through 250 different enterprise resource planning (ERP) systems.

Unilever's Global ERP Vice President Marc Bechet has pointed out that the company's worldwide business runs on ERP systems. Every transaction for each order it receives, material it produces, item it ships, and invoice it issues runs through Unilever's backbone ERP systems. Trying to run a global business that was doubling its transaction volume with 250 systems proved too challenging.

Instead of adding layers of IT infrastructure to prepare for rapid business growth, Unilever's globalization strategy involved the exact opposite action. For the past two decades, Unilever has been consolidating and simplifying its technology platform so that it would support the company operating as a single global entity. Unilever transitioned to running its worldwide business on only four instances of SAP ERP, with the ultimate goal of managing these landscapes as one global platform by 2015.

By 2008, the rollout of the Western European regional SAP ERP system was complete with three more regional centers to come. North America was online by the beginning of 2012. Return on this investment was already notable by 2013. IT research and advisory firm, Gartner ranked Unilever fourth on its Supply Chain Top 25 list, and revenue had increased €10 billion, already one quarter of the way towards its 2020 goal.

With transactions slated to reach the 60,000 per minute range, Unilever was still investigating additional tools to increase transaction processing speed. To remain a leader in modern demand-driven supply chain management, Unilever began adding SAP HANA (High-Performance Analytic Appliance) software to some of its key SAP ERP applications at the end of 2012. HANA is an in-memory data platform (see Chapter 6) that is deployable as an on-premise appliance, or in the cloud. It is very well suited for performing real-time analytics and processing extremely large numbers of transactions very rapidly.

One of Unilever's first projects was implementing SAP CO-PA (Controlling-Profitability Analysis) Accelerator powered by SAP HANA. The enhanced financial analysis software reduced the number of days to produce the month-end close from three to just one. This experience was valuable for Unilever on several levels. It allowed the company to start with a single critical business process that could easily be rolled back into a traditional database if necessary, gain experience, and lay the groundwork for future HANA implementations. The success of this project and its enthusiastic embrace by end users convinced Unilever that other business processes could indeed benefit from the addition of the SAP HANA in-memory computing platform.

The second tangible benefit was the ability to input raw material costs and quickly calculate product price. Understanding its margins—the percent profit after all costs have been deducted—enabled Unilever to analyze ways to improve

them. Production cost analysis confirmed for Unilever that HANA's ability to accelerate business processes was well worth the investment, substantially improving real-time decision making.

Unilever's Enterprise Data Warehouse (EDW) system extracts, transforms, and integrates ERP transaction data with external data for use in reporting and data analysis. The next target of the SAP HANA initiative was to accelerate, simplify, and harmonize all ERP transaction systems so that the data being fed into its global EDW was of the highest quality possible. Valuable business insights depend on real-time analysis of accurate data. The profitability analysis accelerator analyzes reams of financial data and outputs valuable statistics about cost and profit drivers. By mid-2013, the SAP CO-PA Accelerator had been added to all four regional ERP centers over a 16 week timeframe and was being managed as a single global platform. Each region now runs a 27 terabyte relational database using 30 gigabytes of HANA in-memory system. Two hundred million records are now processed in 30 seconds, down from 440.

Cost Center assessment time was reduced 39 percent, pushing this data into CO-PA in 6.7 hours rather than 11 hours and speeding profitability reporting. Overall, controlling and profitability reports were produced ten times more quickly. The Material Ledger Accelerator reduced runtime for period-end closing reports by 66 percent, and cost reduction opportunities were identified by the Overall Equipment Effectiveness (OEE) Management platform. Four and a half billion records for General Ledger line items and over 400 million controlling and profitability analysis records are now run through the CO-PA Accelerator.

Next, SAP Cash Forecasting was added to SAP ERP Financials to minimize liquidity risk and maximize the use of working capital and cash. Product Cost Planning (CO-PC-PCP) was incorporated to help Unilever plan the costs for materials independently from orders; set prices for materials, operations, production lines, and processes; analyze the costs of manufactured materials; and assess product profitability. The time to analyze the approximately 150 million records produced each month was halved, and product cost forecasts could be generated in 30 seconds, down from seven minutes.

On the macro level, the SAP HANA initiative transformed Unilever's attitude towards IT. Until HANA, IT pushed solutions to functions in need of modernization. Now, optimized functions pinpoint business opportunities and stakeholders ripe for HANA solutions. Unilever's Global Director of Finance Thomas Benthien believes this swing from push to pull is a driver for innovation and a growth agenda. Proofs of concept (prototypes used for feasibility testing) were conducted to add the HANA in-memory platform to many components of Unilever's SAP Business Suite, including the SCM (Supply Chain Management) application. Other tests involved components of the Enterprise Performance Management (EPM) system, SAP Advanced Planning & Optimization (APO), SAP Business Planning and Consolidation, and SAP Trade Promotion Management.

Unilever wanted to maximize product availability on store shelves during new product launches and promotional campaigns. Since trade promotion processes drive a significant portion of its sales, Marc Béchet wanted to enhance the speed and efficiency with which they could be planned, budgeted, and executed and in how stock was allocated. Previously, Unilever used a process in which stock was sequentially assigned to orders as they were received. There was no mechanism for assigning limited stock between customers running a promotion and those who were not. Using HANA-accelerated trade promotion management tools, different inventory matching scenarios are instantly available. Allocation options can be compared and the most profitable chosen. Inventory shortfalls can be handled while safeguarding current promotions to the maximum extent possible.

Plans are now underway to add in-memory technology to the rest of the SAP Business Suite. SAP released the first version of SAP Business Suite powered by HANA in January 2013. Unilever is weighing its options so that the risk of adoption to one of the largest SAP ERP systems in the industry is minimized, but it is likely to switch to the newest product before 2015.

By significantly cutting the time it takes to calculate product costs, the HANA in-memory database accelerators fast-track raw material sourcing decisions and pricing analysis. Unilever estimates that time spent tracking raw materials has declined by 80 percent. Improved understanding of the supply chain, in turn, supports managerial decision-making to both improve efficiency and reduce environmental impact. Without the analytics solution it devised and implemented, Unilever would have had a difficult time tracking the 10,000 home and personal care products that use the 2,000 different chemicals that must be reduced to meet the European Union's REACH (Registration, Evaluation, Authorization and Restriction of Chemicals) regulations and its own more stringent sustainability goals. Consolidation of its ERP platforms and the transaction and processing speed of the HANA platform are the keys to improved performance, reporting, and scalability that will enable Unilever to fulfill its ambitious growth, social impact, and environmental goals.

Sources: "Customer Journey: Unilever," www.sap.com, accessed September 16, 2014; "Our Compass Strategy," unilever.com, accessed September 16, 2014; Ken Murphy, "Unilever Goes Global with a Transformative SAP HANA Project," SAP insider PROFILES, July 1, 2013; Fred Pearce, "Unilever Plans to Double Its Turnover While Halving Its Environmental Impact," telegraph.co.uk, July 23, 2013; Joe Mullich, "Unilever Improves Sustainability Through Analytics," Bloomberg BusinessWeek, July 2013; and Cliff Saran, "Unilever Prepares for Global HANA Roll-out," computerweekly.com, December 5, 2012.

CASE STUDY QUESTIONS

15-11 What management problems typical of global systems was Unilever experiencing? What management, organization, and technology factors were responsible for those problems?

15-12 How did Unilever's new systems and use of SAP HANA support its business strategy? How effective was the solution chosen by the company?

15-13 How did Unilever's new systems improve operations and management decision-making?

15-14 What influence does the global business environment have on firms like Unilever and how does that affect its choice of systems?

Chapter 15 References

Accenture. "Technology Not Widely Used in Global Companies' Emerging Market Supply Chains, Study Says" (September 16, 2014).

Biehl, Markus. "Success Factors For Implementing Global Information Systems." *Communications of the ACM* 50, No. 1 (January 2007).

Bisson, Peter, Elizabeth Stephenson, and S. Patrick Viguerie. "Global Forces: An Introduction." McKinsey Quarterly (June 2010).

Burtch, Gordon, Anindya Ghose, and Sunil Watta." Cultural Differences and Geography as Determinants of Online Prosocial Lending." *MIS Quarterly* 38, No. 3 (September 2014).

Cox, Butler. *Globalization: The IT Challenge.* Sunnyvale, CA: Amdahl Executive Institute (1991).

Davison, Robert. "Cultural Complications of ERP." *Communications of the ACM* 45, No. 7 (July 2002).

Deans, Candace P., and Michael J. Kane. *International Dimensions of Information Systems and Technology.* Boston, MA: PWS-Kent (1992).

Dewhurst, Martin, Jonathan Harris, and Suzanne Heywood. "The Global Company's Challenge." *McKinsey Quarterly* (June 2012).

Dou, Eva. "Timeline of China's Social Media Crackdowns." *Wall Street Journal* (August 8, 2014).

Ghislanzoni, Giancarlo, RistoPenttinen, an David Turnbull. "The Multilocal Challenge: Managing Cross-Border Functions." The *McKinsey Quarterly* (March 2008).

Ives, Blake, and Sirkka Jarvenpaa. "Applications of Global Information Technology: Key Issues for Management." *MIS Quarterly* 15, No. 1 (March 1991).

Ives, Blake, S. L. Jarvenpaa, R. O. Mason, "Global business drivers: Aligning Information Technology to Global Business Strategy," IBM Systems Journal Vol 32, No. 1, 1993.

King, William R. and Vikram Sethi. "An Empirical Analysis of the Organization of Transnational Information Systems." *Journal of Management Information Systems* 15, No. 4 (Spring 1999).

Kirsch, Laurie J."Deploying Common Systems Globally: The Dynamic of Control." *Information Systems Research* 15, No. 4 (December 2004).

Krishna, S., Sundeep Sahay, and Geoff Walsham. "Managing Cross-Cultural Issues in Global Software Outsourcing." *Communications of the ACM* 47, No. 4 (April 2004).

Martinsons, Maris G. "ERP In China: One Package Two Profiles," *Communications of the ACM* 47, No. 7 (July 2004).

McKinsey&Company. "Lions Go Digital: The Internet's Transformative Potential in Africa. (November 2013).

Pew Research Global Attitudes Project. "Emerging Nations Embrace Internet, Mobile Technology." (February 13, 2014).

Quelch, John A., and Lisa R. Klein. "The Internet and International Marketing." *Sloan Management Review* (Spring 1996).

Roche, Edward M. *Managing Information Technology in Multinational Corporations.* New York: Macmillan (1992).

Soh, Christina, SiaSiewKien, and Joanne Tay-Yap. "Cultural Fits and Misfits: Is ERP a Universal Solution?" *Communications of the ACM* 43, No. 3 (April 2000).

Tractinsky, Noam, and Sirkka L. Jarvenpaa. "Information Systems Design Decisions in a Global Versus Domestic Context." *MIS Quarterly* 19, No. 4 (December 1995).

Glossary

3-D printing Uses machines to make solid objects, layer by layer, from specifications in a digital file. Also known as additive manufacturing.

3G networks Cellular networks based on packet-switched technology with speeds ranging from 144 Kbps for mobile users to over 2 Mbps for stationary users, enabling users to transmit video, graphics, and other rich media, in addition to voice.

4G networks The next evolution in wireless communication is entirely packet switched and capable of providing between 1 Mbps and 1 Gbps speeds; up to ten times faster than 3G networks.

acceptable use policy (AUP) Defines acceptable uses of the firm's information resources and computing equipment, including desktop and laptop computers, wireless devices, telephones, and the Internet, and specifies consequences for noncompliance.

acceptance testing Provides the final certification that the system is ready to be used in a production setting.

accountability The mechanisms for assessing responsibility for decisions made and actions taken.

advertising revenue model Web site generating revenue by attracting a large audience

affiliate revenue model an e-commerce revenue model in which Web sites are paid as "affiliates" for sending their visitors to other sites in return for a referral fee.

agency theory Economic theory that views the firm as a nexus of contracts among self-interested individuals who must be supervised and managed.

agent-based modeling Modeling complex phenomena as systems of autonomous agents that follow relatively simple rules for interaction.

agile development Rapid delivery of working software by breaking a large project into a series of small sub-projects that are completed in short periods of time using iteration and continuous feedback.

analytic platform Preconfigured hardware-software system that is specifically designed high-speed analysis of large datasets.

analytical CRM Customer relationship management applications dealing with the analysis of customer data to provide information for improving business performance.

Android A mobile operating system developed by Android, Inc. (purchased by Google) and later the Open Handset Alliance as a flexible, upgradeable mobile device platform.

antivirus software Software designed to detect, and often eliminate, computer viruses from an information system.

application controls: Specific controls unique to each computerized application that ensure that only authorized data are completely and accurately processed by that application.

application server Software that handles all application operations between browser-based computers and a company's back-end business applications or databases.

apps Small pieces of software that run on the Internet, on your computer, or on your cell phone and are generally delivered over the Internet.

artificial intelligence (AI) The effort to develop computer-based systems that can behave like humans, with the ability to learn languages, accomplish physical tasks, use a perceptual apparatus, and emulate human expertise and decision making.

attribute A piece of information describing a particular entity.

augmented reality A technology for enhancing visualization. Provides a live direct or indirect view of a physical real-world environment whose elements are augmented by virtual computer-generated imagery.

authentication The ability of each party in a transaction to ascertain the identity of the other party.

automation Using the computer to speed up the performance of existing tasks.

autonomic computing Effort to develop systems that can manage themselves without user intervention.

backward chaining A strategy for searching the rule base in an expert system that acts like a problem solver by beginning with a hypothesis and seeking out more information until the hypothesis is either proved or disproved.

balanced scorecard method Framework for operationalizing a firms strategic plan by focusing on measurable financial, business process, customer, and learning and growth outcomes of firm performance.

bandwidth The capacity of a communications channel as measured by the difference between the highest and lowest frequencies that can be transmitted by that channel.

behavioral models Descriptions of management based on behavioral scientists' observations of what managers actually do in their jobs.

behavioral targeting Tracking the click-streams (history of clicking behavior) of individuals across multiple Web sites for the purpose of understanding their interests and intentions, and exposing them to advertisements which are uniquely suited to their interests.

benchmarking Setting strict standards for products, services, or activities and measuring organizational performance against those standards.

best practices The most successful solutions or problem-solving methods that have been developed by a specific organization or industry.

big data Datasets with volumes so huge that they are beyond the ability of typical relational DBMS to capture, store, and analyze. The data are often unstructured or semi-structured.

biometric authentication Technology for authenticating system users that compares a person's unique characteristics such as fingerprints, face, or retinal image, against a stored set profile of these characteristics.

bit A binary digit representing the smallest unit of data in a computer system. It can only have one of two states, representing 0 or 1.

blade server Entire computer that fits on a single, thin card (or blade) and that is plugged into a single chassis to save space, power and complexity.

blog Popular term for Weblog, designating an informal yet structured Web site where individuals can publish stories, opinions, and links to other Web sites of interest.

blogosphere Totality of blog-related Web sites.

Bluetooth Standard for wireless personal area networks that can transmit up to 722 Kbps within a 10-meter area.

botnet A group of computers that have been infected with bot malware without users' knowledge, enabling a hacker to use the amassed resources of the computers to launch distributed denial-of-service attacks, phishing campaigns or spam.

broadband High-speed transmission technology. Also designates a single communications medium that can transmit multiple channels of data simultaneously.

bugs Software program code defects.

bullwhip effect Distortion of information about the demand for a product as it passes from one entity to the next across the supply chain.

business continuity planning Planning that focuses on how the company can restore business operations after a disaster strikes.

business driver A force in the environment to which businesses must respond and that influences the direction of business.

business ecosystem Loosely coupled but interdependent networks of suppliers, distributors, outsourcing firms, transportation service firms, and technology manufacturers

business functions Specialized tasks performed in a business organization, including manufacturing and production, sales and marketing, finance and accounting, and human resources.

business intelligence Applications and technologies to help users make better business decisions.

business model An abstraction of what an enterprise is and how the enterprise delivers a product or service, showing how the enterprise creates wealth.

business performance management Attempts to systematically translate a firm's strategies (e.g., differentiation, low-cost producer, market share growth, and scope of operation) into operational targets.

business process management Business process management (BPM) is an approach to business which aims to continuously improve and manage business processes.

business process redesign Type of organizational change in which business processes are analyzed, simplified, and redesigned.

business processes The unique ways in which organizations coordinate and organize work activities, information, and knowledge to produce a product or service.

business-to-business (B2B) electronic commerce Electronic sales of goods and services among businesses.

business-to-consumer (B2C) electronic commerce Electronic retailing of products and services directly to individual consumers.

byte A string of bits, usually eight, used to store one number or character in a computer system.

cable Internet connections Internet connections that use digital cable lines to deliver high-speed Internet access to homes and businesses.

capital budgeting The process of analyzing and selecting various proposals for capital expenditures.

carpal tunnel syndrome (CTS) Type of RSI in which pressure on the median nerve through the wrist's bony carpal tunnel structure produces pain.

case-based reasoning (CBR) Artificial intelligence technology that represents knowledge as a database of cases and solutions.

cell phone A device that transmits voice or data, using radio waves to communicate with radio antennas placed within adjacent geographic areas called cells.

change agent In the context of implementation, the individual acting as the catalyst during the change process to ensure successful organizational adaptation to a new system or innovation.

change management Managing the impact of organizational change associated with an innovation, such as a new information system.

chat Live, interactive conversations over a public network.

chief data officer (CDO) Responsible for enterprise-wide governance and utilization of information to maximize the value the organization can realize from its data.

chief information officer (CIO) Senior manager in charge of the information systems function in the firm.

chief knowledge officer (CKO) Senior executive in charge of the organization's knowledge management program.

chief privacy officer (CPO) Responsible for ensuring the company complies with existing data privacy laws.

chief security officer (CSO) Heads a formal security function for the organization and is responsible for enforcing the firm's security policy.

choice Simon's third stage of decision making, when the individual selects among the various solution alternatives.

Chrome OS Google's lightweight computer operating system for users who do most of their computing on the Internet; runs on computers ranging from netbooks to desktop computers.

churn rate Measurement of the number of customers who stop using or purchasing products or services from a company. Used as an indicator of the growth or decline of a firm's customer base.

classical model of management Traditional description of management that focused on its formal functions of planning, organizing, coordinating, deciding, and controlling.

click fraud Fraudulently clicking on an online ad in pay per click advertising to generate an improper charge per click.

client The user point-of-entry for the required function in client/server computing. Normally a desktop computer, workstation, or laptop computer.

client/server computing A model for computing that splits processing between clients and servers on a network, assigning functions to the machine most able to perform the function.

cloud computing Web-based applications that are stored on remote servers and accessed via the "cloud" of the Internet using a standard Web browser.

collaboration Working with others to achieve shared and explicit goals.

co-location a kind of Web site hosting in which firm purchase or rent a physical server computer at a hosting company's location in order to operate a Web site.

community provider a Web site business model that creates a digital online environment where people with similar interests can transact (buy and sell goods); share interests, photos, videos; communicate with like-minded people; receive interest-related information; and even play out fantasies by adopting online personalities called avatars.

communities of practice (COPs) Informal social networks of professionals and employees within and outside the firm who have similar work-related activities and interests and share their knowledge.

competitive forces model Model used to describe the interaction of external influences, specifically threats and opportunities, that affect an organization's strategy and ability to compete.

complementary assets Additional assets required to derive value from a primary investment.

component-based development Building large software systems by combining pre-existing software components.

computer abuse The commission of acts involving a computer that may not be illegal but are considered unethical.

computer crime The commission of illegal acts through the use of a computer or against a computer system.

computer forensics The scientific collection, examination, authentication, preservation, and analysis of data held on or retrieved from computer storage media in such a way that the information can be used as evidence in a court of law.

computer hardware Physical equipment used for input, processing, and output activities in an information system.

computer literacy Knowledge about information technology, focusing on understanding of how computer-based technologies work.

computer software Detailed, preprogrammed instructions that control and coordinate the work of computer hardware components in an information system.

computer virus Rogue software program that attaches itself to other software programs or data files in order to be executed, often causing hardware and software malfunctions.

computer vision syndrome (CVS) Eyestrain condition related to computer display screen use; symptoms include headaches, blurred vision, and dry and irritated eyes.

computer-aided design (CAD) Information system that automates the creation and revision of designs using sophisticated graphics software.

computer-aided software engineering (CASE) Automation of step-by-step methodologies for software and systems development to reduce the amounts of repetitive work the developer needs to do.

consumer-to-consumer (C2C) electronic commerce Consumers selling goods and services electronically to other consumers.

consumerization of IT New information technology originating in the consumer market that spreads to business organizations.

controls All of the methods, policies, and procedures that ensure protection of the organization's assets, accuracy and reliability of its records, and operational adherence to management standards.

conversion The process of changing from the old system to the new system.

cookies Tiny file deposited on a computer hard drive when an individual visits certain Web sites. Used to identify the visitor and track visits to the Web site.

cooptation Bringing the opposition into the process of designing and implementing a solution without giving up control of the direction and nature of the change.

copyright A statutory grant that protects creators of intellectual property against copying by others for any purpose for a minimum of 70 years.

core competency Activity at which a firm excels as a world-class leader.

core systems Systems that support functions that are absolutely critical to the organization.

cost transparency the ability of consumers to discover the actual costs merchants pay for products.

counterimplementation A deliberate strategy to thwart the implementation of an information system or an innovation in an organization.

cross-selling Marketing complementary products to customers.

crowdsourcing Using large Internet audiences for advice, market feedback, new ideas and solutions to business problems. Related to the 'wisdom of crowds' theory.

culture The set of fundamental assumptions about what products the organization should produce, how and where it should produce them, and for whom they should be produced.

customer lifetime value (CLTV) Difference between revenues produced by a specific customer and the expenses for acquiring and servicing that customer minus the cost of promotional marketing over the lifetime of the customer relationship, expressed in today's dollars.

customer relationship management (CRM) Business and technology discipline that uses information systems to coordinate all of the business processes surrounding the firm's interactions with its customers in sales, marketing, and service.

customer relationship management systems Information systems that track all the ways in which a company interacts with its customers and analyze these interactions to optimize revenue, profitability, customer satisfaction, and customer retention.

customization The modification of a software package to meet an organization's unique requirements without destroying the package software's integrity.

customization In e-commerce, changing a delivered product or service based on a user's preferences or prior behavior.

cyberlocker Online file-sharing service that allows users to upload files to a secure online storage site from which the files can be synchronized and shared with others.

cybervandalism Intentional disruption, defacement, or destruction of a Web site or corporate information system.

cyberwarfare State-sponsored activity designed to cripple and defeat another state or nation by damaging or disrupting its computers or networks.

data Streams of raw facts representing events occurring in organizations or the physical environment before they have been organized and arranged into a form that people can understand and use.

data administration A special organizational function for managing the organization's data resources, concerned with information policy, data planning, maintenance of data dictionaries, and data quality standards.

data cleansing Activities for detecting and correcting data in a database or file that are incorrect, incomplete, improperly formatted, or redundant. Also known as data scrubbing.

data definition DBMS capability that specifies the structure and content of the database.

data dictionary An automated or manual tool for storing and organizing information about the data maintained in a database.

data element A field.

data flow diagram (DFD) Primary tool for structured analysis that graphically illustrates a system's component process and the flow of data between them.

data governance Policies and processes for managing the availability, usability, integrity, and security of the firm's data.

data inconsistency   The presence of different values for same attribute when the same data are stored in multiple locations.

data management technology   Software governing the organization of data on physical storage media.

data manipulation language   A language associated with a database management system that end users and programmers use to manipulate data in the database.

data mart   A small data warehouse containing only a portion of the organization's data for a specified function or population of users.

data mining   Analysis of large pools of data to find patterns and rules that can be used to guide decision making and predict future behavior.

data quality audit   A survey and/or sample of files to determine accuracy and completeness of data in an information system.

data redundancy   The presence of duplicate data in multiple data files.

data visualization   Technology for helping users see patterns and relationships in large amounts of data by presenting the data in graphical form.

data warehouse   A database, with reporting and query tools, that stores current and historical data extracted from various operational systems and consolidated for management reporting and analysis.

data workers   People such as secretaries or bookkeepers who process the organization's paperwork.

database   A group of related files.

database (rigorous definition)   A collection of data organized to service many applications at the same time by storing and managing data so that they appear to be in one location.

database administration   Refers to the more technical and operational aspects of managing data, including physical database design and maintenance.

database management system (DBMS)   Special software to create and maintain a database and enable individual business applications to extract the data they need without having to create separate files or data definitions in their computer programs.

database server   A computer in a client/server environment that is responsible for running a DBMS to process SQL statements and perform database management tasks.

decisional roles   Mintzberg's classification for managerial roles where managers initiate activities, handle disturbances, allocate resources, and negotiate conflicts.

decision-support systems (DSS)   Information systems at the organization's management level that combine data and sophisticated analytical models or data analysis tools to support semistructured and unstructured decision making.

deep packet inspection (DPI)   Technology for managing network traffic by examining data packets, sorting out low-priority data from higher priority business-critical data, and sending packets in order of priority.

demand planning   Determining how much product a business needs to make to satisfy all its customers' demands.

denial of service (DoS) attack   Flooding a network server or Web server with false communications or requests for services in order to crash the network.

Descartes' rule of change   A principle that states that if an action cannot be taken repeatedly, then it is not right to be taken at any time.

design   Simon's second stage of decision making, when the individual conceives of possible alternative solutions to a problem.

digital asset management systems   Classify, store, and distribute digital objects such as photographs, graphic images, video, and audio content.

digital certificate   An attachment to an electronic message to verify the identity of the sender and to provide the receiver with the means to encode a reply.

digital dashboard   Displays all of a firm's key performance indicators as graphs and charts on a single screen to provide one-page overview of all the critical measurements necessary to make key executive decisions.

digital divide   Large disparities in access to computers and the Internet among different social groups and different locations.

digital firm   Organization where nearly all significant business processes and relationships with customers, suppliers, and employees are digitally enabled, and key corporate assets are managed through digital means.

digital goods   Goods that can be delivered over a digital network.

Digital Millennium Copyright Act (DMCA)   Adjusts copyright laws to the Internet Age by making it illegal to make, distribute, or use devices that circumvent technology-based protections of copy-righted materials.

digital subscriber line (DSL)   A group of technologies providing high-capacity transmission over existing copper telephone lines.

direct cutover   A risky conversion approach where the new system completely replaces the old one on an appointed day.

disaster recovery planning   Planning for the restoration of computing and communications services after they have been disrupted.

disintermediation   The removal of organizations or business process layers responsible for certain intermediary steps in a value chain.

disruptive technologies   Technologies with disruptive impact on industries and businesses, rendering existing products, services and business models obsolete.

distributed denial-of-service (DDoS) attack   Numerous computers inundating and overwhelming a network from numerous launch points.

documentation   Descriptions of how an information system works from either a technical or end-user standpoint.

domain name   English-like name that corresponds to the unique 32-bit numeric Internet Protocol (IP) address for each computer connected to the Internet

Domain Name System (DNS)   A hierarchical system of servers maintaining a database enabling the conversion of domain names to their numeric IP addresses.

domestic exporter   Form of business organization characterized by heavy centralization of corporate activities in the home county of origin.

downtime   Period of time in which an information system is not operational.

drill down   The ability to move from summary data to lower and lower levels of detail.

drive-by download   Malware that comes with a downloaded file a user intentionally or unintentionally requests.

due process   A process in which laws are well-known and understood and there is an ability to appeal to higher authorities to ensure that laws are applied correctly.

dynamic pricing   Pricing of items based on real-time interactions between buyers and sellers that determine what a item is worth at any particular moment.

e-government Use of the Internet and related technologies to digitally enable government and public sector agencies' relationships with citizens, businesses, and other arms of government.

efficient customer response system System that directly links consumer behavior back to distribution, production, and supply chains.

electronic business (e-business) The use of the Internet and digital technology to execute all the business processes in the enterprise. Includes e-commerce as well as processes for the internal management of the firm and for coordination with suppliers and other business partners.

electronic commerce The process of buying and selling goods and services electronically involving transactions using the Internet, networks, and other digital technologies.

electronic data interchange (EDI) The direct computer-to-computer exchange between two organizations of standard business transactions, such as orders, shipment instructions, or payments.

e-mail The computer-to-computer exchange of messages.

employee relationship management (ERM) Software dealing with employee issues that are closely related to CRM, such as setting objectives, employee performance management, performance-based compensation, and employee training.

encryption The coding and scrambling of messages to prevent their being read or accessed without authorization.

end-user development The development of information systems by end users with little or no formal assistance from technical specialists.

end-user interface The part of an information system through which the end user interacts with the system, such as on-line screens and commands.

end users Representatives of departments outside the information systems group for whom applications are developed.

enterprise applications Systems that can coordinate activities, decisions, and knowledge across many different functions, levels, and business units in a firm. Include enterprise systems, supply chain management systems, and knowledge management systems.

enterprise content management systems Help organizations manage structured and semistructured knowledge, providing corporate repositories of documents, reports, presentations, and best practices and capabilities for collecting and organizing e-mail and graphic objects.

enterprise software Set of integrated modules for applications such as sales and distribution, financial accounting, investment management, materials management, production planning, plant maintenance, and human resources that allow data to be used by multiple functions and business processes.

enterprise systems Integrated enterprise-wide information systems that coordinate key internal processes of the firm.

enterprise-wide knowledge management systems General-purpose, firmwide systems that collect, store, distribute, and apply digital content and knowledge.

entity A person, place, thing, or event about which information must be kept.

entity-relationship diagram A methodology for documenting databases illustrating the relationship between various entities in the database.

ergonomics The interaction of people and machines in the work environment, including the design of jobs, health issues, and the end-user interface of information systems.

e-tailer Online retail stores from the giant Amazon to tiny local stores that have Web sites where retail goods are sold.

ethical "no free lunch" rule Assumption that all tangible and intangible objects are owned by someone else, unless there is a specific declaration otherwise, and that the creator wants compensation for this work.

ethics Principles of right and wrong that can be used by individuals acting as free moral agents to make choices to guide their behavior.

evil twins Wireless networks that pretend to be legitimate to entice participants to log on and reveal passwords or credit card numbers.

exchange Third-party Net marketplace that is primarily transaction oriented and that connects many buyers and suppliers for spot purchasing.

executive support systems (ESS) Information systems at the organization's strategic level designed to address unstructured decision making through advanced graphics and communications.

expert system Knowledge-intensive computer program that captures the expertise of a human in limited domains of knowledge.

explicit knowledge Knowledge that has been documented.

Extensible Markup Language (XML) General purpose language that describes the structure of a document and XML can perform presentation, communication, and storage of data, allowing data to be manipulated by the computer.

external integration tools Project management technique that links the work of the implementation team to that of users at all organizational levels.

extranet Private intranet that is accessible to authorized outsiders.

Fair Information Practices (FIP) A set of principles originally set forth in 1973 that governs the collection and use of information about individuals and forms the basis of most U.S. and European privacy laws.

fault-tolerant computer systems Systems that contain extra hardware, software, and power supply components that can back a system up and keep it running to prevent system failure.

feasibility study As part of the systems analysis process, the way to determine whether the solution is achievable, given the organization's resources and constraints.

feedback Output that is returned to the appropriate members of the organization to help them evaluate or correct input.

field A grouping of characters into a word, a group of words, or a complete number, such as a person's name or age.

file transfer protocol (FTP) Tool for retrieving and transferring files from a remote computer.

file A group of records of the same type.

firewall Hardware and software placed between an organization's internal network and an external network to prevent outsiders from invading private networks.

folksonomies User-created taxonomies for classifying and sharing information.

foreign key Field in a database table that enables users find related information in another database table.

formal control tools Project management technique that helps monitor the progress toward completion of a task and fulfillment of goals.

formal planning tools Project management technique that structures and sequences tasks, budgeting time, money, and technical resources required to complete the tasks.

forward chaining A strategy for searching the rule base in an expert system that begins with the information entered by the user and searches the rule base to arrive at a conclusion.

franchiser Form of business organization in which a product is created, designed, financed, and initially produced in the home country, but for product-specific reasons relies heavily on foreign personnel for further production, marketing, and human resources.

free/fremium revenue model an e-commerce revenue model in which a firm offers basic services or content for free, while charging a premium for advanced or high value features.

fuzzy logic Rule-based AI that tolerates imprecision by using nonspecific terms called membership functions to solve problems.

Gantt chart Visually representats the timing, duration, and resource requirements of project tasks.

general controls Overall control environment governing the design, security, and use of computer programs and the security of data files in general throughout the organization's information technology infrastructure.

genetic algorithms Problem-solving methods that promote the evolution of solutions to specified problems using the model of living organisms adapting to their environment.

geoadvertising Delivering ads to users based on their GPS location.

geographic information system (GIS) System with software that can analyze and display data using digitized maps to enhance planning and decision-making.

geoinformation services Information on local places and things based on the GPS position of the user.

geosocial services Social networking based on the GPS location of users.

global culture The development of common expectations, shared artifacts, and social norms among different cultures and peoples.

Golden Rule Putting oneself in the place of others as the object of a decision.

Gramm-Leach-Bliley Act Requires financial institutions to ensure the security and confidentiality of customer data.

green computing Refers to practices and technologies for designing, manufacturing, using, and disposing of computers, servers, and associated devices such as monitors, printers, storage devices, and networking and communications systems to minimize impact on the environment.

grid computing Applying the resources of many computers in a network to a single problem.

group decision-support system (GDSS) An interactive computer-based system to facilitate the solution to unstructured problems by a set of decision makers working together as a group.

hacker A person who gains unauthorized access to a computer network for profit, criminal mischief, or personal pleasure.

Hadoop Open-source software framework that enables distributed parallel processing of huge amounts of data across many inexpensive computers.

hertz Measure of frequency of electrical impulses per second, with 1 Hertz equivalent to 1 cycle per second.

high-availability computing Tools and technologies ,including backup hardware resources, to enable a system to recover quickly from a crash.

HIPAA Law outlining rules for medical security, privacy, and the management of health care records.

hotspot A specific geographic location in which an access point provides public Wi-Fi network service.

HTML (Hypertext Markup Language) Page description language for creating Web pages.

HTML5 Next evolution of HTML, which will make it possible to embed images, video, and audio directly into a document without add-on software.

hubs Very simple devices that connect network components, sending a packet of data to all other connected devices.

hybrid AI systems Integration of multiple AI technologies into a single application to take advantage of the best features of these technologies.

hybrid cloud Computing model where firms use both their own IT infrastructure and also public cloud computing services.

hypertext transfer protocol (HTTP) The communications standard used to transfer pages on the Web. Defines how messages are formatted and transmitted.

identity management Business processes and software tools for identifying the valid users of a system and controlling their access to system resources.

identity theft Theft of key pieces of personal information, such as credit card or Social Security numbers, in order to obtain merchandise and services in the name of the victim or to obtain false credentials.

Immanuel Kant's Categorical Imperative A principle that states that if an action is not right for everyone to take it is not right for anyone.

implementation All the organizational activities surrounding the adoption, management, and routinization of an innovation, such as a new information system.

in-memory computing Technology for very rapid analysis and processing of large quantities of data by storing the data in the computer's main memory rather than in secondary storage.

inference engine The strategy used to search through the rule base in an expert system; can be forward or backward chaining.

information Data that have been shaped into a form that is meaningful and useful to human beings.

information asymmetry Situation where the relative bargaining power of two parties in a transaction is determined by one party in the transaction possessing more information essential to the transaction than the other party.

information density The total amount and quality of information available to all market participants, consumers, and merchants.

information policy Formal rules governing the maintenance, distribution, and use of information in an organization.

information requirements A detailed statement of the information needs that a new system must satisfy; identifies who needs what information, and when, where, and how the information is needed.

information rights The rights that individuals and organizations have with respect to information that pertains to themselves.

information system Interrelated components working together to collect, process, store, and disseminate information to support decision making, coordination, control, analysis, and visualization in an organization.

information systems audit Identifies all the controls tht govern individual information systems and assesses their effectiveness.

information systems department The formal organizational unit that is responsible for the information systems function in the organization.

information systems literacy Broad-based understanding of information systems that includes behavioral knowledge about organizations and individuals using information systems as well as technical knowledge about computers.

information systems managers Leaders of the various specialists in the information systems department.

information systems plan A road map indicating the direction of systems development: the rationale, the current situation, the management strategy, the implementation plan, and the budget.

information technology (IT) All the hardware and software technologies a firm needs to achieve its business objectives.

information technology (IT) infrastructure Computer hardware, software, data, storage technology, and networks providing a portfolio of shared IT resources for the organization.

informational roles Mintzberg's classification for managerial roles where managers act as the nerve centers of their organizations, receiving and disseminating critical information.

informed consent Consent given with knowledge of all the facts needed to make a rational decision.

input The capture or collection of raw data from within the organization or from its external environment for processing in an information system.

instant messaging Chat service that allows participants to create their own private chat channels so that a person can be alerted whenever someone on his or her private list is on-line to initiate a chat session with that particular individual.

intangible benefits Benefits that are not easily quantified; they include more efficient customer service or enhanced decision making.

intellectual property Intangible property created by individuals or corporations that is subject to protections under trade secret, copyright, and patent law.

intelligence The first of Simon's four stages of decision making, when the individual collects information to identify problems occurring in the organization.

intelligent agent Software program that uses a built-in or learned knowledge base to carry out specific, repetitive, and predictable tasks for an individual user, business process, or software application.

intelligent techniques Technologies that aid human decision makers by capturing individual and collective knowledge, discovering patterns and behaviors in large quantities of data, and generating solutions to problems that are too large and complex for human beings to solve on their own.

internal integration tools Project management technique that ensures that the implementation team operates as a cohesive unit.

international information systems architecture The basic information systems required by organizations to coordinate worldwide trade and other activities.

Internet Global network of networks using universal standards to connect millions of different networks.

Internet of Things Pervasive Web in which each object or machine has a unique identity and is able to use the Internet to link with other machines or send data. Also known as the Industrial Internet.

Internet Protocol (IP) address Four-part numeric address indicating a unique computer location on the Internet.

Internet Service Provider (ISP) A commercial organization with a permanent connection to the Internet that sells temporary connections to subscribers.

Internet2 Research network with new protocols and transmission speeds that provides an infrastructure for supporting high-bandwidth Internet applications.

interorganizational systems Information systems that automate the flow of information across organizational boundaries and link a company to its customers, distributors, or suppliers.

interpersonal roles Mintzberg's classification for managerial roles where managers act as figureheads and leaders for the organization.

intranet An internal network based on Internet and World Wide Web technology and standards.

intrusion detection system Tools to monitor the most vulnerable points in a network to detect and deter unauthorized intruders.

investment workstation Powerful desktop computer for financial specialists, which is optimized to access and manipulate massive amounts of financial data.

iOS Operating system for the Apple iPad, iPhone, and iPod Touch.

IPv6 New IP addressing system using 128-bit IP addresses. Stands for Internet Protocol version 6.

IT governance Strategy and policies for using information technology within an organization, specifying the decision rights and accountabilities to ensure that information technology supports the organization's strategies and objectives.

iterative A process of repeating over and over again the steps to build a system.

Java Programming language that can deliver only the software functionality needed for a particular task, such as a small applet downloaded from a network; can run on any computer and operating system.

Joint Application Design (JAD) Process to accelerate the generation of information requirements by having end users and information systems specialists work together in intensive interactive design sessions.

just-in-time Scheduling system for minimizing inventory by having components arrive exactly at the moment they are needed and finished goods shipped as soon as they leave the assembly line.

key field A field in a record that uniquely identifies instances of that record so that it can be retrieved, updated, or sorted.

key performance indicators Measures proposed by senior management for understanding how well the firm is performing along specified dimensions.

keylogger Spyware that records every keystroke made on a computer to steal personal information or passwords or to launch Internet attacks.

knowledge Concepts, experience, and insight that provide a framework for creating, evaluating, and using information.

knowledge base Model of human knowledge that is used by expert systems.

knowledge discovery Identification of novel and valuable patterns in large databases.

knowledge management The set of processes developed in an organization to create, gather, store, maintain, and disseminate the firm's knowledge.

knowledge management systems Systems that support the creation, capture, storage, and dissemination of firm expertise and knowledge.

knowledge network system Online directory for locating corporate experts in well-defined knowledge domains.

knowledge workers People such as engineers or architects who design products or services and create knowledge for the organization.

knowledge work systems Information systems that aid knowledge workers in the creation and integration of new knowledge into the organization.

learning management system (LMS) Tools for the management, delivery, tracking, and assessment of various types of employee learning.

legacy system A system that has been in existence for a long time and that continues to be used to avoid the high cost of replacing or redesigning it.

legitimacy The extent to which one's authority is accepted on grounds of competence, vision, or other qualities. Making judgments and taking actions on the basis of narrow or personal characteristics.

liability The existence of laws that permit individuals to recover the damages done to them by other actors, systems, or organizations.

Linux Reliable and compactly designed operating system that is an offshoot of UNIX and that can run on many different hardware platforms and is available free or at very low cost. Used as alternative to UNIX and Windows NT.

local area network (LAN) A telecommunications network that requires its own dedicated channels and that encompasses a limited distance, usually one building or several buildings in close proximity.

location-based services GPS map services available on smartphones.

location analytics Ability to gain insights from the location (geographic) component of data, including loation data from mobile phones, output from sensors or scanning devices, and data from maps.

long tail marketing Refers to the ability of firms to profitably market goods to very small online audiences, largely because of the lower costs of reaching very small market segments (people who fall into the long tail ends of a Bell curve).

machine learning Study of how computer programs can improve their performance without explicit programming.

mainframe Largest category of computer, used for major business processing.

maintenance Changes in hardware, software, documentation, or procedures to a production system to correct errors, meet new requirements, or improve processing efficiency.

malware Malicious software programs such as computer viruses, worms, and Trojan horses.

managed security service provider (MSSP) Company that provides security management services for subscribing clients.

management information systems (MIS) Specific category of information system providing reports on organizational performance to help middle management monitor and control the business.

managerial roles Expectations of the activities that managers should perform in an organization.

market creator An e-commerce business model in which firms provide a digital online environment where buyers and sellers can meet, search for products, and engage in transactions.

market entry costs The cost merchants must pay to bring their goods to market.

marketspace A marketplace extended beyond traditional boundaries and removed from a temporal and geographic location.

mashups Composite software applications that depend on high-speed networks, universal communication standards, and open-source code.

mass customization The capacity to offer individually tailored products or services using mass production resources.

massive open online course (MOOC) Online course made available via the Web to very large numbers of participants.

menu costs Merchants' costs of changing prices.

metric A standard measurement of performance.

metropolitan area network (MAN) Network that spans a metropolitan area, usually a city and its major suburbs. Its geographic scope falls between a WAN and a LAN.

microblogging Blogging featuring very short posts, such as using Twitter.

micropayment Payment for a very small sum of money, often less than $10.

middle management People in the middle of the organizational hierarchy who are responsible for carrying out the plans and goals of senior management.

minicomputer Middle-range computer used in systems for universities, factories, or research laboratories.

mobile Web app Internet-enabled app with specific functionality for mobile devices that is accesed through a mobile device's Web browser.

mobile commerce (m-commerce) The use of wireless devices, such as cell phones or handheld digital information appliances, to conduct both business-to-consumer and business-to-business e-commerce transactions over the Internet.

modem A device for translating a computer's digital signals into analog form for transmission over ordinary telephone lines, or for translating analog signals back into digital form for reception by a computer.

Moore's Law Assertion that the number of components on a chip doubles each year

multicore processor Integrated circuit to which two or more processors have been attached for enhanced performance, reduced power consumption and more efficient simultaneous processing of multiple tasks.

multinational Form of business organization that concentrates financial management and control out of a central home base while decentralizing

multitiered (N-tier) client/server architecture Client/server network which the work of the entire network is balanced over several different levels of servers.

multitouch Interface that features the use of one or more finger gestures to manipulate lists or objects on a screen without using a mouse or keyboard.

nanotechnology Technology that builds structures and processes based on the manipulation of individual atoms and molecules.

native app Standalone application designed to run on a specific platform and device and is installed directly on the mobile device

net marketplace A single digital marketplace based on Internet technology linking many buyers to many sellers.

network   The linking of two or more computers to share data or resources, such as a printer.

network economics   Model of strategic systems at the industry level based on the concept of a network where adding another participant entails zero marginal costs but can create much larger marginal gains.

network operating system (NOS)   Special software that routes and manages communications on the network and coordinates network resources.

networking and telecommunications technology   Physical devices and software that link various computer hardware components and transfer data from one physical location to another.

neural network   Hardware or software that attempts to emulate the processing patterns of the biological brain.

non-relational database management system   Database management system for working with large quantities of structured and unstructured data that would be difficult to analyze with a relational model.

nonobvious relationship awareness (NORA)   Technology that can find obscure hidden connections between people or other entities by analyzing information from many different sources to correlate relationships.

normalization   The process of creating small stable data structures from complex groups of data when designing a relational database.

object   Software building block that combines data and the procedures acting on the data.

object-oriented development   Approach to systems development that uses the object as the basic unit of systems analysis and design. The system is modeled as a collection o objects and the relationship between them.

offshore outsourcing   Outsourcing systems development work or maintenance of existing systems to external vendors in another country.

on-demand computing   Firms off-loading peak demand for computing power to remote, large-scale data processing centers, investing just enough to handle average processing loads and paying for only as much additional computing power as the market demands. Also called utility computing.

on-line analytical processing (OLAP)   Capability for manipulating and analyzing large volumes of data from multiple perspectives.

online transaction processing   Transaction processing mode in which transactions entered on-line are immediately processed by the computer.

open-source software   Software that provides free access to its program code, allowing users to modify the program code to make improvements or fix errors.

operating system   Software that manages the resources and activities of the computer.

operational CRM   Customer-facing applications, such as sales force automation, call center and customer service support, and marketing automation.

operational intelligence   business analytics that delivers insight into data, streaming events and business operations.

operational management   People who monitor the day-to-day activities of the organization.

opt-in   Model of informed consent permitting prohibiting an organization from collecting any personal information unless the individual specifically takes action to approve information collection and use.

opt-out   Model of informed consent permitting the collection of personal information until the consumer specifically requests that the data not be collected.

organization (behavioral definition)   A collection of rights, privileges, obligations, and responsibilities that are delicately balanced over a period of time through conflict and conflict resolution.

organization (technical definition)   A stable, formal, social structure that takes resources from the environment and processes them to produce outputs.

organizational and management capital   Investments in organization and management such as new business processes, management behavior, organizational culture, or training.

organizational impact analysis   Study of the way a proposed system will affect organizational structure, attitudes, decision making, and operations.

organizational learning   Creation of new standard operating procedures and business processes that reflect organizations' experience.

output   The distribution of processed information to the people who will use it or to the activities for which it will be used.

outsourcing   The practice of contracting computer center operations, telecommunications networks, or applications development to external vendors.

packet switching   Technology that breaks messages into small, fixed bundles of data and routes them in the most economical way through any available communications channel..

paradigm shift   Radical reconceptualization of the nature of the business and the nature of the organization.

parallel strategy   A safe and conservative conversion approach where both the old system and its potential replacement are run together for a time until everyone is assured that the new one functions correctly.

particularism   Making judgments and taking action on the basis of narrow or personal characteristics, in all its forms (religious, nationalistic, ethnic, regionalism, geopolitical position).

partner relationship management (PRM)   Automation of the firm's relationships with its selling partners using customer data and analytical tools to improve coordination and customer sales.

password   Secret word or string of characters for authenticating users so they can access a resource such as a computer system.

patch   Small pieces of software to repair the software flaws without disturbing the proper operation of the software.

patent   A legal document that grants the owner an exclusive monopoly on the ideas behind an invention for 17 years; designed to ensure that inventors of new machines or methods are rewarded for their labor while making widespread use of their inventions.

peer-to-peer   Network architecture that gives equal power to all computers on the network; used primarily in small networks.

personal area network (PAN)   Computer network used for communication among digital devices (including telephones and PDAs) that are close to one person.

personalization   Ability of merchants to target marketing messages to specific individuals by adjusting the message for a person's name, interests, and past purchases.

PERT chart   Network diagram depicting project tasks and their interrelationships.

pharming Phishing technique that redirects users to a bogus Web page, even when an individual enters the correct Web page address.

phased approach Introduces the new system in stages either by functions or by organizational units.

phishing Form of spoofing involving setting up fake Web sites or sending e-mail messages that resemble those of legitimate businesses that ask users for confidential personal data.

pilot study A strategy to introduce the new system to a limited area of the organization until it is proven to be fully functional; only then can the conversion to the new system across the entire organization take place.

pivot table Spreadsheet tool for reorganizing and summarizing two or more dimensions of data in a tabular format.

podcasting Publishing audio broadcasts via the Internet so that subscribing users can download audio files onto their personal computers or portable music players.

portal Web interface for presenting integrated personalized content from a variety of sources. Also refers to a Web site service that provides an initial point of entry to the Web.

portfolio analysis An analysis of the portfolio of potential applications within a firm to determine the risks and benefits, and to select among alternatives for information systems.

post-implementation audit Formal review process conducted after a system has been placed in production to determine how well the system has met its original objectives.

prediction markets An analysis of the portfolio of potential applications within a firm to determine the risks and benefits, and to select among alternatives for information systems.

predictive analytics The use of data mining techniques, historical data, and assumptions about future conditions to predict outcomes of events, such as the probability a customer will respond to an offer or purchase a specific product.

Predictive search Part of a search alogrithm that predicts what a user query is looking as it is entered based on popular searches. Produces a dropdown list of suggested search queries

price discrimination Selling the same goods, or nearly the same goods, to different targeted groups at different prices.

price transparency The ease with which consumers can find out the variety of prices in a market.

primary activities Activities most directly related to the production and distribution of a firm's products or services.

primary key Unique identifier for all the information in any row of a database table.

privacy The claim of individuals to be left alone, free from surveillance or interference from other individuals, organizations, or the state.

private cloud A proprietary network or a data center that ties together servers, storage, networks, data, and applications as a set of virtualized services that are shared by users inside a company.

private exchange Another term for a private industrial network.

private industrial networks Web-enabled networks linking systems of multiple firms in an industry for the coordination of trans-organizational business processes.

process specifications Describe the logic of the processes occurring within the lowest levels of a data flow diagram.

processing The conversion, manipulation, and analysis of raw input into a form that is more meaningful to humans.

product differentiation Competitive strategy for creating brand loyalty by developing new and unique products and services that are not easily duplicated by competitors.

production The stage after the new system is installed and the conversion is complete; during this time the system is reviewed by users and technical specialists to determine how well it has met its original goals.

production or service workers People who actually produce the products or services of the organization.

profiling The use of computers to combine data from multiple sources and create electronic dossiers of detailed information on individuals.

program-data dependence The close relationship between data stored in files and the software programs that update and maintain those files. Any change in data organization or format requires a change in all the programs associated with those files.

programmers Highly trained technical specialists who write computer software instructions.

programming The process of translating the system specifications prepared during the design stage into program code.

project Planned series of related activities for achieving a specific business objective.

project management Application of knowledge, tools, and techniques to achieve specific targets within a specified budget and time period.

project portfolio management software Helps organizations evaluate and manage portfolios of projects and dependencies among them.

protocol A set of rules and procedures that govern transmission between the components in a network.

prototype The preliminary working version of an information system for demonstration and evaluation purposes.

prototyping The process of building an experimental system quickly and inexpensively for demonstration and evaluation so that users can better determine information requirements.

public cloud A cloud maintained by an external service provider, accessed through the Internet, and available to the general public.

public key encryption Uses two keys: one shared (or public) and one private.

public key infrastructure(PKI) System for creating public and private keys using a certificate authority (CA) and digital certificates for authentication.

pull-based model Supply chain driven by actual customer orders or purchases so that members of the supply chain produce and deliver only what customers have ordered.

push-based model Supply chain driven by production master schedules based on forecasts or best guesses of demand for products, and products are "pushed" to customers.

quantum computing Use of principles of quantum physics to represent data and perform operations on the data, with the ability to be in many different states at once and to perform many different computations simultaneously.

query language Software tool that provides immediate online answers to requests for information that are not predefined.

radio-frequency identification (RFID) Technology using tiny tags with embedded microchips containing data about an item and its location to transmit short-distance radio signals to special RFID readers that then pass the data on to a computer for processing.

ransomware Malware that extorts money from users by taking control of their computers or displaying annoying pop-up messages.

Rapid Application Development (RAD) Process for developing systems in a very short time period by using prototyping, fourth-generation tools, and close teamwork among users and systems specialists.

rationalization of procedures The streamlining of standard operating procedures, eliminating obvious bottlenecks, so that automation makes operating procedures more efficient.

real options pricing models Models for evaluating information technology investments with uncertain returns by using techniques for valuing financial options.

record A group of related fields.

referential integrity Rules to ensure that relationships between coupled database tables remain consistent.

relational DBMS A type of logical database model that treats data as if they were stored in two-dimensional tables. It can relate data stored in one table to data in another as long as the two tables share a common data element.

Repetitive Stress Injury (RSI) Occupational disease that occurs when muscle groups are forced through repetitive actions with high-impact loads or thousands of repetitions with low-impact loads.

Request for Proposal (RFP) A detailed list of questions submitted to vendors of software or other services to determine how well the vendor's product can meet the organization's specific requirements.

responsibility Accepting the potential costs, duties, and obligations for the decisions one makes.

responsive Web design Ability of a Web site to automatically change screen resolution and image size as a user switches to devices of different sizes, such as a laptop, tablet computer, or smartphone. Eliminates the need for separate design and development work for each new device.

revenue model A description of how a firm will earn revenue, generate profits, and produce a return on investment.

richness Measurement of the depth and detail of information that a business can supply to the customer as well as information the business collects about the customer.

risk assessment Determining the potential frequency of the occurrence of a problem and the potential damage if the problem were to occur. Used to determine the cost/benefit of a control.

Risk Aversion Principle Principle that one should take the action that produces the least harm or incurs the least cost.

router Specialized communications processor that forwards packets of data from one network to another network.

routines Precise rules, procedures and practices that have been developed to cope with expected situations.

RSS Technology using aggregator software to pull content from Web sites and feed it automatically to subscribers' computers.

SaaS (Software as a Service) Services for delivering and providing access to software remotely as a Web-based service.

safe harbor Private self-regulating policy and enforcement mechanism that meets the objectives of government regulations but does not involve government regulation or enforcement.

sales revenue model Selling goods, information, or services to customers as the main source of revenue for a company.

Sarbanes-Oxley Act Law passed in 2002 that imposes responsibility on companies and their management to protect investors by safeguarding the accuracy and integrity of financial information that is used internally and released externally.

scalability The ability of a computer, product, or system to expand to serve a larger number of users without breaking down.

scope Defines what work is and is not included in a project.

scoring model A quick method for deciding among alternative systems based on a system of ratings for selected objectives.

search costs The time and money spent locating a suitable product and determining the best price for that product.

search engine A tool for locating specific sites or information on the Internet.

search engine marketing Use of search engines to deliver in their results sponsored links, for which advertisers have paid.

search engine optimization (SEO) the process of changing a Web site's content, layout, and format in order to increase the ranking of the site on popular search engines, and to generate more site visitors.

Secure Hypertext Transfer Protocol (S-HTTP) Protocol used for encrypting data flowing over the Internet; limited to individual messages.

Secure Sockets Layer (SSL) Enables client and server computers to manage encryption and decryption activities as they communicate with each other during a secure Web session.

security Policies, procedures, and technical measures used to prevent unauthorized access, alteration, theft, or physical damage to information systems.

security policy Statements ranking information risks, identifying acceptable security goals, and identifying the mechanisms for achieving these goals.

Semantic Web Ways of making the Web more "intelligent," with machine-facilitated understanding of information so that searches can be more intuitive, effective, and executed using intelligent software agents.

semistructured decisions Decisions in which only part of the problem has a clear-cut answer provided by an accepted procedure.

senior management People occupying the topmost hierarchy in an organization who are responsible for making long-range decisions.

sensitivity analysis Models that ask "what-if" questions repeatedly to determine the impact of changes in one or more factors on the outcomes.

sentiment analysis Mining text comments in an e-mail message, blog, social media conversation, or survey form to detect favorable and unfavorable opinions about specific subjects.

server Computer specifically optimized to provide software and other resources to other computers over a network.

service level agreement (SLA) Formal contract between customers and their service providers that defines the specific responsibilities of the service provider and the level of service expected by the customer.

service-oriented architecture Software architecture of a firm built on a collection of software programs that communicate with each other to perform assigned tasks to create a working software application

shopping bot Software with varying levels of built-in intelligence to help electronic commerce shoppers locate and evaluate products or service they might wish to purchase.

six sigma A specific measure of quality, representing 3.4 defects per million opportunities; used to designate a set of methodologies and techniques for improving quality and reducing costs.

smart card A credit-card-size plastic card that stores digital information and that can be used for electronic payments in place of cash.

smartphone Wireless phone with voice, text, and Internet capabilities.

sniffer Type of eavesdropping program that monitors information traveling over a network.

social business Use of social networking platforms, including Facebook, Twitter, and internal corporate social tools, to engage employees, customers, and suppliers.

social CRM Tools enabling a business to link customer conversatins, data, and relationships from social networking sites to CRM processes.

social engineering Tricking people into revealing their passwords by pretending to rrbe legitimate users or members of a company in need of information.

social graph Map of all significant online social relationships, comparable to a social network describing offline relationships.

social networking sites Online community for expanding users' business or social contacts by making connections through their mutual business or personal connections.

social search Effort to provide more relevant and trustworthy search results based on a person's network of social contacts.

social shopping Use of Web sites featuring user-created Web pages to share knowledge about items of interest to other shoppers.

sociotechnical design Design to produce information systems that blend technical efficiency with sensitivity to organizational and human needs.

sociotechnical view Seeing systems as composed of both technical and social elements.

software-defined networking (SDN) Using a central control program separate from network devices to manage the flow of data on a network.

software localization Process of converting software to operate in a second language.

software package A prewritten, precoded, commercially available set of programs that eliminates the need to write software programs for certain functions.

spam Unsolicited commercial e-mail.

spoofing Tricking or deceiving computer systems or other computer users by hiding one's identity or faking the identity of another user on the Internet.

spyware Technology that aids in gathering information about a person or organization without their knowledge.

SQL injection attack Attacks against a Web site that take advantage of vulnerabilities in poorly coded SQL (a standard and common database software application) applications in order to introduce malicious program code into a company's systems and networks.

storage area network (SAN) A high-speed network dedicated to storage that connects different kinds of storage devices, such as tape libraries and disk arrays so they can be shared by multiple servers.

strategic information system Information system that changes the goals, operations, products, services, or environmental relationships of an organization to help gain a competitive advantage.

strategic transitions A movement from one level of sociotechnical system to another. Often required when adopting strategic systems that demand changes in the social and technical elements of an organization.

streaming A publishing method for music and video files that flows a continuous stream of content to a user's device without being stored locally on the device.

structure chart System documentation showing each level of design, the relationship among the levels, and the overall place in the design structure; can document one program, one system, or part of one program.

structured Refers to the fact that techniques are carefully drawn up, step by step, with each step building on a previous one.

structured decisions Decisions that are repetitive, routine, and have a definite procedure for handling them.

structured knowledge Knowledge in the form of structured documents and reports.

Structured Query Language (SQL) The standard data manipulation language for relational database management systems.

subscription revenue model Web site charging a subscription fee for access to some or all of its content or services on an ongoing basis.

supply chain Network of organizations and business processes for procuring materials, transforming raw materials into intermediate and finished products, and distributing the finished products to customers.

supply chain execution systems Systems to manage the flow of products through distribution centers and warehouses to ensure that products are delivered to the right locations in the most efficient manner.

supply chain management systems Information systems that automate the flow of information between a firm and its suppliers in order to optimize the planning, sourcing, manufacturing, and delivery of products and services.

supply chain planning systems Systems that enable a firm to generate demand forecasts for a product and to develop sourcing and manufacturing plans for that product.

support activities Activities that make the delivery of a firm's primary activities possible. Consist of the organization's infrastructure, human resources, technology, and procurement.

switch Device to connect network components that has more intelligence than a hub and can filter and forward data to a specified destination.

switching costs The expense a customer or company incurs in lost time and expenditure of resources when changing from one supplier or system to a competing supplier or system.

system testing Tests the functioning of the information system as a whole in order to determine if discrete modules will function together as planned.

systems analysis The analysis of a problem that the organization will try to solve with an information system.

systems analysts Specialists who translate business problems and requirements into information requirements and systems, acting as liaison between the information systems department and the rest of the organization.

systems design Details how a system will meet the information requirements as determined by the systems analysis.

systems development The activities that go into producing an information systems solution to an organizational problem or opportunity.

systems life cycle A traditional methodology for developing an information system that partitions the systems development process into formal stages that must be completed sequentially with a very formal division of labor between end users and information systems specialists.

T lines High-speed guaranteed service level data lines leased from communications providers, such as T-1 lines (with a transmission capacity of 1.544 Mbps).

tablet computer Mobile handheld computer that is larger than a mobile phone and operated primarily by touching a flat screen.

tacit knowledge Expertise and experience of organizational members that has not been formally documented.

tangible benefits Benefits that can be quantified and assigned a monetary value; they include lower operational costs and increased cash flows.

taxonomy Method of classifying things according to a predetermined system.

teams Teams are formal groups whose members collaborate to achieve specific goals.

teamware Group collaboration software that is customized for teamwork.

technology standards Specifications that establish the compatibility of products and the ability to communicate in a network.

technostress Stress induced by computer use; symptoms include aggravation, hostility toward humans, impatience, and enervation.

telepresence Telepresence is a technology that allows a person to give the appearance of being present at a location other than his or her true physical location.

Telnet Network tool that allows someone to log on to one computer system while doing work on another.

test plan Prepared by the development team in conjunction with the users; it includes all of the preparations for the series of tests to be performed on the system.

testing The exhaustive and thorough process that determines whether the system produces the desired results under known conditions.

text mining Discovery of patterns and relationships from large sets of unstructured data.

token Physical device similar to an identification card that is designed to prove the identity of a single user.

Total Cost of Ownership (TCO) Designates the total cost of owning technology resources, including initial purchase costs, the cost of hardware and software upgrades, maintenance, technical support, and training.

Total Quality Management (TQM) A concept that makes quality control a responsibility to be shared by all people in an organization.

touch point Method of firm interaction with a customer, such as telephone, e-mail, customer service desk, conventional mail, or point-of-purchase.

trade secret Any intellectual work or product used for a business purpose that can be classified as belonging to that business, provided it is not based on information in the public domain.

transaction costs Costs incurred when a firm buys on the marketplace what it cannot make itself.

transaction cost theory Economic theory stating that firms grow larger because they can conduct marketplace transactions internally more cheaply than they can with external firms in the marketplace.

transaction fee revenue model An online e-commerce revenue model where the firm receives a fee for enabling or executing transactions.

transaction processing systems (TPS) Computerized systems that perform and record the daily routine transactions necessary to conduct the business; they serve the organization's operational level.

transborder data flow The movement of information across international boundaries in any form.

Transmission Control Protocol/Internet Protocol (TCP/IP) Dominant model for achieving connectivity among different networks. Provides a universally agree-on method for breaking up digital messages into packets, routing them to the proper addresses, and then reassembling them into coherent messages.

transnational Truly global form of business organization with no national headquarters; value-added activities are managed from a global perspective without reference to national borders, optimizing sources of supply and demand and local competitive advantage.

Trojan horse A software program that appears legitimate but contains a second hidden function that may cause damage.

tuple A row or record in a relational database.

two-factor authentication Validating user identity with two means of identification, one of which is typically a physical token, and the other of which is typically data.

Unified communications Integrates disparate channels for voice communications, data communications, instant messaging, e-mail, and electronic conferencing into a single experience where users can seamlessly switch back and forth between different communication modes.

unified threat management (UTM) Comprehensive security management tool that combines multiple security tools, including firewalls, virtual private networks, intrusion detection systems, and Web content filtering and anti-spam software.

uniform resource locator (URL) The address of a specific resource on the Internet.

unit testing The process of testing each program separately in the system. Sometimes called program testing.

UNIX Operating system for all types of computers, which is machine independent and supports multiuser processing, multitasking, and networking. Used in high-end workstations and servers.

unstructured decisions Nonroutine decisions in which the decision maker must provide judgment, evaluation, and insights into the problem definition; there is no agreed-upon procedure for making such decisions.

user interface The part of the information system through which the end user interacts with the system; type of hardware and the series of on-screen commands and responses required for a user to work with the system.

user-designer communications gap The difference in backgrounds, interests, and priorities that impede communication and problem solving among end users and information systems specialists.

Utilitarian Principle Principle that assumes one can put values in rank order of utility and understand the consequences of various courses of action.

value chain model Model that highlights the primary or support activities that add a margin of value to a firm's products or services where information systems can best be applied to achieve a competitive advantage.

value web Customer-driven network of independent firms who use information technology to coordinate their value chains to collectively produce a product or service for a market.

virtual company Organization using networks to link people, assets and ideas to create and distribute products and services without being limited to traditional organizational boundaries or physical location.

Virtual Private Network (VPN) A secure connection between two points across the Internet to transmit corporate data. Provides a low-cost alternative to a private network.

Virtual Reality Modeling Language (VRML) A set of specifications for interactive three-dimensional modeling on the World Wide Web.

virtual reality systems Interactive graphics software and hardware that create computer-generated simulations that provide sensations that emulate real-world activities.

virtualization Presenting a set of computing resources so that they can all be accessed in ways that are not restricted by physical configuration or geographic location.

visual web Refers to Web linking visual sites such as Pinterest where pictures replace text socuents and where users search on pictures and visual characteristics.

Voice over IP (VoIP) Facilities for managing the delivery of voice information using the Internet Protocol (IP).

war driving Technique in which eavesdroppers drive by buildings or park outside and try to intercept wireless network traffic.

wearable computer Small wearable computing device such as a smartwatch, smartglasses, or activity tracker.

Web 2.0 Second-generation, interactive Internet-based services that enable people to collaborate, share information, and create new services online, including mashups, blogs, RSS, and wikis.

Web 3.0 Future vision of the Web where all digital information is woven together with intelligent search capabilities.

Web beacons Tiny objects invisibly embedded in e-mail messages and Web pages that are designed to monitor the behavior of the user visiting a Web site or sending e-mail.

Web browser An easy-to-use software tool for accessing the World Wide Web and the Internet.

Web hosting service Company with large Web server computers to maintain the Web sites of fee-paying subscribers.

Web mining Discovery and analysis of useful patterns and information from the World Wide Web.

Web server Software that manages requests for Web pages on the computer where they are stored and that delivers the page to the user's computer.

Web services Set of universal standards using Internet technology for integrating different applications from different sources without time-consuming custom coding. Used for linking systems of different organizations or for linking disparate systems within the same organization.

Web site All of the World Wide Web pages maintained by an organization or an individual.

Wi-Fi Standards for Wireless Fidelity and refers to the 802.11 family of wireless networking standards.

Wide Area Network (WAN) Telecommunications network that spans a large geographical distance. May consist of a variety of cable, satellite, and microwave technologies.

wiki Collaborative Web site where visitors can add, delete, or modify content, including the work of previous authors.

WiMax Popular term for IEEE Standard 802.16 for wireless networking over a range of up to 31 miles with a data transfer rate of up to 75 Mbps. Stands for Worldwide Interoperability for Microwave Access.

Windows Microsoft family of operating systems for both network servers and client computers. The most recent version is Windows Vista.

Windows 8 Most recent Microsoft Windows operating system, which runs on tablets as well as PCs, and includes multitouch capabilities.

Wintel PC Any computer that uses Intel microprocessors (or compatible processors) and a Windows operating system.

wireless sensor networks (WSNs) Networks of interconnected wireless devices with built-in processing, storage, and radio frequency sensors and antennas that are embedded into the physical environment to provide measurements of many points over large spaces.

wisdom The collective and individual experience of applying knowledge to the solution of problems.

wisdom of crowds The belief that large numbers of people can make better decisions about a wide range of topics or products than a single person or even a small committee of experts (first proposed in a book by James Surowiecki).

World Wide Web A system with universally accepted standards for storing, retrieving, formatting, and displaying information in a networked environment.

worms Independent software programs that propagate themselves to disrupt the operation of computer networks or destroy data and other programs.

Index

Name Index

Organizations Index

Subject Index